Introduction to the Law for Paralegals

McGraw-Hill Business Careers Paralegal Titles

MCGRAW-HILL PARALEGAL TITLES: WHERE EDUCATIONAL SUPPORT GOES BEYOND EXPECTATIONS.

Building a solid foundation for a successful paralegal career is becoming more challenging as the needs of students and instructors continue to grow. The McGraw-Hill paralegal texts offer the solution to this ever-changing environment. Integrated real-world applications in each chapter teach students the practical skills needed for a thriving career in the field. A common vocabulary among all McGraw-Hill titles ensures consistency in learning. Up-to-date coverage of the available technology used in a legal setting and a purposefully designed set of pedagogical features with shared goals across the list provide the systems needed for students to fully grasp the material and apply it in a paralegal setting. With a thorough set of ancillaries and dedicated publisher support, these texts will facilitate active learning in the classroom and give students the skills sets desired by employers.

Introduction to Law & Paralegal Studies
Connie Farrell Scuderi
ISBN: 0073524638
© 2008

Introduction to the Law for Paralegals
Deborah S. Benton
ISBN: 007351179X
© 2008

Basic Legal Research, Second Edition
Edward Nolfi
ISBN: 0073520519
© 2008

Basic Legal Writing, Second Edition
Pamela Tepper
ISBN: 0073403032
© 2008

Legal Research and Writing
Neal Bevans
ISBN: 007352462X
© 2008

Contract Law for Paralegals
Linda Spagnola
ISBN: 0073511765
© 2008

Civil Law and Litigation for Paralegals
Neal Bevans
ISBN: 0073524611
© 2008

Wills, Trusts, and Estates for Paralegals
George Kent
ISBN: 0073403067
© 2008

Legal Terminology Explained
Edward Nolfi
ISBN: 0073511846
© 2008

The Law Office Reference Manual
Jo Ann Lee
ISBN: 0073511838
© 2008

The Paralegal Reference Manual
Charles Nemeth
ISBN: 0073403075
© 2008

The Professional Paralegal
Allan Tow
ISBN: 0073403091
© 2008

Titles to come:

Ethics for Paralegals
Linda Spagnola
© 2008

Real Estate Law for Paralegals
George Kent
© 2008

Introduction to the Law for Paralegals

Deborah S. Benton, J.D.

Boston Burr Ridge, IL Dubuque, IA Madison, WI New York San Francisco St. Louis
Bangkok Bogotá Caracas Kuala Lumpur Lisbon London Madrid Mexico City
Milan Montreal New Delhi Santiago Seoul Singapore Sydney Taipei Toronto

The McGraw·Hill Companies

INTRODUCTION TO THE LAW FOR PARALEGALS

Published by McGraw-Hill/Irwin, a business unit of The McGraw-Hill Companies, Inc., 1221 Avenue of the Americas, New York, NY, 10020.

This book is printed on acid-free paper.

1 2 3 4 5 6 7 8 9 0 QPD/QPD 0 9 8 7 6

ISBN 978-0-07-351179-5
MHID 0-07-351179-X

Editorial director: *John E. Biernat*
Publisher: *Linda Schreiber*
Sponsoring editor: *Natalie Ruffatto*
Developmental editor: *Tammy Higham*
Editorial coordinator: *Peter Vanaria*
Marketing manager: *Keari Bedford*
Lead producer, Media technology: *Aliya Haque*
Senior project manager: *Susanne Riedell*
Production supervisor: *Gina Hangos*
Lead designer: *Matthew Baldwin*
Senior media project manager: *Rose M. Range*
Cover design: *Studio Montage*
Cover Image: *© Getty Images*
Typeface: *10/12 Times New Roman*
Compositor: *GTS—New Delhi, India Campus*
Printer: *Quebecor World Dubuque Inc.*

Library of Congress Cataloging-in-Publication Data

Benton, Deborah S.
Introduction to the law for paralegals / Deborah S. Benton.
p. cm. -- (Mcgraw-Hill business careers paralegal titles)
Includes index.
ISBN-13: 978-0-07-351179-5 (alk. paper)
ISBN-10: 0-07-351179-X (alk. paper)
1. Law--United States. 2. Legal assistants--United States--Handbooks, manuals, etc. I. Title.
KF386.B37 2008
349.73--dc22

2006026021

www.mhhe.com

Dedication

To Doug and Diane, who are always at the center of the universe.

About the Author

Deborah S. Benton is an attorney, a professional educator, and a writer. Ms. Benton has taught for five years in a paralegal studies degree program and presently teaches at William Jewell College in Liberty, Missouri. She has extensive experience teaching all paralegal courses, including Introduction to Law, the first class taken by paralegal students. Ms. Benton received a B.A. degree in English and Economics from Sweet Briar College in Virginia and a J.D. from The John Marshall Law School in Chicago and is currently completing a Masters in Education degree. She has been a licensed professional attorney in Illinois since 1983. Ms. Benton has written for various legal practice publications and has extensive experience as both an editor and writer in the publishing field.

Preface

Many paralegal studies programs begin with an introductory course in the law. Typically, these first-semester courses present an overview of the basic aspects of the law, followed by a preview of each substantive area of the law to be studied in depth in a subsequent program offering. Often, students entering a paralegal degree program have some basic knowledge of legal topics, largely due to the significant increase in television programs related to the law, particularly court television shows that resolve disputes between "actual litigants" in a half hour. What is lacking in the knowledge that students bring to an introductory law course is an understanding of how legal principles are applied to different fact situations. This book is an innovative and engaging textbook written for the student who is just starting a paralegal studies degree program.

Many textbooks have been written that provide definitions of legal terminology and rules of law, suggesting that rote memorization is the key to learning about the topic. Little guidance is provided in how those rules of law are relevant to new legal issues and cases. In writing this book, I approached the manuscript with the theory that students do not learn best by rote memorization, but by practicing critical thinking skills that require the student to apply rules of law to various fact patterns. By being asked to compare cases, conduct Internet research, and predict the likely outcome of a hypothetical case, students will complete a first-semester introduction to the law course with a greater understanding of basic legal principles and practical strategies useful in approaching legal issues they will encounter in subsequent legal classes. This book strives to encourage students in the development of critical thinking skills necessary to a successful paralegal career.

In developing legal analysis and critical thinking skills, students need practical guidance and practice in fundamental exercises such as identifying the legal issue, determining the applicable legal principles, and applying them to the facts of a case. This textbook provides such application and practice, through several unique pedagogical features. It provides simple and concise explanations of legal concepts and topics, encouraging students to develop critical thinking skills by applying the legal principles to numerous problems and exercises contained in each chapter. This book introduces students to the major substantive areas of law that will be covered in depth in subsequent courses.

I wrote this book as a result of my experience in how students learn and understand complex legal issues; students develop critical legal analysis skills by a hands-on approach to the subject. Introductory legal textbooks present legal rules in a format that asks students to memorize concepts and principles. This textbook presents the topics and then provides numerous examples, carefully selected court cases, and exercises that ask students to use problem-solving skills, applying the law to hypothetical fact patterns. Some of the unique features of this book are the critical thinking exercises that present hypothetical cases based on the material in that chapter, as well as challenging "You Be the Judge" cases throughout every chapter. There are opportunities for the student to do Internet research using the selected Web sites contained in each chapter, as well as further legal research involving their own jurisdiction's statutes. This book is easy to read, yet provides a solid foundation for not only a study of substantive legal courses in the future but also to help develop students' legal reasoning skills. This book achieves a balance between a concise, thorough overview of legal concepts with extensive pedagogical features, making this book easy to use for both instructor and student. My goal in writing this book was to provide a textbook that any instructor, even with limited advance preparation time, can use to present thorough, engaging lessons that accommodate all learning styles.

A Guided Tour

Introduction to the Law for Paralegals

This book is an innovative and engaging textbook written for the student who is just starting a paralegal degree program. It provides simple and concise explanations of legal concepts and topics, encouraging students to develop critical thinking skills by applying the legal principles to numerous problems and exercises contained in each chapter. This book introduces students to the major substantive areas of law that will be covered in depth in subsequent courses. The pedagogy of the book applies three goals:

1. Learning outcomes (critical thinking, vocabulary building, skill development, issues analysis, writing practices)
2. Relevance of topics without sacrificing theory (ethical challenges, current law practices, technology applications)
3. Practical application (real-world exercises, portfolio creation, team exercises)

Chapter Objectives introduce the concepts students should understand after reading each chapter as well as provide brief summaries describing the material to be covered.

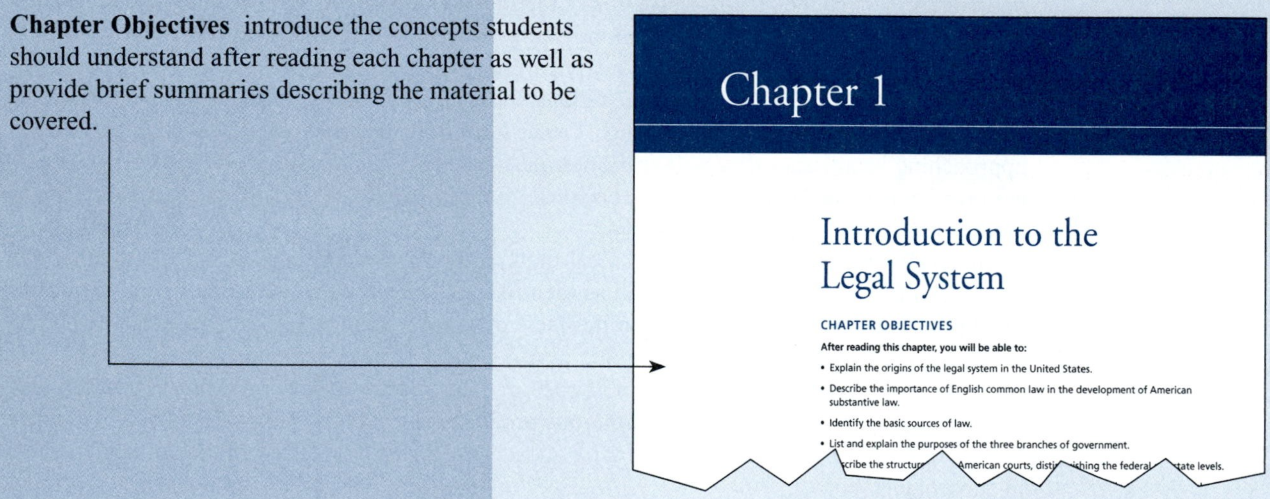

Chapter 1

Introduction to the Legal System

CHAPTER OBJECTIVES

After reading this chapter, you will be able to:

- Explain the origins of the legal system in the United States.
- Describe the importance of English common law in the development of American substantive law.
- Identify the basic sources of law.
- List and explain the purposes of the three branches of government.

Case In Point presents real cases, connecting students to real-world examples and documents that further develop the information presented in the chapter.

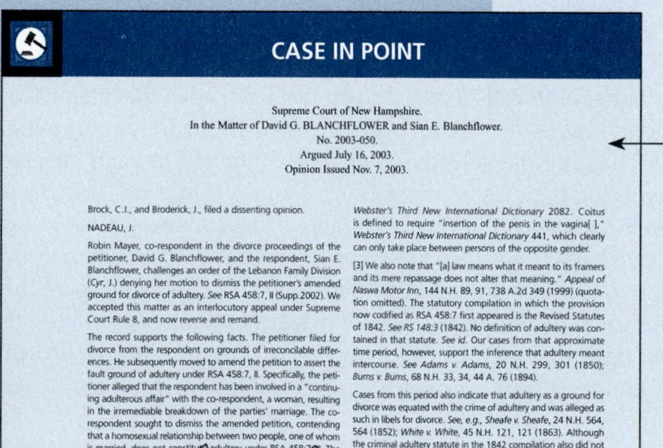

CASE IN POINT

Supreme Court of New Hampshire.
In the Matter of David G. BLANCHFLOWER and Sian E. Blanchflower.
No. 2003-050.
Argued July 16, 2003.
Opinion Issued Nov. 7, 2003.

Brock, C.J., and Broderick, J., filed a dissenting opinion.

NADEAU, J.

Robin Mayer, co-respondent in the divorce proceedings of the petitioner, David G. Blanchflower, and the respondent, Sian E. Blanchflower, challenges an order of the Lebanon Family Division (*Cyr*, J.) denying her motion to dismiss the petitioner's amended ground for divorce of adultery. *See* RSA 458:7, II (Supp.2002). We accepted this matter as an interlocutory appeal under Supreme Court Rule 8, and now reverse and remand.

The record supports the following facts. The petitioner filed for divorce from the respondent on grounds of irreconcilable differences. He subsequently moved to amend the petition to assert the fault ground of adultery under RSA 458:7, II. Specifically, the petitioner alleged that the respondent has been involved in a "continuing adulterous affair" with the co-respondent, a woman, resulting in the irremediable breakdown of the parties' marriage. The co-respondent sought to dismiss the amended petition, contending that a homosexual relationship between two people, one of whom is married, does not constitu

Webster's Third New International Dictionary 2082. Coitus is defined to require "insertion of the penis in the vagina[ ]," *Webster's Third New International Dictionary* 441, which clearly can only take place between persons of the opposite gender.

[3] We also note that "[a] law means what it meant to its framers and its mere repassage does not alter that meaning." *Appeal of Naswa Motor Inn*, 144 N.H. 89, 91, 738 A.2d 349 (1999) (quotation omitted). The statutory compilation in which the provision now codified as RSA 458:7 first appeared is the Revised Statutes of 1842. *See RS 148:3* (1842). No definition of adultery was contained in that statute. *See id.* Our cases from that approximate time period, however, support the inference that adultery meant intercourse. *See Adams v. Adams*, 20 N.H. 299, 301 (1850); *Burns v. Burns*, 68 N.H. 33, 34, 44 A. 76 (1894).

Cases from this period also indicate that adultery as a ground for divorce was equated with the crime of adultery and was alleged as such in libels for divorce. *See, e.g., Sheafe v. Sheafe*, 24 N.H. 564, 564 (1852); *White v. White*, 45 N.H. 121, 121 (1863). Although the criminal adultery statute in the 1842 compilation also did not define adultery,

Research This! engages students to research cases in their jurisdiction that answer a hypothetical scenario, reinforcing the critical skills of independent research.

RESEARCH THIS!

Compare the facts and reasoning in the following cases. Prepare a memorandum of law summarizing the holdings in these cases:

Raethz v. Aurora University, 346 Ill.App.3d 728, 805 N.E.2d 696 (2004).
Bender v. Alderson-Broaddus College, 212 W.Va. 502, 575 S.E.2d 112 (2002).
Lemmon v. University of Cincinnati, 112 Ohio Misc.2d 73, 750 N.E.2d 668 (2001).
Swartley v. Hoffner and Lehigh University, 734 A.2d 915 (1999).

Cyber Trip provides a list of relevant Web sites that students should visit in order to learn more about the topics presented in the chapter. Often, questions are posed to the students in order to help them determine how these Web sites could help in the everyday life of a paralegal.

CYBER TRIP

Have a look at the Web site of the Library of Congress in Washington, DC. What are some of the features of this site that might help you in your research of a case?
www.loc.gov

case law in New York, and then, if necessary, expanding yo
eral circuit cases that include New York.

Keep in mind that precedent is the opinions of the court
the application of legal principles to a specific factual sit
cludes court decisions that interpret statutes, which are not
by legislature and codified. Therefore, precedent builds u
that for purposes of fairness and continuity, judges will de
tive reasoning in those prior cases, so long as a similar fact

The extent to which a court will rely on precedent in pr
limitations of the court in a certain region, whether it is a s
The necessity to research the law by looking for cases or st
cussed in depth in Chapters 3 and 4.

Courts are required to follow precedent if it is a decisio
jurisdiction or from the U.S. Supreme Court, whose decis
nation. If a court is bound to follow the decision of anoth
is referred to as *mandatory* or *binding authority*. Court de
the same jurisdiction are mandatory authority. Thus, if a d
Supreme Court, that decision is binding authority for all lo
of Appeals for the Seventh Circuit decides a case, that o
other decisions within the seventh circuit. Based on the con

Eye on Ethics raises legitimate ethical questions and situations attorneys and paralegals often face. Students are asked to reference rules governing these issues and make a decision.

Eye on Ethics

The American Bar Association's Model Code of Professional Responsibility and the Model Rules of Professional Conduct are the basis for most states' ethical codes of conduct for attorneys. The Model Code of Professional Responsibility, known simply as the "Model Code," consists of nine canons. They set forth both disciplinary rules regarding the practice of law, as well as ethical considerations. You may access them via the ABA's Web site at www.abanet.org.

A Guided Tour

You be the Judge places the students in the role of a judge as they form opinions about relevant legal issues. Students will think critically on the subjects of the chapter and make legal decisions about the hypothetical scenarios presented.

You Be the Judge

Abe, Ben, and Cain are partners in a real estate development company. Their objective is to purchase depressed property or derelict land, redevelop the property, and then resell it in a few months at a huge profit. During one of their partnership meetings, Abe proposes foregoing the opportunity to purchase a large tract of vacant land, suggesting that the land is in an undesirable location and would be difficult to develop. Cain, who had been out late the night before, falls asleep during the meeting and thus misses most of Abe's discussion. Cain wakes up long enough to vote in favor of Abe's recommendation, though he doesn't understand what it is all about. Ben is suffering from hay fever and is unable to concentrate on the discussion, and so also supports Abe's recommendation. One month later, Cain discovers that Abe had purchased this tract of land for himself and then resold it at a profit to the Dinky World Entertainment Corporation which plans to build a large theme park on the land. What, if anything, can Cain do regarding this situation? Explain.

Chapter Summary provides a quick review of the key concepts presented in the chapter.

Summary

Property ownership rights are fundamental to our society, forming the basis for our econom
As such, people are not only keenly interested in acquiring property, but in ensuring that the
ownership rights are protected under the law. Property law sets forth who owns what, a
what rights are associated with that ownership interest. Property law exists for the purpose
protecting the right of owners to sell, use, control, and dispose of their property as they wi
without interference or trespassing by others. Property law ensures that this is accomplishe
without owners taking the law into their own hands and guarding their property with shotguns
building moats around their land.

In beginning an analysis of a property law question, you should first ascertain whether t
subject matter concerns real property or personal property. Sometimes this classification change
depending on the nature of the property, as in minerals in the ground. Issues that arise in proper
law often focus on whether the property has been legally transferred to another. If property h
been transferred, an examination of the rights of ownership is often necessary in resolving
property law issue.

A Day in the Life of a Real Paralegal

In your work as a paralegal for a firm that primarily has corporate clients, you will frequently be dealing with issues surrounding the formation of business entities as well as the ongoing business of those organizations. For this area of work, your greatest challenge might be keeping abreast of the ever-changing rules and regulations applicable to the formation and operation of businesses. Having an eye for detail and being able to ensure that documents are prepared accurately, under your attorney's supervision, is the key to success in this legal area. Knowing the basics of the acts mentioned in this chapter, such as the UPA or the MBCA, will go a long way to you gaining confidence in this field. Corporations frequently have in-house legal departments that employ paralegals, and therefore it is useful to understand the duties and responsibilities of the officers and directors and their accountability to the shareholders.

Some of the tasks that paralegals typically undertake in this field include drafting partnership agreements and articles of incorporation, preparing summaries of meeting minutes, and preparing documents related to the dissolution of business entities (the "winding up") and litigation. Therefore,

A Day in the Life of a Real Paralegal, found in Chapters 7-13, gives students a real-world look at a career as a paralegal, discussing issues they will face in the workplace.

Key Terms used throughout the chapters are defined in the margin and provided as a list at the end of each chapter. A common set of definitions is used consistently across the McGraw-Hill paralegal titles.

Key Terms

Abandoned property
Adverse possession
Bailee
Bailment
Bailor
Chattel
Deed
Donee
Donor
Easement
Estate in land
Fee simple absolute
Fee simple defeasible
Fixtures
Freehold estate
Future interest
Gift
Gift causa mortis
Gift inter vivos
Grantee
Grantor
Intangible property
Joint te...

Landlord
Life estate
Lost property
Marketable title
Mislaid property
Mutual benefit bailment
Non-freehold estate
Periodic tenancy
Quitclaim deed
Real property fixtures
Remainder
Reversion
Right of survivorship
Survey
Tangible property
Tenancy by the entirety
Tenancy for years
Tenancy in common
Tenant
Title insurance policy
Title search
Trade fixtures
W...nty deed

Discussion Questions and **Exercises** ask students to apply critical thinking skills to the concepts learned in each chapter. The Discussion Questions focus on more specific legal topics and promote dialogue among students. The Exercises introduce hypothetical situations, and students will determine the correct answers using their knowledge of topics presented in the chapter. Both sets of questions are found at the end of each chapter.

Discussion Questions

1. Contact your local paralegal association. Inquire as to what is necessary to become a member of the association. Find out if the association maintains salary surveys for y... market.
2. Find out what your state's rules are regarding certification of legal assistants.
3. What do you think are the most important attributes that a paralegal ought to possess
4. Distinguish the difference between attributes and skills. Which do you think are mor... important for a paralegal in his or her first job as a legal assistant?
5. Locate the classified job advertisements in your local newspaper and search for legal professional jobs. What types of positions are open in your area and how many of th... offered through a legal staffing agency? What other options exist for job searches in ... area? How many require certification?
6. Discuss the advantages and disadvantages of working at a small firm versus a large f... then compare it to a corporate legal department. Which do you prefer?
7. List some reasons why internships are a valuable component of a formal legal educat... Explain how you might search for an internship.
8. Discuss what might occur if neither attorneys nor paralegals were licensed or regulat... the practice of law in your state. Do you think formal licensing and regulation of par... is a good idea?
9. Explain what is meant by a "Chinese wall" and give a factual example of this.

Exercises

1. Barney was the owner in fee simple of Blackacre Farm, which comprised a lar... and garden, and the farm lands, which consisted of two large tracts commonly ... to as the "East Tract" and "West Tract." His will contained the following: "I be... house and the garden to my daughters, Ann, Betty, and Charlotte. I bequeath E... West Tract to be shared by my sons Abel and Ben. Barney died in 2002. All fi... continued to live in the house and the two sons farmed the land. In 2003, Ann ... Germany and needed money, so her sisters each gave her $100,000, agreeing i... was in exchange for her share of the inheritance. Meanwhile, Abel married Di... married Esther. They all lived in the house until quarrels occurred, at which ti... Diane moved out, into town. Ben farmed the land alone until his death in 2004 ... took over the farm. Last month, Betty died. Who now has ownership of the ho... farm?
2. Dudley owns a large area of land, in fee simple, that includes a former hotel w... courts and a barn. The only access to the barn is via a path that runs across the ... to the main road in front of the hotel. In 1995, Dudley sold the barn to Smedle... moving in, Smedley has been using the path every day at 6 a.m. to access the ... main road, without any complaints from Dudley. In April of 2005, Dudley gra... by deed, the right to use the tennis court for 10 years. In May of 2005, Dudley ... courts to Smedley. In June of 2005, Dudley sold the rest of his property, includ... hot... and the remaini... land to Mortimer. Mortimer immediately erects a larg...

A Guided Tour

Crossword puzzles at the end of each chapter utilize the key terms and definitions to help students become more familiar using their legal vocabulary.

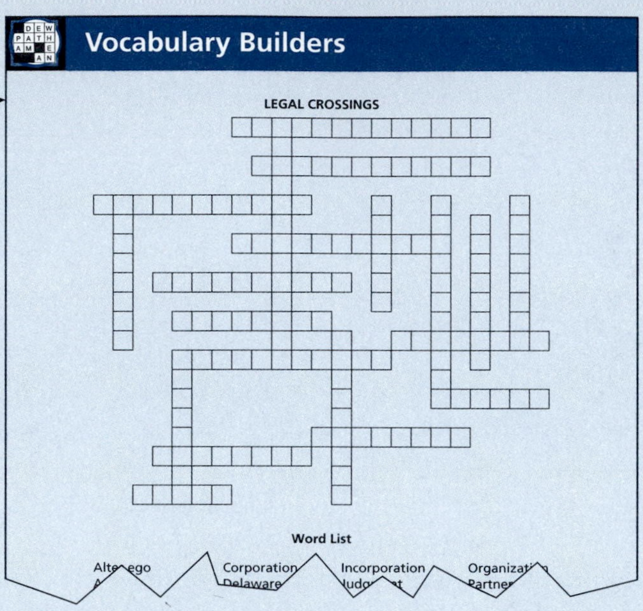

Vocabulary Builders

LEGAL CROSSINGS

Word List

Corporation

Incorporation

SUPPLEMENTS

Instructor's Resource CD-ROM

An **Instructor's Resource CD-ROM (IRCD)** will be available for instructors. This CD provides a number of instructional tools, including PowerPoint presentations for each chapter in the text, an instructor's manual, and an electronic test bank. The instructor's manual assists with the creation and implementation of the course by supplying lecture notes, answers to all exercises, page references, additional discussion questions and class activities, a key to using the PowerPoint presentations, detailed lesson plans, instructor support features, and grading rubrics for assignments. A unique feature, an instructor matrix, is also included which links learning objectives with activities, grading rubrics, and classroom equipment needs. The activities consist of critical thinking and application questions and exercises, research projects, and scenarios with sample legal forms. Instructors will be able to add questions or exercises to the activities and print these as worksheets for the students. The electronic test bank will offer a variety of multiple choice, fill-in-the-blank, true or false, and essay questions, with varying levels of difficulty, and page references.

Online Learning Center

The **Online Learning Center (OLC)** is a Web site that follows the text chapter by chapter. OLC content is ancillary and supplementary material germane to the textbook—as students read the book, they can go online to review material or link to relevant Web sites. Students and instructors can access the Web sites for each of the McGraw-Hill paralegal texts from the main page of the Paralegal Super Site: www.mhhe.com/paralegal. Each OLC has a similar organization. An Information Center features an overview of the text, background on the author, and the Preface and Table of Contents from the book. Instructors can access the instructor's manual and PowerPoint presentations from the IRCD. Students see the Key Terms list from the text as flashcards, as well as additional quizzes and exercises.

The OLC can be delivered multiple ways—professors and students can access the site directly through the textbook Web site, through PageOut, or within a course management system (for example, WebCT, Blackboard, TopClass, or eCollege.)

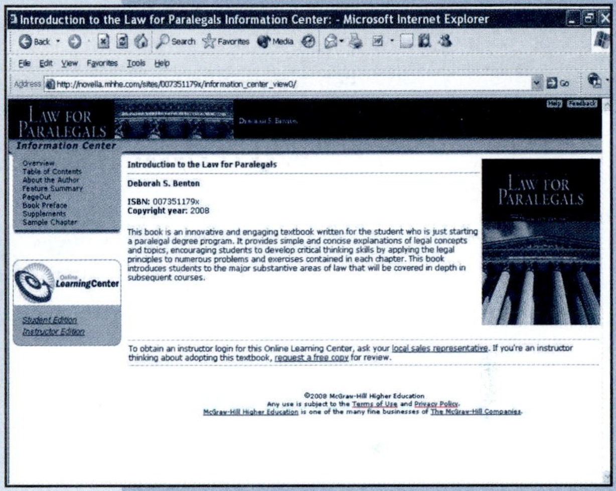

PageOut: McGraw-Hill's Course Management System

PageOut is McGraw-Hill's unique point-and-click course Web site tool, enabling you to create a full-featured, professional-quality course Web site without knowing HTML coding. With PageOut you can post your syllabus online, assign McGraw-Hill Online Learning Center or eBook content, add links to important off-site resources, and maintain student results in the online grade book. You can send class announcements, copy your course site to share with colleagues, and upload original files. PageOut is free for every McGraw-Hill/Irwin user and, if you're short on time, we even have a team ready to help you create your site! To learn more, please visit www.pageout.net.

Acknowledgments

In the preparation of the manuscript for this book, I am grateful to the highly talented staff at McGraw-Hill and at Carlisle Publishing Services for their dedication and confidence in this project. The insight and suggestions provided by everyone from the developmental editor to the reviewers set a high mark and goals that contributed immensely to this work. In particular, I thank the following reviewers for their contributions and suggestions for improvement of the work:

Joyce Becker
Villa Julie Community College

Marisa Campbell
Meredith College

Kay Rute
Washburn University

Melody Schroer
Maryville University

Kathleen Reed
University of Toledo

Sheila Huber
University of Washington

Elizabeth Eiesland
Western Dakota Technical Institute and National American University

Amy Feeney
Wilmington College

Chris Whaley
Roane State Community College

Ernest Davila
San Jacinto College North

Laura Barnard
Lakeland Community College

Carol Halley
National American University

Leslie Miron
Mercy College

Richard Patete
Keiser College—Sarasota Campus

Finally, a special thanks to all my students, whose skillful ability to go "off topic" simply made this entire experience so much more enjoyable. They are a remarkable group of students, inspiring me to write this book and to get it done in the same timely manner in which their assignments were generally completed. Well done!

Deborah S. Benton

Brief Contents

Table of Contents

Chapter 1

Introduction to the Legal System

CHAPTER OBJECTIVES

After reading this chapter, you will be able to:

- Explain the origins of the legal system in the United States.
- Describe the importance of English common law in the development of American substantive law.
- Identify the basic sources of law.
- List and explain the purposes of the three branches of government.
- Describe the structure of the American courts, distinguishing the federal and state levels.

There are many reasons why students decide to undertake a study of the law and choose to enter into a prelaw or a paralegal degree program. Many students are simply interested in the subject, having encountered some aspect of the law from sources such as newspaper articles, high-profile court cases, personal experience, or one of the increasingly popular television shows that feature several court cases decided in a one-hour time slot by a judge. However, many students who seek a formal study of the subject have an intellectual desire to understand the legal rules and principles that govern our society. In acquiring a general understanding of the legal system, students will gain knowledge about the role of paralegals in assisting attorneys, as well as develop skills useful in the legal reasoning process. In approaching this subject, this book presents a synopsis of the basis for the law, provides practice in the method of legal analysis, and then guides the student through an outline of the substantive and procedural areas of the law that will later be studied in depth, in subsequent legal courses. This book has something for everyone. As an introductory text, it presents a highly readable and concise overview of various legal topics, using and developing the student's level of critical thinking necessary to a basic understanding of the subject. Moreover, the key steps to legal analysis that are essential to further study of the law are cultivated throughout this text, using multiple examples and reasoning strategies. As a result, students' research and writing skills are enhanced through the use of the practical exercises in this text.

WHY STUDY THE LAW?

Recognizing that the study of the law is much more than rote memorization of legal rules and principles, this book endeavors to encourage the first-time student of the subject to learn how to think about the law, to apply legal maxims to hypothetical fact situations, and to solve problems. Learning legal rules might seem extremely difficult, but learning legal theory may seem insurmountable. It is one of the objectives of this book to dispel the myth in some students' minds that one must be very adept at memorization in order to be successful in the study and practice of law.

Certainly, one should possess a natural affection for words, as studying the law requires a great amount of reading. In addition, students should be comfortable in their writing skills, and this textbook aims to guide students in their development of clear, concise writing in various styles and formats. However, it is important to emphasize here that it is not necessary to memorize legal tenets, but rather to know how and where to find the relevant law. Then, the student must be able to apply that law to the fact situation at hand. The study of the subject does not, in fact, require an exceptional memory, but rather a sophisticated understanding of how critical thinking skills are necessary to predict the likelihood of success in virtually any legal problem encountered in the future. Therefore, the primary goal of this textbook is to develop the critical thinking skills of the first-time student of the law, while introducing the primary fundamental legal principles that are at the heart of our legal system. In essence, this textbook presents a short explanation of why the law matters, an overview of the key problems arising within the framework of our laws, and the ways in which such problems are resolved.

The starting point for this book is to present a brief introduction to the historical basis for our legal system. This naturally leads to an examination of the sources of law today, as well as who is directing the future development of the law, in terms of the three branches of government. Finally, this introductory chapter gives the student a summary of the courts and their respective functions.

Although there are multiple reasons to study the history of our legal system, in an introductory course the chief reason is to gain perspective on the foundation for our present court system, the relationship between the areas of law, as well as the basis for the legal protections granted under the United States Constitution. In examining each of these concepts individually, one will see that collectively they represent the foundation of American jurisprudence.

WHAT IS "LAW"?

law
A set of rules and principles that govern any society.

Before beginning to understand its origins, it is necessary to define what is meant by the term **law**. In essence, it is a set of rules and principles that govern any society. It is a compilation of rights and duties, providing rules on how people should behave and the remedy for when something happens as a result of not following such rules. Laws serve to govern the conduct of people in society and to provide some formal framework in which to enforce the rules and impose remedies. In sum, its function is to promote justice and correct conduct in a society and to provide the process and set of rules in which to settle disputes.

One might assume that, surely, by now, all aspects of the law are well established, clearly defined principles and therefore there is little discretion and interpretation remaining. Such is not the case. It is necessary to keep in mind that the law is not stagnant, but rather constantly changing in response to societal needs and customs. It is easy to imagine the law as a living, growing thing. Ordinary, reasonable people may accept that "this is a plant," but may not agree on what kind of a plant it is, the plant's classification, or the proper care of the plant. Similarly, ordinary, reasonable people may clearly accept that it is the law to not wear inappropriate clothing in public. However, there may be different interpretations as to specifically what clothing may be inappropriate, the definition of clothing itself, and whether the law applies at all in precise factual situations that require interpretation of the word *public*. A seemingly clearly worded law might provoke different responses; therefore, it should become readily apparent that a study of the law is not for the faint-hearted. Students who expect the "law" to be black and white will be dismayed to discover that the legal profession necessitates living with a certain degree of ambiguity. If this were not the case, and if all legal rules were perfectly unambiguous and easily understood, then the legal profession would be unnecessary, for the law could be simply applied in every given fact situation.

CASE IN POINT

United States District Court,
S.D. Illinois.
Karen BENTLEY, Plaintiff,
v.
Charles SLAVIK and Rosemary Slavik, Defendants.
No. 86-3373.
June 24, 1987.

MEMORANDUM AND ORDER

STIEHL, District Judge:

This cause was tried before the Court, without a jury, on May 26 and 27, 1987. Having heard and considered the evidence and arguments of all parties, the Court makes the following findings of fact and c onclusions of law as required by Rule 52(a) of the Fed.R.Civ.P.

FINDINGS OF FACT

Plaintiff, Karen Bentley, is a citizen of the State of Indiana. Defendants, Charles Slavik and Rosemary Slavik, are citizens of the State of Illinois, who reside within the Southern District of Illinois.

During January, 1984, plaintiff observed, on a bulletin board located at Indiana University, a notice which the defendant, Charles Slavik, asked to be placed there. In the notice, Slavik represented that he had for sale an Auguste Sebastien Philippe Bernardel violin made in 1835 with an appraised value ranging from $15,000 to $20,000.

In response to the notice, plaintiff contacted Slavik by telephone to inquire about the violin. During the telephone conversation, Slavik again represented that he had an authentic 1835 Bernardel violin with an appraised value ranging from $15,000 to $20,000, and invited the plaintiff to visit the defendants at their home in Edwardsville, Illinois, to see the violin.

On January 28, 1984, plaintiff travelled to defendants' home, saw the violin, played and inspected it for at least two hours. During the plaintiff's visit, Charles Slavik again represented to the plaintiff that the violin was an authentic 1835 Auguste Sebastien Philippe Bernardel violin, and further showed her Certificate No. 5500 from one Robert Bernard Tipple dated September 21, 1980, which certificate estimated that the violin was an authentic Auguste Sebastien Philippe Bernardel violin, which had a value of $15,000 to $20,000. Tipple, since deceased, was a violin maker, authenticator, ***738** and appraiser in Mount Vernon, Illinois.

In reliance upon the representations of Slavik, and the certificate presented by him, plaintiff purchased the violin from defendant, Charles Slavik, for $17,500. At that time, plaintiff paid Charles Slavik $15,000 by check, and agreed to pay the balance of $2,500 by February 15, 1984. The bill of sale signed by Slavik referred to the sale of "One Bernardel A.S.P. Violin." The second payment was made by check dated February 13, 1984, mailed from Indiana. A letter which accompanied the $2,500 check expressed the plaintiff's pleasure with the violin. From the date of purchase until the end of 1985, the plaintiff played the violin for an average of eight hours a day.

Sometime in April of 1985, plaintiff became aware that the violin might not be a genuine work of Auguste Sebastien Philippe Bernardel made in 1835. Shortly after the plaintiff became aware the violin might not be a genuine Bernardel, plaintiff made demand upon Charles Slavik to return the purchase price and offered to return the violin, but Slavik refused to do so. Despite this, the plaintiff continued to play the violin until December of 1985.

During the plaintiff's use of the violin it required serious repair. In November of 1984, the top of the violin was removed, a procedure considered "major surgery" in the bowed-stringed-instrument community. The repair was poorly done, and the violin now has adhesive residue visible on its exterior. At this time, the violin has a crack near the fingerboard and a crack under the chin rest. The neck of the violin was recently broken in transit, although it has since been reattached. Finally, the Court finds from the testimony of Professor R. Kent Perry that the violin has a "buzz" due to either the poor repair or the poor condition of the instrument. The Court finds that the violin is in poorer condition now than it was when purchased by the plaintiff.

Although the defendants presented this evidence of the changed condition of the violin with fervor, they presented a theme without a resolution. No evidence was introduced to establish the extent to which the damage and repairs decreased the value of the violin. By failing to complete the theme, the defendants, in effect, leave the Court to speculate as to the measure of the diminution in the value of the violin and thereby improvise the final passage. The Court must, however, decline this offer.

On the crucial question of authenticity, the plaintiff presented the testimony of Lowell Gene Bearden, and the evidence deposition of Frank Passa, both experts in the authentication and appraisal of violins. Bearden, of St. Louis, learned his craft from his father, and has operated his own violin shop for 24 years, where he has crafted three violins. He is a member of the International Society of Violin and Bow Makers, of which there are fewer than 25 members in this country. Frank Passa, of San Francisco, has operated a violin shop for 56 years, serving mostly members of major symphony orchestras. His skill also came under the tutelege of family members. Passa is also a member of the International Society of Violin and Bow Makers, and founded the American Federation of Violin and Bow Makers. Bearden and Passa, while not members of the academic music community, make their living in part from, and have based their reputations on, their ability to correctly identify, authenticate and appraise violins made centuries ago. These men examined the violin in question, and both asserted unequivocally that the instrument is not a Bernardel. They placed its value at between $750 and $2,000.

As counterpoint, defendants offered the testimony of R. Kent Perry, Ph.D., professor of violin and chamber music at Southern Illinois University—Edwardsville. Professor Perry supplemented his testimony by playing brief excerpts from the classics on the violin in question, thereby both educating and entertaining the Court, as had plaintiff at the conclusion of her testimony. While the evidence presented by Professor Perry was helpful to the Court, it is clear that he is not an expert in the field of authenticating violins.

Additional evidence as to the authenticity of the violin as a Bernardel came in the form of the certificate of authenticity issued by Tipple and introduced as a joint exhibit of the parties. Tipple's certificate was less than compelling; it merely stated that it was his "estimation" the violin was a Bernardel.

Defendants also presented the evidence of Mr. Slavik's daughter, Suzanne von Frasunkiewicz, a concert violinist from Brazil, who testified that she had played the violin on tour, found it to be a fine instrument, and believed it to be a Bernardel. Her belief was primarily based on what she had heard over the years in her father's home, and she admitted that she had had no training or experience in authenticating or appraising violins.

The Court finds the evidence presented by plaintiff on the determinative question of authenticity to be the more credible, and finds from a preponderance of the evidence that the violin is not the work of Auguste Sebastien Philipe Bernardel, and that its value at the time of sale was $2,000.

Despite this, the Court finds that Charles Slavik neither purposefully nor willfully misrepresented the maker or value of the violin, though he referred to the instrument as a Bernardel both orally and on the Bill of Sale. Slavik is neither an expert on the masters of violins, nor is he in the business, occupation or vocation of selling violins.

[1] The Court further finds that there has been no evidence that defendant, Rosemary Slavik, had any ownership interest in the violin, nor that she played any role in the sale of the violin to plaintiff. In other words, the sale of this violin was not a duet by the defendants, but rather a solo by Charles Slavik.

CONCLUSIONS OF LAW

This Court has diversity jurisdiction over this action pursuant to 28 U.S.C. § 1332. The amount in controversy exceeds $10,000.

In a diversity action, the choice of law rules of the state in which the district court sits are applied. *Klaxon Co. v. Stentor Electric Mfg.* Co., 313 U.S. 487, 61 S.Ct. 1020, 85 L.Ed. 1477 (1941); *Pittway Corp. v. Lockheed Aircraft Corp.*, 641 F.2d 524, 526 (7th Cir.1981). In contract cases, the Illinois rule is that the law of the place of execution applies when the contract is to be performed in more than one state. *P.S. & E., Inc. v. Selastomer Detroit, Inc.*, 470 F.2d 125, 127 (7th Cir.1972). Because the second payment from Bentley was made from Indiana, the "place of execution" rule will be followed in this case, and Illinois law will be applied by the Court.

[2] The plaintiff alleges in Count I that there were misrepresentations made by the defendants to the plaintiff in violation of the Illinois Consumer Fraud and Deceptive Business Practices Act, (Consumer Fraud Act), Ill.Rev.Stat. ch. 121 1/2, para. 261-272 (1983). After consideration of the Act and relevant case law, it appears the Consumer Fraud Act does not apply to this dispute. Because there was no purposeful misrepresentation on the part of Charles Slavik, the initial portion of Section 2 of the Act does not apply. Ill.Rev.Stat. ch. 121 1/2 , para. 262 (1983). The portion of Section 2 in which the Uniform Deceptive Trade Practices Act (the Uniform Act) is incorporated also does not apply because any alleged violation as described in Section 2 of the Uniform Act must be done by someone "in the course of his business, vocation or occupation. . . ." Ill.Rev.Stat. ch. 121 1/2 , para. 312 (1983).

While there appears to be no case law directly on point, courts have interpreted both the Consumer Fraud Act and the Uniform Act as protecting consumers such as Bentley only "against fraud, unfair methods of competition and deceptive *business* practices." *Frahm v. Urkovich*, 113 Ill.App.3d 580, 69 Ill.Dec. 572, 575, 447 N.E.2d 1007, 1010 (1983), *quoting Scott v. Association for Childbirth at Home, Int'l.*, 88 Ill.2d 279, 288, 58 Ill.Dec. 761, 430 N.E.2d 1012 (1982). From the testimony presented to the Court, there appears to be no evidence that Charles Slavik was in the business of selling violins, nor that he sold the violin to Bentley in the course of his business, vocation or occupation. This being so, the Court must conclude that Section 2 of the Uniform Act does not apply to the plaintiff's allegations, and, therefore, she may not recover under the Consumer Fraud Act on Count I.

[3] In Count II, plaintiff alleges that misrepresentations made by Charles Slavik violated the Illinois Uniform Deceptive Trade Practices Act, Ill.Rev.Stat. ch. 121 para. 312 (1983). A review of the statute and case law shows that the Uniform Act provides only for injunctive relief, *Beard v. Gress*, 90 Ill.App.3d 622, 46 Ill.Dec. 8, 413 N.E.2d 448 (1980), and that attorneys' fees may only be awarded if the Court finds the defendant willfully engaged in deceptive trade practices. The Court has determined in its Findings of Fact that Charles Slavik did not willfully misrepresent the violin's worth to plaintiff. Bentley has not requested injunctive relief. For these reasons the plaintiff may not recover under the Uniform Act on Count II.

The plaintiff alleges in Count III that defendants breached the contract by not delivering a Bernardel. The defendants deny this, and assert that Charles Slavik delivered the violin bargained for and that the contract was ratified through a letter written by the plaintiff on February 13, 1984. Under the Illinois Uniform Commercial Code, Ill.Rev.Stat. ch. 26, para. 2- 313(1)(b) (1983), an express warranty is created at time of sale that the goods sold by a seller will conform to any description of the goods that is a part of the basis of the bargain. The plaintiff, in effect, asserts that the certificate of authentication issued by Tipple and the sellers' reference to the violin as a Bernardel, both orally and in the bill of sale, as well as in the announcement letter posted on the bulletin board, was an express warranty by Charles Slavik to plaintiff.

In a similar dispute arising more than 50 years ago, a California Court of Appeals found that a bill of sale reciting the sale of two violins, a "Stradivarius" and a "Guarnerius," served as a warranty from the seller to the buyer that the violins sold were, in fact, Stradivarius and Guarnerius violins. *Smith v. Zimbalist*, 2 Cal. App.2d 324, 38 P.2d 170 (1934), *hearing denied* by California Supreme Court.

To determine whether a warranty was created under Illinois law, the Court must examine the intent of the parties as expressed in the bill of sale and in the circumstances surrounding the sale itself. *Alan Wood Steel Co. v. Capital Equipment Enterprises, Inc.*, 39 Ill. App.3d 48, 349 N.E.2d 627 (1976). This determination is generally considered a question of fact. *Redmac, Inc. v. Computerland of Peoria*, 140 Ill.App.3d 741, 95 Ill.Dec. 159, 489 N.E.2d 380 (1986). When examining ¶ 2-313(1)(b) of the Illinois Uniform Commercial

Code, courts have used a "basis of the bargain" test which looks to the descriptions or affirmations forming the basic assumption of the bargain between the parties. *Alan Wood*, at 632.

[4][5] From the evidence presented to the Court, it is clear that the description of the violin as a Bernardel, the affirmation created by the seller's repeated use of the term "Bernardel," and the presentation of a certificate of authentication support the conclusion that there existed a basic assumption that the transaction concerned a 1835 Auguste Sebastien Philippe Bernardel violin. The Court finds that ¶ 2-313(1)(b) applies to this dispute, and that a warranty under the statute was created by Charles Slavik. Consistent with the findings of fact, the Court concludes that an Auguste Sebastien Philippe Bernardel violin was not delivered by Charles Slavik to Bentley, and therefore Slavik breached the contract with plaintiff.

[6] The Court further concludes that Bentley's letter to the Slaviks dated February 13, 1984, did not ratify the contract. The concept of ratification includes an understanding and full knowledge of the facts necessary to an intelligent assent. *Black's Law Dictionary* (4th ed. 1968), citing Coe v. Moon, 260 Ill. 76, 102 N.E. 1074, 1076 (1916). There has been no evidence that at the time of the February 13, 1984, letter Bentley knew or had reason to know the violin was not a Bernardel. Therefore, no ratification occurred when plaintiff expressed pleasure with the "Bernardel" in February, 1984.

[7] In defendants' Proposed Findings of Fact and Conclusions of Law, counsel asserted that Bentley should be estopped from rescinding the contract because of her 16 month delay in having the violin inspected. Defendants may assert estoppel against Bentley only if they can show they changed position and suffered a detriment as a result of their reliance on the acts and representations of Bentley. *DeProft v. Heydecker*, 297 Ill. 541, 548, 131 N.E. 114 (1921); *Courson v. The Industrial Commission*, 98 Ill.2d 1, 74 Ill.Dec. 48, 455 N.E.2d 78 (1983). In this case, it is possible that the plaintiff's letter may have misled Slavik into believing she had had the violin authenticated. However, there has been no evidence of any reliance or changed position on the part of Slavik. For this reason, estoppel has not been shown.

[8] The plaintiff claims $20,000 in damages for the breach of contract allegation of Count III. The Court has concluded there was a breach of contract resulting from the warranty created by Slavik. Under Ill.Rev.Stat. ch. 26 ¶ 2-714(2) (1983), "the measure of damages for breach of warranty is the difference at the time and place of acceptance between the value of the goods accepted and the value they would have had if they had been as warranted. . . ." *Id*. The Court has found the violin had a value of $2,000 when sold, and that it was sold for $17,500, a value it would have had were it a Bernardel as warranted.

In this case, the sale may be over, but the warranty lingers on. The plaintiff's measure of damages under Count III, therefore, is $15,500.

Count IV was amended at the close of plaintiff's evidence to allege mutual mistake on the part of buyer and seller. Mutual mistake, as defined in Restatement (Second) of Contracts § 152 (1981), has been recognized in Illinois courts as recently as November, 1986, *Hagenbuch v. Chapin*, 149 Ill.App.3d 572, 102 Ill.Dec. 886, 500 N.E.2d 987 (1986). If a mistake by both parties as to "a basic assumption on which the contract was made has a material effect on the agreed exchange of performance, the contract is voidable by the adversely affected party. . . ." Restatement (Second) of Contracts § 152 (1981). The *Hagenbuch* decision also provides the adversely affected party with the remedy of the return of the excess purchase price. *Hagenbuch*, 102 Ill.Dec. at 890, 500 N.E.2d at 991. It is this relief the plaintiff appears to request.

[9] From the facts already discussed, it appears there did exist a mistake by both parties as to the maker of the violin sold to plaintiff by defendant Charles Slavik. Moreover, it is clear the basic assumption that the violin was a Bernardel materially affected the agreed price, the exchange of performance. Yet it must be determined whether either party assumed the risk of mistake referred to in § 152(1) and explained in § 154, comment c of the Restatement (Second) of Contracts (1981). This Court concludes that neither party assumed the risk.

[10] While the conclusion that Slavik did not assume the risk of mistake is apparent from the facts, a similar conclusion as to plaintiff merits further discussion. Thorough examination of § 154(b) and comment c therein reveals that plaintiff did not bear the risk the violin was not a Bernardel. "Conscious ignorance" is defined in comment c as an awareness of a contracting party prior to agreement that it is unknowledgeable about certain facts that later become the basis for the mutual mistake claim. The party that was aware of the uncertainty prior to the contract may not assert mutual mistake of fact, according to comment c.

The Illinois Supreme Court has long recognized that mutual mistakes of fact may make contracts voidable. *Harley v. Magnolia Petroleum Co.*, 378 Ill. 19, 37 N.E.2d 760 (1941). It is further stated that mutual mistakes must have been unknown at the time the contract is made, and that neither party may have borne the risk of any unknown facts. *Harley*, at 765. It is this voluntary bearing of the risk of unknown facts that the Restatement refers to as "conscious ignorance." The court describes this as a "conscious present want of knowledge of facts" which a party has manifestly concluded will not influence the decision to contract. *Harley*, at 765. Another court has referred to it as an "attitude of indifference." *Southern National Bank of Houston v. Crateo, Inc.*, 458 F.2d 688, 698 (5th Cir.1972). Regardless of the terms used, the Fifth Circuit and the Illinois Supreme Court require a showing that the ignorant party is willing to bear the risk of the unknown facts before that party will be barred from asserting mutual mistake of fact. *Harley*, at 765 and *Southern National Bank*, at 693.

The evidence presented before the Court gives no reason for finding that plaintiff exhibited a willingness to bear the risk that the violin was not a Bernardel. The evidence shows she would not have purchased the violin for the price paid had she not been convinced the violin was a Bernardel. She was not consciously ignorant of, nor did she exhibit an attitude of indifference about, the authenticity of the violin when she purchased the instrument. For these reasons, the Court concludes plaintiff did not bear the risk of mistake under § 154 or § 152 of the Restatement (Second) of Contracts (1981).

[11] The Court therefore concludes that there existed a mutual mistake of fact between defendant, Charles Slavik, and plaintiff, Karen Bentley, and that plaintiff is entitled to return of the excess purchase price paid due to the mutual mistake. The excess price is $15,500, the difference between the $17,500 purchase price, and the value of the violin at the time it was sold, $2,000.

CADENZA

This case gave the Court an insight into the relationship classical musicians develop with their instruments. The plaintiff referred to violins as "living," "breathing" and possessing "souls."

Mr. Slavik spoke of his care of the violin over 33 years of ownership with pride and intensity. It is clear that this dispute concerned more than a simple commercial transaction. The defendant felt his integrity attacked; the plaintiff felt victimized.

While sympathetic, the law is ill-equipped to soothe such emotions. The Court must examine the matter with detachment. Yet, it is this detachment that gives the law a timeless quality similar to that of the music the litigants so love. The law's disinterest gives it consistency, and its consistency, in turn, gives it endurance. It is this enduring quality that the law and great music share. Just as many classic works of music are based on a simple melody, the law of this case is based on a consistent rule: that a seller's description of an item amounts to a warranty that the object sold is as described. Returning to an earlier refrain: the sale may be over, but the warranty lingers on.

FINALE

In summary, the Court finds in favor of defendant, Rosemary Slavik, and against plaintiff, Karen Bentley, on all four counts of plaintiff's complaint. The Court finds in favor of defendant, Charles Slavik, and against plaintiff, Karen Bentley, on Counts I and II of plaintiff's complaint. The Court finds in favor of plaintiff, Karen Bentley, and against defendant, Charles Slavik, on Counts III and IV of plaintiff's complaint, and awards damages in favor of plaintiff, Karen Bentley, and against defendant, Charles Slavik, in the amount of $15,500. The Clerk of the Court is hereby ORDERED to enter judgment accordingly.

IT IS SO ORDERED.

Source: Bentley v. Slavik, 663 F.Supp. 736 (St. Paul, MN: Thomson West). Reprinted with permission from Westlaw.

Consider the United States Constitution, which will be discussed in greater detail later in this chapter. The Constitution sets forth fundamental, legally enforceable rights. Although it was written to clearly articulate basic, fixed rights of the people, it is hard to find any point in the history of court decisions since its inception where judges plainly and consistently defined the law, without some degree of judicial debate as to the interpretation of the words and their application. Because society is constantly changing, questions about the scope of established constitutional rights are continually being posed to the United States Supreme Court for resolution. For example, is there a fundamental, legally enforceable constitutional right to marry someone of the same sex? Consider whether the right to bear arms means that all citizens are free to carry concealed weapons in public at any time. Now, add into the mix the practical reality of an aging judiciary, where at some point, judges must be replaced. Because the political and ideological composition of the nine justices on the Supreme Court is also changing, there is always critical consideration of the interpretation and application of the words in the Constitution.

RESEARCH THIS!

Read the following U.S. Supreme Court opinion: www.law.cornell.edu/supct/pdf/04-1152P.ZO 547 U.S. ________ (2006)

Summarize the holding (the decision) in this case. Consider how the composition of the court influenced the decision reached.

HISTORICAL FOUNDATION OF THE LAW

common law
Judge-made law, the ruling in a judicial opinion.

In England, the "law of the land" is referred to as **common law.** Common law is simply judge-developed law, formulated as cases are decided and legal opinions are issued in these cases. Thus, common law is based on court decisions, as opposed to a formal set of written laws such as statutes. The origin of law in this country is English common law. The appellate courts in the United States have established common law through their published written decisions of cases decided in their jurisdiction.

One interesting account of the history of the common law in England, which provides perspective on how our system of law developed in America, was written by Matthew Hale in the year 1713. Matthew Hale was the lord chief justice of England, a celebrated lawyer, and a dedicated historian. One of his most important legal works was the *History of the Common Law of England*. Excerpted from this work, Hale sets forth the development of common law and then the effect of judicial opinions:

> *The Laws of England may aptly enough be divided into two Kinds, viz. Lex Scripta, the written Law: and Lex non Scripta, the unwritten Law: For although (as shall be shewn hereafter) all the Laws of this Kingdom have some Monuments or Memorials thereof in Writing, yet all of them have not*

their Original in Writing; for some of those Laws have obtain'd their Force by immemorial Usage or Custom, and such Laws are properly call'd Leges non Scriptae, or unwritten Laws or Customs.

Those Laws therefore, that I call Leges Scriptae, or written Laws, are such as are usually called Statute Laws, or Acts of Parliament, which are originally reduced into Writing before they are enacted, or receive any binding Power, every such Law being in the first Instance formally drawn up in Writing, and made, as it were, a Tripartite Indenture, between the King, the Lords and the Commons; for without the concurrent Consent of all those Three Parts of the Legislature, no such Law is, or can be made: But the Kings of this Realm, with the Advice and Consent of both Houses of Parliament, have Power to make New Laws, or to alter, repeal, or enforce the Old. And this has been done in all Succession of Ages. . . .

And when I call those Parts of our Laws Leges non Scriptae, I do not mean as if all those Laws were only Oral, or communicated from the former Ages to the later, merely by Word. For all those Laws have their several Monuments in Writing, whereby they are transferr'd from one Age to another, and without which they would soon lose all kind of Certainty. . . .

The Matters indeed, and the Substance of those Laws, are in Writing, but the formal and obliging Force and Power of them grows by long Custom and Use, as will fully appear in the ensuing Discourse.

For the Municipal Laws of this Kingdom, which I thus call Leges non Scriptae, are of a vast Extant, and indeed include in their Generality all those several Laws which are allowed, as the Rule and Direction of Justice and Judicial Proceedings, and which are applicable to all those various Subjects, about which Justice is conversant. I shall, for more Order, and the better to guide my Reader, distinguish them into Two Kinds, viz.

First, The Common Law, as it is taken in its proper and usual Acceptation.

Secondly, Those particular Laws applicable to particular subjects, Matters or Courts . . .

First, The Common Law does determine what of those Customs are good and reasonable, and what are unreasonable and void. Secondly, The Common Law gives to those Customs, that it adjudges reasonable, the Force and Efficacy of their Obligation. Thirdly, The Common Law determines what is that Continuance of Time that is sufficient to make such a Custom. Fourthly, The Common Law does interpose and authoritatively decide the Exposition, Limits and Extension of such Customs. . . .

Judicial Decisions. *It is true, the Decisions of Courts of Justice, tho' by Virtue of the Laws of this Realm they do bind, as a Law between the Parties thereto, as to the particular Case in Question, 'till revers'd by Error or Attaint, yet they do not make a Law properly so called, (for that only the King and Parliament can do); yet they have a great Weight and Authority in Expounding, Declaring, and Publishing what the Law of this Kingdom is, especially when such Decisions hold a Consonancy and Congruity with Resolutions and Decisions of former Times; and tho' such Decisions are less than a Law, yet they are a greater Evidence thereof than the Opinion of any private Persons, as such, whatsoever.*

To a certain degree, this account may be compared with the development of our legal system in America. English common law was the precursor of common law here. Common law is judicial or case law, derived from the opinions of courts—it is judge-made law. As such, the published appellate court opinions are "common law."

While English common law was adopted to a great extent by our founding fathers, modern law has developed based on written constitutions, statutes, and judicial decisions. When the colonies in America were first settled, before the Revolutionary War, many of the people came from England and thus brought with them the legal philosophies and structure that existed in England at that time. Although they had a basic mistrust and desire to become self-sufficient from their home countries, the settlers nevertheless maintained the basic tenets of English law. American law developed out of the influence of English common law to the extent that the settlers adapted those rules that suited society at that time, discarding that which infringed on their desired rights to be free of burdensome taxation and British military. After the Revolutionary War ended, the colonies worked to establish their own government, balancing the needs of fair representation and the needs of individuals with an effective federal government.

During the Federal Convention in 1787, the delegates planned their new government to include a national judiciary. Article III of the Constitution established a Supreme Court and granted Congress the express authority to decide what other federal courts would be necessary, and the extent of their jurisdiction. The Judiciary Act of 1789 established a federal court system and instituted a three-tier judiciary system: district, appellate, and Supreme Court. Significant to this Act was the establishment of this multitier system, operating alongside state courts. The Act acknowledged the legitimate scope of powers of the state court system, but retained the supremacy of the federal judiciary. Since 1789, Congress has created various courts, established judicial circuits with fixed boundaries, and set up administrative support agencies.

BRANCHES OF GOVERNMENT

Students with a basic foundation in history or politics will recall that there are three branches of government. The U.S. Constitution established the three branches of government, from which a substantial body of substantive and procedural laws have developed. The three branches are: executive, legislative, and judicial. Each of these branches of government is separate and unique, in order to ensure adequate checks and balances are in place, so as to prevent overreaching or an inordinate concentration of power in any one individual branch. This doctrine of **separation of powers** ensures, as our founding fathers wished, that no one branch of government becomes too powerful or overreaching on the rights of the people.

separation of powers
The doctrine that divides the powers of government among the three branches established under the U.S. Constitution.

While the federal government derives its powers from the U.S. Constitution, the state governments have authority under each state's own constitution. States have generally modeled their constitutions on the U.S. Constitution. If there is a conflict between a state law and a right under the U.S. Constitution, the state law is deemed unenforceable; similarly, local laws are subordinate to state laws. The Tenth Amendment to the U.S. Constitution grants all other powers to the states that are not expressly reserved to the federal government.

The Constitution is the fundamental basis for essential human rights, such as life, liberty, and property. Some of the basic protections afforded citizens under the Bill of Rights include the Fourth Amendment—the right to be free of unreasonable search and seizure—and the Fifth Amendment's right against self-incrimination. It has often been argued by constitutional scholars that the protections afforded citizens under the Bill of Rights are not simple technicalities but rather serious procedural safeguards that must be jealously guarded throughout the criminal justice process.

The executive branch of the federal government, established under Article II of the Constitution, consists of the president, who is assisted by numerous established administrative agencies that perform the bulk of the duties concerned with enforcing the law. The president has the power to influence laws in two significant ways. First, the president has the authority to veto legislation that is passed by the legislative branch (Congress). Second, the judges of the Supreme Court are nominated by the president, though their selection must first be confirmed by the Senate body of the legislature prior to confirmation. Since federal judges hold their offices for lifetime tenure, it should be readily apparent that the powers of the executive branch are significant in shaping the course of American jurisprudence. Political ideology may impact judicial decision making, and whether the majority of the bench is conservative or liberal greatly influences the legal reasoning and judicial interpretation, and subsequent decisions rendered on issues ranging from the environment, gun control, to right to life.

The legislature, established under Article I of the Constitution, consists of Congress, which comprises the House of Representatives and the Senate, at the federal level. State governments have similar legislative bodies. Their primary function is to make laws. In theory, legislatures represent the entire population, and therefore the laws passed reflect the customs and needs of society.

Statutes are laws passed by Congress or the state legislatures, as well as local ordinances which are passed by city councils. An example of a statute might be the maximum allowable speed on Highway 83 in the state of Illinois. Another example of a statute might be establishing that it is illegal to carry a concealed weapon. Once the language of a particular statute is approved by the legislature and enacted into law, it is fixed. The statute itself cannot be overruled or amended by the courts; however, courts may construe the meaning of the statute's language. Although statutes are intentionally drafted so as to minimize judicial discretion, the end result is often that some meanings may not be readily understood. Technical language in the statute may be complex, may present ambiguous applications, or may simply use awkward, vague, or intricate language. This may be the result of sloppy drafting by the legislators, or it may be the use of intentionally vague word choices to allow for flexibility of application to unforeseen scenarios. Hence, lawyers flourish, as cases brought into court sometimes hinge on the meaning of a particular statute. The interpretation of the law is reserved to the third branch of government, the judiciary.

Supreme Court of New Hampshire.
In the Matter of David G. BLANCHFLOWER and Sian E. Blanchflower.
No. 2003-050.
Argued July 16, 2003.
Opinion Issued Nov. 7, 2003.

Brock, C.J., and Broderick, J., filed a dissenting opinion.

NADEAU, J.

Robin Mayer, co-respondent in the divorce proceedings of the petitioner, David G. Blanchflower, and the respondent, Sian E. Blanchflower, challenges an order of the Lebanon Family Division (*Cyr*, J.) denying her motion to dismiss the petitioner's amended ground for divorce of adultery. *See* RSA 458:7, II (Supp.2002). We accepted this matter as an interlocutory appeal under Supreme Court Rule 8, and now reverse and remand.

The record supports the following facts. The petitioner filed for divorce from the respondent on grounds of irreconcilable differences. He subsequently moved to amend the petition to assert the fault ground of adultery under RSA 458:7, II. Specifically, the petitioner alleged that the respondent has been involved in a "continuing adulterous affair" with the co-respondent, a woman, resulting in the irremediable breakdown of the parties' marriage. The co-respondent sought to dismiss the amended petition, contending that a homosexual relationship between two people, one of whom is married, does not constitute adultery under RSA 458:7, II. The trial court disagreed, and the co-respondent brought this appeal.

Before addressing the merits, we note this appeal is not about the status of homosexual relationships in our society or the formal recognition of homosexual unions. The narrow question before us is whether a homosexual sexual relationship between a married person and another constitutes adultery within the meaning of RSA 458:7, II.

RSA 458:7 provides, in part: "A divorce from the bonds of matrimony shall be decreed in favor of the innocent party for any of the following causes: ... II. Adultery of either party." The statute does not define adultery. *Id*. Accordingly, we must discern its meaning according to our rules of statutory construction.

[1][2] "In matters of statutory interpretation, this court is the final arbiter of the intent of the legislature as expressed in the words of a statute considered as a whole." *Wegner v. Prudential Prop. & Cas. Ins. Co.*, 148 N.H. 107, 108, 803 A.2d 598 (2002) (quotation omitted). We first look to the language of the statute itself and, where terms are not defined therein, "we ascribe to them their plain and ordinary meanings." *Id.*

The plain and ordinary meaning of adultery is "voluntary sexual intercourse between a married man and someone other than his wife or between a married woman and someone other than her husband." *Webster's Third New International Dictionary 30* (unabridged ed.1961). Although the definition does not specifically state that the "someone" with whom one commits adultery must be of the opposite gender, it does require sexual intercourse.

The plain and ordinary meaning of sexual intercourse is "sexual connection esp. between humans: COITUS, COPULATION." *Webster's Third New International Dictionary* 2082. Coitus is defined to require "insertion of the penis in the vagina[ ]," *Webster's Third New International Dictionary* 441, which clearly can only take place between persons of the opposite gender.

[3] We also note that "[a] law means what it meant to its framers and its mere repassage does not alter that meaning." *Appeal of Naswa Motor Inn*, 144 N.H. 89, 91, 738 A.2d 349 (1999) (quotation omitted). The statutory compilation in which the provision now codified as RSA 458:7 first appeared is the Revised Statutes of 1842. *See RS 148:3* (1842). No definition of adultery was contained in that statute. *See id*. Our cases from that approximate time period, however, support the inference that adultery meant intercourse. *See Adams v. Adams*, 20 N.H. 299, 301 (1850); *Burns v. Burns*, 68 N.H. 33, 34, 44 A. 76 (1894).

Cases from this period also indicate that adultery as a ground for divorce was equated with the crime of adultery and was alleged as such in libels for divorce. *See, e.g., Sheafe v. Sheafe*, 24 N.H. 564, 564 (1852); *White v. White*, 45 N.H. 121, 121 (1863). Although the criminal adultery statute in the 1842 compilation also did not define adultery, *see RS 219:1* (1842), roughly contemporaneous case law is instructive: "Adultery is committed whenever there is an intercourse from which spurious issue may arise...." *State v. Wallace*, 9 N.H. 515, 517 (1838); *see also State v. Taylor*, 58 N.H. 331, 331 (1878) (same). As "spurious issue" can only arise from intercourse between a man and a woman, criminal adultery could only be committed with a person of the opposite gender.

[4] We note that the current criminal adultery statute still requires sexual intercourse: "A person is guilty of a class B misdemeanor if, being a married person, he engages in sexual intercourse with another not his spouse or, being unmarried, engages in sexual intercourse with another known by him to be married." RSA 645:3 (1996). Based upon the foregoing, we conclude that adultery under RSA 458:7, II does not include homosexual relationships.

We reject the petitioner's argument that an interpretation of adultery that excludes homosexual conduct subjects homosexuals and heterosexuals to unequal treatment, "contrary to New Hampshire's public policy of equality and prohibition of discrimination based on sex and sexual orientation." Homosexuals and heterosexuals engaging in the same acts are treated the same because our interpretation of the term "adultery" excludes all non-coital sex acts, whether between persons of the same or opposite gender. The only distinction is that persons of the same gender cannot, by definition, engage in the one act that constitutes adultery under the statute.

The petitioner also argues that "[p]ublic policy would be well served by applying the same law to a cheating spouse, whether the promiscuous spouse chooses a paramour of the same sex or the opposite sex." This argument is tied to the premise, as argued by the petitioner, that "[t]he purpose underlying [the adultery] fault ground is based upon the fundamental concept of marital loyalty and public policy's disfavor of one spouse's violation of the marriage contract with another."

[5][6] We have not, however, seen any such purpose expressed by the legislature. As noted above, the concept of adultery was premised upon a specific act. To include in that concept other acts of a sexual nature, whether between heterosexuals or homosexuals, would change beyond recognition this well-established ground for divorce and likely lead to countless new marital cases alleging adultery, for strategic purposes. In any event, "it is not the function of the judiciary to provide for present needs by an extension of past legislation." *Naswa Motor Inn*, 144 N.H. at 92, 738 A.2d 349 (quotation and brackets omitted). Similarly, "we will not undertake the extraordinary step of creating legislation where none exists. Rather, matters of public policy are reserved for the legislature." In the *Matter of Plaisted & Plaisted*, 149 N.H. 522, 526, 824 A.2d 148 (2003).

The dissent defines adultery not as a specific act of intercourse, but as "extramarital intimate sexual activity with another." This standard would permit a hundred different judges and masters to decide just what individual acts are so sexually intimate as to meet the definition. The dilemma faced by Justice Stewart and his fellow justices applying their personal standards to the issue of pornography in movies demonstrates the value of a clear objective definition of adultery in marital cases. *See Jacobellis v. Ohio*, 378 U.S. 184, 84 S.Ct. 1676, 12 L.Ed.2d 793 (1964).

We are also unpersuaded by the dissent's contention that "[i]t is improbable that the legislature intended to require an innocent spouse in a divorce action to prove the specific intimate sexual acts in which the guilty spouse engaged." Citing *Jeanson v. Jeanson*, 96 N.H. 308, 309, 75 A.2d 718 (1950), the dissent notes that adultery usually has no eyewitnesses and therefore "ordinarily must be proved by circumstantial evidence." While this is true, it does not support the dissent's point. For over a hundred and fifty years judges, lawyers and clients have understood that adultery meant intercourse as we have defined it. It is an act determined not by the subjective test of an individual justice but by an objective determination based upon the facts. What must be proved to establish adultery and what evidence may be used to prove it are separate issues. Adultery cases have always required proof of the specific sexual act engaged in, namely, sexual intercourse. That circumstantial evidence may be used to establish the act does not negate or undermine the requirement of proof that the act actually occurred. "*Jeanson* is no authority for the proposition that evidence justifying nothing more than suspicion will suffice to prove the adultery suspected." *Yergeau v. Yergeau*, 132 N.H. 659, 663, 569 A.2d 237 (1990)....

Reversed and remanded.

DALIANIS and DUGGAN, J.J., concurred; BROCK, C.J., and BRODERICK, J., dissented.

BROCK, C.J., and BRODERICK, J., dissenting.

We agree with the majority that this appeal is "not about the status of homosexual relationships in our society or the formal recognition of homosexual unions." These issues are not remotely before us. We respectfully dissent because we believe that the majority's narrow construction of the word "adultery" contravenes the legislature's intended purpose in sanctioning fault-based divorce for the protection of the injured spouse. *See Appeal of Mikell*, 145 N.H. 435, 439-40, 764 A.2d 892 (2000).

To strictly adhere to the primary definition of adultery in the 1961 edition of *Webster's Third New International Dictionary* and a corollary definition of sexual intercourse, which on its face does not require coitus, is to avert one's eyes from the sexual realities of our world. While we recognize that "we first look to the plain and ordinary meaning of words to interpret our statutes [,] ... it is one of the surest indexes of a mature and developed jurisprudence not to make a fortress out of the dictionary; but to remember that statutes always have some purpose or object to accomplish." *Appeal of Ashland Elec. Dept.*, 141 N.H. 336, 341, 682 A.2d 710 (1996) (citations and quotation omitted).

New Hampshire permits both fault-based and no-fault divorces. No-fault divorces are governed by RSA 458:7-a (Supp.2002), which permits divorce "irrespective of the fault of either party, on the ground of irreconcilable differences which have caused the irremediable breakdown of the marriage." RSA 458:7 (Supp.2002) governs fault-based divorce. Unlike no-fault divorces, a fault-based divorce presumes that there is an innocent and a guilty spouse, and permits divorce "in favor of the innocent party" for any of nine possible causes, including impotency, adultery, extreme cruelty, felony conviction for which a party has been imprisoned, habitual drunkenness, and abandonment. RSA 458:7, I-IV, VII, IX. Under our fault-based law, the innocent spouse is entitled to a divorce because the guilty spouse has breached a marital covenant, such as the covenant to be sexually faithful. *Cf.* 3 C. Douglas, *New Hampshire Practice, Family Law* § 2.14, at 46 (3d ed.2002).

The purpose of permitting fault-based divorces is to provide some measure of relief to an innocent spouse for the offending conduct of a guilty spouse. *See Robinson v. Robinson*, 66 N.H. 600, 610, 23 A. 362 (1891). The law allows the court to consider fault in assessing the equitable division of the marital assets, *see* RSA 458:16-a, II(*l*) (1992), and in so doing, as in the case of adultery, seeks to justly resolve the unseemly dissolution of a confidential and trusting relationship. We should therefore view the purpose and fabric of our divorce law in a meaningful context, as the legislature presumably intended, and not so narrow our focus as to undermine its public goals. *See S.B. v. S.J.B.*, 258 N.J.Super. 151, 609 A.2d 124, 126 (1992).

From the perspective of the injured spouse, the very party fault-based divorce law is designed to protect, "[a]n extramarital relationship . . . is just as devastating . . . irrespective of the specific sexual act performed by the promiscuous spouse or the sex of the new paramour." *Id.* Indeed, to some, a homosexual betrayal may be more devastating. Accordingly, consistent with the overall purpose of New Hampshire's fault-based divorce law, we would interpret the word "adultery" in RSA 458:7, II to mean a spouse's extramarital intimate sexual activity with another, regardless of the specific intimate sexual acts performed, the marital status, or the gender of the third party. *See id.* at 127.

The majority intimates that to construe adultery to include homosexual conduct invades the exclusive province of the legislature to establish public policy. We recognize that questions of public policy are reserved for the legislature. *See Minuteman, LLC v. Microsoft Corp.*, 147 N.H. 634, 641-42, 795 A.2d 833 (2002). Questions of statutory interpretation are our domain, however. *See Cross v. Brown*, 148 N.H. 485, 486, 809 A.2d 785 (2002). We do not intend to add a new cause of action for divorce, which is a purely legislative responsibility. *See S.B.*, 609 A.2d at 126.

Defining the word "adultery" to include intimate extramarital homosexual sexual activity by a spouse is consonant with the decisions of other courts that have considered this issue. *See Patin v. Patin*, 371 So.2d 682, 683 (Fla.Dist.Ct.App.1979); *Owens v. Owens*, 247 Ga. 139, 274 S.E.2d 484, 485- 86 (1981); S.B., 609 A.2d at 126-27; *RGM v. DEM*, 306 S.C. 145, 410 S.E.2d 564, 566-67 (1991). In *Patin*, 371 So.2d at 683, for instance, the court ruled that there was "no substantial distinction" between homosexual extramarital sexual activity and heterosexual extramarital sexual activity "because both involve extra-marital sex and therefore marital misconduct." Similarly, in S.B., 609 A.2d at 127, the court concluded that sexual intimacy with another, regardless of whether the intimacy is with a person of one's own or a different gender, constitutes adultery.

The decision in *RGM* is particularly instructive. The law at issue there, like the divorce law at issue in this case, included adultery as a ground for divorce, but did not define it. South Carolina followed "the common-law concept of adultery as illicit intercourse between two persons, at least one of whom is married to someone other than the sexual partner." *RGM*, 410 S.E.2d at 566. This concept is similar to the New Hampshire Criminal Code definition of adultery. The appellant in *RGM* argued that her lesbian conduct was not adulterous because it was homosexual. *See id.* at 566-67. The court rejected this argument "as unduly narrow and overly dependent upon the term sexual intercourse." *Id.* at 567. The court ruled that explicit extramarital sexual activity constituted adultery, regardless of whether it is of a homosexual or heterosexual nature. We find this reasoning persuasive.

The majority suggests that to define "adultery" so as to include intimate extramarital homosexual sexual activity by a spouse is to propose a test so vague as to be unworkable. Apparently, a similar test has been adopted in the three jurisdictions previously cited and remains good law. Further, while such a definition is more inclusive than one reliant solely upon heterosexual sexual intercourse, we do not believe that "intimate extramarital sexual activity" either requires a more explicit description or would be subject to such a widely varying judicial view. As Justice Stewart stated with regard to defining the term "hard-core pornography,"

> I shall not today attempt further to define the kinds of material I understand to be embraced within that short-hand description; and perhaps I could never succeed in intelligibly doing so. But I know it when I see it....

Jacobellis v. Ohio, 378 U.S. 184, 197, 84 S.Ct. 1676, 12 L.Ed.2d 793 (1964) (Stewart, J., concurring).

We believe that the majority's interpretation of the word "adultery" is overly narrow in scope. It is improbable that our legislature intended to require an innocent spouse in a divorce action to prove the specific intimate sexual acts in which the guilty spouse engaged. There are usually no eyewitnesses to adultery. *See Jeanson v. Jeanson*, 96 N.H. 308, 309, 75 A.2d 718 (1950). It ordinarily must be proved by circumstantial evidence. *See id.* Nor does it seem reasonable that the legislature intended to allow a guilty spouse to defend against an adultery charge by arguing that, while he or she engaged in intimate sexual activity with another, the relationship was not adulterous because it did not involve coitus. It is hard to comprehend how the legislature could have intended to exonerate a sexually unfaithful or even promiscuous spouse who engaged in all manner of sexual intimacy, with members of the opposite sex, except sexual intercourse, from a charge of adultery. Sexual infidelity should not be so narrowly proscribed.

It is much more likely that our legislature intended the innocent spouse to establish adultery through circumstantial evidence showing, by a preponderance of the evidence, that the guilty spouse had engaged in intimate sexual activity outside of the marriage, regardless of the specific sexual acts involved or the gender of the guilty spouse's lover. Under our fault-based divorce law, a relationship is adulterous because it occurs outside of marriage and involves intimate sexual activity, not because it involves only one particular sexual act. Accordingly, we respectfully dissent.

Source: In the Matter re: Blanchflower, 150 N.H. 226, 834 A.2d 1010 (St. Paul, MN: Thomson West). Reprinted with permission from Westlaw.

While it is important for the legislature to represent the population as a whole, so that justice is served in balancing the rights and duties of the people, it is equally imperative that fairness prevails when such laws are applied and administered. The power to interpret and apply the law rests with the judicial branch, established under Article III of the Constitution. One of the most significant functions of the U.S. Supreme Court is to ensure that laws passed by Congress are in conformity with the U.S. Constitution; if not, then the law is invalid. Again, the federal courts operate alongside state courts, and therefore, the decision as to which court has the authority to decide a case is largely governed by the powers reserved to the federal government by the Constitution. Sometimes, both federal and state courts have concurrent authority to decide a particular case, and this situation will be addressed in Chapter 2, "Jurisdiction." The judiciary branch of government gives power to the judges to resolve disputes, either by illuminating existing legal doctrines or by adding to the increasingly large body of case law.

Whether the Constitution is interpreted narrowly or broadly by the U.S. Supreme Court largely depends on the background and ideologies of the nine justices that make up the court. As noted previously, the composition of the court greatly influences the manner and direction in which laws are read. When the framers of the Constitution drafted its provisions, there was a delicate balance in choosing the precise language that would be read by future generations. In this sense, the Constitution has sometimes been called "a living document." Some of the provisions in the

Constitution leave little room for judicial interpretation, and thus have withstood scrutiny and amendment over the years. Other provisions were drafted such that significant judicial discretion was possible. Practically speaking, the framers could not have possibly foreseen every factual situation that might give rise to a question of rights. Thus, when drafting certain provisions in general terms, the framers allowed for flexibility and possible multiple interpretations, based on changing societal customs and circumstances. For example, it is unlikely that the Constitutional fathers would have foreseen the possibility of wiretapping and electronic surveillance of citizens. However, such a question arises today in the context of a citizen's right to privacy balanced against the need for homeland security, in the aftermath of the September 11 tragedy. The composition of the Supreme Court will affect the answer to such a question. One Court may use a literal construction of the Constitution to determine the answer, whereas another Court may utilize a broader interpretation of the same document.

SOURCES OF LAW

case law
Published court opinions of federal and state appellate courts.

stare decisis
The judicial process of adhering to prior case decisions.

precedent
The holding of past court decisions that are followed in future judicial cases where similar facts and legal issues are present.

statutory law
Primary source of law consisting of the body of legislative law.

statutes
Written laws enacted by the legislative branches of both federal and state governments.

United States Constitution
The fundamental law of the United States of America, which became the law of the land in March of 1789.

administrative law
The body of law governing administrative agencies, that is those agencies created by Congress or state legislatures, such as the Social Security Administration.

uniform statute
Model legislation drafted by the National Conference of Commissioners on Uniform State Laws, dealing with areas of the law such as sales transactions.

Students who have seen some of the "court television" programs that are popular during daytime television programming may have considered how these television judges decide the cases. Viewers are reminded that these are actual cases with real litigants, who have chosen to dismiss their court cases and have their disputes settled in the television court forum. This court is presided over by a judge, but how are these disputes settled in a time slot averaging less than 15 minutes? Surely, we say, actual court cases are typically long, drawn-out trials that may take days or weeks to resolve. So, one may assume that the cases are decided by the judges based on nothing more than the likeability or credibility of the parties. Instead, however, these cases are actually decided on established legal principles, from the relevant jurisdiction, derived from one of the primary sources of law in today's legal systems—case law.

There are essentially five sources of law. **Case law** is one primary source of law, and it is the basis for the doctrine of legal **precedent,** or **stare decisis. Stare decisis** literally means "to stand by the decision." This doctrine will be discussed in Chapter 4. Judicial decisions, or "case law," are simply legal opinions issued by appellate courts, at both the state and federal levels. Such opinions either interpret statutory law, administrative regulations, or otherwise clarify the laws where legal principles have not been codified in statutes.

Laws are drafted so as to anticipate the social needs and actions of the citizens, and thus criminal law, for example, is codified into statutes. **Statutory law** is the *second* primary source of law. **Statutes** are but one formal written enactment of laws that are drafted by the legislature. Federal statutes are drafted by Congress, whereas state statutes originate in each state's legislature. Like common law, statutes serve the purpose of defining limits and governing the acts of people in a society.

The **United States Constitution** is the *third* primary source of law and is sometimes referred to as the supreme law of the land because its provisions take priority over any other law or statute. This is expressly noted in Article VI of the Constitution. In addition, states also have their own constitutions, modeled after the U.S. Constitution, but enumerating provisions that will not conflict with it. Essentially, there are three sources for state law: the state's constitution, statutes, and common law, otherwise referred to as case law in that state's jurisdiction.

A *fourth* source of law is **administrative regulations** or codes. Administrative agencies are sometimes called the fourth branch of government, and are established to assist the president in governing the country and enforcing laws. Examples of administrative agencies include the Social Security Administration and the Equal Employment Opportunity Commission. It has been said that rules and regulations promulgated by various agencies are often written in language that requires an expert in the field to interpret. Administrative law judges conduct hearings on behalf of the various government agencies.

Finally, the *fifth* source of law is **uniform statutes** adopted by many states in order to maintain consistency in enforcement of laws in areas such as sales and contracts. These uniform statutes are not law until they are formally adopted by the state legislature. Each state legislature has the ultimate power: it may decide to adopt the uniform act in whole, modify it, adopt some of it, or adopt none of it. Once some or all of a code or act is adopted, it is then incorporated into that state's code, such as the Illinois Revised Statutes. Examples of this fifth source of law include the Uniform Commercial Code and the Model Business Corporation Act.

HIERARCHY OF COURTS

Courts, as a component of the judicial branch of government, provide the mechanism by which to settle disputes between parties. The structure of the court system is similar at both the federal and state levels. Indeed, in terms of the naming of the levels, the only difference comes at the lowest court level. In most states, and in all federal courts, it is a three-tier system, composed of the trial court, court of appeals, and supreme court. The trial court is ordinarily where all cases begin, and thus it is said that this court has original jurisdiction. **Original jurisdiction** simply means the authority of a court to hear a particular case when it is filed; that is, it is heard there first. At this level, the court is responsible for determining the facts and then applying the relevant law to the established facts. When cases go to trial, questions of fact are in dispute. In other words, the courts are asked to ascertain what actually occurred that precipitated the case and to then weigh the credibility of the evidence presented by both sides. If a judge is hearing the case, this is referred to as a **bench trial**; if a jury is determining the facts, then it is a **jury trial**. In either situation, the judge is ultimately responsible for settling questions of what is the applicable law in the given fact situation. This necessitates ruling on what is the relevant law and how it must be applied to the facts at hand. In a jury trial, the judge instructs the jury on the relevant rules of law to be applied to the case they are deciding.

original jurisdiction
Authority of a court to hear a case first.

bench trial
Case is decided by the judge.

jury trial
Case is decided by a jury.

At the state level, the lowest court is simply the trial court or circuit court. At the federal level, the lowest court is called the U.S. District Court. This court is in essence the trial court, as nearly all federal cases begin at this level. Every state has at least one federal district court, with larger states having several courts, and there are a total of more than 90 United States district courts. These courts, being courts of limited jurisdiction, may hear only those cases that are specifically designated and authorized under the Constitution. These courts were created by Congress and adhere to the legal precedents established by the highest federal courts. They hear cases ranging from diversity (between citizens of different states) to cases between states. Further discussion of jurisdiction is in subsequent chapters.

The next level of court is the **appellate court**, or the court of appeals. In some states which have a two-tier legal system, there is only one higher court of appeals. The function of the appellate court is limited to reviewing the trial court proceedings to ascertain whether any errors of law were made by the trial court. At this level, no evidence may be heard or received, as the trial court has sole responsibility to determine the facts and weigh the evidence. The appellate court may only look at the process used in the determination of the case at the lower court level. In other words, it may only examine the questions of law, reviewing the trial court record. This court is not permitted to consider questions of fact, so it only considers procedural errors that warrant reversal of the trial court decision, or remand for consideration of designated procedural issues.

appellate court
The court of appeals that reviews a trial court's record for errors.

When cases originate in federal district courts, such cases are appealed to a federal court of appeals, of which there are 13, including the appeals court for the federal circuit. This court only hears appeals involving claims against the federal government, patents, and federal employment cases. As noted in the map in Figure 1.1, the country is divided into thirteen circuits. A **circuit** is the term formally applied to the U.S. Courts of Appeal, and commonly used by the numerical designation, as in the Court of Appeals for the 2nd Circuit. However, in general, the term circuit simply means one of several courts in a specific jurisdiction. See Figure 1.1 for a map showing the boundaries of the U.S. Courts of Appeals and the U.S. District Courts.

circuit
One of several courts in a specific jurisdiction.

In every instance, each court acts independently of other state courts, or other federal circuits, with the exception of the U.S. Supreme Court, whose decisions are binding on all other courts. Otherwise, the decisions rendered by the highest court in any given jurisdiction are binding on

You Be the Judge

Road Runner owns Acme Dynamite Company and owns the United States patent for an exploding barrel. Road Runner agrees to license the exploding barrel to Coyote Productions for a term of three months, in exchange for a share of the profits generated by this licensing agreement. When the three months is over, Coyote refuses to pay Road Runner its profit share. If Road Runner sues Coyote in federal district court, is this the proper court to hear the case? Explain.

CYBER TRIP

Here are some interesting Web sites that are hosted by the federal government:
www.usdoj.gov
www.fedcir.gov
www.house.gov
www.uscourts.gov

writ of certiorari
Granting of petition, by the U.S. Supreme Court, to review a case.

all lower courts within that same jurisdiction. This concept of jurisdiction and authority will be discussed further in Chapter 2.

It should be noted that when cases are heard in the federal circuit, it is generally the U.S. Court of Appeals that issues the final decision in the matter. It is extremely rare that cases get past this level, as the U.S. Supreme Court is seldom required to review a case on appeal. If requested to consider a case, the Court requires the appellant (the party appealing the decision from a lower court) to petition for a **writ of certiorari**. This is a request for the Court to review the matter, but by and large the case must present a unique legal issue or involve constitutional rights for the Court to agree to hear it. Practically speaking, there are just nine justices and only one U.S. Supreme Court, and therefore the Court is extremely limited in the number of cases it can accept in any given year. Five out of nine justices must agree to hear a particular case, and approximately 150 cases are decided each year by the Court.

Thus, the principal types of cases that may be heard in the U.S. Supreme Court are:

- Cases of original jurisdiction (described below).
- Cases on appeal from lower federal courts, if granted by writ of certiorari.
- Cases on appeal from state supreme courts involving unique federal issues or issues regarding constitutional rights.

It is necessary to recognize that the federal court system is separate and independent of each state's court system. (See Figure 1.2 for a flowchart showing the federal court system, and see Figure 1.3 for a flowchart showing the state court system.) Therefore, cases that begin in the lowest court of each system are appealed to the next highest court in that system. The third level, the highest court in the state court system, is the state supreme court. Again, no new testimony or evidence may be heard at this level, and decisions rendered at this level are final.

FIGURE 1.1 **Geographic Boundaries of the U.S. Courts of Appeals and the U.S. District Courts**

Source: From the U.S. Courts Web site: www.uscourts.gov/images/CircuitMap.pdf.

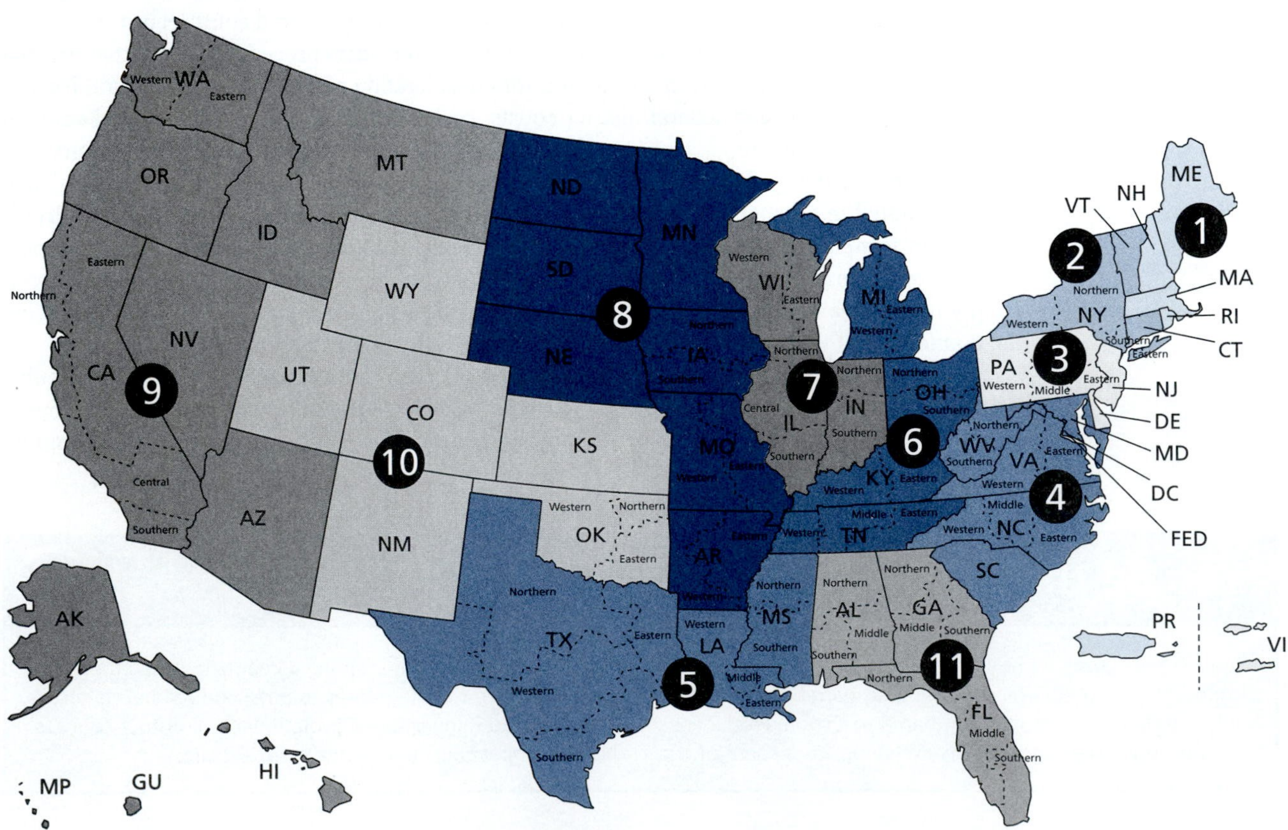

The U.S. Supreme Court has original jurisdiction in certain cases. Such cases involve the U.S. government, where one of the parties to the case is a state or public official, such as an ambassador. In any event, it is possible that there is concurrent jurisdiction, which means that a case has the possibility to be heard in either a federal or a state court; this topic will be discussed in detail in Chapter 2.

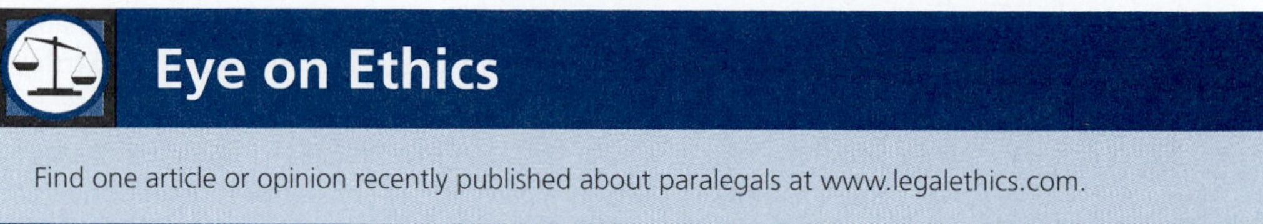

Find one article or opinion recently published about paralegals at www.legalethics.com.

FIGURE 1.2
Federal Court System

United States Supreme Court
Article III of the U.S. Constitution created this highest appellate court. Hears appeals from federal courts and also state courts if a federal question is involved. Nine justices sit en banc and hear approximately 150–200 cases each year. Judges appointed for life tenure by the President of the United States. See www.supremecourtus.gov/ or www.uscourts.gov/.

U.S. Courts of Appeals
Intermediate-level appellate court, twelve regional circuits. These courts decide questions of law after reading briefs and hearing oral arguments.

U.S. Court of Appeals for the Federal Circuit
Created by Congress in 1982. Hears appeals from specialty courts and administrative agencies.

Federal Agencies
Equal Employment Opportunity Commission, Environmental Protection Agency, and other administrative agencies.

U.S. Claims Court
Hears federal cases over $10,000.

U.S. Court of International Trade

Administrative Law Judges
Conduct hearings and submit reports and recommendations to administrative boards or agencies.

Administrative Agencies
Social Security Administration, Patent and Trademark Board, and other agencies.

U.S. District Courts
Courts of general jurisdiction, trial court level, 94 districts. Authority to hear all types of civil and criminal cases. Minimum of one district court for each of the 50 states.

U.S. Magistrate Judges
Supervise court calendars, handle procedural matters, and hear minor criminal and civil cases.

Bankruptcy Judges
Hear bankruptcy cases, enter final judgment; in some cases, submit findings to district.

Which cases are heard in federal court, rather than in a state court, depends on the type of issue and parties involved. Generally, the three fact situations where a case will be heard in federal court are:

- Issues involving a federal question, such as constitutional rights, for example, matters involving one's freedom of speech.
- Controversies in which the parties have diversity of citizenship and the matter in dispute exceeds $75,000. (Note: *Diversity of citizenship* is when the parties to the case are residents of two different states or a foreign country.)
- Crimes or suits in which the U.S. government is a litigant. For example, if one robs the local bank, the United States is a party to the suit, since it regulates banking laws.

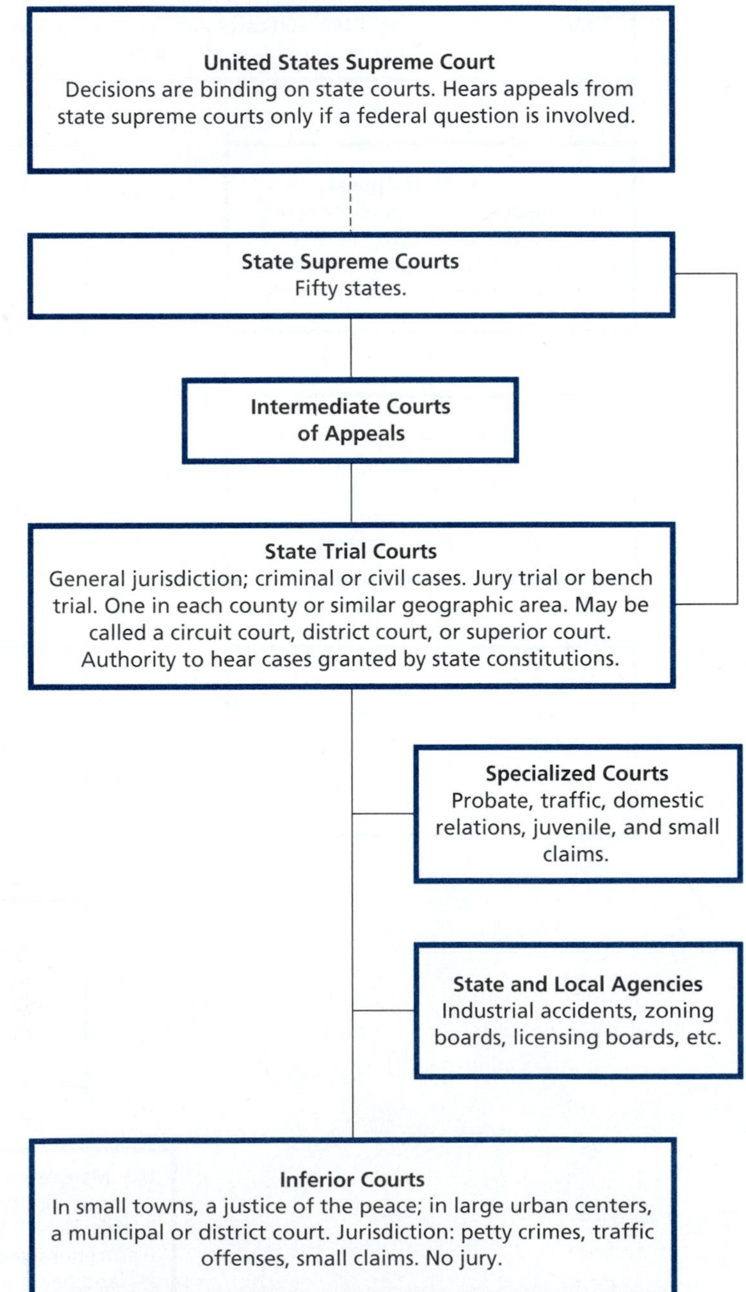
United States Supreme Court
Decisions are binding on state courts. Hears appeals from state supreme courts only if a federal question is involved.
State Supreme Courts
Fifty states.
Intermediate Courts of Appeals
State Trial Courts
General jurisdiction; criminal or civil cases. Jury trial or bench trial. One in each county or similar geographic area. May be called a circuit court, district court, or superior court. Authority to hear cases granted by state constitutions.
Specialized Courts
Probate, traffic, domestic relations, juvenile, and small claims.
State and Local Agencies
Industrial accidents, zoning boards, licensing boards, etc.
Inferior Courts
In small towns, a justice of the peace; in large urban centers, a municipal or district court. Jurisdiction: petty crimes, traffic offenses, small claims. No jury.

FIGURE 1.3
State Court Systems
Most states have a three-tiered judicial system, but some states maintain only one level of appellate court, rather than two levels. The name of the highest court of a state is generally the "state supreme court," although a few states call their highest court the "court of appeals." Appeals to the highest state court may be either discretionary or by right, depending on the type of case.

In terms of jurisdiction of the federal courts, the United States is divided into 13 geographic regions, and these are referred to as the federal judicial circuits. (See the judicial map in Figure 1.1.) The power to hear specific cases that is not reserved for the federal courts is left to each state's court system.

Although the federal government must get its power directly from a specific constitutional article or amendment, such as the express power to collect taxes, the states are free to make any laws necessary for its citizens' welfare, so long as the laws don't conflict with any law under the Constitution. Hence, the state courts are able to hear any type of case. Approximately 95 percent of all court cases originate in the state trial courts. Certain courts of limited jurisdiction are established in each state, such as probate courts (to settle wills and estates) and domestic relations courts (to hear divorces and other legal family issues). Otherwise, cases in the state system are decided by judges in either criminal courts or civil courts. Distinctions between these two primary areas of the law are discussed in Chapter 3.

Summary

Legal education necessarily begins with an introduction to the development of law in this country. By understanding where one finds the law and the nature of the legal structure, one may begin to classify legal problems and know how to analyze them, in the context of our present legal framework. In doing so, students will develop those skills necessary to support sophisticated legal analysis of both case opinions as well as hypothetical fact situations. This is at the heart of the legal profession and will be emphasized throughout this textbook. It is important to remember that the influence of the judiciary in shaping American law is linked to the composition of the court. Understanding that judicial interpretation affects past and future court decisions helps illuminate the concept of the law being a living thing: it constantly changes to reflect society's needs and the uniqueness of the present economic and political structure.

Key Terms

Administrative law
Appellate court
Bench trial
Case law
Common law
Circuit
Jury trial
Law
Original jurisdiction
Precedent
Separation of powers
Stare decisis
Statutes
Statutory law
Uniform statute
United States Constitution
Writ of certiorari

Discussion Questions

1. Explain the doctrine of *separation of powers.* Do you think its principles are adequately reflected in the U.S. Constitution?
2. Identify the difference between *precedent* and *stare decisis.*
3. Explain the importance of the composition of the U.S. Supreme Court in considering the concept of electronic surveillance of private citizens.
4. Explain why law may be described as a "living thing," and give an example that illustrates this concept.
5. Should U.S. Supreme Court justices be subject to term limits, similar to elected officials, rather than have a lifetime appointment to the bench?

Exercises

1. Identify which of the five sources of law might be the best basis for resolving the legal dispute in the following cases:
   a. Mary is speeding down the interstate highway in Nebraska.
   b. John is injured at his factory job in Iowa because his employer failed to provide him with safety goggles.
   c. Lillian wants to work as a greeter at the local discount store, but the store manager tells her that she is too old to be working and won't hire her.
   d. Charles is injured when the safety mechanism on his chain saw malfunctions, causing the blade to detach from the handle.
   e. Loulou deducts from her income tax return the cost of six pairs of high-heeled boots as an unreimbursed job-related expense in working as a prostitute.
2. Assume that John is driving home from his job after working a 12-hour shift at the local hospital. He is extremely tired, and his erratic driving results in a state highway trooper doing a traffic stop. The trooper suspects that John has been drinking, which he has not, and asks to search John's car for liquor. What source of law governs John's rights regarding a search of his car?
3. Mary wants a divorce from her husband, Sam. Mary and Sam were married in the state of Kansas, but Sam has been living with his mother in Missouri for the last two months. Specifically in which court should Mary file a petition for dissolution of marriage?
4. Henrietta slips and falls in the lobby of a post office in Chicago, Illinois. Specifically in which court should Henrietta file a lawsuit for negligence, and who is the defendant in her lawsuit?
5. Smedley is arrested for stealing the automatic teller machine (ATM) from the sidewalk outside of the Second National Bank of Georgia. Who are the parties in this case, and specifically in which court will Smedley's trial occur?
6. Assume that a jury in the case in Exercise 5 finds Smedley not guilty. May the prosecutor appeal this decision, and if so, to which court?

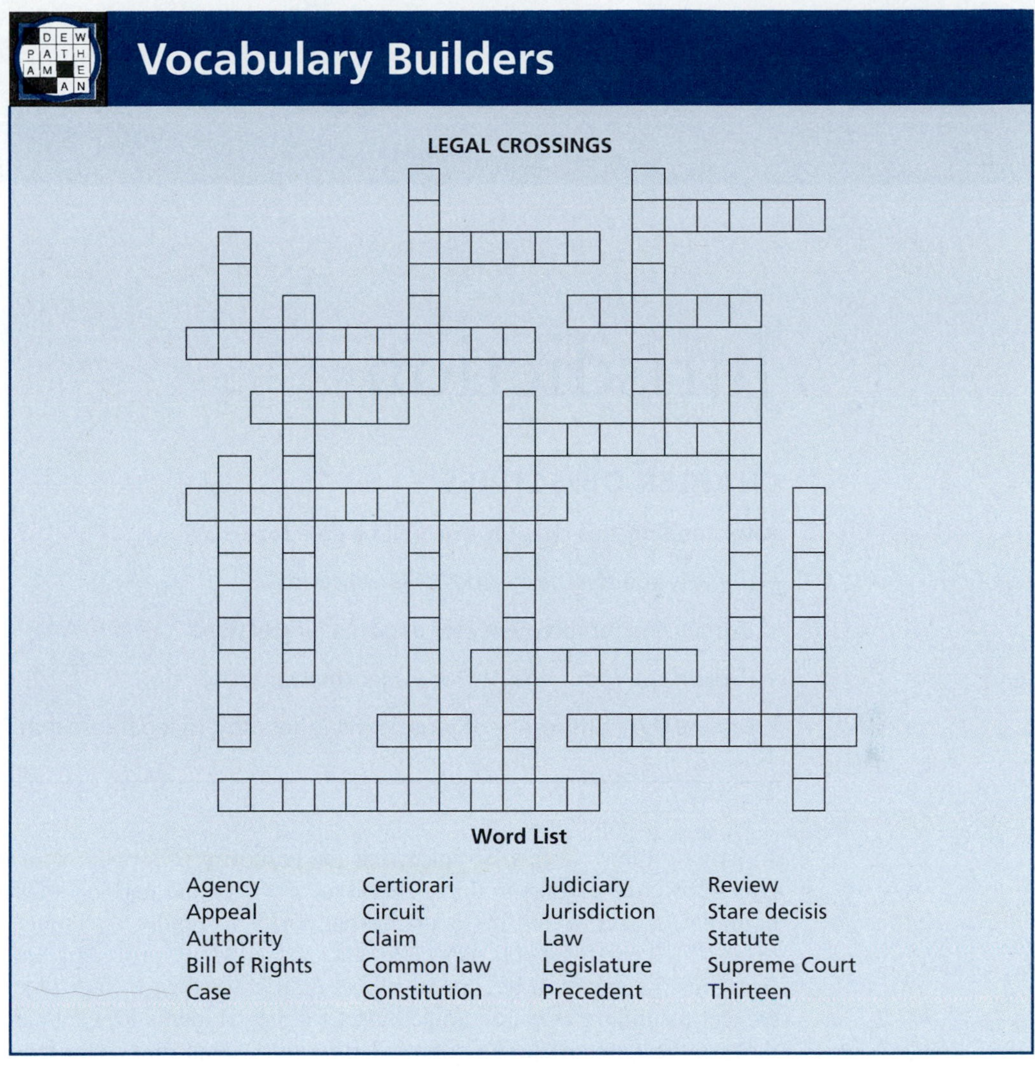
Vocabulary Builders
LEGAL CROSSINGS
Word List
Agency
Appeal
Authority
Bill of Rights
Case
Certiorari
Circuit
Claim
Common law
Constitution
Judiciary
Jurisdiction
Law
Legislature
Precedent
Review
Stare decisis
Statute
Supreme Court
Thirteen

Chapter 2

Jurisdiction

CHAPTER OBJECTIVES

After reading this chapter, you will be able to:

- Identify the two basic types of jurisdiction.
- Explain the requirements for personal jurisdiction.
- Explain the requirements for subject matter jurisdiction.
- Discuss the significance of jurisdiction in relation to legal research.

Jurisdiction may simply be defined as the authority of a court to hear and decide a case. It is the power of a court to decide the issue between the parties, and the specific geographic boundaries over which the court has authority to render decisions. Careful consideration must be given to several aspects of this topic. Many problems are presented by what, at first blush, appears to be a relatively straightforward case. Indeed, errors in identifying the correct forum are common at the outset for new students to legal analysis. This chapter will discuss the types of jurisdiction, whether more than one court may have jurisdiction, and how this is an important consideration in conducting legal research.

WHY IS JURISDICTION IMPORTANT?

First, it is significant because one must decide in which court to initiate a lawsuit. Second, it is important when undertaking legal research, as precedent determines the impact that prior case law or statutory law has on a particular decision.

Let's consider a hypothetical client, Mary, who comes to your law firm seeking advice. Assume that John Smith is a resident of Missouri and had to travel to a business meeting in Illinois. As John was driving through Illinois, he stopped off at a bar and had a few drinks. Ignoring his intoxication, John decided to continue on to his destination, and shortly after leaving the bar, crossed the centerline of Illinois Highway 59 and collided with another car, driven by Mary, a resident of Iowa. Mary sustained multiple injuries and wants to sue both John and his employer. One of the first questions that Mary's attorney must ask is, "In which court do I file this case?" Assume that you are the paralegal in this firm and asked this question: Who has the right, or jurisdiction, to decide this case? Several points should be considered in determining the appropriate forum.

Jurisdiction is relevant because it ensures that the court's resources are properly utilized in protecting the interests of the citizens within its geographic boundaries and realm of authority. It supports the rights of the people in its locale, who are most impacted by the court's decisions. As a result, jurisdiction determines the limits and power of courts to decide particular cases relying on previous judicial decisions. After determining the specific court in which to file a lawsuit, the next step in the legal problem-solving process is to locate the relevant legal rules and principles that apply to your particular fact situation. Remember, it is not imperative that you memorize all the legal principles and laws you will learn in this course, but you should be able to properly identify and locate the law, as well as be able to reasonably predict the outcome of your case, based on the law and the facts at hand. In order to do this, you must be careful to find the law that is applicable in *your* jurisdiction, or where the case is going to be filed.

TYPES OF JURISDICTION

binding authority (mandatory authority)
A source of law that a court must follow in deciding a case, such as a statute or federal regulations.

persuasive authority
A source of law or legal authority that is not binding on the court in deciding a case but may be used by the court for guidance, such as law review articles.

Jurisdiction is imperative because it determines which prior court decisions *must* be followed and which previous decisions *may* be followed by the present court in resolving the impending legal issue. It is a matter of the distinction between **binding** versus **persuasive authority.** These two distinctions will be discussed later in this chapter, but briefly they concern whether a prior court decision is relevant to deciding the case at hand. When considering a question of jurisdiction, it is necessary to identify the types of jurisdiction. The two basic kinds of jurisdiction are personal jurisdiction and subject matter jurisdiction—over the parties or the property at issue. A court must have both types of jurisdiction in order to have the power to hear and decide a case.

Eye on Ethics

Assume that you are a paralegal for the law firm of Shake and Bake, L.L.C., located in Georgia. One day, a client consults your firm regarding an automobile accident in which she was involved while on vacation in New Jersey. Following the initial client interview with your supervising attorney, the client telephones your firm the following day and asks you in which court her case likely will be filed. Is this a "procedural" question in which you may give a response, or must you refer her question to your supervising attorney?

See if any of these Web sites help you with this response:

www.legalethics.com
www.findlaw.com

PERSONAL JURISDICTION

in personam jurisdiction
A court's authority over a party personally.

in rem jurisdiction
A court's authority over claims affecting property.

minimum contacts
The test, based on the case *International Shoe v. Washington,* that courts use to ascertain if a defendant has some contact with the state of which he or she is not a resident.

First, a court must have **in personam** (or personal) **jurisdiction.** This means that the court must have authority to compel the personal appearance of the parties. A court cannot exercise authority over persons with whom it has absolutely no connection whatsoever. In essence, it has no right to enforce the rights of citizens or over issues where there is no connection to that state or within the relevant geographic boundaries if it is a federal matter. Personal jurisdiction means that the court has the authority to award damages or other relief against a party personally.

A court's jurisdiction over the parties and to decide a case may also result from **in rem jurisdiction.** Literally, this means "jurisdiction over the thing." This means that the court has jurisdiction to decide an issue arising out of property, and thus requires that the property is in fact in that forum state, or at least has some relationship to that state. A court may have authority because it has jurisdiction over some property that is the subject of a lawsuit. For example, a buyer who lives in Illinois and is purchasing a farm in Iowa from a seller who lives in Oklahoma may bring suit in Iowa, if there is a dispute regarding some ownership interest in this farm.

Refer to the hypothetical case at the start of this chapter. John is a resident of Missouri and Mary is a resident of Iowa, but the accident took place in Illinois. Mary may wish to sue John in the state of Iowa, because that is where she lives and it would be convenient for her to be a litigant close to home. However, since John does not live in Iowa, Mary would be unable to sue him there, as he lacks any **minimum contacts** *with* Iowa. Similarly, Mary has no minimum contacts with Missouri, and thus the court in Missouri would lack personal jurisdiction over her. However, since the accident occurred in Illinois, Mary has the option to sue John in state court there, as this incident satisfies the minimum contacts needed for an Illinois court to have personal jurisdiction over both parties. A single contact with Illinois, the forum state, results because Mary's claim for negligence arises out of the car accident in Illinois, satisfying the minimum contact requirement to sue in that state.

United States District Court,
D. North Dakota,
Southwestern Division.
Patrick ZIDON, Plaintiff,
v.
Linda PICKRELL, Defendant.
No. A1-04-113.
Nov. 8, 2004.

ORDER DENYING MOTION TO DISMISS

HOVLAND, Chief Judge.

Before the Court is defendant Linda Pickrell's Motion to Dismiss filed on October 20, 2004. On October 25, 2004, the plaintiff, Patrick Zidon, filed a motion opposing dismissal. For the following reasons, the Defendant's motion is denied.

I. BACKGROUND

The plaintiff, Patrick Zidon, is a North Dakota resident. The defendant, Linda Pickrell, is a resident of Colorado. Zidon and Pickrell cultivated a romantic relationship after meeting online in September 2000. Zidon ended the relationship in March 2004. Zidon, in a complaint filed on September 21, 2004, alleged that Pickrell created a Web site entitled "Monster of Love: Surviving Love/Sex Addicts and Spiritual Predators" at the domain name www.patrickzidon.com following their breakup, where she posted allegedly defamatory statements. In addition, Zidon alleges Pickrell e-mailed a hyper link to the Web site to persons in the Bismarck, North Dakota, area as well as the public at large. In his complaint, Zidon sets forth claims for defamation and intentional infliction of emotional distress.

II. LEGAL DISCUSSION

Pickrell requests dismissal citing lack of jurisdiction over the person and improper venue pursuant to Rules 12(b)(2) and (3) of the Federal Rules of Civil Procedure.

A. PERSONAL JURISDICTION

[1][2][3] The initial inquiry is whether the Court has personal jurisdiction over the defendant, Linda Pickrell. The Motion to Dismiss was filed pursuant to Rule 12(b)(2) of the Federal Rules of Civil Procedure for lack of jurisdiction over the party. "To defeat a motion to dismiss for lack of personal jurisdiction, the nonmoving party need only make a prima facie showing of jurisdiction." *Epps v. Stewart Information Services Corp.*, 327 F.3d 642, 647 (8th Cir.2003) (citing *Falkirk Min. Co. v. Japan Steel Works, Ltd.*, 906 F.2d 369, 373 (8th Cir.1990); *Watlow Elec. Mfg. v. Patch Rubber Co.*, 838 F.2d 999, 1000 (8th Cir.1988)). "The plaintiff's prima facie showing must be tested, not by the pleadings alone, but by the affidavits and exhibits presented with the motions and in opposition thereto." *Dever v. Hentzen Coatings, Inc.*, 380 F.3d 1070, 1072 (8th Cir.2004). The party seeking to establish the court's in personam jurisdiction carries the burden of proof, and the burden does not shift to the party challenging jurisdiction. *Epps*, 327 F.3d 642, 647 (citations omitted).

[4] As a preliminary matter, it should be noted that this action is in federal court based on diversity jurisdiction. See 28 U.S.C. § 1332(a). Under Rule 4(k)(1)(A) of the Federal Rules of Civil Procedure, a federal district court in a diversity action will have personal jurisdiction to the same extent as a state court of the state in which that federal district court sits. *Dean v. Olibas*, 129 F.3d 1001, 1003 (8th Cir.1997). Therefore, when this Court sits in diversity, the analysis for personal jurisdiction involves two steps: (1) the court must determine whether the State of North Dakota would accept jurisdiction under the facts of this case; and (2) the court must determine whether the exercise of jurisdiction comports with constitutional due process restrictions. *Lakin v. Prudential Securities, Inc.*, 348 F.3d 704, 706-707 (8th Cir.2003) (citing *Sondergard v. Miles, Inc.*, 985 F.2d 1389, 1392 (8th Cir.1993)). To satisfy the first step of the jurisdictional analysis, the Court will address the relevant North Dakota provisions governing personal jurisdiction over non-resident defendants.

[5] The jurisdiction of North Dakota courts is governed by the North Dakota long-arm statute set forth in Rule 4(b)(2) of the North Dakota Rules of Civil Procedure. The North Dakota Supreme Court has held that Rule 4(b)(2) "authorizes North Dakota courts to exercise jurisdiction over non-resident defendants to the fullest extent permitted by due process. . . ." *Hansen v. Scott*, 645 N.W.2d 223, 230 (N.D.2003) (citing *Auction Effertz, Ltd. v. Schecher*, 611 N.W.2d 173 (N.D.2000); *Hust v. Northern Log, Inc.*, 297 N.W.2d 429, 431 (N.D.1980)). The Eighth Circuit has held that when a state construes its long-arm statute to grant jurisdiction to the fullest extent permitted by the Constitution, the two-step test collapses into a single question of whether the exercise of personal jurisdiction comports with due process. *Oriental Trading Co., Inc. v. Firetti*, 236 F.3d 938, 943 (8th Cir.2001); *Bell Paper Box, Inc. v. U.S. Kids, Inc.*, 22 F.3d 816, 818 (8th Cir.1994); see *Hansen v. Scott*, 645 N.W.2d 223, 232 (N.D.2002) (recognizing that a federal court sitting in diversity may collapse the two step framework under North Dakota law).

[6][7] "Due process requires minimum contacts between [a] non-resident defendant and the forum state such that maintenance of the suit does not offend traditional notions of fair play and substantial justice." *Dever v. Hentzen Coatings, Inc.*, 380 F.3d 1070, 1073 (8th Cir.2004) (citing *Burlington Indus., Inc. v. Maples Indus., Inc.*, 97 F.3d 1100, 1102 (8th Cir.1996); *World-Wide Volkswagen Corp. v. Woodson*, 444 U.S. 286, 291-92, 100 S.Ct. 559, 62 L.Ed.2d 490 (1980)). There are two categories of minimum contacts with a state that may subject a defendant to jurisdiction in that forum, i.e., general and specific. With respect to general jurisdiction over a defendant, "a court may hear a

lawsuit against a defendant who has 'continuous and systematic' contacts with the forum state, even if the injuries at issue in the lawsuit did not arise out of the defendant's activities directed at the forum." *Dever,* 380 F.3d 1070, 1073 (quoting *Helicopteros Nacionales de Colombia, S.A. v. Hall,* 466 U.S. 408, 415-16, 104 S.Ct. 1868, 80 L.Ed.2d 404 (1984)). A state has specific jurisdiction over a defendant when the suit arises out of, or is related to, the defendant's contacts with the forum state.

Both categories of minimum contacts require some act by which the defendant purposely avails himself or herself of the privilege of conducting activities within the forum state, and thus invokes the benefits and protections of its laws. If a court determines that a defendant has minimum contacts with the forum state, the court must then consider "'whether the assertion of personal jurisdiction would comport with fair play and substantial justice.'" *Id.* (quoting *Burger King Corp. v. Rudzewicz,* 471 U.S. 462, 476, 105 S.Ct. 2174, 85 L.Ed.2d 528 (1985)).

[8] The Eighth Circuit has established a five-part test for measuring minimum contacts for purposes of asserting personal jurisdiction over a defendant: (1) the nature and quality of [a defendant's] contacts with a forum state; (2) the quantity of such contacts; (3) the relation of the cause of action to the contacts; (4) the interest of the forum state in providing a forum for its residents; and (5) [the] convenience of the parties. *Dever,* 380 F.3d 1070, 1073-74 (citing *Burlington Indus., Inc. v. Maples Indus., Inc.,* 97 F.3d 1100, 1102 (8th Cir.1996)). In determining whether a defendant has sufficient contacts with the forum state to exercise personal jurisdiction, the court must consider all of the contacts in the aggregate and examine the totality of the circumstances. *Northrup King Co. v. Compania Productora Semillas Algodoneras, S.A.,* 51 F.3d 1383, 1388 (8th Cir.1995). The Eighth Circuit affords "significant weight" to the first three factors.

Zidon sets forth several alleged contacts Pickrell has with North Dakota: (1) Pickrell made telephone calls to Zidon; (2) Pickrell sent e-mails and instant messages over the Internet to Zidon; and (3) Pickrell created a Web site and encouraged individuals to visit that site via e-mail and other mediums. Based on those contacts, Zidon contends the Court has authority to exercise personal jurisdiction over Pickrell. Zidon limits his argument to the exercise of specific jurisdiction.

As previously noted, specific jurisdiction requires that the cause of action arise out of or relate to the defendants' contacts with the forum state. *Epps v. Stewart Information Services Corp.,* 327 F.3d 642, 648 (8th Cir.2003). The Court will analyze each of the Pickrell's contacts in relation to the claims raised by Zidon and the factors prescribed by the Eighth Circuit.

1. NATURE AND QUALITY OF CONTACTS

Under this factor, the primary issue is whether the non-resident defendants "have fair warning that a particular activity may subject a person to the jurisdiction of a foreign sovereignty." *Gould v. P.T. Krakatau Steel,* 957 F.2d 573, 576 (8th Cir.1992) (citing *Shaffer v. Heitner,* 433 U.S. 186, 204, 97 S.Ct. 2569, 53 L.Ed.2d 683 (1977)). The fair warning requirement will be satisfied if the defendant has "purposefully directed" his or her activities at the residents of the forum state. *Id.* (citing *Burger King Corp. v. Rudzewicz,* 471 U.S. 462, 472, 105 S.Ct. 2174, 85 L.Ed.2d 528 (1985)). The contact(s) with the forum state must be more than "random, fortuitous, or attenuated." *Id.*

a) ZIDON'S WEB SITE

Zidon alleges that Pickrell's Web site [FN1] provides the Court with specific jurisdiction. Many courts have examined jurisdictional issues involving the Internet and how electronic contacts affect the exercise of personal jurisdiction. See Richard E. Kaye, Annotation, "Internet Web Site Activities of Nonresident Person or Corporation as Conferring Personal Jurisdiction Under Long-Arm Statutes and Due Process Clause," 81 A.L.R.5th 41 (2003). In some jurisdictions, a "sliding scale" test has been adopted in Internet cases to determine whether the courts have personal jurisdiction over a non-resident defendant. This test involves an examination of the active versus passive nature of the Web site. *See Zippo Mfg. Co. v. Zippo Dot Com, Inc.*, 952 F.Supp. 1119, 1124 (W.D.Pa.1997) (utilizing a "sliding scale" test for jurisdiction which considers a Web site's level of interactivity and the nature of commercial activities conducted over the Internet). There are other courts that apply the "effects test" derived from a United States Supreme Court decision entitled *Calder v. Jones*, 465 U.S. 783, 104 S.Ct. 1482, 79 L.Ed.2d 804 (1984) in which a California resident sued several Florida residents, including the author and editor of a National Enquirer article, for libel. The United States Supreme Court held the exercise of jurisdiction was proper because of the foreseeable "effects" in California of the non-resident defendant's activities.

FN1. As quoted in *Zippo Mfg. Co. v. Zippo Dot Com, Inc.*, 952 F.Supp. 1119, 1124 (W.D.Pa.1997), "[a] 'site' is an Internet address that permits the exchange of information with a host computer. *Bensusan Restaurant Corp. v. King*, 937 F.Supp. 295 (S.D.N.Y.1996). The 'Web' or 'World Wide Web' refers to the collection of sites available on the Internet."

[9] In *Lakin v. Prudential Securities, Inc.*, 348 F.3d 704 (8th Cir.2003), the Eighth Circuit discussed whether and how a Web site could provide minimum contacts to invoke personal jurisdiction. The Court recognized that a majority of the circuits have adopted the analytical framework set forth in *Zippo Mfg. Co. v. Zippo Dot Com, Inc.*, 952 F.Supp. 1119, 1124 (W.D.Pa.1997). The Eighth Circuit quoted Zippo and stated "that the likelihood that personal jurisdiction can be constitutionally exercised is directly proportionate to the nature and quality of commercial activity that an entity conducts over the Internet." *Lakin*, 348 F.3d 704, 710 (quoting *Zippo*, 952 F.Supp. 1119, 1124). The Eighth Circuit noted that the federal court in Zippo created a "sliding scale" test to measure the nature and quality of the commercial contacts for assessing the exercise of personal jurisdiction. The Eighth Circuit also restated a portion of the Zippo court's holding that described the "sliding scale" concept:

> At one end of the spectrum are situations where the defendant clearly does business over the Internet. If the defendant enters into contracts with residents of a foreign jurisdiction that involve the knowing and repeated transmission of computer files over the Internet, personal jurisdiction is proper. At the opposite end are situations where a defendant has simply posted information on an Internet Web site which is accessible to users in foreign jurisdictions. A passive Web site that does little more than make information available to those who are interested in it is not grounds for the exercise [of] personal jurisdiction. The middle ground is occupied by interactive Web sites where a user can exchange information with the host computer. In these cases, the exercise of jurisdiction is determined by examining the level of interactivity and commercial nature of the exchange of information that occurs on the Web site.

Lakin, 348 F.3d 704, 710-11 (quoting *Zippo*, 952 F.Supp. 1119, 1124). The Eighth Circuit concluded that the "sliding scale" approach was appropriate in cases of specific jurisdiction. The Court must analyze whether Pickrell's Web site provides the Court with specific jurisdiction.

[10] Both parties seem to agree that Pickrell is not conducting business or entering into contracts with residents of foreign jurisdictions by way of her Web site. According to Zippo, Pickrell's Web site must fall into either the middle ground or the passive end of the "sliding scale" spectrum. Whether jurisdiction can be exercised based on a Web site falling in the middle ground of the "sliding scale" spectrum is based on its level of interactivity.

Zidon characterizes Pickrell's Web site as interactive for several reasons. First, the Web site has an e-mail hyper link. Second, the Web site offers detailed information about Zidon including where he resides. Third, the Web site contains a bulletin board allowing individuals to exchange information. Last, the Web site encourages viewers to contact the Web creator. Based on those characteristics, Zidon contends the Court can exercise jurisdiction over Pickrell based solely on the operation of her Web site. Pickrell disagrees and maintains the Web site should be characterized as passive.

Neither this Court nor the Eighth Circuit have addressed whether a Web site with the characteristics of Pickrell's Web site meets the requisite level of interactivity to exercise jurisdiction. However, the Fifth Circuit declared a similar Web site interactive in the case of *Revell v. Lidov*, 317 F.3d 467 (5th Cir.2002). In Revell, the plaintiff, a Texas resident, brought an action for defamation against multiple non-residents. The action stemmed from comments publicized on an Internet bulletin board maintained by Columbia University. The bulletin board allowed patrons to post their literary works or read the literary works of others. The Fifth Circuit held the Web site was interactive due to the nature of an Internet bulletin board. The court said, "[t]his means that individuals send information to be posted, and receive information that other have posted. . . . the visitor may participate in an open forum hosted by the website. Columbia's bulletin board is thus interactive." *Id.* at 472; see *EDIAS Software Int'l, L.L.C. v. BASIS Int'l Ltd.*, 947 F.Supp. 413, 420 (D.Ariz.1996) (stating "[a] forum resembles a bulletin board where messages can be posted by the page visitor or the page owner. Thus, a Web page with a forum allows interaction between the page visitors and between the owner"). However, the Fifth Circuit ultimately concluded it could not exercise jurisdiction over the non-resident defendants based solely on the "low-level of interactivity of the bulletin board." *Id.* at 476 (reaching that conclusion after assessing the bulletin board under Calder v. Jones). The Fifth Circuit ultimately held that Texas could not exercise jurisdiction over non-resident defendants who posted the article on the Internet because the article did not refer to Texas; the article was not directed at Texas readers; and the defendants did not know the plaintiff was a resident of Texas. *Id.*

Following the decision in Revell, the Court finds Pickrell's Web site is interactive under the "sliding scale" approach adopted by the Eighth Circuit. However, the Court cannot exercise jurisdiction over Pickrell based solely on her creation and maintenance of the Web site. Additional contacts with North Dakota are needed to exercise jurisdiction.

b) THE CALDER "EFFECTS TEST"

As previously discussed, the "effects test" as recognized in the United States Supreme Court case of *Calder v. Jones*, 465 U.S. 783, 104 S.Ct. 1482, 79 L.Ed.2d 804 (1984), may provide an additional basis for exercising personal jurisdiction. In Calder, a California entertainer brought a libel action against Florida residents who were writers and editors of the National Enquirer, a Florida-based weekly newspaper with a nationwide circulation. The Supreme Court held that California could assert jurisdiction over the non-resident defendants because the defendants' intentional actions were aimed at California, they knew the allegedly libelous articles "would have a potentially devastating impact" on the plaintiff, and they knew the "brunt of the harm" would be suffered in California. Based on those facts, the Supreme Court concluded the defendants could "reasonably anticipate being haled into court" in California. 465 U.S. 783, 790, 104 S.Ct. 1482, 79 L.Ed.2d 804 (quoting *World-Wide Volkswagen Corp. v. Woodson*, 444 U.S. 286, 297, 100 S.Ct. 559, 62 L.Ed.2d 490 (1980)).

The Eighth Circuit has recognized the "effects test" as articulated in *Calder v. Jones. See General Electric Capital Corp. v. Grossman*, 991 F.2d 1376, 1387 (8th Cir.1993); *Hicklin Engineering, Inc. v. Aidco, Inc.*, 959 F.2d 738, 739 (8th Cir.1992); *Dakota Indus., Inc., v. Dakota Sportswear, Inc.*, 946 F.2d 1384, 1390-91 (8th Cir.1991). However, the Eighth Circuit has used the "effects test" as merely an additional factor to consider when evaluating a defendant's relevant contacts with the forum state. *See Hicklin Engineering, Inc. v. Aidco, Inc.*, 959 F.2d 738, 739 (8th Cir.1992) (holding that although the defendants' alleged harmful activities may have harmed the plaintiff in the state of Iowa, "absent additional contacts, this effect alone will not be sufficient to bestow personal jurisdiction."); *Dakota Indus., Inc., v. Dakota Sportswear, Inc.*, 946 F.2d 1384, 1390-91 (8th Cir.1991) (stating that "[i]n relying on Calder, we do not abandon the five-part test. . . . We simply note that Calder requires the consideration of additional factors when an intentional tort is alleged.").

[11] Pickrell's comments on her Web site and the e-mail messages sent to individuals in North Dakota may subject her to jurisdiction under the "effects test." *See EDIAS Software Int'l, L.L.C. v. BASIS Int'l Ltd.*, 947 F.Supp. 413, 420 (D.Ariz.1996) (stating "e-mail messages to Arizona and Compuserve Web site which reaches Arizona customers count as additional 'contacts' under a minimum contacts analysis, but additionally confer jurisdiction in Arizona under the 'effects test.'"). It is clear from the record that Pickrell's Internet communications were directed uniquely toward the State of North Dakota. *See Revell v. Lidov*, 317 F.3d 467, 473 (5th Cir.2002) (holding Texas could not exercise personal jurisdiction over non-resident defendants who posted an article on the Internet because the article did not refer to Texas and was not directed at Texas readers, and defendants did not know the plaintiff was a Texas resident); *Young v. New Haven Advocate*, 315 F.3d 256, 263-64 (4th Cir.2002) (finding Virginia could not exercise jurisdiction because the defamatory comments were posted on a Web site which was not designed to attract or serve a Virginia audience); *Barrett v. Catacombs Press*, 44 F.Supp.2d 717, 730-31 (E.D.Pa.1999) (holding Pennsylvania could not exercise jurisdiction over a non-resident because the defamatory statements posted on the Internet did not concern the plaintiff's work activities in Pennsylvania, but were directed at the plaintiff's work outside the state).

The record reveals that Pickrell deliberately and knowingly directed the Web site, e-mail, and Internet comments at the State of North Dakota because North Dakota is Zidon's residence. The following comments, which appear on Pickrell's Web site, shed light on her intentions:

> As a businessman and community leader in Bismarck, North Dakota, few would suspect his double life of deceit, lies and the trail of tears he leaves behind him. A warning, this man plans to pursue a career in psychological therapy. If you have a history with this man you'd like to share, please contact webmaster@ patrickzidon.com. . . .
>
> A business man and community leader in Bismarck, North Dakota, Patrick John Zidon is manager of Bismarck Lumber. He is a father of one grown son, former husband of an artist/medical technician and claims to have been: past president of Dakota Zoo, past president of the Nodak Lumberman's Association, past president of his Catholic church's counsel, past chair of the legislative committee for the Northwestern Lumberman's Association. . . He recently graduated (supposedly in May of 2004) from the University of Mary with degrees in business and psychology. He is a predator.

The Web site reveals that the focus of the Web site was North Dakota. Pickrell knew Zidon was a resident of North Dakota, and knew the "brunt of the injury" would be felt in North Dakota. The Court finds that Pickrell particularly and directly targeted North Dakota with her Web site and e-mails, and specifically targeted North Dakota resident Patrick Zidon. In summary, the Court is satisfied that the requirements of the "effects test" as enumerated in Calder v. Jones have been met.

Based on the aforementioned contacts, this factor weighs in favor of the exercise of personal jurisdiction.

2. QUANTITY OF CONTACTS

It is well-established that specific jurisdiction can arise from a single contact with the forum state. *Fulton v. Chicago, Rock Island & P.R. Co.*, 481 F.2d 326, 334-36 (8th Cir.1973). However, when specific jurisdiction is being alleged the quantity of contacts is not determinative. *West Publishing Co. v. Stanley*, 2004 WL 73590, *4 (D.Minn. Jan.7, 2004); (citing *Marquette Nat'l Bank of Minneapolis v. Norris*, 270 N.W.2d 290, 295 (Minn.1978); *McGee v. Int'l Life Ins. Co.*, 355 U.S. 220, 223, 78 S.Ct. 199, 2 L.Ed.2d 223 (1957); *Marshall v. Inn of Madeline Island*, 610 N.W.2d 670, 674 (Minn.Ct.App.2000)). Thus, the Court is not concerned with the number of contacts made for purposes of whether specific jurisdiction exists.

3. RELATION OF CONTACTS TO CAUSE OF ACTION

The Court recognizes that all of Pickrell's contacts with North Dakota are related to Zidon's claims of defamation and intentional infliction of emotional distress. Each claim arises out of the contacts with North Dakota. This factor weighs in favor of the exercise of personal jurisdiction.

4. INTEREST OF THE FORUM STATE

It is well-established in the Eighth Circuit that the first three factors as outlined above are of "primary importance," and the last two factors are of "secondary importance." *Stanton v. St. Jude Medical, Inc.*, 340 F.3d 690, 694 (8th Cir.2003); *Northrup King Co. v. Compania Productora Semillas Algodoneras*, 51 F.3d 1383, 1388 (8th Cir.1995); *Aaron Ferer & Sons Co. v. American Compressed Steel Co.*, 564 F.2d 1206, 1210 n. 5 (8th Cir.1977). The interest of the forum state is the fourth factor to be considered for purposes of asserting personal jurisdiction.

It stands to reason that North Dakota has an interest in adjudicating these claims and providing a forum for its residents. Therefore, the fourth factor weighs in favor of the exercise of personal jurisdiction. *See Aylward v. Fleet Bank*, 122 F.3d 616, 618 (8th Cir.1997) (quickly dispensing with this part of the test by assuming the forum state has an interest in providing a forum for its residents).

5. CONVENIENCE OF THE PARTIES

The Court understands that Pickrell currently resides in Colorado and it would be burdensome for her to defend the suit in North Dakota. However, equal hardship would be felt by Zidon if he were forced to litigate this matter in Colorado. This factor does not favor either party.

In summary, based on Pickrell's contacts with North Dakota and the totality of the circumstances, the Court finds that exercising jurisdiction over Linda Pickrell comports with due process. *See Northwest Airlines, Inc. v. Astraea Aviation Services, Inc.*, 111 F.3d 1386, 1390 (8th Cir.1997). The exercise of personal jurisdiction does not offend traditional notions of fair play and substantial justice. An application of the "effects test" as derived from Calder v. Jones in the context of Internet communications is appropriate and warranted.

B. VENUE

"[Section 1404(a)] assumes that venue is proper in the court where the action is initially filed, and also that the court has jurisdiction over the person of the defendant." *Knowlton v. Allied Van Lines, Inc.*, 900 F.2d 1196, 1201 (8th Cir.1990). "Change of venue, although within the discretion of the district court, should not be freely granted. Courts are in the business of deciding cases, not playing procedural hockey among available districts at the whim of dissatisfied parties." *In re Nine Mile Ltd.*, 692 F.2d 56, 61 (8th Cir.1982) overruled on other grounds, *Missouri Housing Development Com'n v. Brice*, 919 F.2d 1306, 1311 (8th Cir.1990).

When considering a motion to transfer a civil action to another district or division where it might have been brought, a court is statutorily required to balance three factors: (1) convenience of parties, (2) convenience of witnesses, and (3) interests of justice. 28 U.S.C. § 1404(a). In keeping with the "flexible and multifaceted analysis that Congress intended to govern motions to transfer within the federal system," *Stewart Org., Inc. v. Ricoh Corp.*, 487 U.S. 22, 31, 108 S.Ct. 2239, 101 L.Ed.2d 22 (1988), the evaluation of a transfer motion is not limited to these three factors, but instead, "such determinations require case-by-case evaluation of particular circumstances at hand and consideration of all relevant factors." *Terra Int'l., Inc. v. Mississippi Chemical Corp.*, 119 F.3d 688, 691 (8th Cir.1997), cert. denied, 522 U.S. 1029, 118 S.Ct. 629, 139 L.Ed.2d 609 (1997).

1. CONVENIENCE OF THE PARTIES

[12] Regardless of where this action is venued, one of the parties will claim to be inconvenienced and placed at a disadvantage at trial. In this case, it is more convenient for Pickrell to litigate in Colorado. However, Zidon chose to litigate in North Dakota. His choice must be afforded some deference. *See Hubbard v. White*, 755 F.2d 692, 694-95 (8th Cir.1985), cert. denied, 474 U.S. 834, 106 S.Ct. 107, 88 L.Ed.2d 87 (1985); *Nelson v. Soo Line Railroad Co.*, 58 F.Supp.2d 1023, 1026 (D.Minn.1999). Transferring this action to a district court in Colorado would only serve to shift the alleged inconvenience and hardship from Pickrell to Zidon. *Terra Int'l Inc. v. Mississippi Chem. Corp.*, 119 F.3d 688, 696-97. "Merely shifting the inconveniences from one side to the other . . . is not a permissible justification for a change of venue." *Id*. The Court finds this factor weighs in favor of a North Dakota venue.

2. CONVENIENCE OF THE WITNESSES

The factor generally afforded the greatest weight by courts considering a motion for change of venue is the convenience of the witnesses. Nevertheless, this factor is not dispositive and must still be weighed against the other relevant factors—such as the willingness of witnesses to appear, the ability to subpoena witnesses, and the adequacy of deposition testimony. *See Gulf Oil Corp. v. Gilbert*, 330 U.S. 501, 508, 67 S.Ct. 839, 91 L.Ed. 1055 (1947). The party with the longest list of potential witnesses who reside in their respective district will not necessarily prevail. *See Terra Int'l. Inc. v. Mississippi Chem. Corp.*, 119 F.3d 688 at 696 (noting that "sheer numbers of witnesses will not decide which way the convenience factor tips"). Rather, the Court "must examine the materiality and importance of the anticipated witnesses' testimony and then determine their accessibility and convenience to the forum." *Reid-Walen v. Hansen*, 933 F.2d 1390, 1396 (8th Cir.1991). . . .

. . .

> Just some of the elements which witnesses will be called to testify on include (a) witnesses to establish plaintiff's reputation, character and good standing in the community prior to this website, (b) witnesses to establish that defendant in fact did actively send links to this website to them and to further establish their response and impact upon receiving the e-mails and accessing the *www.patrickzidon.com* website, (c) witnesses testifying as to the impact this has had upon plaintiff's physical and emotional health, and (d) witnesses testifying as to the impact this had upon plaintiff's current reputation in the community.

According to Zidon, these witnesses would all reside in North Dakota. Zidon specifically identifies three North Dakota residents solicited by Pickrell's e-mails as witnesses he would call. [FN4] See Affidavit of Patrick Zidon, ¶ ¶ 7-8. On the other hand, Pickrell intends to call witnesses in her defense and states that all those witnesses reside outside of North Dakota. However, her pleadings seem to suggest that those witnesses would also reside outside of Colorado. [FN5]

FN4. Two of the individuals, Tammy Perry and Susann Cuperus, are professors at the University of Mary in Bismarck, North Dakota. The third individual, Terry Lincoln, is associated with the Dakota Zoo and apparently also lives in Bismarck.

FN5. Pickrell attests that all stories and information on the Web site are "true and personal memories of those who knew him and information he has openly shared with *us* of his own free will." Affidavit of Linda Pickrell, ¶ 6 (emphasis added). Further, Pickrell attests that all quotations appearing on the Web site are statements from Patrick Zidon himself, or "persons in States *other than Colorado or North Dakota* who have shared their stories about Patrick Zidon and his activities." (Emphasis added).

Not surprisingly, both parties have minimized the value of the other's potential witnesses while touting the importance of their own. Pickrell contends that Zidon could present his witnesses by either deposition or live video if the trial were venued in Colorado. Of course, the knife cuts both ways, and the same could be said for the presentation of Pickrell's witnesses in North Dakota. Neither party has suggested witnesses would be unwilling or unable to travel to either venue. With the information available to the Court, this factor weighs in favor of a North Dakota venue.

3. INTERESTS OF JUSTICE

[13] In *Terra Int'l. Inc. v. Mississippi Chem. Corp.*, the Eighth Circuit recognized several factors to consider in the interest of justice for Section 1404(a) purposes: (1) judicial economy, (2) the plaintiff's choice of forum, (3) the comparative costs to the parties of litigating in each forum, (4) each party's ability to enforce a judgment, (5) obstacles to a fair trial, (6) conflict of law issues, and (7) the advantages of having a local court determine questions of local law. 119 F.3d 688, 696 (8th Cir.1997). Regarding the first factor, the Court finds that judicial economy would not be better served by a transfer of venue.

"In general, federal courts give considerable deference to a plaintiff's choice of forum and thus the party seeking a transfer under typically bears the burden of proving that a transfer is warranted." *Terra Int'l. Inc. v. Mississippi Chem. Corp.*, 119 F.3d 688, 695 (8th Cir.1997). "[U]nless the balance is strongly in favor of the defendant, the plaintiff's choice of forum should

The general rule is that both parties must either be a resident of the state or have at least minimum contacts with the state, in order for a court in that state to have personal jurisdiction over the parties.

Mary' s second option is to sue John in federal court. Even though this was a personal injury accident, and thus a negligence cause of action, the fact that John and Mary are residents of different states might permit Mary to sue in federal court, assuming that she is seeking in excess of $75,000 in damages. Recall from Chapter 1 that federal diversity cases require the amount in controversy to exceed $75,000. In other words, the amount must be at least $75,000.01. Nevertheless, if Mary sues in federal court, that court will nonetheless apply Illinois state law, as this was the location of the accident.

You Be the Judge

Loulou lives in California. While shopping at the Help-Yourself Discount Store, Loulou slips and falls on a puddle of spilled shampoo in the store aisle, breaking her leg. After a month of recuperating in bed, incurring over $90,000 in medical bills, Loulou decides to move to Las Vegas to live with her mother, Hortense, who is suffering from arthritis and needs help with daily care. Shortly after moving to Nevada, Loulou files a negligence suit against Help-Yourself Discount Store in federal court. Does the federal court have subject matter jurisdiction?

rarely be disturbed." *Gulf Oil Corp. v. Gilbert*, 330 U.S. 501, 508, 67 S.Ct. 839, 91 L.Ed. 1055 (1947); [FN6] *Reid-Walen v. Hansen*, 933 F.2d 1390, 1396 (8th Cir.1991) (finding that the defendant "must overcome the heavy presumption against disturbing the plaintiff's forum choice"). Zidon currently resides and works in North Dakota. Zidon also states that a substantial part of the events giving rise to this claim occurred in North Dakota.

FN6. Gulf Oil was originally decided in the context of the doctrine of *forum non conveniens*—a precursor to Section 1404(a)—where the U.S. Supreme Court enunciated a general list of private and public interests, which have assisted the Courts in evaluating a motion to transfer venue. Section 1404(a) is not merely a codification of *forum non conveniens*, but rather a modification that eliminated the harsh result of dismissal. As a consequence, the federal doctrine of *forum non conveniens* has continuing application only in cases where the alternative forum is abroad. *American Dredging Co. v. Miller*, 510 U.S. 443, 449 n. 2, 114 S.Ct. 981, 127 L.Ed.2d 285 (1994). "This is not to say that the relevant factors have changed or that the plaintiff's choice of forum is not to be considered, but only that the discretion to be exercised is broader." *Norwood v. Kirkpatrick*, 349 U.S. 29, 32, 75 S.Ct. 544, 99 L.Ed. 789 (1955).

The next factor the Court must consider is the comparative costs to the parties of litigating in each forum. Neither party has offered the court any estimates as to how much more it would cost to try the case in the other party's forum of choice.

Finally, turning to the remaining factors, namely each party's ability to enforce a judgment, obstacles to a fair trial, conflict of law issues, and the advantages of having a local court determine questions of local law, the Court sees no difficulty in either party enforcing a favorable judgment on its claims in either federal forum. Thus, this factor does not weigh in favor of transfer. Additionally, the Court does not find any relative advantages or obstacles to a fair trial for either party in either forum. The Court finds that the balance of the interest of justice factors weighs in favor of a North Dakota venue.

III. CONCLUSION

In summary, the Court finds that Zidon's claims arise out of Pickrell's contacts with North Dakota via the Internet and establish personal jurisdiction. The exercise of personal jurisdiction over Pickrell based on such contacts does not offend due process. An application of the "effects test" derived from *Calder v. Jones*, 465 U.S. 783, 104 S.Ct. 1482, 79 L.Ed.2d 804 (1984), in the context of Internet activity, is appropriate and warranted. The exercise of personal jurisdiction is proper because of the foreseeable "effects" of Pickrell's Internet communications in North Dakota. It is clear that Pickrell's Internet communications were expressly targeted at, and directed to, the forum State of North Dakota. The Web site at issue directly targeted North Dakota, and specifically, North Dakota resident Patrick Zidon. There is no question that the focus of the Web site was directed uniquely toward North Dakota and Patrick Zidon.

This Court also finds that Pickrell has not met her burden of showing that a transfer to Colorado is more convenient for the parties or witnesses, or is in the interests of justice. The Court, in its discretion, expressly finds that a change of venue is neither required nor warranted. Pickrell's Motion to Dismiss (Docket No. 7) is DENIED.

IT IS SO ORDERED.

Source: *Zidon v. Pickrell*, 344 F.Supp.2d 624 (St. Paul, MN: Thomson West). Reprinted with permission from Westlaw.

SUBJECT MATTER JURISDICTION

subject matter jurisdiction
A court's authority over the *res*, the subject of the case.

federal question
The jurisdiction given to federal courts in cases involving the interpretation and application of the U.S. Constitution or acts of Congress.

The second type of jurisdiction that a court must have before deciding a case is **subject matter jurisdiction.** In essence, the court must have authority to hear a particular type of case. Subject matter jurisdiction concerns the actual issue pending between the parties, that is, the subject matter. For example, if Loulou wants to divorce her husband, Dudley, she would not file her case in traffic court. Only a domestic relations/family law court in the applicable state would have subject matter jurisdiction over a divorce proceeding. Similarly, a bankruptcy law judge would not have the power to hear a criminal law case, as subject matter jurisdiction is lacking. State courts cannot hear an antitrust case because only federal courts have this authority. Recall Chapter 1, in which the authority of federal courts is discussed. Federal courts hear diversity cases, as an example. Consider again the hypothetical case at the start of this chapter. In this example, since federal courts may hear both civil and criminal cases, the federal court in Illinois would have subject matter jurisdiction over Mary and John's case. Aside from diversity cases, the other common basis for federal jurisdiction is where there is a **federal question** involved. A federal question is the jurisdiction given to federal courts in cases involving the interpretation

You Be the Judge

Hansel and Gretel have been married for 10 years and have always resided in the same state. Gretel grows weary of living in the woods and moves to a large city in a nearby state. She files for divorce against Hansel in federal court. Their property is in excess of $250,000. Does the federal court have subject matter jurisdiction to hear this case?

CASE IN POINT

Court of Appeals of Kansas.
Roger Alan ANDERSON, Appellant,
v.
STATE of Kansas, Appellee.
No. 85,797.
Sept. 14, 2001.

Before ELLIOTT, P.J., BEIER, J., and PADDOCK, Special Judge.
ELLIOTT, P.J.:

[1] In this K.S.A. 60-1507 proceeding, Roger Alan Anderson claims his conviction of a felony is unconstitutional because Kansas state courts have no jurisdiction to hear felony cases.

The trial court summarily denied the motion and we affirm.

Anderson claims the United States Supreme Court has exclusive jurisdiction for all cases in which the State is a party. Article III, § 2, clause 2 of the United States Constitution states: "In all cases. . . and those in which a State shall be a party, the supreme Court shall have original Jurisdiction."

[2] This grant of original jurisdiction is not exclusive. See *Rhode Island v. Massachusetts*, 37 U.S. (12 Pet.) 657, 9 L.Ed. 1233 (1838). If the parties are willing, these types of cases can be litigated in state courts. *Popovici v. Agler*, 280 U.S. 379, 383, 50 S.Ct. 154, 74 L.Ed. 489 (1930).

[3] The exercise of the United States Supreme Court's original jurisdiction is not obligatory; rather, it is discretionary. See *Texas v. New Mexico*, 462 U.S. 554, 570, 103 S.Ct. 2558, 77 L.Ed.2d 1 (1983).

[4][5] Original jurisdiction is to be honored "only in appropriate cases. And the question of what is appropriate concerns, of course, the seriousness and dignity of the claim; yet beyond that it necessarily involves the availability of another forum where there is jurisdiction over the named parties, where the issues tendered may be litigated, and where appropriate relief may be had. We incline to a sparing use of our original jurisdiction so that our increasing duties with the appellate docket will not suffer. [Citation omitted.]" *Illinois v. City of Milwaukee*, 406 U.S. 91, 93-94, 92 S.Ct. 1385, 31 L.Ed.2d 712 (1972).

Further, the regulation and punishment of crimes not involving interstate commerce "has always been the province of the States." *United States v. Morrison*, 529 U.S. 598, 618, 120 S.Ct. 1740, 146 L.Ed.2d 658 (2000).

As near as we can discover, only once in its history has the United States Supreme Court heard an original criminal case. See *United States v. Shipp*, 214 U.S. 386, 29 S.Ct. 637, 53 L.Ed. 1041 (1909) (criminal contempt of the United States Supreme Court).

Article 3, § 6(b) of the Kansas Constitution grants our district courts with jurisdiction as shall be provided by law. K.S.A. 22-2601 grants our district courts with exclusive jurisdiction to try all felony and other criminal cases.

The trial court did not err in dismissing Anderson's K.S.A. 60-1507 motion.

Affirmed.

Source: *Anderson v. State*, 29 Kan. App.2d 782, 31 P.3d 322 (St. Paul, MN: Thomson West). Reprinted with permission from Westlaw.

and application of the United States Constitution or acts of Congress. However, the complaint must arise under the Constitution or laws of the United States.

Note that Mary's attorney has the option to sue John in either state court in Illinois or in federal court, based on **diversity jurisdiction.** This is the authority of the federal court to hear a case where the parties are citizens of different states and the amount at issue is in excess of $75,000. Courts will look at the **domicile** of the parties in order to determine if diversity jurisdiction applies. Domicile refers to the citizenship of each party at the time the action is filed, not at the time the action arose. In this hypothetical case, assume that John's travel to the business meeting in Illinois is at the direct request of his employer, and thus he is "in the course of business" at the time the accident occurred. In this situation, Mary will likely sue John, as well as John's employer. The domicile of a corporation may be one of two places: the state in which it was incorporated or the state in which it principally conducts its business.

If Mary can sue John in either federal or state court, then it is said that these two courts have **concurrent jurisdiction**; that is, the state court has overlapping jurisdiction. Most federal courts have concurrent jurisdiction, unless it is statutorily prohibited. For example, federal statutes specify that subject matter involving copyright cases, bankruptcy, antitrust, and certain other substantive areas are the **exclusive jurisdiction** of federal courts. This means that state courts cannot hear these types of cases. Exclusive jurisdiction implies that there is no other court that can hear a certain case.

diversity jurisdiction
Authority of the federal court to hear a case if the parties are citizens of different states and the amount at issue is over $75,000.

domicile
The place where a person maintains a physical residence with the intent to permanently remain in that place; citizenship.

concurrent jurisdiction
Jurisdiction over the subject matter exists in both state and federal court, unless statutorily prohibited.

RESEARCH THIS!

Locate the case *Erie v. Tompkins* either in a law library or on the Internet. Discuss the significance of this case to the concept of forum shopping.

exclusive jurisdiction
Only one court has the authority to hear the specific case; for example, only a federal court can decide a bankruptcy case.

forum shopping
Plaintiff attempts to choose a state with favorable rules in which to file suit.

Mary's attorney may choose which court to initiate the lawsuit, keeping in mind that John's attorney may file a motion to *remove* the case to the other court. Factors that would be evaluated by parties in selecting a forum include evidentiary rules, filing procedures, favorability of the law in a particular jurisdiction, and convenience. Note that if the court lacks subject matter jurisdiction, and neither party raises the issue, the court itself must nevertheless consider its own authority and still may refuse to hear the case, even if neither party has previously objected. However, courts will ordinarily discourage **forum shopping**, which means intentionally trying to circumvent jurisdictional issues by looking for a court favorable to one's side, without valid cause.

Consider the possibility in our hypothetical case that John is employed by the Internal Revenue Service, rather than by a private-sector employer, and is traveling on official business to a meeting in Illinois when the accident occurs. By virtue of the fact that Mary may sue both John and his employer, the appropriate forum would be federal court, as John is a government employee and the United States would be a potential litigant in the case. It can be said that the federal court would have *exclusive jurisdiction* if the United States is a defendant in the case. In other words, only a federal court would have subject matter jurisdiction if the case involved a suit against the United States.

VENUE

venue
County in which the facts are alleged to have occurred and in which the trial will take place.

Once the proper jurisdiction is determined, the final step is to locate the proper venue. **Venue** is the specific place within the jurisdiction in which the trial will take place. It is the county in which the facts are alleged to have occurred and in which the trial will take place. For example, if Illinois is the forum state, then venue refers to the specific county that is the appropriate place for the trial, as in Cook County or DuPage County. For federal courts, venue is the determination of which of the 13 districts is the appropriate place for trial. Thus, jurisdiction refers to the authority of a court to hear a case, whereas venue is the proper place within that jurisdiction where the trial takes place. State statutes determine the correct venue.

SIGNIFICANCE OF JURISDICTION TO PRECEDENT

Perhaps it is helpful to consider how the judges on the court television shows decide cases. Do they base their rulings on whim, on whether they like the appearance of a litigant, or on their own personal values? The answer should be no. If this were true, and judges were able to decide cases independently of one another, then litigants would be at the mercy of the courts. It would be impossible to predict the consequences of one's actions, and there would be no fairness or consistency in decisions from one case to the next. Fortunately, this is not the basis of our legal system. Lawyers rely on case law to establish whether there is a reasonable basis for pursing a legal claim on behalf of a client. By examining precedent, lawyers can predict with some

You Be the Judge

Mortimer lives in Leawood, Kansas, but regularly travels across the state line to get to his job in Kansas City, Missouri. One day, while walking down the street near his office in Kansas City, Mortimer trips on a cracked sidewalk in front of a grocery store and sustains a broken leg. The grocery store is part of a chain that has stores located in both Kansas and Missouri. Mortimer sues the store in federal court in Kansas. What is the area of substantive law that would be applied in this case? Does the federal court have proper jurisdiction here?

CASE IN POINT

Supreme Court of the United States
The FEDERAL REPUBLIC OF GERMANY et al.,
v.
UNITED STATES et al.
No. 127, Orig. (A-736).
March 3, 1999.

Justice Souter filed a concurring opinion in which Justice Ginsburg joined.

Justice Breyer filed a dissenting opinion in which Justice Stevens joined.

PER CURIAM.

The motion of the Federal Republic of Germany, et al. (plaintiffs) for leave to file a bill of complaint and the motion for preliminary injunction against the United States of America and Jane Dee Hull, Governor of the State of Arizona, both raised under this Court's original jurisdiction, are denied. Plaintiffs' motion to dispense with printing requirements is granted. Plaintiffs seek, among other relief, enforcement of an order issued this afternoon by the International Court of Justice, on its own motion and with no opportunity for the United States to respond, directing the United States to prevent Arizona's scheduled execution of Walter LaGrand. Plaintiffs assert that LaGrand holds German citizenship. With regard to the action against the United States, which relies on the *ex parte* order of the International Court of Justice, there are imposing threshold barriers. First, it appears that the United States has not waived its sovereign immunity. Second, it is doubtful that Art. III, § 2, cl. 2, provides an anchor for an action to prevent execution of a German citizen who is not an ambassador or consul. With respect to the action against the State of Arizona, as in *Breard v. Greene*, 523 U.S. 371, 377, 118 S.Ct. 1352, 140 L.Ed.2d 529 (1998) (*per curiam*), a foreign government's ability here to assert a claim against a State is without evident support in the Vienna Convention and in probable contravention of Eleventh Amendment principles. This action was filed within only two hours of a scheduled execution that was ordered on January 15, 1999, based upon a sentence imposed by Arizona in 1984, about which the Federal Republic of Germany learned in 1992. Given the tardiness of the pleas and the jurisdictional barriers they implicate, we decline to exercise our original jurisdiction.

Justice SOUTER, with whom Justice GINSBURG joins, concurring.

I join in the foregoing order, subject to the qualification that I do not rest my decision to deny leave to file the bill of complaint on any Eleventh Amendment principle. In exercising my discretion, I have taken into consideration the position of the Solicitor General on behalf of the United States.

Justice BREYER, with whom Justice STEVENS joins, dissenting.

The Federal Republic of Germany et al. (Germany) has filed a motion for leave to file a complaint, seeking as relief an injunction prohibiting the execution of Walter LaGrand pending final resolution of Germany's case against the United States in the International Court of Justice (ICJ)—a case in which Germany claims that Arizona's execution of LaGrand violates the Vienna Convention. Germany also seeks a stay of that execution "pending the Court's disposition of the motion for leave to file an original bill of complaint after a normal course of briefing and deliberation on that motion." Motion for Leave to File a Bill of Complaint and for a Temporary Restraining Order or Preliminary Injunction 2 (Motion). The ICJ has issued an order "indicat[ing]" that the "United States should take all measures at its disposal to ensure that Walter LaGrand is not executed pending the final decision in these [ICJ] proceedings." ¶ 9, *id.*, at 6-7.

The Solicitor General has filed a letter in which he opposes any stay. In his view, the "Vienna Convention does not furnish a basis for this Court to grant a stay of execution," and "an order of the International Court of Justice indicating provisional measures is not binding and does not furnish a basis for judicial relief." The Solicitor General adds, however, that he has "not had time to read the materials thoroughly or to digest the contents." Letter from Solicitor General Waxman filed Mar. 3, 1999, with Clerk of this Court.

Germany's filings come at what is literally the eleventh hour. Nonetheless, Germany explains that it did not file its case in the ICJ until it learned that the State of Arizona had admitted that it was aware, when LaGrand was arrested, that he was a German national. That admission came only eight days ago, and the ICJ issued its preliminary ruling only today. Regardless, in light of the fact that both the ICJ and a sovereign nation have asked that we stay this case, or "indicate[d]" that we should do so, Motion 6, I would grant the preliminary stay that Germany requests. That stay would give us time to consider, after briefing from all interested parties, the jurisdictional and international legal issues involved, including further views of the Solicitor General, after time for study and appropriate consultation.

The Court has made Germany's motion for a preliminary stay moot by denying its motion to file its complaint and "declin[ing] to exercise" its original jurisdiction in light of the "tardiness of the pleas and the jurisdictional barriers they implicate." *Ante*, at 1017. It is at least arguable that Germany's reasons for filing so late are valid, and the jurisdictional matters are arguable. Indeed, the Court says that it is merely "*doubtful* that Art. III, § 2, cl. 2, provides an anchor" for the suit and that a foreign government's ability to assert a claim against a State is "without *evident* support in the Vienna Convention and in *probable* contravention of Eleventh Amendment principles." *Ante*, at 1017 (emphasis added). The words "doubtful" and "probable," in my view, suggest a need for fuller briefing.

For these reasons I would grant a preliminary stay.

Source: *Germany v. United States*, 526 U.S. 111, 119 S.Ct. 1016 (St. Paul, MN: Thomson West). Reprinted with permission from Westlaw.

stare decisis
General legal principle in which a court abides by the prior decisions in settling cases.

certainty the likelihood of success in their case, by comparing the outcomes of similar cases in their jurisdiction. This is the basis for the concept of **stare decisis**. The phrase literally means "to stand by that which is decided." Thus, when a court television judge decides a case, he or she is relying on the precedent of cases in the jurisdiction in which the court sits.

In resolving legal disputes, courts are required to consider the decisions of previous courts in deciding the current case, comparing identical legal issues in a similar fact situation. This is referred to as examining precedent in one's jurisdiction. Supreme Court Justice Thurgood Marshall defined this concept as the "means by which we will ensure that the law will not merely change erratically, but will develop in a principled and intelligible fashion." Similarly, Justice William Rehnquist affirmed this concept in a recent court case, asserting that stare decisis "carries such persuasive force that we have always required a departure from precedent to be supported by some special justification." In the same vein, Justice Clarence Thomas exclaimed, "stare decisis provides continuity to our system, it provides predictability, and in our process of case-by-case decision making, I think it is a very important and critical concept."

It may be said that stare decisis requires the courts to not alter well-established precedent without significant reason, and that it is far preferable to uphold precedent, so long as it is not in conflict with current societal customs and values. Keep in mind that society's morality and ethical values are constantly changing, and thus the legal system is also evolving. For example, the landmark case of *Plessy v. Ferguson*, which upholds segregation, would still be valid law were it not for the power and authority of the court to reverse or disturb laws that are no longer constitutionally correct or reasonable.

Once courts have decided a particular issue in a certain way, then other courts in the same jurisdiction, faced with similar facts and the same issue, customarily decide future cases in the same way, unless change is justified. Here is the significance of identifying the correct jurisdiction. In order to apply the correct legal principles to a present fact situation, one must first identify the applicable legal rules, and precedent, in that jurisdiction. Legal analysis involves finding prior court decisions, called *precedent*, and then applying them to the facts, but this legal research must be undertaken using the law in the appropriate jurisdiction. It is relatively useless to research negligence law in Iowa if your case involves a negligence action in New York, where both parties reside and the cause of action arose. You must begin your research by examining case law in New York, and then, if necessary, expanding your search to include the relevant federal circuit cases that include New York.

CYBER TRIP

Have a look at the Web site of the Library of Congress in Washington, DC. What are some of the features of this site that might help you in your research of a case?
www.loc.gov

Keep in mind that precedent is the opinions of the court that interprets, explains, or modifies the application of legal principles to a specific factual situation. Moreover, precedent also includes court decisions that interpret statutes, which are not common law, but rather laws enacted by legislature and codified. Therefore, precedent builds upon the existing body of case law, so that for purposes of fairness and continuity, judges will decide similar cases using the authoritative reasoning in those prior cases, so long as a similar factual situation is presented.

The extent to which a court will rely on precedent in prior cases is limited to the geographic limitations of the court in a certain region, whether it is a specific state, region, or federal circuit. The necessity to research the law by looking for cases or statutes in your jurisdiction will be discussed in depth in Chapters 3 and 4.

Courts are required to follow precedent if it is a decision from a higher court within the same jurisdiction or from the U.S. Supreme Court, whose decisions are binding on *all* courts in the nation. If a court is bound to follow the decision of another court in the same jurisdiction, this is referred to as *mandatory* or *binding authority*. Court decisions that are from a higher court in the same jurisdiction are mandatory authority. Thus, if a decision is handed down by the Illinois Supreme Court, that decision is binding authority for all lower courts in Illinois. If the U.S. Court of Appeals for the Seventh Circuit decides a case, that opinion is mandatory authority for all other decisions within the seventh circuit. Based on the concept of stare decisis, it is essential that precedent be cited that is mandatory authority for the court who will hear your case. Unless you have a **case of first impression**, in which you have a new or undecided legal question before the court, then finding controlling authority means that you can predict the likely outcome of your case.

case of first impression
A case in which no previous court decision with similar facts or legal issue has arisen before.

On the other hand, court opinions that are issued from a higher court outside your jurisdiction are relevant only insofar as it is deemed to be *persuasive authority* in fact situations that are new or unique in your jurisdiction. These decisions are not binding, but may be cited in the same manner as secondary authority, such as legal encyclopedias. Courts may consider the legal reasoning in such cases and look to that decision for guidance, but they are not obligated to follow the decision and reach the same conclusion in a similar case. For example, if a decision from the Missouri Supreme Court is issued, the Kansas Supreme Court is not required to reach the same conclusion in a case with similar legal issue and similar facts. It may be persuasive authority only if there has been no such similar case as yet decided in the state of Kansas. Thus, it can be seen that jurisdiction limits the reach of precedent, as the geographical boundaries determine when a legal outcome is binding.

Summary

Legal analysis requires resolving the jurisdictional issue before going any further in the research process. One must define the appropriate forum to initiate a lawsuit, based on the requirements of subject matter jurisdiction and personal jurisdiction. If one files a suit in the wrong court, it is likely that the case will be summarily dismissed for lack of jurisdiction. Indeed, when filing a case in federal court, one is required to file a "statement of jurisdiction," referring to the specific circumstances that warrant the case being heard in federal court.

Likewise, one must also define the appropriate jurisdiction in order to locate the relevant law applicable to the client's fact situation. In the following chapters, the process of legal analysis, and the practice of applying law to hypothetical fact situations, will be explored in depth.

Key Terms

Authority
Binding authority (mandatory authority)
Case of first impression
Concurrent jurisdiction
Diversity jurisdiction
Domicile
Exclusive jurisdiction
Federal question
Forum shopping
In personam jurisdiction
In rem jurisdiction
Minimum contacts
Persuasive authority
Stare decisis
Subject matter jurisdiction
Venue

Discussion Questions

1. Distinguish concurrent jurisdiction and exclusive jurisdiction.
2. If your client's case may be brought in either federal court or your state court, what are some of the considerations you will have in determining where to file the claim?
3. Since the U.S. Supreme Court only has original jurisdiction on limited matters, but yet receives thousands of petitions for certiorari, discuss whether there is sufficient opportunity for parties to have their case heard, given that the Court only decides between 100 to 150 cases each term.
4. With the increasing popularity of the Internet, new issues arise regarding the determination of jurisdiction, since there are no physical boundaries in cyberspace. Discuss what standards the courts might consider in determining whether they have jurisdiction over a Web site operator.
5. Explain what might happen if clients had the opportunity to choose the court in which they could file a lawsuit, without any jurisdictional requirements or limitations.
6. Domestic relations cases typically involve matters such as divorce and custody. Explain what jurisdiction a state court has over family law matters and whether federal courts have jurisdiction over any domestic relations cases.

Exercises

1. You have filed a negligence lawsuit in the trial court of the state of California. Which of the following cases are binding on the California court?
   a. Decision of the New York Supreme Court.
   b. Decision from the U.S. Supreme Court.
   c. Decision from the federal circuit court of appeals for California.
2. You have filed a negligence lawsuit, in a case with damages exceeding $75,000 in the U.S. District Court for the Northern District of Illinois. Which of the following cases are binding on your court?
   a. Decision from the New Jersey Supreme Court.
   b. Decision from the Illinois Supreme Court.
   c. Decision from the U.S. Appellate Court for the Seventh Circuit.
3. Suppose that the Kansas Supreme Court issued a decision which held that all owners of scooters are liable for the injuries caused to pedestrians who are run over by people riding scooters on sidewalks. Subsequently, a similar case arises in Colorado, where this is a case of first impression. May the Colorado court consider the holding of the Kansas case in deciding this case?
4. Rapunzel is extremely wealthy and owns a castle in California, a mansion in Florida, and a beach house in Maine. She spends about four months of the year at each of her residences. If a court is trying to determine Rapunzel's domicile, and she can have just one, what will be the result?
5. Nate, a professional basketball player, resides in Philadelphia during basketball season, maintaining a permanent residence there, and then lives in Phoenix in the off-season, where his family resides and his children attend school. For purposes of personal jurisdiction, what is Nate's domicile?

CERTIORARI: asking the Supreme court to review the decision of a lower court.

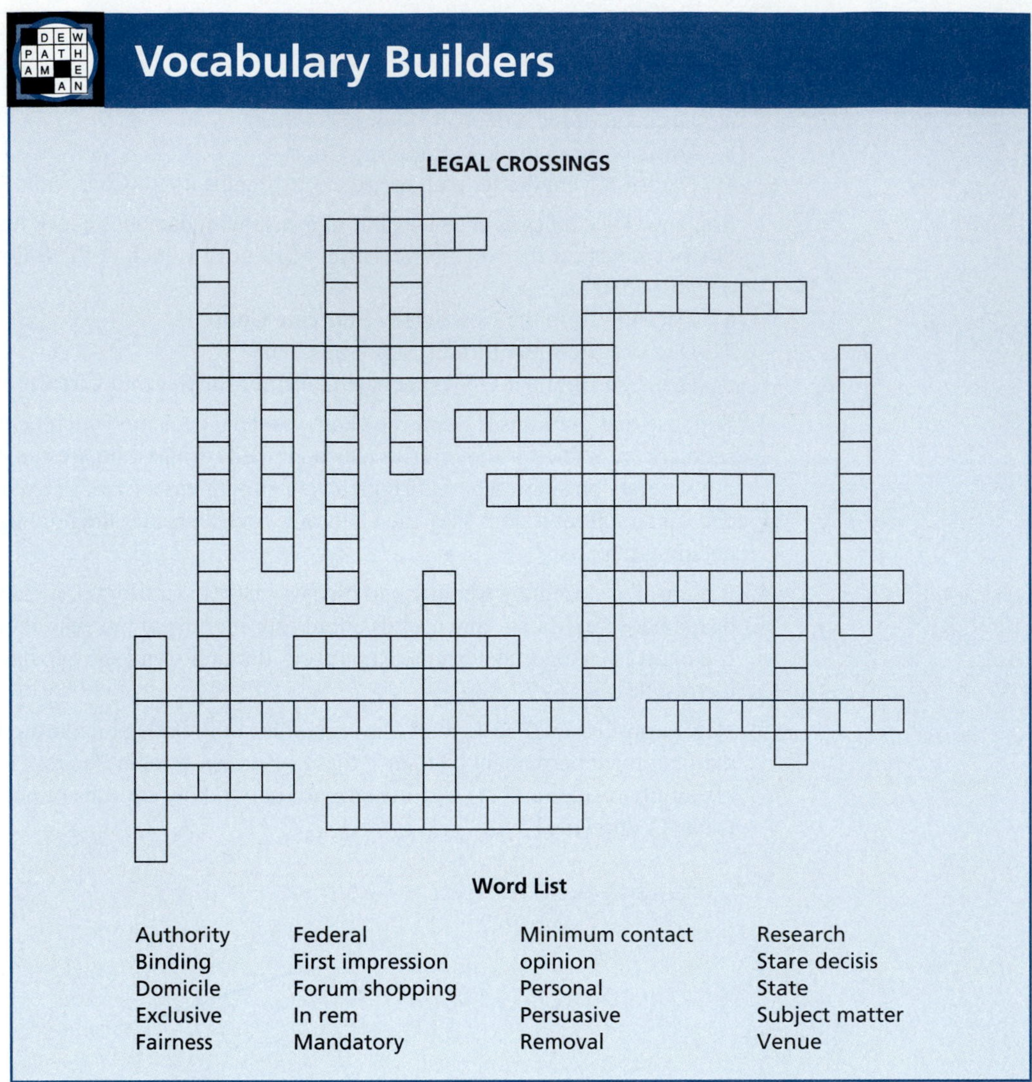

Vocabulary Builders

LEGAL CROSSINGS

Word List

Authority	Federal	Minimum contact	Research
Binding	First impression	opinion	Stare decisis
Domicile	Forum shopping	Personal	State
Exclusive	In rem	Persuasive	Subject matter
Fairness	Mandatory	Removal	Venue

Chapter 3

Categorization of the Law

CHAPTER OBJECTIVES

After reading this chapter, you will be able to:

- Define the goals of classifying cases before undertaking legal research.
- Explain the three steps involved in categorizing cases.
- Describe the importance of legal precedent in the reasoning process.

One of the primary objectives of an introductory course in the law should be to promote the development of the skills of legal analysis. As previously noted in Chapter 1, studying the law does not demand basic memorization of a set of legal rules, but rather an understanding of how to apply the rules and use basic methods of legal reasoning to predict the outcomes of virtually any given case. The legal reasoning process will be discussed in depth in Chapter 4 and implemented throughout this textbook by critical thinking assignments labeled as *You Be the Judge*. This chapter will introduce you to the foundations of legal analysis. Judges decide cases based upon identification of the legal issue, the material facts, and the controlling authority for the case. Subsequently, they must apply the relevant law to the case in order to answer the issue that is presented. The initial step in legal analysis, especially for the student first learning how to analyze a case, is to identify the material facts and determine how they fit into specific categories of the law. You should be able to organize the legal problem by making three preliminary decisions:

- Do the facts encompass *substantive law* or *procedural law*?
- Do the facts involve *civil law* or *criminal law*?
- Do the facts require the application of *state law* or *federal law*?

Once these initial determinations have been made, then you are on track to analyzing the case at hand. These classifications enable you to select the correct source of law, legal issue, and relevant jurisdictional authority that are important in predicting the likely outcome of the case at hand.

SUBSTANTIVE AND PROCEDURAL LAW

To understand the law and be able to classify any legal problem, you must know the difference between substantive law and procedural law. Intertwined with these two categories of the law is distinguishing between civil law and criminal law. This distinction will be addressed later in this chapter. Your ability to differentiate between these concepts directly impacts your mastery of the skill of legal reasoning and analysis.

substantive law
Legal rules that are the content or substance of the law, defining rights and duties of citizens.

Substantive law is the subject or content area of the law. Content areas of the law are the basis for any legal issue. For example, contracts, torts, and criminal law are all content areas. In order to pinpoint the legal issue of any fact situation, legal professionals must discern the relevant area of the law. This includes identifying whether the facts involve substantive versus procedural issues. Substantive law consists of the substance or content of the laws, which define and create legal rights and duties in society. It is the substance or body of law that provides guidance on how people in society must behave, and the results of errant conduct. Substantive law is constantly changing, adapting to current societal trends and evolving morality and ethical values. It is not simply a system based on threats on how to behave, backed up by force—penalties for failure to conform to the conduct required in society. Rather, substantive law also seeks to protect one's individual rights, to promise to uphold one's legal rights without permitting infringement on another citizen's rights. It is this balance of rights that is at the heart of our legal system.

procedural law
The set of rules that are used to enforce the substantive law.

Procedural law is the set of rules that courts and parties follow in taking a case from origination to conclusion. It is the rules that guide the court and the parties fairly through the legal process. The goal of procedural law is to ensure that the laws, whether civil or criminal, are fairly applied and that all necessary steps are properly followed throughout all aspects of the legal system. Procedural law involves such matters as the proper time frame for filing a lawsuit, notifying the other party of the legal proceedings, trial procedures, the evidence that may be presented, discovery methods and rules, and the rules related to the appeals process.

The distinction between substantive and procedural law is readily illustrated using the content area of criminal law. Murder, robbery, and arson are all defined by statute and are specific examples of substantive law. The state criminal statutes delineate each of these unlawful acts and also set forth particular penalties for committing these unlawful acts. On the other hand, an example of procedural law might be the type of evidence that can be introduced at a murder trial.

The constitutional guarantee of "due process of law," found in the Fifth and Fourteenth Amendments of the U.S. Constitution, serves as a source of substantive and procedural criminal law. These amendments proscribe both the states and the federal government from depriving "any person of life, liberty or property, without due process of law."

Trial procedures must be fair, and it is important to society that government officials be unbiased and preserve individual rights. However, these requirements must be detailed and thus are spelled out in codes of criminal procedure. Rules regarding criminal investigations and trials are specifically outlined, so as to provide some measure of predictability and protections for the accused.

Concerns about demanding proper procedures is still a slippery slope for the courts, as due process means much more than just guaranteeing that technicalities are followed. Courts are constantly asked to decide if the procedural fairness of the legal system has been satisfied. Where the government is found to have violated procedural due process, the result may potentially be a reversal of a criminal conviction, or grounds for an appeal.

On the other hand, in a civil case, such as involving a customer who slips and falls in the produce section of a grocery store, substantive law may include the duty of a shopkeeper to maintain the premises so as to avoid injury to an invited guest of the shop. An example of procedural law in a civil case might be the statute of limitations dictating how long a store customer has to sue an errant shopkeeper who failed to maintain the premises. Procedural law encompasses such mandates as the rules in filing lawsuits and in which court to file. In adhering to the rules, the parties are equitably guided throughout the legal process. Procedural laws may include the rules of evidence as well as rules of appellate procedure, such as how long a losing party has to file a notice of appeal. It should be noted that there is an overlap between substantive

RESEARCH THIS!

Read the case *Schiavo ex rel Schindler v. Schiavo*, 358 F.2d 1161 (Fl. 2005). Summarize the case, focusing on the distinction between substantive and procedural due process.

CASE IN POINT

Supreme Judicial Court of Massachusetts,
Worcester.
COMMONWEALTH
v.
Eric W. NEILSON.
Argued March 6, 1996.
Decided June 25, 1996.

Before LIACOS, C.J., and WILKINS, ABRAMS, LYNCH and GREANEY, JJ.

LYNCH, Justice.

The defendant, Eric W. Neilson, is charged with illegal possession of marihuana and cultivating and distributing marihuana, in violation of G.L. c. 94C, § § 32C, 34 (1994 ed.). A District Court judge allowed the defendant's motion to suppress evidence and contraband obtained in a search of his dormitory room at Fitchburg State College. A single justice of this court granted the Commonwealth's application for an interlocutory appeal from the allowance of the defendant's motion and transmitted the case to the Appeals Court. We transferred the case here on our own initiative and now affirm the decision of the District Court.

1. *Facts*. The motion judge did not recite the detailed findings, but there is no dispute as to the following facts. At the time of his arrest, the defendant was a twenty-three year old student living in a dormitory at Fitchburg State College, a public institution. Before moving into the dormitory, the defendant signed a residence hall contract, which stated, in relevant part, that "[r]esidence life staff members will enter student rooms to inspect for hazards to health or personal safety." . . .

On the morning of April 30, 1993, a maintenance worker heard a cat inside a dormitory suite containing four bedrooms, including the defendant's. He reported the information to college officials, who visited the suite and informed one of the residents (not the defendant) that any cat must be removed pursuant to the college's health and safety regulations. That afternoon, a college official posted notices on all four bedroom doors of the suite, informing the students of the possible violation of college policy and alerting them that a "door to door check" would be conducted by 10 P.M. that night to ensure that the cat had been removed.

That night, the officials returned; the defendant was not present. While searching the defendant's bedroom, the officials noticed a light emanating from the closet. The officials, fearing a fire hazard, opened the closet door. There, they discovered two four-foot tall marihuana plants, along with lights, fertilizer, and numerous other materials for marihuana cultivation and use.

The officials stopped their investigation at that point, and requested the assistance of the Fitchburg State College campus police, who have powers of arrest. G.L. c. 22C, § 63 (1994 ed.). The police arrived at the suite, entered the bedroom, and observed the marihuana plants and other apparatus. They took photographs of the evidence and then, with the help of the college officials, removed it from the room. At no time did the police seek, obtain, or possess a warrant for the search.

2. *Discussion*. The District Court judge ruled that the warrantless search of the dormitory room by the campus police violated the defendant's constitutional rights and that all evidence obtained as a result of the search should be suppressed. We affirm that conclusion for the reasons set forth below.

[1][2][3][4] The right [FN2] to be free from unreasonable searches and seizures as guaranteed by the Fourth Amendment to the United States Constitution applies when the police search a dormitory room in a public college. See *Morale v. Grigel*, 422 F.Supp. 988, 997 (D.N.H.1976) ("dormitory room is a student's home away from home"); *Commonwealth v. McCloskey*, 217 Pa.Super. 432, 435, 272 A.2d 271 (1970) ("dormitory room is analogous to an apartment or a hotel room"). See also *Tinker v. Des Moines Indep. Community Sch. Dist.*, 393 U.S. 503, 506, 89 S.Ct. 733, 736, 21 L.Ed.2d 731 (1969) (students do not "shed their constitutional rights . . . at the schoolhouse gate"). To be reasonable in the constitutional sense, a search usually must be supported by probable cause and be accompanied by a search warrant, unless there are circumstances excusing the use of a warrant. See *Pasqualone v. Gately*, 422 Mass. 398, 401-402, 662 N.E.2d 1034 (1996); *Commonwealth v. Viriyahiranpaiboon*, 412 Mass. 224, 226, 588 N.E.2d 643 (1992). [FN3]

FN2. The defendant made no argument below that his rights under the Massachusetts Declaration of Rights were greater than those provided under the Constitution of the United States and therefore any such argument has been waived. *Commonwealth v. Carey*, 407 Mass. 528, 531 n. 3, 554 N.E.2d 1199 (1990).

FN3. "Probable cause for Fourth Amendment purposes means that there is reason to believe that a crime has been committed and that evidence of the crime will be found in the place to be searched." *Commonwealth v. Snyder*, 413 Mass. 521, 527 n. 4, 597 N.E.2d 1363 (1992).

[5][6] The probable cause and warrant requirements are relaxed, however, in the case of searches that occur in elementary and secondary public schools. See *New Jersey v. T.L.O.*, 469 U.S. 325, 341-342, 105 S.Ct. 733, 733-734, 83 L.Ed.2d 720 (1985); *Commonwealth v. Carey*, 407 Mass. 528, 533- 534, 554 N.E.2d 1199 (1990). There is no constitutional violation when a high school official conducts a warrantless search that is "reasonable in all the circumstances." *Id.* at 533, 554 N.E.2d 1199. This reduced standard was prompted by "[c]oncerns about school officials' vital responsibility to preserve a proper educational environment" and "'[t]he special need for an immediate response to behavior that threatens either the safety of schoolchildren and teachers or the educational process itself . . .'" *Id.*, quoting *Coffman v. State*, 782 S.W.2d 249, 251 (Tex.Ct.App.1989). See *New Jersey v. T.L.O., supra* at 339–340, 105 S.Ct. at 741–742. See generally *Camara v. Municipal Court of San Francisco*, 387 U.S. 523, 534–539, 87 S.Ct. 1727, 1736–1737, 18 L.Ed.2d 930 (1967) (setting out Fourth Amendment balancing test for administrative searches).

[7] The Commonwealth urges us to extend the lesser protections afforded to high school students into the collegiate arena. Although the courts that have examined the issue are split on whether the Fourth Amendment requires probable cause and a warrant in college searches when police are involved and the evidence obtained is to be used in a criminal proceeding, courts generally require probable cause and a warrant, absent express consent or exigent circumstances. See *Piazzola v. Watkins*, 442 F.2d 284, 289 (5th Cir.1971); *People v. Cohen*, 57 Misc.2d 366, 369, 292 N.Y.S.2d 706 (N.Y.Dist.Ct.1968); *Commonwealth v. McCloskey, supra* at 434–436, 272 A.2d 271. Cf. *People v. Haskins*, 48 A.D.2d 480, 484, 369 N.Y.S.2d 869 (N.Y.1975) ("A more strict standard would certainly apply if the search had been instigated by law enforcement officials or if law enforcement personnel had participated in the search to any significant degree, thereby directly tainting the search by the school official with State action"); *State v. Hunter*, 831 P.2d 1033, 1037 (Utah Ct.App.1992) ("Nor did university officials attempt to delegate their right to inspect rooms to the police, which would result in the circumvention of traditional restrictions on police activity"). See also *New Jersey v. T.L.O., supra* at 341 n. 7, 105 S.Ct. at 743 n. 7 (not deciding whether probable cause and a warrant might be required when police are involved in a high school search); *Picha v. Wielgos*, 410 F.Supp. 1214, 1219–1221 (N.D.Ill.1976) (junior high school search by police required probable cause). . . .

. . .

[8] The defendant does not contend (and the District Court judge did not find) that the initial search of the dormitory room by college officials was improper. The defendant consented to reasonable searches to enforce the college's health and safety regulations when he signed the residence contract. See *Boston Hous. Auth. v. Guirola*, 410 Mass. 820, 827–828, 575 N.E.2d 1100 (1991). The hunt for the elusive feline fit within the scope of that consent. See *Commonwealth v. Cantalupo*, 380 Mass. 173, 178–179, 402 N.E.2d 1040 (1980). Similarly, when the college officials opened the closet door they were reasonably concerned about health and safety. Thus, the initial search was reasonable because it was intended to enforce a legitimate health and safety rule that related to the college's function as an educational institution. [FN5] See *Piazzola v. Watkins, supra* at 289 (search must further legitimate educational function); *Morale v. Grigel, supra* at 998 (same); *Smyth v. Lubbers*, 398 F.Supp. 777, 790 (W.D.Mich.1975) (same). See generally Annot., 31 A.L.R.5th 229, 337–338 (1995).

FN5. The college officials could have reported their observations to the police, who could have used the information to obtain a warrant.

[9] Instead, the crux of the defendant's argument is that constitutional violation occurred when the campus police searched the room and seized evidence. We agree. The police entered the room without a warrant, consent, or exigent circumstances. This search was unreasonable and violated the defendant's Fourth Amendment rights. The Commonwealth contends that, since the college officials were in the room by consent, and observed the drugs in plain view while pursuing legitimate objectives, the police officers' warrantless entry was proper. Furthermore, the Commonwealth argues, the police action was lawful because it did not exceed the scope of the prior search and seizure by college officials. We disagree.

First, there was no consent to the police entry and search of the room. "The [defendant's] consent [was] given, not to police officials, but to the University and the latter cannot fragmentize, share or delegate it." *People v. Cohen, supra*. While the college officials were entitled to conduct a health and safety inspection, they "[c]learly . . . had no authority to consent to or join in a police search for evidence of crime." *Piazzola v. Watkins, supra* at 290.

Second, the plain view doctrine does not apply to the police seizure, where the officers were not lawfully present in the dormitory room when they made their plain view observations. *Commonwealth v. Lewin (No. 1)*, 407 Mass. 617, 627, 555 N.E.2d 551 (1990). Cf. *Commonwealth v. Franco*, 419 Mass. 635, 641, 646 N.E.2d 749 (1995); *Commonwealth v. Viriyahiranpaiboon, supra* at 227-228, 588 N.E.2d 643. While the college officials were legitimately present in the room to enforce a reasonable health and safety regulation, the sole purpose of the warrantless police entry into the dormitory room was to confiscate contraband for purposes of a criminal proceeding. An entry for such a purpose required a warrant where, as here, there was no showing of express consent or exigent circumstances. . . .

We conclude that, when the campus police entered the defendant's dormitory room without a warrant, they violated the defendant's Fourth Amendment rights. All evidence obtained as a result of that illegal search was properly suppressed by the judge below.

Judgment affirmed.

Source: *Commonwealth v. Neilson*, 423 Mass. 75, 666 N.E.2d 984 (St. Paul, MN: Thomson West). Reprinted with permission from Westlaw.

criminal law
The legal rules regarding wrongs committed against society.

and procedural issues. For example, criminal statutes delineate the penalties for failure to adhere to required standards of conduct in society, and this is the substantive legal standard; procedural law addresses the rules that must be followed in applying those penalties for failure to comply with societal demands.

CRIMINAL AND CIVIL LAW

civil law
The legal rules regarding offenses committed against the person.

In its simplest terms, **criminal law** may be defined as the legal rules regarding wrongs against society, whereas **civil law** may be described as the legal rules regarding offenses against the person. A crime is a public wrong, but a civil offense, such as a tort, is a private wrong. There may be overlap between the two categories, and the identical fact situation may give rise to both a civil suit for damages and a criminal prosecution. However, the two wrongs are considered separately, and it is possible for the malefactor to pay compensation to the victim as well as be punished by the state.

For example, in the highly publicized case of O. J. Simpson's alleged murder of Nicole Simpson and Ron Goldman, the defendant was prosecuted in a California criminal case and acquitted. Subsequently, a wrongful death action was brought against Simpson in a civil suit by the family of the victims. In this case, he was found liable for monetary damages. A similar result occurred in the case of the actor Robert Blake's alleged murder of his ex-wife. Blake was acquitted in the criminal case against him but was found civilly liable to his ex-wife's family for her wrongful death.

Examples of a criminal wrong are burglary, murder, and arson. Even though the victim is a private person, the crime is still prosecuted by the state, and it is still the state that punishes the defendant if he or she is found guilty. If Mary robs the First National Bank of Gidget and is subsequently arrested, she will be prosecuted by the U.S. government, since it regulates banking. If convicted, the punishment will be enforced by the government, and she will likely be sentenced to the federal penitentiary. If Mary robs the local convenience shop instead, the victim is still a private person, in this case the shop owner, but Mary will still be prosecuted by the government, although in this case, it will be the state or county prosecutor rather than the federal government.

Examples of a civil offense are failing to shovel snow on your doorstep, and then your neighbor, an invited guest, slips on your doorstep and falls, or hitting a baseball through your neighbor's bedroom window. Assume that John drives recklessly home from a party late one evening, and his car collides with Mary's car. Though it is possible to be criminally charged with reckless driving, it is Mary who is the victim, and she may seek to recover monetary damages from John as a consequence of his negligent driving. Note that if John was driving while intoxicated, and the state has determined certain acts to be a wrong against society as a whole, and not just the victim, then the state legislature will enact law, for example, to make driving while intoxicated a criminal act.

The initial step in the legal analysis of any case is to accurately categorize the set of facts as a criminal or civil issue. Figure 3.1 compares the major differences between these two legal

FIGURE 3.1
Comparison of Criminal and Civil Law

	Criminal Law	Civil Law
Type of offense	Crime against society	Private wrong against person
Parties involved	Government/prosecutor vs. defendant	Plaintiff vs. defendant
Burden of proof	Beyond a reasonable doubt	By a preponderance of the evidence
Source of law	Criminal statutes (state or federal)	Common law or case law
Outcome of case	Guilty or not guilty	Liable or not liable
Remedy	Prison, death, or restitution	Damages
Right to appeal?	State: No Defendant: Yes	Either party: Yes

classifications by outlining the essential components of each system of law. Finding the applicable rules of law begins with the identification of the legal issue and the area of law.

Upon examining the chart in Figure 3.1, it should become apparent how seemingly disparate conclusions were reached in the O. J. Simpson case. Even though both the criminal and civil cases were established on the exact same set of facts, several factors may have influenced the outcome. First, since the burden of proof is different, the types and amount of evidence that may be introduced or allowed in each type of case is different. There is a lower standard of proof in civil cases. "By a preponderance of the evidence" essentially means "more likely than not" that the defendant is liable, based on the facts. However, the standard "beyond a reasonable doubt" is very high, primarily because of what is at stake. The outcome of the criminal trial may result in deprivation of a defendant's life or liberty, and therefore the state must be careful to balance the needs of society with the fairness accorded the accused under the Constitution. The Sixth Amendment guarantees the accused the right to a fair trial. Second, the remedy in each area of the law is different, and third, the level of evidence admissible at a criminal trial is different than at a civil trial. For example, if Mary is charged with robbery of the convenience store, the state may not be allowed to introduce evidence that Mary has been thrice convicted of robbery in the past. The rationale for excluding this evidence is that such testimony would be prejudicial to Mary receiving a fair trial. The fact that she has been convicted of robbery three times in the past is not valid proof that she has committed robbery for a fourth time. It should be remembered that the defendant in a criminal case need not prove anything. The defendant is presumed innocent until proven guilty, since the procedural safeguards of due process require the government to ensure fundamental fairness under the law. Hence, the juries in each of the Simpson cases may have heard different evidence and were instructed as to a different standard of proof required in order to hold Simpson accountable.

Regarding the trial itself, there is no guaranteed right to a trial by jury in a state court for a civil matter, although the state may allow this under certain circumstances, and this is detailed in each state's code of civil procedure. Ordinarily, one would not have a jury trial in a probate court or in a divorce proceeding. However, in a criminal case, the Sixth and Fourteenth Amendments guarantee the accused a right to a jury trial. Specifically, the Sixth Amendment requires the accused the right to a fair trial by an impartial jury.

As previously discussed in Chapters 1 and 2, determining which cases are heard in federal court as opposed to state court depends on the type of issue and the parties involved. The authority to hear specific cases not reserved for the federal court is left to each state's court system. In general, federal courts derive their power from the U.S. Constitution (the Supreme Court), and

You Be the Judge

Assume there is a statute in Arkansas that states: "Burglary is defined as breaking and entering into the dwelling of another with the intent to commit a felony therein."

In each of the following examples, state whether you think William has violated this statute.

1. William goes to Mabel's house at 7 p.m. when he is certain she will be home, with the intention of stealing her purse from her when she enters her house. William waits in the bushes by her front door until 8 p.m., but she never comes home, so he leaves.
2. William goes to Helga's house when he is certain she won't be home and enters the house through an unlocked front door, only to find Helga's husband, Bert, at home. William demands Bert's wallet, which Bert quickly hands over, and then leaves.
3. William sees a lawn mower left sitting in the middle of Dudley's backyard. Late at night, William walks into the unfenced yard, takes Dudley's mower, and leaves.
4. William climbs through an open window of a detached shed in the back of Mortimer's house, takes his toolbox, and leaves.
5. William goes to his girlfriend's house, where he watches television with her for several hours. When she leaves William alone in the room, he reaches inside her purse, takes her watch and diamond ring, and leaves.

CASE IN POINT

United States Court of Appeals,
Third Circuit.
BUDGET RENT-A-CAR SYSTEM, INC.
v.
Nicole CHAPPELL; Joseph Powell, III
Nicole Chappell, Appellant
No. 04-1931.
Argued Feb. 15, 2005.
Filed May 5, 2005.

Before: SLOVITER, AMBRO and ALDISERT, Circuit Judges.

OPINION OF THE COURT

AMBRO, Circuit Judge.

We apply Pennsylvania's choice-of-law rules to determine which state's substantive law (New York's, Michigan's or Pennsylvania's) governs the extent of vicarious liability of Budget Rent-a-Car System, Inc. ("Budget"), the owner of a vehicle involved in an accident that rendered Nicole Chappell ("Chappell"), a New York resident, permanently paralyzed. The accident occurred in Pennsylvania as Chappell and her boyfriend, Joseph Powell, III ("Powell"), a Michigan resident, were driving from New York to Michigan in a car Powell had rented from Budget in Michigan (and previously driven to New York).

Because the State of New York has the greatest interest in the application of its law to this dispute, we conclude that its law should apply. The contrary judgment of the District Court is reversed.

I. **Pertinent Facts and Procedural History**

On the morning of February 12, 2002, Powell rented a Nissan Xterra from Budget in Michigan. Later that day, he drove eight hours to New York to visit Chappell. Powell stayed with Chappell in New York for the rest of that week. On the evening of February 15, after Chappell completed her work week, she and Powell left New York in the Xterra, planning to drive to Michigan to spend the weekend together there.

While driving through Pennsylvania early the next morning, Powell fell asleep at the wheel. The car drifted from the left lane of Interstate 80 across the right lane and into the right guardrail, causing it to flip over. Powell escaped the crash without substantial physical injury. However, the force of the impact ejected Chappell from the Xterra, causing severe injuries. Shortly after the accident, a helicopter transported her to Mercy Hospital in Pittsburgh, where doctors diagnosed, among other injuries, spinal trauma that has rendered Chappell permanently paraplegic.

Budget initiated this action in the United States District Court for the Eastern District of Pennsylvania, seeking a declaratory judgment against Powell and Chappell and asking the Court to determine which state's substantive law governed its vicarious liability as the owner of the vehicle. [FN1] Budget argued that Michigan law should apply, capping its liability at $20,000. Chappell brought two counterclaims against Budget (vicarious liability and negligent entrustment) and a cross-claim against Powell. She argued that Budget faced unlimited vicarious liability under New York law.

FN1. The District Court exercised diversity jurisdiction pursuant to 28 U.S.C. § 1332. As noted, Chappell is a New York resident and Powell is a Michigan resident. Budget Systems, Inc. was a Delaware corporation that maintained its principal place of business in Illinois. Subsequent to the accident, it was acquired by Budget, which was and remains a Delaware corporation with its principal place of business in New Jersey.

The parties cross-moved for summary judgment on the choice-of-law issue, and the District Court granted summary judgment to Budget, holding that Pennsylvania law applied. Chappell moved for a certification of the issue and entry of a final judgment under Fed.R.Civ.P. 54(b). After the District Court granted that motion and entered a final judgment, Chappell timely appealed. We exercise appellate jurisdiction to review the District Court's final judgment under 28 U.S.C. § 1291.

II. Legal Framework

A. Pennsylvania Choice-of-Law

[1][2] To determine which state's substantive law governs, we must refer to the choice-of-law rules of the jurisdiction in which the District Court sits, here Pennsylvania. *Klaxon Co. v. Stentor Electric Mfg. Co.*, 313 U.S. 487, 496, 61 S.Ct. 1020, 85 L.Ed. 1477 (1941); *Melville v. American Home Assur. Co.*, 584 F.2d 1306, 1308 (3d Cir.1978). Under Pennsylvania law, we begin with an "interest analysis" of the policies of all interested states and then—based on the result of that analysis—characterize the case as a true conflict, false conflict, or unprovided-for case. *LeJeune v. Bliss-Salem, Inc.*, 85 F.3d 1069, 1071 (3d Cir.1996); *Lacey v. Cessna Aircraft Co.*, 932 F.2d 170, 187 & n. 15 (3d Cir.1991).

[3][4] A true conflict exists "when the governmental interests of [multiple] jurisdictions would be impaired if their law were not applied." *Lacey*, 932 F.2d at 187 n. 15. If a case presents a true conflict, Pennsylvania choice-of-law rules "call for the application of the law of the state having the most significant contacts or relationships with the particular issue." *In re Estate of Agostini*, 311 Pa.Super. 233, 457 A.2d 861, 871 (1983). As explained in the Second Restatement of Conflict of Laws,

> the factors relevant to the choice of the applicable rule of law include (a) the needs of the interstate and international systems, (b) the relevant policies of the forum, (c) the relevant policies of other interested states and the relative interests of those states in the

determination of the particular issue, (d) the protection of justified expectations, (e) the basic policies underlying the particular field of law, (f) certainty, predictability and uniformity of result, and (g) ease in the determination and application of the law to be applied.

Restatement (Second) of Conflict of Laws § 6 (1971).

[5][6] "A false conflict exists if only one jurisdiction's governmental interests would be impaired by the application of the other jurisdiction's law." *Lacey*, 932 F.2d at 187. If there is a false conflict, we must apply the law of the only interested jurisdiction. *See, e.g., Kuchinic v. McCrory*, 422 Pa. 620, 222 A.2d 897, 899–900 (1966); *Griffith v. United Air Lines, Inc.*, 416 Pa. 1, 203 A.2d 796, 807 (1964).

[7][8] Finally, an unprovided-for case arises when no jurisdiction's interests would be impaired if its laws were not applied. *Lex loci delicti* (the law of the place of the wrong—here Pennsylvania) continues to govern unprovided-for cases. *See, e.g., Miller v. Gay*, 323 Pa.Super. 466, 470 A.2d 1353, 1355–56 (1983).

With this background, we turn to the competing state laws we consider applying.

B. Relevant State Law Provisions on Vicarious Liability

1. New York

[9] New York law imposes unlimited vicarious liability on the owners of vehicles. It provides that "[e]very owner of a vehicle used or operated in [that] state shall be liable and responsible for . . . injuries to person[s] . . . resulting from negligence in the use or operation of such vehicle . . . " N.Y. Veh. & Traf. Law § 388(1) (McKinney 2002). By passing § 388(1), the New York "[l]egislature intended that the injured party be afforded a financially responsible insured person against whom to recover for injuries." *Plath v. Justus*, 28 N.Y.2d 16, 319 N.Y.S.2d 433, 268 N.E.2d 117, 119 (1971).

It is beyond dispute that § 388(1) has extraterritorial scope, that is, it can apply to accidents occurring beyond New York's borders. *Farber v. Smolack*, 20 N.Y.2d 198, 282 N.Y.S.2d 248, 229 N.E.2d 36, 40 (1967) (holding that "[t]o the extent . . . earlier decisions declined to give extraterritorial effect to [§ 388], they are overruled"). This dispute requires us to assess the *extent* of the extraterritorial scope of § 388(1). The New York Court of Appeals has held that "vicarious liability imposed by section 388(1) does not extend to owners of *vehicles that have never been registered, used, operated or intended for use within [New York]*." *Fried v. Seippel*, 80 N.Y.2d 32, 587 N.Y.S.2d 247, 599 N.E.2d 651, 654 (1992) (emphasis added). We later address whether (under New York law) the Xterra in our case falls within that exclusion.

2. Michigan

[10][11] Michigan also imposes vicarious liability on the owners of vehicles. Its law provides that "[t]he owner of a motor vehicle is liable for an injury caused by the negligent operation of the motor vehicle . . . [if] the motor vehicle is being driven with his or her express or implied consent or knowledge." Mich. Comp. Laws § 257.401(1) (2003) ("Subsection 1"). Liability is capped, however, in certain circumstances: "[The liability of] a person engaged in the business of leasing motor vehicles who is the lessor of a motor vehicle under a lease providing for the use of the motor vehicle by the lessee for a period of 30 days or less . . . is limited to $20,000.00 because of bodily injury to or death of 1 person in any 1 accident...." Mich. Comp. Laws § 257.401(3) (2003) ("Subsection 3"). In effect, vicarious liability is imposed on an owner when the driver's negligence causes an accident in another state so long as the owner-driver relationship was entered into in Michigan. *Sexton v. Ryder Truck Rental, Inc.*, 413 Mich. 406, 320 N.W.2d 843, 856 (1982).

At the time of Chappell's accident, Michigan law provided that it was a misdemeanor for "an owner knowingly [to] permit to be operated, upon any highway, a vehicle required to be registered . . . unless there is attached to and displayed on the vehicle . . . a valid registration plate issued for the vehicle . . . . " Mich. Comp. Laws § § 257.255(1), (2) (2001). [FN2]

FN2. The parties presented (and the District Court relied on) several legal arguments implicating the significance of this provision, all involving events that took place before Powell rented the vehicle. For reasons explained below, we need not reach these arguments. For the sake of completeness, however, we set out the pertinent pre-rental facts.

Assuming that Budget followed its regular procedures, after the Xterra arrived in Romulus, Michigan (on or about January 30, 2002), a Budget fleet clerk obtained Michigan license plate NVQ532 and placed that plate on one of the Xterra's seats. A "lot person" later removed the plate from the Xterra's seat and affixed it to the vehicle.

After placing the plate in the Xterra, the fleet clerk wrote license plate number "NVQ532" at the top of the vehicle's certificate of origin and took the certificate to the office of Michigan's Secretary of State. Someone unknown crossed out the fleet clerk's initial reference to "NVQ532" and wrote "PHS756" next to it.

Michigan license plate NVQ532 was registered for use with a 2001 Ford with Vehicle Identification Number 1FAFP55201G235610 that Team Fleet Financial Corporation ("Team Fleet") owned. Team Fleet leased its vehicles to Budget. Budget's fleet clerk had access to a plate registered to a vehicle that Team Fleet owned.

An employee at the Secretary of State's office used the certificate of origin, including the handwritten annotation for the license plate, to register the Xterra and to create an Application for Michigan Vehicle Title for it. The Michigan Secretary of State's office registered the Xterra with Michigan license plate PHS756 and prepared a title application for the transfer of Michigan license plate PHS756 to the Xterra.

3. Pennsylvania

[12] Pennsylvania follows the common law rule that, absent an employer-employee relationship, an automobile's owner is not vicariously liable for the negligence of its driver. *Solomon v. Commonwealth Trust Co.*, 256 Pa. 55, 100 A. 534, 535 (1917); *Shuman Estate v. Weber*, 276 Pa.Super. 209, 419 A.2d 169, 172 (1980).

III. Analysis

A. District Court Opinion

The District Court's opinion is a plot-twister. The case starts simply enough: "the parties [sought] a declaratory judgment. . . whether the law of *New York* or *Michigan* governs the extent of Budget's vicarious liability to Chappell. . . ." *Budget Rent-A-Car System, Inc. v. Chappell*, 304 F.Supp.2d 639, 644 (E.D.Pa.2004) (emphases added). "[M]indful" of what it described as "[a] delicious irony in how the parties briefed this case," *id.* at 650 n. 17, the District Court "concluded that *Pennsylvania* law controls the resolution of the issues," *id.* at 651 (emphasis added).

This conclusion unfolds as follows. The Court assessed New York and Michigan's respective vicarious liability provisions, reaching the following two intermediate determinations. First, it "predict[ed] that the New York Court of Appeals" would "avoid the serious [federal] constitutional questions" it perceived in § 388(1) by concluding that the statute's "reference to 'vehicle[s] used or operated' in New York [does not] cover vehicles that are registered outside of New York and that were not being used or operated in New York at the time of an accident," *id.* at 647–48. Second, it decided that Budget could not invoke Michigan's limitation of liability for short-term lessors of cars in Subsection 3 because "the lease between Budget Systems and Powell was 'founded on' a misdemeanor—Budget Systems's grant of permission to operate the Xterra without a valid license plate—" and is therefore a "nullity" under Michigan law, *id.* at 650.

Having determined that neither New York's nor Michigan's substantive legal provisions would apply in this case, the District Court reasoned that neither state had an interest in applying its law. *Id.* at 650-51. That is, the Court characterized this dispute as an unprovided-for case. *Id.* at 651. As a result, it held that the rule of *lex loci delicti* governed, Pennsylvania's substantive law applied, and thus Budget did not face vicarious liability. *Id.*

In sum, the District Court's choice-of-law ruling rested on its limiting interpretations of New York and Michigan substantive law. Before turning to the choice-of-law inquiry, we address the propriety of those legal interpretations.

B. Does New York's § 388(1) Apply to This Dispute?

The District Court predicted that the State of New York would not construe § 388(1) to apply to this case. Our review of this prediction is plenary. *Nationwide Mut. Ins. Co. v. Buffetta*, 230 F.3d 634, 637 (3d Cir.2000). We disagree with the District Court's analysis and conclude that this case falls within the scope of § 388(1) as that statute has been construed by New York's courts.

[13] Our core query is what does the phrase "used or operated in [New York]" in § 388(1) mean? Fortunately, New York's Court of Appeals has addressed this question on several occasions.

In *Farber v. Smolack*, the Court of Appeals implied that § 388(1) has as broad a scope of *substantive* application as would be consistent with New York's *choice-of-law* principles. [FN3] When "New York is . . the jurisdiction having 'the most significant relationship' with the issue presented," § 388(1) applies. *Farber*, 282 N.Y.S.2d 248, 229 N.E.2d at 40 (citations omitted). While this formulation is unfortunate inasmuch as it conflates—or at least equates—the substantive law question (the scope of the statute) with the choice-of-law issue (the extent of New York's interest in applying the statute), [FN4] this early precedent nonetheless sets the principle that New York will broadly apply § 388(1), perhaps as broadly as is permissible under constitutional choice-of-law principles.

FN3. *Farber* involved the following facts and disposition. Robert Smolack loaned his automobile to his brother, Arthur, so that Arthur could drive his family to Florida and back. While in North Carolina, Arthur's negligence caused an accident in which his wife was killed and his two sons were seriously injured. Representatives of the wife's estate and of the children sued Robert under § 388(1), but the trial court dismissed the claim, holding that the provision did not apply. The Court of Appeals reversed, stressing that "[all parties] were citizens and domiciliaries of New York; the car was registered in New York; arrangements for its use had been made in New York; and it was on its way back to New York when the accident occurred." *Id.* at 38.

FN4. The District Court in our case recognized the important distinction between these questions, explaining that when it "focus[ed] first on the issue of whether Section 388 covers these facts," it "[would] not address the myriad cases that have considered the applicability of that statute based on choice-of-law principles." *Budget*, 304 F.Supp.2d at 646 n. 12.

Eight years later, in *Sentry Ins. Co. v. Amsel*, 36 N.Y.2d 291, 367 N.Y.S.2d 480, 327 N.E.2d 635 (1975), the New York Court of Appeals again stressed the broad scope of the statute, explaining that "[t]he legislative history of [§ 388(1)] indicates that the Legislature intended to enlarge the vehicle owner's vicarious liability and not to draw the line at the border." *Id.* at 637.

Most recently, in *Fried v. Seippel*, the Court of Appeals directly addressed the scope of the statute and held that the "vicarious liability imposed by section 388(1) does not extend to owners of vehicles that have *never been registered, used, operated or intended for use within [New York].*" 587 N.Y.S.2d 247, 599 N.E.2d at 654 (emphasis added). In *Fried*, Avis (which operated in New York) owned a Jamaican car rental company that rented a vehicle of Jamaican registry to Seippel, a New York resident. Seippel and Fried (also a New York resident) were in the car in Jamaica when one of them[5] negligently caused a head-on collision. Fried died in the accident. His representatives sued Avis under § 388(1), and the trial court denied Avis" motion for summary judgment based on the Jamaican company's ownership of the vehicle. Putting aside the issue whether Avis should be deemed the vehicle's owner, the Court of Appeals held that § 388(1) did not apply because the car "ha[d] never been registered, used, operated or intended for use within [New York]." *Fried*, 587 N.Y.S.2d 247, 599 N.E.2d at 654. . . .

1. Scope of the Statute

Noting that "[t]he facts here fall in the middle ground between *Farber* and *Fried* because the Xterra was not registered in New York but Powell did drive it there," the District Court interpreted these cases to mean that "New York courts would conclude that the New York legislature did not intend . . . to cover vehicles that are registered outside of New York and that were not being used or operated in New York at the time of an accident." *Budget*, 304 F.Supp.2d at 647-48. We disagree with this creative legal interpretation.

The *Fried* Court stated that "the holding in *Farber* ha[d] little bearing on the statutory construction problem presented [in *Fried*], since, *by virtue of its prior 'use . . . or operat[ion] in [New York],' the accident vehicle in Farber was indisputably within section 388's substantive coverage. . . .*" *Fried*, 587 N.Y.S.2d 247, 599 N.E.2d at 654 (emphasis added). This statement by New York's highest Court is irreconcilable with the District Court's view and is arguably sufficient of itself to settle the statutory construction issue before us. As in *Farber*, by virtue of its prior use and operation in New York, the accident vehicle here is indisputably within § 388's substantive coverage.

Yet we need not labor, as the District Court did, to discern the scope of New York's law from the disposition of its precedents, for the *Fried* Court explicitly drew a line for us: "vicarious liability imposed by section 388(1) does not extend to owners of vehicles that have *never been registered, used, operated or intended for use within this State*." *Fried*, 587 N.Y.S.2d 247, 599 N.E.2d at 654 (emphasis added). The vehicle in this case was used, operated *and* intended for use within New York.

[14][15] Lest we be left with doubt as to the meaning of the seemingly clear rule announced in *Fried*, we refer to New York's intermediate courts for further guidance. "Where an intermediate appellate state court rests its considered judgment upon the rule of law which it announces, that is a datum for ascertaining state law which is not to be disregarded by a federal court unless it is convinced by other persuasive data that the highest court of the state would decide otherwise." *West v. Am. Tel. & Tel. Co.*, 311 U.S. 223, 237, 61 S.Ct. 179, 85 L.Ed. 139 (1940). In *Vasquez v. Christian Herald Ass'n*, 186 A.D.2d 467, 588 N.Y.S.2d 291, 292 (N.Y.App. Div.1992), only five months after *Fried*, the First Department of

the Appellate Division of New York's Supreme Court cited *Fried* as authority for the applicability of § 388(1) to facts similar to this case. [FN6] Leave to appeal the intermediate appellate court's decision in *Vasquez* was denied by the Court of Appeals. [FN7]

FN6. In *Vasquez* one plaintiff was a New York resident (the other an Ohio resident), the owner of the vehicle was a Pennsylvania resident (a co-defendant was a New York resident), and the accident took place in Pennsylvania. The Court explained that the "[d]efendant . . . erroneously relie[d] upon . . . *Fried* . . . [because] [an agent of the *New York* defendant (not the owner)] had operated the subject van to and from New York with [the New York defendant]'s permission." *Id*. The use of the car in New York was enough to extend liability under New York law to the Pennsylvania *owner* of the vehicle notwithstanding that the accident took place in Pennsylvania.

We also note that the United States District Court for the Eastern District of New York has decided, albeit in a not precedential opinion we cite solely as persuasive authority, that § 388(1) applied to an out-of-state accident involving a car not registered in New York on the basis of prior use and operation of the vehicle in the State. *Roberts v. Xtra Lease, Inc*., No. 98 CV 7559, 2001 WL 984872, at *7 (E.D.N.Y. June 25, 2001). . . .

. . .

In short, the District Court's conclusion that § 388(1) does not "cover vehicles that are registered outside of New York and that were not being used or operated in New York at the time of an accident," *Budget*, 304 F.Supp.2d at 648, runs afoul of New York's precedent. To the contrary, the provision applies unless the accident vehicle "ha[s] *never* been registered, used, operated or intended for use within [New York]." *Fried*, 587 N.Y.S.2d 247, 599 N.E.2d at 654 (emphasis added). Thus, the provision applies to our case.

2. Constitutional Concerns

[16] The District Court's construction of § 388(1) was premised on its perception that applying the statute in this case would implicate federal constitutional problems. It predicted that the New York courts would adopt its specific limiting construction of the statute in order "[t]o avoid the serious constitutional questions that interpreting Section 388 to cover the facts of this case would raise . . . ." *Budget*, 304 F.Supp.2d at 648. That is, the District Court interpreted New York law to require that a court invoke the doctrine of constitutional avoidance in order to sidestep potential constitutional problems raised by the application of the statute in this case. It further predicted that the New York courts would adopt a limiting construction imposing its bright-line registration requirement. We have already disagreed with the District Court's construction of the statute. We now address the constitutional concerns it perceived.

To be technical, the Court did not actually hold that application of § 388(1) would be unconstitutional. It simply predicted that the courts of New York "would recognize that the United States Supreme Court has held that due process forbids states from regulating extraterritorial activities with which they have 'slight' or 'casual' connection" and avoid the issue altogether by narrowing the statutory scope. *Id*. at 647-48 (citing *Hartford Accident & Indem. Co. v. Delta & Pine Land Co*., 292 U.S. 143, 54 S.Ct. 634, 78 L.Ed. 1178 (1934); *Home Ins. Co. v. Dick*, 281 U.S. 397, 50 S.Ct. 338, 74 L.Ed. 926 (1930)). Having parted from the District Court's statutory interpretation, we ask simply whether application of the statute in this case under the *Fried* rule would violate the Constitution (as opposed to asking whether New York courts would perceive the application of the statute in this case as a potential constitutional problem they should avoid by adopting the District Court's construction).

The Supreme Court has spoken on this issue since 1934, when the most recent case cited by the District Court was decided. In fact, the precedent that gave rise to the District Court's constitutional apprehensions is widely recognized to be irrelevant under modern law. As Chappell points out, *Delta* and *Dick* were decided before the modern states' interest framework for choice-of-law analysis began to dominate. The plurality opinion in *Allstate Ins. Co. v. Hague*, 449 U.S. 302, 101 S.Ct. 633, 66 L.Ed.2d 521 (1981), for example, noted that *Delta* has "scant relevance for today" because "[i]t implied a choice-of-law analysis which, for all intents and purposes, gave an isolated event . . . controlling constitutional significance, even though *there might have been contacts with another State . . . which would make application of its law neither unfair nor unexpected*." *Id*. at 309 n. 11, 101 S.Ct. 633 (emphasis added). *See also Clay v. Sun Ins. Office, Ltd*., 377 U.S. 179, 84 S.Ct. 1197, 12 L.Ed.2d 229 (1964); *Watson v. Employers Liab. Assurance Corp*., 348 U.S. 66, 75 S.Ct. 166, 99 L.Ed. 74 (1954).

In *Hague* the Supreme Court stated that in order for the substantive law of a state "to be selected in a constitutionally permissible manner, the state must have a significant contact or significant aggregation of contacts, creating state interests, such that choice of its law is neither arbitrary nor fundamentally unfair." 449 U.S. at 312–13, 101 S.Ct. 633. In that case, a Wisconsin resident who had three automobile insurance policies was killed in an accident in Wisconsin by an uninsured motorist. Suit was filed in Minnesota by the decedent's personal representative to recover under the uninsured motorist endorsements of the three policies. Minnesota permitted the stacking of policies, while Wisconsin did not. The Supreme Court affirmed the application of Minnesota law on the basis of three contacts that it found, in aggregate, constitutionally sufficient:

> First, . . . Mr. Hague was a member of Minnesota's work force, having been employed by a Red Wing, Minn., enterprise for the 15 years preceding his death. . . . Mr. Hague's residence in Wisconsin does not . . . constitutionally mandate application of Wisconsin law to the exclusion of forum law. . . . Second, Allstate was at all times present and doing business in Minnesota. By virtue of its presence, Allstate can hardly claim unfamiliarity with the laws of the host jurisdiction and surprise that the state courts might apply forum law to litigation in which the company is involved. . . . Third, respondent became a Minnesota resident prior to institution of this litigation.

Id. at 313-18, 101 S.Ct. 633. We have no doubt that this case passes the *Hague* standard for a constitutionally permissible choice of law. All three of the factors the Court relied on in *Hague* are present here, plus many more. As a result, we see no constitutional problem with the choice of New York's substantive law to govern this dispute.

We note an additional problem we perceive with the District Court's analysis. The Court viewed *Hague's* forbears as a limitation on the permissible interpretation of the scope of New York's *substantive* law. Yet, as best illustrated by *Hague*, the relevant issue is the constitutionality of a *choice* of substantive law (not constitutional limitations on the permissible scope of a state's substantive law). In our case we must ask whether New York's substantive law would constitutionally apply to the facts we review, not whether New York could permissibly choose to apply its law (the choice of which substantive law to apply being an issue reserved to Pennsylvania law). Put colloquially, applying choice-of-law principles to the analysis of the constitutional scope of New York's substantive law mixes apples and oranges. For our purposes, it is sufficient to conclude that there is no constitutional bar to the application of New York law to this dispute.

C. Does Michigan's Subsection 3 Apply to this Dispute?

As noted, the District Court concluded that Budget could not invoke Michigan's limitation of liability for short-term lessors of cars in subsection 3 because "the lease between Budget Systems and Powell was 'founded on' a misdemeanor—Budget Systems's grant of permission to operate the Xterra without a valid license plate—" and was therefore a "nullity" under Michigan law. *Budget*, 304 F.Supp.2d at 650. The parties vigorously dispute the propriety of this holding. Because we conclude below that New York's interest in applying its law far outweighs any interest Michigan might have in applying subsection 3 (that is, assuming subsection 3 *would* apply), we find it unnecessary to address the competing, complex statutory interpretation arguments presented by the parties. [FN8] Instead, we leave the construction question to the State of Michigan and assume without holding that Michigan's subsection 3 would apply and limit Budget's liability in this case. Under this assumption, we turn to New York and Michigan's competing interests.

FN8. If Michigan's subsection 3 does not apply to this case, then only New York has an interest in applying its law and this case would be a "false conflict." New York law would clearly apply. If subsection 3 does apply, Michigan has an interest in applying its law and we must weigh the "true conflict" between its interest and that of New York. Because we conclude that New York's interest trumps in any event, we need not settle the construction of Michigan law because we reach the same result under either construction.

D. Identification and Weighing of State Interests

[17][18] In choosing between Michigan and New York law, [FN9] we consider, *inter alia*, "the relevant policies of [the] interested states and the relative interests of those states in the determination of the particular issue." Restatement (Second) of Conflict of Laws § 6 (1971). New York's § 388(1) "was enacted to ensure access by injured persons to a financially responsible [party] against whom to recover for injuries and to change th[e] common-law rule and to impose liability upon the owner of a vehicle for the negligence of a person legally operating the car with the permission, express or implied, of the owner." *Hassan v. Montuori*, 99 N.Y.2d 348, 756 N.Y.S.2d 126, 786 N.E.2d 25, 27 (2003) (internal quotations omitted); *Morris v. Snappy Car Rental*, 84 N.Y.2d 21, 614 N.Y.S.2d 362, 637 N.E.2d 253, 255 (1994). "Another . . . interest is in assuring that New York vendors who furnish medical and hospital care to injured parties are compensated . . . Finally, New York has a public fiscal interest in assuring that . . . New York State can recoup its welfare expense[s] from [victims'] recover[ies]." *Bray v. Cox*, 39 A.D.2d 299, 333 N.Y.S.2d 783, 785-86 (N.Y.App.Div.1972).

FN9. It is clear that Pennsylvania does not have an interest in applying its law to this dispute. But for the chance occurrence of the accident in Pennsylvania, there is no connection between the Commonwealth and the parties. Pennsylvania has no interest in securing a recovery for Chappell nor in limiting Budget's liability. The District Court held that Pennsylvania law applied by default under the rule of *lex loci delicti* because neither New York nor Michigan had an interest in applying its law. We have already stated our disagreement with those predicate determinations.

Describing Michigan's subsection 3, the District Court explained that "[i]n response to car rental companies' complaints that Subsection 1 [—which provides for unlimited vicarious liability—] was 'inhibiting the growth of the [rental car] industry and threatening to drive some companies out of the state,' the Michigan legislature amended the law in June of 1995 [to add subsection 3]." *Budget*, 304 F.Supp.2d at 648 (quoting *DeHart v. Joe Lunghamer Chevrolet, Inc.*, 239 Mich.App. 181, 607 N.W.2d 417, 420 (1999)). That is, subsection 3 was codified to advance Michigan's interest in preventing rental car companies from deciding not to do business (or to do less business) in the State of Michigan for fear of unlimited vicarious liability.

Having identified the competing state policies implicated by this dispute, we turn to the states' relative interests in those policies. New York's interest is clear, direct and compelling. Chappell is a New York resident receiving treatment and care from medical providers in New York with the aid of New York-administered welfare programs. Each of New York's policy justifications for enacting § 388(1) is directly implicated by this case, and New York's interest runs to the full extent of Chappell's recovery, dollar for dollar. It has an interest in (1) Chappell's full recovery from a financially responsible party, (2) the compensation of New York vendors who furnish medical and hospital care to Chappell, and (3) recouping the State's welfare expenses.

Michigan, unlike New York, does not have an interest in securing a recovery for an injured citizen in this case (or associated state medical expenses). Its only interest lies in the extent of Budget's liability (or, put another way, in the potential application of subsection 3's liability cap). We doubt that Michigan's interest in the application of subsection 3 is implicated at all in this case. Is it plausible that Budget will decide not to do business in the State of Michigan if it is held liable under New York law for an accident that occurred in Pennsylvania involving a car rented in Michigan? In fact, the application of New York's more stringent law in this case likely *advances* Michigan's interest in making it a relatively attractive place for rental car companies to do business by highlighting the value of Michigan's liability cap. And if potential liability in other fora would undermine Budget's decision to do business in Michigan, there are steps it can take to preserve the value of Michigan's liability cap short of pulling out of the State. For example, Budget is free to limit to intrastate travel the permissible use of vehicles it rents in Michigan. It is similarly free contractually to bar its customers from operating its vehicles in the State of New York. (We note that, far from restricting the use of vehicles in New York, Budget actually rents vehicles in that State, calling into question the necessity of a liability cap to induce rental car companies to do business in a state.) In short, Michigan's interest in this particular dispute is uncertain and tenuous at best.

We thus conclude that New York's interest in the application of its law to this dispute clearly trumps that of Michigan. Thus, under Pennsylvania's choice-of-law rules, New York law is to be applied.

IV. Conclusion

The District Court erred in its conclusion that the facts of this case do not fall within the scope of New York's § 388(1). Because § 388(1) does apply to this case, and because New York's interest in applying that provision clearly outweighs any interest Michigan might (or might not) have in applying its liability cap, under Pennsylvania's choice-of-law rules New York law governs this dispute and Budget faces unlimited vicarious liability. The District Court's judgment is accordingly reversed.

Source: *Budget Rent-a-Car v. Chappell*, 407 F.3d 166 (St. Paul, MN: Thomson West). Reprinted with permission from Westlaw.

Congress (federal district courts). Article III, Section 2, of the U.S. Constitution establishes the authority of the federal courts. These courts may hear cases involving:

- Issues regarding a federal question, such as constitutional rights.
- Controversies in which the parties have diversity of citizenship and the matter in dispute exceeds $75,000. (Note: Diversity of citizenship is when the parties to the case are residents of two different states or a foreign country.)
- Crimes or suits in which the U.S. government is a party.

CYBER TRIP

Locate the Web site www.courts.net. This Web site provides a national directory of all courts. Find your state and determine what information is available about the federal and state courts located in your jurisdiction. Do any of these courts in your state have their own Web site?

In ascertaining whether a particular case is a federal issue, students should begin by examining the types of cases in the preceding list and then consider whether there might potentially be an applicable federal statute. For example, if the facts of a case concern a job applicant who wants to sue a prospective employer for discrimination based on race, the student will discover that there are relevant federal statutes regarding equal employment opportunities.

In deciding if a particular set of facts concerns state law, students might focus on whether the case covers certain content areas of the law, such as torts and contracts. Generally, states are free to enact laws that anticipate and protect the health and welfare of its citizens. Therefore, so long as there is no conflict with federal laws, state law will cover a wide range of unique areas, including family law and probate law. In many cases, states have moved in the direction of adopting uniform codes that affect such areas of the law as business transactions and sales. Such uniform laws make it easier for citizens to know what to expect if doing business in more than one state. An example is the Uniform Commercial Code, which governs commercial sales transactions in many states.

In certain situations, the facts in a particular case may be decided by either a federal or a state court. As noted in Chapter 2, courts may have concurrent jurisdiction. In such cases, the party initiating the lawsuit has the option to decide in which court to file the claim.

LEGAL REASONING PROCESS

legal issue
The point in dispute between two or more parties in a lawsuit.

Once you have worked through the three steps of categorizing a case, you are ready to begin your legal research and identify cases that may have precedential value to your factual and legal issues. A **legal issue** is the point in dispute between two or more parties in a lawsuit. In examining previous cases decided in your jurisdiction, you will be able to develop some measure of predictability as to the outcome of your case. This process of legal reasoning, applying established legal principles to your case, is the foundation and cornerstone of our legal system. This process will be examined in depth in Chapter 4.

Eye on Ethics

Access the Web site for the National Association of Legal Assistants: www.nala.org.

Find the section on this site that discusses what a paralegal does. May a paralegal perform legal investigations? May a paralegal conduct legal research and summarize the law for a client in a phone conversation?

Summary

The process of categorizing or classifying a case is the first step in legal analysis. Once you are able to identify facts and make a judgment regarding each of the three classifications discussed in this chapter, the procedure of identifying the applicable law and legal issue becomes far simpler. First, you should determine if the issue relates to a procedural or a substantive topic. Second, it must be decided if the facts concern a criminal matter or a civil matter. Finally, you should decide if the facts support the application of state or federal law. After these initial determinations are resolved, you can identify the legal issue and determine applicable law that will help solve the issue. Being able to narrow down a specific legal question and find the relevant legal rules is the key to success in developing the critical thinking skills needed to master legal analysis. The following chapters address the process of case analysis.

Key Terms

Civil law
Criminal law
Legal issue
Procedural law
Substantive law

Discussion Questions

1. Discuss the advantage that a paralegal will have in being able to categorize a legal problem prior to undertaking research on the case at hand.
2. What are some techniques that a paralegal might use to improve the legal analysis process when confronted with a set of facts that poses an unfamiliar legal issue?
3. Explain the importance of identifying whether a case is governed by state or federal law. Discuss how your answer may differ if the courts have concurrent jurisdiction.
4. What are some sources of law that you might consult, once you have classified a case as a criminal matter that involves federal law?
5. In the cases of Robert Blake and O. J. Simpson, each defendant was prosecuted in criminal court, and subsequently was sued by the victim's family in civil court, based on the same set of facts. Discuss why two trials involving the same set of facts does not violate the double jeopardy clause under the U.S. Constitution.

Exercises

1. Identify whether each of the following are civil or criminal cases:
   a. Mary robs the QuickMart convenience store on the way home from work.
   b. John fails to stop at a red light and hits a pedestrian in the crosswalk.
   c. Larry is backing out of his driveway and runs over his neighbors' cat.
   d. Betty is backing out of a parking space at the Price Cutter grocery store and collides with another car in the parking lot.
   e. Dudley is fed up with his neighbor's oak tree blocking his view of the ocean and cuts down the tree.
2. Identify whether each of the following cases involve substantive or procedural issues:
   a. James is making popcorn in his microwave oven, when the oven suddenly catches fire, causing serious burns to James. The statute in James's state specifies that product liability cases must be filed within two years. James sues three years after the accident.
   b. Susan signs a contract in March to have David paint her house in July. In August, David still has not painted her house, but has kept Susan's deposit for the work. Susan sues David.
   c. Elaine has heart surgery in 1998 and seems to recover nicely. The statute in Elaine's state specifies that negligence cases must be filed within two years. Elaine begins to have trouble breathing in 2003, and her new doctor discovers a medical sponge has been left in her abdomen, causing her breathing problems. Elaine sues the heart surgeon in 2003.
   d. Mark is arrested for burglary and is taken to the police station for questioning. Mark is advised of his Miranda rights, and he chooses to not answer questions. The following day, Mark is asked several questions by a police detective investigating a different burglary from a month ago.
3. Determine whether each of the following cases should be filed in a state court or in federal court:
   a. Dudley is in need of some extra cash and stops off at the QuickMart on his way home from work and robs the clerk.

b. Dudley is in need of a lot of extra cash and stops off at the First National Bank of Pleasant and robs the teller.

c. Loulou is in need of extra cash. She decides to work as a prostitute for one evening and is arrested by an undercover police detective.

d. Mary needs to buy stamps and trips on the rug in the lobby of the post office, sustaining a broken wrist.

e. Henrietta is on vacation in California from her home state of Nebraska and trips on the rug in the lobby of a popular fast-food place that has restaurants nationwide.

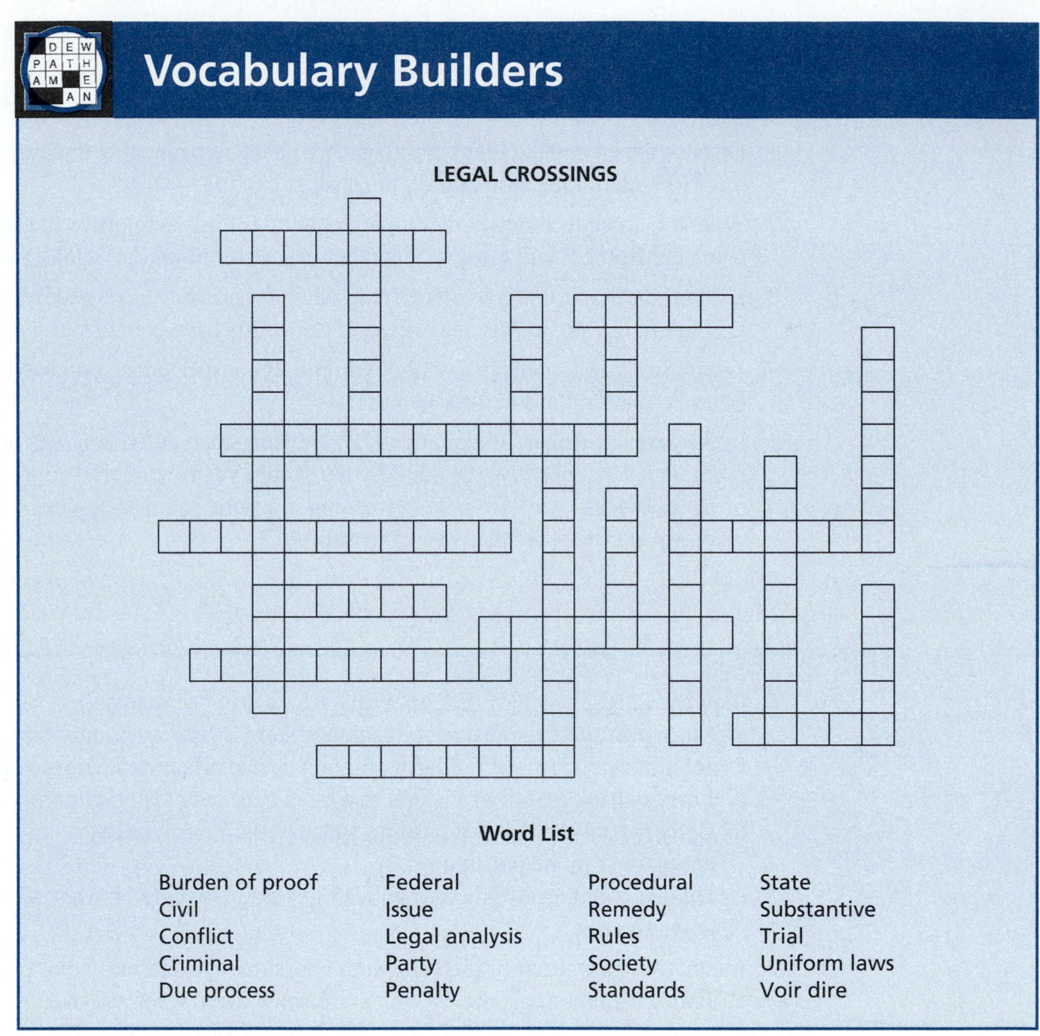

Vocabulary Builders
LEGAL CROSSINGS
Word List
Burden of proof
Civil
Conflict
Criminal
Due process
Federal
Issue
Legal analysis
Party
Penalty
Procedural
Remedy
Rules
Society
Standards
State
Substantive
Trial
Uniform laws
Voir dire

Chapter 4

Reading the Law

CHAPTER OBJECTIVES

After reading this chapter, you will be able to:

- Identify the parts of a court opinion.
- Explain the importance of judicial precedent.
- Explain the process of briefing cases.
- Apply the method of legal analysis to hypothetical fact patterns.
- Discuss the rules of statutory construction.
- Apply a statute to hypothetical fact patterns.

Paralegals undertake a variety of assignments, many of which commonly involve some kind of legal writing. Legal writing includes drafting client correspondence, internal office memoranda, discovery documents, and pleadings. Chapter 6, "The Role of the Paralegal," discusses the types of work that paralegals might do in a typical day, one of which involves legal research and writing. This chapter focuses on the skill of reading the law and on utilizing that skill in one specific kind of legal writing assignment, the legal memorandum. In this chapter, you will be introduced to the process of applying the relevant law to the facts of a case. In order to understand how the law is applied, it is important to be able to read a case or statute. This chapter establishes the significant factors in analyzing judicial opinions and statutes. You will explore the importance of case law in our legal system and then begin to learn the method for analyzing cases. To support your study of the substantive law topics that are discussed in subsequent chapters, such as torts and contracts, this chapter will aid you in developing your critical thinking skills, teaching you how to *apply* the legal principles you will learn in subsequent chapters to hypothetical fact patterns. Remember from Chapter 1 that anyone can memorize legal rules and definitions, but the legal profession necessitates analytical skills, knowing how to summarize cases and apply the law to the facts of the client's case.

WHAT IS CASE LAW?

The foundation of our legal system, as noted in previous chapters, is grounded in common law. In the development of law, judicial opinions are issued that interpret statutes and common legal principles. In the study and practice of law today, the legal principles that are discussed in subsequent chapters have evolved from the application of the law to numerous factual scenarios. **Case law** consists of the published opinions, or judicial decisions, of the courts, as was explained in Chapter 3. When an appellate or U.S. District Court issues its ruling, or decision, in a particular case, a written opinion is delivered. Some of these judicial opinions are not published, but many of them are. As soon as the appellate court decision (or U.S. Circuit Court decision) is filed and approved for publication, it becomes law. At such time as a significant number of opinions in a specific jurisdiction have been issued and "published," these cases are compiled and bound into books commonly called **case reporters.** The cases found in these volumes of reporters comprise what is ordinarily referred to as "case law."

case law
Judge-created law in deciding cases, set forth in court opinions.

case reporters
Sets of books that contain copies of appellate court opinions.

WHERE DO YOU FIND CASE LAW?

official reporters
Government publications of court decisions (for example, 325 Ill.3d 50).

unofficial reporters
Private publications of court decisions (for example, 525 N.E.2d 90).

It is important to note that there are two categories of case reporters: official and unofficial. **Official reporters** are the governmental publications of case decisions. **Unofficial reporters** are the publications of case decisions by private entities, such as West. The texts of the opinions published in both types of reporters are the same, but there are editorial features, such as a case summary and headnotes, that are added at the beginning of the cases in the unofficial reporters. This distinction is significant to note because you should never rely on or quote from these editorial features in legal memoranda, as they are not part of the official court opinion. The sample court opinion (see Figure 4.1) contained in this chapter denotes these features.

There is certain essential information that is found in every judicial opinion as shown in Figure 4.1. Aside from general details such as the parties' names, the specific court that issued the decision, and the date of the court's opinion in that case, you will find three important components of every opinion. First, you will read the court's statement or summary of the facts of the original case heard in the trial court. Second, you will find a statement of the legal issue or issues that are being appealed to the higher court. Third, you will read a discussion of the court's reasoning and its ultimate ruling, or disposition, of the case on appeal. Note that these three components of the case are located within the official opinion, beginning just after the name of the judge who wrote the opinion. At the beginning of cases in unofficial reporters are editorial features written by the private publisher. For example, **headnotes** are numbered summaries of each of the key legal points of a case. The **syllabus** is a short summary of the court's opinion and its decision. Although, as previously mentioned, these features should never be quoted in legal memoranda or appellate briefs, they nevertheless serve a useful purpose in the preliminary stages of legal research. Generally, you might begin by reading the syllabus at the start of each opinion and then skimming the headnotes to determine if the case might be relevant to your client's case. You can use these editorial features to decide if you want to read the entire case or continue with your legal research. Bear in mind that reading the syllabus is not a substitute for reading the case, if in fact you decide that the case has precedential value for the client's case.

headnotes
An editorial feature in unofficial reporters that summarizes a single legal point or issue in the court opinion.

syllabus
An editorial feature in unofficial reporters that summarizes the court's decision.

GENERAL WRITING TIPS

CYBER TRIP

Government publications contain a wealth of information on using plain English and writing well. Visit some of these sites:

- www.sba.gov/plain/whatis.html
- www.sec.gov/pdf/handbook.pdf
- www.plain-language.gov
- www.archives.gov/federal_register/drafting_legal_documents/drafting_legal_documents.html

Although this chapter focuses on reading the law and its application, writing ability is an important consideration in the legal writing that follows. While it will be assumed that you have studied writing style and structure in other classes, certain guidelines are relevant specifically to effective legal writing. It cannot be emphasized enough how the ability to write well is important to practicing in the legal profession. As a paralegal, you will likely be asked to draft a variety of documents and correspondence. Well-written documents will not only demonstrate your abilities but will also reflect well on the firm for whom you work. Therefore, it is in your best interests to strive to be a better legal writer, using proper grammar and appropriate style and sentence structure.

Certain guidelines regarding legal writing should be kept in mind. First, try to avoid legalese. Although certain legal terminology, such as the phrase *Miranda rights,* is generally accepted and understood by people outside of the law, you should try to avoid other legal jargon in your writing, such as the use of words like *hereby* and *wherefore*. In general, plain, simple English should always be used. This doesn't mean that the correct legal terms should be avoided when writing a legal memorandum, since you are preparing this document for your supervising attorney, who is knowledgeable about legalisms. Using plain English simply means using precise language that informs and explains your points.

Second, use an appropriate writing style for the document you are preparing. Note that one section of the Certified Legal Assistant (CLA) examination tests you on your communication skills. To this end, the administrator of the exam, the National Association of Legal Assistants (NALA), has adopted Strunk and White's *The Elements of Style*, as its chief reference on communications. This book is commonly used in many English composition classes and is a useful reference for your legal writing. In writing legal memoranda, you may adopt a formal writing style that presents an objective and thorough summary of the facts and relevant law. A persuasive writing style might be more appropriate for other documents, but not necessarily for an internal document that you are writing for your supervising attorney.

FIGURE 4.1 **Sample Marked-up Case with Notations**

Source: Case is from Westlaw. Reprinted with permission.

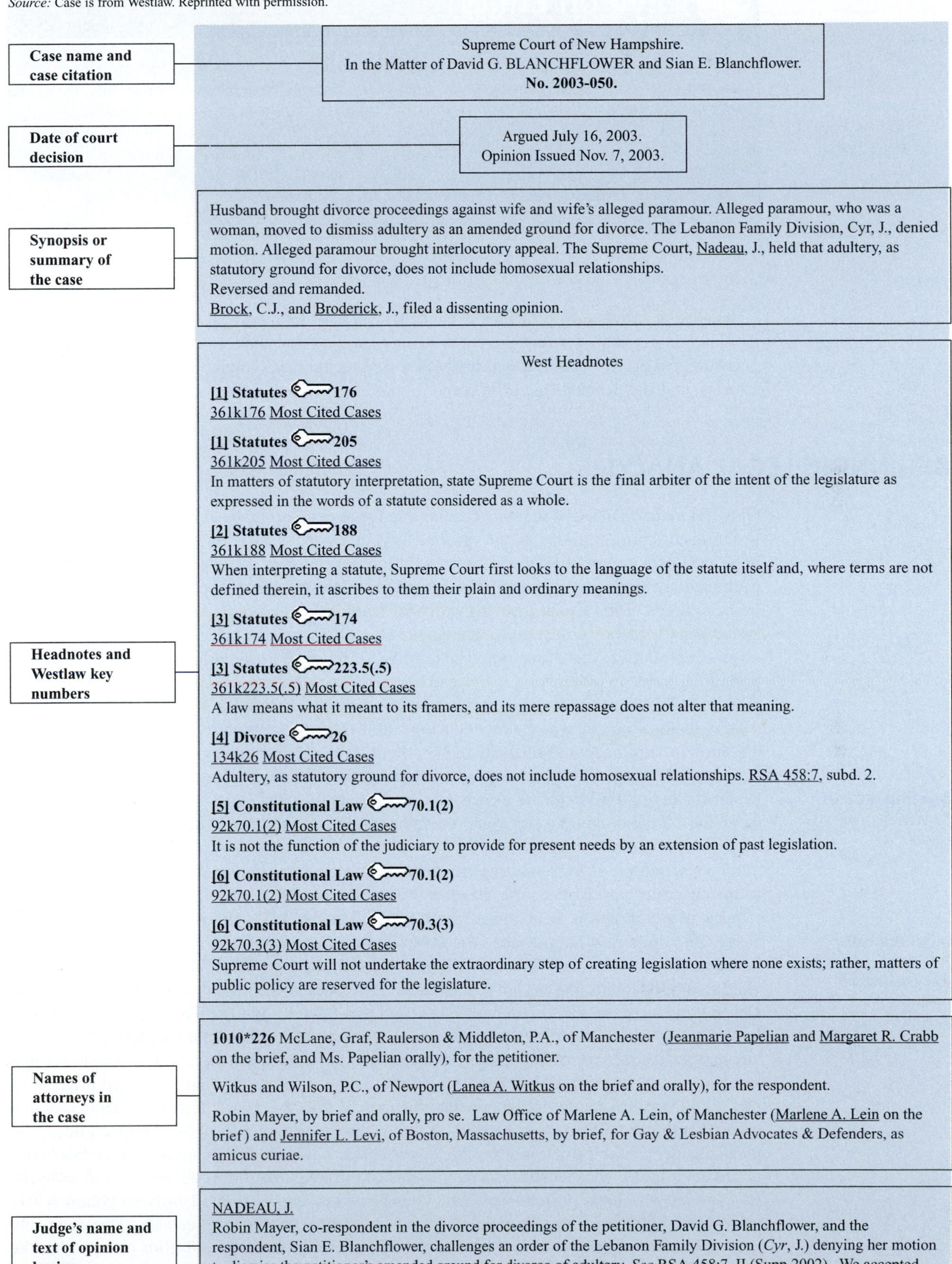

Supreme Court of New Hampshire.
In the Matter of David G. BLANCHFLOWER and Sian E. Blanchflower.
No. 2003-050.

Argued July 16, 2003.
Opinion Issued Nov. 7, 2003.

Husband brought divorce proceedings against wife and wife's alleged paramour. Alleged paramour, who was a woman, moved to dismiss adultery as an amended ground for divorce. The Lebanon Family Division, Cyr, J., denied motion. Alleged paramour brought interlocutory appeal. The Supreme Court, Nadeau, J., held that adultery, as statutory ground for divorce, does not include homosexual relationships.
Reversed and remanded.
Brock, C.J., and Broderick, J., filed a dissenting opinion.

West Headnotes

[1] Statutes 176
361k176 Most Cited Cases

[1] Statutes 205
361k205 Most Cited Cases
In matters of statutory interpretation, state Supreme Court is the final arbiter of the intent of the legislature as expressed in the words of a statute considered as a whole.

[2] Statutes 188
361k188 Most Cited Cases
When interpreting a statute, Supreme Court first looks to the language of the statute itself and, where terms are not defined therein, it ascribes to them their plain and ordinary meanings.

[3] Statutes 174
361k174 Most Cited Cases

[3] Statutes 223.5(.5)
361k223.5(.5) Most Cited Cases
A law means what it meant to its framers, and its mere repassage does not alter that meaning.

[4] Divorce 26
134k26 Most Cited Cases
Adultery, as statutory ground for divorce, does not include homosexual relationships. RSA 458:7, subd. 2.

[5] Constitutional Law 70.1(2)
92k70.1(2) Most Cited Cases
It is not the function of the judiciary to provide for present needs by an extension of past legislation.

[6] Constitutional Law 70.1(2)
92k70.1(2) Most Cited Cases

[6] Constitutional Law 70.3(3)
92k70.3(3) Most Cited Cases
Supreme Court will not undertake the extraordinary step of creating legislation where none exists; rather, matters of public policy are reserved for the legislature.

1010*226 McLane, Graf, Raulerson & Middleton, P.A., of Manchester (Jeanmarie Papelian and Margaret R. Crabb on the brief, and Ms. Papelian orally), for the petitioner.

Witkus and Wilson, P.C., of Newport (Lanea A. Witkus on the brief and orally), for the respondent.

Robin Mayer, by brief and orally, pro se. Law Office of Marlene A. Lein, of Manchester (Marlene A. Lein on the brief) and Jennifer L. Levi, of Boston, Massachusetts, by brief, for Gay & Lesbian Advocates & Defenders, as amicus curiae.

NADEAU, J.
Robin Mayer, co-respondent in the divorce proceedings of the petitioner, David G. Blanchflower, and the respondent, Sian E. Blanchflower, challenges an order of the Lebanon Family Division (*Cyr*, J.) denying her motion to dismiss the petitioner's amended ground for divorce of adultery. *See* RSA 458:7, II (Supp.2002). We accepted this matter as an interlocutory appeal under Supreme Court Rule 8, and now reverse and remand.

Eye on Ethics

Drafting legal documents is one of the primary tasks performed by paralegals. However, many of the documents include legal correspondence that utilizes a law firm's official letterhead and stationery. You must be careful not to sign certain correspondence that requires an attorney's signature, such as an opinion letter. An opinion letter is a formal advisory letter from an attorney to a client that contains a legal opinion of a client's legal question or claim. Other kinds of correspondence may be signed by you, so long as you clearly identify yourself as a paralegal. Find information about this subject by accessing the Web site www.nala.org.

Finally, be sure to edit your final document. Check for grammatical and spelling errors using the function available for this on your computer. At the same time, review the entire document to ensure that proper legal citations are used. Legal memoranda commonly contain references to case law and statutes that should be correctly cited.

BEGINNING LEGAL ANALYSIS

One of the practical skills that this chapter intends to develop is the ability to apply the law, be it statutes or court opinions, to the specific facts of a client's case. Subsequent chapters in this book will provide an overview of important legal principles in seven key substantive areas of the law. Learning how to apply those legal principles to various sets of facts is this book's primary focus. The critical thinking skills for legal analysis require learning how to identify and compare facts, issues, and legal rules. This chapter contains numerous exercises that utilize hypothetical fact situations. The purpose of these short hypothetical fact patterns is to provide practice in identifying issues and key facts and then in predicting the outcome of that case, based on a given specific legal principle or statute. This is the foundation for preparing a legal memorandum, which is a document used to provide your supervising attorney with a complete summary and analysis of the client's case. Drafting legal memoranda for your supervising attorney is just one use of these analytical skills. You may also be asked to perform a task called **briefing a case,** which is to summarize a court opinion. Case briefs may be an individual document that you prepare or may be incorporated into the reasoning section of your legal memorandum.

briefing a case
Summarizing a court opinion.

The starting point for analyzing any client's case, and predicting the probable outcome, is to review what has come before. In other words, the answer to any legal problem will likely require an examination of previous case law. This process of scrutinizing previously decided cases and comparing them to the case at hand is commonly referred to as **legal analysis.** To better understand this sophisticated skill performed in the legal field, imagine this situation. A child is warned by his parents not to jump on the bed because he might fall off and hurt himself. Despite this warning, the child jumps on the bed and falls off, bumping his head on the wall. It is likely that this child will refrain from jumping on the bed in the future, as he will recall the unhappy consequences of engaging in this activity. Or, consider a situation in which a driver receives a speeding ticket for driving 15 miles over the speed limit. That individual driver may rely on this experience to decide how fast she can drive in the future. If she is a passenger in a car with a driver who does not receive a ticket when going five miles over the speed limit, she may consider this information when she drives again. This idea of relying on prior experiences to predict a future consequence is a simple way of thinking about the concept of legal analysis. In a similar way, legal professionals gain knowledge and expertise in identifying common fact situations and legal issues in parallel cases, and learn how to compare such cases to reasonably predict the likely result in a new factual scenario. This consideration of prior cases forms the basis for legal research and legal analysis.

legal analysis
The process of examining prior case law and comparing it to your case.

SIGNIFICANCE OF LEGAL ANALYSIS

Legal professionals develop the skill, with extensive practice, of identifying similarities in both issues and facts when comparing cases. When analyzing cases, you need to have the ability to determine the facts and legal issues of the cases and then to apply the applicable laws in prior cases to a different set of facts in the new case. It is essential to consider not only the facts and legal issue in each case, but also the jurisdiction in which the case was decided. The doctrine of **judicial precedent** provides that if an earlier case is similar to the case before you, in terms of both facts and issue, then the court's decision in that earlier case may apply to your case In essence, you have discovered the probable outcome and have a reasonably good indicator of what should happen in your case, given the experience and knowledge gained from that previous case. In deciding whether a prior court's decision is applicable, you need to look at three elements when comparing that case with yours. The applicability of that earlier case's ruling to your case is dependent on the prior case being decided in the same jurisdiction, the existence of similar facts, and the same legal issue.

judicial precedent
A court decision in which similar facts are presented; provides authority for deciding a subsequent case.

Same Jurisdiction

The legal effect of prior court decisions is defined by the concept of **stare decisis.** In essence, the doctrine of stare decisis maintains that courts decide pending cases by analyzing and comparing cases previously decided in that jurisdiction. Literally, stare decisis means "the decision stands." Stare decisis has specific limitations that delineate when the court is bound to follow the precedent, or earlier court decision.

stare decisis
The doctrine of precedent whereby once a court has decided a specific issue one way in the past, it and other courts in the same jurisdiction are obligated to follow that earlier decision in deciding cases with similar issues in the future.

In order for a prior case to be binding or controlling, in deciding a present dispute, the case must first have been decided in the same jurisdiction. For a prior case to be "binding" authority on the court, it is necessary that the same court or a higher court within that jurisdiction decided the previous case. Chapter 2 of this textbook discusses jurisdiction and jurisdictional issues. Note, for example, that the Kansas Supreme Court is not bound by the decisions of lower courts in Kansas, nor is it bound by decisions of the Illinois Supreme Court. Similarly, the U.S. Court of Appeals for the Seventh Circuit is not bound by decisions of the Third Circuit. However, courts are free to take into account the rulings of other courts outside its jurisdiction, and this is referred to as persuasive authority, meaning that the current court may choose to follow the reasoning of a court outside its jurisdiction, where no similar case in its own jurisdiction has previously been decided. A **case of first impression** exists where a legal issue is presented in a case that has not yet been considered by a court in a specific jurisdiction.

case of first impression
A case with a legal issue that has not been heard by the court before in a specific jurisdiction.

Similar Facts

Second, the prior case must necessarily have similar facts to your case. This does not mean that your case must factually be *exactly* the same as the previous case, but rather should bear a substantial or significant similarity. The prior decision must be sufficiently analogous, rather than being distinguishable on the facts alone. *Analogous* means "similar," whereas *distinguishable* means "different."

Consider, for example, a case involving a negligence action by a customer who finds a dead beetle in the bottom of his mug at a coffee house. It is quite unlikely that you will find a previously decided case in your jurisdiction involving precisely this identical set of facts. That is, it would be unusual to find another case in your jurisdiction in which another customer had also found a dead beetle in the bottom of his coffee cup at that specific coffee house. However, it is possible that you will locate an earlier court decision involving a customer finding a decomposed insect in a different food product sold at a restaurant. These two cases bear substantial or significant similarity so as to meet the criteria for the second component of this test for "precedent." It can be said that these two cases are sufficiently analogous so as to be precedent for the current case before the court.

Same Legal Issue

Third, the earlier case must have some degree of similarity regarding the legal issue or question that is to be decided in your case. Consider, for example, a case in which a child is struck by a car in the parking lot of the Kiddieland Daycare. If the issue in this case is whether a day care

CASE IN POINT

Court of Appeal of Louisiana, Fifth Circuit.
Angel K. POPLAR
v.
DILLARD'S DEPARTMENT STORES, INC. and ABC Insurance Company.
No. 03-CA-1023.
Dec. 30, 2003.

Panel composed of Judges EDWARD A. DUFRESNE, JR., JAMES L. CANNELLA and WALTER J. ROTHSCHILD.

EDWARD A. DUFRESNE, JR., Chief Judge.

This is an appeal by Dillard Department Stores, Inc., defendant-appellant, from a $16,617.40 judgment in favor of Angel Poplar, plaintiff-appellee, who broke several teeth when she bit into a foreign object in a shrimp po-boy at defendant's restaurant. Because we find neither legal nor manifest factual error in the judgment we affirm.

The facts are straightforward. At the time of the incident in question here, plaintiff had an upper dental bridge which consisted of two center false front teeth attached to the natural teeth on either side. She was eating a shrimp po-boy at defendant's restaurant when she bit into a hard object which she later described as being about one inch long. She said that she felt her bridge come loose in her mouth and that she swallowed the object without reflecting on what was happening. She immediately informed the restaurant manager and went into the ladies room to see what had happened. She discovered then that the two side supporting teeth had broken off at the gum line and the entire bridge had thus come loose.

After a bench trial, plaintiff was awarded $4,711.00 for dental bills, $1,906.40 in lost wages, and $10,000.00 in general damages. No reasons for judgment appear in the record. Defendant now appeals.

[1] The only issue before this court on appeal is whether the trial judge properly found the defendant restaurant liable for plaintiff's injuries. The defendant relies on *Porteous v. St. Ann's Cafe & Deli*, 97-0837 (La.5/29/98), 713 So.2d 454, for the proposition that in restaurant harmful food cases the duty-risk analysis is the applicable law. It further urges that under this analysis the plaintiff in the present case failed to prove a specific act of negligence which would establish its liability to her. While we agree that *Porteous, supra*, is the law, we disagree that plaintiff failed to prove her case.

Factual determinations are reviewed on appeal under the manifest error standard. In the present case the trial judge found that plaintiff was credible in testifying that she bit into a foreign substance in the sandwich and that it broke her bridge. Because these findings are based on the trier of fact's assessment of the veracity of the witness, and in the absence of other evidence which would render the testimony implausible, we must affirm those findings. *Stobart v. State through DOTD*, 617 So.2d 880 (La.1993).

That being established, the next issues are whether the defendant had a duty to protect its patrons from such foreign substances, and if so, whether it breached that duty. In *Porteous, supra*, the court stated that:

> A food provider, in selecting, preparing, and cooking food, including the removal of injurious substances, has a duty to act as would a reasonably prudent man skilled in the culinary art in the selection and preparation of food. (at 457)

[2][3] Defendant's position here is that unless a plaintiff can show some specific act constituting a breach of the above duty on the part of the restaurant, she can not prevail. We hold otherwise. In our opinion the doctrine of res ipsa loquitur is applicable on the facts of this case. That doctrine is a rule of circumstantial evidence which permits the fact finder to infer negligence where 1) the circumstances surrounding the event are such they would not normally occur in the absence of negligence on someone's part, 2) the instrumentality was in the exclusive control of the defendant, and 3) the negligence falls within the duty of care owed the plaintiff. However, even where the doctrine is applicable, the inference of a breach of duty is only one aspect of the totality of the evidence in a case, and this inference may be overcome by contrary evidence. *Cangelosi v. Our Lady of the Lake Medical Ctr.*, 564 So.2d 654 (La.1989).

[4] All three elements are present here. There is no question that the presence of a foreign object in prepared food is a circumstance from which it can be inferred that someone was negligent in the preparation of that food. It is equally clear that the ingredients of the sandwich were in the control of the restaurant staff. Finally, the negligent act of serving food with a foreign object in it is within the ambit of the duty owed to customers. Thus an inference of negligence on defendant's part was supportable.

The final part of the analysis is whether there was other countervailing evidence sufficient to produce a result different from the inference. This of course is a factual determination subject to the manifest error rule. Here the trial judge tacitly concluded that the inference of breach of duty was not outweighed by other evidence, and therefore found the defendant liable. We find no manifest error in this finding and so must affirm it.

We finally note that in *Porteous, supra,* the defense showed that its kitchen procedures would filter out most foreign objects, but that the pearls in oysters could not be detected without undertaking extraordinary procedures. The court there stated that when objects are innate to the food itself the duty to eliminate such objects is less demanding. It held that the restaurant had not breached its duty in failing to detect the pearl. In the present case there was no showing by defendant that shrimp sometimes contain hard foreign objects and therefore that it had a lesser duty to watch for such objects.

For the foregoing reasons, the judgment is hereby affirmed.

AFFIRMED.

Source: *Poplar v. Dillard's Department Stores*, 864 So.2d 789 (St. Paul, MN: Thomson West). Reprinted with permission from Westlaw.

operator might be liable for the negligent supervision of a child in the parking lot of the facility, your case should involve the same legal question. So, if your case involves a child falling off a specific piece of playground equipment on the premises of a day care facility, the issue in your case might specifically be whether a day care operator might be liable for the negligent supervision of a child at the facility's playground. The relevant key facts involving injury to a child at a day care facility is present, in conjunction with the key legal issue of "negligent supervision" by a day care operator.

WHY IS PRECEDENT IMPORTANT?

When comparing an earlier court decision to your case, if all three elements are satisfied, then it can be said that the prior case is "precedent" and thus is binding authority on the current court. The goal of judicial precedent is to facilitate efficiency in the administration of justice, as well as to promote the concept of equity and fairness, in the sense that similar litigants should be treated alike. If one party's case is decided based on a particular set of legal principles, then a similarly situated party in a subsequent case might have reasonable expectation of a similar outcome to his or her case as in the earlier court decision.

case on point
A case involving similar facts and issues to the present case.

case on all fours
A case in which facts, issues, parties, and remedies are analogous to the present case.

In conducting legal research, you are looking for cases that are *on point*. A **case on point** is one in which the facts and the legal issue are analogous to that of the present case. Ideally, you might find a **case on all fours.** In this situation, all elements of the case, including the parties and the remedies sought, are similar to that of your case.

Stare decisis is important because it is a reasonably valid predictor of the outcome of any given hypothetical fact situation. It is significant because it is the equivalent of experience in the sense that what happened in the past, assuming all three elements are present, is logically what should happen again. The legal reasoning in a prior court's decision is sound guidance in anticipating outcomes of future legal cases. However, it should be noted that disputes are not strictly identical in terms of the legal issue and the facts, and therefore a degree of analysis and judgment is necessary in determining whether the current dispute is sufficiently similar to a prior case. Often, courts will consider the arguments of both sides in defining and clarifying the holdings of prior cases, or distinguishing the disputes. Courts may overrule a prior case, even if it is precedent, if this is reasonable, given the changes in social or economic contexts in which the previous decision had been rendered. For example, prior courts may not have formerly recognized the viability of frozen embryos, but if current medical science characterizes them as viable "property" with distinct value, then a court may be justified in overruling a previous decision that did not assign property interests or value to such matter. Furthermore, courts might deviate from prior decisions of higher courts within their jurisdiction where it becomes apparent that an alternate conclusion must be reached in light of current interpretation and understanding of legislature.

Searching for the intended meaning of statutes or determining the scope of constitutional powers and limits is governed by a distinct set of rules of judicial construction. Judicial interpretation of a statute begins with direct analysis of the specific language used, and the determination of the "plain meaning" of the statute often requires that the words are truly unambiguous. Often, courts may be obliged to look beyond the statute itself in evaluating legislative intent. For example, prior court decisions based on the interpretation of First Amendment rights may be reversed in light of current social policy and interpretation of such rights in cases such as the legality of same-sex marriages or the legitimacy of arguments involving religious symbols in public places. At the time that legislatures enacted certain statutes, specific individual fact situations may not have been contemplated or anticipated; thus, courts are presented with the opportunity to interpret statutory language in light of developing realities of society.

In summary, stare decisis requires a court to be consistent in deciding cases, in accordance with the aforementioned criteria. Where the case at hand is not substantially similar, a lower court may depart from the higher court rulings and distinguish it; otherwise, the court may only depart from established precedent and overrule a prior controlling decision if social or economic circumstances support this decision.

CASE IN POINT

Supreme Court of Kansas.
Sunny R. CRIST, Appellee,
v.
HUNAN PALACE, INC., and De Tong Chen,
and
Utica National Insurance Group, Utica National Assurance Company (Garnishee),
Appellants.
No. 89,326.
May 14, 2004.

Brazil, Senior Judge, dissented and filed opinion joined by McFarland, C.J., and Gernon, J.

SYLLABUS BY THE COURT

1. Interpretation of a written insurance contract is a question of law over which appellate courts have unlimited review.

2. Exceptions, limitations, and exclusions to insurance policies require narrow construction on the theory that the insurer, having affirmatively expressed coverage through broad promises, assumes the duty to define any limitations on that coverage in clear and explicit terms. If an insurer intends to restrict or limit coverage, it must use clear and unambiguous language in doing so, otherwise the insurance policy will be liberally construed in favor of the insured. The burden is on the insurer to prove facts which bring a case within the specified exception.

3. Under the facts of this case, a general exclusion for damages arising from use of an automobile did not exclude coverage for damages arising from the negligent hiring and supervision of an employee who was driving an automobile at the time plaintiff was injured.

4. It is recognized under the doctrine of stare decisis that once a point of law has been established by a court, that point of law will generally be followed by the same court and all courts of lower rank in subsequent cases where the same legal issue is raised. Stare decisis operates to promote system-wide stability and continuity by ensuring the survival of decisions that have been previously approved.

5. A court of last resort is not inexorably bound by its own precedents but will follow the rule of law which it has established in earlier cases, unless clearly convinced that the rule was originally erroneous or is no longer sound because of changing conditions and that more good than harm will come by departing from precedent.

6. Considerations in favor of stare decisis are at their acme in cases involving property and contract rights, where reliance interests are involved. . . .

. . . . . .

The opinion of the court was delivered by LUCKERT, J.:

This is a garnishment action arising out of a personal injury lawsuit filed by Sunny Crist against Hunan Palace, Inc. (Hunan) and its delivery driver. The matter was tried upon stipulations resulting in judgment in Crist's favor, and Crist instituted garnishment proceedings against Hunan's commercial general liability insurance carrier which had refused to defend the suit. The district court granted Crist's motion for summary judgment and denied the insurer's motion for summary judgment. The insurer appealed, and the Court of Appeals affirmed in an unpublished opinion. *Crist v. Hunan Palace, Inc.*, No. 89,326, 73 P.3d 779, unpublished opinion filed July 25, 2003. This court granted the insurer's petition for review pursuant to K.S.A. 20-3018.

Three issues are presented on appeal: (1) Did the Court of Appeals correctly uphold the district court's grant of summary judgment to Crist on the ground that Crist's automobile accident personal injury claims were covered by the insurer's commercial general liability policy? (2) Should this court reverse the four-to-three decision in *Marquis v. State Farm Fire & Cas. Co.*, 265 Kan. 317, 961 P.2d 1213 (1998)? and (3) Did the Court of Appeals correctly uphold the district court's judgment as comporting with due process?

The case arises from an accident which occurred in July 1999 when De Tong Chen, acting within the scope of his employment as a delivery driver for Hunan, crossed over the centerline and struck Crist's vehicle. Crist filed suit against Hunan and Chen for (1) Chen's negligent operation of his vehicle; (2) negligence imputed to Hunan under the theory of respondeat superior; and (3) Hunan's negligent training and supervision of Chen. Hunan's business automobile liability policy had lapsed. Hunan requested a defense and coverage from its commercial general liability insurance carrier, Utica National Insurance Group, Utica National Assurance Company (Utica). Utica refused to provide a defense or indemnify Hunan because of an automobile exclusion in the general liability policy.

Chen and Hunan reached an agreement with Crist resolving the matter through the presentation of stipulations and testimony of Crist. Chen and Hunan agreed to factual stipulations demonstrating their negligence, and Crist agreed not to execute on the real or personal property of Chen, Hunan, or Hunan's owner, Yuhua Bai. As relevant to this appeal, the journal entry of judgment set out the following stipulations:

> 6. The parties stipulate that on or about July 9, 1999, Defendant De Tong Chen was operating his motor vehicle on the Fort Riley Military Reservation within the scope of his employment with Defendant Hunan Palace, Inc. and crossed over the center line thereby striking Plaintiff's motor vehicle. . . .
>
> 8. The parties stipulate that Plaintiff would provide testimony from military policemen who were then

> assigned to the Fort Riley Military Reservation that Defendant De Tong Chen had been observed on many occasions to operate Defendant De Tong Chen's motor vehicle in an unsafe manner and to [*sic*] fast for conditions.
>
> 9. Neither Defendant stipulates to the fact that Defendant Hunan Palace, Inc. negligently retained or supervised Defendant De Tong Chen. However, the parties do stipulate that a finder of fact would find by a preponderance of evidence that Defendant Hunan Palace, Inc. knew or should have known Defendant De Tong Chen operated his vehicle in an unsafe manner on many occasions and, therefore, an undue risk of harm to others existed as a result of Defendant De Tong Chen's employment by Defendant Hunan Palace, Inc. Therefore, a finder of fact would find Defendant Hunan Palace, Inc. was negligent in its retention and supervision of Defendant De Tong Chen.

The district court found that Hunan had breached its duty of care and was negligent in failing to provide proper training and supervision of Chen, as alleged in Count III of Crist's petition. The court entered judgment in favor of Crist.

Crist then initiated garnishment proceedings against Utica. Utica moved to set aside the underlying judgment and moved for summary judgment on the basis of the automobile exclusion in the general liability policy. The district court denied both of Utica's motions. Instead, the court granted Crist summary judgment on her garnishment claim against Utica, ruling that the general liability policy provided coverage for Hunan under the authority of *Marquis*, 265 Kan. 317, 961 P.2d 1213 and *Upland Mutual Insurance, Inc. v. Noel*, 214 Kan. 145, 519 P.2d 737 (1974).

The Court of Appeals, in affirming the district court, ruled that Utica could not collaterally attack the validity of the underlying civil judgment as a defense in the garnishment proceeding. The Court of Appeals also found that the district court did not err in denying Utica summary judgment and in granting Crist summary judgment. In so ruling, the court relied on *Marquis* for the premise that an automobile exclusion does not exclude coverage for claims of negligent supervision, hiring, or retention because " 'the theory of liability rather than the cause of the accident governs coverage.' " Slip op. at 10 (quoting *Marquis*, 265 Kan. at 328-29, 961 P.2d 1213).

We granted review of all issues. . . .

. . . .

[5] We agree with the Court of Appeals that there is no basis to distinguish the holding in *Marquis,* and under that precedent the district court correctly determined that the automobile exclusion did not apply to Crist's claim of negligent supervision and training, which was a separate and distinct theory of recovery from the use of an automobile.

SHOULD THIS COURT REVERSE THE FOUR-TO-THREE DECISION IN *MARQUIS V. STATE FARM*?

Utica urges this court to reverse the four-to-three decision in *Marquis*. Utica notes that a comprehensive argument for why the decision should be reversed was presented in the concurring and dissenting opinion, which was written by Justice Larson. Chief Justice McFarland and Justice Six joined in the concurring and dissenting opinion. See *Marquis*, 265 Kan. at 335-40, 961 P.2d 1213. Utica builds upon the dissent and argues that the authority underlying the majority's rationale has been further weakened and a significant conflict has developed in Kansas cases.

As the dissent in *Marquis* noted, the authority cited in *Upland* has been "distinguished almost out of existence" or significantly limited in application. *Marquis*, 265 Kan. at 336, 961 P.2d 1213. This trend has continued. See *Calvin v. Janbar Enterprises, Inc.*, 856 So.2d 88, 91 (La.App.2003) (questioning *Smith v. USAA Cas. Ins. Co.*, 532 So.2d 1171, 1174 [La. App.1988], one of the cases supporting the majority); *Society for Christian Activities, Inc. v. Markel Ins. Co.*, 440 Mass. 1006, 795 N.E.2d 545 (2003) (distinguishing *Barnstable County Mut. Fire Ins. Co. v. Lally*, 374 Mass. 602, 606, 373 N.E.2d 966 [1978], another case supporting the majority); *Allstate Ins. Co. v. Moraca*, 244 N.J.Super. 5, 12, 581 A.2d 510 (1990) (distinguishing *McDonald v. Home Ins. Co.*, 97 N.J.Super. 501, 235 A.2d 480 [1967], cited by majority because of difference in language of exclusionary clause); *Scarfi v. Aetna Cas. & Sur. Co.*, 233 N.J.Super. 509, 516-19, 559 A.2d 459 (1989) (distinguishing and disagreeing with *McDonald); Mt. Vernon Ins. Co. v. Creative Housing Ltd.*, 88 N.Y.2d 347, 351, 645 N.Y.S.2d 433, 668 N.E.2d 404 (1996) (limiting *Lalomia v. Bankers & Shippers Insurance Company*, 35 App. Div.2d 114, 312 N.Y.S.2d 1018 [1970], to its facts); *New Hampshire Ins. Co. v. Jefferson Ins. Co. of New York*, 213 App. Div.2d 325, 329, 624 N.Y.S.2d 392 (1995) (same). It is clear that what was the majority rule in 1998 when *Marquis* was decided continues to be the majority rule today. See Annot., *Construction and Effect of Provision Excluding Liability for Automobile-Related Injuries or Damage from Coverage of Homeowner's or Personal Liability Policy*, 6 A.L.R.4th 555.

Utica also argues, as noted by Justice Larson in his dissent, that the *Upland* rule has been disregarded to some extent by the Court of Appeals. The dissenting opinion in *Marquis* cited *United Services Auto. Ass'n v. Morgan*, 23 Kan.App.2d 987, 939 P.2d 959, *rev. denied* 262 Kan. 969 (1997) (intentional act of insured causally connected to use of car, automobile exclusion of homeowner's policy applies, *Upland* not mentioned); *Newton v. Nicholas*, 20 Kan.App.2d 335, 887 P.2d 1158, *rev. denied* 257 Kan. 1093 (1995) (*Upland* not mentioned, negligent acts were failure to inspect and secure water tank on truck, directly connected to use, no coverage); and *Farmers Ins. Co. v. Rosen,* 17 Kan.App.2d 468, 839 P.2d 71, *rev. denied* 252 Kan. 1091 (1992) (negligent instruction claimed, *Upland* distinguished, theory of liability test ignored, no coverage found). 265 Kan. at 340, 961 P.2d 1213.

Utica points out two other Court of Appeals decisions which ignored or declined to extend the "theory of liability" approach: *Bush v. Shoemaker-Beal*, 26 Kan.App.2d 183, 987 P.2d 1103, *rev. denied* 268 Kan. 885 (1999), and *State Farm Mut. Auto. Ins. Co. v. Cummings*, 13 Kan.App.2d 630, 637, 778 P.2d 370, *rev. denied* 245 Kan. 786 (1989).

Finally, Utica argues that this court's decision in *First Financial Ins. Co. v. Bugg*, 265 Kan. 690, 962 P.2d 515 (1998), issued just more than 1 month after *Marquis*, is irreconcilable with *Marquis* and *Upland*. In his dissenting opinion in *Brumley v. Lee*, 265 Kan. 810, 831, 963 P.2d 1224 (1998), Justice Six opined that the *Upland* rule had not been consistently followed in Kansas, citing *Bugg.* See *State Farm Ins. Co. v. Gerrity*, 25 Kan.App.2d 643, 646, 968 P.2d 270 (1998), *rev. denied* 267 Kan. 887 (1999) ("theories of liability are irrelevant when injuries occur from intentional acts"; *Marquis* and *Upland* involved negligence claims).

In her response to Utica's petition for review, Crist argues that this case is not the proper vehicle for overturning *Marquis* since Utica denied coverage and refused to defend Hunan. According to Crist, an insurance carrier wishing to overturn *Marquis* should recognize its duty to tender a defense, subject to a reservation of rights, while filing a declaratory judgment action which would allow sufficient facts to be developed to allow this court to decide whether *Marquis* should be reconsidered.

In a related argument, Crist contends that under the doctrine of stare decisis, this court should not change settled principles of law simply because there is a change in the composition of the court. Crist argues the importance of stare decisis is that it gives parties the ability to predict the legal consequences of their actions.

We agree. In reaching the holding in *Marquis*, the majority impliedly relied upon the doctrine of stare decisis, noting that the law in Kansas was clearly established at the time the insurance contract was entered into. With the additional precedent of *Marquis* in 1998 and the passage of the additional time, stare decisis considerations are even stronger.

[6][7] In *Samsel v. Wheeler Transport Services, Inc.*, 246 Kan. 336, 356, 789 P.2d 541 (1990), *overruled on other grounds Bair v. Peck*, 248 Kan. 824, 844, 811 P.2d 1176 (1991), we discussed the basis for the doctrine of stare decisis and its importance:

> It is recognized under the doctrine of stare decisis that, once a point of law has been established by a court, that point of law will generally be followed by the same court and all courts of lower rank in subsequent cases where the same legal issue is raised. Stare decisis operates to promote system-wide stability and continuity by ensuring the survival of decisions that have been previously approved by a court. . . . The application of stare decisis ensures stability and continuity—demonstrating a continuing legitimacy of judicial review. Judicial adherence to constitutional precedent ensures that all branches of government, including the judicial branch, are bound by law.
>
> . . . The general American doctrine as applied to courts of last resort is that a court is not inexorably bound by its own precedents but will follow the rule of law which it has established in earlier cases, unless clearly convinced that the rule was originally erroneous or is no longer sound because of changing conditions and that more good than harm will come by departing from precedent. [Citation omitted.]

Although Utica cites additional authority in support of the dissent in *Marquis*, it does not make a new argument or point to any factor not considered and rejected by the majority in *Marquis*. There is no "changing condition" requiring us to abandon the prior authority of *Marquis*.

[8] In addition, more harm than good is likely to come from a departure from precedent on this issue. We are mindful that "[c]onsiderations in favor of stare decisis are at their acme in cases involving property and contract rights, where reliance interests are involved." *Payne v. Tennessee*, 501 U.S. 808, 828, 111 S.Ct. 2597, 115 L.Ed.2d 720 (1991). For many years the law in Kansas has been clear that an insurance exclusion for damage or injury arising from an automobile will not exclude a claim based upon negligent supervision. Insurers have been clearly advised that if they wish to have such an exclusion, the policy should include clear language stating an exclusion such as was used in the homeowner's policy at issue in *Marquis*. Insureds and insurers alike have relied upon *Marquis* and *Upland.* As such we decline to overrule such precedent. . . .

. . . .

Affirmed.

BEIER, J., not participating.

BRAZIL, S.J., assigned. [FN1]

BRAZIL, S.J.:

I respectfully dissent. I would adopt the well-reasoned concurring and dissenting opinion written by Justice Larson in *Marquis v. State Farm Fire & Cas. Co.*, 265 Kan. 317, 335-40, 961 P.2d 1213 (1998). The majority opinion in this case perpetuates an inconsistency in Kansas law. See *Brumley v. Lee*, 265 Kan. 810, 825-34, 963 P.2d 1224 (1998) (Six, J., dissenting); *First Financial Ins. Co. v. Bugg*, 265 Kan. 690, 962 P.2d 515 (1998). We should not blindly adhere to the doctrine of stare decisis in light of such an inconsistency, especially where the authority underlying *Marquis* has weakened.

McFARLAND, C.J., and GERNON, J., join in the foregoing dissent.

Source: *Crist v. Hunan Palace*, 277 Kan. 706, 89 P.3d 573 (St. Paul, MN: Thomson West). Reprinted with permission from Westlaw.

It is worth noting here that the art of using precedent to solve legal problems is a skill that builds over time. Many students have difficulty synthesizing cases. This chapter is intended to give you practice in the skills of analyzing cases, using precedent to predict the outcome of any hypothetical case; distinguishing cases; and applying the law to the facts.

BRIEFING CASES

In analyzing cases, you develop critical thinking skills by distinguishing cases. It is necessary to compare and contrast prior cases based on both the facts and the issue presented in order to persuade the court that a particular case should or should not be applicable to your case. This skill of constructing an argument based on how and why a particular case should or should not have precedential value is cultivated throughout this text. The first step in comparing and contrasting prior cases is to prepare a synopsis of each case. This task is commonly called briefing a case. As noted previously in this chapter, briefing a case simply means summarizing a case. Case briefs summarize a particular court decision. You may ultimately utilize these briefs in preparing legal memoranda about a client's legal issue for your supervising attorney.

In preparing a synopsis of a judicial opinion, there is a particular method of briefing a case that is beneficial in organizing your arguments and reasoning. The practice of briefing, or summarizing, cases enables you to put into a formal, organized writing a synopsis of the legal analysis and reasoning that you may have already formulated in thinking about the case.

Summarizing a case might be simply preparing the synopsis of a specific court case. After reading the full court opinion, you can begin to prepare the synopsis. The standard procedure in briefing a case involves the following components:

- *Case citation*. Example: *Smith v. Jones,* 123 Ill.3d 500 (2001).
- *Facts*. Background of the case: what happened to whom, and what is the factual basis for the arguments of each party?
- *Procedural history*. What was the trial court decision? Was there another appellate-level decision (other than the present case you are briefing)?
- *Issue*. The legal question before the court.
- *Decision*. The court's answer to the legal question.
- *Holding*. The concise rule of law contained in the case.
- *Reasoning*. Brief summary of the court's rationale and law applied in reaching its decision.

This format for briefing court opinions forms the basis for the method of legal analysis that will be utilized in this chapter and throughout this textbook. The procedure for briefing cases noted here should be distinguished from the FIRC format that will be used for the critical thinking exercises here. Briefing cases is done because you have conducted legal research about a client's case, and you have found three or four cases that seem to meet the three criteria of precedent listed previously in this chapter. In order to present a succinct and organized document summarizing your research to your supervising attorney, you may find it helpful to brief each of the three or four cases so that your findings can be easily compared and utilized.

On the other hand, the FIRC format that will be taught in this chapter is the method this author prefers to use in helping students learn how to analyze cases. In this book, you will be given hypothetical fact situations and the relevant rule of law, and then will be asked to apply that established rule of law to those facts. By doing this, you will gain practice in summarizing what happened in your own words, spotting the legal issue, and then using reasoning skills to apply the law to the facts.

By following a particular legal analysis method, the consistency of the structure of the format provides an easy process to improve persuasive argument skills and apply the substantive legal principles and rules learned. Learning how to draft this unique type of document improves critical thinking skills. This organized approach to analyzing cases and applying the law to the facts is an effective tool for understanding legal principles and developing skills utilized in legal method courses. It must be pointed out that there is more than one format that can be used for legal analysis, but all of them contain essentially the same information, perhaps in a different order. Many textbooks and lawyers are familiar with the format commonly called IRAC. This acronym, representing issue, rule of law, analysis, and conclusion, contains the same components as the FIRC format preferred by this author. Its purpose is simply to improve your legal reasoning skills, an essential aspect of solving legal problems and organizing information gathered in the legal research process.

INTRODUCTION TO THE FIRC LEGAL ANALYSIS FORMAT

In this textbook, the method used will consistently be identified by the acronym FIRC, which consists of four parts. This method of analyzing cases contains similar components as when you brief a published court opinion. Remember, the purpose of preparing a case brief is to identify key facts, main issues, and significant legal principles used in the court's rationale and decision in that case. By summarizing a court case, you are able to condense the judicial opinion (hence, "brief") and more readily be able to compare that case, based on the synopsis, with the facts and issue of a present case being considered.

In a similar fashion, and in order to improve your analytical skills, you will now learn to prepare a case analysis based on hypothetical fact patterns. The purpose of this exercise is to develop your skills in identifying issues and key facts, as well as to teach you how to apply what you learn in the seven substantive chapters that follow to any set of facts. There is much to be gained from this practice. Consider the typical client who walks in your office door. As discussed in Chapter 6, paralegals often have the duty of interviewing prospective clients. Let's take the example of Samantha Stevens. She is in your office for the first time, and she proceeds to tell you why she needs a lawyer. The problem is she talks for over an hour, not only telling you why she is there, but all about what she had for dinner last night and why she dislikes the supervisor at her workplace. When she is finished, you have three pages of handwritten notes about all she has just told you. From this, you must decide what the material facts are and those that are irrelevant to the potential lawsuit. In addition, you will need to discuss with your supervising attorney the possible legal issues of Samantha's case. Finally, you will need to know where to begin your research into the applicable law. In this scenario, the ability to clearly summarize material facts, spot the legal issue, and apply the relevant law to these facts in order to predict the likely outcome is an invaluable asset for a paralegal.

	FIRC FORMAT
F	Statement of the facts (summarizes the facts of the underlying dispute).
I	Statement of the issue (legal questions addressed by the court).
R	The reasoning that supports the holding.
C	The conclusion, or holding, on the issue.

The primary goal in following this method is to develop a consistent structure or framework for the analysis of cases and synthesis of issues. Learning the legal principles in the substantive law areas that follow is not difficult, as students may well be able to memorize the rules of law. However, learning how to apply those rules to numerous disparate fact situations is a challenge that is only met with practice. It is anticipated that following a prescribed format in comparing and analyzing cases will guide you in using legal authority to best interpret a case and argue your position. Each of the four elements of this format will be discussed in turn.

Facts

The *facts* section of your case summary is a brief statement of the facts presented in a case. In a court opinion, the facts section is typically clearly demarcated by the court; it is sometimes called the syllabus or synopsis. The facts might include both what happened in the case, as well as procedural facts, that is, the history of the proceedings up to that point.

However, in comparison, the facts section of your case analysis should be a restatement of the occurrence facts, in your own words. You should be certain to provide enough details of the events so that someone reading the facts section of your paper would have sufficient understanding of what happened. Being able to identify the key legally significant facts ensures that the application of the law will be consistent with cases involving a similar set of facts. The importance of this section cannot be stressed enough. Too often, it is tempting to rush through with a general paraphrasing of the facts contained in a hypothetical fact pattern. In doing so, you may include irrelevant facts in your summary and exclude those key facts that might determine the applicability of the rule of law. In a client's case, the outcome of a case may hinge upon even one minor fact, so it is important to present an accurate restatement of all the relevant facts. Thus, in writing a fact summary of a hypothetical case, it is necessary to include all material facts that pertain to the legal issue of the case.

Diligent paralegal students who acquire the skill of restating the key facts in their own words will benefit in the future, because the initial stages of litigation require the compilation of

You Be the Judge

Read the following hypothetical fact situation and determine what the key facts are here:

Loulou is shopping at her local discount store, and having completed her purchase of hand lotion, aspirin, and socks, leaves the store to walk to her compact car in the adjacent store parking lot. There are two streetlights in the parking lot, but one of the lights is burned out. While walking to her car, Loulou notices a red purse lying in the road near the entrance to an adjoining shoe store. Loulou walks over to the shoe store, and while leaning over to pick up the purse, Loulou is attacked from behind by an unknown person. Loulou's recent purchases are stolen, as well as her own purse. Loulou sues the discount store for negligence.

thorough facts. As noted previously, and again in Chapter 6, paralegals often assist in the client interview process, as well as undertake the task of summarizing various documents associated with a case. If you develop the skill of identifying key facts and summarizing important points now, then you will find it easier to sift through information obtained in a client interview and ensure that nothing is omitted at the outset. Extraneous facts, facts of minor importance, and characterizations of the facts should be omitted from the summary. The importance of this section must not be minimized.

In the You Be the Judge hypothetical case, a lot of information is presented about Loulou's actions leading up to the assault. What are the key facts in this example? In determining the important facts, it is necessary to separate out irrelevant information, which bears little significance to the outcome of the case. In identifying the key facts in this hypothetical fact pattern, you would first need to know that this is a negligence case and that there are four elements of this cause of action that must be established. The four elements of a **prima facie case** of negligence are: duty, breach of duty, proximate cause, and damages. The first element needed to establish negligence—the basis of Loulou's lawsuit—is that the defendant owes a duty of care to the injured party. The existence and scope of that duty is a legal question for the courts to determine.

prima facie case
The elements of the plaintiff's (or prosecutor's) cause of action; what the plaintiff must prove.

In considering the first element of negligence, that a duty is owed, some of the key facts might include: Loulou is a customer of the discount store; the parking lot is adjacent to the store; the presence of street lights in the lot. It is irrelevant that the purse was red or that it was in front of a *shoe* store, as these facts do nothing to support a showing of duty or impact a claim for negligence. Additional key facts, critical to proving the other elements of a negligence claim, include the lack of one street light and Loulou's proximity to the discount store.

Your goal in summarizing the facts of a case is to include all critical details that establish or relate to the specific elements of the appropriate cause of action. Since the law is applied to the facts of a case, it is important to pay particular attention to details that support the relevant rule of law. In subsequent chapters, where substantive rules of law and legal principles are studied, you will discover that the technique of applying legal standards to the facts may depend upon finding supporting facts for each and every element of the rule of law. For example, in the preceding hypothetical fact pattern, you would need to find facts that support each of the four elements of negligence in order for Loulou to win in her lawsuit. Your statement of facts should be accurate and complete but cannot be presented in a misleading or argumentative manner. Take care also to distinguish opinions from facts. For example, you should avoid characterizing Loulou as a hapless woman or an innocent shopper, as these adjectives are opinion, and not fact. Using active

RESEARCH THIS!

Locate the court opinion in the case *Sullivan v. The Boston Architectural Center, Inc.*, 57 Mass.App.Ct. 771, 786 N.E.2d 419 (2003).

What are the material facts of this case?

How did you determine these facts?

verbs and specific, vivid detail when it is in your favor, in chronological order, may impact the tone and effect of your statement of facts.

The rule of law that forms the basis for the second section of your case analysis is a statement of the issue.

Issue

Determining the *legal issue* is one of the most important steps in the legal analysis process. Identifying the legal issue is sometimes confused with determining factual issues. It is essential to understand the difference between these two, as lower courts are concerned with resolving factual issues, such as whether John was driving the car, whereas higher courts resolve legal issues, such as whether John was negligent in driving the car. Note that precise rules of law are the foundation for legal issues.

The legal issue is generally the question presented for consideration, the question that needs to be answered. Like the game show *Jeopardy,* the issue is always written in the form of a question. For example, "whether the contract between A and B to install a roof is valid" or "whether Dudley is liable to Mary for assault" are both legal issues to be resolved. Examples of factual issues are "whether Smith's dog bit Mary's leg" or "whether Jones painted the wrong house." In drafting the issue, students should keep in mind that the elements of the rule of law are critical to the precise, narrow issue presented, and thus the question raised by the facts of the case should reflect the specific situation. For instance, it is not enough to simply say, "whether the day care operator is liable for negligence" or "whether there is a valid contract." It is more precise to pose the legal question, "whether a day care operator is liable for the negligent supervision of a child injured in the parking lot of the facility" or "whether the contract was executed under duress by a homeowner suffering from insomnia."

There should be a relationship between the facts of the case and the issue presented, such that the applicable law that governs the dispute can be precisely raised in the key facts. The issue is like a topic sentence in that it is usually just one simple, clear sentence that sets forth what will be discussed in the subsequent sentences. It lets the reader know exactly why the parties are in dispute and the applicable rule of law. The issue focuses on resolving a dispute fundamental to a general field of substantive law that you will study in subsequent chapters, such as contracts or torts.

At first, it may be easiest for you to adopt a rigid format that requires little more than "filling in the blanks." For example, suppose that Miller has been arrested and charged with burglary. The issue can be modeled after the following format:

Whether (defendant's name) is (guilty/liable) of/for (rule of law).

Thus, here the issue may be "whether Miller is guilty of burglary." You can then amend this legal issue to include the precise facts that narrow the issue, as in "whether Miller is guilty of burglarizing the Smith residence if he entered the home through an open door." The issue would not be "whether Miller broke a window to enter Smith's house," as this is a factual issue.

In framing the legal issue, be as precise as possible, applying the specific part of the legal rule to the exact facts. It is not a valid issue to state "whether the trial court erred," as this issue could apply to any set of facts and legal standards. Note that fact scenarios might present multiple legal questions; each issue must be addressed separately, as your analysis must involve a discussion of each legal cause of action, citing specific statutes or rules of law. Similarly, if a hypothetical fact scenario presents issues involving multiple parties, the issues must also be addressed separately regarding each individual party. After determining the key facts and issue, the third section of your legal analysis is the reasoning.

Reasoning

The *reasoning* section of the case brief is your opportunity to tell why the dispute was resolved in a specific way. The purpose of this section is to identify in clear terms the rationale of the court in reaching its decision. If you are writing a legal analysis based on a hypothetical fact situation, then this is the part of your paper in which you develop the skill of summarizing and explaining the legal principles supporting your own conclusion about the outcome of the hypothetical case. Your goal for this section is to explain the precise reasons that justify the conclusion, using the specific language contained in the applicable rules of law.

The first half of this reasoning section presents the applicable law, setting forth the legal principles governing the case. Too often, it is easy to omit this part of your legal analysis. Identifying the applicable law is crucial to discussing your reasoning in the second half of this section, where the law is actually applied to the facts. Keep in mind that the law may include specific elements that must be proved in order to state a claim for that cause of action. For example, list the elements of negligence when stating the applicable law in the first part of this section. Then, you are more likely to be focused on how the law applies to the facts of your case, as you will be addressing each element of the law individually. For example, in the hypothetical case previously noted, Loulou's cause of action for negligence against the discount store depends on her proving each of the elements of negligence in turn. Thus, one would argue that the store owed a duty of care to Loulou to keep the premises safe for its customers. It is relevant that the parking lot is adjacent to the store. Next, one must prove that the store breached its duty of care by failing to ensure that adequate security and lighting was provided in the parking lot. Loulou's case depends on the argument that the store breached its duty. Finally, Loulou must demonstrate that her injuries were the proximate result of this breach of duty, and thus one can argue that had the lighting been sufficient and the store patrolled by security guards, then the assault, and subsequent injury to Loulou, may not have occurred.

The reason that the applicable law must be stated in the reasoning section of your legal analysis is to specifically note the relevant legal context in which the facts of the case must be construed. When stating the applicable law in the first part of the reasoning section, you should do this without comment or annotation. If a statute is involved, the statute should be quoted. If the rule of law is legal principles, the definition or rule should be stated objectively, identifying the key elements with specificity.

The second part of the reasoning section involves your legal reasoning. Legal reasoning is applying general rules of law to a specific factual situation. Each element of the statute or applicable rule of law must be applied to the facts of the case, to determine whether the facts satisfy the rule of law. Keep in mind that this reasoning process does not ensure that the "correct" answer or result is achieved, for as you will soon discover, the law is not so black and white, but rather depends on the persuasive abilities and relative strengths and weaknesses of opposing arguments. Law may involve pure logical reasoning, but the disputes are not resolved with mathematical certainty, by virtue of the fact that personal viewpoints, bias, and other extrinsic factors ultimately impact final decisions. One can predict the *likely* result, but this is oversimplified.

Thus, it should be readily apparent that the key goal of this section of your legal analysis based on a hypothetical fact situation is to apply the law and the applicable legal principles to the facts. If you have taken extreme care to present an accurate summary of the facts and the issue, then your task in the reasoning section is to identify how the legal principles were applied to these narrow, specific facts in this hypothetical case.

Conclusion

Finally, the last step in this method of legal analysis is the *conclusion.* This section consists of one sentence, a simple answer to the legal question presented in the issue section of your paper. It requires you to take a firm position, to predict, to decide how the case is likely to be resolved. The conclusion and the issue are obviously mirror images of each other, the conclusion answering the question posed in the issue statement.

Thus, if your issue is "whether the day care operator is liable for the negligent supervision of a child in the parking lot of its facility," the conclusion might simply be either "the day care operator is liable" or "the day care operator is not liable." Since this section is your conclusion, it should reflect that outcome in the reasoning section of your paper. Many students are tempted to explain or list reasons why they have reached this decision in the conclusion section of the paper. Resist this temptation! Emphasize the period at the end of the sentence, so that you do not state, "the day care operator is liable because he failed to have three staff members supervising the class at recess." It helps to consider which road you are heading down when writing the reasoning section so that it persuasively leads to the decision expressed in your conclusion. Hence, you should mentally consider the position you will assume in your conclusion prior to formulating your legal theories in the reasoning section. However, by the time your reader has reached this final part of your legal analysis, there should be no doubt as to what this final sentence will say—the bottom line should have been obvious by this point.

You Be the Judge

Bert needs money and plans to break into Isabel's house at night while she is asleep and steal her diamond ring, valued at $5,000. On the selected night, Bert goes to Isabel's home at midnight, only to find the front door unlocked and wide open. The statute in Bert's state defines burglary as "the breaking and entering in the night of a dwelling with the intent to commit a felony therein." Under this statute, if Bert steals the ring, will he be convicted of burglary in his state?

ANALYZING STATUTORY LAW

Reading the law encompasses not only case law but statutory law as well. Many legal issues, particularly in the substantive area of criminal law, involve statutes. You should take care to locate the relevant statute in your state, especially in the areas of family law and criminal law, before analyzing the holding of any particular case. Statutes should be read carefully, as every word may have profound significance on its relevance and applicability to your fact scenario. In general, keep in mind that the purpose of statutes is to permit, regulate, or prohibit conduct. Therefore, a first reading of a statute should be to determine its overall purpose.

rules of construction
The rules that control the judicial interpretation of statutes.

It is helpful to note the tools that judges use when they are interpreting statutes. These tools are commonly referred to as **rules of construction.** For example, judges might examine legislative history in order to ascertain the intent of the legislators in drafting the statute. They will look to see if the legislative history reveals whether the drafters intended the statute to include the regulation of the fact situation currently under consideration by the court.

plain meaning rule
Courts will use the traditional definition of terms used if those terms are not otherwise defined.

Some judges have emphasized that legislative history is not a valid step in interpreting statutes and that the **plain meaning rule** should apply. In essence, this means that the language of the statute is clear on its face and that this is the interpretation the court will give to it. The statute's words were intentionally chosen by the legislators, and therefore the common meaning of each word should be used when interpreting the language. Proponents of the plain meaning rule argue that since the meaning of the statute is clear on its face, then therefore no additional inquiries ought to be made. The United States Supreme Court has stated that courts should always presume that a legislature says in a statute what it means to say, and means in a statute what it says there. Thus, it is assumed that the legislature intentionally and purposely included language in one section of a statute, but omitted it elsewhere in that statute. However, it becomes apparent when examining statutes that certain words, taken at face value, are inconsistent with the surrounding text and therefore are subject to alternate meanings.

Every question regarding statutory interpretation begins with the language of the statute itself. In addition, courts may rely on previous judicial interpretation of a statute in order to apply statutory provisions to the case before them. Recall the rules of judicial precedent discussed earlier in this chapter. Once a court has interpreted legislative intent, they will not go through this tedious exercise again, but will enforce the statute as it has been previously interpreted by the prior court. Annotated versions of state or federal codes supply cases that interpret specific provisions of a statute and should be consulted when researching a case.

Summary

The process of learning to read the law is a crucial step in your development of legal method and analysis. In order to be an effective paralegal, you must acquire the skills of summarizing cases, organizing ideas, and applying the applicable rules of law. The concept of judicial precedent and stare decisis is important in legal analysis. The method of writing summaries of hypothetical fact scenarios, as well as preparing briefs of judicial opinions, is similar. They are a way to develop analytical skills by providing a precise framework within which to organize ideas. By requiring students to clarify the facts, issue, and holding in a case, it is then easier to apply the law to the facts of a case. Application of the legal principles discussed in subsequent chapters is accomplished in the context of sample cases, and more complex fact patterns will be presented as a challenge to improve your critical thinking and legal analysis skills.

Key Terms

Briefing a case
Case law
Case of first impression
Case on all fours
Case on point
Case reporters
Headnotes
Judicial precedent
Legal analysis
Official reporters
Plain meaning rule
Prima facie case
Rules of construction
Stare decisis
Syllabus
Unofficial reporters

Discussion Questions

1. Explain the difference between a case on point and a case on all fours.
2. Why is it important to present a clear and accurate statement of the facts when writing a legal analysis or case brief?
3. What is the difference between case law and statutory law?
4. Discuss the significance of the plain meaning rule.
5. Summarize each of the sections of the FIRC format.
6. Access the Web site www.abanet.org/cpr/ethicopinions.html. This Web site of the American Bar Association posts summaries of ethical opinions. Choose one of the opinions and discuss the summary.
7. What is the advantage to preparing case briefs of court opinions you intend to use in a legal memorandum?

Exercises

For each of the following hypothetical fact patterns, prepare a legal analysis of the case using the FIRC method. Use the definition of burglary contained in the preceding You Be the Judge exercise.

1. *Hypothetical case*. Ben is in need of extra money to support his drug habit. He learns that his neighbor, Sally, will be working the night shift at the hospital and will not be home all night, so Ben decides to break in to Sally's house and steal her jewelry. Unknown to Ben, Sally becomes suddenly ill from food poisoning and will not be working that night. At around midnight, Ben goes to Sally's house and discovers the back door open. He enters the house, and finds Sally sitting in her living room; taken by surprise at Sally's presence, Ben instead waves a knife at Sally, demands her purse, and then runs out the back door with the purse. (For this case, compare your answer to that of the sample analysis following Exercise 2.)
2. *Hypothetical case*. Mary needs extra money to support her gambling habit. She works at the Dainty Door Motel as a housekeeper. While cleaning a guest's room, she notes a diamond necklace that is left out on a coffee table in the room. At the time she is cleaning the room, the guest is present, so Mary is not able to pocket the necklace, but she plans to return to the room when the guest is out to dinner. At 6 p.m., Mary sees the guest leave and reenters the room with her passkey, for the purpose of stealing the necklace. She finds the necklace in the same place on the table, puts it in her pocket, and leaves.

   Sample legal analysis:

   FACTS: Ben plans to burglarize his neighbor's house, but when he goes to the house at midnight, he discovers the door is open and his neighbor is home. He waves a knife at the neighbor, demands her purse, and then runs out with the purse.

   ISSUE: Whether Ben is guilty of burglary.

   REASONING: Burglary is the breaking and entering in the night of the dwelling of another with the intent to deprive the owner of her property. Here, Ben does not break into the victim's house because the door is left open and he is able to walk in. Although he enters the house at night, he is confronted by the homeowner and uses a deadly weapon to take the homeowner's purse directly from her, before leaving. Ben may have committed robbery, as he took the purse from another person by force.

CONCLUSION: Ben is not guilty of burglary.

3. In order to try out your newly acquired synopsis skills, the following is a court opinion from a recent case. Utilizing the method described in this chapter, read the following opinion and summarize this case, using the standard procedure. This practice will help you in subsequent assignments throughout this book that involve the summary of cases concerning complex subject matter and will help develop your skills of organization.

   As a general guideline, the recommended length of a brief for most cases assigned in this book is approximately 400 words. Considering the fact that both the issue and the conclusion part of your brief should be one sentence each, it is easy to see that the reasoning section of the paper will represent the bulk of your synopsis.

Court of Appeals of Georgia.
WIKE
v.
The STATE.
No. A03A1160.

July 17, 2003.

BARNES, Judge.

Following his jury conviction for misdemeanor battery and the subsequent denial of his motion for new trial, Randy Wike appeals, contending that the trial court erred in declining to give his charge on defense of habitation. Upon finding that the evidence did not support a charge on defense of habitation, we affirm.

Construed to support the conviction, the evidence demonstrates that on January 15, 2001, when Wike brought his son home after a weekend visit, the victim was working in the front yard. The victim is married to Wike's ex-wife. When his son got out of the car, Wike began to yell obscenities at the victim. The victim told Wike to leave, but Wike would not; instead he continued to yell insults and obscenities at the victim. When the victim told Wike for the third time to leave his property, Wike jumped out of his car, approached the victim, and hit him behind his left ear. The victim had a shovel in his hands, which he had picked up with the intent of protecting himself, but when Wike hit him, he dropped the shovel. Wike drove away but was later arrested for battery.

Wike argues that the trial court erred by not giving his requested charge on defense of habitation. He asserts that the victim threw dirt on his vehicle and that created a jury question as to whether his actions after that point constituted defense of habitation.

[1] Pursuant to OCGA § 16-3-23, "[a] person is justified in threatening or using force against another when and to the extent that he reasonably believes that such threat or force is necessary to prevent or terminate such other's unlawful entry into or attack upon a habitation." The term "habitation" also includes a motor vehicle. OCGA § 16-3-24.1. But, defense of habitation is not available where there is no evidence that the victim was attempting to enter or attack a habitation when he was injured. See *Terrell v. Hester,* 182 Ga.App. 160(3), 355 S.E.2d 97 (1987).

[2] Here, Wike testified that after he dropped his son off at the victim's house, the victim cursed him, told him to get off his property, and then threw a shovel of dirt on his Jeep. He said that when he got out of the car to inspect for damage, the victim continued to verbally assault him. Wike testified that he struck the victim only after the victim pushed him with the shovel.

Because Wike's own testimony establishes that the victim was not directing any threats upon the vehicle at the time Wike struck him, OCGA § 16-3-23 is not applicable to the facts of this case. If, in fact, dirt was thrown on Wike's vehicle, the attack had ended before he exited his Jeep to inspect it. Indeed, that Wike's first inclination was to inspect the vehicle, rather than protect it by restraining the victim from committing further violence against his Jeep, belies any argument that any action was needed on his part to stop the victim from attacking his truck.

"In this case, . . . it is evident from [Wike's] testimony that [his] defense was self-defense, not defense of habitation. Thus, the court's failure to instruct the jury on the defense of habitation was not error." *Benham v. State,* 260 Ga. App. 243, 245(3)(a), 581 S.E.2d 586 (2003).

Judgment affirmed.

ANDREWS, P.J., and ADAMS, J., concur.

Source: *Wike v. State*, 262 Ga.App. 444, 585 S.E.2d 742 (St. Paul, MN: Thomson West). Reprinted with permission from Westlaw.

4. Read the following fact scenario. List potential factual issues. Spot possible legal issues.
   Mortimer is a pedestrian at a crosswalk at a busy intersection that is controlled by both stoplights and walk signals. Mortimer steps off the curb and is in the middle of the far right lane when he is struck by a car driven by Dudley. Dudley has previous convictions for driving while under the influence; at the time of this incident, Dudley had consumed exactly one can of beer.
5. For each of the following three hypothetical fact patterns, list the similarities (analogies) and differences (distinctions) in facts among the three cases, including your reasons why, if any, those comparisons matter in determining precedent.
   a. Smith lived in an apartment over his garage. One month, some tools were stolen out of his garage. Later, he noticed that the lock on his garage door had been bent and that there were pry marks on the door. Smith had tools stolen from his garage a second time, one week after the first incident. Smith then set up a trap gun, which would fire when someone opened the garage. Three weeks after doing this, two 15-year-old boys, both unarmed, pried the lock off the garage door. When one boy opened the garage door, he was shot in the face by the trap gun.
   b. Jones was trying to steal the windshield wipers off of Peterson's car. While Jones was in the process of removing the wipers from the car, Peterson ran into his house and retrieved a gun. After warning Jones to stop, Jones still continued. Peterson warned Jones that if he took one more step, he would shoot him. Jones advanced toward Peterson. Peterson then shot Jones in the face.
   c. Harris is a game warden for the National Park Service. Harris spied Long illegally fishing in a lake, which Harris routinely patrolled. Harris arrested Long for illegal fishing. Long attempted to escape arrest by fleeing in his boat. Harris pursued him, and Long began to beat Harris with his oar. Harris then shot Long in the arm.

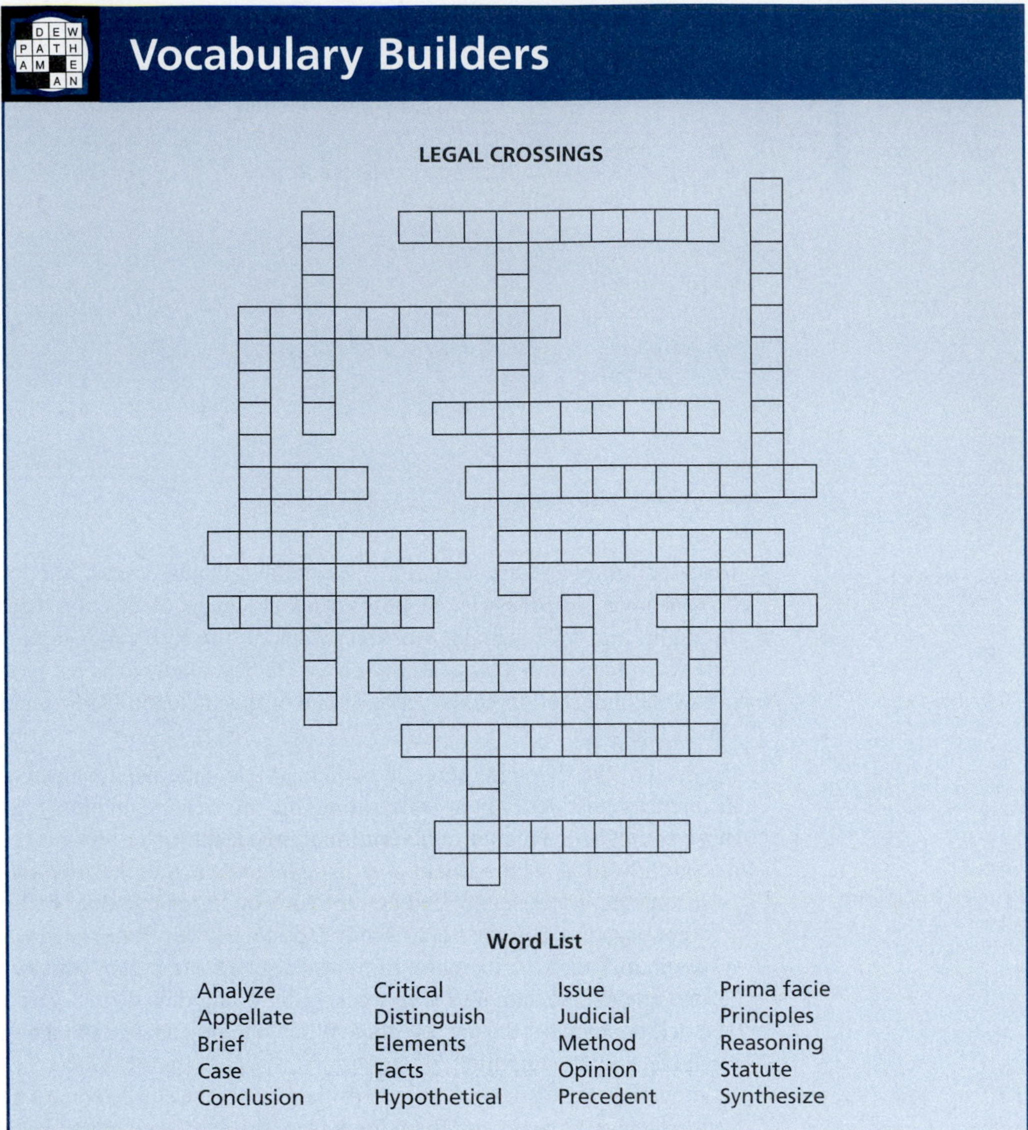
Vocabulary Builders
LEGAL CROSSINGS
Word List
Analyze
Appellate
Brief
Case
Conclusion
Critical
Distinguish
Elements
Facts
Hypothetical
Issue
Judicial
Method
Opinion
Precedent
Prima facie
Principles
Reasoning
Statute
Synthesize

Chapter 5

Procedural Law

CHAPTER OBJECTIVES

After reading this chapter, you will be able to:

- Identify the stages of the litigation process prior to trial.
- Discuss the importance of voir dire.
- Describe the stages of a trial.
- Explain the significance of the Federal Rules of Civil Procedure.
- Distinguish the procedural issues arising from both civil and criminal cases.

---

substantive law
Legal rules that are the content or substance of the law, defining rights and duties of citizens.

procedural law
The set of rules used to enforce substantive law.

In previous chapters, the distinction between substantive and procedural law was discussed. As a reminder, **substantive law** defines the rights and duties of individuals with respect to society. It is the content area of the law. **Procedural law** defines the manner in which these rights and duties are enforced. It is the set of rules that guides the parties through the litigation process. This chapter will further discuss aspects of procedural law, as the overview of substantive law topics will be covered in Chapters 7-13.

Once a dispute arises between parties, and a decision is made to seek legal recourse, there is a basic sequence of steps that are followed in order to achieve resolution of this dispute by formal methods. In this chapter, you will explore the path by which a case may proceed to trial, and the procedural distinctions that arise depending on whether the subject matter of the dispute is civil or criminal in nature. In certain situations, as noted in previous chapters, there may be an overlap between these two areas of the law; therefore, the same set of facts gives rise to both a civil and criminal case. You will be introduced to the unique characteristics of criminal procedure and features of a criminal case, which will be discussed in depth in Chapter 7. Rules of civil and criminal procedure, based on state statutes and the Federal Rules of Civil Procedure, are in place so as to ensure that parties receive a fair trial and that every suit progresses in a similar way through the legal system.

STAGES OF LITIGATION

litigant
A party to a lawsuit.

There is an explicit process with specific steps that are followed once a person intends to seek legal recourse to resolve a dispute. As noted in Chapter 1, society generally prefers that parties settle their differences by legal means, rather than by taking the law into their own hands. These parties to a suit are commonly referred to as **litigants.** The civil litigation process is complex, and there are three distinct stages in this process: pretrial, trial, and appeal. There are also precise elements of a trial itself, should the legal matter ultimately reach this stage. Trials are expensive and time consuming, so everyone involved has an indisputable interest in avoiding trial. The process is different in a civil case as compared to a criminal matter, so let's begin with the civil litigation process.

Assume the hypothetical case of Mary, a postal carrier for the U.S. Post Office. One evening, on her way home from work, Mary stops to buy bananas and milk at her local grocery store, when she slips and falls on a puddle of water in the produce section. As a result of her fall, Mary suffers a broken leg and incurs medical bills in excess of 10,000 dollars. Furthermore, she is unable to maintain her postal delivery route for two months while she recovers from the injury.

If Mary wants the grocery store to pay her medical bills and reimburse her for time lost from work, she is essentially seeking to recover **compensatory damages** and therefore she must notify the store owner that she intends to file a lawsuit against the grocery store. It is said that Mary has a **civil cause of action** against the store. A civil cause of action is a claim for damages that is based on the relevant substantive area of law, and its facts support a judicial resolution. After consulting her local attorney, Mary decides to move forward with her case and file a negligence suit against the store. However, Mary needs to follow a specific set of procedural laws that govern how the various aspects of her case will lead to ultimate settlement of this dispute. She begins on the path to resolution at what is commonly called the **pretrial stage.**

compensatory damages
A payment to make up for a wrong committed and return the nonbreaching party to a position where the effect of the breach has been neutralized.

civil cause of action
A claim for damages that is based on the relevant substantive area of law and has facts that support a judicial resolution.

pretrial stage
The steps in the litigation process before trial, to accomplish discovery and encourage settlement.

As the **plaintiff**—the person instituting legal action and bringing suit against the store—Mary is responsible for initiating the legal process. This is referred to as commencement of the action. The purpose of this stage is to prepare a formal, written statement that essentially advises the other party—in this hypothetical case, the grocery store—of the nature of the action (what allegedly happened), the legal theory underlying the case, a statement of the applicable law, and finally the demand for relief that the party is seeking. The obvious necessity of this initial stage of litigation is to give notice to the other party, the **defendant**, that something has happened and that the plaintiff is claiming that he or she is accountable. The defendant is the party against whom a lawsuit is brought. Logically speaking, the other party (the grocery store) may not have any prior notice that someone is demanding compensation unless informed of this. So, at this point, the plaintiff's attorney initiates the process, first determining the correct court in which to file suit (the jurisdiction, discussed in Chapter 2) and then ascertaining who should be sued. Keep in mind that since the litigation process is expensive and time consuming, the plaintiff's attorney will likely contact the defendant's attorney in order to explore **alternative dispute resolution (ADR)** methods. This is the most  important feature of the pretrial stage. ADR methods are options that the parties have to settle their disputes outside of court.

plaintiff
The party initiating legal action.

defendant
The party against whom a lawsuit is brought.

alternative dispute resolution (ADR)
Method of settling a dispute before trial in order to conserve the court's time.

ADR methods include arbitration, mediation, and traditional out-of-court settlement. At this point, the parties are seeking a compromise, and often they may agree on the basic facts and liability but differ on the amount of damages that is appropriate to the specific case. The primary distinction between arbitration and mediation is that arbitration is frequently court-ordered and the arbiter's decision is typically binding on the parties, whereas mediation is usually voluntary and the mediator's recommendation is not binding. The advantages to utilizing ADR include saving the parties the expense and time of trial, as well as conserving the court's time. In addition, the litigants who settle outside of court may achieve greater satisfaction in the outcome if it is something they have worked out for themselves. If a resolution is not immediately achieved in the initial pretrial stage, then the plaintiff's attorney will move forward with the formal written documents that were prepared at the start of the litigation process. These documents are referred to as pleadings.

Pleadings are the documents that are drafted by both parties, served on the opposing party, and filed with the court. Since the plaintiff has the burden to prove his or her case, then it is the plaintiff who begins by advising the opposing party of the lawsuit, in a document that states the alleged facts and the legal basis (cause of action). This is referred to as the **complaint** (see the end of the chapter for a sample complaint). Imagine if a complaint were not drafted or filed. How would the grocery store owner ever be aware of the fact that Mary was hurt in the store and is demanding compensation for her injuries? The plaintiff files a copy of the complaint with the clerk of the court, as well as information on serving the defendant (the store) with a copy of the complaint. The grocery store receives a copy of the complaint, and a **summons** telling it in which court the cause of action has been filed and a notice to appear. The summons is a notice to appear in court, informing the defendant of the complaint, and is typically served on the party by either the sheriff or a process server. After service, the store's attorney will draft an **answer** or response.

pleadings
The complaint, answer to complaint, and reply.

complaint
The document that states the allegations and the legal basis of the plaintiff's claims.

answer
The defendant's response to the plaintiff's complaint.

summons
The notice to appear in court, notifying the defendant of the plaintiff's complaint.

As this litigation process begins, the parties must be cognizant of the applicable procedural law—the rules—that guides them through the process. Examples of the rules that must be followed include time limitations on filing suit, the time within which complaints must be answered, and specific information that must be included in court documents. Even though the federal and state court systems have different rules, the specific set of rules that is

RESEARCH THIS!

Locate the rules of civil procedure for your state at www.findlaw.com. Are there any additional court rules in your jurisdiction that must be followed?

Federal Rules of Civil Procedure
The specific set of rules followed in the federal courts

followed in the federal courts—the **Federal Rules of Civil Procedure**—is the basis for most of the states' codes. According to the federal rules, for example, a complaint must contain a jurisdictional statement, a concise statement of the claim demonstrating that the plaintiff is entitled to relief, and a demand for judgment (Rule 8). Although the majority of states have modeled their state codes on the federal rules, there are other rules that are written by the courts in some states, as well as local rules that must be followed. You should take care to know the specific rules in your jurisdiction.

The complaint and summons are issued following the specific provisions and particulars, including the time limitations, set forth in the applicable rules of civil procedure. The defendant will file an answer that may deny any duties or obligations, admit or deny the facts alleged, raise applicable affirmative defenses, or state any procedural errors in the complaint warranting dismissal. This is the basis of the defendant's written response to the complaint. In drafting the response, the defendant should take care to address each allegation raised in the complaint, by specifically admitting or denying each one. If an allegation is not specifically denied in the answer, then the allegation is deemed to be admitted, even if this is not expressed in the response. If the defendant fails to file an answer within the time specified in the applicable rules, a **default judgment** may be entered against him or her.

default judgment
A judgment entered by the court against the defendant for failure to respond to the plaintiff's complaint.

Several rounds of pleadings may occur, as the documents may be amended and other claims filed. Note that a licensed attorney is required to sign all pleadings. In addition, a counterclaim or a cross-claim may be filed. A **counterclaim** is a countersuit by the defendant against the plaintiff. A **cross-claim** is where one or more of the defendants are suing each other or where plaintiffs are suing each other. For example, in our hypothetical case of Mary's slip and fall, the defendant grocery store may elect to file a cross-claim against the company that maintains the produce department's sprinkler system, alleging its negligent maintenance causes the accumulation of water on the floors. Finally, a **third-party claim** might be filed, which is where the defendant sues someone not originally a party to the plaintiff's lawsuit. For example, the defendant store might file a third-party claim against the sprinkler system manufacturer if Mary's attorney had not named it as a party in her original complaint.

counterclaim
A countersuit brought by the defendant against the plaintiff.

cross-claim
Plaintiffs or defendants suing each other.

third-party claim
A suit filed by the defendant against a party not originally named in the plaintiff's complaint.

Keep in mind that at any time during the litigation process, the parties may continue to try alternative dispute resolution methods, even if the initial attempts at reaching an out-of-court settlement have failed. At the same time, the parties might file motions during this pretrial stage. A **motion** is a procedural request or application presented by the attorney in court. Examples of motions include dismissal of the complaint for failure to state a valid cause of action, time-barred complaint, or motions to establish certain facts or limit issues in the suit. Rule 12 of the federal rules specifically pertains to the form of the pleadings. Rule 12(b)(6) is a motion to dismiss the plaintiff's suit because the pleadings fail to state a claim upon which relief can

motion
A procedural request or application presented by the attorney in court.

Eye on Ethics

Jim's passenger in his truck was killed when Jim fell asleep while driving and his truck struck a concrete barrier on the side of the highway. The passenger's family consults your law firm, seeking to file a wrongful death suit against Jim. Anne is a secretary at this law firm and types all the documents prepared for court filing. She collects the complaint from the desk of the attorney who reviewed the document, not noticing that he had not yet signed the complaint. Anne files this document with the court clerk. What is the likely result and why?

CASE IN POINT

Commonwealth Court of Pennsylvania.
Thomas E. DAVIES, Appellant
v.
SOUTHEASTERN PENNSYLVANIA TRANSPORTATION AUTHORITY.
Argued Nov. 1, 2004.
Decided Jan. 3, 2005.

OPINION BY Judge SMITH-RIBNER.

Thomas Davies appeals from an order of the Court of Common Pleas of Philadelphia County granting the motion for summary judgment filed by Southeastern Pennsylvania Transportation Authority (SEPTA) and dismissing with prejudice Davies' complaint. In his complaint, filed pursuant to the act popularly known as the Federal Employers' Liability Act, 45 U.S.C. §§ 51-60 (1986), Davies alleged that he suffered repetitive stress injuries and cumulative trauma disorders, including but not limited to carpal tunnel syndrome, during his employment with SEPTA, an employer engaged in the furtherance of interstate commerce within the meaning of the federal act.

Davies raises two questions for review. They include whether one of the Philadelphia County Court of Common Pleas' local rules for mass tort litigation contravenes Pa. R.C.P. No. 1035.3 and whether the trial court erred in determining that Davies' suit was barred by the three-year statute of limitations set forth in 45 U.S.C. § 56. The challenged local rule requires a party to respond to a motion for summary judgment within seven days while Rule 1035.3 allows a party to respond within thirty days after service of the motion.

I

Davies commenced his employment with SEPTA in 1975. In 1978 he became a locomotive engineer for SEPTA, which required him to use his hands in a physically exerting fashion in order to control the train's brakes, throttle and other devices. In June 1996 Davies went to the Lansdale Medical Group with complaints of nighttime awakening caused by numbness and tingling in his hands. Dr. John Motley, Davies' family physician, diagnosed Davies with probable bilateral carpal tunnel syndrome. Davies continued working, but in June 2000 he met with Dr. Scott Fried, a board-certified orthopedic surgeon, who diagnosed Davies as suffering from repetitive stress injury with cumulative trauma disorder to the hands and wrists. Davies ceased working for SEPTA in September 2000, and in December 2000 and in June 2001 Dr. Fried performed surgery on Davies, which alleviated his symptoms. In an August 2003 report, Dr. Fried concluded that Davies suffered permanent disability and that he could not return to his position.

On August 21, 2001, Davies filed his suit against SEPTA alleging that his injuries were caused by SEPTA's negligence in failing to provide safe working conditions. After extensive discovery, on December 22, 2003 SEPTA filed a motion for summary judgment, asserting that Davies' action was barred by the three-year statute of limitations set forth in 45 U.S.C. § 56 because Davies' cause of action accrued in June 1996 when Dr. Motley initially diagnosed Davies with carpal tunnel syndrome. On December 29, 2003, Davies filed a response to the motion stating that in June 1996 he was not advised by Dr. Motley that his condition was work-related, and so the issue of when his action accrued was a disputed issue of material fact that should preclude summary judgment.

By order dated January 7, 2004, the trial court granted SEPTA's motion for summary judgment and dismissed with prejudice Davies' claims against SEPTA. In an opinion dated January 30, 2004, the court explained that the evidence showed that during the June 1996 examination Davies and Dr. Motley discussed Davies' work and the fact that his work placed a great deal of stress on his hands, that Davies was advised that he had carpal tunnel syndrome and therefore that from June 1996 Davies "knew or should have known, in the exercise of reasonable diligence, the essential facts of injury and cause." Opinion of the Trial Court at 3 (citing the standard set forth in *Fries v. Chicago & Northwestern Transp. Co.*, 909 F.2d 1092 (7th Cir.1990), and *Drazan v. United States*, 762 F.2d 56 (7th Cir.1985)). [FN1]

FN1. This Court's review of the trial court's order granting summary judgment is limited to determining whether the trial court abused its discretion or committed an error of law. *Greenleaf v. Southeastern Pennsylvania Transportation Authority*, 698 A.2d 170 (Pa.Cmwlth.1997). Summary judgment is appropriate only when, after review of the record in the light most favorable to the nonmoving party, it is determined that no genuine issue of material fact exists and that the moving party is entitled to judgment as a matter of law. *Id.*

II

Initially, the Court must address the threshold issue regarding the Philadelphia County Court of Common Pleas local rule setting a seven-day time limit for responses to motions in mass tort litigation. That rule is contained in the court's "Revised Mass Tort Motion Procedures," which provides in relevant part:

> Following is the Mass Tort Motion Procedure as revised January 22, 2002. All prior motion procedures are to be considered obsolete.
>
> 1. The motion should be in letter-brief rather than motion package format. It's [sic] caption must specify the type of litigation and name opposing counsel. Facts, issues, and pertinent case law should be briefly outlined. Each motion must include a proposed order, a self-addressed stamped envelope, and a signed Attorney Certification of Good Faith. . . .
>
> . . . .
>
> 4. Motions must be filed by 4:30 p.m. on a Monday or they will be deemed filed the following Monday. The opponent must receive a copy that same day by facsimile or hand delivery. The stamped original motion should be sent or delivered to the Complex Litigation

Center, 679 City Hall, Philadelphia, PA, attention Motions Clerk.

5. If the motion is *opposed*, the opponent must answer in the format stated in Paragraph 1 by the following Monday at 4:30 p.m. This answer should be sent or delivered directly to Motions Clerk, 679 City Hall, Phila., PA 19107. No fee need be paid for a response. The movant and all other parties must receive a copy that same day by facsimile or hand delivery. . . .

. . . .

8. Oral argument on motions will be scheduled by the court as needed.

Plaintiff's Response to SEPTA's Motion for Summary Judgment, Exhibit A.

Davies argues that the rule in paragraph 5, which in this case required him to respond to SEPTA's summary judgment motion within seven days, impermissibly conflicts with Pa. R.C.P. No. 1035.3, which sets forth the following requirements for responses to summary judgment motions:

> (a) Except as provided in subdivision (e), the adverse party may not rest upon the mere allegations or denials of the pleadings but must file a response within thirty days after service of the motion identifying
> (1) one or more issues of fact arising from evidence in the record controverting the evidence cited in support of the motion or from a challenge to the credibility of one or more witnesses testifying in support of the motion, or
> (2) evidence in the record establishing the facts essential to the cause of action or defense which the motion cites as not having been produced.
> (b) An adverse party may supplement the record or set forth the reasons why the party cannot present evidence essential to justify opposition to the motion and any action proposed to be taken by the party to present such evidence.

Davies essentially argues that he suffered unfair prejudice as he was not afforded the thirty days allowed by Rule 1035.3(a) in which to supplement the record or to otherwise respond more fully to SEPTA's motion, e.g., he was not permitted to depose Dr. Motley in opposition to the motion. Also Davies stated in his response to the motion that no medical note or deposition testimony existed to establish when he discovered the etiology of his carpal tunnel syndrome condition.

[1] The courts of common pleas may adopt local rules that "shall include every rule, regulation, directive, policy, custom, usage, form or order of general application, however labeled or promulgated, which is adopted and enforced by a court of common pleas to govern civil practice and procedure." Pa. R.C.P. No. 239(a). *See also* Section 323 of the Judicial Code, 42 Pa.C.S. § 323; *Byard F. Brogan, Inc. v. Holmes Electric Protective Co. of Philadelphia*, 501 Pa. 234, 460 A.2d 1093 (1983). However, a local rule must not conflict with the Pennsylvania Rules of Civil Procedure, and a local rule will be held invalid if it abridges, enlarges or modifies substantive rights of litigants. *Byard F. Brogan, Inc.; City of Philadelphia v. Silverman*, 91 Pa.Cmwlth. 451, 497 A.2d 689 (1985); *Dillon by Dillon v. National R.R. Corp. (Amtrak)*, 345 Pa.Super.126, 497 A.2d 1336 (1985). Thus appellate courts have invalidated numerous local rules after determining that they directly conflicted with or were in some manner inconsistent with the requirements contained in statutory law or in the Rules of Civil Procedure.

III

An array of Pennsylvania appellate court decisions demonstrate the wide range of local rules that have been held to be in conflict with statutory law or with the Rules of Civil Procedure. . . .

. . . .

More particularly, in *Eaddy v. Hamaty,* 694 A.2d 639 (Pa.Super.1997), the Superior Court addressed a case in which the trial court had granted a defendant's motion for summary judgment on the ground that the plaintiff had failed to make out a *prima facie* case of medical malpractice. The trial court conducted a hearing on the motion two weeks after it was filed, and at the hearing the court denied the plaintiff's request for a continuance in order to supplement the record with additional expert testimony. The court then granted the motion for summary judgment, and it justified in part the decision to refuse the continuance request by reference to the court's "Day Backward" program, a set of procedural guidelines designed to expedite litigation and to reduce the court's case backlog. In its opinion, the court failed even to acknowledge the newly enacted rules of civil procedure governing motions for summary judgment, Rules 1035.1-1035.5.

The Superior Court vacated the trial court's order granting summary judgment in *Eaddy* based on the fact that the trial court did not apply the new rules governing summary judgment motions, and it expressly noted that the trial court did not afford the appellant thirty days in which to respond to the defendant's summary judgment motion. The Superior Court observed as follows:

> At the September 4, 1996 hearing, appellant requested a continuance to supplement his expert report as contemplated by Rule 1035.3(b). We acknowledge that the decision to permit supplementation appears to be within the discretion of the trial court. The trial court in this case did not appear to recognize that such a decision was within its province. Instead, it based its refusal to continue the case to allow plaintiff an opportunity to supplement the record solely on its need to comply with the "Day Backward" program. We concede that the trial court may have reached the same result had it applied the new rules. That fact does not alter the conclusion that the trial court failed to apply the correct rules to the motion before it. By failing to apply the new rules governing summary judgment motions and to follow proper legal procedures, the trial court committed an abuse of discretion.
>
> *Eaddy*, 694 A.2d at 643-644 (citations omitted).

[2] The Superior Court's reasoning in *Eaddy* applies with equal force to the situation in this case. Paragraph 5 of the Revised Mass Tort Motion Procedures allows what would typically be only seven days to respond to a motion for summary judgment, a time limit at odds with and substantially less than the thirty days permitted by Rule 1035.3. As case precedents make clear, in such a case the applicable rule of civil procedure must prevail. Notwithstanding the fact that allowing Davies thirty days to respond to SEPTA's summary judgment motion might not have changed the trial court's ultimate decision, the court nevertheless must apply the applicable rule of civil procedure

and allow Davies thirty days in which to respond to SEPTA's summary judgment motion. [FN2] Accordingly, the order of the trial court is vacated, and this case is remanded to that court for further proceedings for the reasons articulated herein. Based on the disposition reached, the Court need not address Davies' substantive arguments regarding the applicability of the three-year statute of limitations.

FN2. *See Gerrow v. John Royle & Sons,* 572 Pa. 134, 813 A.2d 778 (2002) (plurality opinion) (emphasizing that Rule 1035.3 is intended to permit supplementation of record with additional expert reports).

ORDER

AND NOW, this 3rd day of January, 2005, the order of the Court of Common Pleas of Philadelphia County is vacated, and this case is remanded for further proceedings in accordance with the foregoing opinion.

Jurisdiction is relinquished.

Source: Davies v. Southeastern Pennsylvania Transportation Authority, 865 A.2d 290 (St. Paul, MN: Thomson West). Reprinted with permission from Westlaw.

be granted. In making this motion, the defendant is essentially asserting that there is no basis for the plaintiff's claim and that the court cannot possibly find in favor of the plaintiff, even if all the facts the plaintiff alleges in his or her complaint are true. This is not the same as a **motion for summary judgment.** Summary judgment motions may be made by either party, unlike Rule 12(b) motions which are made by defendants. Either party is asserting that, based on *all* the documents, not just the pleadings, the trial court must find in the movant's favor. Motions may be made at various times in the litigation process. Some motions are made in the pretrial stage in order to minimize the time it takes to try a case. For example, a **motion in limine** might be filed that affects what evidence may be presented at trial. A motion in limine is a motion requesting that certain evidence not be raised at trial, such as prejudicial, irrelevant, or legally inadmissible evidence.

motion for a summary judgment
A motion by either party for judgment based on all court documents.

motion in limine
A request that certain evidence not be raised at trial, as it is arguably prejudicial, irrelevant, or legally inadmissible evidence.

The next stage in the civil litigation process is called **discovery**. Discovery is the process of investigation and collection of evidence. The function of this pretrial stage is for the parties to exchange information and gather as much factual information as possible about the opposing party's case. The goal is for each party to be able to fairly evaluate the merits of the case and hopefully to encourage an out-of-court settlement. Remember that throughout the pretrial process, settlement discussions may occur at any time. In essence, both the court and the parties are still searching for the means of avoiding the costly expenses and time in bringing any case to trial. There are various discovery tools available to accomplish this purpose.

discovery
The process of investigation and collection of evidence by litigants.

Discovery may take such forms as **interrogatories,** which are written questions posed to the opposing party; **depositions**, which involve the attorney taking the sworn, oral testimony of either the litigant or witnesses; as well as written statements from witnesses and experts who may be called upon at trial to testify as to specific elements of the case. In many types of cases, interrogatories contain standard questions and are frequently prepared by paralegals. A few general purposes of interrogatories are to establish some basic facts, locate possible witnesses, and discover medical history. Since the answers to interrogatories are scrutinized by the attorney before being returned to the other side, this form of discovery has a somewhat limited purpose. Although it is essential for gathering key information, it lacks the advantage of spontaneity of answers obtained when taking the deposition of an opposing party's witness. Therefore, depositions can be useful in obtaining possibly conflicting or unexpected testimony from a witness that can later be used against the opponent in court. Again, applicable rules of civil procedure are followed here. Remember, you should take care to consult the federal rules and applicable procedural laws in your jurisdiction.

interrogatories
A discovery tool in the form of a series of written questions that are answered by the party in writing.

deposition
A discovery tool in a question-and-answer format in which the attorney verbally questions a party or a witness under oath.

You Be the Judge

Mortimer has been drinking extensively before going to Loulou's house to pick her up for a night at the movies. While driving to Loulou's house, Mortimer crosses the center lane of the highway, striking a vehicle driven by Isabel. She suffers multiple fractures and her left leg is severed in the accident. In a negligence lawsuit by Isabel against Mortimer, Isabel's attorney is eager to illustrate to the jury the severity of the accident. Her attorney wants to show Isabel's severed leg to the jury at trial, as evidence of the magnitude of the collision. Should the leg be admitted into evidence at trial? What should Mortimer's attorney do?

Other discovery tools include requests for the production of documents and requests for the undertaking of physical examinations of the party. The purpose of these discovery methods is to collect such things as medical records; evidence of the medical diagnosis and its import, as alleged in the demand for relief; and information that substantiates claims or defenses. It is important at this stage in the process to gather lists of witnesses and be prepared to interview them in relation to the occurrence. Often, in the process of gathering records, for example, it becomes readily apparent that a prospective witness will be needed to clarify or explain the records or documents. In addition, in many cases, the investigation stage will reveal the need to secure an expert witness. Such witnesses are necessary where it is otherwise impossible to verify the standard duty of care of a particular kind of defendant, such as a medical doctor.

pretrial conferences
The meeting between the parties and the judge to identify legal issues, stipulate to uncontested matters, and encourage settlement.

Another kind of discovery tool is a request for admission. This is a request that the parties stipulate to certain information that is not in dispute, so as to conserve the court's time (see the sample stipulation at the end of the chapter).

If at the conclusion of discovery, there is still no resolution between the parties, then the case proceeds to trial. At **pretrial conferences,** the attorneys meet with the judge in order to focus on contested issues, identify the key issues, and preferably agree to certain matters. The advantage gained at these conferences is to conserve the court's time and also encourage settlement. If still not settled, then trial will begin.

bench trial
A case heard and decided by a judge.

voir dire
The process of selecting a jury for trial.

Some trials are **bench trials,** in which the dispute is heard and decided by a judge. In this situation, the judge is acting as both the fact finder as well as the interpreter of the law. Other trials may be heard by a jury. If this is the case, then this process begins with **voir dire,** which is the process of questioning potential jurors to determine if anyone is not fit for serving on that specific case, and then selecting the jury. From a group of qualified candidates in the jurisdiction where the trial will take place, the parties must agree to a jury to hear the case. The purpose of the jury is to determine the facts of the case. It is perhaps one of the most important steps in the litigation process to ensuring a fair trial. Each side is ideally looking for 12 people who are just like their client. Note that not all trials involve 12 jurors, and thus the applicable procedural laws for that state apply. Assume, for example, that a case involves a lawsuit by a mother whose child was killed by a drunk driver. It is likely that the plaintiff (the mother) will want to have as many mothers, or at least parents, as possible sitting on the jury On the other hand, the defendant would certainly not want jurors who have been personally impacted by a drunken driving incident. To get just the right jury, attorneys will occasionally hire jury consultants. One of the key roles of a jury consultant is to prepare a profile of the ideal juror and then prepare a questionnaire that helps to eliminate those people who may not clearly reveal a bias during voir dire. For example, in our hypothetical case of Mary and the slip in the grocery store, a prospective juror may be eliminated if that juror presently is employed by the same grocery store. Similarly, a prospective juror may be challenged if that juror admits to sustaining a fall in a different store and indicates a strong desire to strongly reprimand store owners who fail to maintain their premises.

CYBER TRIP

Access the Web site www.txed.uscourts.gov/jhandbook.htm. What is some of the information you can find about juries from this federal site?

challenge
An attorney's objection, during voir dire, to the inclusion of a specific person on the jury.

peremptory challenge
An attorney's elimination of a prospective juror without giving a reason; limited to a specific number of strikes.

Ideally, the jury ought to represent a cross section of the community and be composed of jurors who have pledged to be unbiased and open-minded. When selecting the jury, both sides have the opportunity to question the jurors individually, as both parties must agree to accept a person for the jury. Each party, according to the applicable code of civil procedure, has the limited right to excuse a juror either for cause or for no cause. **Challenges** for cause are unlimited on either side, as jurors with bias are excluded from the jury. In addition, jurors are excluded who have a connection to any party or expected witness in the case. Excusing a juror without cause is referred to as a **peremptory challenge.** A specific number of peremptory challenges are given to each attorney, which essentially means that the attorney may decline to pick a potential juror without giving reason to the court. Once the requisite number of jurors is chosen, along with alternates, and confirmed by the judge, trial begins.

STAGES OF TRIAL

Regardless of whether it is a civil or criminal case, the trial process follows similar steps. If you have had the opportunity to see some of the television shows or movies that portray courtroom drama, you should easily see why settling a case before trial is generally preferred by both parties. Litigation is a costly and emotional process, and therefore out-of-court settlements occur in a great number of cases. Once the jury has been selected, the following steps occur.

opening statement
An initial statement by a party's attorney explaining what the case is about and what that party's side expects to prove during the trial.

The first step in the trial is **opening statements.** Since the plaintiff always has the burden of proof, it is the plaintiff that goes first. In our hypothetical case against the grocery store, Mary's attorney will begin by summarizing the facts of the case and how he will prove the defendant store's negligence. The purpose of opening statements is to provide the jury a brief explanation of the nature of the case and to let the attorneys for each side set forth what it is they hope to prove, somewhat like a preview of what is to come. After both sides have given their opening statements, then the case in chief begins, with each side having the opportunity to call witnesses. Again, the plaintiff's side presents its case first, before the defendant's side puts on its case. Witnesses are asked to testify in open court and generally must have knowledge about some specific, relevant aspect of the case. The witnesses have been asked to appear through the issuance of a **subpoena.** A subpoena is an order issued by the court clerk directing a person to appear in court. While the party calling the witness conducts direct examination, or questioning, of that witness, the opponent is allowed to conduct cross-examination, or questioning, of that same witness.

subpoena
An order issued by the court clerk directing a person to appear in court.

Once the plaintiff's side has completed its case in chief, the defendant's side, as a matter of course, asks the judge to grant a **motion for a directed verdict.** This is a formal request to the court, claiming that since the plaintiff's side failed to prove its case, the defendant is entitled to an immediate verdict, as no legal issue remains. Seldom is this motion granted, as normally the extent of pretrial work and settlement discussions would have precluded the possibility that no valid legal issue exists.

motion for a directed verdict
A request by a party for a judgment because the other side has not met its burden of proof.

After the defendant's side presents its case in chief, then both sides give **closing arguments.** This is the opportunity for each party to summarize the case and hopefully convince the jury that they have proved each and every element that they promised to present in opening arguments. At the end of closing arguments, the judge is now in the position to give **jury instructions.** The purpose of this stage of the proceedings is to inform the jury about the applicable rules of law. For example, the judge might say, "If, after considering the facts of this case, you decide that the defendant did in fact break into the house of the victim in the night with the intent to deprive the victim of his cash and jewelry, then you must find the defendant guilty."

closing argument
A statement by a party's attorney that summarizes that party's case and reviews what that party promised to prove during trial.

jury instructions
The relevant laws that the jury uses to apply to the facts of a case.

The jury is then sent off to a private room to deliberate the case and arrive at a consensus. Once a verdict has been reached, it is read aloud in open court. Note that the jury arrives at a verdict, whereas it is the judge that announces the **judgment** in the case. This is the court's final decision regarding the rights and claims of the parties in the case.

judgment
The court's final decision regarding the rights and claims of the parties.

The final stage in the civil litigation process is the appellate stage. At this point, the losing party at the trial court level may decide to appeal the case to the next level, alleging some procedural error at trial. It is important to note, as discussed in Chapter 2 that the function of the appellate court is to solely review the case for procedural errors and not to review the facts. Only the lower court has the fact-finding capability. The appellate court may review whether the proper law was applied but may not revisit the facts or hear any new evidence. In addition, there is no jury at the appellate level, but rather a panel of judges reviews the trial court decision.

CRIMINAL AND CIVIL CASES

In Chapter 3, the distinctions between the two categories of law—civil and criminal—were discussed. Chapter **7** will address the substantive area of criminal law, as well as the substantive areas that are part of civil law, such as property and torts. Here, the differences between civil and criminal procedures will be noted. In the first part of this chapter, the stages of litigation pertaining to a civil case were outlined. Although a criminal case follows somewhat similar stages, there are slight distinctions. Keep in mind that even though the federal and state court systems follow different processes, the specific set of rules followed in the federal courts is the Federal Rules of Civil Procedure, which is the basis for the states' codes. However, the stages in a criminal case and details of criminal procedure in each state may vary greatly, and you should take care to consult the rules of criminal procedure for your jurisdiction.

arrest
The formal taking of a person, usually by a police officer, to answer criminal charges.

Initially, once a crime has allegedly occurred, and a possible defendant arrested, the investigation centers on the police work of investigation, arrest, and booking. At this stage, when an **arrest** occurs, the defendant will be advised of his or her legal rights to counsel and the right to remain silent. These are commonly referred to as "Miranda rights."

The manner in which a defendant is arrested and ordered to appear in court depends to a large extent on the nature of the crime and how and when the defendant is arrested. The defendant must be brought before a judge at his initial court appearance, shortly after being placed in custody, to be formally advised of the charges against him. Depending on the circumstances, and the nature of the offense, the defendant will have bail set at this initial appearance. A police officer, or a prosecutor, files a criminal complaint, which officially charges that person with a crime. Criminal complaints differ from civil complaints in that it is not necessary for the police officer to possess direct personal knowledge of the facts but may rely on witnesses and victims, whose affidavits are typically attached to the criminal complaint.

indictment
A written list of charges issued by a grand jury against a defendant in a criminal case.

The next stage, which occurs in felony cases, consists of determining if there is sufficient probable cause and evidence to support a criminal case against the defendant. This stage may be either a preliminary hearing or a grand jury. In either case, the purpose of this stage is to ascertain whether there is sufficient evidence to bring this defendant to trial. Which method is used is determined by an individual state's code of criminal procedure. It is simply a means of testing the strength of the prosecutor's case before a formal **indictment**, or presentation of the charges, is issued.

arraignment
A court hearing where the information contained in an indictment is read to the defendant.

If a criminal trial is to proceed, then the defendant attends an **arraignment**, in which the information contained in the indictment is read to the defendant. The defendant must enter a plea at this stage; if she pleads guilty here, she has waived her right to a trial and the opportunity to examine state witnesses. The judge may decide to sentence the defendant at a special sentencing hearing at a future time or accept the recommendation of the prosecution at that time. If the defendant pleads not guilty, then the case moves forward to trial.

CYBER TRIP

Look at the Web sites www.law.cornell.edu/rules/fre/, a reference for the Federal Rules of Evidence, and http://straylight.law.cornell.edu/rules/frcrmp/, a reference for the Federal Rules of Criminal Procedure.

If the case goes forward, then another distinction between civil and criminal cases rests in the manner of discovery that takes place. As previously noted, discovery in a civil case assumes two primary forms: interrogatories and depositions. In criminal cases, the prosecution would have already been required to conduct an investigation, obtain witness statements, and locate evidence; otherwise, the case would not have gone through a preliminary hearing or formal indictment. Still, the prosecution will want to secure lists of witnesses that the defendant intends to call at trial. Misdemeanors generally are processed quicker since they do not require a formal indictment.

It is the defendant who generally avails himself the most of discovery at this point, as he is entitled to receive all the information that the prosecution intends to rely upon at trial. This might include copies of witness statements, transcripts, and access to physical evidence obtained, such as weapons. Various evidentiary issues arise, particularly in relation to the manner in which a confession or evidence might have been obtained. Some of these issues will be addressed in Chapter 7 on criminal law.

Finally, numerous motions may be requested by either party, such as limiting evidence at trial, the motion in limine discussed earlier in this chapter, and a motion for change of venue. Venue refers to the location of the trial, and the defendant may decide that it is impossible to obtain a fair trial in the jurisdiction in which the crime occurred.

Summary

Procedural law refers to the set of rules that must be followed by the parties in the legal process. This chapter examined the different stages of litigation, from pretrial to the specific steps in a trial. You should take care to note that each state has its own procedural rules, although generally all states have modeled their codes to a large extent on the Federal Rules of Civil Procedure. However, there may be other relevant court-written rules or local procedural rules in your particular jurisdiction. It should be obvious at this point that due to the costly and time-consuming process of bringing a case to trial, every effort should be made to settle the dispute out of court. Effectively utilizing discovery tools and motion practice assists in this regard amd conserves the court's time in handling cases.

The criminal procedural rules vary greatly from state to state, and thus it is necessary to examine the precise set of rules in your state. Substantive issues pertaining to the types of cases brought in both civil and criminal courts are discussed in future chapters.

Key Terms

Alternative dispute resolution (ADR)
Answer
Arraignment
Arrest
Bench trial
Challenge
Civil cause of action
Closing arguments
Compensatory damages
Complaint
Counterclaim
Cross-claim
Default judgment
Defendant
Deposition
Discovery
Federal Rules of Civil Procedure
Indictment
Interrogatory
Judgment
Jury instructions
Litigant
Motion
Motion for a directed verdict
Motion for a summary judgment
Motion in limine
Opening statement
Peremptory challenge
Plaintiff
Pleadings
Pretrial conference
Pretrial stage
Procedural law
Substantive law
Subpoena
Summons
Third-party claim
Voir dire

Discussion Questions

1. Consider the use of discovery in a case involving an injury to a plumber, who trips on a cracked sidewalk leading up to Mervin's front door. In this case, would you prefer to use depositions or interrogatories, and why?
2. Consider the use of discovery in a case involving an accident in which the warning lights and barrier gate failed to activate, resulting in a train slamming into the side of a car crossing the railroad tracks. In this case, would you prefer to use depositions or interrogatories, and why?
3. Who must sign all pleadings and what is the rationale for this requirement?
4. What is the primary goal of a Rule 12(b)(6) motion, and how does it differ from a summary judgment motion?
5. Explain the significance of the court's desire to settle cases prior to trial in light of the increase in litigation in today's society.
6. If you are the plaintiff in a lawsuit against a negligent manufacturer of electric power saws, what would be your preferred alternative dispute resolution method?

Exercises

1. Sam, an elderly man, slipped and fell in a discount store parking lot. Sam claims that the parking lot was uneven and not properly maintained by the store owner. Sam's attorney wants to find out whether any other people have experienced a similar occurrence in this parking lot. What might be the best method of discovery to find out this information?
2. Assume that Sam's case in Exercise 1 proceeds to trial. What would be a profile of the ideal juror for Sam's attorney? What would be the ideal juror for the defendant store?
3. Molly is leaving class to drive home when another student accidentally backs her car into Molly, knocking her to the ground. There are many other students around who see this happen. Molly sustains a broken leg. Prior to this accident, Molly had recent knee surgery at which time her doctors informed her that she would always walk with a limp. The broken leg does not aggravate this preexisting injury, though it makes it inconvenient for her to drive to school. If your firm is representing the defendant driver, what type of discovery would be extremely beneficial to your defense of this negligence action?
4. Dudley is operating a chain saw when the handle slips, causing the saw to slice his arm. Dudley has surgery and is expected to recover fully from his injury. If your firm represents

Dudley against the saw manufacturer, what would be the most significant goal of discovery in your case?

5. Assume that the saw manufacturer in Exercise 4 admits the facts and its negligent safety standards but disputes the amount of damages it believes should be granted in this case. Is alternative dispute resolution a good idea for Dudley, and why?

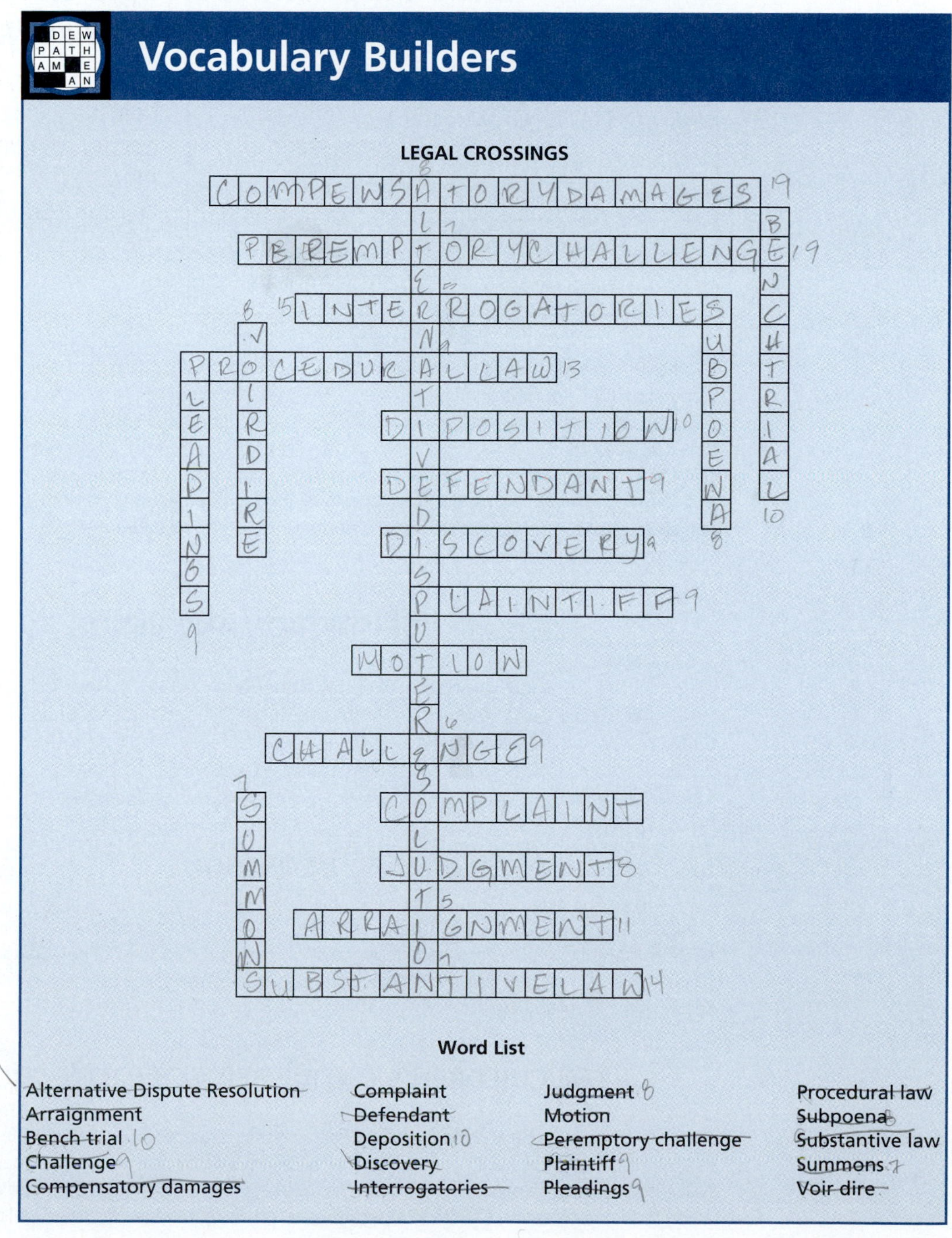

SAMPLE COMPLAINT

KENNETH E. MELSON
United States Attorney
By:
Assistant United States Attorney
2100 Jamieson Ave.
Alexandria, VA 22214
(703) 299-3700

IN THE UNITED STATES DISTRICT COURT FOR THE EASTERN DISTRICT OF VIRGINIA

UNITED STATES OF AMERICA, Plaintiff, v. LISA FRANK, INC., a corporation, Defendant.	Civil Action No. ______________ COMPLAINT FOR CIVIL PENALTIES, INJUNCTIVE, AND OTHER RELIEF

Plaintiff, the United States of America, acting upon notification and authorization to the Attorney General by the Federal Trade Commission ("FTC" or "Commission"), for its Complaint alleges that:

1. Plaintiff brings this action under Sections 1303(c) and 1306(d) of the Children's Online Privacy Protection Act of 1998 ("COPPA"), 15 U.S.C. §§ 6501-6506, §§ 6502(c), 6505(d), and Sections 5(a)(1), 5(m)(1)(A), 13(b), and 16(a) of the Federal Trade Commission Act ("FTC Act"), 15 U.S.C. §§ 41-58, §§ 45(a)(1), 45(m)(1)(A), 53(b), 56(a), to obtain monetary civil penalties, a permanent injunction, and other equitable relief for defendant's violations of the Commission's Children's Online Privacy Protection Rule (the "Rule"), 16 C.F.R. Part 312.

JURISDICTION AND VENUE

2. This Court has jurisdiction over this matter under 28 U.S.C. §§ 1331, 1337(a), 1345, and 1355, and under 15 U.S.C. §§ 45(m)(1)(A), 53(b) and 56(a). This action arises under 15 U.S.C. §§ 45(a)(1) and 6502(c).

3. Venue in this District is proper under 15 U.S.C. § 53(b) and 28 U.S.C. §§ 1391(b)-(c) and 1395(a).

DEFINITIONS

4. For purposes of this Complaint, the terms "child," "collects," "collection," "Commission," "delete," "disclosure," "Internet," "operator," "parent," "person," "personal information," "verifiable consent," and "website or online service directed to children," are defined as those terms are defined in Section 312.2 of the Rule, 16 C.F.R. § 312.2.

THE CHILDREN'S ONLINE PRIVACY PROTECTION RULE

5. Congress enacted the Children's Online Privacy Protection Act ("COPPA"), 15U.S.C. §§ 6501-6506, in 1998 to protect the safety and privacy of children online by prohibiting the unauthorized or unnecessary collection of children's personal information by Internet website operators. The Act directed the FTC to promulgate a rule implementing COPPA. The Commission promulgated the Children's Online Privacy Protection Rule

("Rule"), 16 C.F.R. Part 312, on November 3, 1999 under Section 1303(b) of COPPA, 15 U.S.C. § 6502(b), and Section 553 of the Administrative Procedure Act, 5 U.S.C. § 553. The Rule went into effect on April 21, 2000.

6. The Rule applies to any operator of a commercial website or online service directed to children that collects online, uses, and/or discloses personal information from children, or any operator that has actual knowledge that it is collecting or maintaining a child's personal information.

7. The Rule requires a subject website operator to meet specific requirements prior to collecting online, using, or disclosing personal information from children, including but not limited to:

a. Posting a privacy policy on its website providing clear, understandable, and complete notice of its information practices, including what information the website operator collects from children online, how it uses such information, its disclosure practices for such information, and other specifically required disclosures;

b. Providing clear, understandable, and complete notice of its information practices directly to parents when required by the Rule;

c. Obtaining verifiable parental consent prior to collecting online, using, and/or disclosing personal information from children;

d. Giving parents the option to consent to the collection and internal use of their children's personal information without consenting to the disclosure of that information to third parties;

e. Providing a reasonable means for parents to review the personal information collected from their children and to refuse to permit its further use or maintenance;

f. Not conditioning children's participation in an activity upon children disclosing more personal information than is reasonably necessary to participate in that activity; and

g. Establishing and maintaining reasonable procedures to protect the confidentiality, security, and integrity of personal information collected from children.

8. Pursuant to Section 18(d)(3) of the FTC Act, 15 U.S.C. § 57a(d)(3), a violation of the Rule constitutes an unfair or deceptive act or practice, in violation of Section 5(a)(1) of the FTC Act, 15 U.S.C. § 45(a)(1). *See* also COPPA, 15 U.S.C. § 6502(c).

DEFENDANT

9. Defendant Lisa Frank, Inc. is an Arizona corporation with its principal office or place of business located at 6760 S. Lisa Frank Ave., Tucson, Arizona 85706.

10. Since at least April 21, 2000, defendant has been the operator of www.lisafrank.com, a website on the Internet ("the website"). Via this website, defendant advertises and sells products to girls, including girls' toys, school supplies, and similar items, throughout the United States. The shopping area within this website has a separate web address, shop.lisafrank.com.

11. The acts and practices of defendant alleged in this complaint have been in or affecting commerce, as "commerce" is defined in Section 4 of the FTC Act, 15 U.S.C. § 44.

DEFENDANT'S COURSE OF CONDUCT

12. Defendant has collected and/or maintained personal information from children through its operation of the website and thus is an "operator" as defined in the Rule. This website is directed to children, as that term is defined in the Rule.

Defendant's Information Collection, Use, and Disclosure Practices

13. During the period April 21, 2000 through January, 2001, the home page of defendant's website, www.lisafrank.com, featured links to web site areas entitled "shop," "share," "the.club," and others. Exhibit A. A visitor who clicked on "the.club" hyperlink was presented with a "join today" button. If she clicked on this button, she was invited to click on the hyperlink entitled "Add this item to shopping cart." If she clicked on this button, she was presented with a page stating that before she could add items to a shopping cart, she needed to register for shopping, and she was presented with a hyperlink to a registration form located in the shopping area of the site, shop.lisafrank.com. Exhibit B 1 - 3.

14. Similarly, a visitor to the lisafrank.com home page who searched for an item sold by Lisa Frank was presented with pictures of items available for purchase. If she clicked on the "Add this item to shopping cart" hyperlink, she was told that she needed to first register for shopping, and was presented with a hyperlink to the registration form. Exhibit C 1- 2.

15. A child who clicked on a hyperlink to the registration form was taken to the shopping area of the site, shop.lisafrank.com, and presented with a registration page seeking personal identifying information. Exhibit C 1 - 2. This registration form depicted a young girl. It stated "Welcome to the Lisa Frank on-line shopping center! To shop our site all you need to do is complete the information below." The form that followed collected the visitor's first and last name, complete street

address, email address, phone number, specification of the visitor's favorite color, season and Lisa Frank characters, and birth date. The birth date selection was made by entering the day and month of birth, and selecting a year from a pull-down chart. The pull-down chart required the visitor to select the year 1986 or earlier. Exhibit C 1 - 2.

16. A child who visited the lisafrank.com home page and clicked the "shop" hyperlink was taken to the homepage of the shopping area of the site with the URL shop.lisafrank.com. This page had a menu on the left hand column. The first item on the menu was a "register" button. Exhibit D. A child who clicked the "register" hyperlink was taken to the registration form described above and asked to provide her personal identifying information. Exhibit C 1 - 2.

17. Thus, despite the fact that its website is directed to children, defendant collected information from children without first obtaining consent from their parents, as required by the Rule. Rule, Sections 312.3 and 312.5.

NOTICE TO PARENTS

18. During the period April 21, 2000 through January, 2001, defendant did not provide direct notice to parents, stating that it wished to collect information from their children, that parental consent was needed for that collection, and making disclosures related to those practices, as required by the Rule. Rule, Section 312.4(c).

DEFENDANT'S PRIVACY POLICY

19. During the period April 21, 2000 through January, 2001, defendant posted a privacy policy on its website, but the policy did not clearly, understandably, or completely disclose its information collection, use, and disclosure practices, and it did not make disclosures about those practices as required by the Rule. Exhibit E. Rule, Sections 312.4(a) and (b)(2)(i)-(vi).

20. During the period April 21, 2000 through January, 2001, defendant's privacy policy also made the following false or misleading statements:

a. "In order to participate in certain areas of our Web site, such as ... e-commerce, users are required to register and obtain a screen name ("User-ID"). Children 13 years or younger will require parental consent before being able to register and participate ..."

b. "In the areas that require registration, all registrants receive e-mail confirming their registration. In addition, when a guest 13 years or younger registers, his/her parent or guardian will be required to fill out and sign a registration form..."

Exhibit E. As set forth above, the Lisa Frank site did not require parental consent before allowing children 13 or under to complete the registration page.

DEFENDANT'S VIOLATIONS OF THE CHILDREN'S ONLINE PRIVACY PROTECTION RULE

21. Defendant is an operator of a website directed to children and/or has had actual knowledge that it is collecting or maintaining personal information from children.

22. In numerous instances, including the acts and practices described above, defendant collected or used personal information from children in violation of the Rule, 16 C.F.R. Part 312, including:

a. Failing to obtain verifiable parental consent before any collection or use of personal information from children, in violation of Rule, Sections 312.3 and 312.5, 16 C.F.R. §§ 312.3, 312.5;

b. Failing to provide direct notice to parents about its desire to collect personal information from children, that parental consent is required for the collection, how it uses such information, its disclosure practices, and all other required content, in violation of Section 312.4(c) of the Rule, 16 C.F.R. § 312.4(c); and

c. Failing to make required disclosures on the website about the fact that an operator is prohibited from conditioning a child's participation in an activity on the child's disclosing more personal information than is reasonably necessary to participate in such activity, in violation of Rule Section 312.4(b)(2)(v), 16 C.F.R. § 312.4(b)(2)(v), and about the right of a parent to review and have deleted their child's personal information, in violation of Section 312.4(b)(2)(vi) of the Rule, 16 C.F.R. § 312.4(b)(2)(vi).

DEFENDANT'S UNFAIR OR DECEPTIVE ACTS OR PRACTICES IN VIOLATION OF THE FTC ACT

23. Section 5(a) of the FTC Act, 15 U.S.C. § 45(a), provides that "unfair or deceptive acts or practices in or affecting commerce are hereby declared unlawful."

24. Pursuant to Section 18(d)(3) of the FTC Act, 15 U.S.C. § 57a(d)(3), a violation of the Rule constitutes an unfair or deceptive act or practice violation of Section 5(a)(1) of the FTC Act, 15 U.S.C. § 45(a)(1). *See* COPPA, 15 U.S.C. § 6502(c).

25. By and through the acts and practices described in paragraph 22, defendant has violated Section 5(a)(1) of the FTC Act, 15 U.S.C. § 45(a)(1).

26. During the period April 21, 2000 through January, 2001, defendant represented in its privacy policy that it would obtain parental consent before permitting visitors under the age of 13 to complete the registration form.

27. In truth and in fact, defendant did not obtain parental consent before permitting visitors under the age of 13 to complete the registration form. Therefore, the representation set forth in paragraph 26 was false and misleading.

28. Defendant's false and misleading statement constitutes a deceptive act or practice in or affecting commerce in violation of Section 5(a) of the FTC Act.

CIVIL PENALTIES, INJUNCTION AND OTHER RELIEF

29. Defendant has violated the Rule as described above with knowledge as set forth in Section 5(m)(a)(A) of the FTC Act, 15 U.S.C. § 45(m)(1)(A).

30. Each collection or use of a child's personal information from April 21, 2000 through the filing of this Complaint, in which defendant has violated the Rule in one or more of the ways described above, constitutes a separate violation for which plaintiff seeks monetary civil penalties.

31. Section 5(m)(1)(A) of the FTC Act, 15 U.S.C. § 45(m)(1)(A), as modified by Section 4 of the Federal Civil Penalties Inflation Adjustment Act of 1990, 28 U.S.C. § 2461, and Section 1.98(d) of the FTC's Rules of Practice, 16 C.F.R. § 1.98(d), authorizes this Court to award monetary civil penalties of not more than $11,000 for each such violation of the Rule, 16 C.F.R. Part 312.

32. Under Section 13(b) of the FTC Act, 15 U.S.C. § 53(b), this Court is authorized to issue a permanent injunction against defendant's violations of the FTC Act, as well as such ancillary relief as may be just and proper.

PRAYER

WHEREFORE, plaintiff requests this Court, pursuant to 15 U.S.C. §§ 45(a)(1), 45(m)(1)(A), 53(b) and 57b, and the Court's own equitable powers to:

(1) Enter judgment against defendant and in favor of plaintiff for each violation alleged in this Complaint;

(2) Award plaintiff monetary civil penalties from defendant for each violation of the Rule, 16 C.F.R. Part 312;

(3) Permanently enjoin defendant from violating the Rule, 16 C.F.R. Part 312;

(4) Permanently enjoin defendant from violating Section 5 of the FTC Act in connection with representations about its online information collection and privacy practices; and

(5) Award plaintiff such additional relief as the Court may deem just, proper, or necessary to redress injury to consumers resulting from defendant's violations of the Rule, 16 C.F.R. Part 312.

DATED:

OF COUNSEL:	FOR THE UNITED STATES OF AMERICA:
C. LEE PEELER Associate Director Division of Advertising Practices Bureau of Consumer Protection Federal Trade Commission	ROBERT D. McCALLUM, JR. Assistant Attorney General Civil Division U.S. Department of Justice

MARY K. ENGLE
Assistant Director
Division of Advertising Practices
Bureau of Consumer Protection
Federal Trade Commission

KENNETH E. MELSON
United States Attorney

By: ______________________
Assistant United States Attorney
2100 Jamieson Ave.
Alexandria, VA 23219
(703) 299-3700

JANET EVANS ELIZABETH DELANEY
Attorneys
Division of Advertising Practices
Bureau of Consumer Protection
Federal Trade Commission
600 Pennsylvania Avenue, NW
Washington, DC 20580

EUGENE M. THIROLF
Director
Office of Consumer Litigation

By: ______________________
Elizabeth Stein
Office of Consumer Litigation
Civil Division
U.S. Department of Justice
Washington, D.C. 20530
(202) 307-0486

Source: *United States of America v. Lisa Frank, available at www.ftc.gov/os/2001/10/lfcmp.pdf.*

SAMPLE STIPULATION

UNITED STATES DISTRICT COURT
FOR THE MIDDLE DISTRICT OF FLORIDA
Tampa Division

UNITED STATES OF AMERICA,

Plaintiff,

v.

FEDERATION OF CERTIFIED SURGEONS AND SPECIALISTS, INC., and PERSHING, YOAKLEY & ASSOCIATES, P.C.,

Defendants.

Case No. 99-167-CIV-T-17F

STIPULATION AS TO DEFENDANT
PERSHING, YOAKLEY & ASSOCIATES, P.C.

It is stipulated by and between the undersigned parties, by their respective attorneys, that:

1. The Court has jurisdiction over the subject matter of this action and over each of the undersigned parties hereto, and venue of this action is proper in the Middle District of Florida;

2. The undersigned parties consent that a Final Judgment in the form hereto attached may be filed and entered by the Court, upon the motion of either party, or upon the Court's own motion, at any time after compliance with the requirements of the Antitrust Procedures and Penalties Act, 15 U.S.C. §16, and without further notice to either party or other proceedings, provided that plaintiff has not withdrawn its consent, which it may do at any time before the entry of the proposed Final Judgment by serving notice thereof on defendant and by filing that notice with the Court; and

3. Pershing, Yoakley & Associates, P.C., ("PYA") agrees to be bound by the provisions of this proposed Final Judgment pending its approval by the Court. Within ten days from the execution for this Stipulation, defendant PYA agrees to provide to all of its shareholders, its agents, representatives, employees, officers, and directors (in such capacities only) who provides, or supervises the provision of,

services to competing physicians with offices in Hillsborough, Pinellas or Pasco County, Florida, copies of the proposed Final Judgment; and

4. If plaintiff withdraws its consent, or if the proposed Final Judgment is not entered pursuant to the terms of the Stipulation, this Stipulation shall be of no effect whatsoever, and the making of this Stipulation shall be without prejudice to either party in this or in any other proceeding.

Dated: January 21, 1999

FOR PLAINTIFF
UNITED STATES OF AMERICA:

/S/
Joel I. Klein
Assistant Attorney General

/S/
Donna Patterson
Deputy Assistant Attorney General

/S/
Rebecca P. Dick
Deputy Director of Civil
Non-Merger Enforcement

/S/
Gail Kursh, Chief
Health Care Task Force

/S/
David C. Jordan, Ass't. Chief
Health Care Task Force

/S/
Denise E. Biehn
Steven Kramer
Edward D. Eliasberg
Attorneys U.S. Dept. of Justice
325 7th Street, N.W.
Room 400, Liberty Place Bldg.
Washington, D.C. 20530
(202) 305-2738

FOR DEFENDANT PERSHING,
YOAKLEY & ASSOCIATES, P.C.:

/S/
John J. Miles
E. John Steren
Ober, Kaler, Grimes & Shriver
1401 H Street, N.W., 5th Floor
Washington, D.C. 20005-2110

Source: *Complaint of Employment Discrimination available at www.ilnd.uscourts.gov/PUBLIC/Forms/empdiscrcmpt.pdf.*

Chapter 6

The Role of the Paralegal

CHAPTER OBJECTIVES

After reading this chapter, you will be able to:

- Identify the qualifications a paralegal ought to possess.
- Distinguish the typical places in which paralegals might be employed and the respective advantages of each type of employer.
- Describe the ideal character traits of a successful paralegal.
- Identify the organizations that govern what a paralegal does and the professional associations to which paralegals might belong.
- Explain the duties of a paralegal, given the ethical considerations and applicable rules governing the practice of the profession today.

It is indisputable that the legal profession encompasses much more than just attorneys and judges. Even the terminology applied to the different personnel within the legal field is subject to slight distinctions. Although the legal profession has been in existence for thousands of year, the profession has significantly evolved in accordance with business, economic, cultural, and sociological changes. Lawyers have always functioned as advocates in the legal arena. This chapter will highlight some of the changes that have occurred as a result of the invaluable assistance that support staff such as paralegals provide in the effective delivery of legal services to the client. As a result of these changes, various legal roles have been established and redefined in the constantly evolving legal system, and these roles will be examined, specifically the role of the paralegal. In examining the ethical obligations that one assumes by practicing in the legal profession, it is necessary to examine the interaction among legal professionals, and their respective roles in the advocacy and representation of clients. This chapter provides an introduction to these members of the legal profession, an overview of their respective roles, and discussion of various issues that may arise in the context of ethics and the law.

LEGAL PROFESSIONALS: ATTORNEYS

Generally, the terms used to describe a legal advocate are *attorney, lawyer,* and *attorney at law*. In the broadest use, these terms simply describe a person who has the authority to represent and act on behalf of another. A lawyer is normally required to possess a bachelor's degree in any subject, and then an advanced degree in legal education, generally attained within three years if pursued full-time. In California, one may take the bar exam without having received a formal legal education. Following traditional legal education, a lawyer is required to attain a passing score on any state's bar exam, pass a moral and character background check, and formally apply for admission as a member of the bar of his or her chosen state of practice. If all these requirements are satisfied, the lawyer is granted a license to practice law before the courts of that state. Admission to the bar of the federal court system is an additional step that a lawyer may take, requiring similar fulfillment and procedures.

Historically, the legal profession has operated for thousands of years, but the role of lawyers has changed. Traditionally, lawyers had sole responsibility for providing counsel to lawmaking bodies, interpreted the meaning of the laws once enacted, and advocated on behalf of individuals in the proper application of such laws. Lawyers represented people and gave advice on their individual legal concerns, analyzing the relevant laws and giving opinions on how those laws should be used. Numerous factors contributed to the development of paraprofessionals and modification of the traditional definition of a lawyer's duties.

As technology and population increased in the early twentieth century, several changes occurred that placed a greater demand on lawyers for their services. The ability of businesses to communicate effectively through technological means such as facsimile machines and computer e-mails resulted in commercial activity increasing rapidly, the emergence of global businesses, and increased demands placed on all aspects of the economy. Consequently, parallel growth emerged in areas such as commercial law, corporation law, and contract law. Similarly, the population growth contributed to corresponding increases in criminal behavior, coupled with societal pressures in the family, resulting in increased demand for domestic relations lawyers. As a result of this inevitable transformation of American society, the primary function of lawyers in the legal system underwent an upheaval as well. Increased demand for affordable legal services and the need to deliver those services to individuals as efficiently as possible led to the evolution of the demand for more paraprofessionals. While legal secretaries were available to assist attorneys in the time-consuming and tedious tasks of preparing legal forms and organizing evidence, they were relatively untrained to be able to take on more complex tasks beyond basic clerical matters. Demands on the attorney's time swelled so greatly that a legitimate need emerged for individuals with greater expertise and training to perform nonclerical legal tasks.

Trained paraprofessionals were embraced by lawyers as a viable solution to the need to delegate increasingly complex tasks. In addition, the need to save costs compelled lawyers to seek greater help from paralegals in performing certain legal jobs essential to the practice of law. Within the last five years, the paralegal profession has become one of the fastest growing in the United States. Tasks of a more complex nature could now be delegated to these paraprofessionals, and their roles could be distinguished from that of the legal secretary. Although the emergence of this new role in the legal profession has been very appealing to lawyers, as will be discussed later in this chapter, it has also created a new dilemma in terms of what work can be legally performed by a paralegal and what is meant by "the practice of law."

American Bar Association (ABA)
A national organization of lawyers, providing support and continuing legal education to the profession.

The **American Bar Association (ABA)** is the national organization of lawyers that generally provides support to the legal profession. It is the ABA that promulgated the rules of behavior that govern the profession: the Model Rules of Professional Conduct. Prior to this set of rules, the ABA had developed the Model Code of Professional Responsibility, which includes nine canons. The interpretation of these canons is sometimes difficult in any given situation. This is due to the fact that the rules do not always offer definitive solutions to specific individual situations. There is certainly specific guidance in the Code and Rules, but one must keep in mind that they were written to guide ethical behavior, and actually stand as a set of rules that dictates how to avoid discipline by the state bar, rather than what is the proper moral action in a given situation.

Although the canons in the ABA Model Code specifically apply to attorneys, they are a guideline for what is expected of other professionals in the legal profession. Remember that

Eye on Ethics

The American Bar Association's Model Code of Professional Responsibility and the Model Rules of Professional Conduct are the basis for most states' ethical codes of conduct for attorneys. The Model Code of Professional Responsibility, known simply as the "Model Code," consists of nine canons. They set forth both disciplinary rules regarding the practice of law, as well as ethical considerations. You may access them via the ABA's Web site at www.abanet.org.

the Rules and Code serve as a guide to how to ethically act in certain situations, so as to avoid disciplinary proceedings, but they do not necessarily provide firm answers to moral dilemmas.

WHAT IS A PARALEGAL?

legal assistant
Individual qualified to assist an attorney in the delivery of legal services.

paralegal
A person qualified to assist an attorney, under direct supervision, in all substantive legal matters with the exception of appearing in court and rendering legal advice.

National Association of Legal Assistants (NALA)
A legal professional group that lends support and continuing education for legal assistants.

There is sometimes confusion between the terms *legal assistant* and *paralegal* as these terms have been used interchangeably. It is not easy to identify a one-size-fits-all definition of this legal professional. It is easier to describe what this person does and the typical qualifications of such a person. In a general sense, a paralegal is deemed to have advanced training, meaning a degree in paralegal education, either a two-year associate's or a four-year bachelor's degree in paralegal studies. A **legal assistant** may have taken the exam to become a "certified legal assistant" (CLA), but may not have completed the formal degree program that a paralegal would have done. The definition of a *legal assistant*, as promulgated by the American Bar Association's Standing Committee on Legal Assistants, and approved as an official policy statement, uses the terms interchangeably, but generally adopted the common term, *paralegal.* Simply, the **paralegal** is a person who is qualified to assist an attorney, under direct supervision, in all substantive legal matters with the exception of appearing in court and rendering legal advice. The **National Association of Legal Assistants (NALA),** one of the primary legal professional groups, defines a legal assistant as someone, qualified through education, training, or work experience, who assists attorneys in the delivery of legal services. According to NALA's Web site, "through formal education, training, and experience, legal assistants have knowledge and expertise regarding the legal system and substantive and procedural law which qualify them to do work of a legal nature under the supervision of an attorney." Paralegals are qualified either through education, work experience, or a combination of both.

QUALIFICATIONS OF A PARALEGAL

CYBER TRIP

Visit the following Web sites of professional paralegal organizations and compare the descriptions and definitions of a paralegal:
www.nala.org
www.aafpe.org
www.paralegals.org
www.nals.org

Because paralegals are not required to be licensed in any state in order to work in the profession, there are not clear and detailed rules similar to the requirements of an attorney to practice law. Although there are not specific formal requirements or licensing required by individual states in order to hold oneself out as a paralegal, as is required of attorneys, nevertheless the job market is becoming such that paralegals often find they must have—at a minimum—an associate's degree from an ABA-approved paralegal program, in order to find employment with most firms and corporate legal departments. The Certified Legal Assistant (CLA) exam is not required, but more employers are now seeking this certification as further evidence of a paralegal's qualifications. Thus, even though it is possible for any person to be hired as a legal assistant, or as a paralegal, since most states don't require any formal training, the occupational outlook for this professional person is demanding further education and experience. NALA has written *Model Standards and Guidelines for Utilization of Legal Assistants,* which establishes the role that legal assistants assume in the delivery of legal services by an attorney to the client. It also denotes specific minimum qualifications a paralegal or legal assistant should possess as a legal professional in the field. The following list of qualifications is taken from this NALA document.

- Successful completion of the CLA exam of the NALA.
- Graduation from an ABA-approved program of study for legal assistants.
- Graduation from a course of study for legal assistants that is institutionally accredited though not ABA approved, involving at least 60 semester hours of classroom study.
- Graduation from another course of legal study not contained in the preceding, but also including at least six months of in-house training.
- Baccalaureate degree in any field plus at least six months in-house training as a legal assistant.
- Minimum of three years of law-related experience under attorney supervision, including at least six months of in-house training as a legal assistant; or
- Two years of in-house training as a legal assistant.

CASE IN POINT

Court of Appeals of Arizona,
Division 1, Department C.
CONTINENTAL TOWNHOUSES EAST UNIT ONE ASSOCIATION, an Arizona corporation;
Vincent Territo; Dorothea Waxman; and Jill Sampson, Plaintiffs-Appellees,
Cross Appellants,
v.
Roy R. BROCKBANK and Rita Brockbank, husband and wife, d/b/a Roy Brockbank
Enterprises, Defendants-Appellants, Cross Appellees.
No. 1 CA-CIV 8582.
Aug. 5, 1986.
Reconsideration Denied Dec. 5, 1986.
Review Denied March 11, 1987.

CONTRERAS, Presiding Judge.

This appeal and cross-appeal followed the trial court's remittitur of damages awarded by a jury for the defendant-appellant's breach of the implied warranty of workmanship and habitability in the construction of the plaintiffs-appellees' townhouse roofs. Among the issues we resolve on appeal is whether an award of attorneys' fees under A.R.S. § 12-341.01 may include the cost of legal services performed by legal assistants. We conclude that the cost of such services may be included.

I. BACKGROUND OF THE CASE

Continental Townhouses East Unit One Association (the "Association") filed a complaint on December 16, 1981, against Roy Brockbank, the builder and seller of approximately 40% of the units in the Continental Townhouses condominium development in Mesa, Arizona. The complaint alleged that Brockbank had breached the implied warranty of workmanlike construction in building the condominium roofs. The complaint also alleged that Brockbank had breached his agreement to construct and repair various amenities and facilities within the development's common areas.

Nearly two years later, the trial court ordered that the individual homeowners, rather than the Association, were the real parties in interest. The court's minute entry referred to the Association's Covenants, Conditions and Restrictions, which provided that the homeowners pay the Association an assessment for improvement and maintenance of the homes, and concluded that "though Plaintiff [Association] has a duty to maintain and repair the roofs of the homeowners, the expense of such maintenance and repair is actually born [sic] by the homeowners through the assessment." The court also noted that recovery by the Association might not protect Brockbank from further suits by individual homeowners, and that privity between the Association and Brockbank, required at the time under Arizona law, was lacking. Thus, the court dismissed the complaint "as to those items in controversy which are not part of the 'Common Area' under the management and control of the Plaintiff Association," but "without prejudice in that a new Complaint may be filed by the individual homeowners."

An amended complaint was filed the following month, and in August, 1984, plaintiffs' Motion for Class Certification was granted. The certified class was defined as "any past, present, or future members of the plaintiff association who have paid, who will pay, or who are obligated to pay for any repairs to roofs for which defendants are found liable. . . ." The plaintiff representatives of the class were townhouse owners and Association members; one of the class representatives owned a Brockbank-built unit.

On January 23, 1985, after a six day trial, a jury awarded the plaintiff-class $312,454.91 on the roof damage claim and $17,047.91 to the Association on the common areas claim.

In March of 1985, the trial judge granted Brockbank's motion for remittitur on the roof claim, reducing the amount of the jury verdict to $128,853.00, plus interest from June 2, 1981. Attorneys' fees were awarded to the Association on the common areas claim and to the class in a reduced amount on the roof damage claim. The class elected to accept the remittitur. Appellant Brockbank has not appealed from the judgment on the common areas claim or the award of attorneys' fees in favor of the Association. This appeal, therefore, concerns only the roof damage claim brought by the class and its award of attorneys' fees.

...

[8] The amount of a jury verdict should be reduced only for "the most cogent reasons." *Young Candy & Tobacco Co. v. Montoya,* 91 Ariz. 363, 372 P.2d 703 (1962). It has not been shown on appeal that the jury mistakenly applied the wrong principles in determining the damages or that the jury acted with improper motives or bias. *Id*. The jury was instructed properly on damages and the verdict was within the limits of the evidence. *See also Muccilli v. Huff's Boys' Store, Inc.,* 12 Ariz.App. 584, 473 P.2d 786 (1970). We conclude that it was erroneous for the trial judge to order a remittitur and therefore we reinstate the original jury verdict in the amount of $312,454.91.

B. *Attorneys' Fees.*

We address two important issues regarding the attorneys' fee award at issue in this case:

(1) Whether the value of legal work performed by legal assistants may be recovered as an element of attorneys' fees under A.R.S. § 12-341.01; and

(2) The effect of the original contingency fee contract between counsel and the Association on the recovery of fees by the class.

The class requested an award of attorneys' fees under A.R.S. § 12-341.01(A). [FN6] It sought 40% of the jury verdict, or $124,981.96, pursuant to a contingency fee agreement signed by counsel and the President of the Association, the original plaintiff in the litigation. Counsel for the class contends that the same contingency fee agreement was expected to apply between it and the class when the class replaced the Association as plaintiff.

FN6. A.R.S. § 12-341.01(A) provides in part that "[i]n any contested action arising out of a contract, express or implied, the court may award the successful party reasonable attorney's fees." A.R.S. § 12-341.01(B) adds, "The award of reasonable attorney's fees awarded pursuant to subsection A should be made to mitigate the burden of the expense of litigation to establish a just claim or a just defense. It need not equal or relate to the attorney's fees actually paid or contracted, but such award may not exceed the amount paid or agreed to be paid."

The request for attorneys' fees included an itemization of hourly rates and time expended by counsel and legal assistants, totalling $73,977.00. The trial court awarded the class $58,485.00, and later increased the award to $61,795.00. All amounts requested for the legal tasks performed by legal assistants and law clerks were denied by the trial court. The trial judge set forth his reason:

> Absent specific Arizona authority to the contrary, this Court will not award attorney fees for work performed by non-lawyers. The only authorities cited to the Court are United States District Court holdings which are divided on the issue.

Until now, Arizona courts have not directly ruled on the recoverability of fees for legal work performed by legal assistants and law clerks. See the discussion in Stahl and Smith, *Paralegal Services and Awards of Attorneys' Fees Under Arizona Law,* Ariz. B.J., Oct.-Nov. 1984, at 21.

Courts which have permitted paralegal services to be recovered as an element of attorneys' fees have recognized that doing so promotes lawyer efficiency and reduces client costs. The Ninth Circuit has permitted recovery of paralegal services as part of the recovery of attorneys' fees under the Longshoremen's and Harbor Workers' Compensation Act for the assistance rendered by a claimant's lay representative to the claimant's attorney:

> One of the necessary incidents of an attorney's fee is the attorney's maintaining of a competent staff to assist him. . . . Paralegals can do some of the work that the attorney would have to do anyway and can do it at substantially less cost per hour, resulting in less total cost billed. . . .

Todd Shipyards Corp. v. Director, Office of Workers' Compensation Programs, 545 F.2d 1176, 1182 (9th Cir.1976).

The Arizona federal district court has agreed:

> Paralegal time has been included [in this case] as a part of the lodestar [fee] calculation rather than being allowed as costs . . . I realize this is an issue as to which courts differ. The use of paralegals, if properly supervised and directed, can be cost effective. It is reasonable to recognize and encourage a continuation of paralegal usage in appropriate circumstances.

State of Arizona v. Maricopa County Medical Society, 578 F.Supp. 1262, 1270 (D.Ariz.1984). *See also Pacific Coast Agricultural Export Assoc. v. Sunkist Growers, Inc.,* 526 F.2d 1196, 1210 n. 19 (9th Cir.1975), *cert. denied,* 425 U.S. 959, 96 S.Ct. 1741, 48 L.Ed.2d 204 (1976). [FN7] The Arizona federal district court has also refused to authorize compensation for lawyers performing services that could have been performed by a legal assistant, as well as for excessive or duplicated time incurred by both lawyers and legal assistants on routine tasks. *Metro Data Systems, Inc. v. Durango Systems, Inc.,* 597 F.Supp. 244 (D.Ariz.1984).

FN7. Several other cases and relevant articles are cited in the Arizona Appellate Handbook, vol. 1, ch. 1, p. 2 (Supp.1986).

[9] We conclude that legal assistant and law clerk services may properly be included as elements in attorneys' fees applications and awards pursuant to A.R.S. § 12-341.01, both in the trial court and on appeal. The purpose of awards based on that statute is to "mitigate the burden of the expense of litigation." A.R.S. § 12-341.01(B). Properly employed and supervised **legal assistants** and law clerks [FN8] can decrease litigation expense and improve lawyers' efficiency.

FN8. Lawyers' **professional** responsibilities regarding supervision of nonlawyer **assistants** are stated in Rule of **Professional** Conduct 5.3.

Lawyers should not be required to perform tasks more properly performed by **legal assistants** or law clerks solely to permit that time to be compensable in the event an attorneys' fees application is ultimately submitted. Requiring such a misallocation of valuable resources would serve no useful purpose and would be contrary to the direction to interpret the Rules of Civil Procedure to serve the "just, speedy, and inexpensive determination of every action." Rule 1, Arizona Rules of Civil Procedure. Instead, proper **use** of **legal assistants** and law clerks should be encouraged to facilitate providing the most cost-effective **legal** services to the public. If compensation could not be obtained for **legal assistant** and law clerk services in appropriate cases, the fee-shifting objective of A.R.S. § 12-341.01 would also not be accomplished.

Use of **legal assistants** nationally has significantly increased in recent years. *See* Law Poll, 69 A.B.A.J. 1626 (1983); Ulrich, ***Legal Assistants*** *Can Increase Your Profits,* 69 A.B.A.J. 1634 (1983). **Legal assistants** are being employed increasingly both in Arizona and elsewhere, in many law practice categories, particularly in large firms. *See generally* Stahl and Smith, *supra;* National Law Journal, Sept. 30, 1985, at S4-S18; *Working with* ***Legal Assistants,*** *passim* (P. Ulrich and R. Mucklestone ed. 1980, 1981). Authoritative projections suggest the number of such positions will nearly double during the next years, from an estimated 53,000 in 1984 to 104,000 in 1995. U.S. Dept. of Labor, Bureau of Labor Statistics, *Occupational Outlook Quarterly,* at 19 (Spring 1986). Legal assistants have thus now become an essential element of legal services provided by many law offices. Lawyers have also employed law clerks for as long as there have been law students. They also can provide valuable assistance, particularly in legal research and preparing documents under the lawyer's supervision.

We do not believe such services should be considered part of taxable court "costs." They are instead properly considered as a component of attorneys' fees, since an attorney would have performed these services if a legal assistant was not employed instead. It also cannot be assumed legal assistant services are automatically included in lawyers' hourly billing rates as a standard law office operating expense. Instead, such services are often itemized and billed separately. Ulrich, *supra.* Moreover, lawyers should not be required to inflate their hourly rates to include **legal**

assistant time as a general overhead component. Doing so would make fair allocation of the cost of such services impossible, since some clients and matters may require a much higher proportion of **legal assistant** and law clerk services than others.

The question then arises as to what categories of persons or tasks should be considered "**legal assistant**" for purposes of attorneys' fees applications. [FN9] In this regard, we believe the definition of "**legal assistant**" formulated by the American Bar Association's Standing Committee on **Legal Assistants** and approved as an official policy statement by its Board of Governors in February, 1986, is appropriate:

FN9. We **use** the terms **legal assistant**, paralegal, and law clerk interchangeably in this opinion, and believe the ABA definition encompasses each of these titles.

> A **legal assistant** is a person, qualified through education, training, or work experience, who is employed or retained by a lawyer, law office, governmental agency, or other entity in a capacity or function which involves the performance, under the ultimate direction and supervision of an attorney, of specifically-delegated substantive legal work, which work, for the most part, requires a sufficient knowledge of legal concepts that, absent such assistant, the attorney would perform the task.

Clearly, since the legal assistant must perform legal work and be supervised by an attorney, the fee application must contain enough details to demonstrate to the court that these requirements have been met, thereby comporting with the spirit of *Schweiger v. China Doll Restaurant, Inc.*, 138 Ariz. 183, 673 P.2d 927 (App.1983).

[10] Finally, we reiterate and emphasize the discretionary power of the trial judge in awarding attorneys' fees under A.R.S. § 12-341.01. *See, e.g., Associated Indemnity Corp. v. Warner,* 143 Ariz. 567, 694 P.2d 1181 (1985); *Solar-West, Inc. v. Falk,* 141 Ariz. 414, 687 P.2d 939 (App.1984). The trial judge is not required to, but may, consider the value of services rendered in a case by **legal assistants,** law clerks, and paralegals, applying the same standards as are **used** in evaluating lawyers' time.

Not only must this case be remanded to give the trial judge the opportunity to consider inclusion of **legal assistants'** services in the attorneys' fee award, but further evidence must be considered in order to determine whether the contingency fee agreement between counsel and the Association applies in favor of the class.

In the retainer agreement, the client agreed to pay counsel 40% of the net amount recovered if the case was tried. The client in the agreement was Continental Townhouses East Unit One Association. The client on appeal is the class of homeowners, represented by three individual homeowners. It is not clear to this court following oral argument whether the signed retainer agreement was intended to apply between counsel and the current plaintiff. The trial court is in a better position to determine, perhaps by way of further proceedings, the understanding between the parties with regard to the contingency fee agreement, and therefore whether it would be appropriate to award attorneys' fees pursuant to the fee agreement.

Thus, we remand with the following directions.

1. The original jury verdict must be reinstated, without prejudgment interest.
2. The court should consider evidence of the parties' understanding with counsel regarding the continued viability of the retainer agreement after the lawsuit was converted to a class action.
3. If the court is convinced that the 40% fee recovery under the retainer agreement applies between counsel and the class, it *may* award *up to* 40% of the verdict as attorneys' fees. [FN10] The 40% figure operates as a ceiling on the amount of attorneys' fees that may be recovered; the court need not agree that 40% of the recovery is a reasonable sum for attorneys' fees in this case and may award less. In determining the amount to be awarded as attorneys' fees, the court may, in its discretion, consider and include the value of time spent by **legal assistants** on **legal** tasks. The hourly rate charged for time spent by **legal assistants** should reflect reasonable community standards of remuneration.

FN10. Cross-appellant's argument in its brief that the court "may award fees in an amount even greater than a contingent fee agreement specifies" cannot be supported by the case cited for the proposition, which involved a distinctly different set of facts. *(Prendergast v. City of Tempe,* 143 Ariz. 14, 691 P.2d 726 (App.1984).

4. If the court determines that the retainer agreement was not intended to control the fee paid by the class, it may rely upon the itemized fee request submitted by counsel and also, in its discretion, consider the amounts requested for time spent on legal tasks by legal assistants.

Finally, the class requests an award of attorneys' fees on appeal pursuant to A.R.S. § 12-341.01. We grant the request. The class may establish the amount of its award by complying with Rule 21(c), Arizona Rules of Civil Appellate Procedure, and our decision in *Schweiger v. China Doll Restaurant, Inc.,* 138 Ariz. 183, 673 P.2d 927 (App.1983). In accordance with our decision today, the request for fees on appeal may include the value of legal work performed by legal assistants, if any.

The judgment of the trial court is affirmed in part, reversed in part and remanded with the foregoing directions.

GRANT, J., and ULRICH [FN*], J. Pro Tem., concur.

Source: *Continental Townhouses East Unit One Association v. Brockbank,* 152 Ariz. 537, 733 P.2d 1120 (St. Paul, MN: Thomson West). Reprinted with permission from Westlaw.

Paralegals perform a wide variety of functions, usually dependent upon their level of education, work experience, and specific expertise. The role that paralegals play in the legal profession has dramatically increased in the last 30 years, largely because of the significant increase in the number of colleges and universities that now offer formal degree programs in paralegal studies. Indeed, the paralegal profession is one of the fastest growing occupations in the United States, as the reliance on these legal professionals increases.

WHERE DO PARALEGALS WORK?

One of the reasons for the increase in the use of paralegals or legal assistants arises out of the economic advantages to both the firm and the client in utilizing other personnel to perform certain legal tasks. Besides paralegals, other legal support staff include law clerks, legal secretaries, law librarians, and law office administrators. Attorneys generally work with all these personnel, often directly supervising them.

So long as the paralegal is working under the direct supervision of a licensed, practicing attorney, the paralegal is able to perform a multitude of labor-intensive tasks requiring specialized skills, but ultimately saving time and costs. As the utilization of paralegals increases, the number and type of job opportunities for them correspondingly increases, as employers seek to efficiently deliver legal services to a wide variety of clients.

Paralegals have traditionally found the greatest number of job opportunities with law firms of all sizes. However, paralegals work in a variety of professional settings, ranging from traditional law firms to corporations and governmental agencies.

In-house corporate legal departments employ paralegals in a variety of jobs, with duties involving the preparation of financial reports, the planning of corporate meetings, and drafting contracts. In working in a corporate environment, you will enjoy a professional atmosphere that is typically less stressful, with fewer deadlines for work product, and less "billable hours" for attorneys and thus the paralegal. Compensation for paralegals employed by corporations may be higher than for those working for a small or medium-sized law firm. However, the opportunity for advancement in a smaller corporation employing minimal in-house legal staff might be somewhat limited.

Paralegals are frequently employed by various governmental agencies, such as the Environmental Protection Agency or the Internal Revenue Service. The advantages of working for the government include higher starting salaries and significant job security. However, the scope of your duties may be relatively limited, depending on the type of agency for which you work.

In determining which type of employer is the best fit for you, it is advisable that you seek out internships during your formal legal education training, as well as network through the various professional associations that meet locally in your area, such as NALA. You will be able to explore the type of law that interests you, as well as the kind of employer that best suits your personality. Some paralegals like the closeness of the employees in small law firms , while perhaps limiting their scope of duties and career advancement. Other paralegals place greater emphasis on compensation and advancement opportunities. In addition, other factors to consider are the range of duties you will be expected to perform and your long-term goals.

WHAT DO PARALEGALS DO?

Suppose Mary, Susan, and Evelyn are three women who all work for a different law firm. Mary types letters, answers the telephone, and handles all billing and accounting matters. Susan

RESEARCH THIS!

Access the Web site for the Legal Assistant Management Association: www.lamanet.org. Locate salary history information, and research salaries according to the paralegal's area of specialty. See if there are compensation surveys that compare salary averages both nationally and locally in your specific state.

prepares real estate contracts and closing documents, and organizes complex files. Evelyn often works online with a computerized legal research site, searching for relevant case law and statutes, but also interviews firm clients and conducts legal investigations. What might be each of these women's job titles? Each of them might be called a "paralegal" or a "legal assistant." This example illustrates the fact that paralegal work may involve a broad range of duties and responsibilities and thus is fairly dependent on the type of employer and one's level of experience. Overall, the kinds of work performed will also depend on the kind of law in which the firm is engaged. Paralegals for a firm that practices primarily real estate law may devote a large amount of time to preparing forms and conducting title searches. If you work for a personal injury firm, you may be asked to do legal research, interview witnesses, and conduct legal investigation.

Some of the legal tasks paralegals do are

- Conduct client interviews
- Keep clients apprised of the status of their case
- Locate witnesses
- Conduct legal investigations using public records and other sources
- Interview witnesses
- Maintain client files
- Conduct legal research
- Draft pleadings, contracts, and other legal documents
- Attend depositions
- Prepare discovery

Again, these duties will vary depending on where a paralegal works. A small firm may ask paralegals to perform other duties that are largely clerical in nature, such as filing, photocopying, or answering telephones. Paralegals working in a large office may likely find that support staff is hired specifically to perform those functions previously listed. They may also have a support person to whom they can assign tasks, such as Internet searches for specific witnesses. In general, paralegals will be responsible for case management, which involves document management, calendaring and tracking deadlines, and summation of key information. They will also be responsible for legal research and drafting, and all manners of trial preparation, including preparing jury instructions and managing discovery.

Whereas "legal assistants" once performed primarily secretarial or clerical duties, today the experienced and educated paralegal is able to undertake complex tasks including research and document preparation that most attorneys once exclusively performed. Paralegal degree programs not only instruct students in the substantive and procedural areas of the law, but additionally teach skills that allow attorneys to delegate greater amounts of responsibility to these legal professionals. Performing online and traditional legal research is a specialized skill that is not readily taught at a law firm but is usually a required course in formal paralegal degree programs. The ability to perform this skill enhances the marketability of that paralegal. Paralegals also perform duties that attorneys have ordinarily never done, such as computerized billing, timekeeping, and records management. Law office administrators may sometimes share duties and similar responsibilities as a paralegal. In any case, the scope of duties that a paralegal may perform is determined by what is legally authorized under the Model Code and professional association ethical rules.

You Be the Judge

Rapunzel has worked as a legal assistant for an attorney, Jesse Verdi, for 10 years. While Jesse is away on vacation, Mortimer calls the office and tells Rapunzel that he needs legal advice right away because his wife, Loulou, has filed for divorce. Rapunzel gets the name of Loulou's attorney and talks to him, trying to ascertain the immediate seriousness of the situation. Rapunzel tells the attorney that her firm is representing Mortimer. Has Rapunzel committed any ethical violations?

ATTRIBUTES OF A PARALEGAL

Being a successful paralegal requires much more than meeting the minimum qualifications noted at the beginning of this chapter. While it is desirable to pass the CLA exam administered by NALA, which will demonstrate your knowledge of legal substantive topics, there is more to success than simply the mastery of certain concepts and skills. In a demanding career that requires interaction with a variety of people and an ability to balance many job tasks, it is easy to see that certain traits are essential to achieving success and job satisfaction.

Here are some attributes that will increase your marketability as a paralegal in a competitive job market:

- *Effective listening skills*. It is an active process requiring you to listen to the client or a witness, sift through that which is not pertinent, and recognize when to redirect the speaker back on topic.
- *Superior writing skills*. Paralegals must be able to communicate legal concepts and key facts in a clear and concise document that incorporates relevant issues and arguments. Legal terminology is a whole other language, and if you master key concepts and meanings, you will be able to draft documents that accurately reflect the important points.
- *Advanced analytical ability*. Successful paralegals are able to dissect a complex set of facts and conduct research and investigation that clearly identifies the legal issues and the applicable legal theories.
- *Good verbal communication skills*. It is helpful to both the attorney and the client if you are able to discuss the results of your investigation or research using precise and proper words that accurately convey your information and ideas.
- *Significant organizational skills*. Many attorneys insist that their work is much more efficiently undertaken when they have a legal assistant who is adept at managing cases, tracking deadlines, and following trial preparation procedures that ensure successful office management.
- *Computer skills*. Paralegals perform much of their work using computers and technology, including but not limited to basic word processing, client billing software, and Internet searches.
- *Professional demeanor*. Proficiency in technical skills is of nominal value if the paralegal is unable to maintain confidentiality, act responsibly and honestly, and be able to interact with a wide variety of people from different backgrounds. Paralegals need to be able to work independently, but must also communicate in various settings that demand a professional attitude.
- *Desire for continuing education*. In order to maintain a high degree of competence, staying current on new developments in the legal field, paralegals should have the initiative to continue attending professional seminars and workshops, as well as actively participate in legal association meetings.

Competence is the ability and possession of the expertise and skill in a field that is necessary to do the job. Legal assistants acquire competence through formal education as well informal education through the interaction undertaken on the job in consultation with the attorney. Competence is also enhanced by attendance at professional seminars and other continuing education opportunities. Competence in the legal field demands a constant acquisition of current knowledge and practice, as the law is not stagnant but constantly evolving. Therefore, legal assistants should strive to stay abreast of developments and changes in the law, including maintaining an active participation in their local paralegal association and reading professional literature published by some of the national and state professional organizations mentioned throughout this chapter. Not only must legal assistants maintain a high degree of competence in their work, but they must also take care to perform their duties in an ethical context.

ETHICAL CONSIDERATIONS

In determining the scope of the boundaries of what a paralegal can do, it is generally accepted that activities that are merely preparatory in nature do not cross the line into legal tasks that only an attorney is permitted to perform. For example, paralegals today often perform advanced legal research, draft a variety of legal documents, assist in the client interview process, and organize documents and exhibits in preparation for trial. They may also perform more administrative and secretarial tasks such as filing papers in court, proofreading documents, and filling out simple legal forms. However, a word of caution: the duties that can be performed by a paralegal are not precise, and every state has numerous cases that endeavor to define these boundaries. **Ethics** are the standards by which conduct is measured. Sets of written rules, referred to as codes, establish ethical and limits for legal professionals. The ABA Model Rules of Professional Conduct and the NALA Code of Ethics, mentioned earlier in this chapter, establish guidelines for paralegals.

ethics
Standards by which conduct is measured.

The ABA Model Rules of Professional Conduct govern the professional practice of licensed attorneys and are the basis for statutes in each state that set forth ethical standards and rules regarding the unauthorized practice of law. Supplementing the ABA Code is the NALA Code of Ethics, which specifically governs legal assistants. NALA promulgated the Model Standards and Guidelines for the Utilization of Legal Assistants, adopted substantially by the ABA and many state bar associations. This code is designed to set forth the scope of a legal assistant's work. Your own state's code is the governing authority for attorney conduct in your state.

Paralegals are directly accountable to a supervising attorney. You cannot go out and hire a paralegal on your own, as the paralegal is not licensed to give legal advice or provide any form of legal representation without the supervising attorney. Therefore, it is essential to understand a few of the key ethical obligations and issues that may arise. Here are the three primary areas where ethical considerations generally arise:

1. *Duty of competence*. The attorney and paralegal must not cause harm to the client through incompetence. Adequate supervision of paralegal work is required.
2. *Duty of confidentiality*. All information concerning the client and representation of that client must be kept in confidence and not disclosed to third parties (on or off the job). The client may consent to disclosure or the court may order the attorney to reveal information.
3. *Duty to avoid conflict of interest*. Lawyers are prohibited from representation if it will adversely affect the interests of another client, past or present.

In addition, ethical considerations arise where a paralegal performs duties that constitute the unauthorized practice of law.

Unauthorized Practice of Law

The greatest concern arises from what constitutes "the unauthorized practice of law." While paralegals are legally able to perform numerous tasks in support of the supervising attorney—tasks that are preparatory in nature—such tasks like interviewing clients may be uncomfortably close for some states to crossing the line in engaging in the unauthorized practice of law. Simply interviewing clients and witnesses, conducting research, or drafting documents may not be practicing law, but using such information gained through these tasks might be defined as advocacy, a function reserved for licensed attorneys. It might be argued that in the process of interviewing a client, the paralegal may be perceived as giving counsel or exercising legal judgment in the presentment of questions to the client. Fortunately, the various paralegal

You Be the Judge

Bertha has been a client of the Dudley Law Firm for 10 years, as Bertha buys distressed properties, renovates the homes, and then sells them for a profit, with Dudley handling the real estate closings for Bertha. One day, Dudley is out of the office, and Bertha comes in to discuss her will that Dudley had prepared five years ago. Samantha, the legal assistant in the office, assists Bertha in making minor changes to her will. Is this ethically permissible for Samantha to do?

CASE IN POINT

Supreme Court of South Carolina.
The HOUSING AUTHORITY OF THE CITY OF CHARLESTON, Petitioner,
v.
Willie A. KEY, Respondent.
No. 25545.
Submitted Sept. 17, 2002.
Decided Oct. 28, 2002.
Certiorari Denied March 24, 2003.

Justice MOORE:

We accepted this case in our original jurisdiction to determine whether respondent has engaged in the unauthorized practice of law. We find he has and enjoin him from further engaging in such conduct.

FACTS

Petitioner (Housing Authority) commenced this action seeking to enjoin respondent Key from the unauthorized practice of law. We appointed the Honorable John W. Kittredge as special referee to hear evidence and make recommendations. Based on the uncontested facts set forth below, Judge Kittredge concluded respondent had engaged in the unauthorized practice of law and recommended an injunction be issued. No objections to the referee's report have been filed.

Respondent has a paralegal certificate and worked as a paralegal at a law firm in Charleston for three years. He has been unemployed since 2000 and has no address or telephone number. Respondent volunteers at an office referred to as the Fair Housing Office in Charleston advising people who call with landlord complaints. He is not paid. No attorney supervises the office.

In 2001, on behalf of Jacqueline Sarvis and Derotha Robinson, respondent prepared and filed a complaint in federal court alleging unlawful evictions. [FN1] He appeared at a status conference before the federal magistrate. Respondent also prepared pleadings filed in circuit court alleging an unlawful termination of public assistance rental benefits for Joan Whitley and assisted Ms. Whitley at the hearing in circuit court. [FN2] Respondent did not sign any of the pleadings he prepared but had them signed by the plaintiffs as *pro se* litigants. He accepted no payment and in fact paid the filing fees out of his own pocket. Respondent did not obtain leave of court to represent any of these clients. [FN3]

FN1. This action was ultimately dismissed as frivolous except for one cause of action; the appeal was dismissed for failure to prosecute.

FN2. This action was dismissed for lack of subject matter jurisdiction.

FN3. Under former S.C.Code Ann. § 40-5-80 (1986), a citizen could represent another with leave of the court. This section was recently amended to omit a citizen's right to defend or prosecute the cause of another effective June 5, 2002.

DISCUSSION

Respondent defends his conduct on the ground he was not paid and he had the clients' permission to represent them. . . . [1][2][3] The practice of law includes the preparation of pleadings and the management of court proceedings on the behalf of clients. *Doe v. Condon,* 351 S.C. 158, 568 S.E.2d 356 (2002). Respondent's activities on behalf of Whitley, Robinson, and Sarvis constituted the practice of law. The fact that respondent accepted no remuneration for his services is irrelevant. Our purpose in regulating the practice of law is to protect the public from the negative consequences of erroneously prepared legal documents or inaccurate legal advice given by persons untrained in the law. *Linder v. Ins. Claims Consultants, Inc.,* 348 S.C. 477, 560 S.E.2d 612 (2002). We note respondent has shown no indication he intends to discontinue his practice of representing others in court.

We hereby adopt the referee's findings and enjoin respondent from further engaging in the unauthorized practice of law.

INJUNCTION ISSUED.

Source: *Housing Authority of the City of Charleston v. Key,* 352 S.C. 26, 572 S.E.2d 284 (St. Paul, MN: Thomson West). Reprinted with permission from Westlaw.

organizations noted elsewhere in this chapter have accomplished much in raising the standards of paralegal education and promoting ethics in its members.

Paralegals may not render legal advice to any person nor may they appear in court on behalf of another person. To do so is engaging in the unauthorized practice of law. Should this be done with the knowledge of the attorney, or if the attorney had reason to know that this is occurring, the attorney may be held accountable. In addition, generally paralegals cannot accept new clients or establish fees for legal representation by the attorney. Attorneys are ultimately responsible for the authorized work performed by their legal assistant under their supervision and must maintain a direct relationship with the client.

CASE IN POINT

Supreme Court of Ohio.
CLEVELAND BAR ASSOCIATION
v.
COATS, d.b.a. Paramount Paralegal Services.
No. 2002-2118.
Submitted Feb. 12, 2003.
Decided April 9, 2003.

PER CURIAM.

{¶ 1} On two occasions since 1995, respondent, Andra Coats, d.b.a. Paramount Paralegal Services, assisted others in their claims before the Ohio Bureau of Employment Services and appeared as their representative. He has also drafted divorce complaints and judgment entries for filing on behalf of pro se litigants. Respondent has a college degree with a major in paralegal studies; however, he has never been licensed to practice law in Ohio, and he did not provide this representation under a licensed attorney's supervision.

{¶ 2} On July 9, 2001, relator, Cleveland Bar Association, filed a complaint charging respondent with having engaged in the unauthorized practice of law and sought to permanently enjoin this conduct. Respondent was served with the complaint but did not answer. He was also served notice of a December 19, 2001 hearing to be held before the Board of Commissioners on the Unauthorized Practice of Law, but he did not appear.

{¶ 3} The board found, mainly on the basis of his testimony during an investigative deposition, that respondent's filings, appearances, and preparation of documents, all of which were completed without a licensed attorney's supervision, constituted the unauthorized practice of law. As the board explained, "The unauthorized practice of law consists of rendering legal services for another by any person not admitted to practice in Ohio," citing Gov.Bar R. VII(2)(A). Moreover, the practice of law includes conducting cases in court, preparing and filing legal pleadings and other papers, appearing in court cases, and managing actions and proceedings on behalf of clients before judges, whether before courts or administrative agencies. *Richland Cty. Bar Assn. v. Clapp* (1998), 84 Ohio St.3d 276, 278, 703 N.E.2d 771; *Cincinnati Bar Assn. v. Estep* (1995), 74 Ohio St.3d 172, 173, 657 N.E.2d 499. Accord *Cleveland Bar Assn. v. Picklo,* 96 Ohio St.3d 195, 2002-Ohio-3995, 772 N.E.2d 1187, at ¶ 5.

{¶ 4} The board recommended that we find that respondent engaged in the unauthorized practice of law, that we enjoin such conduct, and that we order the reimbursement of costs and expenses incurred by the board and relator. We adopt, in the main, the board's findings [FN1] and its recommendation. Accordingly, respondent is hereby enjoined from all further conduct on another's behalf, whether it involves preparing a legal document, filing, or appearing before a tribunal, that constitutes the unauthorized practice of law. All expenses and costs are taxed to respondent.

FN1. The board also made a factual finding that respondent had represented clients in proceedings before the Social Security Administration. We do not adopt this finding because relator abandoned this aspect of its case during the board hearing.

Judgment accordingly.

MOYER, C.J., RESNICK, FRANCIS E. SWEENEY, SR., PFEIFER, COOK, LUNDBERG STRATTON and O'CONNOR, JJ., concur.

Source: *Cleveland Bar Association v. Coats,* 98 Ohio St.3d 413, 786 N.E.2d 449 (St. Paul, MN: Thomson West). Reprinted with permission from Westlaw.

Competence

competence
The ability and possession of expertise and skill in a field that is necessary to do the job.

One of the duties of an attorney is to represent the client "vigorously." Interpretation of this rule often hinges on basic principles of professional responsibility. **Competence** is the ability and possession of expertise and skill in a field that is necessary to do the job. Attorneys must advance the cause of their clients with an educated degree of expertise in their field, supported by reasonable investigation of both the facts and the law.

Since paralegals have assumed many of the preliminary duties associated with initiating a lawsuit, it is easy to see that paralegals are often responsible for conducting client interviews, fact-gathering tasks, and research of the law. Thus, attorneys must be certain that paralegals possess the skills and expertise to conduct investigation into the law and the facts and ensure that a cause of action is not brought "for an improper purpose." Filing a frivolous lawsuit may result in sanctions against the attorney by the court. At the same time, the attorney must be careful to properly supervise the paralegal while conducting preliminary investigations and fact-gathering tasks, so as to ensure that the line of client representation and advocacy is not unintentionally crossed.

You Be the Judge

Wolfgang's relatives all know he has been a legal assistant for 10 years. Every holiday gathering, his relatives regularly try to elicit Wolfgang's opinions on various matters of a legal nature. Since his relatives do not pay him any legal fees, is it ethically permissible for Wolfgang to give his legal advice to his relatives on matters such as reviewing Aunt Martha's will that she wrote herself?

Confidentiality

confidentiality
Lawyer's duty not to disclose information concerning a client.

Another significant issue that may arise involves issues of **confidentiality.** Attorneys have a duty to not disclose confidences shared by the client to the attorney, according to the attorney-client privilege. Likewise, information that paralegals learn in conjunction with their duties and employment is confidential and may not be disclosed. It is a serious breach of professional ethics if a legal professional should divulge information that is obtained from the client once a professional relationship has been established. Paralegals are prohibited from discussing the client or the client's case in social settings outside the office. In addition, lawyers and their legal assistants must avoid the disclosure of the fact of the representation of a client, identification of the client, or any portion of the client's files to any third parties or visitors in the office, including other clients, night cleaning crew, or those waiting in the reception area.

Confidentiality is a significant issue and is defined in Rule 1.6 of the ABA Model Rules of Professional Conduct: "a lawyer cannot disclose information concerning the representation of a client unless the client consents or unless the disclosure is necessary to carry out the representation."

Suppose that Ellen works at a law firm that regularly handles divorce proceedings. One day, a new client walks in the door that Ellen recognizes as the mother of one of Ellen's daughter's classmates. Ellen has heard from other school mothers certain gossip that might be detrimental to this new client's case. Ethical considerations would arise if Ellen shares the knowledge that this new client has come to her law firm seeking a divorce, and this is not common knowledge with the other parents with whom Ellen converses. Indeed, the attorney will be held accountable for any breach of confidentiality of one of his employees, under the Code of Professional Conduct.

In one case, *Richards v. Jain,* 168 F.Supp.2d 1195 (W.D. Wash. 2001), the court was presented with the issue as to whether a paralegal who was privy to confidential documents should be held to a different standard of ethical conduct than an attorney in the same fact situation. The *Richards* court determined that a law firm's paralegal should not be held to a lower standard of ethical behavior than one of its attorneys. Basing its decision on the Washington Rules of Professional Conduct, the court noted that RPC 5.3 charges attorneys with the responsibility of ensuring that nonattorney staff members follow the same ethics rules that apply to attorneys. The *Richards* court went on to conclude that the Washington RPC regarding confidential information applies equally to paralegals as to attorneys. "Applying a lower standard to the conduct of paralegals would undercut the rules applicable to attorneys."

In a similar case regarding confidentiality, *Zimmerman v. Mahaska Bottling Co.,* 270 Kan. 810, 19 P.3d 784 (Kan. 2001), under the Kansas Rules of Professional Conduct, nonlawyer

You Be the Judge

Mary Smith is represented by your firm in her divorce. Proceedings are going slowly, and one day Mary contacts Dorothy, the legal assistant, telling her that she is going to hire a hit man to murder her husband, Milton. Mary tells Dorothy that she is tired of the divorce process and wants to move on, and this is the only option. If Dorothy is positive that Mary is serious, may she ethically disclose this information to the police?

CASE IN POINT

District Court of the Virgin Islands, Division of St. Croix.
Eunice LAMB, Plaintiff,
v.
PRALEX CORPORATION, Zenith Goldline Pharmaceuticals and Ivax Corporation d/b/a
Ivax Biosciences, Defendants.
No. CIV.2000/145.
July 12, 2004.

ORDER REGARDING DEFENDANTS' MOTION TO DISQUALIFY PLAINTIFF'S COUNSEL

CANNON, United States Magistrate Judge.

THIS MATTER came for consideration on defendants' motion to disqualify counsel. Plaintiff filed an opposition to the motion, and defendants filed a reply.

RELEVANT FACTS

The plaintiff in this case is represented by Lee J. Rohn ["Rohn"] of the Law Offices of Lee J. Rohn. Defendants are represented by Kevin Rames, Esq. ["Rames"] of the Law Offices of Kevin Rames. This motion revolves around Eliza Combie ["Combie"] who worked as a paralegal at the Rames law office from October 30, 2000 to March 26, 2004. Her work at Rames' office involved working with several litigation matters, including this case.

On March 26, 2004, Combie began work with the Rohn law firm. Combie, Rohn and K. Glenda Camero, Esq. ["Cameron"], an associate at the firm, assert that they discussed the possible conflicts raised by Combie's possible employment. They also aver that at the initial interview, Combie acknowledged that there were cases in which she was conflicted at which time she was informed that, should she accept employment with the Rohn firm, she would be barred from contact with those cases.

Rohn and Cameron also state that on Combie's first day of work with Rohn, she submitted the list of cases. The list was circulated to all employees and a memo informing employees to refrain from discussing those cases in her presence was circulated and posted in common areas of the office. Combie, Rohn and Cameron all aver that no-one in the office has discussed any of the relevant matters with Combie. They also state that Combie is locked out of the electronic files and does not work in close proximity to them or to Rohn.

Rames invokes ABA Rules of Professional Conduct 5.3, 1.9, 1.16, and 1.10 [FN1] to argue that Rohn and her entire law firm must be disqualified because during Combie's previous employment with Rames she obtained confidential information regarding pending matters which she may divulge to Rohn. Rohn denies any impropriety and assures the court that no confidences have been disclosed, and that a "scrupulous" screening procedure has been implemented to shield Combie from contact with the conflicted cases. Rames argues that such "self-serving" statements are insufficient to stave off disqualification.

...

DISCUSSION

[1][2] A motion to disqualify counsel requires the court to balance the right of a party to retain counsel of his choice and the substantial hardship which might result from disqualification as against the public perception of and the public trust in the judicial system. *Powell v. Alabama,* 287 U.S. 45, 53, 53 S.Ct. 55, 77 L.Ed. 158 (1932). The underlying principle in considering motions to disqualify counsel is safeguarding the integrity of the court proceedings; the purpose of granting such motions is to eliminate the threat that the litigation will be tainted. *United States Football League v. National Football League,* 605 F.Supp. 1448, 1464 (S.D.N.Y.1985). The district court's power to disqualify an attorney derives from its inherent authority to supervise the professional conduct of attorneys appearing before it. *Richardson v. Hamilton Intern. Corp.,* 469 F.2d 1382, 1385-86 (3d Cir.1972), *cert denied* 411 U.S. 986, 93 S.Ct. 2271, 36 L.Ed.2d 964.

[3] Disqualification issues must be decided on a case by case basis and the party seeking disqualification of opposing counsel bears the burden of clearly showing that the continued representation would be impermissible. *Cohen v. Oasin,* 844 F.Supp. 1065, 1067 (E.D.Pa.1994) *citing Commercial Credit Bus. Loans, Inc. v. Martin,* 590 F.Supp. 328, 335-36 (E.D.Pa.1984). Courts are required to "preserve a balance, delicate though it may be, between an individual's right to his own freely chosen counsel and the need to maintain the highest ethical standards of professional responsibility." *McCarthy v. Southeastern Pennsylvania Transportation Authority,* 772 A.2d 987 (Pa.Super.2001). This balance is essential if the public's trust in the integrity of the Bar is to be preserved. *Id.* The Court was unable to find a Third Circuit decision on this precise issue. However, several courts have addressed it.

[4][5] ABA Rule 5.3 addresses the responsibilities of attorneys who employ non-lawyer assistants. It encompasses the protection of client confidences communicated to a nonlawyer assistant, such as a paralegal or secretary. *Daines v. Alcatel, S.A.,* 194 F.R.D. 678, 681 (E.D.Wash.2000); The rule imposes a duty on the supervising attorney to ensure that the non-lawyer adheres to professional obligations. Thus, a trial court has the authority, in a litigation context, to disqualify counsel based on the conduct of a nonlawyer assistant that is incompatible with the lawyer's ethical obligations. *Smart Industries Corp. Mfg v. Superior Court in and for County of Yuma,* 179 Ariz. 141, 876 P.2d 1176, 1181 (1994). Moreover, such disqualification may be imputed to the entire law firm. *Leibowitz v. The Eighth Judicial District Court of the State of Nevada,* 78 P.3d 515, 523 (Nev.2003).

[6] The issue is whether plaintiff's counsel should be disqualified because a paralegal formerly employed by defendants' attorney

and who was involved in litigation concerning defendants is now employed by plaintiff's counsel. The Standing Committee on Ethics and Professional Responsibility, pursuant to the ABA Model Rules of Professional Conduct, hold that a law firm that hires a paralegal formerly employed by another law firm may continue to represent clients whose interests conflict with the interests of clients of the former employer on whose matters the paralegal has worked, so long as the employing firm screens the paralegal, and as long as no information relating to said clients is revealed to the employing firm. *Informal Opinion 88-1526 BNA Lawyers' Manual on Professional Conduct 901:318 (June 22, 1988).* The Committee reasoned as follows:

> it is important that nonlawyer employees have as much mobility in employment opportunity consistent with the protection of clients' interests. To so limit employment opportunities that some nonlawyers trained to work with law firms might be required to leave the careers for which they have been trained would disserve clients as well as the legal profession. Accordingly, any restrictions on the nonlawyer's employment should be held to the minimum necessary to protect confidentiality of client information.

...

A Court faced with such a motion must first determine whether confidential information has been divulged. Rames claims that Combie participated in all of the cases in which his firm was litigation counsel; that he "shared with Combie litigation strategies and tactics"; and that Combie was "privy to the firm's entire case load as she worked on the vast majority of cases that were and are pending in the Rames law office." Rames maintains that Combie's possession of confidential client information gives Rohn an unfair advantage, and violates the notions of fairness and integrity in the judicial process, requiring disqualification of Rohn and her entire law firm. Combie's affidavit, annexed to Rohn's opposition, counters that Combie "never participated in any discussions or meetings with Attorney Rames", and was never privy to any strategy and tactical deliberation with regard to any opposing counsel. Combie avers that her duties revolved around filing of pleadings and correspondence and that information was transmitted to her on an "as needed" basis. Rames dismisses these statements as self-serving and untrue.

The Court finds that Combie was exposed to confidential information at the Rames law firm. It is reasonable for paralegals to handle confidential client information in order for the law firm employer to render efficient and cost-effective service. Combie is described as an experienced and competent worker. Therefore, it is conceivable that based on her skills, she was given substantial responsibility with the cases, including this case. By virtue of her working on the cases, it is also conceivable that she and Rames shared confidential information regarding them.

[7] However, the fact that Combie has acquired confidential information in a former job is not sufficient by itself to require disqualification of her new employer. *Rivera v. Chicago Pneumatic Tool Co.,* 1991 WL 151892 *4 (Conn.Super. Aug.5, 1991); *Leibowitz,* 78 P.3d at 523; *In Re Complex Asbestos Litigation,* 232 Cal.App.3d 572, 592, 283 Cal.Rptr. 732 (1991). Imputed disqualification is considered a hard remedy that "should be invoked if, and only if, the [c]ourt is satisfied that the real harm is likely to result from failing to invoke it." *Leibowitz,* 78 P.3d at 521, *citing Hayes v. Central States Orthopedic,* 51 P.3d 562, 565 (Ok.2002).

[8] The hiring of a nonlawyer who possesses confidential information of an adversary puts such confidential information at risk. As a result, a rebuttable presumption arises that the information will be disclosed to the new employer. *Zimmerman v. Mahaska Bottling Co.,* 270 Kan. 810, 19 P.3d 784 (2001); *Liebowitz,* 78 P.3d at 521; *Kapco Mfg. v. C & O Enterprises, Inc.,* 637 F.Supp. 1231, 1237 (N.D.Ill.1985). The presumption serves to strike a balance between protecting confidentiality and the right to counsel of one's choice. *Liebowitz,* at 522. A party is able to rebut the presumption that confidential client information has been used or disclosed, by presenting evidence of effective screening mechanisms to shield the employee from the cases. *Rivera,* 1991 WL 151892 at *6; *Daines,* 194 F.R.D. at 682. In other words, the challenged attorney has the burden of showing that the practical effect of formal screening has been achieved and that the employee has not had and will not have any involvement with the litigation or any communication concerning the litigation. *In re Complex Asbestos Litigation,* 232 Cal.App.3d at 597, 283 Cal.Rptr. 732. In this jurisdiction, the erection of a "Chinese Wall" [FN2] is recognized in this regard. *David v. Bank of Nova Scotia,* Terr.Ct. Civ. No. 37/2000 (Order dated December 19, 2001); *Island Management Group, Inc. v. The Bank of Nova Scotia,* Dist.Ct. Civ. No.1999/104 (Order dated November 17, 2000); *Rennie v. Hess Oil Virgin Islands Corp.,* 981 F.Supp. 374, 378 (D.Vi.1997).

FN2. A "Chinese Wall" is a screening mechanism to protect a former client's confidences so that the current client may be represented by lawyers of its own choosing.

Rohn states, and Combie and Cameron aver, that during her interview the parties discussed the fact that she was previously employed with Rames who is an adversary of Rohn and is opposing counsel in this case. They further state that upon Combie's disclosure of the conflicted cases, "they advised her that were an offer of employment extended, she would be prohibited from and have no access to the electronic or physical files for those cases on which she would be conflicted." A list of the cases was circulated to all employees and posted in common areas; Combie has not been near the files and does not know their location; the employees have been instructed not to discuss the cases in her presence; and she has been locked out of the electronic filing system with regard to those cases.

The evidence of screening provided by Rohn was not directly contradicted by Rames. Although the Court understands his chagrin, more is required before a court will be forced to relieve a litigant of his counsel of choice. A majority of courts have endorsed screening procedures similar to the ones implemented in this case, under similar circumstances. Additionally, Rohn's office employs several individuals and there is little likelihood that Combie will be *required* to work on the conflicted cases. The Court is satisfied that the procedures employed by Rohn's office to shield Combie from the files, supports a finding that any information obtained at the Rames law firm will not be disclosed.

CONCLUSION

In light of the foregoing, disqualification is not warranted. In addressing ethical problems created by non-lawyers changing employment from a law firm representing one party to a law firm representing an adverse party, courts must fashion rules which strike a balance between the public policy of protecting the confidentiality of attorney-client communications and a party's right to representation by chosen counsel. *See, Saldana v. Kmart,*

260 F.3d 228 (3d Cir.2001); *Leonard v. University of Delaware,* 1997 WL 158280, *3 (D.Del. April 20, 1997). Accordingly, any restrictions on the non-lawyers employment should be held to the minimum necessary to protect confidentiality of client information.

A prophylactic rule which requires the employing firm to establish procedures which ensure that confidential information has not and will not be disclosed to the employing firm safeguards the competing interests. The Court finds that plaintiff's counsel has rebutted the presumption of improper disclosure by presenting evidence of the "Chinese Wall" implemented in that regard. Accordingly, disqualification is not warranted and the defendants' motion will be denied at this time.

Now therefore it is hereby

ORDERED that the defendants' motion to disqualify plaintiffs' counsel is DENIED WITHOUT PREJUDICE. Defendants may refile their motion if there is credible evidence that confidential client information has been disclosed.

Source: *Lamb v. Pralex Corporation,* 333 F.Supp.2d 361 (St. Paul, MN: Thomson West). Reprinted with permission from Westlaw.

employees of a firm are held to the same standards as lawyers in matters concerning issues of confidentiality and disqualification. In *Zimmerman,* the court noted,

> *It is no secret that paralegals and other nonattorney staff members are regularly exposed to confidential client information as part of their everyday work. Whether by such means as the filing of a confidential client letter in a case file or attendance at a strategical meeting, nonattorneys often acquire sensitive information about their clients. To allow such employees to change firms at random and without concern for the information they have acquired would be to undercut the rules applicable to attorneys.*

The court noted exceptions to applying mandatory disqualification of a firm whenever a nonlawyer moves to another firm where the two firms are in pending litigation and representing adverse parties, but reiterated the necessity of following the Kansas RPC.

Conflict of Interest

Another key issue for legal assistants and attorneys is the rule regarding the representation of parties that have adverse interests, known as the conflict of interest rule.

Rule 1.7 states, "A lawyer cannot represent opposing parties in a legal matter unless (1) the lawyer reasonably believes that the representation will not affect either party adversely and (2) each party consents."

This rule applies to both lawyers and legal assistants who perform services on a contractual basis for different law firms, as well as those who leave the employment of one firm to work at another. Conflicts of interest arise because the representation of one client adversely impacts the zealous representation of another client with adverse interests. When an employee switches jobs, and now works at a firm that represents interests adverse to those of a former client, then the new employer uses procedures to screen and shield the new employee from information about a case in which there is a conflict of interest. This is sometimes referred to as an ethical wall or a **Chinese wall.** In essence, the new employee is walled off from others in the firm regarding this specific client or file. In every case, attorneys run a **conflict check.** This is a procedure to determine if taking on the new client will result in a conflict of interest. The attorney will check the name of a prospective client in the firm's database to see if there are any adverse interests or parties or legal issues involved that will prevent her representation.

Chinese wall
The shielding, or walling off, of a new employee from a client in the new firm with whom there may be a conflict of interest.

conflict check
A procedure to verify potential adverse interests before accepting a new client.

RESEARCH THIS!

Various associations support the role and profession of the paralegal. In addition, many state bar associations provide links to information on a local level.

Locate your state bar association on the Internet, and identify the information available regarding the utilization of paralegals.

Selected legal Web sites, not previously noted in this chapter, that you may consult include:

www.alanet.org
www.paralegals.org/development/modelcode.html
www.nala.org/stand.htm

Summary

As the use of legal professionals besides attorneys continues to grow, there is a recognized need to establish standards and redefine the role of paralegals. It is indisputable that paralegals provide a valuable resource to the legal profession, as their specialized skills enable attorneys to offer cost-effective representation to a larger number of clients. Formal training programs have dramatically increased in recent years, and some courses offering paralegal training or law office administration have established methods of ensuring that minimum competencies are satisfied before the paralegal is certified as qualified. This is good news for the general public, as the degree of contact that one might have with a paralegal as opposed to an attorney has shifted dramatically in recent years. Paralegals perform many of the preparatory tasks necessary in the litigation process, as well as in many other substantive legal fields, such as real estate closings and settling estates. In essence, they are providing services just short of advocacy or the giving of legal advice, as this unauthorized practice of law is illegal in all states. It is likely that the trend of allowing paralegals greater responsibilities, yet also holding them to the same ethical standards as attorneys, will continue and will only serve to further develop and redefine the profession in our legal system.

Key Terms

American Bar Association
Chinese wall
Competence
Confidentiality
Conflict check
Ethics
Legal assistant
National Association of Legal Assistants (NALA)
Paralegal

Discussion Questions

1. Contact your local paralegal association. Inquire as to what is necessary to become a student member of the association. Find out if the association maintains salary surveys for your local market.
2. Find out what your state's rules are regarding certification of legal assistants.
3. What do you think are the most important attributes that a paralegal ought to possess?
4. Distinguish the difference between attributes and skills. Which do you think are more important for a paralegal in his or her first job as a legal assistant?
5. Locate the classified job advertisements in your local newspaper and search for legal professional jobs. What types of positions are open in your area and how many of them are offered through a legal staffing agency? What other options exist for job searches in your area? How many require certification?
6. Discuss the advantages and disadvantages of working at a small firm versus a large firm and then compare it to a corporate legal department. Which do you prefer?
7. List some reasons why internships are a valuable component of a formal legal education. Explain how you might search for an internship.
8. Discuss what might occur if neither attorneys nor paralegals were licensed or regulated in the practice of law in your state. Do you think formal licensing and regulation of paralegals is a good idea?
9. Explain what is meant by a "Chinese wall" and give a factual example of this.

Exercises

For each of the following questions, consult your state's rules as well as the NALA Code of Ethics and the ABA Model Rules.

1. Campbell has worked as a legal assistant on a complex employment law case for almost two years. Finally, the case ends, and the firm's client is extremely pleased with the outcome. As a token of appreciation, the client sends Campbell a set of four tickets to an upcoming sporting event that has long been sold out. Must Campbell return the tickets to the client or give the tickets to his supervising attorney, or may he keep them for himself?

2. Sam works as a legal assistant at a large law firm that regularly handles family law cases. The firm often advertises its services in the area of family law, including a prominent ad in the telephone book. One day, Sam is surprised to see Meredith Brown in the reception area, as he recognizes her as the parent of a child in his son's class at the local elementary school. At the next PTA meeting, Sam mentions to another parent, Richard, that Meredith was in his firm's office last week. Has Sam committed any ethical violations?
3. Assume the same facts as in Exercise 2, except that now Sam learns Meredith is seeking a divorce from her husband, Peter. At a classroom back-to-school night, Sam and Meredith casually chat, and Meredith mentions during this conversation that she is hiding assets from Peter in a secret bank account that she opened without Peter's knowledge. Sam is aware that his supervising attorney, handling Meredith's divorce, has no knowledge of this account, which contains half a million dollars. Should Sam keep this information to himself, since he received the information in a social setting, or must he disclose this information to the attorney?
4. Mary works as a legal assistant at a small firm that uses a general fee scale to handle legal matters such as the preparation of a will or representation at a real estate closing. Tom Thumb comes to Mary's office while all the attorneys are at lunch, inquiring about the preparation of a will and trust. Mary meets with Tom and informs him that it should cost $250 to do the work for Tom, and he readily agrees to have the firm represent him. Has Mary committed any ethical violations?
5. Hubert is an experienced legal assistant who has worked in the legal profession with several different attorneys. Hubert sees the need to provide legal services to low-income parties seeking to divorce, and thus he compiles a book that contains necessary forms and information, entitled *Divorce: You Can Do It Yourself.* He markets the book online. The book cautions people about using the forms and to seek a licensed attorney for legal advice. Has Hubert engaged in the unauthorized practice of law?
6. Assume the same facts as in Exercise 5, except that Hubert also has a Web site. The link is contained in the back of the book. It offers suggestions, for an additional fee, to buyers of his book on how to choose the correct forms and how to complete the standard forms. Has Hubert engaged in the unauthorized practice of law?

Vocabulary Builders

LEGAL CROSSINGS

Word List

AAfPE	Confidentiality	Expertise	Professional
ABA	Corporate	Legal assistant	Representation
Canons	Deposition	Model rules	Salary
Client	Discovery	NALA	Training
Competence	Ethics	Paralegal	Unauthorized practice

Chapter 7

Criminal Law

CHAPTER OBJECTIVES

After reading this chapter, you will be able to:

- Explain the significance of the Model Penal Code.
- Distinguish between general intent and specific intent.
- Identify the two essential elements of a criminal offense.
- Explain the difference between burglary and robbery.
- Describe the defenses available in most criminal cases.

In Chapter 5, students reviewed one central aspect of criminal law—criminal procedure, which addresses the rules that must be followed in both initiating and maintaining a criminal action. This chapter discusses the other significant aspect of criminal law—substantive criminal law, which defines and classifies the kinds of conduct that constitute a crime. A crime is defined as an act, or failure to act, that is expressly proscribed by written public law. Referring to the chart in Chapter 3, criminal law is characterized by legal wrongs that are committed against society, as opposed to private wrongs committed against individuals and/or their property (civil action, or tort).

Systems of law endeavor to promote stability and security among citizens. Therefore, the state, or society, acts to enforce certain standards of conduct, defining that behavior which society deems to be harmful, objectionable, or disruptive to the whole community. In order for members of the community to live peacefully, in a cohesive society, the state enacts appropriate legislation that identifies this criminal conduct, as well as outlines the penalties imposed on those persons who violate the prescribed laws. Federal, state, and local governments share the common goal of keeping undesirable conduct and wrongdoing within limits, encouraging decent standards of conduct that promote coexistence. Criminal statutes are enacted by legislatures in order to provide incentives for people to act reasonably, to deter people from undesirable behavior that affects society, and to provide consistent, impartial penalties for those who break the laws. The plaintiffs are fundamentally the people of the state or nation, represented by the designated individual, usually the prosecuting attorney for that state or the United States.

This chapter will identify the essential elements of a crime, discuss a select number of certain crimes in depth, and review basic criminal defenses. Furthermore, jurisdiction and ethical issues related to criminal law will be addressed.

JURISDICTION

In Chapter 2, "Jurisdiction," the distinction between civil and criminal law was explained. The criminal law system in the United States may be described as a system that both looks to the future as well as the past. Legislatures have defined those acts that are deemed undesirable to an orderly society, intending to deter persons from violating those acts in the present. Society enacts laws intending to provide incentives for people to act reasonably in the future, because ultimately society has an interest in preserving people's lives, property, and the safety of the entire community. In addition, the legal system looks to the past because it provides consistent, specific remedies for those who commit legal wrongdoing, failing to abide by society's rules.

If a person breaches a duty that is owed to society, committing an act that violates a particular criminal statute, the lawsuit is brought by the government, even if the actual victim is a private individual, as in the crimes of murder or robbery. If convicted, the defendant is punished by the government, as opposed to the victim seeking redress directly from the wrongdoer. However, it should be recognized that there is occasionally overlap between criminal and civil law. The same set of circumstances may be regarded as a wrong against society, but the actual victim may also commence a civil suit in tort, to recover compensation for the harm caused by the wrongdoer. So, while the criminal system of law provides punishment of a wrongdoer, the victim may also choose to pursue a civil remedy, claiming money as compensation for the injury suffered as a proximate result of the wrongdoer's conduct. This concept is discussed in Chapter 3.

CYBER TRIP

For criminal justice links and topics of interest in criminal law, visit this Web site sponsored by the United States Department of Justice: www.ncjrs.gov/.

Under the United States Constitution, the right to impose liability for criminal acts is primarily left to the states. In making particular conduct a crime, the Constitution grants jurisdiction to the federal government in limited areas, reserving jurisdiction to the states in most areas, and sometimes resulting in concurrent jurisdiction in limited situations. Federal jurisdiction is applicable to crimes involving federal government property, the District of Columbia, citizens abroad, and conduct or activities within states where power is expressly granted by the Constitution, as in the conduct of federal officials or interstate commerce. An example of crimes in which the federal government retains jurisdiction includes a murder that occurs inside a federal building or a case in which a child is kidnapped and taken across state lines. Concurrent jurisdiction, where both federal and state authorities have authority to prosecute, might involve a case where a bank teller is murdered in the process of a defendant robbing a bank.

The state, through the prosecutor, initiates the suit, based on whether the particular conduct is adjudged to be proscribed by that state's criminal code. The essential foundation for criminal liability today is the Model Penal Code, the basis for modern criminal statutes, which will be discussed in the next section. Since each state's criminal code is different, it is recommended that you consult your jurisdiction's code to determine the elements of each crime discussed in subsequent sections of this chapter.

SOURCES OF LAW

Rules used to define criminal acts are formally set forth in state statutes, and therefore you should take care to consult relevant criminal statutes in your respective jurisdiction. In essence, there are 50 sets of criminal codes, in addition to the federal criminal code that covers all states and the code of the District of Columbia. Furthermore, the U.S. Constitution, as noted in Chapter 3, defines criminal procedural rights, as well as reserving certain powers to impose criminal liability in matters of an exclusive federal interest, such as crimes committed on military bases. Criminal codes define in detail the acts constituting crimes, including the elements of each offense that must be proved by the state beyond a reasonable doubt. Since there are significant differences in the precise language, as well as interpretation, of the criminal statutes in each state, it is difficult to present here a comprehensive statement of the definitive rules of criminal law. Therefore, this chapter will present a synopsis of general substantive criminal law principles, based on the common law. As noted in previous chapters, criminal law principles originate from common law. However, modern statutes are, to a large extent, based on the **Model Penal Code (MPC).** This is a comprehensive body of criminal law, defining criminal activity and penalties, that was compiled by the **American Law Institute,** a nongovernmental body consisting of distinguished lawyers and judges in the United States, and adopted, in whole or in part, by the majority of states. The purpose of this code was to aid state legislatures in assessing substantive penal law by a modern, reasoned judgment. Since its adoption in 1962 by the American Law Institute, the Code has prompted vast revision and codification of the substantive criminal law in the United States.

Model Penal Code (MPC)
A comprehensive body of criminal law, adopted in whole or in part by most states.

American Law Institute
A nongovernmental organization composed of distinguished judges and lawyers in the United States.

There are additional sources of law in the area of criminal law. Federal criminal law encompasses statutes, in addition to the rules delegated to administrative agencies or the U.S. Constitution. Title 18 of the U.S. Code defines federal crimes, such as illegal conduct or activities arising out of interstate commerce or involving or concerning federal officials. Administrative agencies, such as the Securities and Exchange Commission, define criminal conduct pertaining to

RESEARCH THIS!

Locate the Model Penal Code in your law library. Locate the criminal code for your state in the library. Are the codes organized the same? What comparisons can you make just by scanning the sections of each?

CYBER TRIP

Visit the Web site: http://straylight.law.cornell.edu/rules/frcrmp/. This site sets forth the Federal Rules of Criminal Procedure.

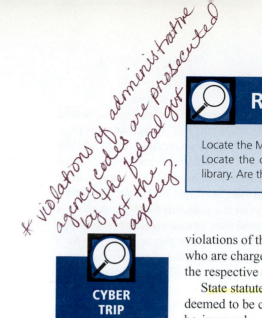

violations of their agency rules. However, it should be noted that prosecution of those individuals who are charged with violation of agency rules is reserved to the federal court system, and not to the respective administrative agency.

State statutes are the key source of criminal law. A state's penal code classifies in detail actions deemed to be crimes and prescribes the penalties for committing the crime. The penalties that may be imposed generally comprise imprisonment, fines, or both. Society's rationale for imposing imprisonment rests on the principles that the criminal must be prevented from harming others in society, while deterring the criminal, and others, from committing crimes in the future. Furthermore, punishment such as imprisonment serves to remove the offender from society, preventing the victim from seeking personal retribution and thereby committing further criminal activity. At the same time, it is hoped that imprisonment will serve to rehabilitate the criminal, motivating the individual to abide by society's rules in the future. This latter theory of punishment has been the source of controversy, as criminal justice scholars debate the efficacy of imprisonment for many criminals.

CLASSIFICATION OF CRIMES

All crimes are classified according to the gravity of the offense, with the most serious crimes resulting in severe punishment. In general, crimes may be categorized as either felonies or misdemeanors.

felony
A crime punishable by more than a year in prison or death.

A **felony** is the most serious crime, for which punishment may result in death or lengthy imprisonment. Statutes define the mandatory sentencing for commission of such crimes, and such prescribed punishment varies from one state to another. Typically, felonies are punishable by imprisonment of a year or more. Many states will define varying degrees of crimes, with according penalties for each degree, such as first- and second-degree murder. Types of crimes that are generally characterized as felonies typically include most crimes against the person such as murder and rape. At common law, crimes such as burglary and arson were also classified as felonies. It should be noted that which crimes are defined as felonies varies in every jurisdiction, and thus a misdemeanor in one jurisdiction may very well be a felony in another jurisdiction. For this reason, a comprehensive laundry list of felonies cannot be provided here, and the student should consult relevant state statutes. Thus, the majority of states, having adopted the Model Penal Code, in whole or in part, provide consistency in defining criminal conduct.

misdemeanor
A lesser crime punishable by less than a year in jail and/or a fine.

A **misdemeanor** is less serious than a felony and is typically characterized by a maximum punishment of less than a year and/or a fine. Under common law, those crimes not specifically classified as felonies were designated misdemeanors. Today, under modern criminal statutes, misdemeanors might include crimes against property, such as burglary, as well as traffic violations. Typical misdemeanors in most jurisdictions might be drunkenness in public and disturbing the peace.

malum prohibitum
An act that is prohibited by a rule of law.

malum in se
An act that is prohibited because it is "evil in itself."

In classifying a crime, one might consider the offensive act to be legally wrong, or morally wrong, or both. In situations where the crime is not inherently evil, but is conduct deemed wrong because the state legislature says it is wrong, such a crime may be characterized as **malum prohibitum.** An example of a malum prohibitum crime is riding a motorcycle without a helmet. Some states have specifically required a helmet, not because it is morally wrong but because it is against the law to not wear a helmet in that particular jurisdiction. Conversely, an act may be wrong not only because it is prohibited in a specific jurisdiction, but also because society in general deems it morally wrong. This involves conduct that is considered inherently bad by society, such as murder, and this is referred to as a crime **malum in se.** These crimes are both legally and morally wrong; examples are murder and rape.

ESSENTIAL ELEMENTS OF A CRIME

actus reus
The guilty act.

mens rea
"A guilty mind"; criminal intent in committing the act.

Prosecutors must establish each and every single element of the crime, as defined by the statute, in order to secure a conviction. As noted in Chapter 5, "Procedural Law," the prosecutor must also establish the facts necessary to satisfy each element "beyond a reasonable doubt." While every criminal statute will specify the requisite elements of each crime, in nearly all criminal cases, the prosecution must generally prove two essential elements in order for the accused to be found guilty. These two elements are **actus reus** and **mens rea.** In simple language, this means that the prosecution must show that the defendant actually did the prohibited act (actus reus, or guilty act) and that the accused actually possessed the required state of mind (mens rea, or guilty mind). The specific terms for these two elements originate from the Latin phrase, *actus non facit reum nisi mens sit rea,* which translates as "the act itself does not constitute guilt unless done with a guilty mind." Note, too, that the specific elements of each crime, as defined by statute, must be proven.

Actus Reus

actually commit the act.

The first element, the actus reus, requires that the defendant either did the prohibited act or failed to act when the law required action. The failure to act constitutes an omission that fulfills the requisite physical element. The actus reus is some physical act. An example of an act that satisfies this first element would be the physical motion in swinging one's arm and striking someone in the face. This action of punching someone in the face comprises the action forming the basis for criminal assault and battery, where actual harm is caused. An example of an omission that satisfies this first element may be the failure of a parent to attempt to rescue her child who is drowning in the swimming pool. The law asserts that by virtue of the relationship between parent and child, the parent has a duty to act, and therefore the failure to do so establishes the actus reus.

Certain restrictions apply when determining whether this first element is present. In every situation, the prosecution must prove that the defendant's act or omission was voluntary. Thus, if a defendant lacks control over his bodily movements, then it cannot be said that the actus reus was committed. For example, if a driver loses control of his car and strikes a pedestrian, in most cases, the act of physically driving the motor vehicle typically satisfies the requisite actus reus. However, if the driver suffers a heart attack while driving, and had no previous history of a heart condition, then it could not be said that striking the pedestrian with his car was a voluntary act. Similarly, reflex actions or the actions of a third person might be involuntary conduct, demonstrating that the defendant lacked control over her actions, and thus did not commit the actus reus. For instance, if the defendant is violently sneezing, propelling her body forward into the person in front of her on a downward escalator, causing the person to lose his balance and tumble down the steps, this ordinarily cannot be deemed a voluntary act giving rise to criminal conduct, as the reflex action in sneezing is wholly involuntary. Likewise, if the defendant is pushing a shopping cart through a crowded grocery store, and another person plows a cart into the defendant's body, causing the defendant to strike the victim with his own cart, resulting in bodily injury to the victim, the action would not be considered voluntary, as the defendant's conduct was involuntary.

Regarding the duty to act, the law generally recognizes several categories that are sufficient to constitute the actus reus where the defendant has a duty, but fails to act (the omission). For instance, the relationship between parent and child creates a duty in the parent to act, as evidenced in the preceding example. Similarly, the duty to act is created by virtue of one's employment. If Darren is a police officer, then Darren has a duty to act when witnessing an attack by Snidely upon Winnie on the street corner. Ordinarily, if one is unrelated to the victim, the law does not impose a duty to act, and therefore there is no criminal liability for walking away from a violent crime taking place. However, an omission, or failure to act, is sufficient for the actus reus element where one is a public officer charged with the duty to perform, as in police or fire department personnel. Employment may also create a duty to act, as in the case of a bridge tender, who has the duty to warn cars and lower the barriers when a bridge is being raised to permit boats to cross under the bridge. If the bridge tender, Matt, observes an approaching barge, and sees cars traveling toward the bridge entrance, then Matt must act in time to activate warning signals and prevent the cars from attempting to cross the bridge while it is being raised for the passing barge.

Another category in which the omission is sufficient to prove actus reus is where a dangerous situation has been created or set into motion by the defendant. For example, if an apartment resident is smoking in bed, and his bed catches fire, he has a duty to try to put out the fire, or at least summon help; he cannot just walk away and leave the mattress burning without further action.

Finally, if a person voluntarily undertakes a duty that is not created by law, then once that person agrees to assume a duty, it must be fulfilled. An example might be where an adult agrees to take responsibility for the care of an elderly relative. Once the duty of care is undertaken, the adult cannot fail to properly care for this relative, as the omission to act may constitute the actus reus. For instance, if the elderly relative falls out of her wheelchair, the defendant cannot continually step over her every day for weeks until she dies of malnutrition as this voluntary conduct will satisfy the first element of the crime in proving manslaughter.

It must be noted that a criminal act requires that there is actual performance of the act or a definitive failure to act. It is not enough to be merely contemplating the commission of some crime, as the actus reus is lacking. In other words, as much as some people believe that they know what others are thinking, the law does not punish mere evil thoughts; there must be some *conduct.* You might surmise that a person is having bad thoughts, but you can't punish that person unless he or she chooses to act on them. Thus, in analyzing any factual situation, you should consider whether there was any *conduct,* and then ask whether that conduct involved a *voluntary* act. Even if there is no voluntary act, you must still consider whether the facts lead you to conclude that there was a legal *duty* to act and whether the person's omission thereby constitutes the "act."

Mens Rea

To be found guilty, one must also have the requisite evil intent, or mens rea. Note that *all* crimes have an actus reus, but only *most* crimes have a mens rea. Each specific crime has its own mens rea that must be proven. In every case, the prosecution has the burden of proof in establishing the mens rea for the particular crime charged against the accused. The defendant must be found to have had at least the minimum level of mental state that is required by the offense charged. In other words, you might have a general kind of "guilty" mind, but you may not have the *right* kind of "guilty" mind necessary to be convicted of a particular offense.

The four levels of mens rea, or mental state, are

- Intentionally
- Recklessly
- With criminal negligence
- Strict liability

specific intent
The mental desire and will to act in a particular way.

When finding that the defendant committed a prohibited act at the first level, it is said that the defendant acted with **specific intent.** According to common law and the Model Penal Code, a defendant is presumed to have acted with specific intent where he knowingly and intentionally committed the prohibited act. The defendant is said to have had the desire to bring about a certain result and acted with the intention to purposefully achieve that result. This is the highest level of culpable mental state. Even if the defendant did not anticipate an exact result, it is sufficient if the defendant's actions were plainly certain to cause that specific harm, and the defendant knew that this harm would occur. For example, firing a gun into a crowd of people inside a shopping mall satisfies the mens rea as it can be said that the defendant knowingly and intentionally fired a gun, with virtual certainty that people would be struck by the bullets and suffer bodily harm as a result of that action. It does not matter if the defendant later argues that he only wanted to scare people, as the serious bodily harm or death of shoppers was the natural and probable consequence of the defendant's actions.

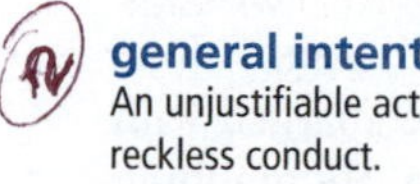

general intent
An unjustifiable act; reckless conduct.

In comparison, **general intent** is found where the defendant assumes an unjustifiable risk in her actions, and this demonstration of recklessness, though a lesser level of mental culpability, nevertheless satisfies the second element—the mens rea.

This requires that the prosecution prove that the defendant realized the risk involved, and it is a risk that a reasonably prudent person would recognize, but ignores the risk and acts in reckless disregard of the likely consequences. This is a subjective test, and generally the facts and circumstances surrounding the action determine whether the mens rea has been shown. Unless the prosecution can prove the required mens rea with respect to *each* element of an

CYBER TRIP

If you are looking for specific help deciphering the meanings of some common legal words, consult one of these online browsable dictionaries of basic terminology:

http://jurist.law.pitt.edu/dictionary.htm#sectA

http://dictionary.lp.findlaw.com/

www.law.harvard.edu/library/services/research/guides/united_states/basics/one_l_dictionary.php

offense, then generally it will be said that no crime has occurred. In some cases, a person's conduct, though reckless, may only be considered to be negligent conduct, rather than criminal. Negligent conduct would encompass the creation of a risk for which the person should be aware of such risk.

For example, if a person is intoxicated, and elects to drive a motor vehicle, is it deemed to be reckless behavior? In other words, is this conduct that constitutes criminal behavior? So long as the defendant is aware of the obvious risk involved in driving while under the influence, and then performs that act of driving without much concern for the risk involved, then it can be said that the reckless behavior, intending to endanger life, was likely and thus may be sufficient for establishing the requisite mens rea. The defendant may not have intended to cause bodily harm when his drunk driving causes him to strike a pedestrian, but his reckless disregard for the probable consequences of his action may satisfy the test of criminal recklessness and the required mental state.

Negligent conduct is established where the defendant shows a lack of regard for life or the safety of others. Manslaughter can be committed where the defendant is guilty of gross negligence, as in the case of the drunk driver in the preceding situation. It should be noted that individual criminal statutes in every state will specify what level of criminal intent is necessary for a particular crime. In every case, if the mens rea proven is for a different offense than the charge brought against the accused, then the defendant may not be found guilty, as the mental state required is identified in each statutory offense.

Finally, some offenses are strict liability statutes, in which criminal liability is imposed even in the absence of mens rea. So long as the actus reus is proven, no mental state need be shown. An example of a strict liability crime may be public nuisance crimes, as in violating specific regulatory standards in disposing of harmful chemicals. In these limited cases, the prosecution need only show that the prohibited act was voluntarily committed, with no requirement of proving an evil intent.

CRIMES AGAINST THE PERSON

One of the attributes of the Model Penal Code is its systematic structure, organizing and grouping offenses according to related subcategories. Therefore, offenses against property are grouped together, and likewise offenses against the person are organized in one group. Offenses against the person are organized into four articles. In general, crimes against the person may be subdivided into crimes involving death of the victim and nonfatal offenses against the person. As stated previously in this chapter, felonies are the most serious type of crime, typically being homicides and rape. Statutory definitions of homicide or **murder** include the unlawful killing of another human being, with death caused by either an act or an omission. The mens rea required for murder is described as **malice aforethought.** Essentially, this means that the defendant had either the intention to kill (*express*) or the intention to cause serious bodily harm (*implied*). It is irrelevant whether the accused intended the specific result (death), but more importantly that the consequences were likely to occur and that the defendant intended or brought about such consequences as a result of her actions or omissions.

murder
The killing of a human being with intent.

malice aforethought
The prior intention to kill the victim or anyone else if likely to occur as a result of the actions or omissions.

Specific intent to kill may be inferred from the use of a deadly weapon in a manner likely to cause death or serious bodily harm. In addition, intent to kill will be viewed in light of the surrounding circumstances and the nature of the attack. For example, assume that John is stopped by a police officer for making an illegal left turn at an intersection. John becomes belligerent and the officer asks him to step out of the car. As John walks to the side of the car, he strikes the officer on the arm, takes the officer's gun, and immediately fires a shot. As the two struggle for control of the gun, John fires several more shots, shouting, "I'm going to kill you!" None of the shots actually hit the officer, and eventually John is restrained. John will be charged with attempted murder, because he attempted to intentionally kill another human being. By grabbing the officer's gun, firing the gun, and stating he is going to kill the officer, John will be said to have engaged in conduct that constituted a substantial step toward intentionally killing another human being. In this case, intent to kill may be established by John's use of a deadly weapon against the officer coupled with a verbal intention to kill. Furthermore, discharging a weapon in the general direction of a victim may be substantial evidence from which a jury can infer the

You Be the Judge

Assume the relevant section of the criminal code in your state reads: "A person is guilty of a misdemeanor if he or she initiates or circulates a report or warning of an impending bombing, knowing that the report or warning is false or baseless and that it is likely to cause evacuation of a building or to cause public inconvenience or alarm."

What state of mind is applicable to the circulation or initiation of a bomb threat called in to the local high school by a student? What if the bomb threat is posted on a popular teen chat Web site instead?

requisite intent to kill. It is not necessary for any of the shots to actually hit the victim, because that fact alone does not demonstrate that John lacked the intent to kill the officer.

manslaughter
The unlawful killing of a human being without premeditation.

Besides murder, other offenses within the category of homicide include voluntary and involuntary **manslaughter.** In cases where the killing of another human being has occurred, but circumstances in the situation support findings of diminished responsibility or impaired state of mind, then manslaughter is typically charged against the accused as opposed to murder. In order to prevail on a manslaughter charge, the prosecution must prove the defendant killed another human being, but particular defenses raised by the accused are mitigating factors lessening the charge to manslaughter. Such defenses, discussed later in this chapter, may include proof that the defendant lacked the ability to distinguish right from wrong or did not rationally understand the consequences of his actions that a reasonably prudent person would comprehend. In the same respect, the defendant may also prove that he was impaired in some way, such as by intoxication, thereby substantially lacking sound mental judgment at the time of the killing. Finally, the defendant may raise the defense of provocation, also enabling the reduced charge of manslaughter in the killing of another human being.

In distinguishing between voluntary and involuntary manslaughter, there are several points that should be recognized. First, involuntary manslaughter charges may be brought where an unlawful act has been committed, but it is gross negligence or recklessness on the part of the defendant that caused the death. Reckless manslaughter cases typically involve the defendant's operation of a motor vehicle. Second, involuntary manslaughter may involve a defendant who owes the victim a duty of care, but performs an act, or fails to act, in a way that constitutes gross negligence. For example, if Dr. Butcher is treating a patient, but in the middle of surgery, needs to take a coffee break, resulting in the patient bleeding to death, this may amount to gross negligence supporting an involuntary manslaughter conviction. Similarly, charges of involuntary manslaughter may be brought against a railway shipper who is aware of the fact that illegal immigrants routinely try to stow away in its boxcars, yet does nothing to either decisively prevent this practice or alternatively ensure adequate outside air vents are affixed in the boxcars, resulting in the deaths of a group of stowaways who suffocate from the intolerable heat conditions inside the train.

assault
The threat or attempt to cause a touching, whether successful or not, provided the victim is aware of the danger.

Nonfatal offenses against a person encompass crimes such as assault and battery. Although these two offenses are routinely mentioned together and often combined as if they were one, in fact these are two distinctly separate offenses and in which one can occur without the other. **Assault** is the intent to cause immediate apprehension or fear of an unlawful or unwanted touching. The actus reus required for this offense may be words or some act that puts the victim in imminent fear of a touching. For example, telling a classmate that you will strike her on the head with your textbook at the conclusion of class may be sufficient to constitute assault. No act of physical touching need occur, but simply the imminent fear of that touching. It is not enough to threaten to strike a classmate on the head with your book at the end of the year, if it is only January. There is no imminent fear. It should also be noted that the victim must be aware of the threat or words in order to constitute assault. It is not enough if the victim finds out the following day that he was threatened in class the day before, but didn't hear the defendant's words because the victim fell asleep during class. If no physical act occurred the day before and the victim did not hear the defendant utter the threat to be supposedly carried out at the end of that class, then no crime has occurred. An assault can occur without a battery if the defendant threatens bodily harm, but never actually touches the victim or carries out the threat.

You Be the Judge

Ronald is 16 years old and has been evaluated at school as learning disabled, reading at the sixth grade level. On Halloween night, while out trick-or-treating, Ronald knocks on the door of Hortense, an elderly woman, demanding candy. Hortense apologizes for not having any Halloween treats, as she is unable to get to a grocery store on her own, and relies on neighbors to bring her meals. Ronald becomes angry at leaving her house empty-handed and vows to get even. The next night, Ronald returns to her house late in the evening, takes a large gnome from her garden and hurls it through the living room window. The window shatters, and Hortense is struck in the eye with flying glass, causing blindness in her right eye. What are possible criminal charges against Ronald and the likely result? (Use the criminal code in your state to answer this question.)

battery
The actual intentional touching of someone with intent to cause harm, no matter how slight the harm.

Battery is the intentional voluntary action of the defendant that results in an unwanted touching. The body of the defendant need not directly touch the plaintiff, as long as it is the defendant's intentional act that causes the unwanted touching. For example, it is sufficient to prove a battery if the shopping cart pushed by Laura strikes the back of Richard's legs, if the intent to cause this unlawful touching (the mens rea) can be proven. Since the cart strikes Richard from behind, it is unlikely that Laura can be convicted of assault, since Richard would not have had any apprehension or fear of an unwanted touching; if Richard is in front of Laura and no words were spoken prior to the offensive touching—the ramming of the cart into his legs—then he had no threat or fear prior to the unwanted contact.

It is also a battery even if the unwanted touching does not in fact hurt or involve any physical violence. If the defendant knows that the victim does not like to be patted on the shoulder, but the defendant persists in doing so, this may constitute a battery, even though no actual physical bodily injury is suffered. However, the normal touching that inevitably and inadvertently occurs as the result of walking through crowded places does not give rise to battery, as the unwanted touching is to be expected from such circumstances found in normal life. In other words, overly sensitive people may not routinely demand that battery charges be brought if such unwanted touching is unintentional or the result of unavoidable circumstances, such as during the airport screening process where people must occasionally submit to pat-down searches before a flight.

The victim need not be aware of the touching at the time it occurred in order to have battery charges brought against the defendant. Assume three roommates share an apartment, and one roommate, Ben, kisses Mary on the cheek while she is sleeping, and this act is observed by the third roommate, Hubert. It is sufficient to bring a battery charge if the victim, Mary, learns about this unwanted touching from Hubert on the following day, as even the slightest touching, if unwanted, is enough.

Other nonfatal offenses against a person may include various sexual offenses, such as rape. These elements of these offenses, like those previously described, are specifically set forth in each state's criminal statutes. Note that this specific area of criminal law as contained in the Model Penal Code necessitates a modern interpretation, in light of today's society. For example, some state codes have adopted gender-neutral language when defining sexual offenses, and other common law approaches to sexual offenses, such as marital rape, have been updated in certain state codes. Therefore, again you are urged to consult your respective jurisdiction's criminal statutes with respect to defining sexual offenses.

CRIMES AGAINST PROPERTY

The most common types of crimes committed against property are robbery, burglary, and larceny, sometimes combined in states as the crime of theft.

burglary
Breaking and entering into a structure for the purpose of committing a crime.

Common law **burglary** is defined as the breaking and entering of the dwelling of another at night with the intent to commit a felony therein. However, statutes have expanded this definition to include any unauthorized entry into the dwelling of another, regardless of the time of day, and irrespective of whether the door is locked or not. Whether the crime of burglary has occurred is dependent upon first, whether the accused is a trespasser, or even goes beyond the permission granted to be in the building, thus going from being a guest to being a trespasser. Secondly, it depends on whether the person entered the building with the intent to steal or commit bodily

Supreme Court of Washington,
En Banc.
STATE of Washington, Respondent,
v.
Antonio B. CANTU, Petitioner.
No. 76198-1.
Argued Oct. 25, 2005.
Decided April 20, 2006.

CHAMBERS, J.

[1] ¶ 1 Seventeen-year-old Antonio B. Cantu was convicted of residential burglary following allegations he entered his mother's home, broke into her dead bolt-locked bedroom door, and took some of her possessions. We are again asked to interpret a statute that could be construed to impermissibly shift the burden of persuasion to the accused and relieve the State of its obligation to prove each element of the crime. [FN1]

¶ 2 We held in *State v. Deal,* 128 Wash.2d 693, 699-700, 911 P.2d 996 (1996) (citing *State v. Brunson,* 128 Wash.2d 98, 107, 905 P.2d 346 (1995)), that, under certain circumstances, RCW 9A.52.040 creates a permissive, rather than a mandatory, presumption of criminal intent. A permissive presumption permits but does not require an inference of criminal intent, while a mandatory presumption mandates such inference unless it is rebutted. Permissive presumptions do not necessarily deprive the State of its obligation to prove every element of the crime, and thus the statute is not facially invalid. However, in this case we cannot say that the State bore the burden of proving every element of the crime charged. The record suggests that the court improperly applied a mandatory presumption of criminal intent. We also hold that a child's privilege to enter the family home, or any portion inside, may be expressly or impliedly limited. We reverse, vacate the conviction, and remand for proceedings consistent with this opinion.

I
FACTS

¶ 3 Cantu's mother, Noyola Moncada, lives in Moses Lake with her boyfriend and daughter, Sophia. One morning in February 2003, Corporal Steven Miers of the Moses Lake Police Department responded to a call from the home. Sophia told Miers that Cantu had just left after breaking into their mother's bedroom by kicking in the dead bolt-locked door. Miers saw damage to the bedroom door consistent with Sophia's account. Sophia also reported to Miers that Cantu had taken items, including his own alarm clock, out of their mother's bedroom. [FN2] Shortly afterward, Moncada came home and told Miers that money, beer, and pain pills had been taken from her bedroom. Moncada testified that at the time of the incident, Cantu was not living with her, did not have her permission to enter her bedroom, and that the missing beer, money, and pills were returned by Moncada's nephew later that same day. [FN3]

¶ 4 Cantu testified that he went to his mother's home on February 6, 2003, to pick up some clothes. Cantu explained that while he was inside the house and playing with his dogs, he ran into his mother's bedroom door and accidentally broke the door. Cantu asserted he entered his mother's bedroom only to shut the door and did not remove anything.

¶ 5 Cantu was charged by information with one count each of residential burglary, theft in the third degree, minor in possession of alcohol, and possession of a legend drug. The court found Cantu guilty of residential burglary, but found insufficient evidence existed as to the other three counts. The Court of Appeals affirmed. *State v. Cantu,* 123 Wash.App. 404, 98 P.3d 106 (2004). Cantu's petition to this court for review was granted. [FN4] 154 Wash.2d 1002, 113 P.3d 481 (2005).

II
UNLAWFUL ENTRY

¶ 6 First, we must decide whether a license to enter a dwelling may be impliedly limited. This is a question of law reviewed de novo. *State v. Hanson,* 151 Wash.2d 783, 784, 91 P.3d 888 (2004). Cantu argues that implied limitations are not enough; that his mother did not expressly prohibit him from entering her bedroom, and that the dead bolt-locked door did not give him sufficient notice. . . . The State argues that express limits are not required and that the locked dead bolt was sufficient. We agree with the State.

¶ 7 As part of its proof of residential burglary, the State bore the burden of showing that Cantu entered and remained unlawfully in Moncada's home with the intent to commit a crime against a person or property. RCW 9A.52.025(1). A person "enters or remains unlawfully" when he is not licensed, invited, or otherwise privileged to enter or remain on the premises. RCW 9A.52.010(3).

[2][3] ¶ 8 A juvenile is presumed to have a license to enter his parents' home. *Steinbach,* 101 Wash.2d at 462-63, 679 P.2d 369. Because Cantu was 17 years old at the time, we will presume he had a license to enter Moncada's home. However, even though Cantu may have had a license to be in the home, an unprivileged entry into a locked room may still constitute unlawful entry for purposes of burglary. *Crist,* 80 Wash.App. at 514-15, 909 P.2d 1341; *see generally State v. Collins,* 110 Wash.2d 253, 751 P.2d 837 (1988).

¶ 9 In *Crist,* Division Two of the Court of Appeals found a juvenile unlawfully entered his father's locked room when the juvenile had a license to enter certain parts of the home but was expressly told that he was not to enter his father's room. *Crist,* 80 Wash. App. at 513-16, 909 P.2d 1341. In *Jensen,* Division One of the

Court of Appeals found that there was substantial evidence to support the trial court's finding that a juvenile did not have permission to enter his parents' home in their absence when his parents "'made it very clear that they did not want him in the home unattended.'" *Jensen,* 57 Wash.App. at 506, 789 P.2d 772 (quoting finding of fact). In *Steinbach,* this court found that a juvenile's entry into her mother's home was not unlawful since neither the mother nor the alternative residential placement orders absolutely prohibited the juvenile from being in the home. *Steinbach,* 101 Wash.2d at 462-64, 679 P.2d 369.

[4] ¶ 10 While Cantu is correct that *Crist, Jensen,* and *Steinbach* all involved some sort of express limits, no Washington court has held that to find an unlawful entry, express limits on the juvenile *must* exist. The *Crist* court explained that the privilege could be limited either expressly or impliedly. *Crist,* 80 Wash.App. at 515, 909 P.2d 1341. We agree and hold that a child's license to enter the family home, or any room within, may be limited expressly or by clear implication. Since Moncada's locked bedroom door gave Cantu clear implied notice that any permission to enter the home did not extend to her bedroom, there was sufficient evidence to find an unlawful entry. We find no error.

III
MANDATORY VS. PERMISSIVE INFERENCES

[5][6] ¶ 11 Basic principles of due process require the State to prove every essential element of a crime beyond a reasonable doubt. *Deal,* 128 Wash.2d at 698, 911 P.2d 996 (quoting *State v. Hanna,* 123 Wash.2d 704, 710, 871 P.2d 135 (1994)). Thus, the State bore the burden of proving every element of burglary, including criminal intent. Cantu contends that the trial judge employed an impermissible mandatory presumption, shifting the burden of persuasion to Cantu to show lack of criminal intent. "The burden of persuasion is deemed to be shifted if the trier of fact is required to draw a certain inference upon the failure of the defendant to prove by some quantum of evidence that the inference should not be drawn." *Deal,* 128 Wash.2d at 701, 911 P.2d 996 (citing *Sandstrom v. Montana,* 442 U.S. 510, 517, 99 S.Ct. 2450, 61 L.Ed.2d 39 (1979)). Cantu maintains that the Court of Appeals impermissibly applied a mandatory presumption in this case when it held: "the defense offered no evidence to *rebut* the *statutory inference of* [criminal] *intent.*" *Cantu,* 123 Wash.App. at 410, 98 P.3d 106 (first emphasis added).

[7][8] ¶ 12 The State may use evidentiary devices, such as presumptions and inferences, to assist it in meeting its burden of proof, though they are not favored in criminal law. . . . We have previously approved the permissive inference of intent to commit a crime "whenever the evidence shows a person enters or remains unlawfully in a building.". . . The permissible inference of criminal intent is found in RCW 9A.52.040.

[9] ¶ 13 The statute provides that:

> In any prosecution for burglary, any person who enters or remains unlawfully in a building *may* be inferred to have acted with intent to commit a crime against a person or property therein, unless such entering or remaining shall be explained by evidence satisfactory to the trier of fact to have been made without such criminal intent.

RCW 9A.52.040 (emphasis added). Again, "when permissive inferences are only part of the State's proof supporting an element and not the 'sole and sufficient' proof of such element, due process is not offended if the prosecution shows that the inference more likely than not flows from the proven fact." *Deal,* 128 Wash.2d at 700, 911 P.2d 996 (citing *Brunson,* 128 Wash.2d at 107, 905 P.2d 346).

¶ 14 However, mandatory presumptions are more troubling. While RCW 9A.52.040 contains a constitutionally valid permissive inference, it may also be read to unconstitutionally shift the burden of persuasion to the defendant, as it did when the jury instructions included the specific statutory language, "'unless such entering or remaining shall be explained by evidence satisfactory to the jury to have been made without such criminal intent.'" *Deal,* 128 Wash.2d at 704, 911 P.2d 996; *see* RCW 9A.52.040. We held the inclusion of this language, "essentially requir[ed] the Defendant to either introduce evidence sufficient to rebut the inference that he remained on the premises with intent to commit a crime, or concede that element of the crime." *Deal,* 128 Wash.2d at 701, 911 P.2d 996; *see also* RCW 9A.52.040. "In other words, a reasonable juror could have concluded that once [the defendant's] presence on the premises was shown, a finding that he intended to commit a crime was compelled, absent a satisfactory explanation by [the defendant] as to why he was on the premises." *Deal,* 128 Wash.2d at 701, 911 P.2d 996.

[10] ¶ 15 In this case, while the record is not conclusive, it appears to us that the court applied a mandatory presumption to find Cantu's intent was criminal. We note in passing that the text of RCW 9A.52.040 is unfortunate and, as we explained in *Deal,* can be misleading. *Deal,* 128 Wash.2d at 702, 911 P.2d 996. In his own words, the trial judge seemed to have found Cantu's intent criminal on the belief that Cantu was unable to provide sufficient evidence to rebut the presumption. Statements made by the prosecutor and the judge near the close of the trial support our conclusion that the trial court improperly placed the burden on Cantu to prove his innocence—instead of the State having to prove his guilt. For instance, in discussing the statutory inference provided in RCW 9A.52.040, the prosecutor initially stated, "[RCW] 9A.52.040, and burglary is unique . . . a person [who] . . . enters or remains unlawfully in a building, and [in this case], in the bedroom, may be inferred to have acted with [criminal] intent. And then the burden actually shifts [to Cantu] to show evidence satisfactory that the entry was made without such criminal intent." Report of Proceedings (RP) at 69. Subsequently, the prosecutor corrected herself, saying, "[the] [i]nference of an intent to commit a crim[inal] act from [an] unlawful entry is not shifting the burden because the inference is permissible, not mandatory." RP at 71. However, the prosecutor continued stating, "[s]o, um, it's [a] permissible inference that the court can find that an illegal entry should have some explanation to it. And [Cantu's] explanation at this point in time is lame, Your Honor." *Id*. In addition, in the trial court's oral decision, the judge stated, "The assessment, first off [is that Cantu] broke into his mother's bedroom and he was not living there, [and] . . . did not have permission to be there and [that] he kicked . . . in and ruined the door in . . . [gaining entry to the bedroom]. I pray that the inference is *and it's not been rebutted,* nor has there been any explaining, that [Cantu] didn't go in [the bedroom] without the intent to commit a crime." RP at 73 (emphasis added). Following this statement, the trial judge found Cantu guilty of residential burglary but dismissed the theft, drug, and alcohol charges. A fair interpretation of this statement, along with the prosecutor's discussion of the statutory inference provided in RCW 9A.52.040, leads this court to conclude that the trial judge impermissibly

employed a mandatory presumption of criminal intent, making it incumbent upon Cantu to prove, with sufficient evidence, that his intent was innocent. [FN5]

¶ 16 In *Deal,* we found the error to be harmless because, even though the instruction shifted the burden to the defendant, Deal's own testimony was sufficient to prove he had the requisite criminal intent. *Deal,* 128 Wash.2d at 697, 703, 911 P.2d 996. However, unlike *Deal,* in this case there is no indication that the imposition of a mandatory presumption was harmless. It is the intent to commit a crime not the actual commission of a crime which is an element of residential burglary. *State v. Bergeron,* 105 Wash.2d 1, 15-17, 711 P.2d 1000 (1985); *see also* RCW 9A.52.025(1). Therefore the court's acquittal on the theft charge may be irrelevant. But, given that the court employed a mandatory presumption of criminal intent, we cannot conclude that the error was harmless. [FN6]

IV
SUMMARY AND CONCLUSION

[11] ¶ 17 The permissive inference provided in RCW 9A.52.040 permits the trier of fact to reject the inferred conclusion of criminal intent *regardless* of whether the defendant provides an innocent explanation of the unlawful entry or not. *Deal,* 128 Wash.2d at 702-03, 911 P.2d 996. That is appropriate. Due process requires the State to bear the "'burden of persuasion beyond a reasonable doubt of every essential element of a crime.'" *Deal,* 128 Wash.2d at 698, 911 P.2d 996 (quoting *Hanna,* 123 Wash.2d at 710, 871 P.2d 135). A fair reading of the record leads us to conclude that the trial judge relieved the State of this burden by creating a mandatory presumption of criminal intent which Cantu was required to rebut. We therefore reverse the Court of Appeals, vacate the conviction, and remand for further proceedings consistent with this opinion.

Concurring: ALEXANDER, C.J., C. JOHNSON, SANDERS, BRIDGE, OWENS and FAIRHURST, JJ.

MADSEN, J., concurs in result only.

J.M. JOHNSON, J. (dissenting).

¶ 18 Antonio B. Cantu entered his mother's home and went to her locked bedroom. He broke the dead bolt lock to the bedroom door by kicking in the door. Cantu took some possessions from within the bedroom and immediately fled the scene. He was convicted in a bench trial for residential burglary. Cantu was found guilty in part because the trial judge found unpersuasive Cantu's defense that he had broken the dead bolt lock by accidentally bumping against the lock while playing with dogs.

¶ 19 In drawing the permissible inference that the facts surrounding Cantu's unlawful entry into his mother's bedroom demonstrated intent to commit a crime, the trial court arrived at a reasonable, common sense judgment. Unfortunately, the majority's decision today reverses the Court of Appeals and vacates Cantu's conviction. I dissent.

¶ 20 I concur in the majority's holding that "a child's license to enter the family home, or any room within, may be limited expressly or by clear implication." Majority at ----. Further, I agree with the majority's conclusion that his mother's locked bedroom door "gave Cantu clear implied notice that any permission to enter the home did not extend to her bedroom," thereby providing "sufficient evidence to find an unlawful entry." *Id.* However, I disagree with the majority's conclusion that the trial judge employed an "impermissible mandatory presumption" that shifted the burden of proof requiring Cantu to show lack of criminal intent. *See id.* I would hold that the trial judge permissibly found beyond a reasonable doubt that Cantu committed residential burglary since the trial judge made a permissible inference under that the facts and circumstances of this case that Cantu intended to commit a crime.

STANDARD OF REVIEW

¶ 21 The standard of review for a sufficiency of the evidence claim is whether, after viewing evidence in the light most favorable to the State, any rational trier of fact could have found essential elements of crime beyond a reasonable doubt. . . . Put another way, credibility determinations are for the trier of fact and are not subject to review. *State v. Camarillo,* 115 Wash.2d 60, 71, 794 P.2d 850 (1990); *Jackson,* 129 Wash.App. at 109, 117 P.3d 1182.

***6** ¶ 22 However, a defendant is innocent until proven guilty by the State. Thus, a burden of persuasion wrongly placed upon a defendant implicates constitutional rights of due process of law under the fourteenth amendment to the United States Constitution. . . .

ANALYSIS

¶ 23 Due process requires the State bear the burden of persuasion beyond a reasonable doubt for every essential element of a crime. *Deal,* 128 Wash.2d at 698, 911 P.2d 996; *Hanna,* 123 Wash.2d at 710, 871 P.2d 135. The State may use evidentiary devices, such as presumptions and inferences, to assist it in meeting its burden of proof. *Deal,* 128 Wash.2d at 699, 911 P.2d 996; *Hanna,* 123 Wash.2d at 710, 871 P.2d 135.

¶ 24 The majority wrongly attributes to *Hanna* and to a United States Supreme Court case a disfavor toward presumptions and inferences. In its opinion, the majority writes that "they are not favored in criminal law," majority at ---- (citing *Hanna,* 123 Wash.2d at 710, 871 P.2d 135; and *Sandstrom v. Montana,* 442 U.S. 510, 523-24, 99 S.Ct. 2450, 61 L.Ed.2d 39 (1979)). But the pinpoint cite for *Hanna* simply states: "The State may, however, use evidentiary devices, such as inferences and presumptions, to assist in meeting its burden of proof." *Hanna,* 123 Wash.2d at 710, 871 P.2d 135. *Hanna* does *not* say that presumptions or inferences are disfavored in criminal law. Nor does *Sandstrom*. Both cases stand for the proposition that *mandatory* inferences (or conclusive presumptions) are not favored in criminal law. [FN1]

¶ 25 The State adopts a permissive inference of intent to commit the crime of burglary in RCW 9A.52.040:

> In any prosecution for burglary, any person who enters or remains unlawfully in a building *may* be inferred to have acted with intent to commit a crime against a person or property therein, unless such entering or remaining shall be explained by evidence *satisfactory to the trier of fact* to have been made without such criminal intent.

(Emphasis added.) We have approved the permissive inference of intent to commit a crime "whenever the evidence shows a person enters or remains unlawfully in a building. . . . When permissive inferences are only part of the State's proof supporting an element and not the "sole and sufficient" proof of such element, due process is not offended if the prosecution shows that the inference more likely than not flows from the proven fact. *Deal,* 128 Wash.2d at 700, 911 P.2d 996 (citing *Brunson,* 128 Wash.2d at 107, 905 P.2d 346).

***7** ¶ 26 Here, the record sufficiently supports the trial judge's decision. The trial judge made a permissible inference from Cantu's unlawful entry into his mother's locked bedroom by breaking the door and lock that he intended to commit a crime and did not find Cantu's explanation for his entry into his mother's bedroom to be satisfactory.

¶ 27 The facts and circumstances in the record bolster the trial judge's drawing of the permissible inference that Cantu acted with the intent to commit a crime. The trial judge concluded that Cantu did not have permission to be in his mother's bedroom and that Cantu broke into the bedroom by kicking in the door and ruining it. Report of Proceedings (RP) (July 9, 2003) at 73. The trial judge also noted Cantu's defense that he did not enter the bedroom with intent to commit a crime, claiming that the door was accidentally broken in the course of playing with dogs and that only his possessions were removed.

¶ 28 The trial judge held that he did not believe this defense to be credible. The dogs were not seen by a witness. Items were missing from the bedroom which belonged to Cantu's mother, and Cantu was the only suspect. Cantu also fled the home immediately after he broke into the bedroom. Later, Cantu returned to his mother money that she was missing from the bedroom.

¶ 29 Statements in the record cited by the majority do not demonstrate the trial judge employed any mandatory inference (or shifted the burden to require defendant to disprove an element of the crime). Admitting "the record is not conclusive," majority at ----, the majority asserts that "it appears to us that the court applied a mandatory presumption to find Cantu's intent was criminal." *Id.* The majority cites two statements made by the prosecutor and one statement made by the judge near the close of the trial in support of its contention that "the trial court improperly placed the burden on Cantu to prove his innocence." Majority at ---- - ----.

¶ 30 Discussing RCW 9A.52.040's statutorily permissive inference, the prosecutor stated that "a person [who] . . . enters or remains unlawfully in a building, and [in this case], in the bedroom, *may* be inferred to have acted with [criminal] intent. And then the burden actually shifts [to Cantu] . . . to show evidence satisfactory that the entry was made without such criminal intent." RP at 69 (emphasis added). This statement is itself ambiguous as to whether an inference of criminal intent is permissible or mandatory. The prosecutor stated that such intent "may" be inferred. The prosecutor's subsequent sentence can be read as describing what happens when the permissible inference is actually engaged. *See* RP at 69.

¶ 31 However, the record shows the prosecutor more clearly relating the law moments later. Stating she "misspoke," the prosecutor said "the inference is permissible, not mandatory." She reiterated that "its permissible inference that the court can find that the illegal entry should have some explanation to it." RP at 71.

***8** ¶ 32 Furthermore, to read the trial judge's statement cited by the majority as demonstration that the inference applied was mandatory is a jump to conclusion. More likely, the trial judge simply exercised his discretion and found such an inference. *See* RP at 73. Cantu entered not just into a house where he was no longer a resident, but kicked through a locked door, and entered the room without permission.

¶ 33 The standard of review requires we defer to the trier of fact for purposes of resolving conflicting testimony and evaluating the persuasiveness of the evidence. *Jackson,* 129 Wash.App. at 109, 117 P.3d 1182; *Walton,* 64 Wash.App. at 415–16, 824 P.2d 533. If the trial judge had applied a *mandatory* inference in deciding the case below, his decision would be reversible as a violation of due process. But the trial judge's ruling shows that he understood that the inference was related to the element of intent. In fact the trial judge dismissed charges against Cantu that required proof of commission but found against Cantu on the charge that required only proof of intent. *See* RP at 72.

¶ 34 Judges are presumed to know and apply the law, just as there is a presumption that a trial judge knows the rules of evidence. . . . There is a presumption that a trial judge properly discharges official duties without bias or prejudice . . . Absent a strong showing that the trial judge misunderstood and misapplied the law or that substantial evidence shows that the inference of intent cannot be supported, his ruling on the element of criminal intent should be respected.

CONCLUSION

¶ 35 Here, there is no record showing that the judge misunderstood or improperly applied the law. The decision of the trial judge rested upon a permissible inference of intent, is supported by substantial evidence, and should therefore be affirmed.

¶ 36 Therefore, I dissent.

. . .

FN2. Sophia partially recanted on the stand.

FN3. It is unclear from the record how Moncada's nephew came into possession of the items taken from her bedroom. In addition, Sophia testified that it was Cantu who had returned the missing money to Moncada after the incident.

FN4. While it was not raised as an issue for review, the record does not appear to contain the juvenile court's written findings of fact in support of its judgment on appeal. "The prosecution must submit," and the juvenile court must enter, written findings of fact when a juvenile appeals. JuCR 7.11(d).

FN5. We recognize that this case is not factually on all fours with Deal. However, the underlying principle of Deal and its antecedents is that mandatory presumptions are not favored. See Deal, 128 Wash.2d at 702, 911 P.2d 996 (citing State v. Johnson, 100 Wash.2d 607, 617-20, 674 P.2d 145 (1983) overruled on other grounds by State v. Bergeron, 105 Wash.2d 1, 4, 711 P.2d 1000 (1985)). Since it appears that such mandatory presumption was in fact employed here, that principle applies.

FN6. At the close of the bench trial, the trial judge stated to both counsel, in an apparent inquiry concerning the elements necessary to prove residential burglary, "Do you think I need to actually find that something was stolen from within the bedroom, or do you think that I need to, or do I have to find . . . that there had to be an intent to steal something from the bedroom?" RP at 69.

FN1. The majority strikes at fact finders' ability to reason. Inferences draw their power from their ability to better explain facts and phenomena than other explanations. Triers of fact routinely make inferences in finding or not finding elements of crimes proved beyond a reasonable doubt. This is especially so with criminal intent, which is a state of mind. As discussed below, we allow permissive inferences of intent to burglarize to be drawn. In such cases, intent constitutes an inference to the best explanation in light of the particular facts and our common-sense experience with unlawful entry and burglary.

Source: *State v. Cantu,* 2006 WL 1060827 (Wash.) (St. Paul, MN: Thomson West). Reprinted with permission from Westlaw.

harm upon another person in the building. There must be the requisite mens rea for theft or the infliction of bodily harm upon another person. The intention at the time of entry into the building is relevant to proving this crime. If it can be determined that the defendant actually committed one of the two offenses constituting burglary, intent can be proven by the defendant's actions.

robbery
The direct taking of property from another through force or threat.

Common law **robbery** is defined as the taking of personal property from another by the use of fear or force. The actual theft, or stealing of the property, and the force used must be related, and not two separate, distinct incidents. It is sufficient that the defendant uses even just minimal force, as in bumping into a victim on a crowded subway in order to pick the victim's pocket. This is still robbery. However, if the pickpocket does not use any force whatsoever, but merely removes the wallet from a purse or the victim's pocket, this is not robbery.

Likewise, it is robbery if the defendant threatens a convenience store cashier with a hand in her coat pocket, pretending to have a gun, so long as the cashier is compelled to surrender all the cash in the register based on the reasonable fear that force may be used. It is irrelevant that no force is actually used, or even that the defendant has no weapon, so long as the fear is reasonable and therefore a theft occurs.

larceny
The common law crime of taking property of another without permission.

Common law **larceny** is the wrongful taking of another's property, but neither force nor unlawful entry has occurred. Examples of larceny include removing the car stereo from a car parked in the garage of a shopping mall, or changing the price tags on clothing at a department store and paying the incorrect price for the items. In each case, the incident involves taking the property of another wrongfully or fraudulently with the intent to deprive the owner of his rights to that property.

As noted earlier, burglary, larceny, and robbery have occasionally been combined into the general category of theft in certain statutes. The level of the crime is distinguished primarily based on the value of the goods taken. There are other crimes involving property that will not be discussed here, including arson and handling stolen goods.

INCHOATE OFFENSES

inchoate offenses
Uncompleted crimes.

Certain crimes may be attempted, but for one reason or another, are not completed. Such crimes are called **inchoate offenses.** These are defined as crimes that are incomplete, that involve encouraging others to participate, and that are attempted but are not finished. Under traditional common law definitions, these offenses are those that are committed in preparation of the undertaking of a more serious crime.

solicitation
The crime of inducing or encouraging another to commit a crime.

Solicitation to commit a felony or unlawful act is one kind of inchoate offense. Solicitation is the advising, urging, or inducing another person to commit a felony. The solicitor intends for the other person to actually carry out the felony crime, and as such, the solicitor can be charged with the offense of solicitation even if the other person does not even act or agree to do what is commanded. If the other person should actually go through with the commission of the felony, the solicitor is accountable for the crime as if she had done it herself. Similarly, if the other person has only *attempted* to commit the felony, but failed, the solicitor is charged with attempt, just as the other person would be.

In the same respect, a person may be criminally responsible for a crime committed by someone else if such person intentionally aids, abets, advises, hires, counsels, or procures another person to commit the crime. To establish guilt on the basis of aiding and abetting, it must be shown that the person knowingly associated with the unlawful venture and participated to the extent that he facilitated the venture's success.

conspiracy
By agreement, parties work together to create an illegal result, to achieve an unlawful end.

In considering the offense of **conspiracy**, the prosecution must examine the level of participation of those persons who have entered into an agreement to commit a crime, and whether any or all of those persons have taken substantial steps to fulfill their plan. A conspiracy necessarily involves the plan of at least two people to commit a crime. This goal of committing the crime is a separate crime from the actual crime intended. In order to be found guilty of conspiracy to commit burglary, for example, the defendants must be shown to have intended to agree to burglarize a specific building and actually have the ability to carry out the plan. Assume that Kane, Able, and Sarah are driving to the convenience store, and Sarah believes that their discussion of a possible robbery of the Quikserve store cashier is just a joke. Sarah may not be liable for conspiracy if she does not agree to any plans because she thinks it is a joke, does not take some overt act to attempt the crime, and falls asleep in the back seat of the car en route to the store.

CASE IN POINT

Supreme Court of Kansas.
STATE of Kansas, Appellee,
v.
Marshall J. GREEN, a/k/a Marshall J. Green, Jr., Appellant.
No. 90,912.
Feb. 3, 2006.

The opinion of the court was delivered by LOCKETT, J.:

The State appeals the Court of Appeals' reversal of Green's conviction for voluntary manslaughter based on the majority of the panel's conclusion that the evidence was insufficient to support Green's conviction for voluntary manslaughter as an aider and abetter.

In the early morning hours of June 29, 2002, O.T. Ruffin died after a fight in the parking lot of Harry and Ollie's bar in Wichita. The events leading up to O.T.'s death began when O.T. bumped into Green's sister, Latrina Green, on the bar's dance floor. Latrina was upset and started arguing with O.T. Latrina's boyfriend, Derrick Henderson, became involved and commenced arguing with O.T. O.T.'s brother, Patrick, stepped in front of O.T., told Henderson that they were not looking for trouble, and attempted to calm Henderson. Henderson would not calm down. A group of Henderson's friends began crowding behind Henderson. Latrina's brother, Marshall Green, was one of the individuals that joined Henderson.

O.T. and Patrick were each about 5 feet, 6 inches or 5 feet, 7 inches tall and weighed 170 to 180 pounds. Patrick estimated Henderson's height at approximately 6 feet, 3 inches and his weight at about 220 to 230 pounds. Concerned about Henderson's relative size and afraid that the group was going to jump them, Patrick stated to O.T. that it was time to leave. Patrick then grabbed the front of O.T.'s shirt and commenced pushing O.T. backwards through the bar toward the door. Patrick kept himself between Henderson and O.T. The crowd led by Henderson and Green followed O.T. and Patrick to the bar's front door. When Patrick and O.T. reached the front door of the bar, O.T. stated to the crowd, "I don't want to fight you all."

Green, using both of his fists, responded to O.T.'s statement by shoving O.T. out the door. After being shoved outside the door and into the parking lot, O.T. and Patrick started running towards Patrick's car. Henderson went after O.T., and Green pursued Patrick. A few seconds later, Patrick stopped and looked back. Patrick observed O.T. lying on the ground in the parking lot and several people kicking and stomping on his brother. Patrick testified that when he attempted to go back to help his brother, Green swung at him and prevented him from helping O.T.

A few minutes after Green pushed O.T. outside, a police officer arrived. The officer had been across the street on a domestic violence call and heard neighbors shouting that there was a fight in the bar's parking lot. The officer observed Henderson jumping up and down on O.T.'s back. Green's sisters became aware of the officer and attempted to pull Henderson off of O.T. Henderson then stepped off O.T. and kicked him one last time before backing away. Green and his girlfriend immediately ran to Green's car and left. The officer arrested Henderson, both of Green's sisters, and others. O.T. was rushed to the hospital. Before surgery could be performed, O.T. died from a lack of oxygen to his brain caused by blunt force trauma to his head and chest.

Green spent the rest of the night with his girlfriend. Green dropped her off at her house about 8 a.m. Officers attempted to contact Green at his last known address at approximately 10 a.m., but could not find him. Green missed an appointment with his parole officer on July 1, 2002, and did not contact his parole officer after that date. Neither Green's sister nor his girlfriend saw Green until after Green was arrested in Los Angeles on December 2, 2002.

After Green was returned to Kansas, he was formally charged with and tried for the second-degree murder of O.T. It is important to note that a jury convicted Green of the lesser included offense of voluntary manslaughter. Green appealed to the Kansas Court of Appeals, arguing that the evidence was insufficient to support his conviction. The Kansas Court of Appeals reversed his conviction. *State v. Green,* No. 90,912, 2004 WL 2848615, unpublished opinion dated December 10, 2004. This court granted the State's petition for review of the Court of Appeals' decision.

WAS THE EVIDENCE SUFFICIENT TO SUPPORT A CONVICTION FOR VOLUNTARY MANSLAUGHTER AS AN AIDER AND ABETTER?

[1] The State argued to the Court of Appeals that, based on his participation in the death of O.T. Ruffin, the evidence was sufficient to support Green's conviction for voluntary manslaughter. A majority of the Court of Appeals reversed Green's conviction, concluding that, because he was chasing Patrick, Green was not personally involved in the attack on O.T. The majority of the Court of Appeals further concluded that O.T.'s death was not a reasonably foreseeable consequence of a "bar fight, without weapons or premeditated planning of purposeful life-threatening activity." *Green,* Slip op. at 14.

[2][3][4][5] When the sufficie ncy of the evidence is challenged in a criminal case, the standard of review is whether, after review of all the evidence, viewed in the light most favorable to the prosecution, the appellate court is convinced that a rational factfinder could have found the defendant guilty beyond a reasonable doubt. *State v. Calvin,* 279 Kan. 193, 198, 105 P.3d 710 (2005).

. . .

K.S.A. 21-3205 provides:

> (1) A person is criminally responsible for a crime committed by another if such person intentionally aids, abets, advises, hires, counsels or procures the other to commit the crime.
>
> (2) A person liable under subsection (1) hereof is also liable for any other crime committed in pursuance

of the intended crime if reasonably foreseeable by such person as a probable consequence of committing or attempting to commit the crime intended.

(3) A person liable under this section may be charged with and convicted of the crime although the person alleged to have directly committed the act constituting the crime lacked criminal or legal capacity or has not been convicted or has been acquitted or has been convicted of some other degree of the crime or of some other crime based on the same act.

[6] To establish guilt on the basis of aiding and abetting, the State was required to show that Green knowingly associated with the unlawful venture and participated in such a way as to indicate that he was facilitating the success of the venture. Without other incriminating evidence, mere presence in the vicinity of the crime or mere association with the principals that committed the crime is not sufficient to establish guilt as an aider and abettor. *State v. Bryant,* 276 Kan. 485, 493, 78 P.3d 462 (2003).

Here, the unlawful venture was the beating that resulted in O.T.'s death. Green asserts that he cannot be convicted as Henderson's aider and abettor simply because he was in the vicinity of the beating and associated with Henderson, who actually beat O.T. Green argues that there is no evidence that he participated in beating O.T. or encouraged Henderson to beat O.T.

A majority of the Court of Appeals accepted Green's argument, concluding that Green was involved in "a bar fight with Patrick, not a sustained attack on O.T." *Green,* slip op. at 14. However, this conclusion overlooks the applicable standard of review, which requires an appellate court to review the evidence in the light most favorable to the State. See *Calvin,* 279 Kan. at 198, 105 P.3d 710.

. . .

Viewing the evidence in a light most favorable to the State, there is evidence that Green facilitated the success of the criminal venture in two ways. First, Green initiated the attack on O.T. by pushing O.T. out of the bar and into the parking lot where the beating occurred. Patrick testified that Green pushed O.T. out the door into the parking lot with his fists after both O.T. and Patrick told Henderson, Green, and their other companions that they did not want a fight. Green was the first person to physically contact O.T. Based on that evidence, it was reasonable for the jury to infer that Green's physical contact encouraged or incited others in the crowd to batter O.T. Second, Green also facilitated O.T.'s beating by preventing Patrick from coming to O.T.'s aid. Green admitted to chasing Patrick. Patrick testified that Green pursued him, swung at him, and prevented him from returning to help his brother. The Court of Appeals' majority concluded that the evidence did not link Green with O.T.'s beating is in error.

We note that the New Mexico Supreme Court also applied an aiding and abetting theory to a person who prevents another from giving aid. In *State v. Ochoa,* 41 N.M. 589, 72 P.2d 609 (1937), two defendants, Ochoa and Avitia, were convicted of second-degree murder as aiders and abettors to the shooting death of the local sheriff. Ochoa and Avitia were part of a mob that was attempting to free a prisoner from the sheriff. 41 N.M. at 595, 72 P.2d 609. The sheriff was returning the prisoner to the jail following a court proceeding. The jail was down the alleyway from the courthouse. A mob of people formed in the alley to prevent the sheriff's passage with the prisoner. 41 N.M. at 593–94, 72 P.2d 609. When Sheriff's Deputy Boggess threw a tear gas bomb into the crowd, shooting broke out. 41 N.M. at 594, 72 P.2d 609. Ochoa hit another deputy with a hammer. 41 N.M. at 595, 72 P.2d 609. Ochoa and Avitia then beat and kicked Deputy Boggess. While Deputy Boggess was on the ground, the sheriff was mortally wounded by gunfire. 41 N.M. at 596, 72 P.2d 609. The jury found that Ochoa's and Avitia's actions prevented the sheriff's deputy from coming to the sheriff's aid. The *Ochoa* court upheld defendants' convictions for aiding and abetting. 41 N.M. at 599, 601–02, 72 P.2d 609.

The principle in *Ochoa* applies to this case. Green prevented Patrick from coming to O.T.'s aid. When that evidence is viewed in a light most favorable to the State, there is sufficient evidence to support Green's conviction for voluntary manslaughter based on an aiding and abetting theory.

[10] For his second claim, Green argues that O.T.'s death was not a reasonably foreseeable consequence of simple battery. This argument assumes that bar fights are limited to simple battery. The Court of Appeaaccepted this argument, concluding that a bar fight is not inherently dangerous. According to the majority of the Court of Appeals, a bar fight without "weapons or premeditated planning of purposeful life-threatening activity" is not per se inherently dangerous. *Green,* slip op. at 14. In reaching this conclusion, the majority of the *Green* court observed that, "[c]onsidering the number of fatal bar brawls which occur annually in this country, it is curious that none is cited by either party as support for their position and none have yet to be found by the court to help resolve this issue." *Green,* slip op. at 12.

These statements demonstrate the focus of the majority of the Court of Appeals on a "bar brawl," and implies there must be an agreement by both sides to participate in a fight. This focus does not consider the fact that the Ruffin brothers clearly did not want to participate in a fight. Both O.T. and Patrick made their lack of agreement clear by stating that they did not want to fight or become involved in a bar brawl. In addition, there is no evidence that O.T. threw a punch. The majority's focus on a "bar brawl" does not consider O.T.'s status as a victim rather than a participant. O.T. was kicked and stomped on the head by several individuals while he was lying face down in the bar's parking lot. Neither O.T. nor Patrick attempted to fight. Rather, both chose to flee.

The majority agreed with the State that Green was participating in a "venture," *i.e.,* the crowd action against O.T. and Patrick. *Green,* slip op. at 12. Without stating which specific crime or crimes, the majority concluded, "[W]ere Green charged with mob action or general violent behavior, he would undoubtedly be guilty." *Green,* slip op at 12–13.

In his dissent, Judge Malone agreed with the majority that Green was not responsible for O.T. Ruffin's death just because Green was involved in the melee. However, he noted, there were two concrete facts in evidence supporting the prosecution's claim that Green's actions aided Derrek Henderson in the beating death of O.T. "First, Green pushed O.T. out the tavern door into the parking lot at a time when O.T. was telling the crowd he did not want to fight. Second, Green prevented Patrick Ruffin from helping his brother by swinging his fists at Patrick in the parking lot." *Green,* slip op. at D-1. Judge Malone observed that this evidence supported the prosecution's claim that Green intentionally aided Henderson in O.T.'s beating. He noted that Green may not have intended for O.T.'s death to result, but this was a reasonably foreseeable consequence of his actions. Judge

Malone concluded the evidence against Green as an aider and abettor was legally sufficient for his culpability in the criminal act to become a jury question and the judge would have affirmed Green's conviction of voluntary manslaughter.

The *Green* court's general conclusion that bar fights are not inherently dangerous accepts Green's assumption that bar fights only involve simple battery. Besides this oversimplification of the nature of bar fights, Green's argument to this court presumes that conclusion without considering the facts of each case. It is important to note that Kansas law does not support that presumption.

[11] K.S.A.2004 Supp. 21-3436(b)(6) states that aggravated battery, as defined in K.S.A. 21-3414(a)(1), is an inherently dangerous felony. K.S.A. 21-3414(a)(1) includes any intentional conduct that causes great bodily harm, disfigurement, or death. Kansas courts have defined "great bodily harm" as more than slight, trivial, minor, or moderate harm, and does not include mere bruising, which is likely to be sustained by simple battery. *State v. Moore,* 271 Kan. 416, 419, 23 P.3d 815 (2001). Except for a few specific injuries that have been declared to be great bodily harm as a matter of law, the question of whether an injury constitutes great bodily harm is a question of fact for the jury to decide. 271 Kan. at 419-20, 23 P.3d 815 (referring to gunshot wounds, rape, and sodomy). Thus, if a bar fight involves intentional great bodily harm, it is, by definition, an aggravated battery which is an inherently dangerous felony.

The Court of Appeals' broad statement that bar fights are not inherently dangerous is not supported by Kansas law. Depending on the degree of harm involved, there are instances similar to our case, where a bar fight was found to be inherently dangerous. See, *e.g., State v. Maxfield,* 30 Kan.App.2d 873, 875-76, 54 P.3d 500 *rev. denied* 273 Kan. 1038 (2001) (demonstrating that a defendant may aid and abet a death during a bar fight). The dangerousness of the bar fight is determined by the facts of each case. We therefore conclude it is reasonably foreseeable that any level of harm, ranging from a simple battery to death, can result from a bar fight.

[12][13] Thus, the facts of each case are evaluated to determine whether a bar fight results in great bodily harm. Because that factual determination is within the province of the jury, an appellate court is limited to reviewing the record for evidence to support the jury's decision. *Boone,* 277 Kan. at 218, 83 P.3d 195. Consequently, an appellate court cannot conclude, as a matter of law, that all bar fights involve only simple battery and are not inherently dangerous.

Though not cited by the parties or the Court of Appeals, a prior Kansas Court of Appeals decision supports the State's proposition that bar fights without weapons or preplanning that cause death will support a conviction for voluntary manslaughter. See, *e.g., Maxfield,* 30 Kan.App.2d 873, 54 P.3d 500, (victim died after being chased, falling to the ground, and being hit and kicked in the head and chest by several men in the parking lot of a bar); see also *State v. Jackson,* 258 Neb. 24, 601 N.W.2d 741 (1999) (victim was killed during a fist fight; Jackson's conviction for manslaughter was upheld even though his friend fought and killed the decedent).

Henderson was jumping up and down on O.T.'s back using his full force. The jumping on and kicking of the victim's head lasted approximately 1 minute. Within that short amount of time, O.T.'s death was assured. O.T. suffered more than slight, trivial, minor, or moderate harm. This beating was not a simple battery, and it invalidated the very basis of Green's argument. Here, the evidence supports the jury's conclusion that O.T.'s death during a bar fight was the reasonably foreseeable consequence of an inherently dangerous felony-aggravated battery. Under the circumstances, the majority of the Court of Appeals erred by concluding that a bar fight is not per se inherently dangerous and O.T.'s death was not a reasonably foreseeable consequence of a bar fight.

The evidence, when viewed in a light most favorable to the State, also supports the State's argument that Green recognized the culpability of his actions regarding O.T.'s death. When the police arrived at the bar, Green immediately ran to his car and left. He did not check on his sisters or Henderson. Green did not simply flee the bar parking lot. After spending the night with his girlfriend, Green left Kansas. Officers began looking for Green at his last known addresses as early as 10 a.m. on the day of O.T.'s murder. Green failed to show up for an appointment with his parole officer a few days after O.T.'s murder and did not contact his parole officer after that date. Green was arrested in Los Angeles, California, in December 2002 and returned to Kansas.

While Green was hiding out in California, two of his sisters, Derrick Henderson, and another individual were charged with and convicted of O.T.'s death. Derrick Henderson was convicted of second-degree murder. Green's sister, Latrina, was also convicted of second-degree murder. Green's other sister, Melissa Stanford, was convicted of voluntary manslaughter, and Green's friend, Edwuan Askew, was also convicted of voluntary manslaughter.

After he was arrested and returned to Kansas, Green was charged with second-degree murder under an aiding and abetting theory. The jury convicted Green of the lesser included offense of voluntary manslaughter. This court's review is limited to examining the evidence in a light most favorable to the State to determine if there is evidentiary support for the jury's verdict. See *Boone,* 277 Kan. at 217, 83 P.3d 195. Following that standard, we find that the record supports the jury's verdict. We reverse the Court of Appeals' decision reversing Green's conviction and affirm Green's conviction for voluntary manslaughter.

LOCKETT, J., Retired, assigned. [FN1]

Source: *State v. Green,* 127 P.3d 241 (St. Paul, MN: Thomson West). Reprinted with permission from Westlaw.

CASE IN POINT

Appellate Court of Connecticut.
STATE of Connecticut v. Jerome LEGGETT.
No. 25189.
Argued Nov. 17, 2005.
Decided March 21, 2006.

LAVERY, C.J., and SCHALLER and GRUENDEL, Js. GRUENDEL, J.

The defendant, Jerome Leggett, appeals from the judgment of conviction, rendered after a jury trial, of two counts of robbery in the second degree in violation of General Statutes § § 53a-135 (a) (2) and 53a-8, and one count of conspiracy to commit robbery in the second degree in violation of General Statutes § § 53a-135 (a)(2) and 53a-48 (a). On appeal, the defendant claims that (1) there was insufficient evidence to convict him of (a) conspiracy to commit robbery, (b) robbery of the store clerk and (c) robbery of a customer, and (2) the trial court improperly instructed the jury on (a) the element of intent and (b) *Pinkerton* [FN1] liability. We disagree and affirm the judgment of the trial court.

FN1. Pinkerton v. United States, 328 U.S. 640, 66 S.Ct. 1180, 90 L.Ed. 1489 (1946).

The jury reasonably could have found the following facts concerning this case, which involves the robbery of a 7-Eleven convenience store on Oakwood Avenue in West Hartford by the defendant, James Arnold [FN2] and Reginald Sledge. [FN3] On October 31, 2001, the three men met in Hartford. Arnold and Sledge had previously agreed to commit a robbery that evening [FN4] and obtained a facsimile of a weapon for use in carrying out their plan. [FN5] The defendant accompanied one of the men that evening, and all three gathered in Sledge's car. [FN6] Once together, Arnold asked if Sledge would drive "*them* to go do a score," and Sledge agreed to drive "*them* somewhere to do something." (Emphasis added.)

FN2. Arnold pleaded guilty to one count of robbery in the first degree and one count of robbery in the second degree and received an effective sentence of thirteen years.

FN3. Sledge made a plea agreement under which he was sentenced to twelve years for this robbery, which would be suspended after the fifty-four months he was serving at the time of trial on another charge. An additional robbery charge was nolled.

FN4. Arnold and Sledge had committed another robbery a few days earlier at a nearby Dunkin' Donuts shop.

FN5. The weapon was not an actual gun, but rather a facsimile fashioned to resemble one. The parties disagree as to whether the facsimile weapon was in Sledge's car at the beginning of the evening or whether Arnold obtained it at an abandoned building where the three men went and where Arnold obtained clothing to disguise his appearance for the robbery. It is nevertheless undisputed that the weapon was obtained before the men arrived at the store and that Arnold brandished the facsimile weapon at the time of the robbery.

FN6. The precise circumstances that brought the men together are unclear, as Arnold and Sledge testified to different versions. Arnold testified that the defendant already was in Sledge's car when he arrived, and Sledge told him that the defendant was only there to steal cigarettes and did not commit robberies. In contrast, Sledge testified that the defendant accompanied Arnold and that Arnold introduced the defendant as his "kid brother." The jury reasonably could have believed either scenario and still have found the defendant guilty of the charged offenses.

The three men first obtained some heroin and cocaine, which they mixed and injected. . . . They then proceeded to an abandoned building where Arnold obtained some clothing to disguise his appearance for the robbery. He also returned with some vodka, which the three men consumed. While drinking, Arnold asked Sledge what they could do and where could they go. Arnold suggested the 7-Eleven that they ultimately robbed. Once the men arrived in the vicinity of the 7-Eleven, the defendant and Arnold started bickering over whether one of them was going to "blow everything" and whether they should call off their plans. Sledge warned them to "keep a clear head" because there were police around. Sledge then parked his car on a nearby residential street. Arnold and the defendant exited the car and headed in the direction of the 7-Eleven.

. . .

At about 1 a.m., Nafiou Salaou was working alone as a clerk at the 7-Eleven. Salaou was near the counter speaking with Donna Zuerblis, the only customer in the store at that time. The defendant entered the 7-Eleven first and started walking around the store. Arnold entered the store next, walked in front of the counter and stood next to Zuerblis. [FN8] Arnold then took the facsimile of a gun, pointed it at Salaou and ordered that he open the cash register. After getting the money from the register, Arnold ordered Salaou and Zuerblis to lie down on the floor. Immediately after Arnold announced the robbery, at the same time that he was stealing the money, the defendant went behind the counter and took some cigarettes, which he placed in a plastic bag. The defendant then exited the store, returned to the car where Sledge was waiting and informed him that Arnold was still inside the store with the customer. Arnold remained in the store and took money and jewelry from Zuerblis before exiting.

FN8. A tape from the in-store surveillance camera depicts the two men entering, but their faces cannot be identified from the tape. At trial, Arnold identified the defendant as the first man who entered and himself as the second.

At about the same time the defendant was leaving the store, Sergeant Donald Melanson of the West Hartford police department was on patrol in his marked police cruiser. While driving past the 7-Eleven, Melanson observed the defendant walking away from the store, suspiciously fumbling with the cartons of cigarettes. Melanson then turned his car around to return to the 7-Eleven to investigate. When the defendant and Sledge noticed that a police car was nearby, they departed, leaving Arnold behind at the store. [FN9] When Melanson returned to the store, he observed a car, without headlights, driving away from the property. Melanson then approached the door to the store, encountering Arnold. Arnold ignored Melanson, and proceeded toward where the car had been, yelling something to the effect of "don't leave without me." Salaou then told Melanson that Arnold had robbed him at gunpoint. Arnold was apprehended nearby shortly thereafter.

FN9. Sledge and the defendant continued to a location in Hartford where they sold the stolen cigarettes and divided the money between themselves. They also discussed the possibility of Arnold's arrest and the potential to free him.

. . .

[T]he state charged the defendant with two counts of robbery in the second degree in violation of § § 53a-135 (a)(2) and 53a-8 (a), and one count of conspiracy to commit robbery in the second degree in violation of § § 53a-135 (a)(2) and 53a-48 (a). The defendant entered a pro forma plea of not guilty to all counts. Following trial, on September 29, 2003, the jury returned a verdict of guilty on all three counts. . . . This appeal followed.

I

The defendant's first three claims challenge the sufficiency of the evidence supporting his conviction on each of the three counts charged in the information. We do not find his arguments persuasive.

. . .

A

[1] The defendant first claims that there was insufficient evidence for the jury to find him guilty of conspiracy to commit robbery in the second degree under § § 53a-135 (a)(2) and 53a-48. Specifically, the defendant argues that the state failed to show that he had the intent to agree to commit the robbery and that even if he had the intent to enter the store with Arnold, the state failed to show that he had the intent to use force or threatened force to carry out a larceny. We conclude that there was sufficient evidence for the jury reasonably to have found the defendant guilty of conspiracy to commit robbery in the second degree.

[2][3][4] The essential elements of the crime of conspiracy are well established. "To sustain a conviction under § 53a-48 (a), [FN10] the state needs to prove beyond a reasonable doubt (1) that a defendant intended that conduct constituting a crime be performed, (2) that he agreed with one or more persons to engage in or cause the performance of such conduct and (3) that he or any one of those persons committed an overt act in pursuance of such conspiracy. . . . While the state must prove an agreement, the existence of a formal agreement between the conspirators need not be proved because [i]t is only in rare instances that conspiracy may be established by proof of an express agreement to unite to accomplish an unlawful purpose. . . . [T]he requisite agreement or confederation may be inferred from proof of the separate acts of the individuals accused as coconspirators and from the circumstances surrounding the commission of these acts." (Citations omitted; internal quotation marks omitted.) *State v. Davis,* 68 Conn.App. 794, 798- 99, 793 A.2d 1151, cert. denied, 260 Conn. 920, 797 A.2d 518 (2002); see also *State v. Smith,* 15 Conn.App. 122, 127, 543 A.2d 301 (conspiracy found where defendant arrived with principal, other associates, attempted to distract store owners, left moments before actual theft, attempted to flee with associates), cert. denied, 209 Conn. 805, 548 A.2d 441 (1988).

FN10. General Statutes § 53a-48 (a) provides: "A person is guilty of conspiracy when, with intent that conduct constituting a crime be performed, he agrees with one or more persons to engage in or cause the performance of such conduct, and any one of them commits an overt act in pursuance of such conspiracy."

1

The defendant argues that there is insufficient evidence that he intended to agree to the conspiracy to commit robbery because he expressly disavowed his intent to participate in a robbery. He relies on Arnold's testimony that it was made clear that the defendant ***400** "only steals, he don't do robberies" and that "[h]e wasn't there to do the robbery, he was going out to steal cigarettes." "[W]e must defer to the jury's assessment of the credibility of the witnesses based on its firsthand observation of their conduct, demeanor and attitude." (Internal quotation marks omitted.) *State v. Morgan,* 274 Conn. 790, 800, 877 A.2d 739 (2005). The jury reasonably could have discredited Arnold's testimony of the defendant's intent to commit only larceny. "This court cannot substitute its own judgment for that of the jury if there is sufficient evidence to support the jury's verdict." (Internal quotation marks omitted.) *State v. Flowers,* 85 Conn.App. 681, 692, 858 A.2d 827, cert. granted on other grounds, 272 Conn. 910, 863 A.2d 703 (2004).

[5] The defendant further argues that the state failed to prove that he intended to agree with Sledge and Arnold to the conspiracy to commit robbery. [FN11] The defendant supports his assertion with citations to the record suggesting that he may not have been present for certain conversations between Sledge and Arnold pertaining to plans for the robbery. "A conviction of the crime of conspiracy can be based on circumstantial evidence, for conspiracies, by their very nature, are formed in secret and only rarely can be proved otherwise than by circumstantial evidence." (Internal quotation marks omitted.) *State v. Smith,* 86 Conn.App. 259, 269, 860 A.2d 801 (2004). Here, the jury was presented with sufficient evidence to find that the defendant agreed to the conspiracy to commit robbery. First, the defendant began the evening with either Arnold or Sledge; see footnote 6; who had previously agreed to commit a robbery that night and provided a facsimile weapon to further that purpose. Second, once all three men were present, Arnold asked if Sledge would drive "*them* to go do a score," and Sledge agreed to drive "*them* somewhere to do something." (Emphasis added.) Third, the defendant was present when Arnold returned with the clothes to disguise his appearance and was also present for a conversation about where to carry out the robbery. Fourth, the defendant exited from the same car as Arnold and Sledge, entered the store immediately before Arnold, and waited until Arnold displayed the facsimile weapon to take the cigarettes. Fifth, the defendant returned to the same car, driven by Sledge, to which Arnold intended to return after the robbery.

FN11. The defendant also argues that no agreement may be found because an agreement must provide mutual benefit, with each party agreeing to the other's participation. The defendant, however, offers no case law in support of this proposition. Furthermore, the defendant's argument fails under his own definition. The jury reasonably may have inferred that Arnold and Sledge implicitly agreed to the defendant's participation by continuing to carry out the planned robbery at the same time that the defendant was taking cigarettes. We will address the question of whether the defendant aided his coconspirators in our analysis of the evidence on the count of robbery in the second degree with respect to Salaou.

[6][7] "[I]n viewing evidence which could yield contrary inferences, the jury is not barred from drawing those inferences consistent with guilt and is not required to draw only those inferences consistent with innocence. . . . The jury's conclusion that the defendant intended to agree to the conspiracy is reasonable and logical in light of the evidence before it and the inferences that may be drawn therefrom. Cf. *State v. Elsey,* 81 Conn.App. 738, 747, 841 A.2d 714, cert. denied, 269 Conn. 901, 852 A.2d 733 (2004). [FN12]

FN12. In *Elsey,* this court affirmed the defendant's conviction on the conspiracy charge where "the jury could have reasonably inferred that he was fully aware of the unlawful purpose of [his] companions and . . . [i]n the event of resistance, the [defendant was] ready to render assistance to those actually committing the [crime] and to aid them in making a speedy escape. . . . In addition, the jury could have based at least part of its decision regarding the conspiracy charges on the defendant's decision to come to the scene of the crime with the coconspirators, stay at the scene while the crimes were committed and leave the scene with the coconspirators." (Citations omitted; internal quotation marks omitted.) *State v. Elsey,* supra, 81 Conn.App. at 747, 841 A.2d 714.

[8] The defendant next argues that even if there was sufficient evidence to demonstrate that he intended to agree to the conspiracy, the evidence was insufficient to prove that he intended to commit a robbery because he did not intend to use or threaten the use of physical force. "To sustain a conviction for conspiracy to commit a particular offense, the prosecution must show not only that the conspirators intended to agree but also that they intended to commit the elements of the offense." (Internal quotation marks omitted.) *State v. Davis,* supra, 68 Conn. App. at 799, 793 A.2d 1151. Robbery requires that a larceny be committed by the use or threatened use of immediate physical force. General Statutes § 53a-133. [FN13] "A person commits larceny when, with intent to deprive another of property or to appropriate the same to himself or a third person, he wrongfully takes, obtains or withholds such property from an owner. . . ." General Statutes § 53a-119. The defendant correctly concedes that the evidence "may support a finding that [he] had the intent to commit larceny." We therefore must look only to whether the defendant carried out the larceny through the use or threatened use of physical force. [FN14]

FN13. General Statutes § 53a-133 provides: "A person commits robbery when, in the course of committing a larceny, he uses or threatens the immediate use of physical force upon another person for the purpose of: (1) Preventing or overcoming resistance to the taking of the property or to the retention thereof immediately after the taking; or (2) compelling the owner of such property or another person to deliver up the property or to engage in other conduct which aids in the commission of the larceny."

FN14. The defendant argues that the state must prove separately his intent to use or threaten the use of physical force. This construction, however, misinterprets the statute. The larceny component of robbery, as described in General Statutes § 53a-119, is an intent crime. The use or threatened use of force described in General Statutes § 53a-133, however, has no additional intent element. The state, therefore, need only prove that the defendant intended the larceny and carried it out through the use or threatened use of physical force.

[9] "[I]f the use of force occurs during the continuous sequence of events surrounding the taking or attempted taking, even though some time immediately before or after, it is considered to be in the course of the robbery or the attempted robbery within the meaning of the statute." (Internal quotation marks omitted.) *State v. Ali,* 92 Conn.App. 427, 438, 886 A.2d 449 (2005). The record includes evidence that the defendant entered the store first but waited until Arnold threatened the use of force to take the cigarettes. From this evidence, the jury reasonably could have determined that the defendant had the intent to commit a larceny and did so through the use or threatened use of immediate force. Cf. *State v. Crosswell,* 223 Conn. 243, 256, 612 A.2d 1174 (1992) ("fact that the defendant stood by silently when a gun was displayed in order to gain entry and then to intimidate the occupants of the premises is evidence from which the jury might reasonably have inferred the defendant's acquiescence in this enlarged criminal enterprise").

After examining the evidence presented in the light most favorable to sustaining the verdict, we cannot say that the jury's inferences leading to the defendant's conviction on the count of conspiracy to commit robbery were illogical or unreasonable.

B

[10] The defendant next claims that there was insufficient evidence to convict him, as either a principal or an accessory, of robbery in the second degree as to Salaou, pursuant to § 53a-135. [FN15] Specifically, the defendant argues that he did not intend to threaten the use of immediate force. He further argues that he cannot be held liable as an accessory because he did not intend to aid Arnold in the commission of the robbery of Salaou. We conclude that there was sufficient evidence for the jury reasonably to have found the defendant guilty of robbery in the second degree.

FN15. General Statutes § 53a-135 (a) provides: "A person is guilty of robbery in the second degree when he commits robbery as defined in section 53a-133 and (1) he is aided by another person actually present; or (2) in the course of the commission of the crime or of immediate flight therefrom he or another participant in the crime displays or threatens the use of what he represents by his words or conduct to be a deadly weapon or a dangerous instrument."

[11][12] The state proceeded against the defendant under a theory of accessory liability for the robbery of Salaou. [FN16] "To justify a conviction as an accessory, the state must prove both that the defendant had the intent to aid the principal and that, in so aiding, he had the intent to commit the crime. . . . Mere presence as an inactive companion, passive acquiescence, or the doing of innocent acts which may in fact aid the [principal] must be distinguished from the criminal intent and community of unlawful purpose shared by one who knowingly and willingly assists the perpetrator of the offense in the acts which prepare for, facilitate, or consummate it." (Internal quotation marks omitted.) *State v. McClendon,* 56 Conn.App. 500, 505, 743 A.2d 1154 (2000); see also General Statutes § 53a-8 (a). [FN17]

FN16. We note that "there is no difference between being convicted as a principal or as an accessory"; (internal quotation marks omitted) State v. Smith, supra, 86 Conn.App. at 266, 860 A.2d 801; and accordingly limit our review to whether there was sufficient evidence to convict the defendant of robbery in the second degree as an accessory.

FN17. General Statutes § 53a-8 (a) provides: "A person, acting with the mental state required for commission of an offense, who solicits, requests, commands, importunes or intentionally aids another person to engage in conduct which constitutes an offense shall be criminally liable for such conduct and may be prosecuted and punished as if he were the principal offender."

In examining the sufficiency of the evidence supporting the conviction for conspiracy to commit robbery in the second degree, we already have concluded that the jury reasonably could have found that the defendant had the intent to commit the larceny and accomplished it by the use or threatened use of physical force. We are therefore left to examine whether the defendant had the intent to aid the principal in commission of the robbery. The defendant entered the store before Arnold, yet waited until Arnold announced the robbery to join him near the register and take the cigarettes. From these facts, the jury reasonably could have inferred that the defendant's criminal activity immediately after Arnold announced the robbery was intended to aid Arnold by obtaining additional property from the store. [FN18] Such actions are not passive acquiescence or innocent acts, but rather acts that facilitate and consummate the robbery. See *State v. McClendon,* supra, 56 Conn.App. at 505, 743 A.2d 1154 (defendant found to be accessory where he spent evening with two men following victims; when one man attacked victims, defendant moved behind attacker and alongside other man).

FN18. The defendant further aided a member of the conspiracy when, after fleeing the scene, Sledge received a portion of the profit from the sale of the stolen cigarettes.

[13] The defendant further argues that he lacked the intent to aid Arnold because he left the store while Arnold was still inside robbing Zuerblis. "A defendant may be convicted as an accessory if he intentionally assists in the commission of the crime, regardless of whether he actively participated in every stage of its commission." *State v. Smith,* supra, 86 Conn.App. at 267, 860 A.2d 801. The defendant's liability as an accessory for the robbery of Salaou, therefore, is not alleviated merely because he did not participate actively in the portions of the robbery occurring after he had left the store.

C

[14] The defendant next claims that there was insufficient evidence to convict him of robbery in the second degree of Zuerblis. He argues that the jury reasonably could not have found that he intended to rob Zuerblis or had the intent to aid Arnold in doing so, and, therefore, he cannot be held liable as a principal or accessory because he was a mere passive observer. We conclude that there was sufficient evidence for the jury reasonably to have found the defendant guilty of the robbery of Zuerblis under the *Pinkerton* doctrine. [FN19]

FN19. The defendant argues that principal or accessory liability are the only theories available to the state. He asserts that the court should not have given an instruction on liability under the Pinkerton doctrine because the robbery of Zuerblis was the subject of the original conspiracy charge. We disagree and address that claim with his other challenges to the jury instructions.

[15] We begin by setting forth the scope of *Pinkerton* liability, which our Supreme Court expressly adopted in *State v. Walton,* 227 Conn. 32, 630 A.2d 990 (1993). Under the *Pinkerton* doctrine, "a conspirator may be held liable for criminal offenses committed by a coconspirator that are within the scope of the conspiracy, are in furtherance of it, and are reasonably foreseeable as a necessary or natural consequence of the conspiracy. . . . The rationale for the principle is that, when the conspirator [has] played a necessary part in setting in motion a discrete course of criminal conduct, he should be held responsible, within appropriate limits, for the crimes committed as a natural and probable result of that course of conduct." . . .

The defendant argues that the facts do not support his liability for the robbery of Zuerblis because, for the portion of time that he was present for the robbery, he was a mere passive observer of Arnold's actions. Our Supreme Court has noted that "a factual scenario may be envisioned in which the nexus between the defendant's role in the conspiracy and the illegal conduct of a coconspirator is so attenuated or remote, notwithstanding the fact that the latter's actions were a natural consequence of the unlawful agreement, that it would be unjust to hold the defendant responsible for the criminal conduct of his coconspirator." (Internal quotation marks omitted.) Id., at 493, 820 A.2d 1024. This is not such a case. Here, we have concluded that there was sufficient evidence for the jury reasonably to have concluded that the defendant was guilty of the conspiracy to commit robbery and guilty of the actual robbery of Salaou. The 7-Eleven was open to the public at the time the defendant entered to commit the robbery. Giving deference, as we must, to the reasonable inferences of the jury, it reasonably was foreseeable that a customer might be present at that time and that a coconspirator, already in the act of committing a robbery, might also rob additional persons to obtain more property. Cf. *State v. McFarlane,* 88 Conn.App. 161, 167-68, 868 A.2d 130 (defendant found guilty of larceny in first degree, burglary in third degree, conspiracy to commit larceny in first degree, burglary in third degree, present when burglary planned, served as lookout during commission of crimes, received share of proceeds), cert. denied, 273 Conn. 931, 873 A.2d 999 (2005). Under these circumstances, we conclude that the extent of the defendant's participation was not so attenuated and remote that it would be unjust to hold him responsible for the criminal conduct of his coconspirator, Arnold. See *State v. Garner,* 270 Conn. 458, 486, 853 A.2d 478 (2004) (defendant participated in planning of crimes, was present at scene with knowledge crimes were being committed, acted as lookout).

. . .

The judgment is affirmed.

In this opinion the other judges concurred.

Source: *State v. Leggett,* 94 Conn.App. 392, 892 A.2d 1000 (St. Paul, MN: Thomson West). Reprinted with permission from Westlaw.

attempt
To actually try to commit a crime and have the actual ability to do so.

An **attempt** to commit a crime is intending to commit the offense, taking steps to carry out the crime that are more than merely preparatory in nature, but then failing to actually commit the crime. The prosecution must prove that the defendant has taken some substantial step in the commission of the crime, intends to commit the crime, but for some reason the actus reus is incomplete; the defendant is unable to complete the crime. Recall the example discussed earlier in this chapter involving John grabbing a gun from a police officer and firing it in the officer's direction. The fact that John has bad aim and missed does not negate the fact that John engaged in conduct that constituted a substantial step toward intentionally killing another person.

The intent, or mens rea, that must be proven is the same as that of the completed offense. For example, to be convicted of attempted burglary, the prosecution must show that defendants were caught reaching inside the broken window of a building, but were unable to actually steal

You Be the Judge

Max was driving his battered old car along a narrow road overlooking the coast when he was passed by Ted in his new Mercedes. Max sped up, drew even with the Mercedes, and repeatedly rammed his car into the side of the newer car. After several collisions, the Mercedes was forced off the road, sliding down the cliff for several yards and being kept from falling the several hundred feet onto the rocks and surf below by a large tree. Ted was rescued and Max was charged with attempted murder. At trial, Max testified he was angry because of the arrogant way Ted passed him in his new car, and that his only intent in smashing into Ted's car was to scratch and dent it so that Ted would not be arrogant in the future. What is the likely result?

anything because their arms are wedged between the window frame and broken glass, preventing any theft of property. Similarly, if Elvis is trying to enter his neighbor's house through the roof, but gets stuck halfway down the chimney, Elvis might be charged with attempted burglary, once he is freed from the chimney, of course. Likewise, a person may be found guilty of attempted murder if he threatens to shoot the convenience store clerk, but it is discovered that the gun jammed and could not be fired. However, consider the situation where a person intends to sell widgets on a street corner, believing that it is illegal to sell widgets in public, though in fact it is *not* a crime to sell widgets. If that person attempts to sell the widgets on the corner, but is unable to complete the act because she is struck by a bicyclist when crossing the street, that person cannot be convicted of an attempt to commit a crime, since her actions in fact did not constitute a crime after all, despite her personal belief.

It must be noted that inchoate offenses are merged into the primary offense, as in the case of conspiracy to commit murder and murder. If an intended crime is completed, then the attempt becomes a part of the actual completed crime. Therefore, it is said that the two crimes are *merged* into the more serious of the offenses. The end result is that if the primary crime cannot be proven, it is still possible to convict the defendant on the lesser included offense, the inchoate crime of attempt.

CRIMINAL DEFENSES

Under our legal system, any person charged with a crime is presumed innocent until proven guilty. The prosecution has the burden of proving that the accused is guilty beyond a reasonable doubt. To this end, the defendant has a number of defenses that may possibly be raised in order to negate either the mens rea or the actus reus that is required for conviction on any offense. Certain defenses are available for all crimes, whereas some are limited to crimes of specific intent or not available at all for certain crimes. For example, the defense of **consent** is not available to a defendant charged with murder because societal norms do not recognize the possibility that the victim consented to be killed.

consent
All parties to a novation must knowingly assent to the substitution of either the obligations or parties to the agreement.

In limited situations, the law presumes that certain people are not capable of committing a crime. For example, very young children may be deemed incapable of engaging in criminal conduct, simply because they lack the **capacity** to understand the nature of their conduct or to distinguish right from wrong. Mentally ill people may also raise the defense of lack of capacity to understand the charge against them, or that, at the time of the offense, they lacked substantial mental reasoning that impaired their ability to reason or comprehend the acts.

capacity
Ability to understand or comprehend specific acts or reasoning.

Insanity may be raised as a defense to virtually all crimes. Students should take care to note that this term, as it is used in the context of legal proceedings, does not necessarily imply a specific psychiatric condition, but rather is a specific legal term that may entitle a defendant to an acquittal. There are different standards used to judge whether a defendant may successfully rely on an insanity defense. Some states use the Model Penal Code, whereas other states use the M'Naghten Rule, which will be discussed later in this chapter. Note that a defendant is *presumed* to be sane unless he is able to show that he meets the criteria for raising the **insanity defense.**

insanity defense
A defendant's claim that he or she was insane when the crime was committed, even if temporarily insane.

First, the Model Penal Code supplies a test to determine whether a defendant meets the criteria for relying on the insanity defense, justifying an acquittal. This two-pronged test requires that the defendant prove that she (1) suffers from a mental disease or defect and (2) lacks substantial capacity to understand and appreciate the wrongfulness of certain conduct, or alternately cannot control her actions or behavior to prevent the commission of the criminal act. In essence, the defendant is arguing that some mental infirmity precludes her from conforming to societal expectations of appropriate and lawful behavior.

Second, the **M'Naghten Rule** establishes a traditional standard by which a defendant may allege that he lacks the capacity to form the criminal intent necessary to be guilty of the crime charged. This rule arose from an English case (1843) in which the defendant, M'Naghten, was found not guilty of murder when he tried to kill Sir Robert Peel but actually killed his secretary instead. The rule is sometimes referred to as the "right and wrong" test for criminal responsibility.

M'Naghten Rule
The defendant alleges he or she lacked capacity to form criminal intent.

According to this rule, the person lacks sufficient reasoning ability to be responsible for his crimes. Under this test, the defendant must prove that he has a mental defect or infirmity that

CASE IN POINT

Supreme Judicial Court of Massachusetts, Barnstable.
COMMONWEALTH
v.
Zane A. RASMUSEN.
Argued March 11, 2005.
Decided July 13, 2005.

Present: MARSHALL, C.J., IRELAND, SPINA, SOSMAN, & CORDY, JJ.

CORDY, J.

In the early morning of January 26, 2002, six young men, including the defendant, Zane A. Rasmusen, broke into an apartment in Yarmouth, seeking revenge against another group of young men with whom they had fought at a party earlier in the evening. Rasmusen was armed with a large kitchen knife. Shawn Kimball, a guest in the apartment, was beaten and stabbed several times. Spencer MacLeod, who had not been involved with the earlier fight and was sleeping upstairs when Rasmusen's group forced its way in, joined the fracas and attempted to pull several attackers away from Kimball. He was stabbed in the heart and died. Rasmusen was arrested the next day and later indicted. His principal defense at trial was insanity. A jury convicted him of felony-murder in the first degree for the killing of MacLeod, home invasion, armed burglary, and assault and battery by means of a dangerous weapon for the attack on Kimball. Rasmusen appealed, and we have carefully reviewed the entire record, as is our responsibility under G.L. c. 278, § 33E. Both Rasmusen and the Commonwealth agree that we should reverse Rasmusen's conviction for the felony that underlies the felony-murder conviction as duplicative, and we therefore reverse Rasmusen's conviction for armed burglary. In all other respects, we affirm the convictions.

1. *Background.* The evidence at trial included the following. The altercation that resulted in the death of MacLeod had its origins in the violent feuding of two groups of young men, all of whom lived in the vicinity of Yarmouth and knew each other. On the evening of January 25, 2002, Rasmusen and several friends attended a party at a large summer home near the beach in West Dennis. Earlier, before Rasmusen's arrival, another group, including Germaine Conceptione, had been denied admission to the party. Insults had flown back and forth and a fight had broken out between this group and Rasmusen's friends. The fight was apparently short lived, and Conceptione's group left to assess their injuries and plot strategy at the apartment of a friend on Alewife Circle in Yarmouth, where Shawn Kimball joined them.

FN1. The defendant, Zane A. Rasmusen, and his friends had been drinking beer that evening. Rasmusen himself admitted to consuming one six pack of beer and one shot of hard liquor. Others attending the West Dennis party were also drinking beer.

FN2. Germaine Conceptione testified at trial that one of Rasmusen's friends told his group that they were "not welcome" at the West Dennis party and said, "This is a million dollar house, and you people need to go back to the village where you came from." The comment apparently referred to Swan Pond Village, also known as Alewife Circle, the housing development where Conceptione's group could often be found.

The group, now including Kimball, decided to return to the party in West Dennis and get revenge. They arrived back at the home after midnight, unarmed, and entered through the open garage door. A fight ensued, this time including Rasmusen. During the fight, Conceptione put Rasmusen in a headlock, nearly asphyxiating him. Conceptione eventually released Rasmusen and, with the rest of his group, ran to their vehicles and returned to the Alewife Circle apartment. Rasmusen, wielding a knife he had grabbed from a drawer in the home's kitchen, attempted to pursue Conceptione, slashing the tires of one of the fleeing vehicles. Shortly thereafter, he collapsed on the lawn and vomited violently, apparently from the effects of the headlock.

After recovering, Rasmusen telephoned his girl friend, who picked him up from the party in her Chevrolet Suburban sport utility vehicle. When he got into the Suburban, Rasmusen was carrying a long-bladed kitchen knife. They drove to another home, where Rasmusen's friends reconvened and plotted their own revenge, particularly against Conceptione. A witness to this meeting testified that when one of the participants said, "Let's go fuck them up," Rasmusen responded, "I'm not fucking anyone up. I'm going to kill someone."

Rasmusen's group proceeded to gather garden tools (to be used as weapons) and loaded them into the Suburban. They then drove to the homes of other friends, picking up two pit bull dogs at one, and a baseball bat, a golf club, and a crowbar at another. Fully armed, they headed to the Alewife Circle area to look for Conceptione and his friends. As they drove through the neighborhood, someone spotted Kimball through the window of one of the apartments. Rasmusen and five companions got out of the Suburban, armed themselves with the weapons they had brought, and headed for the apartment.

Kimball saw the group approaching and tried to lock the door. Someone threw a brick through the kitchen window, and four of the group, including Rasmusen, stormed the apartment, breaking through the locked door with such force that they destroyed the door frame. The four men immediately attacked Kimball with their weapons; one member of the group struck him with a golf club, another struck him with a wooden stick, and another with a crowbar. Wielding the knife, Rasmusen stabbed Kimball four times. During these attacks, Kimball eventually fell to the floor.

Conceptione was not in the apartment during the assault, having left before Rasmusen's group arrived. Upstairs, however, two women were feeding the baby of the apartment owner, who was not at home. MacLeod, the boy friend of one of the women, was asleep in another room. Awakened by the fighting, MacLeod came down the stairs and attempted to pull the four men off of Kimball. Those men turned their attention from Kimball to MacLeod. Kimball saw Rasmusen stab MacLeod twice in the chest. Rasmusen and his companions then fled the scene in the waiting Suburban. When his girl friend asked what had happened,

Rasmusen responded, "I stabbed someone." He also expressed regret that Conceptione had not been at the apartment and said that he "fucked [Kimball] up" and then "fucked [MacLeod] up." Sitting in the front passenger seat, Rasmusen cleaned the blood-soiled knife with a t-shirt and directed his girl friend to drive to a nearby pond where he threw the knife into the water.

Meanwhile, those who remained at the Alewife Circle apartment telephoned 911. Shortly after 3 a.m., paramedics arrived and attended to the badly wounded Kimball and MacLeod. MacLeod had a heart rhythm but no pulse or blood pressure. After MacLeod was transported to a local hospital, the emergency room physician discovered that the stab wound had fatally punctured MacLeod's heart; the physician pronounced him dead. When the police arrived at the apartment, Kimball was screaming, naming the men involved in the attack, including Rasmusen. Kimball was transported to the hospital in a second ambulance. He recovered from his injuries.

The next day, Rasmusen was arrested and brought to the police station. After he was booked, advised of his Miranda rights, and detained in a holding cell, Rasmusen asked to speak with a detective investigating the stabbings, Charles Peterson of the Yarmouth police department. During the interview, which lasted nearly two hours, Rasmusen described the previous night's events. He said that his group had gone to the Alewife Circle apartment "to get" Conceptione, and that he had brought a knife with him for that purpose. He admitted stabbing Kimball, but denied knowingly stabbing MacLeod, offering that it was possible he had stabbed MacLeod when MacLeod had tried to break up the fight.

Rasmusen's trial was severed from that of the others charged in the Alewife Circle attack. In his defense, Rasmusen offered the testimony of his mother and a forensic psychiatrist about his long history of psychiatric problems to demonstrate that he lacked criminal responsibility for his conduct on the evening of the attack. Rasmusen's mother described his troubled childhood, which involved witnessing her being beaten by an alcoholic husband from the time he was a toddler, and a violent home invasion and assault when he was twelve years old. After the home invasion, Rasmusen began drinking and using drugs, and he was often violent when intoxicated. His mother testified that when she saw him on the morning after the stabbings, he appeared to be drunk or high. The psychiatrist, who examined Rasmusen, his medical records, and court records, testified that Rasmusen suffered from four (previously undiagnosed) psychological disorders—posttraumatic stress disorder, intermittent explosive disorder, substance induced mood disorder, and a nonspecific learning disorder. The psychiatrist opined that as a result of these disorders, at the time of the stabbings at the Alewife Circle apartment, Rasmusen was experiencing an uncontrolled pathological rage precipitated by Conceptione choking him at the West Dennis party. Therefore, the psychiatrist testified, Rasmusen was unable to appreciate the criminality of his actions and lacked the capacity to conform his behavior to the requirements of law.

[1][2] 2. *Criminal responsibility.* At trial, Rasmusen did not dispute that he was involved in the attack at the Alewife Circle apartment. As exemplified in defense counsel's closing, Rasmusen argued that (1) there was reasonable doubt as to whether Rasmusen was the one that stabbed MacLeod during the altercation ; (2) if the Commonwealth had demonstrated that he stabbed MacLeod, he should be found not guilty of murder by reason of insanity; and (3) if the Commonwealth had demonstrated that he was not insane, he should be found guilty of a lesser degree of homicide than murder in the first degree as a result of his impaired mental condition. On appeal, Rasmusen claims that the Commonwealth failed to prove Rasmusen's sanity beyond a reasonable doubt because it neither offered any expert evidence of sanity to rebut the defense expert's testimony nor requested an instruction on the "presumption of sanity." We find no merit in Rasmusen's argument because the evidence warranted the jury's finding that he was criminally responsible.

FN5. One of the defense theories was that another of the attackers might have stabbed Spencer MacLeod, that Shawn Kimball could not really have seen what was happening because he was wounded and on the floor, and that one of the members of the Rasmusen group who testified for the Commonwealth was lying about incriminating statements Rasmusen made to the group right after the event. There was, however, no evidence that anyone other than Rasmusen was armed with a knife, and MacLeod's wounds were deep and consistent with the knife Rasmusen admittedly brought to the apartment and used to stab Kimball.

. . .

"A person is not responsible for criminal conduct if at the time of such conduct as a result of mental disease or defect he lacks substantial capacity either to appreciate the criminality [wrongfulness] of his conduct or to conform his conduct to the requirements of law." *Commonwealth v. McHoul,* 352 Mass. 544, 546-547, 226 N.E.2d 556 (1967). "When a defendant claims that he is not criminally responsible for his acts, the Commonwealth bears the burden of proving beyond a reasonable doubt that the defendant is sane."

. . .

In this case, the jury had before them expert testimony offered by the defendant that suggested that the defendant lacked criminal responsibility for his conduct . . . In their role as fact finder, the jury plainly rejected Rasmusen's insanity defense, and had an ample basis on which to do so.

> The evidence of Rasmusen's sanity at the time of the attacks was compelling. Angered and humiliated by the earlier fight at the house in West Dennis, Rasmusen and his group of friends discussed, planned, and executed the raid on the Alewife Circle apartment. As described by Kimball, Rasmusen's conduct during the attacks was consistent with deliberate combat. After the raid was over, Rasmusen cleaned and disposed of the knife, and Rasmusen's subsequent interview with the police revealed that he had a clear memory of his involvement in and the purpose of the attack. The jury were warranted in inferring Rasmusen's sanity from this evidence and therefore could have rationally rejected the opinion of Rasmusen's one expert witness, who concluded that Rasmusen was insane at the time of the attacks by describing all of Rasmusen's conduct as consistent with four previously undiagnosed mental disorders.

. . .

[3][4] That the Commonwealth did not request and the judge did not provide a jury instruction on the "presumption of sanity" does not undermine the soundness of the jury's finding that Rasmusen was sane at the time of the attacks. The judge provided extensive instructions to the jury to guide their deliberations on whether the Commonwealth had met its burden to prove

criminal responsibility and the absence of mental impairment. Although we said in *Commonwealth v. Keita,* 429 Mass. 843, 846, 712 N.E.2d 65 (1999), that a "jury instruction concerning the presumption of sanity should be given in every case in which the question of the defendant's criminal responsibility is raised," we have never held that the failure to give such an instruction should be grounds for a new trial or presents a substantial likelihood of a miscarriage of justice. Indeed, the instruction is for the benefit of the Commonwealth, not the defendant. It would be paradoxical for the absence of the instruction to constitute such a grave error when the "presumption" merely reflects our recognition that jurors should be permitted to infer or presume the defendant's sanity from their "common knowledge that a great majority of people are sane, and the probability that any particular person is sane." *Id.* at 846, 712 N.E.2d 65, quoting *Commonwealth v. Brennan,* 399 Mass. 358, 364, 504 N.E.2d 612 (1987). That the Commonwealth secured the convictions without the benefit of a "presumption of sanity" instruction suggests the strength, not weakness, of the Commonwealth's proof of criminal responsibility. The Commonwealth chose not to rely on the "presumption" presenting "evidence of the defendant's conduct before, during, and after the crime, which the 'jury are permitted to weigh in reaching their conclusions on the insanity issue,' and from which they had the right to infer the defendant's mental competency." *Commonwealth v. Lunde, supra* at 48, 453 N.E.2d 446, quoting *Commonwealth v. Walker,* 370 Mass. 548, 581, 350 N.E.2d 678, cert. denied, 429 U.S. 943, 97 S.Ct. 363, 50 L.Ed.2d 314 (1976).

[5] In a related argument, Rasmusen claims that the convictions are illogical and should be reversed pursuant to G.L. c. 278, § 33E, as against the weight of the evidence. This argument is premised on the theory that the jury must have accepted Rasmusen's evidence of insanity because it found Rasmusen not guilty of murder in the first degree by reason of deliberate premeditation and by reason of extreme atrocity or cruelty, despite "fairly overwhelming" evidence suggesting Rasmusen's guilt on those theories. Consequently, Rasmusen contends the jury must have misunderstood how to apply their finding of insanity to the remainder of the charges. We do not agree. There are many possible explanations for the jury's verdicts and no reason to conclude that the instructions were either misunderstood or misapplied to the evidence.

First, MacLeod had had no involvement in the prior altercation, and the jury could well have found that he was not the target of Rasmusen's planned revenge, that his presence at the scene was an unforeseen circumstance, and that his death was unpremeditated and unintended. The jury could also have found that MacLeod's injuries, insofar as they were suffered in the course of breaking up a violent and heated altercation, were not the product of extreme atrocity or cruelty. Such conclusions would not be inconsistent with the jury's finding that Rasmusen was criminally responsible for his conduct during the incident, including planning and executing the vicious assault on Kimball and the predicate felonies of armed burglary and home invasion.

FN8. There was evidence at trial that MacLeod and Rasmusen were acquaintances and that Rasmusen was a good friend of MacLeod's brother. The jury may have considered this evidence in assessing whether Rasmusen had the specific intent to kill MacLeod.

Just as likely, the evidence of Rasmusen's impaired mental capacity may have created doubt in the minds of the jury on the element of premeditation in the killing of MacLeod, and on whether the Commonwealth had sustained its burden of proving that Rasmusen had acted with extreme cruelty or atrocity. It would have been perfectly consistent with that doubt for the jury to conclude that Rasmusen nevertheless had the mental capacity to intend an armed break-in for the purpose of gaining revenge.

. . .

In this case, the issues of criminal responsibility and diminished capacity were "fully and fairly before the jury," and "justice does not require that their verdict be disturbed.

. . .

So ordered.

Source: *Commonwealth v. Rasmusen,* 444 Mass. 657, 830 N.E.2d 1040 (St. Paul, MN: Thomson West). Reprinted with permission from Westlaw.

results in ill-formed reasoning precluding him from exercising sound judgment, understanding the wrongfulness of his conduct, or appreciating the consequences of a particular wrongful act. This rule requires that the defendant lack the capacity to distinguish societal norms and expectations for permissible conduct, not recognizing that certain conduct is unlawful. The defendant must prove that at the time of the crime, he was suffering under such a defect of reason, from a disease of the mind, that he did not know the nature and quality of the act he was doing or that he did not know that what he was doing was morally wrong.

This rule does not excuse a defendant who argues that she had some irresistible impulse or uncontrollable desire to commit a criminal act, unless the impulse arose from some mental disease. You should take care to consult your own state's statute regarding the application or interpretation of this rule in your jurisdiction. Some states have interpreted the phrase "distinguishing right from wrong" and others specifically have interpreted the meaning of "irresistible impulse."

Another possible criminal defense is that the conduct of the defendant comprised *involuntary acts*. This is a defense that relates to the actus reus element of the crime, as the defendant is contending that the act was involuntary, for instance as the result of a muscle spasm or undiagnosed medical condition. However, if the defendant is aware of a medical condition, such as epilepsy, but neglects to take his prescribed medication, and subsequently has an automobile accident, then his reckless behavior in ignoring the risks of driving without proper medication will not permit the raising of this defense in a criminal case of manslaughter.

However, consider the case where Hortense is driving her car in a rural area with the windows rolled down. Assume that a swarm of bees enters through the open car window and attacks her as she is driving. If she subsequently loses control of her car and crosses the centerline, crashing into an oncoming car, Hortense would have a viable defense that her actions were not voluntary. In the same manner, if a truck driver on a busy highway is driving under a bridge at the exact time that a chunk of concrete snaps off the bridge and crashes through his windshield, it cannot be said that his failure to avoid crashing into the car in front of him was a voluntary act. In both of these situations, it should be noted that it is some *external* act or force that prevented the person from exercising proper care and control. Thus, there is no indication that it is *voluntary* conduct or the proper actus reus to sustain a conviction on the charged offense.

Intoxication may be a possible criminal defense if it negates a specific element of a crime. Becoming voluntarily intoxicated and then causing an accident while driving a car will not permit the defense that the acts were not voluntary, as voluntary intoxication is reckless behavior, just like continuing to drive while in an impaired physical state. Involuntary intoxication may occur where the defendant is unaware that she has ingested some intoxicating substance, as in the case where someone has doctored a drink with alcohol or an illegal drug. In this situation, the defendant argues that she lacked the mens rea, the intent to commit the crime, because she did not knowingly engage in the wrongful conduct due to the involuntary impairment caused by the ingestion of some intoxicating substance without her knowledge.

self-defense
A defendant's legal excuse that the use of force was justified.

Another common defense raised is **self-defense.** Persons may allege that they were either protecting themselves, or protecting another person, or property, from serious bodily harm, or acting to prevent a crime. The essence of this defense is that the use of force was justified. This defense may be raised by the accused of any offense. It must be noted that the force used under the circumstances must be reasonable, and that the defendant's belief as to the necessity of using that force must be also reasonable. One cannot use excessive force, but only that amount of force that is reasonably necessary given the fact situation.

Where self-defense is raised, the defendant's conduct is judged based on the surrounding facts, and the action he believed was necessary in the context of that specific situation. However, once the need to use force is no longer necessary, as in a retreating assailant, the defense of self-defense may no longer apply. Therefore, although this is an objective standard by which the defendant's conduct is measured, keep in mind that once the perceived threat or force is gone, the defendant, too, must abandon any use of force. You cannot shoot a burglar in the back if the burglar is halfway down the street, attempting to escape, even if you think that the burglar might return later, because the danger at that time is no longer in existence.

entrapment
An act of a law enforcement official to induce or encourage a person to commit a crime when the defendant expresses no desire to proceed with the illegal act.

In certain situations, the defendant may raise the issue of **entrapment.** Consider, for example, the traveling business executive who becomes lost while navigating through an unfamiliar city. He stops to ask directions, unknowingly inquiring for help from an undercover police officer who is involved in a prostitution sting operation. The officer encourages the businessman to let her show him the route herself, rather than provide directions. He innocently agrees to let her in his car to take him where he needs to be in the city, and then the officer attempts

You Be the Judge

Herman is an alcoholic, who has been seeking treatment for his disease off and on for the last five years. He does not get along with his neighbor, Eddie, and decides that he is going to kill him. As he is thinking about this, Herman consumes 10 bottles of beer. While in a drunken state, Herman looks out the window of his home and sees Eddie in his own backyard, trimming trees. Mistakenly believing that Eddie is about to come over and attack him with the hedge clippers, Herman rushes outside and stabs Eddie with a butcher knife, causing his death.

Herman is charged with murder. What is the likely outcome? (Use your state's criminal code to answer this question.)

You Be the Judge

Sylvester was an avid collector of antique and unusual weapons. He subscribed to various magazines about weapons so that he could add to his collection. In one catalog he received by mail, a particular hunting knife was advertised that was a total of 18 inches long, with the blade measuring 14 inches. Although Sylvester knew the model penal statute in his state prohibited the possession of any knife that was greater than 20 inches total, he did not know that another part of the statute also prohibited any hunting knife with a blade measuring more than 12 inches long. He ordered the advertised knife and when it arrived in the mail, he measured it to confirm its length. While driving to a weapons show in his state, he was stopped for speeding. The police officer saw, lying in plain view on the back seat of Sylvester's car, the hunting knife. Sylvester was arrested for possession of an illegal knife. What is the likely result?

to engage him in provocative conversation and acts. In this situation, the businessman may insist that he was entrapped to commit an unlawful act because the criminal plan originated with the officer and the defendant had no intent to commit any crime when he stopped to ask directions. The officer was not simply providing an opportunity for the defendant to commit an unlawful act because here the defendant was not otherwise predisposed and intending to commit such act.

mistake in fact
An error in assessing the facts, causing a defendant to act in a certain way.

Finally, the defendant may raise **mistake in fact** as a defense in certain cases. Essentially, this defense is based on the assertion that the defendant mistakenly believed certain things to be true and therefore acted accordingly, in what is a reasonable manner assuming that the premises were indeed true. The defendant must have had an honest, genuine belief that the assumptions she made were true. In asserting this defense, the rationale is that the defendant lacked the mens rea for the particular offense. For example, if Dudley leaves an airport with a suitcase that he honestly believes belongs to him, when in fact it is of just similar brand, color, and size, then Dudley lacks the mens rea for theft because he does not deprive the true owner, Loulou, of her property with dishonest intentions. Similarly, if Mortimer points a toy gun at his neighbor, Harriet, as an April Fool's Day prank, and Harriet, fearing that Mortimer truly intends to shoot her, reacts by throwing a brick at Mortimer, knocking him unconscious, it cannot be said that Harriet possessed the requisite mens rea for battery and assault, as she acted under a genuine mistaken belief that Mortimer was aiming a real gun at her. It is important to note that the alleged mistake of fact must directly relate to the mens rea, or intent, that is required for that specific offense.

In summary, where criminal acts occur, there are always explanations offered up by the defendant for her actions. In some cases, these explanations serve as valid defenses that the accused may assert to avoid conviction and punishment for the alleged unlawful, prohibited acts. The defendant may assert that her actions were justified under the circumstances, whether by virtue of self-defense or because of some mistaken belief of fact upon which she relied. It should be noted that while mistake of fact is an accepted defense, mistake of law is generally not a valid excuse. The common maxim applies, that is, ignorance of the law is no excuse. Finally, insanity may be a possible defense.

Eye on Ethics

Read the case on this Web site: www.law.com/jsp/article.jsp?id=1146139204085. In this case, a California Superior Court judge reprimanded a prosecutor for what the attorney wrote in his personal blog about a misdemeanor case he was handling. Discuss the legal ethics of a criminal prosecutor who is writing about an ongoing court proceeding. Does your answer change if it is a paralegal blogging about an ongoing criminal case?

ETHICAL CONSIDERATIONS

In our complex society, it is desirable for the legal system to try to minimize wrongdoing, either by the threat of punishment or by strictly enforcing the law when the rules are broken, setting an example and hopefully acting as a deterrent to future crime. However, even if everyone agrees that it is in the best interests of society to protect individuals and their property from harmful conduct, for the good of the whole society, nevertheless there is some concern that the system of law is overreaching in trying to protect people from themselves. For instance, one may ask whether offenses such as bigamy or prostitution ought to be considered crimes in the same way as battery or burglary. The argument may be set forth that society should not characterize offenses that are primarily moral in nature as criminal acts, for what specific harm does society sustain by these offenses? Do moral offenses threaten to undermine security or stability? Therefore, one can argue that offenses such as the ban on public nudity go too far in terms of maintaining the common good of society. One might ask whether it will soon be possible for a legislature composed of vegetarians to make it a crime to consume meat. This is but one of the ethical issues in criminal law—how far should our system of law go to regulate what is deemed to be acceptable versus unacceptable conduct?

CYBER TRIP

Access this Web site: www.hricik.com/StateEthics.html. Locate your state and see whether there are any ethics opinions in your state related to criminal law and procedure.

Another ethical issue centers on whether there are ever any circumstances whereby a person does not *deserve* to be punished for an act that is expressly prohibited under criminal statutes. For example, euthanasia, or mercy killing, is in the spotlight today, as people are living longer and consequently doctors and caregivers are facing ethical dilemmas as to whether it is ever justifiable to cause the death of another human being, simply to spare that person prolonged suffering. This is a challenge to society that is constantly changing as society itself changes, and subsequently opinions as to what is just conduct.

Finally, people sometimes wonder how it is possible for lawyers to represent a defendant in a criminal law case who they are convinced is guilty. Yet, it is simple to overlook the basic premise in criminal law, repeated often in television reality crime shows: all suspects are innocent until proven guilty in a court of law. As the basic foundation of our legal system, the Constitution stands to protect the accused and guarantee them basic rights, one of which is representation by counsel. Thus, to question how lawyers can represent guilty clients is really ignoring the tenets that are at the root of our system: that these clients are not guilty and are entitled to receive a fair trial by jury. Ethically, criminal defense lawyers are charged with the responsibility of ensuring that their clients receive these basic rights guaranteed under our Constitution.

A Day in the Life of a Real Paralegal

One of the most compelling statistics regarding society today is the increased number of cases entering the criminal justice system. As a result, there is a greater need for paralegals to assist both government attorneys as well as criminal defense lawyers in this challenging area of the law. Working in the criminal justice arena requires a keen desire to engage in continuing legal education opportunities, keeping informed of the current law, as this area is constantly evolving. You should strive to be active in your local and national paralegal associations, such as the National Association of Legal Assistants (NALA). Participation in these organizations, tracking recent court decisions in your jurisdiction, and simply reading the newspaper are all vital elements to remaining current in this field.

Some of the duties performed by paralegals in criminal litigation include undertaking legal research, critically analyzing relevant statutes with cases, and assisting the attorney in preparing a trial notebook. Research in this area of the law may involve investigating procedural issues as well as determining evidentiary rules. For those people who enjoy being involved in every detail of a case, from start to finish, this area offers such opportunities. Paralegals may perform trial preparation duties such as drafting motions, preparing jury questions, and gathering evidence. These tasks, although important in civil cases, take on a different dimension when performed in the area of criminal litigation. Throughout your work, you will constantly be remembering that every person is innocent until proven guilty; therefore, the level of job satisfaction in assisting the attorney to see that justice is served is extremely high, making this a rewarding career path for those individuals who are willing to diligently meet new challenges and employ critical thinking skills on a daily basis.

Summary

For people to peacefully coexist in society, it is necessary to have a system of laws in place to act as both a deterrent to harmful conduct and a punishment for wrongdoers who fail to abide by these laws. This chapter has examined the two specific elements that must be proven in nearly every crime, the mens rea and the actus reus, as well as the characteristics of certain specific criminal offenses, such as burglary and assault. Once the accused has been charged with specific criminal acts, it is the prosecution who bears the burden of proof that the accused did indeed knowingly commit these prohibited acts, the standard of proof being beyond a reasonable doubt. As with any situation, the accused has the right to offer explanations for his or her actions, and some of these may be deemed valid defenses to the specific offense. Certain defenses are available only in limited situations. In analyzing any factual situation, you should always be certain to consult your state's criminal code in order to identify whether the specific conduct is prohibited, whether the facts support each element of the offense, and whether there are any valid defenses available to the defendant.

Key Terms

Actus reus
American Law Institute
Assault
Attempt
Battery
Burglary
Capacity
Consent
Conspiracy
Entrapment
Felony
General intent
Inchoate offenses
Insanity defense
Larceny
Malice aforethought
Malum in se
Malum prohibitum
Manslaughter
Mens rea
Misdemeanor
Mistake in fact
M'Naghten rule
Model Penal Code (MPC)
Murder
Robbery
Self-defense
Solicitation
Specific intent

Discussion Questions

1. In *The Common Law* by Oliver Wendell Holmes (1881), he stated, "It has been thought that to shoot at a block of wood thinking it to be a man is not an attempt to murder, and that to put a hand in an empty pocket, intending to pick it, is not an attempt to commit larceny, although on the latter question there is a difference of opinion." Discuss the meaning of this quotation. Is this statement true if one uses the Model Penal Code?
2. What is the significance of accountability in the application of the criminal code to individuals? What do you think is the significance of morality in the application of the criminal code? If a person lacks any individual moral responsibility or sense of principled or ethical behavior, should that person be punished for criminal conduct in every instance?
3. Read the article on "Character and Content." Summarize the three difficult ethical dilemmas frequently encountered by prosecutors in the criminal justice system. The article can be downloaded for free at http://papers.ssrn.com/sol3/papers.cfm?abstract_id=894931#PaperDownload
4. Discuss whether a person in a state of voluntary intoxication, induced by either drugs or alcohol, should be able to negate criminal liability for an offense. Does it matter to you what the criminal offense is in the availability of this defense?
5. Refer to the Case in Point *State v. Cantu* contained in this chapter, According to the criminal code in your state, can a person be convicted of burglary if he thinks that he is *not* privileged or licensed to enter the premises, but in fact he is? In this situation, can your state's prosecutor prove that the defendant "knows" he is not licensed or privileged to enter?

Exercises

Use the criminal code in your state to answer the following questions.

1. Mortimer is a known drug dealer. One day, his friend, Helen, needs a ride to work at the local discount store and asks Mortimer to drive her there. On the way to Helen's workplace, Mortimer stops off at the local convenience store. While Helen waits in the car, Mortimer goes in and robs the clerk. Helen suspects something is amiss when Mortimer comes dashing out of the store and speeds away. Less than a mile from the store, the police stop Mortimer and arrest both him and Helen. What is the likely result?
2. Loulou and her sister, Annabelle, live in a secluded farm house, several miles from the nearest neighbor. They invite their elderly uncle, Homer, to come visit with them for a month. After about two weeks of having Homer in their house, they become fed up with his presence and demand that he leave. Homer asks to stay another few days, until he can arrange for Aunt Bea to come get him, as Homer doesn't have a car nor is he able to drive. Despite the fact that it is the middle of winter and there is considerable snow on the ground, Loulou and Annabelle insist that Homer leave immediately. Homer has nowhere else to go, but he dutifully packs his bag and starts walking into town, three miles away. An hour later, Homer returns, pleading with Loulou to let him stay because of the frigid weather, but Loulou refuses and locks the door. Homer starts walking again, but collapses in the snow about a mile from town, and dies. Discuss the possible criminal charges against Loulou and/or Annabelle and the result.
3. Late one night, Tim sneaks in through the bedroom window of Sam, assuming that Sam was asleep in bed. Inside Sam's room, Tim fires a gun at the bed, intending to kill Sam. Tim then climbs back out the bedroom window and flees. Unknown to Tim, Sam was in the kitchen fixing nachos in the microwave oven, so he was not harmed. Meanwhile, Sam's neighbor, Molly, sees Tim climbing out the window and calls the police, who apprehend Tim a block from the house. Tim is charged with attempted murder. What is the likely outcome?
4. Lionel works for a dry-cleaning business that has home delivery and pickup service for its customers. One day, Lionel is asked to pick up a mink coat at a customer's residence and bring it to the store for cleaning. Lionel collects the coat and puts it in the dry-cleaner's van, but rather than deliver it to the store, he takes it to his home, intending to give it to his girlfriend as a birthday gift. What criminal charges might be filed, and what is the likely result?
5. Eloise is shopping at a grocery store with her 4-year-old daughter, Hattie. Eloise is trying to finish her shopping quickly, but she is constantly stopping to remove items, such as candy and soda, from her cart that Hattie has placed in it, and put them back them on the grocery shelves. After the sixth such incident, Eloise shouts at Hattie, "if you do that one more time, I will kill you!" Does this statement prove Eloise's intent to kill?
6. Darren enters the Third National Bank of Salem waving a gun and rushes up to the teller window demanding that the bank vault be opened immediately. He takes the teller, Endora, as hostage, shouting, "Unless you open the safe immediately, I will kill you!" Does this statement prove Darren's intent to kill? Is this case similar to Exercise 5, and if not, how would you distinguish them?
7. Sneed and Hook plan to burglarize their neighbor's home. Since their neighbor, Juliet, is nearly 75 years old, the two agree that they will not hurt her and will immediately leave her house if she awakens. Sneed is aware of Hook's violent temper and insists that Hook comply with this agreement. As they carry out the burglary on the selected night, Juliet wakes up and confronts the two. Hook becomes enraged and knocks Juliet unconscious with her cane. Sneed reprimands Hook but continues to load Juliet's jewelry into a pillowcase. The concussion causes Juliet to remain unconscious for four days, whereby she dies from dehydration. A church volunteer, Ellie, normally delivers meals to Juliet every day, but failed to do so for those four days because she went to Las Vegas for a week and didn't arrange a substitute to deliver meals for Juliet. Discuss the criminal liability of Sneed, Hook, and Ellie for Juliet's death.
8. Huey, Dewey, Louie, and Donald plan to break into a shoe warehouse to steal. Huey, Dewey, and Louie know there is a night watchman on duty at all times, but Donald doesn't know this fact. Huey gives Dewey a loaded gun and tells him to not hesitate to use it if necessary. When the four set off to the warehouse, Donald knows that Dewey has a gun, but Louie

doesn't know this fact. As they break into and enter the warehouse, the four are confronted by the watchman, Max. As Dewey is in the act of firing the gun, Huey recognizes the watchman as being his nephew, knocks Dewey's hand to one side and shouts, "Don't shoot!" Huey's act causes the bullet to miss the watchman, but it strikes and kills a policeman who is entering the room at that moment. Discuss the criminal liability of each party.

9. Jack encouraged Richard to kill Victor. Jack gave Richard a substance that both of them believed to be a toxic poison capable of killing Victor. Richard went to Victor's house with a drink containing the poison, intending to make Victor drink it. However, when Richard knocked on the front door, he was met by Victor's uncle, who informed him that Victor had died a week ago. In a state of remorse, Richard confesses his plan to the police, who test the substance and discover it was harmless, incapable of causing death. Discuss the criminal liability of each party.
10. One extremely frigid winter night, Chuck is driving down an isolated country road with Mrs. Smith, with whom he is having an affair. Chuck is distracted by talking to Mrs. Smith, and he knocks down a pedestrian, Dave. Chuck is worried that Mr. Smith will find out about the illicit affair and thus does not stop the car but drives on. Dave is injured and unconscious. He is not discovered until the next morning, but at that point, it is too late, and he has died from exposure to the unusually cold weather. Had he received medical treatment the night of the accident, he would not have died. Discuss the criminal liability of each party.

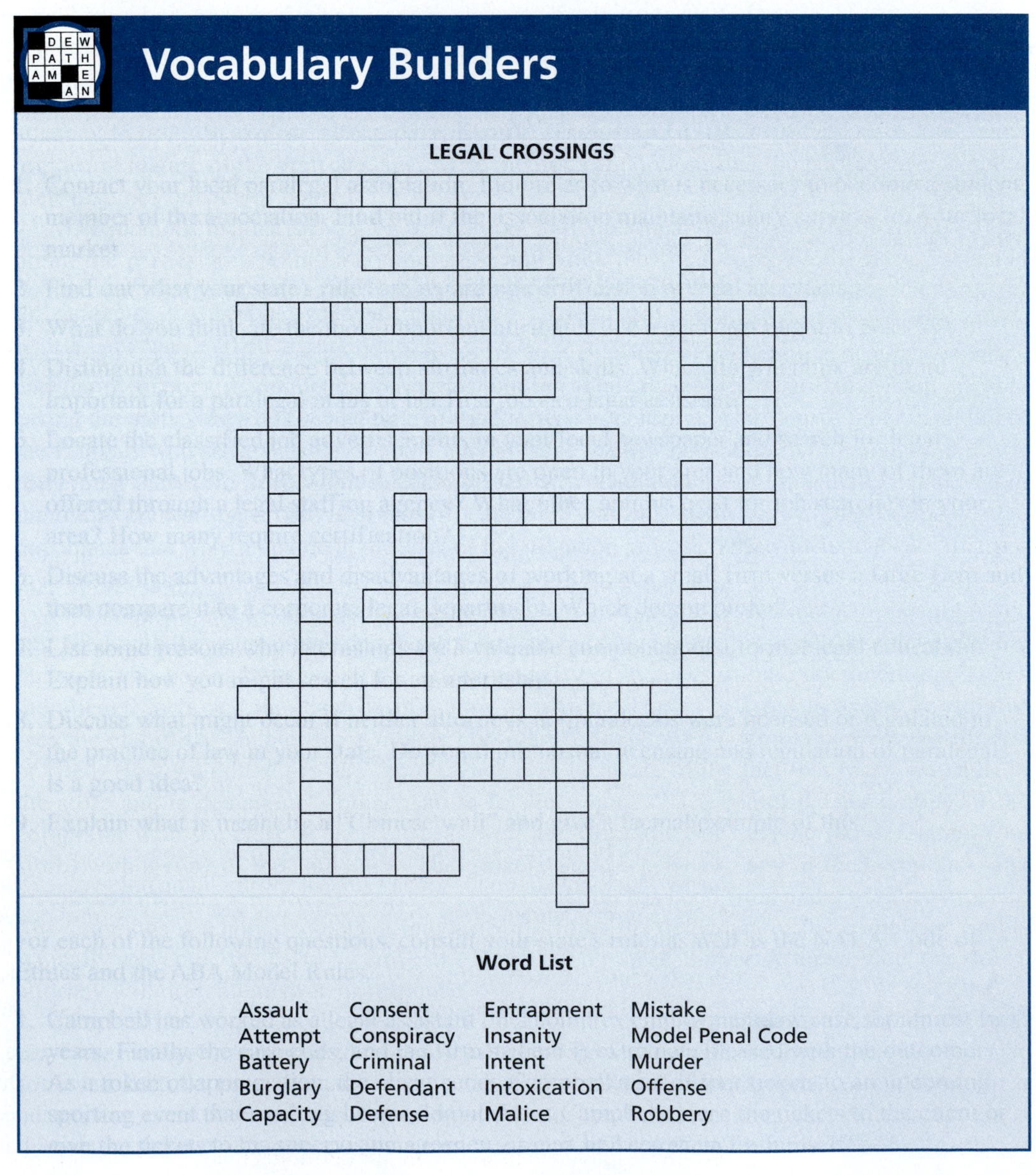

Vocabulary Builders
LEGAL CROSSINGS
Word List
Assault
Attempt
Battery
Burglary
Capacity
Consent
Conspiracy
Criminal
Defendant
Defense
Entrapment
Insanity
Intent
Intoxication
Malice
Mistake
Model Penal Code
Murder
Offense
Robbery

Chapter 8

Contracts

CHAPTER OBJECTIVES

After reading this chapter, you will be able to:

- Define a contract and what it means to have a "meeting of the minds."
- Explain the elements of a contract.
- Describe the defenses to valid contracts.
- Identify remedies available to breach of contract actions.
- Explain the purpose of the Uniform Commercial Code.

Samuel Butler declared, "A lawyer's dream of Heaven: Every man reclaimed his own property at the resurrection, and each tried to recover it from all his forefathers." Contracts affect virtually every aspect of our lives. Every time that we make a purchase at the local grocery store, we are completing a contract, even though we don't think of it in those terms. Imagine what it would be like if the following occurred: you take your shopping cart filled with milk, bread, and bananas to the cash register, and you say to the checkout clerk, "I offer to buy this milk, bread, and bunch of bananas for $5." It's quite likely that the clerk will eye you suspiciously, because even though she bags your purchases, accepts your $5 cash, and hands you the grocery bag, she is not going to respond, "I accept your offer." Yet, this kind of transaction occurs every day, and this agreement to purchase goods is indeed a contract.

WHAT IS A CONTRACT?

contract
A legally binding agreement between two or more parties.

A **contract** is the necessary means by which commerce is conducted in our society. It is simply a legally binding agreement between parties, be they individuals or companies. The agreement may involve the purchase of goods, such as a car or this book, or the sale of services, such as the construction of a building or the painting of a house. As you will soon learn, contract law plays an important part in ensuring that valid agreements are enforced, and this entails an understanding of the myriad of rules defining contract formation, performance, and remedies available when a contract is breached. This chapter discusses the requirements of a valid contract and provides an overview of the specific rules and concepts related to the agreement between the parties. Once you think you have mastered the basic concepts, you will then discover that there are, naturally, exceptions to the rules. Lest you begin to feel confused, consider the notion that contract law centers on the court deciding which agreements ought to be kept and which ones mandate that the excuse or exception should be allowed.

Consider the reason contract law developed in the first instance. Historically, countries needed to reach agreements in order to avoid the conflict of war. Making treaties was a way to minimize disputes and outright aggression. Similarly, values in society today advocate reaching an agreement, and then binding the parties to respect that agreement. For example, assume that John promises to build a house for Martha, and Martha agrees to pay John a set price for his work. Martha relies on his promise, selling her existing home and moving in to an apartment with Mary. In enforcing this agreement between the parties, some people would argue that if you promise to do something, you should honor that commitment, because it is enough that you are morally and ethically bound to do so. Other people trust and rely on those promises and make promises in return. So, the basis for contract law is fundamentally that laws are needed to guarantee that people fulfill their agreements, and it is preferable to have the courts back up these contracts than to have the parties exchange blows and resolve their differences with physical conflict. Of course, there are good reasons why people may be unable to respect their commitments, and hence the law recognizes that in certain situations there is justification for not enforcing those promises.

In this chapter, you will learn the types of contracts, the method of formation, the determination of contract validity, and finally the remedies available if one party is unable to fulfill his commitment under the contract. Exceptions to general contract rules will be reviewed, and finally an overview of the legislation governing business contracts will be presented.

PARTIES TO A CONTRACT

As previously stated, a contract is a legally binding agreement between at least two parties that can be enforced by a court of law or equity. According to the Restatement of Contracts, (2d):

> *A contract is a promise or set of promises for the breach of which the law gives a remedy or the performance of which the law in some way recognizes a duty.*

offeror
The person making the offer to another party.

offeree
The person to whom the offer is made.

The agreement that represents the intent of the two parties as to the substance of their promises is a contract. There must be at least two parties, and they are generally referred to as the **offeror** and the **offeree.** The offeror is the party who is making the offer to enter into a contract. The offeree is the party to whom the offer is made. Note that an offeror can become the offeree and vice versa. For example, if Jack says to Mary, "I offer to sell you my brown leather sofa for $500," Jack is the offeror and Mary is the offeree. But, if Mary replies, "No, that is too much money, but I'll buy it for $400," then Mary is now the offeror and Jack is the offeree. As will be seen later in this chapter, in order to find that there was a binding agreement between the parties, the court must find conclusive evidence of *all* the elements of a contract.

ELEMENTS OF A BINDING CONTRACT

CYBER TRIP

See http://courttv.com/archive/legaldocs/business/pepsi.html. This is a copy of the complaint filed by a man who tried to redeem Pepsi-Cola points in exchange for a Harrier jet (*Leonard v. PepsiCo*). After reading the pleadings, locate the court's decision!

There are three key elements necessary to form a valid contract:

1. Offer
2. Acceptance
3. Consideration

In approaching a contract problem, keep in mind that each element should be taken in turn, so that unless you can find evidence of a valid offer, for example, then there is no need to go further to find manifestation of an acceptance. The first two elements—offer and acceptance—form the basis for the agreement, and the third element is the promise that supports the agreement, representing a bargained-for exchange of something of value that demonstrates the parties did intend to be bound by the terms of their agreement. Again, all three elements must be present in order to form a valid, enforceable contract. As you will learn later in this chapter, even if all three elements are present, there must not be any defenses that would preclude enforcement of the contract terms. A valid offer and a valid acceptance of that offer must be identified, as these form the basis for the agreement. Each element will be discussed here in detail.

Offer

An **offer** is the firm and clear promise to be bound to do something, such as a promise to build you a house or a promise to sell you my car. The offer is made with the condition that the party accepting this offer will do something in return. In order to be a valid offer, section 24 of the Restatement of Contracts specifies that there must be evidence of "the manifestation of willingness to enter into a bargain, so made as to justify another person in understanding that

offer
A promise made by the offeror to do (or not to do) something provided that the offeree, by accepting, promises or does something in exchange.

his assent to that bargain is invited and will conclude it." In order to constitute a valid offer, the following must be present:

1. The offeror must intend to be bound by the terms.
2. The terms of the offer must be definite and clear in substance (have reasonable certainty of terms).
3. The offer must be communicated so that the offeree may accept or reject it.

Imagine if your instructor says to you on the first day of class, "I offer to sell you my law book for $10." You are thinking, what a great deal, because the book you just purchased for your class cost $90. So, you excitedly shout out, "I accept that offer," and hand over $10 to your instructor. At this point, she takes your money, and then reaches into her pocket and hands you in exchange a 15-page paperback book. You would probably be surprised, but would also want your money back, because *it isn't what you expected*. The problem arises because there was no clear communication of definite terms, and thus no **meeting of the minds.** A better offer might be, "I offer to sell you my law book, titled *Law for You*, second edition, published by Smurf, for $10." Here, you probably have a valid offer that is capable of acceptance because it includes clear and definite terms about *which* book the offeror has in mind.

meeting of the minds
A legal concept requiring that both parties understand and ascribe the same meaning to the terms of the contract; a theory holding that both parties must both objectively and subjectively intend to enter into the agreement on the same terms.

In order to be definite in substance, the offer should contain at least these terms:

1. The specific subject matter of the contract.
2. The price.
3. The quantity.
4. Time for performance.

The subject matter of the contract should be a clear description that is not subject to interpretation. For example, saying "I offer to sell you my car for $5,000" is insufficient, especially if you own five cars, because the offer terms do not clearly convey the subject matter. Time for performance becomes important where the subject matter of the contract involves perishable product, or service contracts.

In addition, keep in mind that it should be certain whether the offer has been made to a specific person or to the whole world to accept. For example, if there is only *one* law book that your instructor has to sell, and she makes the offer to the entire class, then it becomes obvious that only one person can accept. In this case it is the first person who signifies assent. Otherwise, the instructor can say, "Mary, I offer to sell you my law book for $10," in which case the *only* person who may accept or reject this offer is Mary. This reflects the third element of offers: the offer must be communicated to the offeree. You cannot accept (or reject) an offer about which you know nothing.

Assume for example that Dudley telephones Mary at home with the intent of offering to sell his car to her for $5,000. Dudley knows that Mary is eager to buy his antique car and has inquired about the possibility often. So, when Dudley calls Mary, he is disappointed to find that Mary is not home. He leaves a message on her answering machine that says, "Mary, I offer to sell my antique car to you for $5,000, but you must let me know by the end of today if you are interested." Unfortunately, Mary has a parakeet that lands on the erase button of the answer machine, and therefore Mary never hears this message. Dudley doesn't receive a response from Mary, assumes she is not interested, and sells his prized car to Mortimer. In this situation, Mary could not accept the offer because it was not communicated to her (she can't accept an offer she didn't know about.)

intent
Having the knowledge and desire that a specific consequence will result from an action.

In ascertaining the validity of an offer, the court considers the terms previously listed, as well as the **intent** of the offeror. It must be obvious to a reasonable person that the person truly intended to be bound by her promise. If it appears that an offer was made in jest, or in anger, then it is unlikely that the court will treat this as an offer capable of acceptance. In addition, certain statements may appear to be offers, but in fact are nothing more than an invitation to make an offer. Some courts refer to this as an **invitation to treat,** which simply means that the person making the statement is expressing willingness to enter into negotiations but is not at the point to actually be bound by anything immediately. For example, most newspaper advertisements are not offers, but merely invitations to the public to come in and make an offer. Technically, advertised products are not really subject to price negotiation, but rather

invitation to treat
A person is expressing willingness to enter into negotiations, inviting another to make an offer.

the merchant is inviting customers to come to the store, select the advertised product, take it to the cashier, and *offer* to purchase it. Typically, store ads or merchandise displayed on a store shelf for sale are merely invitations to make an offer, and the offer is not made until the customer brings it to the cashier for payment. However, consider vending machines, selling soda or snacks. These can be deemed to be making offers, since once you have inserted your money, and the coins are accepted, the transaction is irrevocable, so it is not an invitation to make an offer.

Once an offer has been received, the offeree has several options: the offer can be *accepted,* it can be *rejected,* or it can be amended. However, if the offer terms are changed, that offer is actually no longer "on the table" because the offeree has effectively rejected it by making a **counteroffer.** A counteroffer is when the offeree changes a significant term of the original offer and creates a new offer. For example, assume that Milton offers to sell his set of golf clubs to Homer for $500. Homer might respond, "$500 is way too much. I'll give you $400." Here, the original offer by Milton (the offeror) is terminated, and once it is rejected, it is gone forever. The counteroffer is a new offer, making Homer now the offeror, which gives Milton (now the offeree) the right to accept or reject it. Assume Milton says, "No thanks, $400 is too low, I'll keep my clubs." Now, Homer goes home and thinks about it and decides that maybe $500 wasn't such a bad price after all. He immediately telephones Milton and says, "I changed my mind, I accept your offer." Is Milton obligated to sell the clubs to Homer? The answer is no because once Homer rejected the offer, it is no longer on the table to be accepted. If anything, Homer is free to make a new offer to buy the clubs for $500.

counteroffer
A refusal to accept the stated terms of an offer by proposing alternate terms.

acceptance
The offeree's clear manifestation of agreement to the exact terms of the offer in the manner specified in the offer.

Acceptance

Once a clear offer has been made, the offeree may accept it, reject it, or make a counteroffer, which as we have seen, is technically a new offer. **Acceptance** is basically a clear manifestation of agreement by the offeree to the exact terms of the offer in a manner specified by the offer. Whether an offer has truly been accepted depends on whether the contract is unilateral or bilateral. **Unilateral contracts** are those that can only be accepted by the offeree actually performing the required act. For example, if Steve places a flyer in a store window, advertising a $500 reward for the safe return of his kitty, Fluffy, then this is a unilateral offer. It is only capable of acceptance if the offeree—the person who finds Fluffy—actually returns Fluffy safely to Steve, at which time the reward money may be collected. A **bilateral contract** is accepted when the offeree promises to do something or promises to perform the requested act. This is essentially a promise for a promise, as in "I promise to paint your house if you promise to pay me $1,000 to paint your house."

As in the requirements for an offer, an acceptance must be communicated by the offeree to the offeror. If the offeree does accept, then the **mirror image rule** applies, in which the acceptance must be exactly the same as the offer. Terms cannot be modified, added, or deleted, because then it becomes a whole new offer capable of acceptance and the original offer is now rejected. Likewise, acceptances cannot be made by **unauthorized means.** The offeror has the right to specify how an offer can be accepted. For example, Joe can say, "I offer to sell you my tool box for $100. You must send me a certified letter accepting these terms." David is so excited about

unilateral contract
A contract in which the parties exchange a promise for an act.

bilateral contract
A contract in which the parties exchange a promise for a promise.

mirror image rule
A requirement that the acceptance of an offer must exactly match the terms of the original offer.

unauthorized means
The offeree accepts the offer by a method that is not the same as specified by the offeror.

You Be the Judge

Mario loses his pet dog, Spot. He places a notice in the windows of his local stores and on trees in the park: "Lost schnauzer, answers to the name, 'Spot.' Reward of $200 for his return." One week later, Helga finds the dog in the park while walking home. Although Helga saw the reward notice in the park on the day it was first posted, she has since forgotten about it when she finds Spot. Knowing that Spot belongs to Mario, Helga takes the dog to him and is pleased to get the $200 in return. Unknown to Mario, as he is leaving the house to remove the reward notices from the park and shop windows, Spot runs away again. All the reward notices are taken down. Later that day, Brutus, a policeman, finds the dog running loose down Main Street. Having previously read the reward posters, and unaware that Mario has just now removed all of them, Brutus takes Spot to Mario and asks for the $200 reward. Mario refuses. Analyze the rights of Brutus.

this offer that he picks up the phone and excitedly leaves a message on Joe's answering machine, "I accept." David then proceeds to send the certified letter. The offer has not been accepted when the voice message is left, but only when the letter is received by Joe.

Only the person to whom the offer is made has the power to accept or reject it. Assume that your instructor offers to sell her law book to Mary, who sits beside you in class. Mary says nothing, but you are prepared to buy right now, so you hand over your money to the instructor. The instructor is not bound to sell her book to a third person and create a contract; however, if Mary rejects the offer, then you are free to make an offer to buy the book, creating an offer for the instructor to accept.

Consider the same situation except that this time you overhear the instructor offering to sell Mary her law book for $10. Mary expresses interest and gives the instructor a dollar to keep the offer open for 24 hours while she thinks it over. You know this book is worth much more, so you approach the instructor immediately after overhearing this conversation and offer to buy the book for $25. Since this is a better deal, is the instructor now free to accept your offer? In this example, the answer is no. Mary has given the instructor a dollar to keep the offer open for a specific period of time. This is referred to as an **option contract.** An option contract is where the offeror agrees to not sell the subject matter of the offer to anyone other than the offeree during the time agreed to by both parties, so long as some consideration, or compensation, is paid to the offeror in exchange for keeping the offer open. This gives the offeree time to think about the offer without making an immediate decision but not risking losing the purchase to some other buyer. Now assume the same set of facts except that Mary does not give the instructor a dollar, but merely says, "Let me think about it; I'll let you know tomorrow." You overhear this conversation and immediately offer the instructor $25 for the book. In this case, the instructor is free to accept your offer because an offeror (the instructor) is free to **revoke,** or take back, an offer any time prior to it being accepted—unless consideration or compensation had been paid to keep it open.

option contract
A separate and legally enforceable agreement included in the contract stating that the offer cannot be revoked for a certain time period.

revoke
To take back, as in to retract an offer at any time prior to it being accepted.

Consideration

This is the necessary element to any agreement, as it signifies to a court that the parties intended to be bound by their agreement. **Consideration** is the bargained-for exchange, the thing of value that is given in exchange for a promise. Consideration can be a promise for a promise, or something of value, but each party must give something. It can be money, services, goods, or whatever will demonstrate that each party is receiving some benefit that is to the detriment of the other. The reason that this element is required to form a valid contract centers on the distinction the court makes between making a contract and making a gift. If Loulou gives her daughter a diamond necklace and does not expect, nor receive, anything in return, this is not an enforceable contract, but a gift, which can be revoked by Loulou if she changes her mind later that same day.

consideration
The basis of the bargained for exchange between the parties to a contract that is of legal value.

Consideration becomes a factor where the court is asked to determine if a valid contract exists and there is nothing in writing. Oral contracts are valid so long as they do not violate the **Statute of Frauds.** According to the Uniform Commercial Code, which is the basis for the statute of frauds, certain contracts *must* be in writing. Unless a contract falls into one of the following categories, then the contract may be entirely oral, and this is where courts are compelled to decide if consideration is present to support the finding of a valid contract. Contracts that must be in writing include those where the contract price is over $500, where the subject matter of the contract is real estate, service contracts that can't be completed in less than a year, and agreements to assume the debt of another when not legally required otherwise to do so.

Statute of Frauds
Rule that specifies which contracts must be in writing to be enforceable.

In order for consideration to be present, the court must conclude that both parties exchanged something of value. It has to be detrimental to the party giving it up or beneficial to the party who gets it. For example, if Tina agrees to pay for Mary's college education in exchange for Mary agreeing to give up smoking cigarettes, a court would conclude that this is not valid consideration if Mary has never smoked in the first place and doesn't plan to start. Mary has given nothing up in exchange for receiving a free college education.

Consideration cannot be given for something that is illegal or violates public policy. For example, assume that Ben and Stella have always disliked their daughter's husband, Mike. If Ben and Stella agree to buy their daughter a new house in exchange for the daughter divorcing Mike,

You Be the Judge

In July of this year, Basil contracted in writing to rent out his house overlooking Wrigley Field in Chicago to Tim, for a week in September, for the sum of $800 to be paid in advance. Both parties knew that the Chicago Cubs would surely be in the World Series that year and that at least two games would be played in Wrigley Field that specific week in September, although the contract made no mention of this. Tim paid the money to Basil, who immediately spent half of it on painting the house. Subsequently, the Cubs went on a lengthy losing streak and were eliminated from the playoffs. No games took place that week in September at Wrigley Field.

Analyze the rights of Tim, who did not use the house at all, and now wants his money back. Would your answer be different if the contract to rent was signed in September, after the Cubs had been eliminated?

a court would likely find that this contract is not valid as being contrary to public policy, as the consideration has a negative impact by encouraging divorce in society. Similarly, they could not offer to buy her a house in exchange for murdering Mike, as this is clearly illegal and contrary to public policy.

pre-existing duty
An obligation to perform an act that existed before the current promise was made that requires the same performance presently sought.

Finally, consideration is not valid if one of the parties had a **pre-existing duty.** Assume that you are a very nervous flier, and so as you are boarding EasyGo Airlines, you turn to the pilot and state, "if you land this plane safely at our final destination, I will give you $500." The pilot agrees. At the end of your uneventful plane flight, as you are getting off the plane, the pilot holds out his hand and demands the $500. Are you legally obligated to pay him? The answer is no because the pilot had a pre-existing duty to fly and land planes safely, and thus cannot use that promise as consideration for the promise to pay him $500.

It should be noted that the court only looks at the validity of the consideration, but not at whether both parties got a "good deal." In other words, a party cannot later challenge the validity of the contract based on inadequate consideration, once that agreement has been made. For example, you can't argue that the consideration was inadequate because you made a bad bargain, as in overpaying for a used car. In most cases, the court abides by the maxim *caveat emptor*, "let the buyer beware." Hence, so long as the contract does not fall into one of the exceptions noted later herein, the court will enforce the agreement between the parties if consideration had been given.

implied contract
An agreement whose terms have not been communicated in words, but rather by conduct or actions of the parties.

IMPLIED CONTRACTS

unjust enrichment
The retention by a party of unearned and undeserved benefits derived from his own wrongful actions regarding an agreement.

In some cases, there may not be an actual written contract, but the courts may look to the surrounding circumstances and still conclude that a valid contract exists. In this case, the courts find there is an **implied contract**. Evidence of an implied contract, meaning that the parties intended to be mutually bound, includes a "course of conduct" or prior dealings that are long-standing and fairly regular. Commonly referred to as a *quasi contract*, this is technically a remedy, as it is a legal fiction created by the courts to create a contract so as to avoid one party benefiting at the expense of the other. This theory is called **unjust enrichment.**

You Be the Judge

Sam signs a contract with Pete's Painters, hiring the company to paint his house. On the scheduled day, Pete's employees, Henry and Matt, drive out to Sam's neighborhood and park in the driveway of what they honestly believe to be Sam's house, but actually is Mary's home. Mary is sitting in her kitchen and watches Henry and Matt paint her entire house, without saying a word. Later that day, after they leave, Sam arrives home and discovers that his house has not been painted. Pete's Painters sues Sam for the contract price. What is the likely result?

CASE IN POINT

District of Columbia Court of Appeals.
Harold PEARSALL, Appellant,
v.
Joe ALEXANDER, Appellee.
No. 87-826.

Argued Feb. 28, 1990.
Decided March 22, 1990.

Before NEWMAN, FERREN, and FARRELL, Associate Judges.
NEWMAN, Associate Judge:
In what must be a common development wherever there are state-sponsored lotteries, this is the story of two friends who split the price of a ticket only to have the ticket win and split their friendship.

Harold Pearsall appeals from the dismissal of his complaint against Joe Alexander, in which Pearsall claimed breach of an agreement to share the proceeds of a winning D.C. Lottery ticket worth $20,000. The trial court found that such an agreement did, in fact, exist, but determined that the agreement was invalid under § 1 of the Statute of Anne, as enacted in D.C.Code § 16-1701 (1989 Repl.). We conclude that the trial court erred in applying § 16-1701 to the Pearsall-Alexander agreement and, therefore, we reverse and remand with instructions to enter judgment for the appellant.

I.

Harold Pearsall and Joe Alexander were friends for over twenty-five years. About twice a week they would get together after work, when Alexander would meet Pearsall at the Takoma Metro station in his car. The pair would then proceed to a liquor store, where they would purchase what the two liked to refer to as a "package"—a half-pint of vodka, orange juice, two cups, and two lottery tickets—before repairing to Alexander's home. There they would "scratch" the lottery tickets, drink screwdrivers, and watch television. On occasion these lottery tickets would yield modest rewards of two or three dollars, which the pair would then "plow back" into the purchase of additional lottery tickets. According to Pearsall, the two had been sharing D.C. Lottery tickets in this fashion since the Lottery began.

On the evening of December 16, 1982, Pearsall and Alexander visited the liquor store twice, buying their normal "package" on each occasion. The first package was purchased when the pair stopped at the liquor store on the way to Alexander's home from the Metro station. Pearsall went into the store alone, and when he returned to the car, he said to Alexander, in reference to the tickets, "Are you in on it?" Alexander said "Yes." When Pearsall asked Alexander for his half of the purchase price of the tickets, Alexander replied that he had no money. When they reached Alexander's home, Alexander, expressing his anxiety that Pearsall might lose the tickets, demanded that Pearsall produce them, snatched them from Pearsall's hand, and "scratched" them, only to find that both were worthless.

At about 8:00 p.m. that same evening, Alexander, who apparently had come by some funds of his own, returned to the liquor store and bought a second "package". This time Pearsall, who had been offended by Alexander's conduct earlier in taking both tickets, snatched the two tickets from Alexander and announced that he would be the one to "scratch" them. Intending only to bring what he regarded as Alexander's childish behavior to Alexander's attention, Pearsall immediately relented and gave over one of the tickets to Alexander. Each man then "scratched" one of the tickets. Pearsall's ticket proved worthless; Alexander's was a $20,000 winner.

Alexander became very excited about the ticket and began calling friends to announce the good news. Fearing that Alexander might lose the ticket, Pearsall told Alexander to sign his name on the back of the ticket. Subsequently, Alexander cashed in the ticket and received the winnings; but, when Pearsall asked for his share, Alexander refused to give Pearsall anything.

Pearsall brought suit against Alexander, claiming breach of an agreement to share the proceeds of the winning ticket. Alexander denied that there was any agreement between the two to share the winnings of the ticket and further claimed, *inter alia*, that any such agreement was unenforceable because it was not in writing and contravened public policy.

The trial court dismissed Pearsall's complaint on the public policy grounds raised by Alexander, finding that the enforcement of contracts arising from gaming transactions is barred by the Statute of Anne, as enacted in D.C.Code § 16-1701, even when such contracts concern legalized gambling. Citing *Hamilton v. Blankenship*, 190 A.2d 904 (D.C.1963), for this latter proposition, the trial court went on to determine that § 16-1701 applies to bets placed legally within the District pursuant to D.C.Code § 2-2501 to 2537, which authorizes the D.C. Lottery. The court did not reach the issue of whether such an agreement must be in writing pursuant to the Statute of Frauds, as enacted in D.C.Code § 28:1-206 (1981).

[1] The Statute of 9 Anne, ch. 14, § 1 (1970), as enacted in the District of Columbia, provides, in relevant part, as follows:

FN1. The Statute of Anne, enacted in England in 1710, outlawed certain forms of wagering, permitted losers to recover their gambling losses, and denied winners the use of judicial process to collect from recalcitrant losers. *LaFontaine v. Wilson*, 185 Md. 673, 45 A.2d 729, 732 (1946). This latter goal was addressed in § 1 of the Statute, which declared as void all contracts growing out of gambling transactions. *D.C.Code Encyclopedia*, § 16-1701 (1966). § 1 of the Statute of Anne was adopted in the District of Columbia, D.C.Code, 1961 Ed., § 16-1701 (9 Anne, 14, § 1, 1710; Kilty's Rept., p. 248; Alex.Brit.Stat., p. 689; Comp.Stat. D.C., p. 243, § 12), where it continues to apply, D.C.Code § 16-1701 (1989), *Hamilton v. Blankenship, supra*, 190 A.2d 904, except where it is inconsistent with or repealed by subsequent law. *Wirt v. Stubblefield*, 17 App.D.C. 283 (1900).

§ 16-1701. Invalidity of gaming contracts.

(a) A thing in action, judgment, mortgage, or other security or conveyance made and executed by a person

> in which any part of the consideration is for money or other valuable thing won by playing at any game whatsoever, or by betting on the sides or hands of persons who play, or for the reimbursement or payment of any money knowingly lent or advanced for the purpose, or lent or advanced at the time and place of play or bet, to a person so playing or betting or who, during the play, so plays or bets, is void except as provided by subsection (b) of this section.
>
> D.C.Code § 16-1701. Thus, the statute invalidates only those contracts in which one party agrees either to (1) pay something to another as the result of losing a game or bet, or (2) repay money knowingly advanced or lent for the purpose of gambling. *Hamilton v. Blankenship, supra,* 190 A.2d 904.

Pearsall's cause of action does not involve either of these types of transactions. First, he is not suing Alexander to recover a gambling debt owed by Alexander. Pearsall and Alexander did not wager against one another on the outcome of the D.C. Lottery or any other event, and they did not play against one another at cards, dice, or any other game. Second, Pearsall is not suing to recover money loaned to Alexander for the purpose of gambling. Rather Pearsall and Alexander entered into an agreement to share the winnings of a jointly-purchased lottery ticket, and it is this agreement, and not any gaming contract, that forms the basis of Pearsall's cause of action. Thus, the nature of the Pearsall-Alexander agreement removes it from the ambit of *Hamilton v. Blankenship, id.,* upon which the trial court relied.

FN2. *Hamilton* concerned an agreement by a D.C. resident to repay a Maryland restauranteur the loan of some $1600 in coins knowingly advanced for the purpose of playing slot machines, which were legal in the county where the loan was made. In invalidating this contract, the court applied Maryland's Statute of Anne, which, like our own, expressly voids such contracts

Similarly, we distinguish this case from the Nevada cases cited by the *Hamilton* court, which held that the Statute of Anne remained in force despite the legality of gambling in Nevada. Like *Hamilton,* those cases dealt with the types of contracts expressly invalidated by the Statute of Anne, and thus it was held that the Statute prevented a gambling establishment from suing a customer to recover losses, *West Indies, Inc. v. First Nat'l Bank of Nev.,* 67 Nev. 13, 214 P.2d 144 (1950), a customer from suing a gambling establishment to recover winnings, *Weisbrod v. Fremont Hotel, Inc.,* 74 Nev. 227, 326 P.2d 1104 (1958), and a creditor from recovering funds loaned to another for the purpose of gambling, *Wolpert v. Knight,* 74 Nev. 322, 330 P.2d 1023 (1958). Once again, the Pearsall-Alexander agreement does not fall into any of these categories and, thus, these cases are inapposite.

Moreover, the Pearsall-Alexander agreement is not based upon the type of consideration described in the § 16-1701, *i.e.,* money or valuables won at gambling or knowingly loaned for the purpose of gambling. Rather, each man gave as consideration for the agreement his promise to share the proceeds of the ticket he "scratched." Such consideration does not derive from one man having bested the other in a game of chance. Nor does it derive from any sort of loan.

. . .

Therefore, the agreement that forms the basis of Pearsall's cause of action is not a gaming contract as defined in § 16-1701, and the trial court erred in applying the statute in this case.

FN4. Because we conclude that the trial court misapplied the statute in this case, we do not reach the issue of whether the statute has been repealed or narrowed by the passage of D.C.Code § 2-2501 to 2537 (1988) creating the D.C. Lottery. However, we do note with interest § 2-2520, which is titled "Persons ineligible to purchase tickets or *shares* or receive prizes." (Emphasis added). This reference to shares seems to acknowledge that agreements to share winnings exist. . . .

B.

In addition to concluding that the Pearsall-Alexander agreement does not offend the letter of § 16-1701, we are equally convinced that it gives no offense to the statute's spirit. . . .

Stated differently, denying Pearsall recovery is not going to discourage illegal gambling in this instance, because the gambling involved, betting on the D.C. Lottery, is not illegal. Nor does it make sense to say that denying Pearsall recovery will serve the public policy interest of discouraging gambling in general, whether legal or illegal, when the District is spending money to encourage people like Pearsall and Alexander to gamble on the Lottery in order to serve the public policy behind the Lottery.

We note that other jurisdictions faced with public policy challenges to agreements to share the proceeds of winning lottery tickets have reached the same result we reach today. . . .

We further note that the force of this reasoning is only increased where, as in this situation, the gambling at issue is legal in the court's own jurisdiction. If a jurisdiction surrounded by states with legalized lotteries cannot expect to deter its citizens from betting on such lotteries by prohibiting agreements of this kind, then surely a jurisdiction with its own legalized lottery cannot expect, and more to the point should not be about the business of trying, to deter its citizens from betting on its own lottery by prohibiting such agreements either.

News accounts and personal observations reveal that it is common practice for friends, relatives, and coworkers to pool their resources and purchase large blocks of tickets on those occasions when various state lotteries present exceptionally large prizes. The approach taken by the trial court would make such arrangements perilous indeed, by permitting the unscrupulous holders of winning tickets to renege on their agreement and keep the winnings for themselves. We agree with the Supreme Court of Indiana that such an approach would only reward those who convert the property of others, without conferring any benefit on the citizens of the District.

III.

[2] The record supports the trial court's finding that an agreement existed between Pearsall and Alexander to share equally in the proceeds of the winning ticket at issue.

The conduct of the two men on the evening of December 16, 1982, when the ticket was purchased, clearly demonstrates a meeting of the minds. After purchasing the first pair of tickets, Pearsall asked Alexander if he was "in on it." Not only did Alexander give his verbal assent, but later, when the two reached Alexander's home, Alexander, who had contributed nothing to the purchase price of the tickets, snatched *both* tickets from Pearsall and anxiously "scratched" them. It is evident from this that Alexander considered himself "in on" an agreement to share in the fortunes of the tickets purchased by his friend. It is equally clear that in giving over tickets he had purchased, Pearsall gave his assent to the agreement he had proposed earlier in the car. Moreover, this conduct took place within the context of a long-standing pattern of similar conduct, analogous to a "course of conduct" as described in the Uniform Commercial Code, which included their practice of "plowing back" small returns from winning tickets into the purchase of additional tickets.

FN5. U.C.C. § 1-205(1), adopted in the District of Columbia as D.C.Code § 28:1-205(1) (1981), provides that "[a] course of dealing is a sequence of previous conduct between the parties to a particular transaction which is fairly to be regarded as establishing a common basis of understanding for interpreting their expressions and other conduct."

FN6. In view of this evidence, we reject Alexander's contention that the trial court's finding of an agreement between the two men was clearly erroneous or not supported by sufficient evidence. Furthermore, we see no reason to disturb the trial court's findings on credibility.

[3] It is also clear to us that, by exchanging mutual promises to share in the proceeds of winning tickets, adequate consideration was given by both parties. An exchange of promises is consideration, so long as it is bargained-for. Restatement (Second) Contracts, § 75 (1932). Moreover, consideration may consist of detriment to the promisee. *Clay v. Chesapeake & Potomac Tel. Co.,* 87 U.S.App.D.C., 284 F.8d 995 (1950). The giving over of one-half of the proceeds of a winning ticket would be a detriment to either man. Therefore, Pearsall's promise to share, as expressed in his question to Alexander, "Are you in it?" induced a detriment in Alexander. Likewise, Alexander's promise to share, as contained in his assent, induced a detriment in Pearsall.

FN7. Adequate consideration also may be found by characterizing this agreement as an exchange of mutual promises to forbear. Williston on Contracts, Third Edition § 135 at 567 (1957). Forbearance may be found in each party's promise not to exercise his right to keep to himself the entirety of the proceeds of a winning ticket in his possession

[4] Finally, we find no merit in Alexander's contention that the agreement is unenforceable under D.C.Code § 28:1-206, because it is not in writing. § 28:1-206 provides as follows:

Statute of Frauds for kinds of personal property not otherwise covered.

(1) Except in the cases described in subsection (2) of this section a contract for the sale of personal property is not enforceable by way of action or defense beyond five thousand dollars in amount or value of remedy unless there is some writing which indicates that a contract for sale has been made between the parties at a defined or stated price, reasonably identifies the subject matter, and is signed by the party against whom enforcement is sought or by his authorized agent.

(2) Subsection (1) of this section does not apply to contracts for the sale of goods (section 28:2-201) nor of securities (section 28:8-319) nor to security agreements (section 28:9-203).

D.C.Code § 28:1-206 (1981).

This statute, which applies only to the sale of personal property "beyond" $5000, is inapplicable on its face. The Pearsall-Alexander agreement does not involve the sale of personal property. There was no agreement between the parties for the holder of a winning ticket to "sell" half of his winnings, as personal property, to the other. This was simply an agreement to share the proceeds of a jointly-purchased ticket; no buying or selling as between the parties was contemplated or required.

IV.

In conclusion, we find that there was a valid, enforceable agreement between Pearsall and Alexander to share in the proceeds of the $20,000 ticket purchased by Alexander on the evening of December 16, 1982. Therefore, we reverse and remand with instructions to enter judgment in favor of the appellant.

Reversed and remanded.

FN9. We find no merit in Alexander's argument that we should refuse to enforce the contract because Pearsall allegedly intended to defraud the Internal Revenue Service by permitting Alexander, who allegedly was in a lower tax bracket than Pearsall, to claim the prize. At this point, such allegations are merely speculative and, therefore, are not properly before this court.

Source: *Pearsall v. Alexander,* 572 A.2d 113 (St. Paul, MN: Thomson West). Reprinted with permission from Westlaw.

DEFENSES TO VALID CONTRACTS

Even if all the elements of a valid contract are present, the court may still conclude that the contract is not enforceable. Once each element of a contract is proved, it is up to the party seeking to get out of a contract to prove that he has an excuse why the contract should not be honored. In certain cases, the court will agree and release the party from respecting his promise under that agreement.

capacity
The ability to understand the nature and significance of a contract.

First, a party can claim that either she or the other party to the agreement lacked **capacity** to enter into a valid contract. Here, the basis for the allegation is that the person has been formally adjudicated to be mentally incompetent, was under the influence of some intoxicating substance at the time of entering into the contract, or is not of legal age. It should be noted that the court judges the capacity of the person *at the time* the parties entered into the contract. If one is alleging that being intoxicated prevented him from understanding the nature and import of his actions, the court will examine the surrounding circumstances to decide if this is a valid excuse. Generally, the courts will look to whether the person has a documented illness or a history of substance abuse, and whether the intoxication was self-induced or involuntary, as when the other party intentionally provided substances to confuse the person. Courts are divided on whether self-induced intoxication will be a valid argument for lack of contractual capacity.

Mental incompetence must be demonstrated by proof that some formal proceeding had occurred prior to the contract formation, declaring the person incapable of handling her own affairs. It is not enough to argue that you were crazy at the time or didn't really comprehend what you were doing when you signed the contract.

CASE IN POINT

Supreme Court, New York County, New York,
Special Term, Part I.
Christopher PANDO, an Infant over the age of 14 years, by his father
and natural guardian, John PANDO, Plaintiff,
v.
Daysi a/k/a Daisy FERNANDEZ, New York State Division of the Lottery,
Department of Taxation and Finance, Defendants.
Oct. 19, 1984.

EDWARD J. GREENFIELD, Justice.
The motions of defendant Fernandez to dismiss the complaint for failure to state a cause of action and for summary judgment are consolidated for disposition with plaintiff's motion for sanctions for failure of that defendant to comply with requirements for discovery, and defendant's cross-motion for leave to amend the answer.

Plaintiff, claiming breach of a "partnership agreement", asks the court for a declaratory judgment, for the imposition of a constructive trust, and for an accounting, arising out of his contention that defendant Fernandez, winner of a $2.8 million lottery prize, promised to share her winnings equally with him. The complaint consists of two causes of action. The first alleges that plaintiff, a minor, entered into an oral "partnership agreement" with Mrs. Fernandez, who, believing the youth to be deeply religious and a strong believer in "St. Eleggua", prayers to whom might help her win the prize, promised that if plaintiff took her $4.00 and purchased the tickets and selected the numbers, and any of the tickets he purchased won, they would share the prize equally. One of the tickets he claims to have purchased for her in fact did win a prize of $2.8 million dollars, and plaintiff claims that the refusal to give him 50% of the proceeds constitutes a breach of contract. The second cause of action alleges that despite the agreement Mrs. Fernandez presented the winning ticket to the New York State Division of the Lottery of the Department of Taxation claiming to be the sole owner of the ticket. Plaintiff seeks a declaratory judgment as to the rights of the parties, and asks for the imposition of a constructive trust, so that the proceeds hereafter would be paid equally. He also asks for an accounting for all moneys already paid out and received.

Defendant Fernandez, having answered by interposing a general denial, now moves to dismiss on three grounds: (i) that the alleged oral agreement is barred by the Statute of Frauds because it is incapable of being performed within one year; (ii) that the agreement called upon a minor to do an illegal act, and is therefore unenforceable; and (iii) that it is impossible to prove in a court of law that the conditions precedent to the effectiveness of the contract have taken place.

On the motion addressed to the complaint alone, which does not spell out the controlling facts but alleges a breach of contract in very broad terms, it is difficult to focus on the grounds for the motion to dismiss. However, defendant has also asked for summary judgment, and both sides have seen fit to augment the bare facts of the complaint with factual affidavits which flesh out and clarify the controversy.

Defendant, 38, the mother of three children, who before good fortune befell her was on welfare, vehemently denies that she ever asked plaintiff, a 16 year old friend of her son, to buy lottery tickets or to pick the numbers for her, and she emphatically denies any suggestion that she offered to share her winnings equally with him. Denials, however, as she and her attorney recognize, are properly reserved as issues of credibility for the trial. There are, however, certain undisputed facts set forth in the affidavits which require the court to make legal determinations as to the viability of the cause of action wholly independent of disputes as to credibility.

***226 Statute of Frauds**

Defendant contends that the alleged oral agreement to share the prize equally, even if plaintiff's allegations be accepted as true, runs afoul of the Statute of Frauds, because the prize of $2,877,203.30 is to be paid out by the state Lottery Division in annual installments over a ten year period.

Section 5-701 of the General Obligations Law specifies:

> a. Every agreement, promise or undertaking is void, unless it or some note or memorandum thereof be in writing, and subscribed by the party to be charged therewith, or by his lawful agent, if such agreement, promises, or undertaking:
> 1. By its terms is not to be performed within one year from the making thereof . . .

Defendant contends that the alleged agreement cannot be performed within one year. She relies on the line of cases in which an oral agreement to pay commissions over a period of several years has been held to be unenforceable. . . .

[1] Defendant claims the ten year payout of the total prize here calls for analogous treatment. In this case, however, the contract could be performed well within one year. Defendant was to furnish the funds with which to purchase the ticket. Plaintiff had to purchase the ticket, select the numbers, return it to defendant, and pray. The winning numbers were scheduled to be drawn, and were drawn, within days, and at that time the obligations of the parties became fixed. The defendant would then have to have notified a third party, the state Lottery Division, that all future payments were to be divided equally between herself and the plaintiff, a task which she could perform within days. At that point the obligations of each side would have been performed. (*North Shore Bottling Co., Inc. v. Schmidt & Sons, Inc.*, 22 N.Y.2d 171, 292 N.Y.S.2d 86, 239 N.E.2d 189.) The fact that the payout

would be extended over several years is of no moment, for the liability, if any, was fixed, the amounts known, and all that remained was the ministerial act of having the annual payouts divided. That is quite different from an agreement by a party to pay out a percentage of sales or earnings over a period of years, which may call for future services, and where the amounts cannot be established until well into the future.

. . .

The actual computation of the amount due, even if it were to take more than a year, was of no significance, since this was a mere ministerial act. The controlling criterion is the time at which the obligation becomes, or could become fixed. If all the contingencies can occur, and all conditions precedent can be performed within the one year period, with nothing remaining to be done thereafter except the act of payment, there is no violation of the Statute of Frauds.

The ten year payout of the prize in this case is the measure of the obligation of the State Lottery Division. The alleged obligation of the defendant to share that prize with plaintiff was fixed well within the one year period.

Illegality

Defendant contends that inasmuch as the alleged agreement called upon the plaintiff, who was under 18, to purchase the lottery ticket, it called for the performance of an illegal act, so that the enforcement of the contract by our courts would contravene the public policy of the state prohibiting the encouragement of gambling by minors.

[3] Undeniably, the public policy of the state, as exemplified in its constitution (N.Y.Const., Art. I, Sec. 9[1]), prohibits gambling or lotteries except those operated by the state. Its proceeds are applied to aid education, with appropriate legislation to prevent offenses. The policy of the state disfavors gambling, unless done in accordance with laws and regulations strictly complied with. *Molina v. Games Management Services*, 89 A.D.2d 69, 72, 454 N.Y.S.2d 730, aff'd 58 N.Y.2d 523, 462 N.Y.S.2d 615, 449 N.E.2d 395. Thus a comprehensive statutory scheme was enacted in 1976 to set up a lottery commission to supervise, with standards as to the eligibility and licensing of ticket agents, the sale of lottery tickets, and the distribution of prizes. Tax Law, Secs. 1601–1616. Section 1610 dealt with barring participation by minors. It provides:

> Sec. 1610. Sales to certain persons prohibited
>
> a. No ticket shall be sold to any person under the age of eighteen years, but this shall not be deemed to prohibit the purchase of a ticket for the purpose of making a gift by a person eighteen years of age or older to a person less than that age. Any licensee or the employee or agent of any licensee who sells or offers to sell a lottery ticket to any person under the age of eighteen shall be guilty of a misdemeanor.
> b. No ticket shall be sold to and no prize shall be paid to any of the following persons:
> (i) any member, officer or employee of the division; or
> (ii) any member, officer or employee of the department of taxation and finance whose duties directly relate to the operation of the state lottery; or
> (iii) any spouse, child, brother, sister or parent residing as a member of the same household in the principal place of abode of any of the foregoing persons.

The statute plainly sets forth two categories: (a) those to whom no ticket may be sold, and (b) those to whom no ticket may be sold *and* to whom no prize shall be paid. Persons under 18 are in the first class.

[4][5] Thus it is clear that the prohibition against some degree of participation by those under 18 years of age is not absolute. A gift of a ticket or a prize to a child of any age is permitted, for it is specified that a minor may be the donee of a winning ticket purchased by an adult. See, for example, *Mizrahi v. Mizrahi,* 57 Misc.2d 1021, 293 N.Y.S.2d 964. It is further to be noted that while sellers are not permitted to sell to minors, they are not included in that class of persons to whom no prize may be paid. Had it been the intention of the legislature to prohibit prizes to minors who had illegally purchased tickets, it could have spelled out that intent in Section 1610(b). It did not. Instead, Sec. 1613(b) specifies the procedures for distributing prize money to minors. This differs from the situation in *Johnson v. New York Daily News,* 97 A.D.2d 458, 467 N.Y.S.2d 665, aff'd. 61 N.Y.2d 839, 473 N.Y.S.2d 975, 462 N.E.2d 152, where the 14 year old whose name appeared on a winning "Super Zingo" ticket was barred from recovery because of the restrictive rules specified by the newspaper, as conclusively interpreted by the contest judges.

> If a statute does not provide expressly that its violation will deprive the parties of their right to sue on the contract, and the denial of relief is wholly out of proportion to the requirements of public policy or appropriate individual punishment, the right to recover will not be denied.
>
> *Rosasco Creameries v. Cohen*, 276 N.Y. 274, 278, 11 N.E.2d 908.

I find no pervasive requirement that the protection of public morals calls for denial of enforceability of this alleged contract. "The courts are not free to refuse to enforce a . . . right at the pleasure of the judges, to suit the individual notion of expediency or fairness. They do not close their doors unless help would violate some fundamental principle of justice, some prevalent conception of good morals, some deep-rooted tradition of the common weal" . . . Courts did refuse to enforce an alleged agreement to divide a lottery prize in *Goodrich v. Houghton,* 134 N.Y. 115, 31 N.E. 516, and *Moskowitz v. Cohen,* 158 Misc. 489, 286 N.Y.S. 152, but that was at a time when all lotteries were illegal. Here the lottery was legal, and distribution of a prize to a minor is legal. While the purchase of the ticket was not legal, I hold that, in itself, to be no bar to receipt of a share of the prize. Cf.*Cohen v. Iuzzini,* 25 A.D.2d 878, 270 N.Y.S.2d 278.

Impossibility of Proof

[6] The most intriguing question presented by this case is whether, in a court of law, plaintiff can prove compliance with the conditions of the contract, as he has set it forth. In an affidavit he submitted specifying in greater detail the nature of the alleged contract, and attempting to explain why an adult would ask him to get the tickets and select the numbers, he said:

> . . . Mrs. Fernandez, knowing that I am religious and a strong believer in St. Eleggua asked me, after noticing that the Lotto prize was several million dollars, whether or not I could get my Saint to win the Lottery. I told her that I did not know, but I would try. She thereupon told me that she would give me $4.00 to select four

> different tickets and that if my St. Eleggua made my selection of the Lottery numbers win, she would go equal partners with me on the prize.

Taking plaintiff's description of the agreement on its face, it is apparent that the expressed condition precedent for the sharing of the prize is that his piety and prayer would cause heavenly intervention so that his selections would win. How can plaintiff prove on a trial that "St. Eleggua made my selection of the Lottery numbers win"?

On a trial he can testify as to his version of what defendant said. He can testify that he purchased the tickets, and that he selected the numbers. He can testify that he prayed. Who is going to provide the proof that his prayers were efficacious, and that the saint caused the numbers to win?

It is not a sufficient answer that he prayed, and that one of the tickets he filled out was the winner. That would leave a gap in the proof, which must demonstrate not merely that winning followed prayer, but that plaintiff's prayer was the causative factor in winning. According to his own story, defendant was not relying on him because he was lucky, but because she believed he had the ability through his piety to intercede with the saint, and persuade the heavenly powers to cause his number to win.

FN* In attempting to ascertain the identity of "St. Eleggua", the closest the court could come in its research was a saint with the Latin name of St. Eligius (immortalized on television as St. Elsewhere), the patron saint of goldsmiths, who before his canonization served under French kings in the 7th Century as master of the mint, and who showered his riches on the poor who turned to him in overwhelming numbers. He possessed the gifts of miracles and prophecy, and is reputed to have broken open the chains of prisoners by his prayers. 2A Dictionary of Christian Biography, p. 93, 1967 ed.; Butler's *Lives of the Saints,* rev. ed. of 4 Thurston & Attwater, pp. 455–458. No wonder defendant sought to invoke his aid as the means to overwhelming riches!

[7] In other words, according to the terms of the deal as set forth by plaintiff himself, he was to be rewarded, not if defendant's tickets fortuitously won, but only if his efforts caused her to win. If a party is to receive a sum of money only on the occurrence of a contingent event which he did nothing to bring about, the transaction would be of an aleatory nature and would partake of the elements of an unenforceable wager. Cf. *Liss v. Manuel,* 58 Misc.2d 614, 617, 296 N.Y.S.2d 627; *Irving v. Britton,* 8 Misc. 201, 203, 28 N.Y.S. 529. If defendant was bargaining at all, it was not to afford plaintiff an "all profit-no risk" deal. She wanted something from plaintiff—not his skill in picking the right seller or the right numbers but, because of his piety and devoutness, his "connections" with heavenly powers which would result in divine intervention to cause her to win. In short, she wanted nothing less than a miracle! Plaintiff would have to arrange for a miracle to be brought about by St. Eleggua if he was to share in the winnings. To recover, plaintiff must demonstrate that his prayers caused the miracle to occur.

How can we really know what happened? Is a court to engage in the epistemological inquiry as to the acquisition of knowledge and belief through proof or through faith? Faith is the antithesis of proof. It is a belief which is firmly held even though demonstrable proof may be lacking. It is instinctive, spiritual, and profound, arrived at not through a coldly logical appraisal of the facts but, in Wordsworth's phrase, by "a passionate intuition".

> "Faith is the substance of things hoped for, the evidence of things not seen." Paul, Epistle to Hebrews: xi, 1.

How, then, in a court of law, set up to require tangible proof, in a mundane setting, can a litigant establish that his faith and his prayers brought about a miracle? Perhaps they did, but there is no way to prove that in a modern courtroom.

In ages past, controversies were not determined by marshaling an array of rational probative proof. Under Roman law, there was acceptance of divine testimonies, omens, auguries of oracles and the power of dreams. 1 Wigmore, Evidence, Sec. 9, fn. 6 (Tillers rev. ed. 1983). In Medieval law the demonstration of miracles in the courtroom and a show of divine intervention were grist for the judicial mill, and trial by combat and trial by ordeal constituted proof of God's will. But in those days, the function of the secular and the ecclesiastical courts was not sharply separated, and the distinction was not drawn between the *ius soli,* the law of earth, and *ius poli,* the law of heaven. 1 Pollock and Maitland, History of English Law, Second Ed., p. 112. Up to the 18th Century, testimony of the power of spells was received in cases where a defendant was accused of witchcraft—the charge that invocation of the spirits caused temporal disasters. Goebel & Naughton, Law Enforcement in Colonial New York (1944) pp. 558–559. The question of the efficacy of prayer is just the converse. Are we to accept testimony or argument that invoking the power of Heaven rather than of the nether world, followed by a beneficial rather than a sinister result should result in a court decision? In this more workaday and pragmatic era, shaped by tragic experience, the chasm between the temporal and the spiritual world has become unbridgeable. Theology is to be protected against the law, just as the law is to be protected from theology.

It is incumbent on the plaintiff to prove that under the agreement as he alleged it, every condition which had to occur to entitle him to payment did occur, and thereupon defendant's obligation came into being. The condition was not that the numbers chosen would win, but that the saint was to make the numbers win. Establishing that this occurred is not susceptible to forensic proof. It calls for matters which transcend proof—the existence of saints, the power of prayer, and divine intervention in temporal affairs. "What is faith," said St. Augustine, "unless it is to believe what you do not see?" But judges and jurors must decide based on what they have seen and heard, not on what faith leads them to believe. Beliefs founded on faith cannot readily be tested on motions directed to the sufficiency of the evidence, or on appellate review.

If a rainmaker exacts a promise from a group of farmers to be paid if he makes it rain, he can collect if the trier of facts finds he seeded supercooled clouds with silver iodide and an expert testifies that was the cause of the rain. On the other hand, if the rainmaker performs chants and dances and incantations and it rains within 24 hours, he cannot demonstrate by accepted judicial modes of proof that his acts caused the desired event. The distinction is that in the first example the claimant is shown to have caused something; in the second we do not know if he has.

The distinction must always be made between evidence based on knowledge and conclusions based on belief. This court has no desire to denigrate the power of prayer, matters of spirit, or the workings of the hand of God, but such matters, not susceptible of rational courtroom proof, are for theology and not jurisprudence. Concededly, "there are more things in heaven and in earth . . . than are dream't of in [our] philosophy."

[8] To recapitulate, the agreement as alleged by plaintiff required him to comply with four conditions precedent:

1. He was to buy the lottery tickets with defendant's money.
2. He was to select the numbers.
3. He was to pray to the saint.
4. The saint was to make his selection win.

Condition # 4 is impossible of courtroom proof. What are the consequences? There are two options open:

a Ignore the last condition and enforce the contract.

b Declare the contract unenforceable.

The argument for ignoring the condition essentially is that plaintiff has done all he humanly could. He has performed as completely as he was able, and he should not be penalized because he cannot demonstrate that he brought about heavenly intervention. But heavenly intervention is exactly what defendant bargained for—that her pious young friend would bring about a miracle. It was not an incidental part of the agreement—it was its essence, its very heart and soul. Is she to be deprived of half the return on her investment, and plaintiff rewarded, because she was naive and gullible? Elision of the unprovable condition (tantamount to proof by default) would result in a rewriting of the contract into something other than what the parties intended. Defendant did not bargain for a propitious coincidence but for a miracle. If she believed it to have happened, she was free to show her appreciation or to withhold it, but a court could not compel her to do so. "There are no guarantees in life, and good fortune . . . does not invariably bring with it a life-long annuity." *Trimmer v. Van Bomel,* 107 Misc.2d 201, 213, 434 N.Y.S.2d 82, aff'd. 82 A.D.2d 1023, 441 N.Y.S.2d 762, lv. den. 55 N.Y.2d 602.

Constructive Trust

[9] It was open, of course for defendant, even if not contractually bound, to share her good fortune and shower her bounty upon plaintiff. Without consideration, and without any performance, she could designate plaintiff as the recipient of a gift or the beneficiary of a trust, provided the words or acts are unequivocal and that the only interpretation is that the property is to be held in trust. *Blanco v. Velez,* 295 N.Y. 224, 66 N.E.2d 171; *Matter of Fontanella,* 33 A.D.2d 29, 30, 304 N.Y.S.2d 829. She could do so unconditionally, or she could require that it would occur only upon the happening of a specified condition. A donor may agree to bestow money on a nephew if he gives up smoking (*Hamer v. Sidway,* 124 N.Y. 538, 550, 27 N.E. 256), or give money if a child marries as the father wishes. (*Sarasohn v. Kamaiky,* 193 N.Y. 203, 86 N.E. 20). Conditional gifts, like contractual conditions precedent, require the occurrence of the conditional event, whether within the donee's control or not. The underlying question always is the matter of donative intent.

Thus, in *Mizrahi v. Mizrahi,* 57 Misc.2d 1021, 293 N.Y.S.2d 964, an action was brought to impress a trust on the proceeds of a winning state lottery ticket. There it was held that the circumstances of the case compelled the conclusion that the ticket purchaser intended his wife and two sons to share the prize equally if any of his tickets won, and that given his donative intent, a constructive trust would be declared on the proceeds.

[10] In this case there was no close or confidential relationship between the parties which would call for the imposition of a trust, nor would defendant be unjustly enriched if she retained the full proceeds of her winning ticket. No basis is demonstrated for the establishment of a constructive trust, or the declaration of a trust *ex maleficio*.

For the reasons above stated, the plaintiff has no legally enforceable claim on the proceeds of the winning ticket, and defendant's motion for summary judgment dismissing the complaint is granted. In view of this disposition, plaintiff's discovery motion and defendant's cross-motion for leave to serve an amended answer are deemed moot.

Source: *Pando v. Fernandez,* 127 Misc.2d 224 (St. Paul, MN: Thomson West). Reprinted with permission from Westlaw.

disaffirm
Renounce, as in a contract.

necessaries of life
Generally legally considered to be food, clothing, and shelter; necessities.

Minors also are within the category of lacking capacity to contract. The courts have reasoned that those who have not reached the statutory age of majority do not have the experience or sophistication needed to enter into contracts with adults. In such situations, the minor has the right to **disaffirm** or cancel the contract, regardless of how much time has passed (though only up until they reach the age of majority). It is also irrelevant whether the minor is able to actually return the subject matter of the contract to the other party. However, minors are not able to get out of contracts involving the **necessaries of life.** This entails being required to pay for food, clothing, and shelter, as the courts presume that some minors are emancipated and public policy would encourage merchants to feel confident selling these necessaries to minors without fear of never being paid.

You Be the Judge

One night when Samantha was extremely drunk, she offered to sell her car to Ben for $400. Her parents had spent $40,000 on the car one year before as a 16th-birthday gift for Samantha. A few hours after she made the offer, Samantha returned home. Unbeknownst to Ben, Samantha died shortly after midnight of alcohol poisoning. The next morning, Ben left a voice mail for her, accepting her offer to sell her car. Describe and rank in terms of their strength the arguments that Samantha's estate will make in defending against Ben's suit for breach of contract.

You Be the Judge

Andy sees an attractive necklace in the window of a store one evening while he is out taking a stroll. The next day, he calls the store and asks the price of the necklace. The store owner says "fifty-six twenty." Andy says, "I'll take it. Mail it to me with a bill." When the bill arrives, Andy gasps when he sees the price of $5,620.00. He had assumed that the necklace was $56.20 and was unaware that the stones in the necklace were actually genuine opalites, which are rare, precious stones. Is there an enforceable contract? Explain.

illegal contract
A contract that is unenforceable because the subject matter of the agreement is prohibited by state or federal statutory law and thus void.

The second primary argument or defense that may be raised by a party is that the contract should not be enforced because it is **illegal** or against public policy. For example, Rapunzel is fed up with Prince Charming and hires Geppetto to be the hired killer to murder Prince Charming for $1,000. Assume that Geppetto actually kills the Prince and then asks Rapunzel for the money. If Rapunzel refuses, this agreement could never be enforced because the subject matter of the contract—murder—is illegal.

An example of a contract that is against public policy and thus unenforceable would be highly restrictive covenants not to compete. Although businesses spend a great deal of time and money hiring, training, and assisting their employees to succeed, thus justifying the desire to protect their financial investment in their employees, courts will frown on using covenants not to compete in a heavy-handed manner. For example, assume that a famous violinist signs a contract to play her violin exclusively for the Micronesia Symphony Orchestra and not take her talents elsewhere in the entire world for the next 50 years. Courts would conclude that this provision is highly unreasonable in both time and geographic area and thus would be unwilling to enforce this agreement.

Finally, a third defense that a party may raise in seeking to avoid the enforcement of a contract rests on the argument that there was no real "meeting of the minds" because one of the parties was subject to either fraud, duress, undue influence, or mistake.

fraud
A knowing and intentional misstatement of the truth in order to induce a desired action from another person.

In alleging duress, undue influence, or mistake, the party is claiming that for one of these reasons, they were on "unequal footing" with the other party in the process of forming the contract. **Fraud** is raised as a defense to a contract where one party claims that the other intentionally deceived them, inducing to enter into the contract.

Fraud centers on proving the following elements:

1. An intent to deceive the other party.
2. The deception concerns material facts about the subject matter of the contract.
3. The party justifiably relied on the representations made by the other party.
4. Harm resulted from this reliance.

For example, assume that Carole is not familiar with buying cars and heads off to Pinnochio's Used Cars to buy her first automobile. Pinnochio tells Carole that the 2005 car she is considering is a fantastic vehicle, beautiful model, and has never sustained any damage or harm. In fact, this car, which was recently floating down the river after the recent hurricanes, is a salvaged car, and Pinnochio knew this at the time he told Carole that it had never sustained any damage. Relying

RESEARCH THIS!

Compare the facts and reasoning in the following cases. Prepare a memorandum of law summarizing the holdings in these cases:

Raethz v. Aurora University, 346 Ill.App.3d 728, 805 N.E.2d 696 (2004).
Bender v. Alderson-Broaddus College, 212 W.Va. 502, 575 S.E.2d 112 (2002).
Lemmon v. University of Cincinnati, 112 Ohio Misc.2d 73, 750 N.E.2d 668 (2001).
Swartley v. Hoffner and Lehigh University, 734 A.2d 915 (1999).

CASE IN POINT

Court of Appeals of Utah.
Wesley L. LARSEN, Plaintiff and Appellant,
v.
EXCLUSIVE CARS, INC., a Utah corporation; and Floyd Maestas, an individual,
Defendants and Appellees.
No. 20030086-CA.
July 29, 2004.

Before Judges BILLINGS, JACKSON, and THORNE.

OPINION

THORNE, Judge:

****1** The trial court granted Exclusive Cars, Inc. (Exclusive Cars) and Floyd Maestas's motion for summary judgment on Wesley L. Larsen's fraudulent misrepresentation claim. We reverse.

BACKGROUND

****2** On December 4, 1998, Larsen, a nineteen-year-old high-school graduate with no experience in buying or selling vehicles, purchased a used truck from Exclusive Cars. Floyd Maestas, a car salesman employed by Exclusive Cars, negotiated the sale with Larsen. Prior to purchasing the truck, Larsen test drove the truck twice. On the day that Larsen agreed to purchase the truck, Maestas orally represented to Larsen that the truck had a "new engine." Upon questioning by Larsen, Maestas stated that Dahle Toyota in Logan, Utah, had installed the new engine. Maestas wrote this information on a "post-it note," and handed it to Larsen. After litigation ensued, Maestas admitted that he had told Larsen the truck had a new engine.

****3** Larsen alleges that he agreed to purchase the truck at the stated price only because he had been assured that the truck had a new engine. On December 4, 1998, Larsen executed a motor vehicle contract of sale, and signed a document indicating that he was purchasing the truck "as is" with "no warranty." The latter document explained that Larsen was responsible for any repairs and that "[t]he dealer assumes no responsibility for any repairs regardless of any oral statements about the vehicle." Larsen also signed a document declining the car dealer's warranty plan and a bill of sale stating that "oral promises are not binding on the dealer."

****4** Less than two weeks later, on December 17, 1998, the truck had mechanical difficulties. Larsen then learned that the truck's engine was not new and that repairs would cost between $2500 and $8600. Larsen brought suit against Maestas and Exclusive Cars alleging fraudulent misrepresentation and negligent misrepresentation.

****5** Exclusive Cars and Maestas filed a motion for summary judgment, which the trial court granted. [FN1] . . . The court concluded that Larsen had not reasonably relied on Maestas's representations because the documents he signed negated any oral promises. In its final order, the court stated that

> Wesley L. Larsen did not act reasonably in relying upon the oral representations of co-defendant Floyd Maestas, despite having been provided with many flags and ignoring the same, and [Larsen] was neglectful in failing to follow up in an inquiry to determine the veracity of the information orally presented by co-defendant Floyd Maestas, and having received from co-defendant Exclusive Cars, Inc., the automobile dealer, four separate and distinct documents disclaiming oral representations. . . .

Larsen appeals.

ANALYSIS

****6** Larsen argues that the trial court erred in granting Exclusive Cars and Maestas's motion for summary judgment because it cannot be concluded, as a matter of law, that Larsen acted unreasonably in relying on Maestas's representation regarding the truck's engine. A grant of summary judgment is appropriate only when there is no genuine issue of material fact and the moving party is entitled to judgment as a matter of law. *See* Utah R. Civ. P. 56(c). Here, Larsen argues that if we review the facts in the light most favorable to him, *see Briggs v. Holcomb,* 740 P.2d 281, 283 (Utah Ct.App.1987), the summary judgment must be reversed. We agree.

[1] ****7** The elements of a claim for fraudulent misrepresentation are:

> (1) a representation; (2) concerning a presently existing material fact; (3) which was false; (4) which the representor either (a) knew to be false, or (b) made recklessly, knowing that he had insufficient knowledge upon which to base such representation; (5) for the purpose of inducing the other party to act upon it; (6) that the other party, acting reasonably and in ignorance of its falsity; (7) did in fact rely upon it; (8) and was thereby induced to act; (9) to his injury and damage.

Dugan v. Jones, 615 P.2d 1239, 1246 (Utah 1980); *see also Conder v. A.L. Williams & Assocs.,* 739 P.2d 634, 638 (Utah Ct.App.1987). Thus, to succeed on his claim of fraudulent misrepresentation, Larsen must prove that (1) Maestas made a representation; (2) concerning a presently existing material fact; (3) which was false; (4) which Maestas knew to be false or made recklessly knowing that he had insufficient knowledge upon which to base such representation; (5) for the purpose of inducing Larsen to act upon it; (6) that Larsen acted reasonably and in ignorance of its falsity; and (7) that Larsen relied upon the representation and was thereby injured and damaged.

FN1. Larsen withdrew his claim for negligent misrepresentation and the motion for summary judgment was decided solely on the issue of fraudulent misrepresentation.

[2] **8 The only issue on appeal is whether the trial court erred when it decided, as a matter of law, that Larsen acted unreasonably in relying on Maestas's representation that the truck had a new engine. The trial court's conclusion that Larsen acted unreasonably rested largely upon the fact that Larsen signed several documents purporting to negate all warranties and oral promises.

**9 In *TS 1 Partnership v. Allred,* 877 P.2d 156 (Utah Ct.App.1994), we reversed a grant of summary judgment on similar facts. *See id.* at 159. In that case, the owner of a shopping center sued one of its tenants for breach of contract. *See id.* at 157. In its counter-claim, the tenant raised fraud in the inducement as a defense and argued that it would not have signed the lease agreement had the landlord not promised that it would compensate the tenant for any improvements made on the property. *See id.* at 158–59. Despite these alleged oral promises, the lease explicitly stated that the cost of any improvements would be paid by the tenant. *See id.* The trial court, relying on the lease agreement, granted the landlord's motion for summary judgment. *See id.* at 159. We reversed on appeal, noting that "given [the tenant's] position that she would not have signed the lease . . . absent the fraudulent representations, the trial court's reliance on the lease to grant the motion is misplaced." *Id.*

**10 The same reasoning applies here. Larsen alleges that Maestas's oral representations induced him to purchase the truck. Viewing the facts in the light most favorable to Larsen, *see Briggs,* 740 P.2d at 283, had Maestas not told Larsen that the truck had a new engine he would not have purchased it at the stated price. Had the parties been unable to reach a price acceptable to Larsen, he would not have purchased the truck at all, and would not have signed the sales documents. The trial court erred when it looked chiefly to the sales documents to determine that Larsen's reliance on Maestas's oral representations was unreasonable as a matter of law. *See TS 1 P'ship,* 877 P.2d at 159; *see also Spears v. Warr,* 2002 UT 24,¶ 19, 44 P.3d 742 (noting that fraud is an exception to the rule excluding parol evidence and can be proven by evidence outside the contract).

**11 Viewing the totality of the alleged facts in the light most favorable to Larsen, a jury could find that he acted reasonably. Larsen was a nineteen-year-old high-school graduate purchasing his first vehicle. Maestas unequivocally told Larsen that the truck had a new engine, as well as the name of the dealership that had allegedly installed the new engine. Larsen test drove the truck twice prior to purchasing it, and did not notice anything which would have led him to believe that the truck was mechanically defective or that the engine was not new. Under these circumstances, Larsen might have acted reasonably in concluding that the various disclaimers contained in the sales documents—"as is," "no warranty," "oral promises are not binding on the dealer," etc.—all referred to the truck as described by Maestas, i.e., one having a new engine. [FN2]

FN2. The trial court also concluded that Larsen acted unreasonably because he did not heed the warning of his brother-in-law to get all promises in writing. The weight to be given to this evidence is for the trier of fact to decide and is not a basis for granting a summary judgment.

CONCLUSION

**12 We conclude that an issue of material fact remains in dispute regarding whether Larsen acted reasonably under the circumstances. We reverse the grant of summary judgment and remand for further proceedings.

Source: *Larsen v. Exclusive Cars,* 97 P.3d 714, 2004 UT APP 259 (St. Paul, MN: Thomson West). Reprinted with permission from Westlaw.

on Pinnochio's statements, Carole buys this car, and later discovers that the electrical wiring and the engine all need to be replaced immediately due to water damage. Here, Carole can rescind the contract and get her money back from Pinnochio because of the fraud involved in the contract. **Rescission** of a contract means that the party is allowed to withdraw from the contract due to fraud.

rescission and restitution
A decision by the court that renders the contract null and void and requires the parties to return to the wronged party any benefits received under the agreement.

There have been numerous breach of contract cases involving students who were enrolled at various universities, suing on the basis of fraud or negligence, alleging that the institutions of higher education misrepresented the program, the tuition, or some other aspect of the contract. In most states, courts have been reluctant to interfere with what is deemed to be the academic judgment of higher education institutions. Courts have seldom embraced "educational malpractice" claims based on allegations of fraud, negligence, or misrepresentation. Although not broadly condoning absolute judicial deference with respect to academic decisions made by colleges, courts have preferred to require that the plaintiff prove that the said decisions were arbitrary and capricious. In other words, courts have held that in such breach of contract claims by students against universities, what would make the university liable for breach in the student-university setting is not that the university exercised its academic judgment unwisely, but rather by allegedly failing to properly comply with its own policies and procedures.

undue influence
Using a close personal or fiduciary relationship to one's advantage to gain assent to terms that the party otherwise would not have agreed to.

duress
Unreasonable and unscrupulous manipulation of a person to force him to agree to terms of an agreement that he would otherwise not agree to.

Undue influence and **duress** are two closely related defenses, as both depend on one party alleging that the unequal footing was based on the relationship between the two parties. Undue influence exists when the parties are closely related, as in mother-daughter or uncle-nephew disputes. Because of their relationship, the one party trusted the other to their detriment. For example, assume that Mary has sole responsibility as caretaker for her elderly grandmother Henrietta. Although frail, Henrietta is quite fond of her new luxury convertible car that she uses to get to bingo games every Friday night. Mary envies her and constantly begs Henrietta to sign title to the car over to Mary, but Henrietta constantly refuses. Finally, in exasperation, Mary tells Henrietta that she will stop feeding her until she signs over the title to her convertible. After five days, Henrietta relents and signs the papers. Here, Henrietta has a valid defense of undue influence, as she was induced to sign by her granddaughter.

Duress is similar except that the two parties may not have a special relationship, but still it is alleged that one party did not voluntarily sign a contract. For example, if Joe is holding a gun to Mark's head, ordering him to sign a loan paper, this would clearly be duress, as Mark is not acting voluntarily and the threat used was overwhelming so as to impair his ability to make a free choice.

unconscionable contract
A contract so completely unreasonable and irrational that it shocks the conscience.

Finally, a mistake may be alleged by one party where a contract is so detrimental as to lead the court to conclude that enforcing it would be wrong because the contract is unconscionable. **Unconscionable contracts** arise where no reasonable person, viewing all the facts, would have ever entered into such a contract. An example might be agreeing to mow 50 acres of farmland every week with a push mower for 50 cents a week.

PROMISSORY ESTOPPEL

promissory estoppel
A legal doctrine that makes some promises enforceable even though they are not compliant with the technical requirements of a contract.

According to the Restatement of the Law of Contracts, section 90, "a promise which the promisor should reasonably expect to induce action or forbearance of a definite and substantial character on the part of the promisee and which does induce such action or forbearance is binding if injustice can be avoided only by enforcement of the promise." **Promissory estoppel** is an extension of the basic contract principle that people who make promises must be required to keep them. In order to furnish the basis of an estoppel, a representation or assurance must relate to some present or past fact, as distinguished from a mere promise or expression of opinion as to the future. The doctrine protects against that which resembles fraud in the view of the court. It is based on sound equitable principles which hold that a promise is binding if a promisee has suffered some detriment in reliance on that promise. The offer or promise forming the basis of the estoppel must be reasonably certain and definite. This equitable doctrine is unavailable if there is a written contract between the parties covering the disputed promises.

A plaintiff must satisfy four elements to win on a claim of promissory estoppel:

1. A promise.
2. Reliance on the promise.
3. Injury caused by the reliance.
4. An injustice if the promise is not enforced.

Assume, for example, that your Aunt Martha says to you, "If you don't marry until after you graduate from college, I promise to pay you $50,000." You are eager to get married, but in reliance on your aunt's promise, you don't do it, in anticipation of the money. Upon graduation, your aunt refuses to pay you, citing a lack of contractual consideration for her promise. It is possible the court will conclude that under the doctrine of promissory estoppel, your aunt is estopped (prevented) from raising this argument and therefore her promise to you may be enforced.

BREACH OF CONTRACT

breach of contract
A violation of an obligation under a contract for which a party may seek recourse to the court; a party's performance that deviates from the required performance obligations under the contract.

impossibility of performance
An excuse for performance based upon an absolute inability to perform the act required under the contract.

Sometimes, after a contract has been formed, a party may not raise any defenses to challenge its enforceability but rather may simply decide to just walk away from it. When a party fails to fulfill his duties arising under a contract, as promised, this is called a **breach of contract.** Unlike some of the defenses discussed earlier in this chapter, in which a party challenges a contract's validity by an available legal excuse, here the party simply terminates her duties without legal justification.

For example, Tim agrees to paint the exterior of Monica's house in exchange for a fee of $1,000. Tim proceeds to paint three sides of the house, but since it is extremely hot outside, decides to leave and not return to paint the fourth side. In this situation, Tim has failed to completely perform his contractual duties and has breached the contract. Monica's remedies will be discussed in the next section. Now, assume that Tim has painted three sides of Monica's house, but before he is able to return the following day to paint the fourth side, lightning strikes the house and it is destroyed that night in a fire. In this situation, the courts will say that performance has become impossible. In other words, "it can't be done." This is referred to as **impossibility of performance** and the legal outcome is different. Here, Tim is excused from completing performance due to impossibility.

You Be the Judge

Builder Ben agreed to build a house for Owner Owen, according to Owen's specifications, at a price of $100,000. The house was to be completed by December 15, 2005. On December 1, the house was nearly complete (95 percent) and a dispute that turned into a fistfight broke out between the contractor and Owen's brother. The brother had been hanging around the premises off and on, poking fun at some of the quality of the contractor's work. As a result, Owen refused to allow the contractor to finish, and Owen withheld a $15,000 final progress payment (the rest having been paid). The contractor has about $5,000 of work left to do. He asserts that Owen made a very good deal. Assume that the fair market value of the house, as it stands, is $125,000. What can the contractor recover? Explain your answer.

REMEDIES

compensatory damages
A payment to make up for a wrong committed and return the nonbreaching party to a position where the effect of the breach has been neutralized.

consequential damages
Damages resulting from the breach that are natural and foreseeable results of the breaching party's actions.

liquidated damages
An amount of money agreed upon in the original contract as a reasonable estimation of the damages to be recovered by the nonbreaching party.

specific performance
A court order that requires a party to perform a certain act in order to prevent harm to the requesting party.

In certain contract cases, typically involving the sale of goods or services, plaintiffs may seek to recover monetary damages. There are essentially three kinds of damages that may be awarded in a contract action. **Compensatory damages** are essentially the monetary amount it would take to place the nonbreaching party in the same position had the breach not occurred. The goal of awarding compensatory damages is to place the plaintiff in the position as if the contract had been totally performed. It is said that compensatory damages focus on the *losses* incurred by the plaintiff, whereas restitution is focused on the *gains* of the breaching party. In other words, a plaintiff seeking restitution desires to be put back in the same position as if the breach had not occurred and no contract had been formed.

Consequential damages are also called special damages. This remedy refers to the other losses that the plaintiff might have sustained outside of the contract itself, but were reasonably foreseeable losses if the contract was not fully performed. An example of consequential damages is purchasing a specific trailer for one's business, intending to use it with a particular truck, only to discover that the seller's representation about its compatibility was false, causing subsequent losses from the inability to haul business supplies as scheduled.

Some contracts have provisions for **liquidated damages** in the event of a breach. In this situation, the contract specifies the amount of damages payable if the contract is not performed; these damages are in place of compensatory damages and are for a fixed sum that is agreed upon by the contracting parties at the time of signing. So long as the liquidated damages clause is reasonable, the contract provision will not be set aside by the court.

In certain situations, the nonbreaching party prefers to be made whole by enforcing equitable remedies. One such remedy is **specific performance.** In this case, the party demands that the other party fulfill its contractual obligation. In many cases, the court will award the remedy of specific performance where the subject matter of the contract is unique, such as the sale of a rare Picasso painting or a limited-edition vintage automobile. Parties may also seek the equitable remedy of an **injunction.** This generally requests that the court order the breaching party to refrain from doing a particular act that will cause irreparable harm.

UNIFORM COMMERCIAL CODE

injunction
A court order that requires a party to refrain from acting in a certain way to prevent harm to the requesting party.

The Uniform Commercial Code (UCC) is an act containing rules that govern business sales transactions and has been adopted by individual states to serve as the rules that govern commerce. Only Louisiana has not adopted the Code in full. The purpose of this set of uniform rules is to provide consistent guidance on matters pertaining to sales of goods, banking and negotiable instruments, leases, and other financial investments. Article 2 of the UCC is concerned with the sale of goods, governing title passing between buyer and seller, regardless of the method of payment. Services are not covered under UCC Article 2.

UCC sections 2-106 and 2-102 specifically address the types of contracts covered within the scope of Article 2. It applies to transactions in goods and includes a present sale of goods as well as a contract to sell goods at a future time. A "sale" consists of the passing of title from the seller to the buyer for a price. "Goods" generally means all things that are movable at the time of

CASE IN POINT

United States District Court,
District of Columbia.
GRAHAM, VAN LEER & ELMORE CO., INC., Plaintiff,
v.
JONES & WOOD, INC., Defendant.
Civ. A. No. 85-3984.
April 1, 1987.

DECISION AND ORDER

JACKSON, District Judge.

Plaintiff Graham, Van Leer & Elmore Co., Inc. ("Graham, Van Leer"), a Virginia seller/installer of architectural building products, brings this contract action against defendant Jones & Wood, Inc. ("Jones & Wood"), a District of Columbia mechanical contractor, for the purchase price of six "modified Duralab fume hoods" at a cost of $3,800 each, or a total of $22,800.00, under a written agreement. In its answer and counterclaim Jones & Wood alleges that several months earlier Graham, Van Leer had given it an oral quote over the telephone to supply the hoods for $1,000 each, in reliance upon which it prepared and submitted its formal bid to its client, and that Graham, Van Leer is therefore either contractually bound to that figure or estopped from demanding the higher price. The written purchase order, Jones & Wood explains, was submitted under "economic duress"—Graham, Van Leer being the exclusive distributor of the hoods in the Washington, D.C. area—and is thus voidable at its election. Upon the following facts, as found by the Court in accordance with Fed.R.Civ. P. 52(a) upon trial without a jury, for the reasons stated, the Court will enter judgment for the plaintiff as prayed.

I.

In the fall of 1983, Jones & Wood was preparing a formal bid for a construction project at a Howard University laboratory building calling for modification of an existing hood ventilation and exhaust system. In early December, 1983, John ("Jack") Sis, the Jones & Wood estimator preparing its bid, telephoned Rush H. Elmore, Jr., an employee of Graham, Van Leer, to obtain a price quotation for the fume hoods. There had been no prior contact between the firms with respect to the project, and Elmore, Jr., was unprepared to give an answer. He explained to Sis that he was not qualified to give telephone quotes for Duralab products. He then checked the "bid board," where the company posted completed workups and quotations, found no listing for the Howard University project and no other proposals to furnish the fume hoods, and told Sis that he could give him no figure at that time. Elmore, Jr., later related the inquiry to his father, Rush Elmore, Sr., the company president, who was in the hospital recovering from surgery, and obtained a figure from him which Elmore, Jr., passed on to Sis as a "guesstimate" when he called back several days later. Sis testified, without contradiction by Elmore, Jr. (who doesn't remember the figure he mentioned), that he had been given a "price-not-to-exceed" quote of $1,000 per hood. Jones & Wood submitted its bid to Howard University the same day, allowing in its calculations a sum of $6,000 for six fume hoods.

When it was awarded the Howard University contract, in the amount of about $103,000, in mid-April, 1984, Jones & Wood again contacted Graham, Van Leer regarding the hoods and learned from Elmore, Sr., that it could expect to pay considerably more than $1,000 per hood. In the ensuing weeks, Jones & Wood complained that it had "relied" on the earlier figure and that Graham, Van Leer had not lived up to its "quotation" of December, 1983, but negotiations between them continued, and on August 30, 1984, Graham, Van Leer demanded a firm price of $3,800.00, for each fume hood (being its own cost to obtain them from the Duralab factory), which Jones & Wood, albeit reluctantly, agreed to pay by its written purchase order for six of them at a total price of $22,800, under date of September 4, 1984.

Graham, Van Leer delivered the hoods to the site in April, 1985, where they were installed, and, having paid Duralab for them, billed Jones & Wood for $22,800. To date, Jones & Wood has made no payments to Graham, Van Leer in any amount.

II.

[1] The Court concludes that defendant's purchase order of September, 1984, constitutes a valid and enforceable contract in writing for the sale of goods, governed by Article II of the Uniform Commercial Code pursuant to which it represents the totality of the agreement between the parties, and its terms cannot be contradicted or varied by parol evidence. D.C.Code Ann. § 28:2–202 (1981). [FN1] By its purchase order defendant agreed to buy six fume hoods from plaintiff for a total price of $22,800.00. Plaintiff made (for purposes of this case) a timely delivery of conforming goods to the worksite, and defendant is in breach of the contract by its failure to pay for them.

FN1. The purchase order itself, moreover (on a Jones & Wood form), contains an integration clause providing that "[a]ll prior representations, conversations or preliminary negotiations shall be deemed to be merged into this order. This purchase order, when accepted by the seller, shall constitute the entire agreement between the purchaser and the seller." Purchase Order, para. 8. (Plaintiff's Exhibit 1).

[2] By way of defense, defendant claims that it submitted the purchase order under "economic duress," and that the contract is therefore voidable. The economic duress, according to defendant, is to be found in the fact that Graham, Van Leer was the sole local source for Duralab hoods, [FN2] making it fearful of repercussions, i.e., damages for defective performance or delay, under its own contract with Howard University had it sought to find a cheaper substitute which might not have been acceptable to Howard.

FN2. Graham, Van Leer, as Jones & Wood at all times knew, has been the exclusive distributor of Duralab products in the Washington area since 1968.

The circumstances, however, do not constitute the "economic duress" which is sufficient to relieve a party to a contract of his otherwise voluntary undertaking. *See generally* 13 Williston on

Contracts § § 1603, 1617 (3d ed. 1970). The compulsion to enter into a contract which may later be lawfully avoided must be the result of the other party's *illegal* coercive conduct, not merely the stress of market conditions or the victim's financial exigencies. *Id.; e.g., Business Incentives Co. Inc. v. Sony Corp. of America,* 397 F.Supp. 63, 69 (S.D.N.Y.1975). Exclusive distributorships are a fact of market life; if they do not offend the antitrust laws, they are simply a circumstance to be taken into account by prospective buyers of a commodity who must realize that their economic choices are limited and plan accordingly. And virtually all construction contracts contain performance specifications and call for completion within a time certain. A general contractor who is forced into a harsh bargain with a subcontractor or supplier to meet his obligation to his client is no less bound to that bargain merely because business necessity dictates that he accept the unfavorable terms, unless the subcontractor/supplier has no right to demand such terms in the first place. *See Chouinard v. Chouinard,* 568 F.2d 430, 433-34 (5th Cir.1978).

[3] As evidence of Graham, Van Leer's loss of right to insist upon a higher price for the fume hoods, in its counterclaim defendant asserts that the December, 1983, telephone conversations between Sis and Elmore, Jr., formed an oral contract by which Graham, Van Leer agreed to supply Jones & Wood with Duralab hoods at not more than $1,000 apiece. By either's account of the conversations, however, there was neither an offer, nor an acceptance of an offer, to buy or sell. Sis requested a price "quote" for fume hoods and was given one. He did not purport to obligate his employer, Jones & Wood, to buy any number of them from Graham, Van Leer at any price at any time; conversely, he neither asked for nor was given a commitment by Elmore, Jr., to sell them to him. Thus, whether or not Jones & Wood might be entitled to show an oral agreement at variance with the terms of the written September, 1984, purchase order, the evidence presented simply does not establish any such agreement.

[4] Jones & Wood's principal alternative theory upon which it seeks to hold Graham, Van Leer to a $1,000-per-hood price—promissory estoppel—fails for the same reason: irrespective of any justification for its reliance upon the erroneous quotation, Elmore, Jr., made no promise, express or implied, to sell Duralab hoods to Jones & Wood over the telephone. *See N. Litterio & Co. v. Glassman Constr. Co.,* 319 F.2d 736, 739 (D.C.Cir.1963).

[5] In support of its remaining alternative theories—estoppel *in pais* and negligent misrepresentation—Jones & Wood adduced considerable evidence of "industry custom and practice." It appears that general contractors customarily wait until the final hours preceding the deadline for bid submission before preparing bids, and then usually do so on the basis of telephone inquiries of potential subcontractors and suppliers whose figures are then "shopped" among prospective competitors. Assuming Elmore, Jr., was aware of the custom, and that, on behalf of Graham, Van Leer, he must therefore be presumed to have responded to Sis' query in the light of it, the custom still does not support defendant's theories. A contractor who relies upon a verbal price quotation, which he may then "shop" on the market for a better one, without obtaining a binding commitment from the source of the quotation to adhere to it for the necessary time (by, for example, an option), is not justified in doing so; he relies at his peril. [FN3] By similar reasoning, a contractor who acts upon a price quotation from one who is not bound to honor it cannot complain even if he is negligently misinformed; he is himself contributorily negligent.

FN3. There is evidence that, by industry custom, a quotation which both parties understand to be a "firm bid" justifies reliance notwithstanding it is unsupported by consideration. The Court finds that Elmore, Jr.'s quotation/"guesstimate" was not the "firm bid" contemplated by industry custom.

For the foregoing reasons, therefore, it is, this 1st day of April, 1987,

ORDERED, that judgment be entered on the complaint for plaintiff Graham, Van Leer & Elmore Co., Inc., against defendant Jones & Wood, Inc. for $22,800.00, together with interest at six (6) percent per annum from June 4, 1985, in accordance with D.C.Code Ann. § § 15–108, 28-3302 (1981);[4] interest in accordance with 28 U.S.C. § 1961 (1982) from the date hereof; and costs.

Source: *Graham, Van Leer & Elmore v. Jones & Wood,* 656 F.Supp. 667 (St. Paul, MN: Thomson West). Reprinted with permission from Westlaw.

CYBER TRIP

You may access the Uniform Commercial Code and read Article 2 through this Web site: www.law.cornell.edu/ucc/ucc.table.html.

A Day in the Life of a Real Paralegal

Whether working for a corporation or for a law firm, it is likely that you will be asked to review contracts. For example, a general-practice firm often handles real estate transactions, and this typically entails a real estate contract between the buyer and seller. You may be expected to carefully read contracts that are already prepared using preprinted forms, or you may be asked to draft certain contract provisions on behalf of a client. In either case, it is important to recognize the legal terms in contract law and to be able to identify the client's rights and remedies under the contract. This requires more than a basic understanding of this substantive area of the law.

Some of the skills useful to paralegals practicing in this field include the ability to write well and to communicate contractual issues to their supervising attorney in a concise memorandum. In addition, being able to research case law pertaining to your state's version of the Uniform Commercial Code is important.

CYBER TRIP

Several Web sites have numerous online contract forms that may be downloaded for free and can then be customized for your fact situation and in accordance with your state's sales code, if applicable. You may access this Web site for a variety of forms: www.lectlaw.com/formb.htm.

Eye on Ethics

Assume that your supervising attorney has asked you to draft a contract for the firm's client, who wants to purchase handmade jewelry from individual artisans in New Mexico and then resell the items on an Internet auction site. You are unfamiliar with the types of issues that may arise under this type of a contract, so you download a preprinted form off the Internet. You think to yourself, "why reinvent the wheel?" What else should you do before submitting the draft contract to the attorney?

contract for sale; although at first glance, this may appear to be relatively straightforward, courts are divided as to what constitutes "goods." While animals may be considered goods for purposes of the UCC, assets in the sale of a business may not be goods within the scope of Article 2.

The UCC applies to sales contracts, and its use generally arises in cases where there is some dispute over ambiguous or missing terms. However, the UCC doesn't replace the common law of contracts, as discussed in this chapter, but rather governs where there is a sale of goods. But if the UCC is silent as to any particular principle, then the common law of contracts governs.

Summary

In reviewing the subject of contract law, it is not difficult to imagine the myriad of scenarios that arise when one party challenges the validity of an agreement. Although it is in the best interest of the courts to enforce agreements between parties, nevertheless, the courts will examine situations where for some reason and justifiable excuse, there was a definitive lack of the meeting of the minds. In analyzing any factual pattern involving agreements, you should always begin by determining whether each of the three elements of a contract is present. If you can establish that a valid offer was made, that it was accepted without any changes to the material terms, and that consideration was given, then you may conclude that all the elements of a contract are present. However, there may be circumstances in which the courts will refuse to enforce an agreement. These defenses center on the nature of the subject matter as well as the equitable relationship of the parties. Moreover, certain contracts are governed by the Uniform Commercial Code, and therefore such agreements are evaluated in light of those rules.

Key Terms

Acceptance
Bilateral contract
Breach of contract
Capacity
Compensatory damages
Consequential damages
Consideration
Contract
Counteroffer
Disaffirm
Duress
Fraud
Illegal contract
Implied contract
Impossibility of performance
Injunction
Intent
Invitation to treat
Liquidated damages
Meeting of the minds
Mirror image rule
Necessaries of life
Offer
Offeree
Offeror
Option contract
Pre-existing duty
Promissory estoppel
Rescission
Revoke
Specific performance
Statute of frauds
Unauthorized means
Unconscionable contract
Undue influence
Unilateral contract
Unjust enrichment

Discussion Questions

1. "The law interferes too much in the making of contracts, which should be a private matter between the parties." Discuss.
2. Describe the ways that obligations under a contract differ from the obligations that are imposed under tort law.
3. Compare the claims that people have against a seller of a product, both in tort and in contract law.
4. Explain how the courts have sought to balance the concept that there must be certainty in contract law against the principle that justice should be reached between the parties. How does the "meeting of the minds" influence contract law?
5. Explain the concept of promissory estoppel and whether you believe that some promises are made to be broken.

Exercises

1. Frodo owned a small dog and a large cat, which he wanted to sell. The two animals were about equal in value. Wally and Isabella were Frodo's friends. Frodo did not know that Wally was interested in buying the cat. Wally knew that Frodo had been negotiating to sell the cat to Isabella, and Wally knew that Frodo did not want to sell the cat to Wally, that Frodo hoped to sell the dog to Wally. One day, Frodo, intending to offer his dog to Wally, said: "I'll sell you my cat for $175," a slip of the tongue. Several friends overheard what Frodo said. Wally immediately said: "I accept." Can Wally enforce a contract to purchase the cat?
2. Smedley is an economics professor who is preparing to retire. He is also a bit absentminded, and Longfellow knows of one instance of this 10 years before. Also, Longfellow knows that Smedley has a collection of rare books that he keeps at home. One day, Smedley spoke with Longfellow. Smedley said to him, "I'll sell you my academic library in my office for $20,000, journals and all." Longfellow, after looking over the shelves, said, "It's a deal." At the time that Smedley made the statement, he had forgotten that his favorite copy of How to Get Rich—a rare, valuable first edition—was in his office rather than at his home. Smedley had no intention of selling this book. Longfellow, however, insists that the deal includes this book. Is Longfellow correct? Explain.
3. Jill is accused of obtaining a loan of $500 from her bank by using fraud. The bank tells Jill that unless she immediately repays this loan, the bank will report this to the police for prosecution. Jill is upset and promptly asks her 18-year-old daughter, Eliza, a single mother, for the money, explaining the bank threat to her. She also tells Eliza that unless she gives her this money to repay the bank, that Jill will renege on her existing promise to care for Dudley, Eliza's son, so that Eliza can go to work. Eliza is distraught because she can't lose her job, so she gives Jill this money. Later, Eliza changes her mind and telephones Jill, requesting her money back. What is the likely result? Explain.
4. Ruby enters into a contract with Smurf College to perform a concert at their formal dance which is organized by the student union, in return for a fee of $5,000. According to the terms of the contract, a deposit of $1,000 is due to Ruby at the time the contract is signed. The night before the dance is to occur, the student union building is destroyed by fire. Since no alternative suitable hall can be rented at the last minute, the dance is cancelled. Ruby now demands the balance of $4,000 due her. What is the likely result in a suit against Smurf College? Explain.
5. Laura bought a movie ticket and entered the darkened theater just as the film was beginning. As she walked down the aisle, she slipped on a pile of spilled popcorn. She sustained a broken leg, and as a result of her injury, she was unable to participate in a ballroom dance competition the following week, at which she had been predicted to win the first prize of $10,000. Laura sues the movie theater for breach of contract. Explain her likelihood of success in a contract action.
6. Wally was living in an extremely cold and drafty house and decided to have each of the 50 windows in his house totally replaced. He hired All Windows Company to remove the

50 windows and replace them all with energy-efficient 2-inch-thick windows, at a price of $5,000, payable on completion of the work. One month later, All Windows finished the work and informed Wally that the job was complete. However, upon inspecting the windows carefully, Wally discovered that 5 of the windows had actually not been replaced at all and that another 15 of them still were drafty. In addition, Wally found that another 6 windows were only 1 inch thick instead of 2 inches thick. When Wally noted all this to All Windows, they confirmed that further work needed to be done, but insisted on payment of $2,500 for the 24 windows that were satisfactory, before doing any further work. Wally refuses, citing that all work had to be completed in accordance with the contract terms first before he made payment. What is the likely result?

7. Arthur buys a washing machine from Good Buys Store and pays the store to deliver and install the machine the following day, for one all-inclusive delivery and installation fee of $100. The next day, Dudley comes to Arthur's home and installs the machine, and then asks Arthur to sign a form stating that all work has been completed satisfactorily and that any parts that need repair on the machine will be replaced within three months of the signing. Further, the form states that Dudley accepts no liability for loss or damage caused by his work. Arthur signs the form. The next day, Arthur uses the machine, whereby it floods, causing $1,000 worth of damage to Arthur's carpet. When Arthur tries to turn off the machine and unplug it, he receives an electric shock that severely burns his arm. Discuss the liability of the parties here.
8. Loulou is a prostitute, who attracts clients by sitting on a bar stool near the front bay window of her house. The window was broken after someone threw a brick through it, so Loulou hires All Windows to replace the window with an extra-thick glass and to also enlarge the window opening so that prospective clients will have a better view. All Windows is aware of Loulou's line of work. All Windows finishes the job, at which point, Loulou refuses to pay, claiming that the contract is unenforceable due to illegality. Discuss.

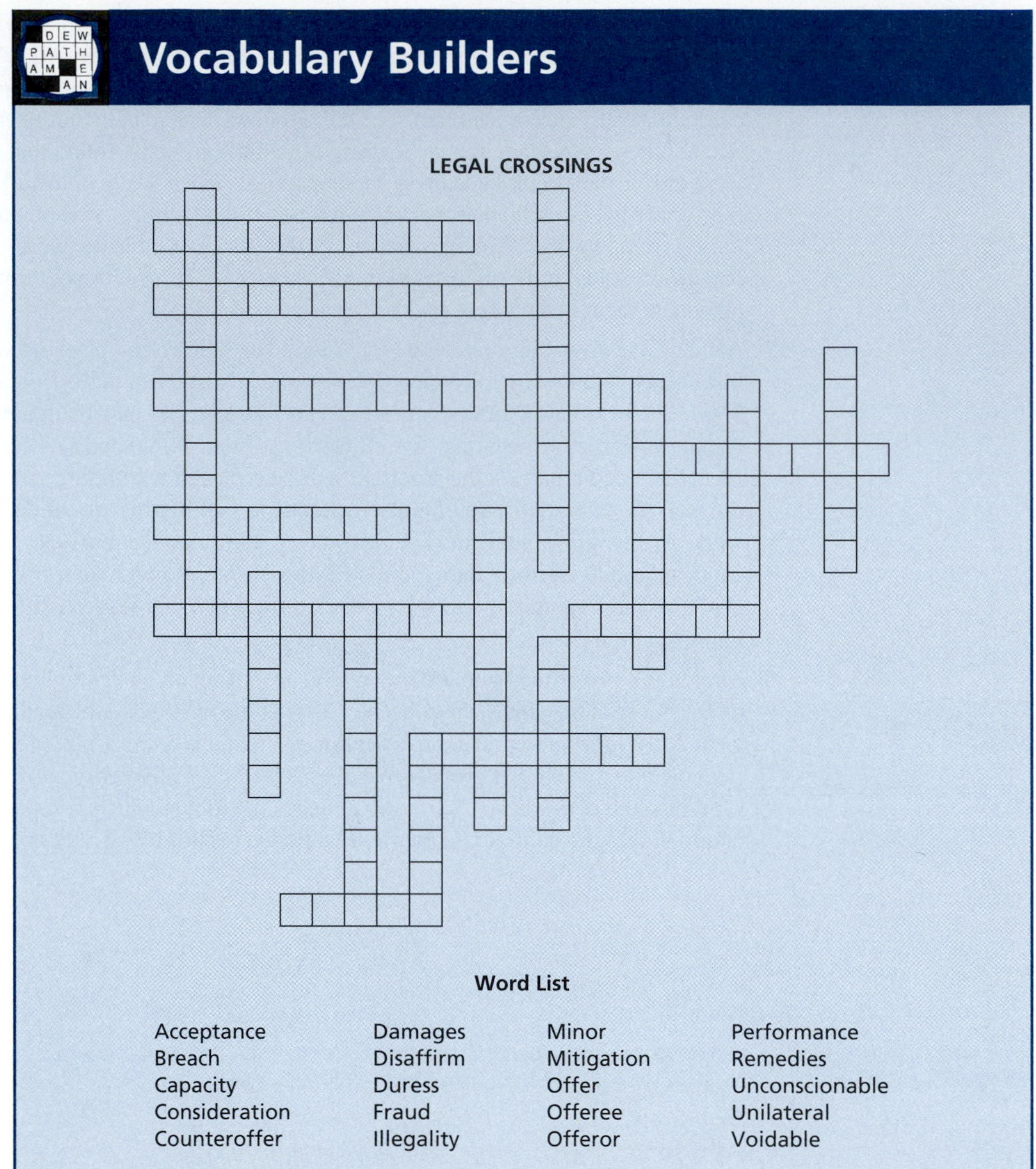
Vocabulary Builders
LEGAL CROSSINGS
Word List
Acceptance
Breach
Capacity
Consideration
Counteroffer
Damages
Disaffirm
Duress
Fraud
Illegality
Minor
Mitigation
Offer
Offeree
Offeror
Performance
Remedies
Unconscionable
Unilateral
Voidable

Chapter 9

Business Law

CHAPTER OBJECTIVES

After reading this chapter, you will be able to:

- Identify and distinguish four common forms of business organizations.
- Explain the advantages of each form of business organization.
- Explain the disadvantages of each form of business organization.
- Discuss the role of the paralegal in the business law field.

business organization
A form of conducting business.

CYBER TRIP

Visit this Web site, which provides links to various business- and corporate-related legal sites: www.katsuey.com/results.cfm?categoryID=4.

Imagine that you have worked as the manager of a dry-cleaning business for five years and believe that you have gained considerable knowledge and experience in those five years, doing everything from pressing shirts to ordering supplies. You are confident that you have the business acumen and expertise to start your own dry-cleaning business, but are unsure as to how to begin. One of the first decisions that you must make concerns whether you want to operate your dry cleaner in one of the most common forms of **business organization** or utilize some alternate legal business option, such as purchasing a franchise. Should you decide to operate your dry cleaner as one of the general forms of business organization, then you will need to select the form that is most suitable, given a thorough consideration of the many factors that influence such a selection.

The major forms of business organization are *sole proprietorships, general partnerships, limited partnerships, limited liability companies, and corporations*. Of these, the most common are sole proprietorship, partnership, and corporation. These three forms will be the focus of this chapter. In examining these unique business enterprises, the characteristics of each form will be compared, as well as the specific factors that influence the selection of a particular form of organization. In comparing the different ways in which a business may operate, this chapter will highlight the general principles of business law, which include the formation, operation, and dissolution of the various business enterprises. In addition, the text will reference relevant sections of the Uniform Partnership Act and the Revised Model Business Corporation Act.

SOLE PROPRIETORSHIP

sole proprietorship
A business owned by one person.

Without a doubt, the simplest and most common form of business organization is the **sole proprietorship.** This form of business organization is created when one person decides to open up his own business. The owner of this business is simply called the sole proprietor. The size of the business operation does not matter, although many sole proprietorships tend to be small businesses, such as the dry cleaner on the corner in your neighborhood or the local flower shop.

A common characteristic of this form of business enterprise typically means one owner who is ultimately responsible for the day-to-day operation of the business. The owner may hire employees to help her assist in the daily operation, but she retains full ownership and decision making concerning the business operation. There is no separate identity for this business, or no distinctive legal entity, as the business is an extension of the owner; they are one.

Another characteristic of the sole proprietorship is that while the owner retains all profits from the business, likewise he is responsible for all losses sustained by the business. From examining these two characteristics, the general advantages and disadvantages in operating a business in this form emerge.

If a person selects a sole proprietorship as the form in which she will operate her business, she has typically weighed several advantages against the equal number of disadvantages. As the sole owner of a business, the person does not have to be accountable to anyone else for its operation or for any decisions made. Forming a sole proprietorship is quite easy and inexpensive, as there is no need to seek formal federal or state government approval to create such a business. However, the owner may still be required to file any paperwork that is normally necessary for that type of a business to legally operate. For example, if Chuck wants to open a tattoo parlor on the corner, he may need to obtain the necessary special license in order to operate a tattoo parlor in his state. Similarly, if Tanisha wants to open a jewelry store that does ear piercing, she may need to obtain a special license to perform ear piercing, as well as a state sales tax license, since she is in the business of selling goods as well. Nevertheless, the formalities in waking up tomorrow and opening up that jewelry store are nominal compared to other forms of business organization that will be discussed later.

Chuck and Tanisha may prefer to operate their businesses as sole proprietorships because they retain the right to make all decisions about how their business is run. For example, they each can decide operating hours, selection of merchandise to sell, and whether to take on any employees to assist them. They also retain the right to keep all the profits generated from their business. However, it should be noted that since the sole proprietorship and the owner are technically one and the same, then for income tax purposes, the owner reports all profits and losses on his personal income tax return. There is no separate income tax filed for the business itself.

From this advantage arises a distinct disadvantage to operating a sole proprietorship. While it is optimistic for the small business owner to assume that the business will operate at a profit, it is quite possible that it may indeed sustain losses. In such a situation, the owner, having no separate identity from the business, is personally liable for all debts. Because of the unlimited personal liability, it is entirely possible for Chuck or Tanisha to lose not just their business assets, but their own personal assets such as their homes and cars as well. In addition, the sole proprietor may find it more difficult to secure capital or loans to open and run the business. Chuck may use the funds in his personal savings account to get the business started, but may also need to secure capital contributions from Uncle Joey or, if lucky, a bank that may be willing to make him a small loan. Should the business fail, Chuck is personally liable to repay the bank loan and all other debts incurred by the business. The likelihood of obtaining loans or financing from the bank will be largely dependent on the personal credit history of the business owner.

Besides financial liability for debts incurred, the sole proprietor must also recognize that she may be personally liable for her torts as well as the torts committed by any employees. For example, assume Chuck hires David to work as a tattoo artist in his store for 10 hours per week. If David assaults a client in the store, Chuck may be personally liable for David's tort. Finally, the duration of a sole proprietorship is unique in that it can be easily sold or permanently closed at the discretion of the owner. For example, if Tanisha is weary of the long hours in operating a jewelry store, she may decide to close the business and sell off its assets. Alternatively, she can sell the entire business to another person. If Tanisha should die, the sole proprietorship is liquidated, as its life is limited to the life of its owner. In such a situation, if Tanisha's niece inherits the store, then the niece becomes the new owner and a new sole proprietorship is created, as the previous one had been dissolved by death.

RESEARCH THIS!

Locate information about starting a business in your state. You may try using this Web site: http://chss.montclair.edu/leclair/LS/students/corporations.html.

Generally, a sole proprietorship has the advantages of being easy to create and having the greatest degree of management decisions, fewest government restrictions, sole profit receipts, and possibly advantageous tax liability. The disadvantages include the extent of personal liability for both finances as well as torts, lack of capital investment, and limited duration of the business itself.

GENERAL PARTNERSHIP

partnership
Business enterprise owned by more than one person, entered into for profit.

Under the Uniform Partnership Act (UPA), section 6(1), adopted by virtually all states, a **partnership** is "an association of two or more persons to carry on as co-owners a business for profit." In forming a partnership, specific rights and duties are created. Note that there are four criteria that must be satisfied in order for a business to qualify as a partnership. First, the partnership must be comprised of at least two persons. Under the UPA, a "person" can include an individual, other partnerships, a corporation, or some other legal association. Second, the persons must intend to operate a business, such as a trade or an occupation. For example, doctors may voluntarily agree to associate in a practice together, forming a partnership, just like law firms. Third, the persons must operate a business as co-owners, and lastly they must do so with the intent to make a profit. The business does not actually have to make a profit, but simply must be formed with that motive in mind. This last criterion necessarily excludes such businesses as charitable organizations, which are not formed as a profit-making venture.

In ascertaining whether the intent to form a partnership is present, the court looks for evidence of one of three methods of creation:

1. By written agreement.
2. By oral agreement.
3. By operation of law.

articles of partnership
Written agreement to form a partnership.

The preferred method for creating a partnership is by execution of a formal, written partnership agreement. In this document, the co-owners of the business should set forth the rights and duties of all the partners. Unless specified otherwise in the partnership agreement, the courts will conclude that contributions, assets, liabilities, and profit sharing are all equally shared among the partners. Therefore, if the partners want the profits or some other factor decided differently, then their intentions must be specifically and clearly stated in the written agreement, in order to avoid the general presumption that everything is equally shared. In addition, the written agreement, sometimes referred to as the **articles of partnership,** is important to clarify any other terms of the business and is useful evidence should some dispute arise. Keep in mind that a written agreement might be required in cases where the state statute of frauds requires certain contracts to be in writing. Otherwise, there are no particular formalities required to form a partnership.

A partnership may be formed simply by oral agreement among the co-owners. For example, Smedley and Loulou may decide to open a flower shop and verbally agree to buy a building together, share in the profits and losses, and have equal decision making. No written agreement regarding their rights and obligations is necessary, although it is certainly wise to have one, for the reasons mentioned earlier. In such situations, the UPA still governs the agreement, just as if provisions had been omitted from a written agreement, in which case the UPA fills in the missing details.

Finally, even if no evidence of an agreement exists, the court may nonetheless find that the intent to create a partnership existed. The intent to form a partnership may be implied. It can be derived from an objective evaluation of the parties' actions. Where there is a dispute as to whether the intent to form a partnership existed, an inference of intent to create a partnership may be presumed by examining several factors. Such factors include evidence that two or more people are sharing business profits, that there is shared management decision making, and there has been some contribution evidencing common ownership. It is the legal effect of the parties' relationship, and not their subjective intent, that determines whether a partnership was formed.

Generally, the courts will look for profit sharing as well as the sharing of control of the business. For example, assume that Mary and John are running a Christmas tree farm. Mary acts as the manager, hiring employees, paying the bills, and purchasing supplies. John plants trees, tends to the farm, and decides which section of the farm is ready for cutting each holiday season. Neither Mary nor John draw a regular salary, but split the profits at the end of each season. In addition, the checking account for Holly Tree Farms is registered in both of their names. In such a situation, a court might conclude that a partnership had been formed without any clear written agreement, simply by operation of law. Normally, evidence that someone has the right to profit sharing and decision making is substantial proof of the existence of a partnership. It should be noted that mere co-ownership of a store or piece of property is insufficient alone to infer that a partnership is created. In most cases, the court will be looking for evidence of all three criteria to determine that a partnership had been formed. It is immaterial that the parties do not realize that they are partners.

The advantages to operating a business as a partnership are varied. For instance, just like a sole proprietorship, it is very easy to form a partnership. Few government formalities or written documents are required. Second, assets of the partnership are only taxed once. In other words, each individual declares his share of the profits or losses on his own personal income tax form. Just like a sole proprietorship, the partnership is generally treated as an aggregate of its partners. This leads to one of the disadvantages of operating a partnership. Each partner can be individually sued and be personally liable for the actions of each other. Yet, courts also state that a partnership can be considered a separate legal entity and may be sued separately, without naming each individual owner. *UPA (15)a.* Thus, the partnership may be jointly and severally liable. Consider the example of three doctors, Moe, Larry, and Harry. While examining a patient, Moe negligently strikes the patient with his book, causing the patient to fall to the floor and break an arm. The patient may sue the partnership as a legal entity and also may sue Moe or any other partners individually. If Moe had committed an intentional tort upon a patient, then it is possible for the other partners to avoid liability if they can show that Moe's action was outside the scope of the partnership business.

Partnerships are automatically dissolved upon the death or withdrawal of any of the co-owners. However, the partnership may continue to operate under the old name, but be re-created under a new written agreement. Technically, a new partnership is created at this point, even if the co-owners continue to operate the business using the original terms contained in the first written agreement. A partnership may also end if all the partners agree to its dissolution. For example, if Abel, Baker, and Cain decide to operate a business developing land at a particular site, they may terminate this partnership upon agreement once the land is fully developed. In this situation, it would be preferable to draft a written dissolution agreement, specifying the terms of the dissolution and the "winding up" of partnership business.

LIMITED PARTNERSHIP

limited partnership
A partnership of two or more persons, consisting of limited partners, who provide only financial backing, and general partners, who manage the business and have unlimited liability.

A **limited partnership** is created by state statute and is formed by two or more persons who desire to include both general and limited partners in the business. *General* partners are typically responsible for providing capital to start up the business, participate in the daily management of the business, and have unlimited liability for partnership debts and losses. *Limited* partners do not participate in the daily management of the business and are not liable for partnership debts beyond their capital contribution. Their primary function is to provide the capital and investment needed to start up the business.

The primary distinction between the general and limited partners is that general partners have unlimited liability for debts whereas limited partners are liable only up to the amount of their capital investment. The Revised Uniform Limited Partnership Act (RULPA), adopted in most states, guides the creation of this type of partnership and specifies the requirements of the certificate that must be filed with the state. This certificate must contain the names and addresses of each partner, the business name of the partnership and its address, the contributions of the partners, and the last date on which the partnership will dissolve. Like general partnerships, the limited partnership may be dissolved if all partners agree. In such a case, RULPA provides a distribution scheme whereby both kinds of partners receive similar treatment. Like general partnerships, the limited partnership also enjoys the benefits of no double taxation. Each partner's profits and losses are reported on the individual's personal income tax return.

CASE IN POINT

Court of Appeals of Mississippi.
Clinton SUMMERS, Appellant
v.
A-1 CASH, INC. and Mickey Russell, Appellees.
No. 2004-CA-00188-COA.
Sept. 27, 2005.

Before BRIDGES, P.J., GRIFFIS and BARNES, JJ.

BARNES, J., for the Court.

¶ 1. Clinton Summers appeals the decision of the Marion County Chancery Court, challenging the court's finding that no partnership existed between him and Mickey Russell with regard to A-1 Cash, Inc., a check-cashing business. Finding no error, we affirm.

SUMMARY OF FACTS AND PROCEDURAL HISTORY

¶ 2. Clinton Summers and Mickey Russell met as business colleagues in 1989 and continued to work together as co-employees in a number of businesses until the spring of 1994. In April of 1994, Summers and Russell met to discuss a plan to open a check-cashing business in Columbia, Mississippi. Summers and his wife testified that, under the plan, Russell would fund the business while Summers would provide labor and day-to-day oversight of the business. Summers and his wife also stated that a verbal partnership agreement existed under which Summers and Russell would split ownership of the business and all profits equally after Russell recouped his start-up capital of $20,000. Russell, however, testified that no partnership agreement existed, and that he merely offered Summers a position as an employee-manager of the proposed business. Both parties testified that under the plan, Summers was to be paid a salary of $400 per week until Russell recouped his initial investment, and that afterward Summers would receive a percentage of the profits. Summers said the agreement was that he would receive fifty percent of all profits; Russell stated that he offered Summers forty percent of the profits, but over time raised Summers's share to fifty percent.

¶ 3. Upon opening the business—named Cash Advance—in May of 1994, the parties established a bank account for the business at Magnolia Federal Bank (now Union Planters Bank) in the name of "Clinton Summers or Mickey Russell JTROS DBA Cash Advance." The style of the account indicated that the parties held the account as joint tenants with the right of survivorship. The tax identification number associated with the account was Summers's social security number. In addition, the parties established telephone and electricity services for the business; these accounts were opened in Summers's individual name. The business quickly became profitable, and by November of 1995 Russell had recouped his initial investment. From that point on, Summers received forty percent and then fifty percent of the business's profits.

¶ 4. The business's success spurred Russell and Summers to open locations in Brookhaven and McComb, and Summers's duties expanded to the oversight of all three branches. Summers and Russell split the profits from all three locations equally. On July 14, 1998, Russell formed a corporation known as A-1 Cash, Inc., naming himself as the sole officer and director, and issuing to himself all shares of stock in the corporation. The bank accounts were re-titled in the name of A-1 Cash, Inc., and a corporate bank account was established at Union Planters Bank to handle the business's day-to-day check-cashing operations. The signature cards for the corporate account indicated Summers and Russell as being co-owners of A-1 Cash. Another account was also opened at Union Planters Bank and titled in the name of "A-1 Cash, Mickey W. Russell and Clinton Summers." Profits from all three branches were deposited into this account, and after employee wages were deducted from the account, Russell and Summers shared the remainder of the money equally. Russell and Summers were both considered employees of A-1 Cash for income tax purposes, and both reported their income on IRS W-2 forms issued by A-1 Cash, Inc.

¶ 5. In March of 2000, Russell prepared a document entitled "Management Personnel." The document has the heading of "A-1 Cash, Inc.," and lists Russell as holding the positions of president, secretary and treasurer. Summers is listed as manager of the Columbia, McComb and Brookhaven locations. Both parties signed the document: Russell signed his name next to the word "owner," and Summers signed his name next to the word "manager." Additionally, documents from the business's workers' compensation insurance policy indicated that Russell was the president of the corporation and that Summers held the position of secretary. Neither Russell nor Summers was covered by the policy.

¶ 6. The business relationship between Summers and Russell continued until January of 2002, when Russell entered the Columbia location and asked Summers to leave. One month later, Summers filed a ***978** complaint in the Marion County Chancery Court to dissolve the partnership and for an accounting. The court bifurcated the trial, first proceeding without a jury to determine whether a partnership existed between Summers and Russell, and, if so, when the partnership ceased to exist. Finding that the parties lacked sufficient intent to form a partnership, that Summers did not exercise sufficient control over the business to be considered a partner and that the profits distributed to Summers were actually wages, the chancellor held that a partnership did not exist between the parties with regard to Cash Advance and A-1 Cash, Inc. Aggrieved, Summers timely appealed to this Court.

¶ 7. On appeal, Summers claims that (1) the chancellor was manifestly wrong in his finding that there was no intent by Summers and Russell to form a partnership; (2) the chancellor was manifestly wrong in finding that Summers failed to exercise control over the business sufficient to indicate a partnership interest in the business; and (3) the chancellor was manifestly wrong in finding that profits from the business paid to Summers were in the form of wages and that thus Summers did not share in the losses and liabilities of the business. Finding that the chancellor applied the correct legal standards and that the evidence, while conflicting, supports the chancellor's determinations of fact, we affirm the lower court's ruling that no partnership existed between Russell and Summers.

. . .

ANALYSIS ¶ 9. Section 79-12-11 of the Mississippi Code defines "partnership" as "an association of two (2) or more persons to carry on as co-owners a business for profit. . . ." Miss.Code Ann. § 79-12-11 (Rev.2001). Additionally, section 79-12-13 sets forth the guidelines for determining whether a partnership exists. It reads:

> In determining whether a partnership exists, these rules shall apply:
>
> (1) Except as provided by section 79-12-31 persons who are not partners as to each other are not partners as to third persons.
> (2) Joint tenancy, tenancy in common, tenancy by the entireties, joint property, common property, or party ownership does not of itself establish a partnership, whether such co-owners do or do not share any profits made by the use of the property.
> (3) The sharing of gross returns does not of itself establish a partnership, whether or not the persons sharing them have a joint or common right or interest in any property from which the returns are derived.
> (4) The receipt by a person of a share of the profits of a business is prima facie evidence that he is a partner in the business, but no such inference shall be drawn if such profits were received in payment:
> (a) As a debt by installments or otherwise,
> (b) As wages of an employee or rent to a landlord,
> (c) As an annuity to a widow or representative of a deceased partner,
> (d) As interest on a loan, though the amount of payment varies with the profits of the business,
> (e) As a consideration for the sale of the goodwill of a business or other property by installments or otherwise.
> (5) Operation of a mineral property under a joint operating agreement does not of itself establish a partnership.

Miss.Code Ann. § 79-12-13 (Rev.2001).

[1][2][3] ¶ 10. While these statutes codify the common law rules of partnership, "[T]he common law is still used to supplement the statute in determining when a partnership exists." *Smith v. Redd,* 593 So.2d 989, 993 (Miss.1991). Although the existence of a written partnership agreement is useful, it is not necessary. *Century 21 Deep South Properties, Ltd. v. Keys,* 652 So.2d 707, 715 (Miss.1995). "A partnership 'may exist as an oral or written, express or implied agreement among its members.'" *Id.* (quoting *Carmichael v. Agur Realty Co.,* 574 So.2d 603, 610 (Miss.1990)).

[4] ¶ 11. The Mississippi Supreme Court held in *Smith* that the three main questions that must be considered in partnership determination are (1) the intent of the parties, (2) participation in the control of the business and (3) profit sharing. *Smith,* 593 So.2d at 994. While the intent and control questions are important, profit sharing is the most important factor. *Century 21,* 652 So.2d at 715. In fact, section 79-12-13(4) of the Mississippi Code provides that "receipt by a person of a share of the profits of a business is prima facie evidence that he is a partner in the business." Miss. Code Ann. § 79-12-13(4) (Rev.2001). Notably, however, section 79-12-13(4)(b) prohibits the inference of partnership when the profits shared are characterized as wages of an employee.

A. Intent

[5] ¶ 12. Because there was no written partnership agreement between the parties, the chancellor looked to the surrounding circumstances in determining whether the parties intended to enter into a partnership. *See Smith,* 593 So.2d at 994. The chancellor was confronted with conflicting testimony as to whether Russell and Summers intended to enter into a partnership with regard to Cash Advance and, later, A-1 Cash, Inc. The lower court noted that while there were some documents in evidence purporting to list Summers as a co-owner of the business, "[T]here was conflicting testimony as to who actually prepared the documents, who provided the information, and who physically filled out portions of the documents." The chancellor took special note of the "Management Personnel" form featuring Russell's signature above the word "owner" and Summers's signature above the word "manager" in determining that the parties had intended Summers to be an employee of the business rather than a partner.

[6] ¶ 13. In attempting to show that the parties had the requisite intent to form a partnership, Summers relies heavily on the fact that the business's original bank account was titled in the name of Russell and Summers as joint tenants with the right of survivorship. While this fact was clearly entitled to some consideration by the chancellor, it does not resolve the question of intent. Section 79-12-13(2) of the Mississippi Code states that joint tenancy "does not of itself establish a partnership, whether such co-owners do or do not share any profits made by the use of the property." Miss.Code Ann. § 79-12-13(2) (Rev.2001). Summers concedes that the chancellor was not required to find that ***980** the parties intended to create a partnership solely because the business's bank account was held in joint tenancy; however, he suggests that "a significant amount of imagination would be required to believe that a sole proprietor, as Russell claims himself to be, would title the only asset of his business in such a manner if he intended anything other than a partnership." While that may be the case, when substantial evidence supports a chancellor's findings, we will not disturb his conclusions, even if we might have found otherwise as an original matter. *See Murphy v. Murphy,* 631 So.2d 812, 815 (Miss.1994). There was sufficient evidence before the chancellor to cast doubt on Summers's claim of partnership; thus we must affirm the chancellor's findings.

[7] ¶ 14. The chancellor's final judgment also noted that Russell and Summers had formerly been partners in a business known as "Mac's Titles for Cash." The chancellor stated in his judgment that "It is undisputed among the two that this was intended to be a partnership, and was evidenced in a formal partnership agreement that had been drafted and properly executed." The chancellor reasoned that in light of the parties' past behavior, the lack of such a writing in the case of the Cash Advance business militated against the finding of a partnership. While the chancellor's reasoning would have been sound had this alleged written agreement been introduced into evidence, no evidence of the prior partnership agreement appears in the record. Neither party submitted the agreement into evidence, and the only testimony elicited on the matter showed that the partnership agreement between Russell and Summers in the Mac's Titles for Cash business had been verbal in nature. Notwithstanding the chancellor's mistake, however, the court still had before it sufficient evidence to find that no intent to create a partnership existed between Russell and Summers. Accordingly, the chancellor's finding of no intent was not clearly erroneous.

B. Control

[8][9] ¶ 15. While control is indicative of the existence of a partnership, "Control by itself is not the exclusive indicator of partnership. 'Partner-like control' may or may not be found depending on the surrounding circumstances, because the circumstances will vary from relationship to relationship." *Century 21,* 652 So.2d at 715 (quoting *Smith,* 593 So.2d at 994). In the instant case, the chancellor found that Summers failed to exercise sufficient control over the business to be considered a partner. In so finding, the court noted that there was no testimony showing any particular incident where Summers exercised authority over business decisions.

¶ 16. The evidence before the chancellor showed that on one particular occasion when Summers filed suit against the Marion County Sheriff on behalf of the business, Russell became furious and forced Summers to drop the suit. Furthermore, testimony from former A-1 Cash employees Lisa Walker and Susan Prine shows that Summers admitted to them that he was only a manager of the business, not the owner. Similarly, Ricky Myers, president of a state check cashers' association, testified that Summers told him he could not attend a convention because Russell was "tight" with the business's money. Lastly, Summers's own testimony belies his contention that he exercised control over the business. When asked whether he did whatever Russell commanded, Summers said, "If he told me something I needed to do I did it." However, when asked whether Russell would follow Summers's orders, Summers responded "I doubt it. He did what he wanted to." While it was shown that Summers exercised some control over the business in conjunction with Russell, it is unclear from the record that his actions were inconsistent with being an employee-manager of the business. The record is replete with evidence that contradicts Summers's claims that he exercised control over the business; thus, we affirm the chancellor's finding.

C. Profit sharing

[10] ¶ 17. The Mississippi Supreme Court stated in *Smith* that "one of the main indicators of a partnership is the right of a party to share profits and losses." *Smith,* 593 So.2d at 994. The court took the analysis further in *Century 21,* holding that profit sharing was the most important factor in the *Smith* analysis. *Century 21,* 652 So.2d at 715. Additionally, under section 79-12-13(4)(b) of the Mississippi Code, "receipt by a person of a share of the profits of a business is prima facie evidence that he is a partner in the business." Miss.Code Ann. § 79-12-13(4)(b) (Rev.2001). However, this inference is destroyed if the profits shared are characterized as wages. *See* Miss.Code Ann. § 79-12-13(4)(b) (Rev.2001). The chancellor found that Summers received his share of profits in the form of wages, and that as a result he did not share in the business's profits in accordance with *Smith*. Summers contends that the chancellor erred in characterizing his earnings as wages and in finding that he did not share in the business's profits and losses.

¶ 18. It was undisputed at trial that Summers and Russell split the profits from Cash Advance and, later, A-1 Cash, Inc. While Summers testified that he received his half of the business's profits in the capacity of partner, Russell testified that he hired Summers as an employee-manager of the business, offering him a share of the profits in order to give him an incentive to work diligently. Russell testified that he had structured a similar plan for an employee at another one of his check-cashing businesses; that employee, Russell testified, received forty percent of the business's profits in return for her service as an employee-manager.

¶ 19. In arguing that he was in fact a partner, Summers relies heavily on the fact that he was excluded from A-1 Cash's workers' compensation policy. Section 71-3-5 of the Mississippi Code provides in pertinent part:

> Any employer may elect . . . to be exempt from the provisions of the Workers' Compensation Law as to its sole proprietor, its partner in a partnership or to its employee who is the owner of fifteen percent (15%) or more of its stock in a corporation, if such sole proprietor, partner or employee also voluntarily agrees thereto in writing.

Miss.Code Ann. § 71-3-5 (Rev.2000).

¶ 20. Summers voluntarily waived coverage under A-1 Cash's workers' compensation policy in order to increase the business's profits. He asserts that under section 71-3-5, he could not have waived coverage were he not a partner alongside Russell. Further, he argues that Russell should not be able to "have his cake and eat it too," claiming that Russell should not be able to disclaim him as a partner while reaping significant savings on policy premiums. However, we refuse to conflate partnership law with the law of workers' compensation. While the chancellor rightly could have considered that Summers's waiver of coverage militated in favor of a finding of partnership, the chancellor was not bound to find a partnership merely because Summers waived such coverage. There was substantial evidence before the chancellor suggesting that Summers's share of the business's profits was in the form of wages, and thus we must affirm his finding.

***982 CONCLUSION** ¶ 21. The chancellor had substantial evidence before him suggesting that Summers and Russell never intended to enter into a partnership, that Summers exercised little control over Cash Advance or A-1 Checking and that Summers's share of the business's profits was in the form of wages. While this Court might have found otherwise as an original matter, we cannot say that the chancellor's findings were manifestly wrong. Thus, we must affirm.

Source: *Summers v. A-1 Cash,* 911 So.2d 975 (St. Paul, MN: Thomson West). Reprinted with permission from Westlaw.

CASE IN POINT

Court of Appeals of Ohio,
Ninth District, Lorain County.
ZELINA, Appellant,
v.
HILLYER, Appellee.
No. 05CA008661.
Decided Nov. 2, 2005.

BAIRD, Judge.

{¶ 1} Appellant, John Zelina, appeals from the judgment of the Lorain County Court of Common Pleas that granted the motion for summary judgment of appellee, Phyllis Hillyer. We affirm.

I

{¶ 2} The parties met in 1991 at the American Slovak Club where Hillyer was working as a bartender and Zelina as a manager. At that time, Zelina was married, and Hillyer was recently widowed. Zelina began experiencing marital problems, so Hillyer allowed Zelina to move in with her at her residence, located at 1303 Narragansett in Lorain, Ohio, in November 1991. In addition to the Narragansett residence, Hillyer owned two rental properties free and clear with no mortgages, one located at 408 Illinois Avenue in Lorain, Ohio, and the other located at 552 Oberlin Avenue in Lorain, Ohio.

{¶ 3} At the death of her husband, Hillyer received funds in various forms, including joint-and-survivorship accounts, life-insurance, bonds, and dependent benefits from her deceased husband's employer. Hillyer was also receiving $900 per month for each of her two children from her husband's pension. In addition, Hillyer owned a few cars, which she sold. During the parties' cohabitation, Hillyer inherited money from her deceased father's and grandmother's estates and also received some gambling winnings. Zelina, on the other hand, made approximately $540 every two weeks working at the American Slovak Club and had a monthly spousal support obligation arising out of a 1992 marriage dissolution decree.

{¶ 4} During their cohabitation, the parties lived at the Narragansett residence and other locations, but Hillyer also acquired rental properties. In order to purchase other rental properties or residences, Hillyer would use proceeds from the sale of one of the properties or other homes as collateral. Zelina's name was on the deed for four of the properties, but he later quitclaimed his interest in three of these properties to Hillyer. The fourth property was sold during the parties' cohabitation.

{¶ 5} The parties never married, and the relationship eventually began to disintegrate. Zelina moved out in 2000 upon Hillyer's request, and the relationship finally ended in the fall of 2001, after approximately ten years.

{¶ 6} On August 2, 2002, Zelina filed a complaint alleging breach of a partnership agreement, asserting a one-half interest in claimed partnership property. Zelina maintained that the parties had entered into an oral agreement to share equally in the assets accumulated during their ten-year cohabitation from the fall of 1991 through 2001. . . .

{¶ 7} On August 27, 2004, Hillyer filed a motion for summary judgment, asserting that the facts did not establish that the parties had entered into an oral partnership.

. . .

{¶ 8} In a judgment dated January 19, 2005, the trial court granted Hillyer's motion for summary judgment, finding that "the evidence which has been presented is insufficient, as a matter of law, with regard to the claims of the plaintiff that an oral contract was made by the parties to enter into a partnership agreement. The Court cannot enforce the alleged partnership agreement, as there is insufficient evidence of a meeting of the minds as to the basic terms and conditions of the claimed partnership." {¶ 9} Zelina timely appealed, asserting one assignment of error for review.

. . .

{¶ 10} In his sole assignment of error, Zelina basically asserts that the trial court erred in granting summary judgment in favor of Hillyer. We disagree.

. . .

[1][2][3][4][5] {¶ 12} In this case, the parties both agree that they had never executed a written agreement regarding the alleged partnership and that property was never placed in any partnership name. However, Zelina maintains that the parties had an oral partnership agreement. The existence of a contract is a question of law. *Telxon Corp. v. Smart Media of Delaware, Inc.*, 9th Dist. Nos. 22098 and 22099, 2005-Ohio-4931, 2005 WL 2292800, at ¶ 40. "'[T]o declare the existence of a contract, the parties to the contract must consent to its terms, there must be a meeting of the minds of both parties, and the contract must be definite and certain.'" Id. at ¶ 41, quoting *Purdin v. Hitchcock* (Jan. 21, 1993), 4th Dist. No. CA 531, 1993 WL 19508, at *3. Essential to valid contract formation is a meeting of the minds by the parties as to the essential terms of the contract, such that "a reasonable person would find that the parties manifested a present intention to be bound to an agreement." *Telxon Corp.* at ¶ 40. An oral contract may be ascertained from the parties' words, deeds, acts, and silence. Id., citing *Kostelnik v. Helper,* 96 Ohio St.3d 1, 2002-Ohio-2985, 770 N.E.2d 58, at ¶ 15.

{¶ 13} In the instant case, the trial court determined that the evidence presented was insufficient to establish Zelina's claim of an oral partnership agreement.

. . .

Hillyer asserted that Zelina based his case on what he thought had occurred between the parties and his own understanding of what the alleged partnership would specifically concern. Hillyer attached an affidavit to her motion, in which she asserted the following: (1) the parties never entered into a partnership agreement to divide any funds from her investments, (2) the parties agreed only that Zelina "came in with one luggage, he left with one luggage," (3) Zelina in fact benefited from her investments and inheritances during the cohabitation, (4) Hillyer performed most of the work on the rental properties and Zelina's contribution was very minimal, and (5) the quitclaim deeds executed by Zelina supported her assertion that the parties never had entered into a partnership agreement.

{¶ 16} In addition, Hillyer appended copies of deeds to the various properties, including the quitclaim deeds that Zelina executed, as well as copies of both parties' depositions, all of which substantiated the statements she made in her affidavit. Specifically, the depositions demonstrated that the parties had inconsistent understandings of Zelina's rights with respect to Hillyer's various property investments and inheritances. Zelina's deposition testimony merely reflected his assumptions regarding his rights to any properties. Hillyer explained during her deposition that the parties had a "precise" arrangement from the beginning of their relationship. Specifically, Hillyer explained, "[Zelina would] move in with a luggage, [he would] move out with a luggage, if I'm generous to put any deeds or any real estate in [his] name, and [Zelina] promised that he would sign off [on the deeds], and he always did." Hillyer stated that she had made it clear to Zelina on several occasions during their ten-year relationship that if the time came, "[Zelina] was taking [his] luggage and that's it." Hillyer also maintained during her deposition that Zelina never contributed any funds towards the purchase of real estate. Hillyer's summary-judgment motion showed that no genuine issue of material fact remained whether the parties had reached a meeting of the minds as to Zelina's rights to Hillyer's assets. See *Telxon Corp.* at ¶ 40.

{¶ 17} Thus, the burden then shifted to Zelina to point to or submit evidentiary materials that showed that a genuine dispute over material facts remained. See *Dresher,* 75 Ohio St.3d at 293, 662 N.E.2d 264. In his brief in opposition to the summary judgment motion, Zelina argued that it was "clearly evident" that an oral contract existed between the parties, asserting that it was while the parties lived at the Tanglewood residence that they reached an agreement to buy and sell/rent real estate. Zelina merely referred to his deposition testimony, which reflected *his own expectation* of what financial arrangement the parties would have and actually illuminated the fact that the parties never reached a meeting of the minds as to the essential nature and terms of the alleged partnership agreement. Zelina explained, "We were doing some work on her house on Illinois, and I remember mentioning it to her to maybe try to sell that house and get something a little better and easier to take care of and rent it out." When asked by counsel whether the parties had any discussion regarding sharing profits and real estate purchases, Zelina responded, "We were together. Well, I thought we'd stay together and I figured everything would be 50/50."

{¶ 18} Thus, the testimony that Zelina refers to only strengthens the fact brought up by Hillyer that this sharing arrangement resided in Zelina's own expectations and assumptions about the parties' relationship. In fact, Zelina admitted in his brief in opposition to the motion, as well as on appeal, that the nature and terms of the alleged agreement were in dispute. Zelina has plainly failed to demonstrate that the parties manifested a meeting of the minds such that an agreement to have a partnership was reached.

[6][7] {¶ 19} Zelina also argues that the doctrine of promissory estoppel applied in this case to enforce an alleged promise made by Hillyer to share in profits. The promissory estoppel doctrine requires an actual reliance to one's detriment on a clear and unambiguous promise that would be objectively reasonable and foreseeable to rely upon. *Telxon* at ¶ 59. However, Zelina did not point to any evidence that Hillyer had clearly and unambiguously promised to share the rent profits and returns on investment that she enjoyed during their ten-year cohabitation. Zelina averred that he had contributed labor and funds towards the purchase of certain properties, that the parties had filed joint tax returns, and that he was a cosigner on some of the mortgages. He asserted that he had contributed funds towards Hillyer's New Jersey property, but he did not produce any evidence to show that the money he deposited in his account had actually been used for this property. Zelina also mentioned that he had purchased a few sheds for the property, but did not produce documentation of these purchases.

{¶ 20} In addition to failing to provide documentary evidence to support these assertions, Zelina has failed to demonstrate that his claimed reliance on an alleged promise had ultimately worked to his detriment. The evidence presented by Hillyer showed that Zelina had in fact benefited from the parties' living arrangement. During their relationship, Hillyer allowed Zelina to live with her, bought him necessities such as clothing, purchased cars for Zelina, and maintained the properties in which they resided. Zelina even stated during his deposition that the extent of work he had performed on the properties consisted of painting and plumbing. In fact, Zelina acknowledged during his deposition that when it came to managing the properties, "[Hillyer] took care of all the renting properties," including collecting rent, paying the bills, and getting proposals for work to be done. He also admitted that he had not contributed any funds towards the payment of outstanding mortgage and home-equity line debts when he left Hillyer in 2001. Zelina did not present any arguments or evidence to contest any of these facts.

[8] {¶ 21} Zelina has also asserted that the parties bought, sold, and rented real property and shared in the profits during their relationship, and that pursuant to the Uniform Partnership Law, R.C. Chapter 1775, this is prima facie evidence of a partnership. See R.C. 1775.06. However, Zelina failed to produce any evidence to demonstrate that the parties had actually shared in profits or that Zelina had received payments from the gross returns of the real property investments. See R.C. 1775.06(C) and (D); R.C. 1775.05.(A). In fact, during his deposition Zelina stated that any proceeds from property sales had been used to pay off home equity lines or invested in other properties; Zelina did not present evidence to refute this fact.

. . .

{¶ 23} Based upon the foregoing, we find that Hillyer was entitled to judgment as a matter of law, and therefore the trial court did not err in granting Hillyer's motion for summary judgment. Although the court appears to have based its ruling on the insufficiency of the evidence presented by Zelina rather than the parties' respective summary-judgment burdens, we nevertheless affirm the judgment of the trial court because it reached the correct result, albeit for the wrong reason.

Judgment affirmed.

SLABY, P.J., and WHITMORE, J., concur.

BAIRD, J., retired, of the Ninth Appellate District, sitting by assignment.

Source: *Zelina v. Hillyer,* 165 Ohio App.3d 255, 846 N.E.2d 68 (St. Paul, MN: Thomson West). Reprinted with permission from Westlaw.

You Be the Judge

Abe, Ben, and Cain are partners in a real estate development company. Their objective is to purchase depressed property or derelict land, redevelop the property, and then resell it in a few months at a huge profit. During one of their partnership meetings, Abe proposes foregoing the opportunity to purchase a large tract of vacant land, suggesting that the land is in an undesirable location and would be difficult to develop. Cain, who had been out late the night before, falls asleep during the meeting and thus misses most of Abe's discussion. Cain wakes up long enough to vote in favor of Abe's recommendation, though he doesn't understand what it is all about. Ben is suffering from hay fever and is unable to concentrate on the discussion, and so also supports Abe's recommendation. One month later, Cain discovers that Abe had purchased this tract of land for himself and then resold it at a profit to the Dinky World Entertainment Corporation which plans to build a large theme park on the land. What, if anything, can Cain do regarding this situation? Explain.

CORPORATION

corporation
An organization formed with state government approval to act as an artificial person to carry on business and issue stock.

shareholder
The owner of one or more shares of stock in a corporation.

dividends
Portion of profits, usually based on the number of shares owned.

The third type of business organization that will be addressed in this chapter is the dominating form of business enterprise—the corporation. A **corporation** is a distinct legal entity, an artificial person, created under state statutes.

Unlike sole proprietorships or partnerships, corporations have complex formalities and documents that must be filed in order to be formed. This may be deemed a disadvantage to this kind of business entity, as there are numerous expenses, steps, and decisions that must be made to ensure compliance with the requisite statutory formalities. Another distinct disadvantage of a corporation is the sting of double taxation. Since the owners of a corporation are the **shareholders,** be it just one individual or thousands of people, the corporate profits are distributed to them as **dividends** and are taxed on their individual income taxes. However, the separate legal entity, the corporation, is also taxed on the profits at the corporate rate, prior to the distribution of dividends ordered by the directors of the company. Despite these two disadvantages, there are many advantages to this form of business organization that many people believe outweigh the disadvantages.

For example, the corporation—as a separate legal entity—has a life of its own, and thus its perpetual existence guarantees that the business will continue even if principal owners of the corporation die or ownership shares are transferred to other people. Second, the investors in a corporation enjoy limited liability, restricted solely to the amount of their investment. Thus, if Mary purchases 25 ownership interests (shares of stock) in Dudley's Widgets Corporation, her liability for corporate debt is limited to that investment in Dudley's Widgets. Should the corporation declare bankruptcy, Mary's personal assets generally cannot be reached by creditors. There may be an exception to this principle, which will be discussed later in this section. Similarly, if the corporation is sued for the negligence of one of its employees, Mary cannot be individually sued or held civilly or criminally liable for the acts of the corporation, except, again, in a specific limited situation. If the corporation is found liable or guilty, then monetary damages are the only option to the plaintiff, as a corporation cannot be imprisoned.

articles of incorporation
The basic charter of an organization, written and filed in accordance with state laws.

A third advantage to this form of business organization is the comparative ease in obtaining additional capital in the form of bank loans or credit. Although most capital is raised through the sale of ownership shares in the company, there may still be a need to secure additional financing because the **articles of incorporation**—the document needed to form a corporation—limits the share structure and number of shares authorized to be issued. Furthermore, the corporation may desire to utilize the deductibility of interest payments on outstanding loans as a way to reduce the sting of double taxation of corporate profits.

Finally, depending on the size of the corporation, it may be advantageous for the shareholders to retain the right to profit sharing without the burden of daily management and decision making of the company. This centralization of management is advantageous in that experts can be hired or elected to promote the success of the company, with just minimal involvement of the shareholders. Shareholders still have some control over the way the corporation is operated, through their voting rights, but this is a topic that will be discussed later in this chapter.

Once the decision is made to incorporate a business, someone must assume the duties and responsibilities of bringing this vision into reality. A group of six people may agree that they want to incorporate their carpet cleaning business, but may lack the expertise and knowledge to ensure

promoter
A person, typically a principal shareholder, who organizes a business.

compliance with statutory formalities. In such a case, the six people may enlist a **promoter,** who takes charge of organizing the business formation, preparing the appropriate documents, securing capital, and following specific incorporation procedures in the selected state of incorporation.

closely held corporation
A business that is incorporated with limited members, typically related family members.

One of the first decisions is the choice of corporate form. If the business is a fairly small carpet-cleaning business, and the six people are all members of the same family, it is likely that this will be incorporated as a **closely held corporation.** In this case, the capital is coming from just the six people, restricting ownership or the sale of shares to outside individuals; they may also have greater management and decision-making involvement than a larger corporation. If a closely held corporation is formed, the shareholders should be careful to hold regular meetings and issue stock so that the line is not blurred between the existences of a corporation versus the similarities in that of a partnership.

publicly held corporation
A business held by a large number of shareholders.

foreign corporation
A business that is incorporated under the laws of a different state, doing business in multiple states.

The opposite of this classification is a **publicly held corporation.** Typically, this type of corporation is owned by a large number of shareholders and the shares may be bought and sold on one of the primary stock exchanges. Examples of a publicly held corporation are McDonald's and Ford Motor Company. A **foreign corporation** is incorporated in one state but does business in one or more other states. For example, a corporation may find the law of Delaware to be advantageous and thus will incorporate in that state but do business in Illinois. In this situation, the company is a foreign corporation in Illinois but a domestic corporation in Delaware. This becomes relevant when jurisdiction needs to be established, as this corporation may be sued in either Delaware or Illinois.

Once the proposed classification of corporation is settled, then the promoter begins working on ensuring that the business is created according to the statutory requirements. The articles of incorporation are drafted, which according to the Revised Model Business Incorporation Act (RMBCA), adopted by most states, should contain the following:

1. The name of the corporation.
2. The intended duration of the company.
3. The purpose(s) for which the corporation is organized (i.e., to operate as a carpet-cleaning business).
4. The name and address of each incorporator (i.e., the six people forming the carpet-cleaning business).
5. The number of authorized shares of stock to be issued.
6. The address of the corporation's registered office and the name and address of each registered agent for the corporation.
7. The names and addresses of each member of the initial board of directors.

board of directors
Policy managers of a corporation, elected by the shareholders, who in turn choose the officers of the corporation.

The RMBCA indicates that once the articles of incorporation are filed with the secretary of state in the appropriate state of incorporation, then the separate legal entity is created. Generally, the next step is to hold the first meeting of the corporation, held by the named board of directors. The **board of directors,** initially designated by the corporation, is responsible for the daily management of the corporation. At this meeting, the necessary steps required to complete the formation are taken, such as opening a corporate bank account, designating stock certificates,

You Be the Judge

Claire is the sole director and shareholder of Widgets to Go. Claire acquires a rival company, Widgets Unlimited, but does not fairly evaluate the new company's net worth and its poor business prospects. Fearing the collapse of Widgets to Go, Claire persuades her friend Molly to invest half a million dollars in her business. Her friend relies on Claire's promises that the investment is a good idea and borrows from her sister, Louise. After buying shares in Widgets to Go, Molly discovers that the company is virtually worthless. She tries to sell her shares but can't find a buyer. Molly is forced to sell her house and work three jobs in order to repay the loan to Louise. Can Molly force Widgets to Go to proceed in an action against Claire to recover the losses incurred by the business as a result of the purchase of the rival company, rendering Widgets to Go insolvent?

bylaws
Corporate provisions detailing management structure and operating rules.

and adopting **bylaws.** Bylaws are the detailed provisions that delineate the management structure; they are the rules that supplement and expand on the articles of incorporation and govern all corporate meetings. Although the bylaws are not filed with the state, they are still binding on the officers, directors, and shareholders of the corporation. After the initial organizational meeting of the corporation, the shareholders thereafter have the right to elect the board of directors. This is an important voting right, as it provides some measure of control over the operation of the corporation. The board of directors, in turn, chooses the officers of the corporation, who generally have the management and business expertise.

An important task to be completed by the board of directors at this initial organizational meeting is the election of officers. While the board of directors is ultimately responsible for the daily management of the company, including investment and policy decisions, the officers are charged with the duty to carry out these decisions, in accordance with policies and the bylaws. Specific duties of the officers, as well as the number of officers, are defined in the bylaws.

At all times, the board and the officers have the duty to act in good faith, in the best interests of the corporation, possessing a fiduciary duty to all shareholders. Officers and directors must undertake their duties as an ordinarily prudent person would do in a similar position in a similar situation. The **business judgment rule** precludes liability of the officers and directors for simply exercising judgment and making an honest mistake or error. In this respect, the shareholders have the power to exercise approval, by voting at annual corporate meetings, deciding on proposed amendments or management resolutions, and electing new board members as often as is specified in the articles of incorporation. Typically, the RMBCA permits shareholders to vote to remove directors without cause prior to the end of their term, unless the corporate articles specifically prohibit this.

business judgment rule
The rule that protects corporate officers and directors from liability for bad business decisions.

CORPORATE LITIGATION

Shareholders have the advantage of limited liability for the debts of the corporation. In addition, they are usually not personally liable for any criminal or civil wrongs committed by the corporation. However, there may be circumstances in which a court may choose to disregard the corporate entity and *reach* individual owners. This doctrine is called **piercing the corporate veil.** This occurs when someone sues a corporation and the court concludes that the business entity should be stripped of its unlimited liability protection because the corporate form is but a sham. The court then treats the individual owners as if they were partners or sole proprietors and reaches their individual personal assets to satisfy any debts or judgments. Another term for this is the **alter ego doctrine.** Sometimes this occurs because the shareholders have failed to exercise sound judgment practice and act with the same duty of care as another ordinary prudent person in a similar position. This does not mean that officers or directors are held accountable for honest mistakes in business decisions.

piercing the corporate veil
To show that a corporation exists as an alter ego for a person or group of individuals to avoid liability.

alter ego doctrine
A business set up to cover or be a shield for the person actually controlling the corporation, and thus the court may treat the owners as if they were partners or a sole proprietor.

Other times, this piercing of the corporate veil occurs simply because the court concludes that the business entity is in fact a sham. As a result, shareholders may be personally liable for a corporation's debts or liabilities, provided the following criteria can be proved:

1. It is a close corporation where the primary shareholders failed to issue stock or hold regular annual meetings.
2. The corporation was *thinly capitalized,* meaning that it was formed with nominal capitalization.
3. The shareholders have commingled personal and corporate assets and failed to establish a corporate bank account.
4. Other factors that indicate intent to form a corporation for improper purposes, such as avoiding debt.

Conversely, a corporation, as a legal entity, has standing to sue and pursue any claims by the corporation, such as unpaid debt by a creditor of the corporation. In many cases, jurisdiction is difficult to ascertain for initiating any such lawsuit on behalf of the corporation, as corporate property may be located in the domestic state as well as a foreign state. In any event, any legal expenses incurred by the board of directors or the officers in defending the corporation are to be paid by the corporation, so long as the individuals had acted in good faith and in the best interests of the corporation in fulfilling their obligations under state statutes.

CASE IN POINT

Court of Appeals of North Carolina.
Jill Womble WOOD, Plaintiff,
v.
McDONALD'S CORPORATION, Johnny Lynn Tart, Johnny Tart Enterprises, Inc., and T & T Management Corporation, Defendants.
No. COA03-953.
Sept. 7, 2004.

McCULLOUGH, Judge.

The issues in this appeal arise from the following undisputed facts: On 4 January 1998, plaintiff went to a McDonald's restaurant (the "restaurant") located in Greensboro, North Carolina. She and her husband were on their way to a matinee movie. Plaintiff's husband remained in the car while she entered the restaurant to purchase a cup of coffee. She entered by way of a single door in the rear of the restaurant and walked towards the front counter. To her left, plaintiff noticed an employee sweeping debris on the floor near the restaurant's side double-door entrance. Plaintiff veered slightly to the right to avoid stepping into any of the debris, and walked to the front of the counter without incident.

After being served her coffee, plaintiff turned to the condiment counter to get cream and sweetener. Finding there to be only cream, which she there added, she returned to the serving counter to get sweetener. Plaintiff was given sweetener, added it, placed a lid on the coffee, and then turned to leave.

She had intended to exit by means of the double doors on the side of the restaurant. She turned to her right from the counter and faced the double doors, but saw that the employee had swept the pile of debris in front of those doors. Plaintiff decided that she would exit from the rear door, by which she had entered, to avoid the debris. With her eyes on the debris so as not to step in it, she rounded the corner of the serving counter. Plaintiff's right foot suddenly shot out from under her and she fell to the floor landing on her back and right elbow. She immediately felt pain in her elbow, and then hot scalding pain as the coffee cup burst onto her stomach.

She lay there for a moment in pain, and saw the employee that had been sweeping the floor looking at her. He dropped his broom and walked past her. She got up and made her way to the serving counter where she spoke to the employee that had served her coffee, and told him what happened. He offered her another cup of coffee. Plaintiff left the store and ran to her car to tell her husband what happened.

Plaintiff's husband went back in the store to get plaintiff napkins to wipe off the coffee. He entered by the back door. Taking the same route to the counter his wife had taken, he saw the coffee spill. Nearby he saw a dirty, floor-colored french fry. The lone, half-mashed french fry was approximately five feet from the principal pile of debris that was blocking the side double doors. He proceeded to the counter and spoke with the manager. He then took the manager to the scene of the accident, and showed her the spot where the french fry remained with what he believed to be his wife's heel print in it.

Plaintiff's husband returned to the car and took her to the hospital where she arrived at approximately 4:00 p.m. On the day of the incident, X-rays showed no fracture. However, it was later determined that she had in fact fractured her elbow, and had median nerve damage. She contracted reflex sympathetic dystrophy.

The McDonald's restaurant in question was purchased outright from McDonald's Corporation by defendant Johnny Tart ("Mr. Tart") on 2 January 1997. He then assigned his ownership to T & T Management Corporation ("T & T").

Mr. Tart had formed T & T on 24 January 1994 for the purpose of assigning McDonald's franchises to the corporation. T & T was a C corporation, and owned everything but the building and land of franchises it was assigned (it owned the cookers, fryers, freezer, etc.). He formed two other C corporations for this same purpose: Tracor, Inc., was formed on 13 July 1994; and Kayln Corporation was formed on 8 March 1995. Additionally, on 3 July 1995, Mr. Tart formed Johnny Tart Enterprises, Inc. ("JT Enterprises"), an S corporation. He formed JT Enterprises for the purpose of charging a fee to his three C corporations for providing administrative services so that these fees would not be taxed as income to the C corporations and instead deductible as business expenses. JT Enterprises and T & T, by signature of Mr. Tart as president of each, entered into a Management Services Agreement ("MSA").

On 25 July 2000, plaintiff filed her complaint against McDonald's Corporation, Kayln Corporation, Mr. Tart individually, and JT Enterprises, alleging she was injured due to their negligence in her slip and fall on 4 January 1998. In their answers, all defendants named T & T as the owner and operator of the McDonald's where the incident occurred. On 30 May 2001, plaintiff filed a motion to amend the complaint to add T & T as an additional defendant.

. . .

Dismissal of Mr. Tart

Plaintiff's second issue on appeal is that the trial court erred in granting summary judgment in favor of Mr. Tart. Plaintiff argues Mr. Tart should remain a party to this action under either the doctrine of "joint venture," or the doctrine of "piercing the corporate veil."

[13][14][15] "Joint venture" is synonymous with "joint adventure." *See Pike v. Wachovia Bank & Trust Co.,* 274 N.C. 1, 8, 161 S.E.2d 453, 460 (1968). For a joint adventure to exist, "'there must be (1) an agreement, express or implied, to carry out a single business venture *with joint sharing of profits,* and (2) an *equal*

right of control of the means employed to carry out the venture.'" *Rhoney v. Fele,* 134 N.C.App. 614, 620, 518 S.E.2d 536, 541 (1999) (quoting *Edwards v. Northwestern Bank,* 39 N.C.App. 261, 275, 250 S.E.2d 651, 661 (1979)), *disc. review denied,* 351 N.C. 360, 542 S.E.2d 217 (2000). "The control required for imputing negligence under a joint enterprise theory is not actual physical control, but the *legal right* to control the conduct of the other with respect to the prosecution of the common purpose." *Slaughter v. Slaughter,* 93 N.C.App. 717, 721, 379 S.E.2d 98, 101, *disc. review allowed,* 325 N.C. 273, 384 S.E.2d 519 (1989), *disc. review dismissed as improvidently allowed,* 326 N.C. 479, 389 S.E.2d 803 (1990).

[16] In the instant case, for a "joint venture" to exist between Mr. Tart and the corporations of T & T and JT Enterprises, our law requires evidence that these corporations had the legal right to control the conduct of Mr. Tart in "prosecution of the common purpose" of running the profitable restaurant where plaintiff was injured. Furthermore, that these corporations were sharing in the profits of the venture. No such evidence has been forecast.

The only evidence of record shows that Mr. Tart was president and 50% shareholder of JT Enterprises and T & T. Furthermore, the evidence shows that Mr. Tart did not "share" in the profits with either of these corporations. With JT Enterprises, a Sub-chapter C corporation, Mr. Tart was both president and an employee, receiving "biweekly" paychecks. With T & T, a Sub-chapter S corporation, Mr. Tart received the monthly profits of T & T flowing to him as personal, taxable income. Mr. Tart stated in his deposition, that, "[i]f at the end of the year there's any [profits] left over, you have an option to either leave it in the business or take a vacation or buy some Christmas presents or what have you." Plaintiff has offered no evidence that T & T is sharing in the corporate profits. Thus, this theory of liability fails.

[17] Plaintiff next attempts to keep Mr. Tart individually as a party to this action by piercing the corporate structure utilized to operate his restaurants and presenting them as a mere instrumentality of himself. We do not believe the evidence as forecast raises an issue of fact as to this theory.

[18] It is well recognized that courts will disregard the corporate form or "pierce the corporate veil," and extend liability for corporate obligations beyond the confines of a corporation's separate entity whenever necessary to prevent fraud or to achieve equity. *Glenn v. Wagner,* 313 N.C. 450, 454, 329 S.E.2d 326, 330 (1985). This Court has enumerated three elements which support an attack on a separate corporate entity:

> " '"(1) Control, not mere majority or complete stock control, but complete domination, not only of finances, but of policy and business practice in respect to the transaction attacked so that the corporate entity as to this transaction had at the time no separate mind, will or existence of its own; and
>
> " '"(2) Such control must have been used by the defendant to commit fraud or wrong, to perpetrate the violation of a statutory or other positive legal duty, or a dishonest and unjust act in contravention of plaintiff's legal rights; and
>
> " '"(3) The aforesaid control and breach of duty must proximately cause the injury or unjust loss complained of." ' "
>
> B-W Acceptance Corp. v. Spencer, 268 N.C. 1, 9, 149 S.E.2d 570, 576 (1966) (citations omitted). Case law has provided a number of factors for a reviewing court to consider when determining whether to pierce the corporate veil:
>
> 1. Inadequate capitalization.
> 2. Non-compliance with corporate formalities.
> 3. Complete domination and control of the corporation so that it has no independent identity.
> 4. Excessive fragmentation of a single enterprise into separate corporations.

Glenn, 313 N.C. at 455, 329 S.E.2d at 331 (citations omitted). No one factor has been deemed dispositive by our Courts, and thus we read the totality of the forecast evidence and of factors set forth in *Glenn* in determining whether an issue of fact exists sufficient to survive summary judgment.

Mr. Tart's undisputed affidavit shows that each of the corporations of which he is president, including JT Enterprises and T & T, adhered with great care to corporate formalities: they keep completely separate records, regular meetings were held of directors and shareholders, minutes were kept for all meetings and corporate actions, and by-laws for each corporation were in place. Additionally, each had obtained the same insurance liability coverage amounting to $26 million dollars. From Mr. Tart's first answer to plaintiff's complaint, he gave clear notice of who he believed was the proper, fully insured defendant:

> [T]his franchise was sold and assigned to T & T Management Corporation by written Assignment and Consent To Assignment effective January 2, 1997. From and after January 2, 1997, the franchise to the McDonald's at this location was owned by T & T Management Corporation which operated this McDonald's restaurant, with management services being provided to T & T management Corporation by Johnny Tart Enterprises, Inc. under a Management Services Agreement . . . dated January 1, 1997.

In light of the forecast evidence, we do not find Mr. Tart has abused the corporate structure, and therefore affirm the lower court's grant of summary judgment in favor of Mr. Tart on all theories of liability.

. . .

Source: *Wood v. McDonald's,* 166 N.C.App. 48, 603 S.E.2d 539 (St. Paul, MN: Thomson West). Reprinted with permission from Westlaw.

CASE IN POINT

District Court of Appeal of Florida,
Fifth District.
Roch CARTER, Appellant,
v.
The ESTATE OF Elizabeth P. RAMBO, Etc., Appellee.
No. 5D05-250.
Feb. 24, 2006.
Rehearing Denied April 7, 2006.

PALMER, J.

Roch Carter appeals the trial court's non-final order denying his motions to quash service of process and to dismiss this action. Concluding that the Estate of Elizabeth P. Rambo (Rambo) failed to establish personal jurisdiction over Carter, we reverse. [FN1]

Rambo filed suit against numerous defendants, including Carter, for injuries allegedly caused by the negligent operation of a nursing home. In the complaint, Carter is described as being a managing member of Partner's Health Group-Florida, LLC (LLC), the entity which operated the nursing home. The complaint alleges that Carter breached or failed to perform the duties of a managing member of the LLC and that said breach or failure constituted recklessness or an act of omission which was committed in bad faith or with malicious purpose or in a manner exhibiting wanton and willful disregard of the rights of others.

Carter filed motions to quash service of process and to dismiss the complaint, arguing that the trial court lacked personal jurisdiction over him. In support of the motions, Carter filed an affidavit asserting that he did not have sufficient minimal contact with the State of Florida to establish personal jurisdiction.

Carter also filed a deposition in support of his motion. In that deposition, Carter admitted that he filed uniform business reports with Florida for the LLC; however, he claimed that he signed the reports in error. A certification at the bottom of the reports set forth as follows:

> I further certify that the information indicated on this report is true and accurate and that my signature shall have the same legal effect as if made under oath; that I am a managing member or manager of the limited liability company or the receiver or trustee empowered to execute this report as required by chapter 608 Florida statutes.

Carter stated that he was authorized to sign on behalf of the company, but knew he was not a managing partner.

The trial court denied Carter's motions on the basis that Carter had signed the uniform business reports filed with Florida as a managing member. The trial court explained as follows:

> COURT: Okay. Guys, I think when you sign under oath that you're a manager or managing member, that you get personal jurisdiction. Now, that doesn't foreclose his ability to go in and show that he wasn't to a jury. But as far as getting personal jurisdiction, I think it's denied. I think you got it.

[1] Carter appeals, arguing that the trial court erred in so ruling because Rambo failed to demonstrate a basis for Florida to have personal jurisdiction over him. We agree.

[2][3][4][5] The question in this appeal is whether the courts in Florida can obtain personal jurisdiction over non-resident Carter in his individual capacity. Two inquiries must be made when deciding whether personal jurisdiction exists over a nonresident: (1) the complaint must allege sufficient facts to bring the action within the ambit of one of the various jurisdictional criteria contained in Florida's long-arm statute, and (2) if the complaint properly alleges long-arm jurisdiction, sufficient minimum contacts must be demonstrated that satisfy the requirements of federal due process. *Law Offices of Sybil Shainwald v. Barro,* 817 So.2d 873 (Fla. 5th DCA 2002). The first prong of this analysis, involves a shifting burden:

> Initially, the plaintiff may seek to obtain jurisdiction over a nonresident defendant by pleading the basis for service in the language of the statute without pleading the supporting facts. Fla.R.Civ.P. 1.070(i); *Jones v. Jack Maxton Chevrolet, Inc.,* 484 So.2d 43 (Fla. 1st DCA 1986). By itself, the filing of a motion to dismiss on grounds of lack of jurisdiction over the person does nothing more than raise the legal sufficiency of the pleadings. *Elmex Corp. v. Atlantic Fed. Savings & Loan Ass'n,* 325 So.2d 58 (Fla. 4th DCA 1976). A defendant wishing to contest the allegations of the complaint concerning jurisdiction or to raise a contention of minimum contacts must file affidavits in support of his position. The burden is then placed upon the plaintiff to prove by affidavit the basis upon which jurisdiction may be obtained.
>
> . . .

Here, Rambo filed a complaint which tracked the language of Florida's long-arm statute and alleged in detail that Carter was an individual doing business in Florida, that he operated a nursing home during Rambo's residence, and that he had committed tortious acts while in Florida. *See* § 48.193(1)(a)(b) & (2), Fla. Stat. (2003). [FN2] In response, Carter submitted an affidavit stating that: (1) he was not a resident of Florida; (2) he did not have any significant personal business interests in Florida; (3) he was not a managing member of the LLC; (4) he was the general counsel and an officer of Extendicare Health Services, Inc; (5) Extendicare Health Services, Inc., at no time established, managed, operated or maintained the nursing home involved in this matter, or provided care to Elizabeth P. Rambo; (6) Extendicare Health Services, Inc., at no time established, managed, operated or maintained a nursing home in Florida, or provided care to Elizabeth P. Rambo; and, (7) he at no time established, managed, operated or maintained the nursing home or provided care to Elizabeth P. Rambo.

Since Carter's affidavit expressly contested each of Rambo's allegations, the burden shifted back to Rambo to prove the alleged basis for personal jurisdiction over Carter. To meet its burden, Rambo relied on Carter's deposition testimony and the authenticated business records attached as exhibits to the deposition. However, Carter maintains that those records only prove that he was acting as a corporate officer and that he is not subject to personal jurisdiction for his activities as a corporate officer, citing to the corporate shield doctrine.

[6] The corporate shield doctrine draws a distinction between a corporate officer acting on his own and a corporate officer acting on behalf of his corporation. *Stomar, Inc. v. Lucky Seven Riverboat Co., L.L.C.,* 821 So.2d 1183 (Fla. 4th DCA 2002). Under the corporate shield doctrine, any activity in one's capacity as a corporate officer or director is exempted from consideration in support of the exercise of long-arm jurisdiction over said officer or director.

Here, Rambo presented no evidence indicating that Carter personally operated a nursing home in Florida or that he personally committed any tortious acts against Rambo in Florida. The deposition evidence indicates that Carter's only contact with Florida was that he signed business reports as a managing member of an LLC in his representative capacity. Furthermore, Rambo also failed to demonstrate that Carter had sufficient "minimum contacts" with Florida to establish personal jurisdiction over him. Accordingly, the trial court erred in denying Carter's dismissal motion. *See Doe v. Thompson,* 620 So.2d 1004 (Fla.1993) (holding that under long-arm jurisdiction statute, personal jurisdiction did not exist over nonresident defendant who was president of corporation which did business in Florida; president stated he did not personally operate business, commit tortious act or cause injury in Florida, and his purportedly negligent actions were not alleged to have been taken outside his duties as corporation's president and chief executive officer).

REVERSED and REMANDED.
THOMPSON and LAWSON, JJ., concur.

FN1. Jurisdiction is proper pursuant to rule 9.130(a)(3)(C)(i) of the Florida Rules of Appellate Procedure.

FN2. Section 48.193 of the Florida Statutes provides:

48.193. Acts subjecting person to jurisdiction of courts of state

1. Any person, whether or not a citizen or resident of this state, who personally or through an agent does any of the acts enumerated in this subsection thereby submits himself or herself and, if he or she is a natural person, his or her personal representative to the jurisdiction of the courts of this state for any cause of action arising from the doing of any of the following acts:
   a. Operating, conducting, engaging in, or carrying on a business or business venture in this state or having an office or agency in this state.
   b. Committing a tortious act within this state.

* * *

2. A defendant who is engaged in substantial and not isolated activity within this state, whether such activity is wholly interstate, intrastate, or otherwise, is subject to the jurisdiction of the courts of this state, whether or not the claim arises from that activity.

Source: *Carter v. Rambo* (St. Paul, MN: Thomson West). Reprinted with permission from Westlaw.

LIMITED LIABILITY COMPANY

limited liability company
A hybrid business formed under state acts, representing both corporation and partnership characteristics.

professional corporation
Business form organized as a closely held group of professional intellectual employees such as doctors.

The final type of business organization to be discussed in this chapter is the form that is a hybrid of both a corporation and a partnership. It is a **limited liability company,** which shares the best characteristics of both a corporation and a partnership. It enjoys the tax benefits of a partnership with the limited liability characteristic of a corporation. It is similar to a **professional corporation,** which is typically closely held by a group of professionals such as doctors or lawyers.

The limited liability company, commonly referred to as an "LLC," was created as the result of LLC acts passed in all 50 states. It offers its owners a corporate kind of shield from liability while permitting the pass-through tax benefits found in partnerships. In order to obtain the benefits of this form of business organization, the owners must ensure that the LLC has the characteristics of a partnership, to prevent the Internal Revenue Service from classifying the business as a corporation. These requisite characteristics include a definite life of the business, as well as no transferability of interests. The owners must draft an LLC agreement that resembles, to a great extent, a partnership agreement. In this agreement, the owners must define the elements of the management of the business, the relationship of the members, and the operating provisions. Generally, this agreement will follow the requirements of the state's LLC act. Paralegals that assist in this field should be aware of their individual state's LLC act. In the absence of a formal LLC agreement, the court will rely on the provisions of that state's act in resolving disputes.

A Day in the Life of a Real Paralegal

In your work as a paralegal for a firm that primarily has corporate clients, you will frequently be dealing with issues surrounding the formation of business entities as well as the ongoing business of those organizations. For this area of work, your greatest challenge might be keeping abreast of the ever-changing rules and regulations applicable to the formation and operation of businesses. Having an eye for detail and being able to ensure that documents are prepared accurately, under your attorney's supervision, is the key to success in this legal area. Knowing the basics of the acts mentioned in this chapter, such as the UPA or the MBCA, will go a long way to you gaining confidence in this field. Corporations frequently have in-house legal departments that employ paralegals, and therefore it is useful to understand the duties and responsibilities of the officers and directors and their accountability to the shareholders.

Some of the tasks that paralegals typically undertake in this field include drafting partnership agreements and articles of incorporation, preparing summaries of meeting minutes, and preparing documents related to the dissolution of business entities (the "winding up") and litigation. Therefore, paralegals in this field should enjoy writing, as well as researching, state corporation laws and relevant acts.

Eye on Ethics

For insight into the ethical issues that may arise in practicing as a paralegal in the corporate legal arena, visit this Web site and identify areas that might be relevant to your duties and responsibilities: www.bizfilings.com.

Summary

Many people may dream about quitting their jobs and starting up their own business. In doing so, there is a multitude of factors that must be considered in weighing which form of business organization is suitable for each situation. In considering these factors, one should keep in mind that each business form has distinct advantages and characteristics which make that form unique. The Uniform Partnership Act and the Revised Model Business Corporation Act provide guidance in relevant procedures and rules to be followed in each state. Similarly, the limited liability act of each state contains rules and guidance in formulating agreements and settling disputes.

Key Terms

Alter ego doctrine
Articles of incorporation
Articles of partnership
Board of directors
Business judgment rule
Business organization
Bylaws
Closely held corporation
Corporation
Dividends
Foreign corporation
Limited liability company
Limited partnership
Partnership
Piercing the corporate veil
Professional corporation
Promoter
Publicly held corporation
Shareholder
Sole proprietorship

Discussion Questions

1. Do you think that the only responsibility of corporate directors should be to run the company in the best interests of the shareholders? Should directors be held accountable for incompetence?
2. Discuss the advantages of forming a limited liability company over a partnership. Consider whether it matters if the business owners are family relatives.
3. Explain how shareholders can exercise control over the operation of a corporation. Be sure to consider both principal as well as minority shareholders.
4. Should states enact laws that require prospective corporate directors to pass an examination that proves their managerial expertise and skills before being able to sit on a board of directors? Explain.
5. Explain the concept of piercing the corporate veil, and the alter ego doctrine.

Exercises

1. Jerry, Ben, and Harvey jointly own land located at the corner of Brand and Hendon road. They decide to pool their own money together and open up a greenhouse where they will sell plants. They decide to buy their supplies to build their greenhouse at HomeBase Improvement Warehouse and split the costs of the materials. Then, they go out to the land and together build the greenhouse. They buy some plants wholesale and start selling them at a markup of 50 percent over cost. They lose money on their venture in the first three months of winter, but start making significant profits during the spring months. In May of that first year, Jerry decides to take the profits and run off to Tahiti. What is the likely result when Jerry returns home?
2. Rather than running off to Tahiti, as he does in Exercise 1, Jerry remains in town, but decides to sell some of the plants out of the greenhouse, on the side, to the nearby Convention Center to decorate the lobby. He sells about a thousand dollars worth of plants out of the greenhouse to the Convention Center, for a profit of 3,000 dollars. Jerry pockets the profits. What is the likely result if Ben and Harvey sue Jerry for a split of those profits?
3. Jerry, from Exercises 1 and 2, now decides that he is in love with one of the customers, Henrietta, who frequents the greenhouse on her way home from work. One day, Jerry hustles the woman into the back storage area of the greenhouse, ostensibly to show her some new ficus trees that have newly arrived, and then forcibly assaults her. What is likely to happen if Henrietta decides to sue?
4. Mary wants to open a dog grooming business, having worked as a groomer for three years at a large chain pet store. She has little money, since she was paid minimum wage, but she has the expertise. Her best friend, Sally, has inherited a large sum of money but is highly allergic to animals and has no interest in working with pets. What might be the preferred form of business organization for Mary and Sally if they decide to work together on this business?
5. Monica, Ruby and Rhonda decide to pool their money and buy a hot dog cart that they will set up on the sidewalk in New York City. They obtain all necessary permits and buy the cart, Monica contributing half the money and Ruby and Rhonda each contributing a fourth of the cash. Assuming they have formed a general partnership, how much will each partner receive if they realize a profit of $30,000 in their first year of operation?
6. June is a wealthy philanthropist who organizes a business solely for the purpose of finding jobs for young adults with learning disabilities. She is the only shareholder and sits on the board of directors with her accountant, Ward, and a young adult, Theodore, who does not understand much of what is discussed at board meetings. Two years after the business is formed, June discovers that Ward has been using company funds to donate money to various businesses in Palm Beach, which Ward asserts was done in order to woo potential benefactors for the business. June is concerned about the future financial stability of the business, which is now near bankruptcy due to Ward's actions. Can June and Theodore be personally liable for the debts of the business, and can June recover the donations that Robert wrongfully made to the various businesses?

Vocabulary Builders

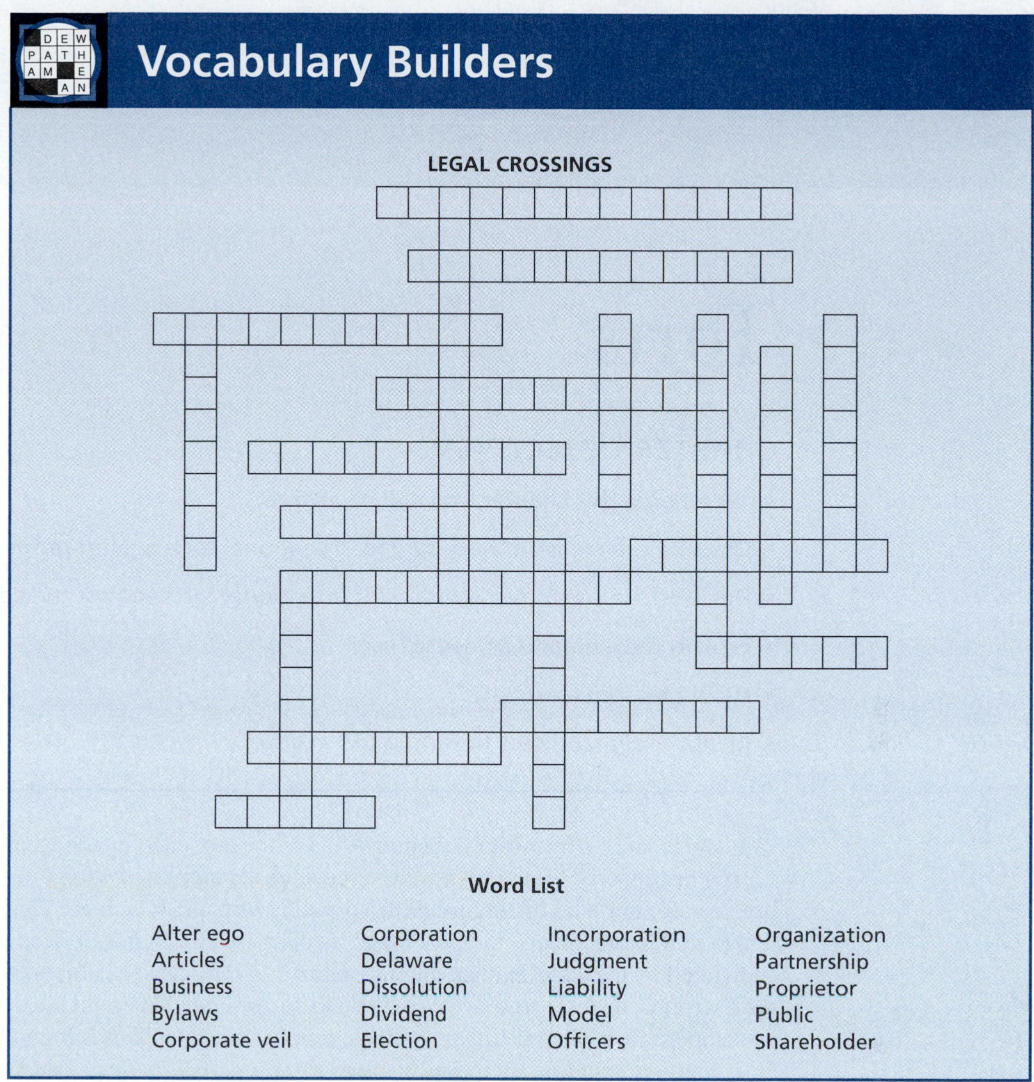

Word List

Alter ego	Corporation	Incorporation	Organization
Articles	Delaware	Judgment	Partnership
Business	Dissolution	Liability	Proprietor
Bylaws	Dividend	Model	Public
Corporate veil	Election	Officers	Shareholder

Chapter 10

Torts

CHAPTER OBJECTIVES

After reading this chapter, you will be able to:

- Describe the elements necessary for intentional torts against property.
- Describe the elements necessary for intentional torts against the person.
- Explain the elements of negligence.
- Define res ipsa loquitur.
- Identify valid defenses to various tort claims.

Tort law is one of the most fascinating areas of the law, encompassing civil wrongs against either person or property. The word *tort* has French roots, meaning "wrong." Such civil wrongs, which are private, must be distinguished from public wrongs, which are characterized by a criminal action that harms others. Public wrongs, as discussed in Chapter 7, lead to the prosecution of the individual by the state, leading to imprisonment if the accused is found guilty. On the other hand, civil wrongs, as discussed here, give rise to an action by one individual against another, leading to compensation or some other equitable relief if the defendant is found liable.

tort
A civil wrongful act, committed against a person or property, either intentional or negligent.

A **tort** is a wrongful act in which a person or property is harmed, due to a breach of a duty established by law, resulting in a legally redressable remedy such as monetary compensation or damages. In assessing whether a civil wrong has occurred, the court relies on common law principles, looking to establish whether the defendant's act or omission caused damage to the plaintiff through the fault of the defendant, and the damage is such that the law provides a remedy in the form of compensation. Society dictates the specific rules of conduct to which a person is expected to conform.

In this chapter, the student will learn about the primary classifications of torts: *intentional torts, negligence,* and *strict liability torts.* Selected intentional torts will be examined, including assault, battery, and false imprisonment and defamation. In addition, this chapter will cover the elements of negligence, as well as potential defenses. Strict liability will be discussed, and finally a review of remedies will be considered.

NATURE OF TORT LAW

Restatement of the Law of Torts, Second
An authoritative treatise that is a compilation of the key principles of tort law.

Tort law is based on common law principles, which have been summarized in a persuasive treatise entitled the ***Restatement of the Law of Torts, Second,*** published by the American Law Institute. This is an authoritative compilation of key principles of tort law. Although it is a secondary source of the law, it is useful to courts when examining case law in this substantive area, as court-created law is constantly adapting and changing, based on unique fact situations and evolving society customs. It is generally helpful when researching a case in a tort area of which you are unfamiliar to begin with the *Restatement* to familiarize yourself with the specific topic.

Tort law is designed to protect individuals' interests in several different areas: personal security, property, reputation, and economic loss. Personal security types of cases involve individuals' right to be free from trespass to their person. Such cases involve torts such as assault and battery as well as actions involving the suffering of emotional distress. Property cases involve protecting an individual's interest in land or chattels. Such cases involve torts like conversion and trespass. Reputation cases involve torts such as defamation and malicious prosecution. Finally, cases involving economic loss center on torts associated with competing businesses.

Tort law demands that the claimant prove that he has suffered some loss which is compensable. Fault must first be established, and then it must be determined whether the victim, or plaintiff, may be placed in the same position as if the tort had not happened. The purpose of remedies in tort actions is to compensate the injured party, but also to provide some measure of deterrence to others.

malice
Person's doing of any act in reckless disregard of another person.

In evaluating whether liability for a tort may be found, the court considers the mental state of the defendant. If a person acts with disregard for another, that person is said to have acted with **malice.** For example, in a nuisance tort, a defendant must be shown to have acted unreasonably under the circumstances. The tort of malicious prosecution requires that proof of actual malice be demonstrated. The second possible state of mind necessary in establishing liability in tort is intention. This must be shown where trespass is alleged, as in the tort of assault. It must also be proven in cases involving fraud, as in defamation, where a defendant knowingly makes statements that are untrue. Finally, the third possible state of mind is negligence. A person is said to have acted with negligence if no reasonable person would have acted similarly in the same situation; this is an objective standard, as the "reasonable man " is sometimes described as the man on the street."

prima facie case
A case with the required proof of elements in a tort cause of action.

One of the keys to understanding tort law is recognizing that each of the kinds of torts has a specific set of *elements* that must be established in order to make out a **prima facie case.** This simply means that each tort requires proof that certain elements existed in a given set of facts. In evaluating sample cases, it is necessary to find proof of each of the elements of that tort in turn. If one element is missing from the factual scenario, then that tort cannot be proven. If all elements of the tort are present, then the next step is to determine whether any possible defenses are applicable. Possible defenses include consent, self-defense, and privilege.

Acts that give rise to tort liability may also form the basis for criminal actions. The same set of facts, and the same conduct by a defendant, may support a civil action as well as prosecution under the criminal statutes. For example, recall the case involving O.J. Simpson, who was accused of murdering his ex-wife and her friend. In that situation, Mr. Simpson was found "not guilty" of criminal murder but was found liable in a subsequent wrongful death suit brought by the family of the victims. The same result occurred in a more recent case involving the actor Robert Blake. Like Simpson, he was acquitted of the alleged murder of his wife, but found civilly liable for her death. Because civil and criminal cases are completely separate, having different standards of proof and remedies, the result in a criminal case has no bearing on the conclusion of a civil case.

INTENTIONAL TORTS

Torts may be classified as intentional where it is shown that the defendant knowingly violated a duty owed to others and that the conduct harmed someone else. One set of facts may create a cause of action for multiple torts, so paralegals should take care to examine the prima facie elements of possible torts. This section will discuss the most common **intentional torts** related to the person, as well as those that intentionally cause harm to a person's property.

intentional torts
An intentional civil wrong that injures another person or property.

Trespass to Land

trespass to land
Intentional and unlawful entry onto or interference with the land of another person without consent.

Trespass to land is perhaps the most common property tort and is defined as the intentional and unlawful entry onto or interference with the land of another without consent. An invasion of your right to possess and enjoy real property is the basis of a trespass to land tort, whereas an invasion of your right to possess and control personal property is classified as trespass to chattels.

The required elements—the prima facie case—of a trespass to land are

- Entering or causing something to enter or to remain
- on the land of another
- without consent.

CASE IN POINT

Court of Appeals of Georgia.
RENAUD
v.
BLACK et al.
No. A01A2399.
Feb. 22, 2002.

JOHNSON, Presiding Judge.

This wrongful death lawsuit was brought after a young child drowned in a backyard swimming pool. Because there is no evidence that the pool owners acted improperly, we affirm the trial court's grant of summary judgment to them.

Angie and Chris Renaud lived with their two sons in a subdivision in Bartow County. On June 22, 1997, Angie Renaud was at home talking on the telephone when she saw her son Stephen, who was three years and ten months old, go out the kitchen door. She hung up the telephone and followed Stephen into the backyard. Ms. Renaud did not find her son there, so she and her husband searched the area. Unable to locate Stephen, the Renauds called the police, who came to search for the child.

Andrew and Cheryl Black and their children lived in the same subdivision as the Renauds. The families, however, lived on different streets and did not know each other. When rescue workers told families to search their own property for the missing child, the Blacks checked the aboveground swimming pool in their backyard, which was enclosed by a four-foot-high chain-link fence. Mr. Black found Stephen's body in the pool.

Angie Renaud sued Andrew and Cheryl Black for the wrongful death of Stephen. She claims that the pool constituted an attractive nuisance, that the Blacks were negligent per se in failing to fully comply with a county ordinance requiring the pool to be fenced in, and that the Blacks were negligent in failing to lock their backyard fence gates. The Blacks moved for summary judgment, and the trial court granted their motion on all three claims. Renaud appeals from the trial court's ruling.

[1] 1. Under the attractive nuisance doctrine, one who possesses land which has an artificial condition upon it is subject to liability when the condition causes physical harm to a trespassing child if: (1) the possessor knows or has reason to know that children are likely to trespass where the condition exists; (2) the possessor knows or has reason to know that the condition involves an unreasonable risk of death or serious harm to trespassing children; (3) children, because of their youth, do not discover the condition or realize its risk; (4) the utility of the condition to the possessor and the burden of eliminating the danger are slight in comparison to the risk to children; and (5) the possessor fails to exercise reasonable care to eliminate the danger or otherwise protect children.

. . .

[2] In the instant case, the trial court correctly found that there is no evidence of either the first or fifth elements required to support an attractive nuisance claim. As to the first element, the Blacks did not know and had no reason to know that children were likely to trespass into their enclosed backyard. The only children whom the Blacks had ever allowed to use the pool were their own daughters, along with their nieces and nephews. They had never allowed neighborhood children to use the pool. And there is no evidence that any neighborhood children had ever tried to gain access to the swimming pool or that the Blacks had ever known of any children coming into their yard without permission. In regard to Stephen Renaud, the Blacks did not know him and he had never been to their house or in their yard. Based on the evidence, the trial court did not err in concluding that the first prong of the attractive nuisance test was not met. [FN2]

FN2. See *Knutzen v. O'Leary,* 210 Ga.App. 590, 593(2), 437 S.E.2d 347 (1993) (first prong of attractive nuisance test not met where child had previously been on landowner's property, but had never been to the pool area where he drowned).

[3] The fifth prong also was not met. The backyard and the pool were enclosed by a four-foot-high fence, free of any defects. The Supreme Court has stated that erecting a fence or other enclosure around a pool is generally all that is required of a landowner in the exercise of reasonable care. [FN3] Here, we find that the Blacks exercised reasonable care to protect children from any danger by having a fence around their backyard pool. [FN4]

FN3. *Gregory,* supra at 155, 289 S.E.2d 232.

FN4. See *Knutzen,* supra at 594(4), 437 S.E.2d 347 (landowner exercised reasonable care where his property, which included a backyard pool, was fenced).

Because there is no evidence supporting two of the requisite elements for an attractive nuisance claim, the trial court did not err in granting summary judgment to the Blacks on that claim.

[4] 2. A county ordinance provided: "Any swimming pool shall be enclosed with a solid or chain link fence not less than four (4) feet in height. . . ." [FN5] Renaud argues that the fence surrounding the Blacks' pool did not comply with this ordinance because it had two gates that latched, but did not lock.

FN5. Bartow County Ordinance § 7.1.7.

[5] We must strictly construe the ordinance and cannot extend it beyond its plain and explicit terms. The plain terms of the ordinance impose no requirement that a fence have gates which lock, and we cannot extend those plain terms to include such a requirement. Instead, we are compelled to find that the Blacks complied with the ordinance because the chain-link fence surrounding their pool was four feet high. Because the Blacks were in compliance with the ordinance, the trial court correctly granted summary judgment to them on Renaud's negligence per se claim. . . . [6][7] 3. "The general rule is that a person who owns or controls property owes no duty to a trespasser upon it, except not to wilfully or recklessly injure him; and this rule applies alike to adults and to children of tender years." [FN8] There is no question that Stephen Renaud was not invited onto the Blacks' property, that they did not know he was there, and that he was a trespasser

on their property. [FN9] Likewise, there is no evidence that the Blacks injured him wilfully or recklessly. On the contrary, they acted with reasonable care by fencing in their backyard pool. Because the Blacks did not violate the duty they owed to the child trespasser, Renaud's claim of ordinary negligence must fail. [FN10]

FN8. (Citation omitted.) *Trammell v. Baird,* 262 Ga. 124, 125, 413 S.E.2d 445 (1992).

FN9. See *Gregory,* supra at 153, 289 S.E.2d 232 (no question that uninvited child was a trespasser).

FN10. See *Bowers v. Grizzle,* 214 Ga.App. 718, 720(4), 448 S.E.2d 759 (1994) (even assuming there was no gate on a fence surrounding an aboveground pool in which a child drowned, summary judgment appropriate because the property owner did not breach duty not to injure child wilfully or wantonly).

Judgment affirmed.

RUFFIN and ELLINGTON, JJ., concur.

Source: *Renaud v. Black,* 254 Ga.App. 31, 561 S.E.2d 183 (St. Paul, MN: Thomson West). Reprinted with permission from Westlaw.

When you possess real property, you have the exclusive right to possession and control of that property, free of unreasonable interference. No proof of actual damages is necessary because it is the mere invasion of your rights to enjoy your land that provides the remedy in the law. Thus, it can be said that this tort is actionable, per se. Trespass to land occurs if a neighbor continually sets up a tent on your property to sleep or if a neighbor lets his cow onto your land to graze. The purpose of this tort is to remove intruders and recover land, as well as to receive compensation for any harm caused by these unwanted intrusions. Thus, beside money damages, equitable relief for this tort may include an injunction, forcibly removing the defendant from your property, as well as a declaration that the property is rightfully yours. It makes no difference if the intrusion or trespass is temporary, fleeting, or occurs even once, keeping in mind the state of mind of the defendant must be established. If the defendant lacks the *intent,* then this cannot be the intentional tort of trespass to land, as, for example, where cattle accidentally break through a boundary fence and graze on your land once before being corralled.

Attractive Nuisance Doctrine

attractive nuisance doctrine
The doctrine that holds a landowner to a higher duty of care even when the children are trespassers, because the potentially harmful condition is so inviting to a child.

The **attractive nuisance doctrine** arises in the context of the duty that a landowner owes to trespassers on the land. Ordinarily, landowners must take reasonable steps to avoid physical harm to those who trespass on their land that has some artificial condition on it. The most common examples are swimming pools or trampolines in one's backyard. Courts have held that homeowners know, or have reason to know, that people may likely trespass onto their property because of the presence of the pool or other "attractive" enticement. Under the attractive nuisance doctrine, if the homeowner has reason to know that children, as opposed to adults, are likely to trespass, then the owner must exercise a reasonable degree of care to eliminate danger to children, by erecting fences or other barriers. This doctrine reflects public policy, which recognizes that a child may be incapable of appreciating all the possible dangers that may be encountered in trespassing. Adults, who can appreciate the risks or dangers involved, are presumed to have capacity to avoid such attractive enticements.

To establish a prima facie case of trespass to personal property, the following elements must be shown:

- Interference with the exclusive possession
- of another
- of personal property

This tort requires that it be shown there is some direct, immediate, and intentional interference with goods belonging to someone else. The contact with the goods must be direct and intentional. Trespass to chattels is a fairly easy tort as it simply protects one's personal property from another who is entitled to immediate possession of the goods.

Conversion, a similar tort, is more complex as it involves taking the personal property of another with the intent of permanently depriving the owner of that property. For example, if Mary takes her college roommate's watch, with the intent of keeping it for her own use, then she may be liable for conversion. Similarly, conversion may occur where someone has been temporarily given possession of a personal item, but then refuses to return it to the rightful owner upon demand. Generally, the remedy available to the injured party here is either money damages,

up to the value of the item, or else an injunction ordering the return of the item, especially if that item is unique. Damages for tangential loss of the goods may also be recovered, even if the goods are returned.

Intentional torts concerning trespass to the person include assault, battery, false imprisonment, and intentional infliction of emotional distress. These torts cause some form of harm to either the person's body or reputation. Furthermore, these torts are frequently the actions that give rise to overlapping criminal actions.

Assault and Battery

Assault and battery are two distinct torts that are often inadvertently linked together, perhaps because of their common association to the criminal offenses of the same name. An **assault** is a separate act, in which the plaintiff must establish the following elements:

assault
Intentional voluntary movement that creates fear or apprehension of an immediate unwanted touching.

- An intentional voluntary movement
- that creates reasonable apprehension or fear
- of an immediate unwanted offensive or harmful touching.

Assault requires that the plaintiff show that he was in fear of an imminent battery, based on impressions of the circumstances, regardless of what the defendant actually does. Examples of assault include any threatening behavior, such as telling another person that you will strike them with a book as soon as the class ends. Words generally should be accompanied by some threatening gesture, as in a raised hand or waving a weapon. The key fact in this tort is to remember that no actual touching need occur. It only requires some active, voluntary behavior on the defendant's part. Defenses to this tort may include consent, necessity, or self-defense. Necessity involves warning someone in a threatening manner so as to keep them away from certain harm, as in scaring someone off from entering a bank that is in the process of being robbed.

battery
An intentional and unwanted harmful or offensive contact with the person of another.

Battery is linked to assault because often it is incorrectly assumed that one tort cannot exist without the other. A prima facie case of battery requires proof of the following elements:

- An intentional and unwanted
- harmful or offensive physical contact with the person of another

It should be noted that battery does not require the touching to be harmful, as it is sufficient that it is unwanted. For example, kissing someone without their consent is technically a battery, even though the contact didn't actually hurt. Also, the contact need not be directly to the person, but may be to something that is physically attached to the person, such as a hat on the head or a backpack on the back. Defenses to this tort include consent, necessity, self-defense, and claiming the battery was a direct result of a lawful arrest. An example of the defense of necessity might be where John sees a car careening down the road and forcibly shoves Mary out of the path of the speeding car. Although John's action in pushing Mary is technically a battery, John has a valid defense in that his action was arguably necessary to save Mary from certain collision with the vehicle.

Assaults may occur without a battery, as where Dudley threatens to punch Mortimer but Mortimer sees the swinging arm coming and ducks just in time. No physical contact occurred, so there can be no battery, only assault. Battery can occur without an assault, as where Dudley sneaks up behind Mortimer and knocks him squarely across the back of his head. Since Mortimer never saw Dudley and Dudley never speaks any threatening words, there can be no assault, as Mortimer was not in fear or apprehension of the knock on the head—he didn't know about it until it actually occurred.

Actual touching of the person need not occur, so long as the defendant's action caused the harm. For example, if Dudley throws a rock at Mortimer's head and the rock strikes Mortimer, causing a concussion, that act is a battery because Dudley put the rock in motion causing the unwanted touching.

transferred intent doctrine
The doctrine that holds a person liable for the unintended result to another person not contemplated by the defendant's actions.

Assume that Dudley swings at the back of Mortimer's head, intending to strike him, but misses and hits Herman instead. According to the **transferred intent doctrine,** Dudley will be liable to Herman for battery, even though he did not intend to specifically harm Herman, because the law specifies that if a person voluntarily and intentionally commits a tortuous act at A, but instead harms B, the intent to act against A is transferred to B.

False Imprisonment

false imprisonment
Any deprivation of a person's freedom of movement without that person's consent and against his or her will, whether done by actual violence or threats.

Another kind of intentional tort is **false imprisonment.** This tort occurs when the defendant intentionally and directly imposes a complete restraint on the movements of the plaintiff. It is the willful detention by another without legal justification and without consent. Submission to the mere verbal direction of another person, unaccompanied by force or threats, is nonactionable.

The prima facie case of this tort requires that the following elements be shown:

- An intentional act
- that caused total restraint or confinement
- through force or the fear of force.

This tort is usually associated with wrongful restraint by a store security guard or by the police. This tort does not exist if the restraint or confinement is not *total.* Thus, if the defendant has some alternate and reasonable means of escape or movement, then this tort will not exist. For example, assume that Diane is shopping in downtown Chicago when she comes upon sidewalk construction directly in her path to the nearest shoe store. In order to access the shoe store a block from where she stands, Diane is obliged to cross the busy street and then cross back again a block later. Diane will not win in a suit against the sidewalk construction crew for false imprisonment, as she has the option to turn around and retrace her steps, or alternately to cross the street to reach her final destination.

It should be noted that liability for this tort may even exist despite the plaintiff being unaware of the confinement. For example, assume you are in your school library and fall asleep at your desk while reading this book. You awake the next morning and only then find out that you were locked in the building overnight. Some courts will conclude that the school committed the tort of false imprisonment, even if you were unaware that you had been confined without your consent. However, you must claim that some harm was sustained as a result of this confinement.

Valid defenses that may be raised for this tort include privilege, consent, or mistake. For example, statutes in most states allow a shopkeeper the limited privilege to protect property, and therefore a shopkeeper may legally detain a suspected shoplifter in a reasonable manner for a reasonable amount of time. This standard of what constitutes a reasonable length of time varies among jurisdictions, but it generally entails an appropriate amount of time to conduct an investigation into the shoplifting suspicion. The purpose is to investigate the ownership of the property. In addition, police making lawful arrests are legally permitted to confine suspects. Note that attorneys consulting with their clients, who happen to be incarcerated, cannot claim false imprisonment because the attorneys consent to being locked in a visiting room or holding cell while advising their clients in prison.

Defamation

defamation
An act of communication involving a false and unprivileged statement about another person, causing harm.

Defamation is simply making false statements about another person, causing that person to suffer some harm. The elements of a prima facie case of defamation are

- The making of a statement about another person
- where the unprivileged statement is published to a third person
- and harm to that person results.

A statement is "published" when it is made to a third party. Most states have statutes that define the specific elements and list available defenses. California laws will be referenced here

RESEARCH THIS!

Compare the following cases, distinguishing the facts and the conclusions reached in the same state:

Dillard Department Stores v. Silva, 106 S.W.3d 789 (TX 2003)
Sears v. Castillo, 693 S.W.2d 374 (TX 1985)

simply by way of example; general legal principles apply, and those will be addressed. According to California Code section 45, in part:

> *Libel is a false and unprivileged communication by writing, printing, picture, effigy or other fixed representation to the eye, which exposes any person to hatred, contempt, ridicule or obloquy, or which causes him to be shunned or avoided, or which has a tendency to injure him in his occupation. If the language is not libelous on its face, and requires some further explanation, then plaintiff must prove special damages, meaning some provable harm.*

Likewise, section 46 of the California Code states, in part:

> *Slander is a false and unprivileged publication, orally uttered, and also communicated by radio or any mechanical or other means which (1) charges any person with crime . . . (2) imputes in him the present existence of an infectious, contagious, or loathsome disease: (3) tends directly to injure him in respect to his office, profession, trade or business . . . (4) imputes to him impotence or want of chastity; or (5) which, by natural consequence, causes actual damage." Defenses include privilege, such as statements made in the discharge of official duty, as in a judge or police officer.*

Intentional Infliction of Emotional Distress

intentional infliction of emotional distress
Intentional act involving extreme and outrageous conduct resulting in severe mental anguish.

The final intentional tort to be discussed here is **intentional infliction of emotional distress.** This tort arose in lieu of claiming trespass to the person, as it involves emotional harm.

As the name of this tort suggests, these are the elements necessary to establish a prima facie case:

- An intentional act
- that is extreme and outrageous
- resulting in
- severe emotional distress.

Keep in mind that overly sensitive people who take grievance at even slightly officious remarks are not protected by this tort. Rather, this tort concerns some traumatic shock or distress that results from either being present at a scene or being at risk of injury to self or family. Some courts may include close friends as a category within this tort, where some immediate personal danger is foreseeable to any of these groups and is witnessed by the plaintiff.

A related tort is the *negligent* infliction of emotional distress. The basis for this cause of action is that as a result of the defendant's negligent conduct, the plaintiff suffered emotional anguish, though the defendant did not intend to cause such distress. Many states have limited recovery for negligent infliction of emotional distress to cases where one was a bystander to an accident or was in fear of personal physical harm. This tort typically does not extend to recovery for serious emotional distress caused by witnessing the negligent injury or destruction of one's property. Courts will generally not recognize companion animals as anything more than property.

CYBER TRIP

See the Web site www.llgeorgetown.edu/research/index.cfm. Try one of the legal research tutorials or consult the in-depth research guide to find tort law in your jurisdiction! This site hosted by Georgetown University's Law Library is useful in guiding you through a legal research question.

Consider, for example, that in today's society, people are becoming increasingly more emotionally attached to their pets. In cases involving the death of a pet, courts in most states have refused to allow recovery of damages for the emotional distress suffered as a result of some negligent act by the defendant. Since the majority of courts typically classify animals as "property," recovery has been restricted to the actual value of the pet. Courts have declined to grant noneconomic damages for the loss of companionship or the emotional distress sustained as a result of the negligence to the pet.

Rescue Doctrine

rescue doctrine
Doctrine in which a tortfeasor is liable for harm caused to a person who is injured while rescuing the original victim.

Questions might arise as to whether rescuers who have a pre-existing duty to treat people at trauma scenes may recover for their emotional distress if they discover a family member at the scene.For example, if a police officer responds to a request for assistance at an automobile accident and subsequently discovers his son is one of the injured drivers, may that officer recover for his emotional distress? Generally, most jurisdictions will require that the claimant be within the zone of impact in order to prevail here. This is not the same factual scenario as arises under the **rescue doctrine.** The *Restatement of Torts, Second,* recognizes a person's duty to aid another who is harmed by his or her conduct. The person is required to exercise reasonable care to prevent

CASE IN POINT

Court of Appeals of Ohio, Second District, Greene County.
OBERSCHLAKE et al., Appellants,
v.
VETERINARY ASSOCIATES ANIMAL HOSPITAL et al., Appellees.
No. 2002-CA-44.
Decided Feb. 28, 2003.

BROGAN, Judge.

{¶ 1} This is the story of "Poopi," a dog who tried to sue for emotional distress and failed. According to the complaint filed by her owners, Poopi was taken to Veterinary Associates Animal Hospital in March 2001 to have her teeth cleaned. Unfortunately, while Poopi was under anesthesia, the veterinarian also tried to spay her, even though she had previously been spayed as a puppy. Consequently, Poopi emerged from anesthesia not only with clean teeth but also with a three-inch closed incision on her abdomen.

{¶ 2} Subsequently, the owners, Sean and Melissa Oberschlake, filed an action on Poopi's behalf, alleging that veterinary malpractice caused Poopi physical pain and suffering, as well as emotional distress. The Oberschlakes asked for damages, including expenses for Poopi's further medical and "psychological" care. They also requested compensatory damages for their own emotional distress. As causes of action, the complaint alleged veterinary malpractice, negligent infliction of emotional distress, and loss of companionship.

{¶ 3} After receiving the complaint, the defendants (the Animal Hospital and Christian Hurst, DVM), filed a motion to dismiss and/or for partial judgment on the pleadings. In the motion, the defendants contended that dogs are personal property under Ohio law. Defendants also argued that claims for negligent infliction of emotional distress and for loss of companionship in connection with personal property would not be permitted. The trial court agreed and granted the motion to dismiss as to these claims.

{¶ 4} The veterinary malpractice claim was referred to an arbitration panel, which awarded the Oberschlakes compensatory damages of $104.28, the costs of the action, and arbitration fees of $250. Subsequently, the court entered judgment against defendants in that amount, and this appeal by the Oberschlakes followed. The Oberschlakes raise the following single assignment of error:

{¶ 5} "The trial court erred and abused its discretion by granting the defendant-appellees' motion to dismiss counts two and three of plaintiffs' complaint regarding the emotional distress and loss of companionship/consortium (noneconomic damages) suffered by 'Poopi's' pet guardians as a result of defendants' malpractice."

{¶ 6} After considering the applicable law, we find the assignment of error without merit. Consequently, the trial court judgment will be affirmed.

{¶ 7} Although plaintiffs classify their quest as one for "clarification," what they are essentially seeking is a change in the law. Plaintiffs concede that dogs are currently classified as personal property under Ohio law and that the law does not recognize noneconomic damages for personal property. Nonetheless, plaintiffs contend that we should "do the right thing" by distinguishing between inanimate property like chairs and tables, and animate property like dogs, cats, birds, and other animals who may serve as companions. Such a change in the law may one day occur, but this is not the proper case for plowing new ground. Furthermore, even if the situation were otherwise, we would have difficulty deviating from current law, since the Ohio legislature has explicitly dictated how dogs are to be classified. Specifically, R.C. 955.03 states:

{¶ 8} "Any dog which has been registered under sections 955.01 and 955.04 of the Revised Code and any dog not required to be registered under such sections shall be considered as personal property and have all the rights and privileges and be subject to like restraints as other livestock."

[1] {¶ 9} Typically, damages for loss of personal property are limited to the difference between the property's fair market value before and immediately after the loss. *Akro-Plastics v. Drake Industries* (1996), 115 Ohio App.3d 221, 226, 685 N.E.2d 246. Due to this standard, damages will seldom be awarded for the loss of a family pet, since pets have little or no market value. See *Ramey v. Collins* (June 5, 2000), Scioto App. No. 99CA2665, 2000 WL 776932, at * 3. In *McDonald v. Ohio State Univ. Veterinary Hosp.* (1994), 67 Ohio Misc.2d 40, 644 N.E.2d 750, the Court of Claims did award $5,000 in damages for a German Shepard pedigree dog who was paralyzed as the result of the admitted malpractice of the state veterinary hospital. The court recognized that market value is the normal standard, but believed that the standard of value to the owner could be used "in exceptional circumstances." Id. at 42, 644 N.E.2d 750. The court then applied that standard based on the dog's unique pedigree and time invested in specialized, rigorous training, which established that a similar dog was not available on the open market. Id. Notably, the court also stressed that sentimentality is not a proper element in determining damages caused to animals. Id. The amount ultimately awarded included damages for the animal's loss, plus potential earnings from stud fees.

[2] {¶ 10} Nothing about the allegations in the complaint suggests that Poopi is unique or that the circumstances of this case are exceptional in any way. While Poopi was a Miniature Poodle, the complaint does not allege that Poopi had a unique pedigree or was used for breeding. In fact, since the dog had been spayed, breeding would not even have been an issue. Consequently, we find nothing to distinguish this case from any other situation where a family pet is injured by the negligent action of a veterinarian. Damages were properly limited to costs connected to the improper surgery, and did not include emotional distress or the pain and suffering of either the animal or its caretakers.

{¶ 11} In attempting to convince us that the law should be changed, plaintiffs cite various articles recognizing a human-animal bond and urging expansion of tort law to allow recovery of noneconomic injuries. For example, one article comments:

{¶ 12} "If a companion animal is wrongfully killed, through veterinary malpractice or otherwise, her human companion suffers an injury that is of the same kind, if not necessarily of the same degree, that she would suffer from the wrongful killing of any other family member. If a human companion witnesses the wrongful killing of, or severe injury to, a companion animal, the injuries he suffers are also of the same kind.

{¶ 13} "The 'animals as property' syllogism arbitrarily, irrationally, unfairly, and formalistically limits recovery of noneconomic damages for the wrongful deaths of companion animals. It ignores the fact that the relationship between a human and his companion animal is no more based upon economics than is any other family relationship. It perversely permits the award of damages for an economic loss that a human companion does not suffer and refuses to compensate for the emotional distress and loss of society and companionship that he actually does suffer." Wise, Recovery of Common Law Damages for Emotional Distress, Loss of Society, and Loss of Companionship for the Wrongful Death of a Companion Animal (1998), 4 Animal Law 33, 93.

{¶ 14} In arguing that a distinction should be made between pets and inanimate objects, the Oberschlakes also rely on *Corso v. Crawford Dog & Cat Hosp., Inc.* (City Civ.Ct.1979), 97 Misc.2d 530, 415 N.Y.S.2d 182, which overruled prior precedent and held that a pet "occupies a special place somewhere in between a person and a piece of personal property." 97 Misc.2d at 531, 415 N.Y.S.2d 182. However, *Corso* has been described as an aberration "flying in the face of overwhelming authority to the contrary." *Gluckman v. Am. Airlines, Inc.* (S.D.N.Y.1994), 844 F.Supp. 151, 158 (declining to follow *Corso*). We likewise decline to follow the approach outlined in *Corso,* particularly since it contradicts the Ohio legislature's classification of dogs as personal property.

[3] {¶ 15} Whether or not one agrees with the view that pets are more than personal property, it is clear that Ohio does not recognize noneconomic damages for injury to companion animals. Moreover, even if noneconomic damages were allowed, Ohio limits recovery for negligent infliction of emotional distress to situations where a plaintiff-bystander observes an accident and suffers "emotional injury that is both severe and debilitating." *Paugh v. Hanks* (1983), 6 Ohio St.3d 72, 78, 6 OBR 114, 451 N.E.2d 759. See, also, *Binns v. Fredendall* (1987), 32 Ohio St.3d 244, 245, 513 N.E.2d 278. The Ohio Supreme Court has described this type of injury as "beyond trifling mental disturbance, mere upset or hurt feelings. * * * [S]erious emotional distress describes emotional injury which is both severe and debilitating. Thus, serious emotional distress may be found where a reasonable person, normally constituted, would be unable to cope adequately with the mental distress engendered by the circumstances of the case." (Citation omitted.) 6 Ohio St.3d at 78, 6 OBR 114, 451 N.E.2d 759.

{¶ 16} In the present case, the allegations in the complaint indicate that neither of the Oberschlakes was a bystander. In fact, the dog was left at the veterinary hospital and was picked up some time after the surgery was performed. As the Ohio Supreme Court has stressed on various occasions, "[t]he only logical definition of 'bystander' is 'one who is at the scene.' 'Bystander' does not include a person who was nowhere near the accident scene and had no sensory perception of the events surrounding the accident." *Burris v. Grange Mut. Cos.* (1989), 46 Ohio St.3d 84, 92-93, 545 N.E.2d 83, overruled on other grounds, *Savoie v. Grange Mut. Ins. Co.* (1993), 67 Ohio St.3d 500, 620 N.E.2d 809. See, also, *Heiner v. Moretuzzo* (1995), 73 Ohio St.3d 80, 85-86, 652 N.E.2d 664.

{¶ 17} As a further point, being "shocked" over improper surgery to a dog does not present the type of severe and debilitating emotional injury required for negligent infliction of emotional distress. Accordingly, even if Ohio law permitted the award of noneconomic damages, negligent infliction of emotional distress would not have been an appropriate cause of action.

[4] {¶ 18} We note that the Oberschlakes have also included a claim for Poopi's own emotional distress. Although Poopi was obviously directly involved in the incident, a dog cannot recover for emotional distress—or indeed for any other direct claims of which we are aware. We recognize that animals can and do suffer pain or distress, but the evidentiary problems with such issues are obvious. As a result, the claims on Poopi's behalf were also not viable.

{¶ 19} We do note that one Ohio court has impliedly indicated that dog owners may present claims for intentional infliction of emotional distress. In *Langford,* a pet owner sued a clinic and pet cemetery that had buried her dog in a mass grave. Summary judgment was granted against the pet owner because she failed to prove that the defendants' conduct was intentional or reckless, or that she had suffered mental anguish beyond her endurance. . . . The implication is that under appropriate circumstances, such a claim might be presented. However, the present case does not involve appropriate circumstances. Moreover, the mental anguish in such situations must be "'so serious and of a nature that no reasonable man could be expected to endure it.'" Even conceding the bond between many humans and their pets, the burden is one that would be very difficult to meet.

{¶ 20} As a final point, we have found no authority in Ohio that would allow recovery for loss of companionship of animals. Other jurisdictions also do not permit recovery in such cases. See, e.g., *Krasnecky v. Meffen* (2002), 56 Mass.App. 418, 777 N.E.2d 1286, 1289-1290 (refusing to allow recovery for loss of companionship of slain sheep, because Massachusetts wrongful-death statutes limit recovery to persons); *Lewis v. Di Donna* (2002), 294 A.D.2d 799, 801, 743 N.Y.S.2d 186 (loss of companionship of pet is not actionable in New York); and *Harabes v. Barkery, Inc.* (2001), 348 N.J.Super. 366, 791 A.2d 1142 (denying recovery for negligent infliction of emotional distress for death of pet dog, due to public-policy considerations).

{¶ 21} Among the public-policy considerations mentioned in *Harabes* were (1) problems with defining the limit of the class of persons who fit within the human companion category, i.e., whether recovery should be allowed for every family member, for the owner of record or primary caretaker; or for even a roommate; (2) problems defining the class of animals for whom recovery would be allowed; (3) the need to ensure fairness of financial burdens on defendants, due to difficulty in quantifying the emotional value of pets; and (4) the risk of opening the "floodgates" of litigation and increasing the burden on courts. 348 N.J.Super. at 371, 791 A.2d at 1145. We agree that these are legitimate public-policy concerns. In particular, the first three items pose significant barriers to a cause of action.

{¶ 22} In light of the preceding discussion, we find no error in the trial court's decision dismissing plaintiffs' claims for negligent infliction of emotional distress and loss of companionship. Accordingly, the single assignment of error is overruled and the judgment of the trial court is affirmed.

Judgment affirmed.

FAIN, P.J., and FREDERICK N. YOUNG, J., concur.,

Source: *Oberschlake v. Veterinary Associates Animal Hospital,* 151 Ohio App.3d 741, 785 N.E.2d 811 (St. Paul, MN: Thomson West). Reprinted with permission from Westlaw.

further harm. The tortfeasor is liable not only to the victim for the harmful conduct, but also to any person who is injured while attempting to rescue that victim. The rationale supporting this doctrine is essentially "danger invites rescue."

NEGLIGENCE

negligence
The failure to use reasonable care to avoid harm to another person or to do that which a reasonable person might do in similar circumstances.

The second category of torts is **negligence.** Generally, people have a duty to use reasonable care to avoid acts or omissions that might reasonably and foreseeably injure another person so closely affected that you should have anticipated the result. There is a wide body of law that covers this substantive area, and often cases turn on either the reasonableness of either the action or the expected result.

Like intentional torts, the tort of negligence has a specific set of elements:

- The defendant owed a duty to the plaintiff or someone similarly situated,
- the defendant breached that duty,
- and the defendant's act or omission proximately caused
- the plaintiff harm.

At common law, negligence was defined quite broadly, encompassing the preceding elements in some fashion, but as cases arose, the law gradually developed, thus refining the meaning of these elements via court-created law. Like intentional torts, each element of negligence must be proven, in turn. If the court does not find that the defendant owed a duty to the plaintiff, then there is no need to examine the existence of the other three elements.

duty
A legal obligation that is required to be performed.

Duty requires that people act reasonably, with due care, to avoid harm or injury to another. Here, case law in your jurisdiction is crucial to identifying who owes a duty and what that duty means. It is necessary to show that there is some relationship that justifies a finding of duty, though all people within society owe a duty to each other to act reasonably to avoid harm to others. For example, if Mary lives in a suburban neighborhood, she owes a duty to her fellow neighbors to not go duck hunting in her backyard, as this is not something an ordinarily prudent person would do who lives in close proximity to other people. Certain professionals have prescribed duties, such as firefighters and doctors. They owe others the duties of safety and assumption of public service and thus are required to act in specific situations.

breach of duty
The failure to maintain a reasonable degree of care toward another person to whom a duty is owed.

reasonable person standard
The standard of conduct of a person in the community in similar circumstances.

Breach of duty occurs whenever a defendant falls below the standard of care appropriate to a particular situation, according to the duty established in that jurisdiction and based on precedent. Here, the **reasonable person standard,** based on that fictitious person on the street, is used to evaluate if the conduct is something that a reasonable, prudent person would not do or would not fail to do, in similar circumstances. Various factors are used to determine the relevant standard of care, such as foreseeability, the magnitude of the risk involved in undertaking that conduct, the practicality involved in taking specific precautions, and whether something is a common practice in that jurisdiction. Thus, the court uses an objective standard to determine if the defendant did what a reasonable person would have done.

res ipsa loquitur
Doctrine in which it is assumed that a person's injuries were caused by the negligent act of another person as the harmful act ordinarily would not occur but for negligence.

Res ipsa loquitur is a doctrine that the plaintiff may raise where circumstances cannot be conclusively proven or where the burden of proving the elements of negligence proves to be too high. This doctrine essentially means that "the thing speaks for itself." In other words, the accident of this type usually does not occur but for some outside negligent act. It must be proven that at all relevant times the thing causing harm or damage to the plaintiff was in the express control of the defendant and that there is no alternate feasible explanation for what occurred other than negligence. For example, if Mary is standing outside of a building window and a beer

CASE IN POINT

Court of Appeal of Louisiana, Fifth Circuit.
Angel K. POPLAR
v.
DILLARD'S DEPARTMENT STORES, INC. and ABC Insurance Company.
No. 03-CA-1023.
Dec. 30, 2003.

Panel composed of Judges EDWARD A. DUFRESNE, JR., JAMES L. CANNELLA and WALTER J. ROTHSCHILD.

EDWARD A. DUFRESNE, JR., Chief Judge.

This is an appeal by Dillard Department Stores, Inc., defendant-appellant, from a $16,617.40 judgment in favor of Angel Poplar, plaintiff-appellee, who broke several teeth when she bit into a foreign object in a shrimp po-boy at defendant's restaurant. Because we find neither legal nor manifest factual error in the judgment we affirm.

The facts are straightforward. At the time of the incident in question here, plaintiff had an upper dental bridge which consisted of two center false front teeth attached to the natural teeth on either side. She was eating a shrimp po-boy at defendant's restaurant when she bit into a hard object which she later described as being about one inch long. She said that she felt her bridge come loose in her mouth and that she swallowed the object without reflecting on what was happening. She immediately informed the restaurant manager and went into the ladies room to see what had happened. She discovered then that the two side supporting teeth had broken off at the gum line and the entire bridge had thus come loose.

After a bench trial, plaintiff was awarded $4,711.00 for dental bills, $1,906.40 in lost wages, and $10,000.00 in general damages. No reasons for judgment appear in the record. Defendant now appeals.

[1] The only issue before this court on appeal is whether the trial judge properly found the defendant restaurant liable for plaintiff's injuries. The defendant relies on *Porteous v. St. Ann's Cafe & Deli,* 97-0837 (La.5/29/98), 713 So.2d 454, for the proposition that in restaurant harmful food cases the duty-risk analysis is the applicable law. It further urges that under this analysis the plaintiff in the present case failed to prove a specific act of negligence which would establish its liability to her. While we agree that *Porteous, supra,* is the law, we disagree that plaintiff failed to prove her case.

Factual determinations are reviewed on appeal under the manifest error standard. In the present case the trial judge found that plaintiff was credible in testifying that she bit into a foreign substance in the sandwich and that it broke her bridge. Because these findings are based on the trier of fact's assessment of the veracity of the witness, and in the absence of other evidence which would render the testimony implausible, we must affirm those findings. *Stobart v. State through DOTD,* 617 So.2d 880 (La.1993).

That being established, the next issues are whether the defendant had a duty to protect its patrons from such foreign substances, and if so, whether it breached that duty. In *Porteous, supra,* the court stated that:

> A food provider, in selecting, preparing, and cooking food, including the removal of injurious substances, has a duty to act as would a reasonably prudent man skilled in the culinary art in the selection and preparation of food. (at 457)

[2][3] Defendant's position here is that unless a plaintiff can show some specific act constituting a breach of the above duty on the part of the restaurant, she can not prevail. We hold otherwise. In our opinion the doctrine of res ipsa loquitur is applicable on the facts of this case. That doctrine is a rule of circumstantial evidence which permits the fact finder to infer negligence where 1) the circumstances surrounding the event are such they would not normally occur in the absence of negligence on someone's part, 2) the instrumentality was in the exclusive control of the defendant, and 3) the negligence falls within the duty of care owed the plaintiff. However, even where the doctrine is applicable, the inference of a breach of duty is only one aspect of the totality of the evidence in a case, and this inference may be overcome by contrary evidence. *Cangelosi v. Our Lady of the Lake Medical Ctr.,* 564 So.2d 654 (La.1989).

[4] All three elements are present here. There is no question that the presence of a foreign object in prepared food is a circumstance from which it can be inferred that someone was negligent in the preparation of that food. It is equally clear that the ingredients of the sandwich were in the control of the restaurant staff. Finally, the negligent act of serving food with a foreign object in it is within the ambit of the duty owed to customers. Thus an inference of negligence on defendant's part was supportable.

The final part of the analysis is whether there was other countervailing evidence sufficient to produce a result different from the inference. This of course is a factual determination subject to the manifest error rule. Here the trial judge tacitly concluded that the inference of breach of duty was not outweighed by other evidence, and therefore found the defendant liable. We find no manifest error in this finding and so must affirm it.

We finally note that in *Porteous, supra,* the defense showed that its kitchen procedures would filter out most foreign objects, but that the pearls in oysters could not be detected without undertaking extraordinary procedures. The court there stated that when objects are innate to the food itself the duty to eliminate such objects is less demanding. It held that the restaurant had not breached its duty in failing to detect the pearl. In the present case there was no showing by defendant that shrimp sometimes contain hard foreign objectsand therefore that it had a lesser duty to watch for such objects.

For the foregoing reasons, the judgment is hereby affirmed.

AFFIRMED.

Source: *Poplar v. Dillard's Department Stores,* 864 So.2d 789 (St. Paul, MN: Thomson West). Reprinted with permission from Westlaw.

You Be the Judge

Two students, Moe and Larry, purchase a course outline book published by Skunk Publishing Company, on the subject of business law, based on the representations on the book cover that this book outlines key business law topics and aids students in passing their class. Both Moe and Larry use the book to get through their college business law class, which has a complicated and difficult-to-understand textbook. The boys study from the Skunk outline book. Unbeknownst to both boys, the book contains a number of significant inaccuracies with respect to one particular topic. The errors in question did come to the attention of Skunk Publishing Company several months ago and were immediately noted and corrected on the company's Web site, which is advertised in the back of the course book. However, neither Moe nor Larry has ever looked at the Web site. Unfortunately, this erroneous topic is covered significantly on their final exams, and both students fail. As a result, they are obligated to retake the class the following semester. If Moe and Larry sue in tort for their losses, what is the likely result? Explain.

keg falls out of a fifth-story window striking her on the head, Mary may allege res ipsa loquitur. Her theory of negligence is based on the presumption that kegs do not normally roll out of building windows but for the negligence of someone.

proximate cause
The defendant's actions are the nearest cause of the plaintiff's injuries.

The third element of negligence, **proximate cause,** requires that the plaintiff show that the defendant's actions are closely related to the cause of the plaintiff's injuries. This element is sometimes referred to as the "but for" test, meaning that but for the negligence of the defendant, the plaintiff's injuries would not have occurred. It is possible that there are multiple causes for what occurred, so the court requires that the plaintiff establish that the defendant's action was a substantial cause of the harm. Proximate cause means that the court must find some continuing and natural casual connection between the actions of the defendant and the harm caused. Like the issue of breach of duty, the issue of foreseeability arises with this element.

Foreseeability is an essential element of both duty and causation in a negligence action. Under the law in most states, the test for establishing that an incident was foreseeable is whether the defendant reasonably should have anticipated an injury. An injury can be said to be proximately caused by the defendant's negligence if the injury was a natural and probable consequence. Note that the plaintiff need not prove the defendant foresaw the exact injury that occurred. Foreseeability simply means that the injury was of a general character that should have been reasonably anticipated.

Finally, as the last element of a prima facie case, the plaintiff must establish some *harm* or resulting injury. Since negligence actions are intended to compensate the party for harm done, it is ineffective to allege the first three elements and then conclude that no harm was done. Liability here depends on some economic loss sustained, be it medical bills or lost wages.

Premises Liability

One of the most common negligence suits involves "slip and fall" cases. In such cases, the outcome often rests on the ability of the plaintiff to prove that the defendant breached a duty to keep the premises safe for the plaintiff's intended use. This duty is based on a property owner's superior knowledge of hazards. If an owner did not cause the hazard, a plaintiff must demonstrate that the hazard must have existed for such time that the defendant, in the exercise of reasonable care, should have known of it. These types of suits are referred to as "premises liability" claims.

RESEARCH THIS!

Compare the following cases. Prepare a memorandum of law, distinguishing the facts and the court's conclusion in each case.

Puffinbarger v. Hy-Vee, Inc., 665 N.W.2d 442 (IA 2003)

Spates v. Wal-Mart Stores, Inc., 144 S.W.3d 657 (TX 2004)

Hampton v. Wal-Mart Stores, Inc., 2004 WL 2492283 (2004)

Kurtz v. Wal-Mart Stores, Inc., 338 F.Supp.2d 620(2004)

They require that the defendant owner had actual or constructive knowledge of some condition of the premises, that the condition posed an unreasonable risk of harm, that the defendant did not exercise reasonable care to reduce or eliminate the risk, and that the defendant's failure to use reasonable care proximately caused the plaintiff's injuries.

Premises liability suits do not always involve some hazard or condition of the premises itself, subjecting the property owner to liability. Suits may also arise as the result of the owner allowing overcrowded conditions in aisles or pathways, causing an unreasonable risk of injuries to patrons, resulting in people tripping over others and sustaining injury. For example, casinos have often been sued by patrons alleging that the congestion inside the casino caused them or others to trip [*see, Green v. Harrahs Casino,* 774 So.2d 1174 (2000)]. Or, in another case, a worshipper at a church, who testified that he was "trotting under the Spirit of the Lord," ran into another praying worshipper, who then sued for her injuries [see *Bass v. Aetna Insurance Company*, 370 So.2d 511 (1979)]. The suit alleged that the church and the pastor negligently failed to maintain safety for its parishioners by not stopping the services to clear the aisles of worshippers engaging in open religious expression (by running or moving "in the Spirit"). Similarly, premises liability suits may arise out of injuries or death resulting from criminal attacks occurring on the property, plaintiffs typically alleging that the defendant owner failed to properly maintain the safety of invited guests.

Defenses

Except in situations involving *gross negligence,* sometimes statutory immunity is granted so that the defendant is not liable in the absence of proof of a deliberate and wanton act or gross negligence. Typically, this immunity from liability may be granted to governmental authorities or other organizations as permitted by the states, sometimes in order to ensure that such organizations are able to obtain insurance or carry out their duties.

In a few jurisdictions, contributory negligence is raised as a defense to an action. Essentially, this entails the argument that each person was to some degree at fault, and therefore the defendant is not liable because the plaintiff to some measure, even if slight, contributed to his own injuries. This doctrine is commonly applied to automobile negligence cases, where it is often difficult to conclude that only one person was absolutely to blame for the accident.

Many states have adopted a comparative negligence method for determining relative negligence, and this may be considered a defense, as damages are assessed according to percentage of fault. Plaintiffs may recover even if their own negligence is deemed to be slight, but they are barred from any recovery if the court concludes that the plaintiff's own negligence amounted to gross negligence.

assumption of the risk
The doctrine that releases another person from liability for the person who chooses to assume a known risk of harm.

Another defense in a negligence action is **assumption of the risk.** The basis for this defense is that the plaintiff voluntarily and knowingly accepted some risk by exposing herself to an activity that she knows to be hazardous, a foreseeable danger. The assumption of the risk doctrine is based on the public policy that one who chooses to take risks will not then be heard later to complain that she was injured by the risks she chose to take. For example, if Mary voluntarily and knowingly gets into the car of John, an intoxicated person, and allows John to drive, should an accident occur, Mary may be considered to have assumed the risk. The basis for this argument is that the person knew the risk of injury, but acted anyway. Therefore, when Mary gets into John's car in the face of a known risk—a drunk driver—then the courts will generally agree that Mary has absolved John from a duty to protect her.

You Be the Judge

Dudley is driving home one night on a dark country road when he is passed on the left by Tom, who is driving at a high rate of speed. Dudley has to swerve violently in order to avoid being clipped by Tom's car as it passes in front of him on a hill, before it speeds off. Ten minutes later, while still upset and shaken over the near accident, Dudley arrives at a horrific scene. The car driven by Tom has crashed into a school bus, and there are bodies lying all over the road. While waiting for the paramedics to arrive, Dudley tries to comfort some of the survivors. Tom is pronounced dead at the scene. Too traumatized to return to work, Dudley takes a leave of absence. Hubert, his boss, tells him that the absence is affecting work. Unable to cope with the pressures, Dudley enters the hospital for clinical depression. What are possible tort actions Dudley might have?

CASE IN POINT

Superior Court of Pennsylvania.
Jason M. ZACHARDY, Appellant,
v.
GENEVA COLLEGE, Appellee.
Argued March 24, 1999.
Filed June 23, 1999.

Before DEL SOLE, JOYCE and BECK, JJ.

JOYCE, J.:

¶ 1 This is an appeal from the final order of the trial court which granted the motion for summary judgment filed by Appellee, Geneva College. For the reasons set forth below, we affirm. Before addressing the merits of this appeal, we will briefly recount the relevant facts.

¶ 2 On April 21, 1994, Appellant, Jason Zachardy, the starting center fielder for Point Park College, and his teammates were scheduled to play a baseball game against Appellee. The game was played on Appellee's baseball field. During the game, Appellant, while in pursuit of a fly ball, stepped in a divot/hole/imperfection in the grass-covered outfield. Appellant's right knee buckled and he sustained severe injury to his right knee.

¶ 3 As a result of the foregoing incident, Appellant filed a complaint alleging that Appellee had a duty to keep and maintain the ball-field in a reasonably safe condition. Appellant asserts Appellee was negligent in failing to maintain this condition. On April 29, 1998, Appellee filed a motion for summary judgment on the grounds that no duty of care was owed because Appellant had assumed the risks associated with playing baseball. Furthermore, Appellee believes these risks were obvious and apparent. Following argument, the trial court granted summary judgment in favor of Appellee. Appellant timely appealed.

[1][2] ¶ 4 Appellant presents the following issue for our review; (1) whether the trial court erred in granting summary judgment finding that Appellee owed no duty of care to Appellant.

. . .

¶ 6 Appellant makes note of the fact that there is substantial uncertainty with respect to the current status of assumption of the risk in Pennsylvania. The Pennsylvania Supreme Court has held that implied assumption of the risk has become part of the duty analysis for the trial court and not as part of the case to be determined by the jury. *Howell v. Clyde,* 533 Pa. 151, 161, 620 A.2d 1107, 1112-1113 (1993) (plurality opinion). Furthermore, the court observed:

> In assumption of the risk types 2 and 3 a plaintiff has voluntarily and intelligently undertaken an activity which he knows to be hazardous in ways which subsequently cause him injury. His choice to undertake this activity may or may not be regarded as negligent. His negligence or lack of negligence, however, is not the operative fact; rather, the operative fact is his voluntary choice to encounter the risk. The theoretical underpinning of these types of assumption of risk is that as a matter of public policy one who chooses to take risks will not then be heard later to complain that he was injured by the risks he chose to take and will not be permitted to seek money damages from those who might otherwise have been liable.

Id. at 161, 620 A.2d at 1112. The court then goes on to explain that: Under this approach the court may determine that no duty exists only if reasonable minds could not disagree that the plaintiff deliberately and with the awareness of specific risks inherent in the activity nonetheless engaged in the activity that produced his injury. Under those facts, the court would determine that the defendant, as a matter of law, owed plaintiff no duty of care.

Id. at 162-163, 620 A.2d at 1113.

[6][7] ¶ 7 The first component of assumption of the risk involves Appellant's knowledge or awareness of the risk or hazard. In the instant case, Appellant testified that prior to the game starting he observed frequent holes, ruts and depressions scattered throughout the outfield. N.T. Appellant Deposition, 8/18/97, at 21, 35. Appellant recalled that one of his teammates commented on the condition of the outfield by stating "someone's going to break an ankle out here today." *Id.* at 25. When questioned by Appellee's attorney, the following dialogue took place:

Q. -depression? Well, you had seen some of the ruts and depressions prior to the game even starting; correct?
A. Correct.
Q. At that time in your life, at that time were you aware that running around the field with ruts or depressions could cause you to trip, fall, lose your balance?
A. Was I aware that it could happen?
Q. Yes.
A. Sure. I was aware that that could possibly happen.
Q. Were you aware that you could get injured?
A. Yes.
Q. And you knew that before the game started?
A. Yes. You know, that—yes. Before any game starts, you are aware you could be injured.

Id. at 98-99. From the facts discussed above, we find no error in the trial court's determination that Appellant knowingly proceeded in the face of an obvious danger.

¶ 8 The second component is that the risk must be faced voluntarily. Citing *Rutter v. Northeastern Beaver County School District*, 496 Pa. 590, 437 A.2d 1198 (1981) (plurality opinion), Appellant questions the voluntariness of his decision to play. In *Rutter*, the plaintiff, a person with limited experience was injured during preseason football practice. Prior to practices beginning, plaintiff's coach had announced that it was unlikely that boys not participating in practice would make the team. The court concluded that given plaintiff's inexperience and the coach's comments, there was at least a question as to the voluntariness of the plaintiff's actions. We do not find the same circumstances in the present case.

[8] ¶ 9 Appellant was an experienced ball-player. He admitted he was aware he could be injured running around the outfield which had ruts and depressions. N.T. Appellant Deposition, 8/18/97, at 98-99. Appellant testified he would not pull himself out of a game because of an unsteady surface. *Id.* at 26. Additionally, Appellant stated he thought his coach "wouldn't have liked it too much" if he decided not to play because of some holes in the outfield. *Id.* at 27. However, Appellant never discussed the holes in the outfield with his coach. *Id.* at 28-29. Furthermore, Appellant never testified that his coach told him his starting position or scholarship was in jeopardy if he did not play that day. Indeed, Appellant never testified he felt his position or scholarship was in danger were he not to play. Therefore, sufficient justification exists to support the trial court's conclusion that Appellant voluntarily faced the risk presented.

[9][10] ¶ 10 Where an appellant voluntarily and with the awareness of specific risks inherent in the activity proceeds in the face of a known risk, he absolves the appellee from a duty to protect him from injuries thus sustained. *Howell v. Clyde*, 533 Pa. 151, 161, 620 A.2d 1107, 1113 (Pa.1993) (plurality opinion). From the facts discussed above, the trial court determined that Appellant voluntarily and knowingly proceeded in the face of an obvious and dangerous condition. We agree. Accordingly, we find Appellee owed no duty to Appellant.

¶ 11 Finally, Appellant admits that while holes on a baseball field may be a normal hazard associated with the game, holes in the outfield large enough to cause this type of injury are not a normal hazard of the game. We note there is no evidence regarding the size, location or appearance of the hole that may have caused this injury. Thus, we find this claim to be without merit. Finding no cause for relief, we affirm.

¶ 12 Order affirmed.

¶ 13 DEL SOLE, J. files Dissenting Opinion.

DEL SOLE, J., dissents:

¶ 1 Because I believe the Majority incorrectly concludes that the issue of voluntariness in the Assumption of the Risk defense has been established, I must dissent.

¶ 2 Initially, I note the Majority holds that because the Appellant did not testify that his baseball "coach told him his starting position or scholarship was in jeopardy if he did not play that day . . . [or that] he felt his position or scholarship was in danger," he has failed to establish the involuntariness of his actions. Majority Op. at 651. This analysis fails for two reasons.

¶ 3 First, since assumption of the risk is an affirmative defense, the appellee has the burden of establishing the appellant's voluntary act. Since the case reaches us following entry of summary judgment, only an admission of Appellant would be sufficient to provide the basis for such a ruling. Having reviewed the deposition of Appellant, there is no admission. The Majority has, I believe, engaged in an impermissive shifting of the burden of proof on the issue.

¶ 4 Second, I contend that *Rutter v. Northeastern Beaver County School District*, 496 Pa. 590, 437 A.2d 1198 (1981) is controlling and requires the issue be submitted to a fact finder. In the lead opinion, now Chief Justice Flaherty cited with approval, the Restatement (Second) of Torts § 496 E and its comments involving voluntariness, particularly comment "c" which prohibits a defendant, by its tortuous act, from forcing a person to give up the exercise of a right or privilege in order to avoid a risk.

¶ 5 As the court in *Rutter* held:

> There is at least a question for the jury as to whether appellant was compelled to accept the risk of playing "jungle football" in order to protect his right or privilege to play (varsity) football (§ 496 E, comment "c"). If he was so compelled, the acceptance of risk was not voluntary, and thus, he was not subject to the bar the rule.

Id. at 605, 437 A.2d at 1205.

¶ 6 Applying this analysis to the present case requires that the issue of voluntariness, at the least, must be submitted to a jury. Further, where the plaintiff believes, even if incorrectly, that he must participate, the defense would not apply.

¶ 7 For these reasons, I dissent and would reverse the entry of summary judgment.

Source: *Zachardy v. Geneva College,* 733 A.2d 648 (St. Paul, MN: Thomson West). Reprinted with permission from Westlaw.

STRICT LIABILITY

strict liability
The defendant is liable without the plaintiff having to prove fault.

The last classification of tort to be discussed in this chapter is **strict liability.** In this case, the courts hold that the defendant is liable "no matter what." Essentially, the plaintiff is able to recover for injuries sustained without having to prove fault. The courts have adopted this tort for policy reasons, as the presumption is that any person who voluntarily engages in ultrahazardous

RESEARCH THIS!

Read these two cases, both related to bears! Compare the court's reasoning in each case relative to the assumption of risk doctrine.

Rubenstein v. United States of America, 338 F.Supp. 654 (CA. 1972)

Maisonave v. The Newark Bears, Gourmet Services, 371 N.J. Super. 129, 852 A.2d 233 (2003)

Eye on Ethics

Read the following case: *Zimmerman v. Mahaska Bottling Company,* 270 Kan. 810, 19 P.3d 784 (2001). Identify the ethical issue raised in this case regarding paralegals, and summarize the court's reasoning.

activities or product should be responsible for any resulting injuries, regardless of actions taken by the defendant to prevent harm to others.

For example, if John owns a dynamite company that is responsible for imploding old casinos in Las Vegas, and someone is injured as a result of viewing such a demolition, the courts may hold John liable to that spectator in strict liability. Voluntarily choosing to use dynamite, an ultrahazardous activity, is sufficient cause for finding liability. Keeping wild animals in one's backyard, in a residential neighborhood, may subject the owner to claims in strict liability if someone is attacked by such an animal, since nondomesticated animals are presumed to have dangerous propensities of which the owner should be aware. In other words, you should not be surprised if the lion cub you keep in your backyard as a pet suddenly attacks your neighbor's child, because lions are a wild animal with known dangerous tendencies. It is irrelevant how high you build your fence and how secure you believe the lion's leash to be, as you will be held liable "no matter what."

Any person who engages in activity considered to be inherently dangerous is said to assume the risk of someone being injured, because such results are foreseeable. It is irrelevant that the defendant did everything possible to act safely and prudently. Often, this doctrine applies to manufacturers in product liability cases.

A Day in the Life of a Real Paralegal

Civil litigation is a fascinating and challenging practice area. Those attorneys who handle tort cases are typically personal injury lawyers. If you work as a paralegal in a litigation firm, you will be expected to stay current in this vast area of law, through reading and participation in events through your national and local paralegal associations. In addition, the Association of Trial Lawyers of America (ATLA) has a separate membership division specifically for paralegals. To join a Listserv for paralegal members of the ATLA, contact paralegal@www.atla.org.

Some of the work you will do involves contact with many different people at all levels. You may be asked to locate and interview witnesses. Witness coordination in preparation for trial is a key task performed by paralegals, and thus those people who are time-management gurus will enjoy this area of the law. You will likely interact also with the opposing counsel's office, expert witnesses, and medical personnel. In addition, you will be in constant contact with the client, who will often call you first to check on the status of the case. Successful paralegals in this field have excellent client-centered interviewing skills, enabling the client to relax but also recall key facts about the subject matter of the case. Paralegals may create time lines for clients so that they may anticipate the next step in the litigation process. Furthermore, you can provide written summaries or abstracts of information for the client to review at home to reinforce office discussions with the attorney.

Finally, paralegals in this practice area will devote a great amount of time to document management. Superior organization skills are essential. You will assist your supervising attorney in creating a trial notebook, organizing exhibits, witnesses, and key evidence. You will be responsible for helping develop a legal theory for the case and gathering relevant facts to support that theory at trial. Many litigation attorneys emphasize that paralegals are best utilized when they are able to understand the big picture. In other words, if you keep in mind the larger issue of the case, then individual assignments related to the case become more relevant when you know how that specific piece fits into the larger puzzle.

REMEDIES

compensatory damages
A payment to make up for a wrong committed and return the nonbreaching party to a position where the effect of the breach has been neutralized.

exemplary damages
Punitive damages, awarded as a punishment and a deterrent.

Once the plaintiff has established that the defendant is liable in tort, then the secondary issue is determining what the damages are as a result of the defendant's actions. Typically, the plaintiff will seek **compensatory damages.** Compensatory damages reimburse the plaintiff for out-of-pocket expenses such as medical bills and lost wages. The plaintiff might also seek to recover **exemplary damages,** also called punitive damages. These are damages awarded where the defendant's willful acts are characterized as malicious, violent, oppressive, fraudulent, wanton, or grossly reckless. Punitive damages might be awarded in the case of tobacco litigation claims or of automobile manufacturers and rollover accidents. These damages are awarded as both a punishment and as a deterrent to others. They are seldom awarded though, because the defendant's actions must amount to truly egregious conduct. Noneconomic remedies are also possible, such as injunctions or restitution.

Summary

While contracts are a substantive area of civil law, torts are a distinct, constantly evolving area of case law that ensures full court dockets. Tort reform measures are constantly being raised to contend with the rising number of cases based in tort. Remember, a tort is any private wrong, involving negligence, strict liability, or intentional wrongs against another. It is essential to keep in mind that prima facie cases exist for each of the torts, based on a requisite set of elements. By identifying each tort's required elements and establishing the facts that support a prima facie case, you will be able to predict the likelihood of success on any given fact scenario, taking into consideration the case law in your jurisdiction.

Key Terms

Assault
Assumption of the risk
Attractive nuisance doctrine
Battery
Breach of duty
Compensatory damages
Defamation
Duty
Exemplary damages
False imprisonment
Intentional infliction of emotional distress
Intentional torts
Malice
Negligence
Prima facie case
Proximate cause
Reasonable man standard
Rescue doctrine
Res ipsa loquitur
Restatement of the Law of Torts, Second
Strict liability
Tort
Transferred intent doctrine
Trespass to land

Discussion Questions

1. Consider a doctor who kills a patient, without actually intending or desiring that result in his patient. How does tort law serve to compensate the victim's family while recognizing the lack of criminal intent in the doctor?
2. Some states, such as Missouri, have enacted tort reform laws that cap the amount of punitive damages that a victim may recover. Discuss the pros and cons of this legislation. Does it matter if fewer cases are being filed because the cost of litigation now outweighs the potential for high recovery of damages once awarded?
3. "The law of torts exists to prevent people from hurting each other." Discuss.

Exercises

1. Marylou, who is six months pregnant, is on vacation at the Waterside Hotel with her two children, Mabel and Ethel. A swimming competition is arranged at the hotel pool by the resort entertainment director. Mabel, 8 years old, enters the race for the 8- to 10-year-olds. Halfway through this race, she suffers from a severe leg cramp. There was no life guard in attendance, and Mabel nearly drowns before being rescued by a spectator, another hotel guest. Mabel is rushed to the hospital and dies the next day. Ethel, who had been watching the race, now suffers serious anxiety and won't swim any more. Marylou, who watched the race from her hotel room, had a miscarriage shortly thereafter. Marylou's husband, Jim, was away at work and heard the news of the accident only the next day, as he was in a coal mine at that time without phone access. He was unable to get to the hospital before Mabel died. Jim is now seriously depressed and is unable to return to his job. Discuss the possible tort causes of action for Marylou, Jim, and Ethel.
2. Harry was driving his car quite fast down a country road when he swerved to avoid Mortimer, a young boy who was riding his bicycle in the middle of the road. Harry's car went out of control, crashed into a tree, and caught fire. Jeeves, a passing pedestrian, rushed to save Harry and sustained burns of his own when he dragged Harry from the car. Then, while Jeeves was at the hospital for burn treatment, an inexperienced nurse applied the wrong ointment to his wounds, causing him permanent disfigurement. He is now unable to work, due to his emotional anxiety about his appearance. Mortimer is traumatized by the events and now refuses to leave the house or ride his bicycle. His grandmother, who witnessed the near collision of her grandson with the car, is seriously depressed. Discuss the possible tort causes of action for each person.
3. Herman plays professional hockey for Chicago and has a reputation for being a dirty and vicious player. During a game, Eddie, a player on the Minnesota team, skated toward Herman at a high rate of speed. Eddie's hockey stick was raised in a threatening manner. Eddie did not want to hurt Herman but just wanted to intimidate him, to let him know how it felt to be threatened by a large player at a fast speed. As Eddie approached Herman, Herman swung his hockey stick into Eddie's face, causing serious injury. What torts are possible causes of action in this scenario?
4. Eric, an eight year old boy, was playing soccer in the street, when he ran out into the middle of the road to retrieve his ball, causing an oncoming truck driver to swerve to avoid him. The truck driver ended up crashing into a telephone pole, killing him instantly. The driver's spouse sues Eric's parents. What is the likely result?
5. Heidi and Jennifer, seven year old girls, are pretending to be pirates and are fencing with plastic rulers on the school playground during recess. One of the rulers snaps in half, and strikes Heidi in the eye, causing permanent blindness in that eye. Discuss the possible tort causes of action by Heidi's parents.
6. David is strolling on a sidewalk which adjoins a public golf course when he is struck on the head by a golf ball that came slicing across the course and over the fence. David suffers a serious concussion and is hospitalized for a week. It is unusual for golf balls to leave this particular course, and in fact only six incidents have occurred as a result of balls hit outside the course in 45 years. If David sues the golf course, what is the likely result?
7. Isabella, a pregnant woman, is working as a clerk in the post office when she sees a truck driving erratically in the parking lot. Shortly thereafter, the driver of the truck crashed through the front window of the post office. Isabella was not injured, but extremely frightened and upset, resulting in the premature birth of her baby. Discuss possible tort causes of action.

Vocabulary Builders

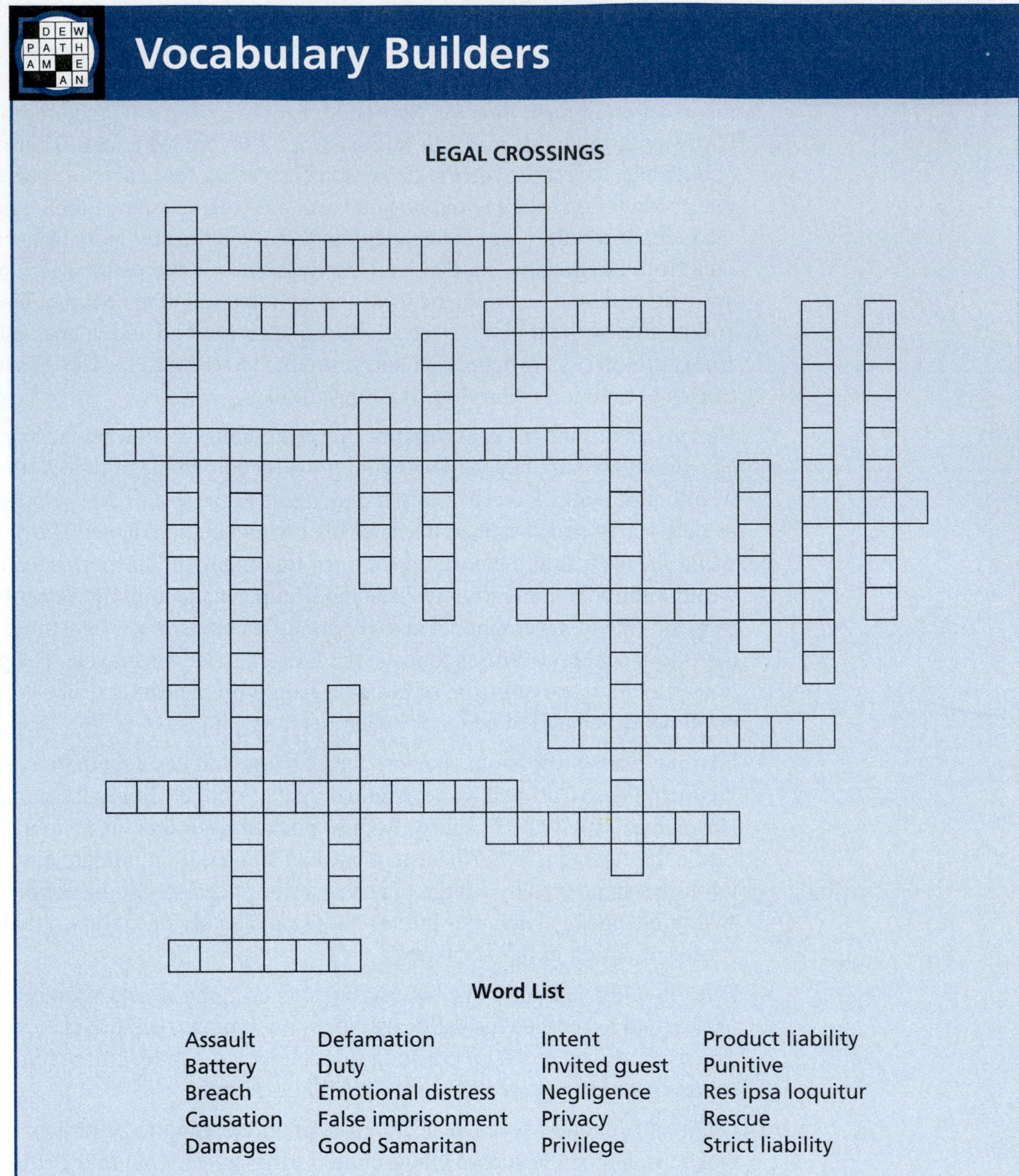

LEGAL CROSSINGS

Word List

Assault	Defamation	Intent	Product liability
Battery	Duty	Invited guest	Punitive
Breach	Emotional distress	Negligence	Res ipsa loquitur
Causation	False imprisonment	Privacy	Rescue
Damages	Good Samaritan	Privilege	Strict liability

Chapter 11

Property

CHAPTER OBJECTIVES

After reading this chapter, you will be able to:

- Distinguish between real and personal property.
- Describe the methods of transferring real property.
- Identify and distinguish the categories of personal property.
- Explain the methods of transferring personal property.
- Discuss the types of leases in landlord-tenant relationships.

According to Lord Mansfield (1728), "possession is nine-tenths of the law." In the widest possible interpretation of property, this legal concept may be defined as anything of monetary value that can be owned or exchanged by a person. It is indisputable that people like to have things, whether it is a house, a car, or this book. Owning property is one of our most basic rights and affects everyone. People enjoy owning, using, and exercising control over their possessions, and having these assets gives people financial security for their future. Indeed, it is the basis for our economic system and therefore it should be no surprise that property law encompasses an impressive range of topics, from acquiring land to transferring ownership interest in a magazine article to another person.

A first glance at this body of substantive law raises several questions regarding property law. First, how exactly should *property* be defined? Second, how does one have an exclusive right to this property; that is, how does one come to own a particular thing? Finally, how is this right to own something protected under the law? This chapter will address the answers to these questions.

Generally, it should be noted that there are two kinds of property: real and personal. Real property generally includes real estate, which consists of land and property that is permanently attached to the land. Personal property is all property other than land and structures attached to the land; it is said to be everything else. It is sometimes called chattel, or movable property, and may be either tangible or intangible goods. This chapter will examine the distinctions between these types of property and will discuss the transfer of both kinds of property.

WHAT IS PROPERTY?

Property is commonly regarded as something tangible—something we can touch or hold in our hands. We can touch the dirt in our garden and the grass growing in our front yard; we can hold this book in our hands. If we are quick, we can touch the butterfly that might land on our fence or pick up the baby bird that has fallen from its nest in the tree. Perhaps a deer might wander into our backyard. We may even think about locking the fence to prevent it from leaving. Even if these tangible objects have some monetary value, can they be possessed? Imagine you are walking through a national forest and spot the perfect Christmas tree, so you return to your truck to retrieve your chain saw. Now, one must ask, are all these things tangible objects—can they be possessed, and therefore can someone have a legitimate property interest in any of them?

If we apply the general definition of property, one might agree that all the aforementioned things have some monetary value. But is that enough? Can a person have a legally recognizable ownership interest and an exclusive right to all the tangible items just noted? The answer is no. Consider the person who owns 100 shares of stock in McDonald's corporation, or the person who has a right of access across his neighbor's property to reach a lake. Or consider the person who has a great idea, the design of a new and improved mousetrap? Can these examples, like that great idea for a better mousetrap, all be considered "property"? We can't hold the right of access in our hands, nor can we physically touch the idea. Yet, someone might have a legal property interest in them. However, one cannot ordinarily consider the butterfly or the deer to be property. It should be readily apparent that it is not so easy to define property.

Although property may in fact be visible or tangible, it can also be simply the exclusive right of interest in something. Property encompasses anything of value that can be exclusively possessed or physically controlled; it can be tangible objects or it can be a group of rights representing a valuable interest in how something is used. Therefore, in the preceding examples, though some of the tangible things have value, the second question is relevant: can one have an exclusive right of ownership in them? Wild animals, until captured, for example, are not in the exclusive possession and control of the person who first sees them, and therefore they are not property.

EXCLUSIVE RIGHTS

If someone has *control* of something, it is said that that person has possession. The law protects the rights of property owners to use, sell, control, or prevent someone else from controlling or using their rights. But the key point first is determining if someone can actually have control or ownership of certain things. In the preceding examples, everything on our land, such as the dirt and grass, is tangible and can be possessed. However, the butterfly, deer, or baby bird, though tangible, are not things that can be owned by us because these are deemed to be "wild" and thus are not considered to be in our exclusive domain, unless they are captured and we attempt to exercise ownership of them *before* someone else claims rights. The example of the tree in the forest is slightly different, as we cannot claim exclusive rights to a tangible object that is in the control of someone else, in this case the United States Parks Service.

intangible property
Personal property that has no physical presence but is represented by a certificate or some other instrument, such as stocks or trademarks.

However, as noted, **intangible property,** such as shares of stock or a great idea, are considered to be property because we have physical control and the exclusive right to them, though they are represented by something tangible, such as a stock certificate or a patent. This kind of property has value, though not in the actual piece of paper, rather in what that piece of paper represents, as in intellectual property. In this situation, the law creates the control giving us the right of ownership of that property interest, as in copyright law or contract law. With this right of ownership comes the right to sell, dispose of, use, or pass on ownership of the object to someone else.

PROTECTION OF OWNERSHIP RIGHTS

If someone has ownership of something, it is said that the owner has the exclusive right of control over the thing for an indeterminate length of time. Depending on the thing owned, it may not be exclusive rights forever. For example, the person with the great idea may seek protection of her ownership in that idea, through patent law, and be rewarded for her initiative, but that protection may be granted for just a limited number of years, in order to encourage fair use and access, but not a monopoly.

You Be the Judge

Homer owned a farm and kept beehives. During the summer months, the bees left the hives and swarmed into a tree on his neighbor's property. Homer followed the swarm onto his neighbor's land and asked for his consent to collect the bees and bring them back to the hives. The neighbor refused to allow Homer on his land, so Homer sues for the loss of the bees. What is the likely result?

Protection of property rights depends on the circumstances surrounding both the owner and the possessor. The original owner of something has exclusive rights to sell, use, or dispose of the thing at will. However, situations occur where the owner did not intend to relinquish property rights but possession of the item has been temporarily lost. In such a situation, the owner's rights to control the item may no longer be paramount as the person who, in good faith and for value, acquired that item and is now in possession. Consider for example the situation where you park your car in the parking lot adjacent to your school and at the end of the day your car is missing. Someone has temporarily taken possession of your car. You have not voluntarily relinquished property rights and control, but yet someone else has possession. In this case, the law protects the owner, and so if your car is found, you can take it back without seeking permission as you still have exclusive property rights. However, consider the situation where Mary steals this textbook from you on Friday, and on Saturday Mary sells your book to John for value, John having no idea that Mary doesn't own this book. You temporarily lost possession of the book when Mary stole it, but you did not voluntarily relinquish ownership. When she sold the book to unsuspecting John, John acquired exclusive ownership rights in that book, paramount to your rights, because he was a good-faith buyer of the book. In this case, he now has exclusive property rights in the book; your recourse is to seek the value of the book from Mary, as you did not voluntarily part with ownership. If the item was unique, it is possible to regain the item, but otherwise only the value of it may be recovered. Thus, possessors of an item may have rights and control of an item superior to that of the original owner. Having considered the way in which the law protects property rights, let us look at the two basic types of property.

REAL PROPERTY

real property
Land and all property permanently attached to it, such as buildings.

fixtures
Personal property that has become permanently attached or associated with the real property.

Real estate law relates to the manner in which real property is acquired, transferred, and used. **Real property** is simply land and any other property that is permanently attached to the land. This includes property that is naturally growing on or beneath the land, as well as human-made structures that are permanently built or affixed to the land. For example, real property includes the fruit trees in your front yard, your house, the detached garage, the in-ground swimming pool, and the shed in the back garden. Further, it also encompasses the **fixtures** that are permanently attached to these structures, such as lighting, security systems, the garden benches, and the barbecue pit that are all built into the concrete patio in your backyard.

FIXTURES

Fixtures are ordinarily personal property but for the fact that they are closely associated or attached with the real property. Most items are easily identifiable as being real property because they are permanently attached to the land, such as the oak tree in the backyard or the kitchen cabinets in the house. Other items are occasionally subject to debate. For example, is the swing set in your backyard real property? It depends. If the swing set is freestanding, then it is probably movable and thus not real property; however, if the legs of the swing set have been grounded in cement, then this would be deemed "permanently" attached to the land, as removal of the item might cause considerable damage to the land or structure to which it is attached. Similarly, objects such as heating systems cannot be easily detached from a building, and therefore would be regarded as a permanent fixture and thus real property. The classification of fixtures becomes important when one is selling real estate, because courts have determined that, unless otherwise provided in the sales contract, such fixtures are automatically included in the sale and therefore cannot be removed by the seller prior to conveying the property. For instance, buyers have the right to assume that the house they just bought includes the wall-to-wall carpeting and the chandeliers, but not the furniture. A property owner will not receive additional compensation for the value of the fixtures left behind, but personal property can be sold separately. Typically, the parties must expressly agree that the sale of the real estate includes personal property found on the property.

Items that may have been personal property become real property because they have been permanently attached to the land. For instance, a furnace is an item of personal property when it is stored in the back of the plumber's truck or in a warehouse. However, once the furnace is installed in a home, it becomes a fixture. Even if it still retains its individual identity as a furnace,

CASE IN POINT

Appeals Court of Massachusetts,
Middlesex.
Julie M. CHAPMAN & others
Ann S. Webster and Carolyn Patti Mijares.
v.
David L. KATZ & others.
The Camera Company, Inc., and Banknorth, N.A.
No. 04-P-1702.
Argued Dec. 14, 2005.
Decided March 29, 2006.

Present: GREENBERG, DOERFER, & KATZMANN, JJ.

KATZMANN, J.

In this commercial lease dispute, all parties appeal from the judgment. A Superior Court judge granted declaratory relief in favor of the plaintiffs (owners) terminating the lease, but at the same time required the plaintiffs to pay restitution to defendant Banknorth, N.A. (Banknorth), a subtenant, for improvements it made to the property. The judge also entered judgment in favor of the defendants on the remaining counts of breach of contract and violation of G.L. c. 93A, § 11. While the parties press a number of claims on appeal, we essentially focus on the central, dispositive question, which requires that we interpret the interplay of the concepts of "trade fixture" and "structure" under the lease in issue.

The owners, as lessors, contend that defendants David L. Katz and The Camera Company, Inc. (collectively tenants), as lessees, breached the lease when they permitted their subtenant, Banknorth, to erect an automated teller machine (ATM) kiosk on the premises without the owners' consent. [FN3] The terms of the lease are generally not in dispute. The tenants were not prohibited from repairing or improving the property under the lease. "[B]uildings, structures, additions, alterations and improvements" made by tenants or subtenants become the property of the owners at the termination of the lease, but "trade fixtures" installed by tenants or subtenants may be removed. Any damage caused by the removal must be repaired by the tenants. The lease permitted an initial structure to be erected on the property, but thereafter prohibited any "future buildings or structures . . . upon the demised premises during the entire term . . . or any subsequent renewal term unless approved in writing by the Lessor, which approval shall not be unreasonably withheld." [FN4] The lease also contained a clause permitting the owners to terminate the lease after providing the tenants with thirty days' written notice of a failure to perform an obligation under the lease, so long as the tenants failed to remedy the default within the thirty days (a so-called "default clause"). As a threshold matter, at the heart of the dispute between the parties regarding the lease is the question whether the ATM kiosk is a "structure," requiring the consent of the owners, or a "trade fixture," which does not require such approval. As constructed, the ATM kiosk is simply an ATM on a concrete pad, under a free-standing canopy, and in the drive-up lane in the parking lot.

FN3. The plaintiffs own the commercial property located on Route 9 in Natick that is the subject of the lease. Defendants Katz and The Camera Company, Inc., are the tenants of the property pursuant to a lease beginning on October 17, 1974, with a term of twenty years, and an option for the tenants to renew for up to four successive ten-year periods. Banknorth currently occupies the property as a subtenant.

FN4. The lease did not require approval for future improvements or alterations to the property.

The owners sued, claiming breach of contract and violation of G.L. c. 93A, § 11, and requesting a declaratory judgment that the lease had been terminated. The owners argued that the defendants materially breached the lease by failing to gain their consent before constructing the ATM kiosk. They also argued that the defendants violated c. 93A by falsely representing to the town of Natick that they were the agents of the owners. There was no evidence of any diminution in use or value of the property due to the construction. A Banknorth employee testified that, upon request, the ATM kiosk would be removed when the bank departed the premises.

The jury answered several special questions, finding that the tenants had materially breached the lease, that the owners had not unreasonably withheld consent, and that the tenants and Banknorth had wilfully or knowingly committed unfair or deceptive business practices. However, the jury that also found no damages resulted from either the breach of contract or the unfair or deceptive behavior. Because there were no damages, the judge entered judgment in favor of the defendants on those two claims (counts II and III, respectively). On the claim for declaratory judgment (count I), the judge ruled that the lease terminated due to the material breach, but also ordered restitution to Banknorth in compensation for the improvements already completed.

[1][2] *Discussion.* At trial and in posttrial motions, the defendants argued that the ATM kiosk is a trade fixture and therefore, under the terms of the lease, not a structure. This, they contended, meant that there was no breach, because the defendants were only required to get the consent of the owners before constructing structures, not trade fixtures. At trial, the judge declined to rule that the ATM kiosk was a trade fixture as matter of law, but allowed the defendants to argue the question to the jury. In her memorandum of law and order, the judge stated that "[t]he court rejected as a matter of law the defendants' claim that the kiosk was not a 'structure' but, rather, a 'trade fixture.'" This was error. Whether the ATM kiosk is a trade fixture or structure is "a mixed question of law and fact." *Leblanc v. Friedman,* 438 Mass. 592, 596, 781 N.E.2d 1283 (2003). Since there was no factual dispute over the nature of the ATM kiosk, the issue resolves itself into a question of contract law for the judge—whether the ATM kiosk is within the definition of trade fixture as used in the lease, and therefore not a structure. Considering that question now, we conclude that the ATM kiosk is a trade fixture. . . .

[3][4] We begin our analysis with the language of the contract. We interpret the language of the contract "as a whole, in a reasonable and practical way, consistent with [the contract's] . . . background[ ] and purpose.". . . Where not inconsistent with the terms of the contract, we give words their ordinary meaning. . . .

The words "trade fixture" are only used once in the lease in section nine, describing what property will stay with the real estate at the termination of the lease and what will remain the property of the tenants. [FN5] Although this section does not explicitly define trade fixture, it does establish a distinction between trade fixtures and structures under the lease. This distinction is crucial because if structure means "not a trade fixture," and if the ATM kiosk is a trade fixture, then the lease did not require the tenants to seek permission from the owners under the section that prevented construction of "future buildings or structures." See *Clark v. State St. Trust Co.,* 270 Mass. 140, 151, 169 N.E. 897 (1930) (in interpreting a contract, "words used in one undoubted sense in one place may be presumed to be used in the same meaning in another place in the writing").

FN5. "All buildings, *structures,* additions, alterations and improvements made by Lessee upon the demised premises shall become and remain the property of Lessor and shall not be removed at the termination of this lease, but shall be delivered up at the end of the term in good repair and condition, reasonable use and wear, and damage by fire or other inevitable accidents only excepted, and free from any and all encumbrances. All *trade fixtures* installed by Lessee or his assigns or subtenants and used in connection with the business conducted by him or them on said demised premises shall remain their property, as the case may be, and may be removed by Lessee from time to time and at the termination of this lease. Any damage, however, caused by such removal shall be repaired by Lessee." (Emphasis added.)

Since the lease provides no further definition of trade fixture, we must apply the ordinary meaning of the phrase to determine if the ATM kiosk is a trade fixture. See, e.g., *Given v. Commerce Ins. Co.,* 440 Mass. 207, 212-213, 796 N.E.2d 1275 (2003) (use of dictionary to determine ordinary meaning of term in insurance policy). The definitions found in several legal and real estate dictionaries are consistent in theme. See, e.g., Black's Law Dictionary 669 (8th ed. 2004) (defining trade fixture as "[r]emovable personal property that a tenant attaches to leased land for business purposes, such as a display counter"); Brownstone & Franck, The VNR Real Estate Dictionary 317 (1981) ("A fixture belonging to a lessee of commercial property, used in the normal course of conducting lessee's business, and considered personal property even though attached to the leased premises)." [FN6] See also Restatement (Second) of Property (Landlord & Tenant) § 12.2, at 432, 448–449 (1977). More significantly, these definitions are consistent with Massachusetts precedent. See, e.g., *Consiglio v. Carey,* 12 Mass.App.Ct. 135, 139, 421 N.E.2d 1257 (1981), quoting from *Hanrahan v. O'Reilly,* 102 Mass. 201, 203 (1869) (twelve-foot high, exterior walk-in freezer, installed on concrete slab and enclosed in plywood shell at rear of restaurant was found to be a trade fixture because it was installed by tenant for his business and could be removed without material injury to the premises and "without losing its essential character or value as a personal chattel"). In *Consiglio v. Carey,* pointing to the vintage of pertinent authorities, the court commented "[t]hat the cited cases are not notably recent is not an indication of their obsolescence but merely shows that settled law breeds little litigation." *Consiglio v. Carey, supra* at 139, 421 N.E.2d 1257. That observation has only been reinforced by the paucity of reported decisions in the years since *Consiglio.*

FN6. See also Friedman, Harris, & Lindeman, Barron's Dictionary of Real Estate Terms 458 (6th ed.2004) ("articles placed in rented buildings by the tenant to help carry out trade or business"); Cox, Cox, & Silver-Westrick, Prentice Hall Dictionary of Real Estate 272 (pocket ed.2001) ("personal property consisting of equipment, furniture, and other systems that are specific to a trade or business that have been placed in or on the premises for a specific purpose associated with the use of the property").

Applying the standard definitions, we conclude that the ATM kiosk is a trade fixture under the terms of the lease. [FN7] As we have noted, the ATM kiosk is simply an ATM on a concrete pad, under a free-standing canopy, and in a drive-up lane in the parking lot. The equipment was installed by Banknorth, is the property of Banknorth, is specific to Banknorth's business, can be removed with little damage to the parking lot, and when removed does not lose its nature as personal chattel. Given these circumstances, the ATM kiosk is within the ordinary meaning of trade fixture. Because the ATM kiosk is a trade fixture under the lease, it cannot also be a structure under the lease, and therefore the tenants were not required to seek the owners' permission before its construction. [FN8] There was no breach of contract, and the lease should not have been terminated. [FN9]

FN7. In *Consiglio v. Carey, supra* at 137, 421 N.E.2d 1257, there was a factual question that needed to be resolved in order to determine whether the item was a fixture or part of the real estate. See *Southern Mass. Broadcasters, Inc. v. Duchaine,* 26 Mass.App.Ct. 497, 499, 529 N.E.2d 887 (1988) (jury resolved factual dispute regarding trade fixture indicia). Here, however, where there is no dispute regarding the attributes of the ATM kiosk, the issue is the legal interpretation under the contract of the concept of trade fixture.

FN8. The owners maintain that it is the definition of the word structure, rather than the term trade fixture, that is important. They contend that the ATM kiosk is a structure under a variety of definitions, including Natick zoning laws, and therefore permission was required. This argument misses the point that, although a broad definition of structure might include many items also considered trade fixtures, the lease specifically distinguishes between the two, meaning that a trade fixture cannot also be a structure under this lease.

FN9. On the breach of contract claim, the judge entered judgment for the defendants essentially based on the jury finding that the owners suffered no damages from the breach of contract. Although we affirm the judgment for the defendants on this claim, we do so for a different reason, that being there was no breach of contract. See *Schwartz v. Travelers Indemnity Co.,* 50 Mass.App.Ct. 672, 673, 740 N.E.2d 1039 (2001) (appellate court may affirm for different reasons).

. . .

Insofar as the judgment terminates the lease and requires the plaintiffs to reimburse the defendant Banknorth, N.A., for the cost of improvements, it is vacated, and a new judgment shall enter as to count I declaring that there was no breach of the lease and therefore the lease remains in full force and effect.

So ordered.

Source: *Chapman v. Katz,* 65 Mass.App.Ct. 826, 844 N.E.2d 270 (St. Paul, MN: Thomson West). Reprinted with permission from Westlaw.

it has now become an integral part of the house. Note that a furnace that is simply stored in the basement, propped up against a wall in the corner, is not attached to the real property and thus is not a fixture; it must be attached in some permanent manner and be used in the way in which it was intended to be used.

Compare this to a piece of wood. The lumber has its own identity when it is stacked in a lumberyard. Yet, once that piece of wood is used to build a house, that exact piece of lumber no longer retains its individual identity; it is indistinguishable from the house and thus is not a fixture. It is simply a part of the house.

trade fixtures
Pieces of equipment on or attached to the property being used in a trade or business.

Fixtures are also important in the context of leasing property. **Trade fixtures** are ordinarily defined as articles annexed to the real property by a tenant for the purpose of carrying on a trade or business. Even if a fixture is large and attached to the premises, it is still considered a trade fixture if the tenant installed the article for the purpose of conducting business. Tenants must remove the fixtures before vacating the premises at the end of the lease, or it is understood that they are giving those fixtures to the landlord. Tenants are required to compensate the property owner for the damage caused by removing any fixtures or else must repair such damage. Examples of trade fixtures include clothes racks or display counters.

REAL PROPERTY RIGHTS

If one owns the land and everything permanently attached to the land, then when you buy a piece of property, you buy the exclusive rights of possession and control over that land, everything above the land, and everything below the land, within reason. Clearly, real estate includes not only the dirt and the grass, but the trees, crops, and that which is below the land, such as oil or minerals. So, if you should be lucky enough to buy vacant land and discover gold, or other valuable natural minerals in the soil, you have exclusive rights to that real property. You also own everything in the airspace above the land you purchase. But, does this mean that you can seek compensation for Wholesome Jet Airlines flying above your home and using your airspace without permission? No, because your right to that airspace above your land is limited to a reasonable distance above the property and not to the height at which airplanes typically fly. However, you can certainly object if the branches of your neighbor's fruit tree are growing over the fence and hanging over your property, in your airspace.

estate in land
An ownership interest in real property.

freehold estate
An estate interest that includes both ownership and possessory interests.

fee simple absolute
A property interest in which the owner has full and exclusive use and enjoyment of the entire property.

fee simple defeasible
An interest in land in which the owner has all the benefits of a fee simple estate, except that property is taken away if a certain event or condition occurs.

If one owns land, the ownership interest in that land is referred to as an **estate in land.** With ownership of the land comes a bundle of legal rights, giving the owner the right to exclusive and unfettered use and enjoyment of the property. Included is the right to transfer this interest in land by deed, will, lease, or any other legal means of transferring ownership rights.

There are several different types of interest in land that an owner may have. Property that is both owned and includes the right of possession is deemed to be a **freehold estate.** The most common, and preferable, ownership interest is called **a fee simple absolute.** This type of ownership gives the person full and exclusive use of the entire property. Words conveying this fee simple state are "to A and his heirs." A derivative of this type of estate in land is a **fee simple defeasible,** in which the owner has all the benefits of a fee simple estate, except that ownership rights may be taken away if a particular condition occurs or fails to occur. If, for example, a wealthy alumnus, Mortimer, conveys land to your school to build another academic building so long as the land is operated as an educational facility, then this fee simple defeasible interest grants your school full use and enjoyment of the land. However, if in five years, your school decides it would be more profitable to operate the facility as a brothel rather than a school, then the school's ownership rights in the land is terminated and the property will revert back to Mortimer or some other person designated in the deed transfer.

You Be the Judge

Rosita owns a large, 20-acre country estate. An aerial photography company flew over Rosita's land and took photographs to be offered for sale to Rosita and others. Rosita objects and demands possession of the photos, alleging trespass to her land. What is the likely result?

life estate
An ownership interest in property for a designated period of time, based on the life of another person.

future interest
Right to property that can be enforced in the future.

reversion
Right to receive back property in the event of the happening of a certain condition.

remainder
Right to receive property interest at some point in the future.

A **life estate** is an ownership interest in real property for a specified period of time. For example, Dudley can transfer his farm to Mary, "for the life of Dudley" and then "to Dudley's son, Mortimer." In this case, Mary owns a life estate in the farm, which transfers to Mortimer upon the death of Dudley. Dudley can also transfer his farm to Mary, "for the life of Endora," and then the farm reverts back to Dudley once Endora dies. These are all deemed to be present interests in land.

It is possible to have a **future interest** or ownership of property, as in a **reversion** or a **remainder.** Referring back to the preceding example, if Dudley transfers his farm to Mary "for the life of Dudley," then it is Dudley's son, Mortimer, who holds a future interest, or in this case a remainder. Mortimer is only entitled to possession of the farm upon the death of Dudley, at which time the farm transfers from Mary to him. A remainder is the right to receive title to property at some future date. It can be either vested or contingent. A vested remainder is the unconditional right to receive the property at some future point. A contingent remainder is where a person is entitled to property if one or more prior conditions are satisfied. For example, if Harry transfers his lakefront cottage to Sam, and then to Mary only if Sam's wife, Sally, predeceases Sam, then Mary is a contingent remainderman. A reversion is where the land returns to the grantor, as where Mortimer specifies that the donation of land is limited to the school so long as it operates as an educational facility. Once the school converts the land into a brothel, the land reverts to Mortimer—the reversion.

TRANSFER OF REAL PROPERTY

Like personal property, real property may be transferred to someone else by sale, gift, donation, inheritance, or unique to land, adverse possession. The sale of real estate is probably the most common way to transfer ownership rights. Typically, the seller lists the property for sale until a buyer is found that is willing to pay a mutually agreed on price for ownership of the property. A real estate broker is commonly engaged to assist in bringing a buyer and seller together. A separate contract is typically signed between the seller and the broker, specifying the length of time that the listing agreement shall remain in effect, as well as the amount of commission that the seller will pay to the broker once the house is sold. Once a contract is signed for the sale of the property, certain steps are taken to ensure that the transfer of title is clear.

survey
A description of the boundaries of a piece of property.

title search
A search of the abstract of title, the short history of a piece of property including ownership interests and liens.

First, a **survey** of the property is conducted, which establishes or confirms the boundaries of the property as well as the accuracy of the recorded legal description. **Title searches** are conducted in order for the buyer to ensure that he is receiving free and unencumbered clear title to the property. Title searches trace the chain of title, or ownership of interest being conveyed, backward from the seller (the current owner) to previous owners, typically traced 50 or more years. A buyer who fails to conduct a title search might discover that she has paid the seller money for land that is subject to unpaid taxes, liens by building contractors for unpaid repair work, and other debts such as mortgages. A seller can only convey that interest in the property that he presently holds, and thus this interest is traced by a title search.

Title searches will reveal a history of all transactions that have occurred affecting that piece of property, so long as the prior owners properly recorded their interests with the local officials, typically the county clerk's office (or the recorder's office). Real estate transactions are documents that are recorded, or filed, including deeds, mortgages, easements, long-term leases, and liens against the property from unpaid judgments. State and local statutes will determine the form of recording, as well as whom must record, and thus you should take care to consult the relevant statutes when real estate transactions are involved.

marketable title
The title transfers full ownership rights to the buyer.

title insurance policy
The insurance provided by a title company; it protects the lender and buyer in case it is discovered that the title is imperfect.

If title to the property is **marketable,** this means that the title search has guaranteed the buyer the full rights of ownership to the property, free of encumbrances or defects in the chain of title to or ownership of that land. The title search will ascertain the owners of the property and in what form the owners have an interest. **Title insurance policies** are purchased by the buyer, normally required by the buyer's lender, to ensure that indeed the buyer is taking marketable title. Title examination is a vital step in the transfer of real property because you want to be sure that the seller has the right to sell the property and to determine whether any claims against the property, such as liens, exist. Title insurance policies protect the buyer and lender in case there is some defect in the title that is undisclosed by the examination.

FORMS OF OWNERSHIP

joint tenancy
The shared ownership of property, giving the other owner the right of survivorship if one owner dies.

right of survivorship
The right of a surviving joint tenant to take ownership of a deceased joint tenant's share of the property.

tenancy in common
A form of ownership between two or more people where each owner's interest upon death goes to his or her heirs.

tenancy by the entirety
A form of ownership for married couples, similar to joint tenancy, where the spouse has right of survivorship.

There are several different forms in which real property may be owned by two or more persons. One of the most common forms of concurrent ownership of land is **joint tenancy.** In this form, the co-owners enjoy the **right of survivorship.** Thus, if one of the joint tenants dies, that person's interest automatically transfers to the surviving joint tenant(s). Typically, determining whether a joint tenancy has been established requires language indicating intent to create this form of property ownership. Common words used are "John Smith and Mary Smith, as joint tenants, with right or survivorship." A joint tenant is free to transfer his interest in the property, but once this is done, the joint tenancy is severed, and the new owner becomes a "tenant in common" with the remaining joint tenant(s).

The second form of concurrent ownership is **tenancy in common.** Here, the interest held by a tenant does not pass to the remaining tenants upon one's death, but rather that interest passes to the deceased tenant's estate. In some states, this form of ownership is presumed unless the parties have specified otherwise in writing. Common words used to establish this form are "John Smith and Mary Smith, as tenants in common, and not joint tenants." The significant distinction is that there is no right of survivorship; the deceased tenant's interest does not transfer to the surviving tenants. Like joint tenants, a tenant in common may transfer her interest in the property to someone else, but the tenancy in common is not severed.

Finally, a third form of concurrent ownership is **tenancy by the entirety.** This form is distinguished in that it only pertains to married couples, as co-owners. Words used to create this tenancy are "John Smith and Mary Smith, husband and wife, as tenants by the entirety." Similar to joint tenancy, the surviving spouse has rights of survivorship, and neither party can transfer his or her interest in the property without consent. This form of co-ownership is not recognized in all states, so you should be sure to ascertain whether this form exists in your state.

TRANSFER OF TITLE BY DEED

deed
The written document transferring title, or an ownership interest in real property, to another person.

grantor
The person transferring the property.

grantee
The person receiving the property.

Contracts for the sale of real property are governed by the common law requirements for a valid contract. The real estate sales agreement typically contains provisions requiring, for instance, a survey, a title search and title insurance, an inspection of the property, and warranties of title. In the exchange of information regarding the property, a third party is usually involved: the escrow agent. This agent acts as an intermediary, holding the deed to the property until the buyer pays the seller the contracted price. Escrow agents are commonly title insurance companies or banks. They facilitate the exchange of documents, such as the survey, and funds required in the transaction. Most significantly, at the closing—the last step in the transfer process—the escrow agent accepts the funds from the buyer, accepts the deed from the seller, and then delivers the money to the seller and the deed to the buyer.

The **deed** is the written document transferring ownership and title, or an interest in real property, to another person. Certain information must be contained in the deed, including a legal description of the property, the names of the parties, and the signature of the grantor. The **grantor** is the person transferring the property, and the **grantee** is the person receiving the property. There are generally two types of deeds: a warranty deed and a quitclaim deed.

You Be the Judge

A and B, a married couple, owned Blackacre in joint tenancy. They conveyed a 10 percent interest in Blackacre to their son, C. Six months later, they conveyed a 10 percent interest in Blackacre to C's wife, D. Assume that Blackacre is located in a state that does not recognize tenancy by the entirety. What is the ownership interest of Blackacre after the conveyances? (Be sure to tell the percentage of ownership A, B, C, and D each has and what kind of ownership interest each has.)

warranty deed
A deed guaranteeing clear title to real property.

quitclaim deed
A deed transferring only the interest in property of the grantor, without guarantees.

A **warranty deed** is the deed to property that guarantees that the grantor owns a clear title that is capable of being conveyed to another person. A **quitclaim deed** is a deed in which the grantor is transferring (conveying) only that interest in the property to which he has title. These types of deeds are often used among family members but are also commonly utilized to clear up title where someone has a possible but unknown interest in the land. Good title is not guaranteed.

Real property may also be conveyed by gift or by inheritance. In these cases, the recipient should still ensure that proper deeds or documents properly conveying ownership to her are executed.

ADVERSE POSSESSION

adverse possession
The legal taking of another's property by meeting the requirements of the state statute, typically open and continuous use for a period of five years.

Title to real property may be acquired by **adverse possession.** Here it is possible for someone to acquire property rights to a rightful owner's land if certain state statutory requirements are met. Technically, the person acquiring these rights is depriving the true owner of exclusive use and enjoyment of his property by wrongfully possessing some part of it, through the elements specified by statutes.

Typically the wrongful possession must have been all the following:

1. Actual and exclusive, meaning the adverse possessor is actually occupying the property.
2. Open and notorious, meaning the adverse possessor is not hiding but occupying in a way that the true owner should notice.
3. Hostile and adverse, meaning without consent of the true owner.
4. For the statutorily prescribed time, usually between 5 and 20 years.

Once the adverse possessor has satisfied these elements, she acquires clear title to the land as if she is the rightful owner, but only to that specific piece or parcel of land.

CYBER TRIP

See the Web site www.scotusblog.com. Find a recent case regarding easements or adverse possession.

easement
A right to use another's property for a specific purpose, such as a right of way across the land.

An **easement** is another form of acquiring an interest in land; it gives a person limited use of another person's land. The difference, though, between an easement and adverse possession, is that title to the land by easement is typically created by an express grant by the owner, though it can also occur by means of prescription, or adverse possession. An example of an easement that is created by grant is where utility companies have the express right to bury cables or power lines under a parcel of land owned by another person. Easements also can be sold, as in the case where someone's land is landlocked, and so in order to gain access to the land, that person purchases a right of egress or ingress across or through the land of another person.

LEASES

landlord
The lessor of property.

tenant
A person, or corporation, who rents real property from an owner; also called a lessee.

Many of us have rented an apartment at some time in our lives and are familiar with the relationship between **landlords** and **tenants.** However, it is not as common to refer to the lease as a **non-freehold estate** in real property, but that is the legal term for this agreement. The lessee (or tenant) has the exclusive right to possess and use the property for a specified period of time, but does not have any ownership interest in that property. A typical lease, having a fixed beginning and ending date, such as one year, is called a **tenancy for years.** The lease expires automatically at the end of that designated period, be it one month or 50 years. It is not necessary to provide

You Be the Judge

In a rural area of Idaho, an underground tunnel owned by the railroad company extends one mile between a coal mine and town and was often used by local villagers, for the last 25 years, as a shortcut into town. One day, a local resident, Leonard, was struck by a train while walking through the tunnel. Leonard sues the railway for damages, claiming that an easement to use the tunnel had been established by adverse possession. The railroad company contends that he was at fault for trespassing on its property. What is the likely result?

CASE IN POINT

Court of Appeals of Mississippi.
J.L. MORAN and Wife, Judy Moran, Appellants,
v.
Billy SIMS, Appellee.
No. 2003-CA-00370-COA.
May 18, 2004.

Before SOUTHWICK, P.J., IRVING and GRIFFIS, JJ.

SOUTHWICK, P.J., for the Court.

¶ 1. The chancellor awarded Billy Sims a prescriptive easement across J.L. and Judy Moran's property. The Morans appeal, but we find no error and affirm.

¶ 2. Sims owns property surrounded on three sides by the Morans. His deed was recorded in 1985, but the property had been in his family for at least fifty years. Sims used the land to raise horses and cattle. He began construction of a home in 1991. The Morans purchased parcels to the north, east, and west of Sims in 1996. The access from the Sims property to a state highway had historically been on a driveway across the property now owned by the Morans.

¶ 3. Sims filed a complaint in 1999 seeking an easement. The court sent the dispute to the Smith County Board of Supervisors so that it could lay out a private road. The parties could not agree on a proposal and the matter was returned to chancery court. A trial was held in 2002. Sims and other witnesses testified that the driveway had been used by Sims or his predecessors for at least the past fifty years. Moran did not appear at trial and presented no witnesses. Sims was found to have a prescriptive easement giving him access from the highway to his property.

DISCUSSION

1. Prescriptive easement

[1][2][3] ¶ 4. An easement may be acquired by ten years possession, just as may fee simple title. *Rutland v. Stewart,* 630 So.2d 996, 999 (Miss.1994). Prescription occurs if there is ten years of use that is open, notorious, and visible; hostile; under a claim of ownership; exclusive; peaceful; and continuous and uninterrupted. *Myers v. Blair,* 611 So.2d 969, 971 (Miss.1992). Permission from the record title owner will make the use permissive and not adverse. *Id.*

[4] ¶ 5. Moran argues on appeal that Sims never proved the negative, that is, never proved that Sims and his predecessors did not have permission to use his property. The elements for a prescriptive easement will be examined individually.

a. Open, notorious and visible

¶ 6. At trial, Sims testified that he had used the driveway running across Moran's property since he purchased the parcel in 1985. His family had used the driveway for at least the past fifty years. Among the testimony was from a school bus driver who testified that he had driven the bus down the driveway to pick up children in 1956–1957. When Moran purchased his property in 1996, the driveway and a house on Sims' land were both in existence. This was sufficient under this factor.

b. Hostile

[5] ¶ 7. Moran argues that Sims and his predecessors had implied permission to use the property. That allegedly is proved by the fact that the owners of the land across which the driveway ran never objected to his use. A prescriptive easement cannot originate from a permissive use of land because it would not be hostile. *Sharp v. White,* 749 So.2d 41, 42 (Miss.1999). However, the absence of an objection is not the equivalent of consent.

¶ 8. Here, there was no evidence that Sims or his predecessors had permission to use the driveway. Consent may be inferred from evidence, but it will not be presumed in the absence of evidence. There is nothing in the record from which such an inference can be drawn. The Morans argue that the very obviousness of the use indicates that it must have been consensual. That is not so. If the use of an easement is inconsistent with the title of the servient estate owner, that is the needed hostility. Consent must be shown. Here it was not.

c. Claim of ownership

¶ 9. Sims presented testimony which showed a claim of ownership, including the fact that he purchased gravel for the driveway. There was testimony on that from the person whom Sims hired to deliver and spread the gravel. This element was properly established.

d. Exclusive

[6] ¶ 10. "Exclusive" use does not mean that no one else used the driveway. Exclusivity here means that the use was consistent with an exclusive claim to the right to use. There was evidence that the driveway was used by the Sims family and those whom they implicitly permitted to do so. The Sims' home was the only home located on the driveway.

e. Peaceful

¶ 11. Sims testified that there was no controversy concerning the driveway prior to Moran's purchase of property. There was no evidence of a dispute with prior owners. By the time that Moran complained, the period of prescription had long since run.

f. Continuous and uninterrupted for ten years

¶ 12. Sims recorded the deed to his property in 1985. His family had owned the property for at least fifty years before. During this time, the driveway had been in use. That is ten years, and more.

¶ 13. The elements of adverse possession were sufficiently proven.

2. Description of easement

[7] ¶ 14. Moran claims that the chancellor erred in granting Sims a prescriptive easement until an accurate description of the easement was determined. The testimony presented at trial

established that the driveway ran across Moran's property from Highway 531 in more or less a straight line to the Sims property. The driveway is approximately 216 feet long and 30 feet wide. There is no factual dispute as to its location. This issue concerns a perceived need to have a certain kind of description prepared before title can be confirmed.

[8][9] ¶ 15. There are a variety of accepted methods of describing real property. A valid means is by reference to monuments. Natural monuments include rivers, lakes, streams, or trees; artificial monuments include such landmarks as fences, walls, houses, streets, or ditches. Descriptions employing monuments may in part also employ a "metes and bounds" description. That method uses a measurement of length (metes) along certain boundary lines (bounds). Monuments, natural or artificial, can disappear or be altered, so there is an inherent danger in long-time use of monuments. The risk does not invalidate the use. What is needed in any description is accuracy and clarity. Descriptions using monuments are valid even when there is no surveyor's angle and distance description, so-called "courses and distances" descriptions. The validity of references to roads as they presently exist has been confirmed by the Supreme Court. *Armstrong v. Itawamba County,* 195 Miss. 802, 818, 16 So.2d 752, 757 (1944). In that case, an easement by prescription was awarded to the public on a road "as it now runs." *Id.* Witnesses testified that there had been no change in the location of the road as far as anyone could remember. This was enough of a description.

¶ 16. The chancellor granted an easement in the "existing road." There was no evidence that the driveway's location had changed over the years. This was sufficient. Should either party now or eventually wish to employ a surveyor so that a different kind of description can be obtained, that is certainly within the rights of landowners. There is no requirement on these facts that the chancellor order such a survey.

¶ 17. **THE JUDGMENT OF THE CHANCERY COURT OF SMITH COUNTY IS AFFIRMED. ALL COSTS ARE ASSESSED TO THE APPELLANTS.**

Source: *Moran v. Sims,* 873 So.2d 1067 (St. Paul, MN: Thomson West). Reprinted with permission from Westlaw.

non-freehold estate
A lease agreement.

tenancy for years
A lease with fixed beginning and ending dates; for example, a lease may be for one year.

periodic tenancy
Tenancy in which the tenant is a holdover after the expiration of a tenancy for years.

the other party with any notice that the lease is terminated, as the duration of the agreement is clearly specified in the lease. If, for some reason, the tenant fails to move out at the end of this tenancy for years but continues to pay rent, which is accepted by the landlord, this becomes indefinitely a **periodic tenancy**. The tenant becomes a trespasser only when the landlord decides to evict the tenant who has "held over" after the expiration of the tenancy for years.

When leasing property, issues may arise regarding the duties and obligations of the landlord and the tenant. Keep in mind that only possession, but not ownership, of the premises is transferred to the lessee. Therefore, the landlord remains responsible for the maintenance of the leased property and owes a duty to keep the premises safe for both the tenants and their invited guests. This concept of premises liability is discussed in Chapter 10, "Torts." In general, the legal theory of negligence, exposing invitees to an unreasonable risk of harm, forms the basis for many suits against landlords involving some personal injury. Sometimes, injury results from pets kept on the premises by tenants, both with and without landlord consent. Note that the general rule in most states is that a landlord out of possession is not liable for injuries caused by animals kept by tenants when the tenant has exclusive control of the premises.

PERSONAL PROPERTY

chattel
A term for tangible personal property or goods.

tangible property
Personal property that can be held or touched, such as furniture or jewelry.

All property that is not classified as real property is personal property, sometimes also called **chattels.** It can be further categorized as either tangible or intangible goods. **Tangible property** is generally that which can be touched or is movable, such as jewelry, books, furniture, and other portable items. Sometimes students might suggest that if you can pick it up and hold it in your hand, then it is personal property. So, can an automobile be considered personal property? Clearly, it is not easily held, yet it is still personal property because the keys to the car represent the ownership of that chattel. Therefore, it is not accurate to say that personal property only includes that which can be held in one's hand.

Eye on Ethics

Identify the key issue in the Case in Point, *Housing Authority of the City of Charleston v. Key,* on page 208. Note the facts and specific cause of action in this case.

CASE IN POINT

Supreme Court of South Carolina.
The HOUSING AUTHORITY OF THE CITY OF CHARLESTON, Petitioner,
v.
Willie A. KEY, Respondent.
No. 25545.

Submitted Sept. 17, 2002.
Decided Oct. 28, 2002.
Certiorari Denied March 24, 2003.

FACTS

Petitioner (Housing Authority) commenced this action seeking to enjoin respondent Key from the unauthorized practice of law. We appointed the Honorable John W. Kittredge as special referee to hear evidence and make recommendations. Based on the uncontested facts set forth below, Judge Kittredge concluded respondent had engaged in the unauthorized practice of law and recommended an injunction be issued. No objections to the referee's report have been filed.

Respondent has a paralegal certificate and worked as a paralegal at a law firm in Charleston for three years. He has been unemployed since 2000 and has no address or telephone number. Respondent volunteers at an office referred to as the Fair Housing Office in Charleston advising people who call with landlord complaints. He is not paid. No attorney supervises the office.

In 2001, on behalf of Jacqueline Sarvis and Derotha Robinson, respondent prepared and filed a complaint in federal court alleging unlawful evictions. [FN1] He appeared at a status conference before the federal magistrate. Respondent also prepared pleadings filed in circuit court alleging an unlawful termination of public assistance rental benefits for Joan Whitley and assisted Ms. Whitley at the hearing in circuit court. [FN2] Respondent did not sign any of the pleadings he prepared but had them signed by the plaintiffs as *pro se* litigants. He accepted no payment and in fact paid the filing fees out of his own pocket. Respondent did not obtain leave of court to represent any of these clients. [FN3]

FN1. This action was ultimately dismissed as frivolous except for one cause of action; the appeal was dismissed for failure to prosecute.

FN2. This action was dismissed for lack of subject matter jurisdiction.

FN3. Under former S.C.Code Ann. § 40-5-80 (1986), a citizen could represent another with leave of the court. This section was recently amended to omit a citizen's right to defend or prosecute the cause of another effective June 5, 2002.

DISCUSSION

Respondent defends his conduct on the ground he was not paid and he had the clients' permission to represent them. [FN4]

FN4. Respondent filed no objections to the referee's report but stated this position when he was deposed.

[1][2][3] The practice of law includes the preparation of pleadings and the management of court proceedings on the behalf of clients. *Doe v. Condon,* 351 S.C. 158, 568 S.E.2d 356 (2002). Respondent's activities on behalf of Whitley, Robinson, and Sarvis constituted the practice of law. The fact that respondent accepted no remuneration for his services is irrelevant. Our purpose in regulating the practice of law is to protect the public from the negative consequences of erroneously prepared legal documents or inaccurate legal advice given by persons untrained in the law. *Linder v. Ins. Claims Consultants, Inc.,* 348 S.C. 477, 560 S.E.2d 612 (2002). We note respondent has shown no indication he intends to discontinue his practice of representing others in court.

We hereby adopt the referee's findings and enjoin respondent from further engaging in the unauthorized practice of law.

INJUNCTION ISSUED.

TOAL, C.J., WALLER, BURNETT and PLEICONES, JJ., concur.

Source: *Housing Authority of the City of Charleston v. Key,* 352 S.C. 26, 572 S.E.2d 284 (St. Paul, MN: Thomson West). Reprinted with permission from Westlaw.

You Be the Judge

Herman was enrolled at the University of Transylvania, having started his degree 16 years ago. At that time, Herman had moved into student housing and has resided there ever since. The university tries to evict Herman since he has only enrolled in one class every other semester and never completed his degree. Herman refuses to leave, claiming he is a valid student, so the university sues for eviction. What is the likely result?

RESEARCH THIS!

Landlords may be liable for injuries sustained by tenants or their guests. Compare these two cases, and explain the different results reached in each case:

Gallick v. Barto, 828 F.Supp. 1168 (1993)
Jackson v. Real Property Services Corporation, 602 S.E.2d 356 (GA. 2004).

CYBER TRIP

Visit and compare these Web sites which detail intellectual property rights:

http://lcweb.loc.gov/copyright
http://uspto.gov
www.ipmag.com
www.ggmark.com

Intangible property includes that which cannot physically be touched or moved, but still is deemed personal property, such as copyrights, bank deposits, and stock certificates. It is unclear whether computer data may be considered intangible personal property. Instruments representing personal property may not have value in and of itself, but it represents the value in the idea or in the money that is acknowledged in that piece of paper. Intangible property comes with the same rights of interest, to use, sell, or control, as tangible property or real property. One of the most complex areas of the law involves intangible property: intellectual property law. Intellectual property centers on patents, trademarks, and copyrights, all of which offer ownership rights to something intangible.

A patent is the grant of a property right for an invention, issued by the Patent and Trademark Office. Patents are granted for a term of 20 years. According to the applicable statute, 35 USC section 101 (1999), a patent grant confers "the right to exclude others from asking, using, offering for sale, or selling the invention in the United States or importing the invention into the United States." A trademark is a word, symbol, or device that is used in trade with goods to indicate the source of the goods to others. Similarly, service marks identify and distinguish the source of a service. Others may produce or sell the same goods, but they must do so under a different mark that is unlikely to cause confusion with the original service's mark. Finally, a copyright protects the authors of original works, such as literary, dramatic, musical, or other creative works, published or unpublished. According to the Copyright Act (1976), copyright owners possess the exclusive right to reproduce, perform, or display the work.

CAN THE CLASSIFICATION OF PROPERTY CHANGE?

Once something is classified as real property or as personal property, can this classification ever change? Consider the fruit trees that are growing in your backyard. The trees are permanently attached to the land, but what happens when the fruit drops off the tree onto the ground? The fruit is now personal property, though the tree is still real property. Similarly, if you discover gold in the soil of your backyard, it is real property, but once you dig out the gold from the ground and load it into a wheelbarrow, that gold is now personal property. In the same respect, the garden bench you buy at the store and haul home in your truck is personal property. However, if you set the garden bench in concrete in the backyard, it now becomes real property, as you have permanently attached the object to the land. Think about that neighbor's fruit tree, whose branches are invading your airspace because they are hanging over the fence. You may not have the right to cut the tree branches and keep the fruit, as this is your neighbor's tree, but you may have the right to keep the fruit that falls off the branches and lands in your yard, as that fruit is now considered to be personal property.

TRANSFER OF PERSONAL PROPERTY

Personal property may be transferred in one of several ways: it can be sold, it can be donated, or it can be devised by will. In these cases, the property is permanently and voluntarily transferred to someone else. In certain situations, property may also be involuntarily transferred, and this will be discussed later in this section. Finally, property may also be temporarily transferred—possession, but not ownership—and this will also be discussed herein.

Transferring personal property by sale of the goods is quite simple, as ordinarily no formal paperwork or words of conveyance are required like there is for real property. If you are selling an automobile or perhaps a live animal, then it is likely that state licensing requirements may require some added documentation of the sale beyond the mere exchange of the item for value.

gift
Bestowing a benefit without any expectation on the part of the giver to receive something in return and the absence of any obligation on the part of the receiver to do anything in return.

Giving property away is similar to selling it, quite simple and straightforward, but this **gift** or voluntary transfer without value, or consideration, has specific characteristics dependent upon the time the gift is made.

Gifts

donor
The person making a gift.

donee
A party to whom a gift is given.

gift inter vivos
Gift made during the lifetime of the donor.

If Debbie gives her diamond necklace to her daughter, Diane, Debbie is called the **donor** and Diane is referred to as the **donee.** This gift, if made while Debbie is still alive, is considered to be an irrevocable transfer of ownership and is called a **gift inter vivos,** or a gift in the lifetime of the donor. A valid gift inter vivos, also called an absolute gift, occurs when (1) the donor intends to make the gift; (2) the transfer of the gift is complete; (3) delivery of the gift by the donor is accomplished, and accepted by the donee; and (4) the gift is immediate. Therefore, once delivery and acceptance of a gift inter vivos occurs, the transfer is irrevocable and title to the gift immediately vests in the donee. However, a conditional gift is one in which it is conditioned upon the occurrence of some event or the performance of some act by the donee.

Sometimes, the issue arises as to whether the gift had any "strings attached." For example, the courts are occasionally asked to consider whether a diamond ring that is given in contemplation of marriage, as an engagement gift, is an irrevocable gift. Many courts consider an engagement ring to be a conditional gift, unless there is some contrary expression of intent by the donor. An engagement ring is a symbol of a couple's agreement to marry, and thus marriage is a condition precedent before title to the ring vests in the donee. The majority of jurisdictions have adopted a fault-based approach in considering the ownership of an engagement ring when the engagement is terminated. Under this approach, the courts conclude that the donor is entitled to the return of the ring if the engagement was broken by mutual agreement or unjustifiably by the donee. The rationale is that the courts will not assist a donor who breaks his promise to marry to regain possession of a ring he would not have recovered had he kept his promise. Jurisdictions that have rejected this fault-based approach contend that once an engagement is broken, that the ring should be returned to the donor, regardless of fault. These courts reason that the fault-based approach places an unreasonable burden on the judiciary to sift through mountains of testimony regarding who was at fault for the termination of the engagement. In some respects, this is the approach favored by states with a no-fault divorce system; the judiciary is not compelled to weigh the evidence of who did what during the marriage or, in this case, in the period of engagement. Thus, the courts conclude that an engagement ring is a conditional gift, and not an inter vivos transfer of property.

gift causa mortis
A gift made by the donor in contemplation of death.

If Mary gives Loulou her necklace as she is lying in a hospital bed, near death, then this is called a **gift causa mortis,** or a gift in contemplation of death. In this situation, Mary's gift takes precedence over any terms stated in a will, so long as the gift was made as death is near from some pre-existing known illness and the donor does in fact soon thereafter die from this illness without first revoking the gift.

Involuntary Transfer of Property

Sometimes ownership of property is transferred without the owner's knowledge or consent. Immediately, the concept of theft comes to mind, as certainly when we park our car on the street in front of our house at night, we expect it will still be there the following morning. But, there are other situations where we involuntarily relinquish our property rights and control over a tangible object. There are three different categories of ways that personal property may be transferred to someone else in this manner.

lost property
Personal property with which a person has involuntarily parted possession.

Assume that you leave class to go home and are walking out to the parking lot. Unknown to you at the time, the clasp on your diamond bracelet is broken, and thus en route to your car, the bracelet falls off your wrist in the parking lot. You do not discover it is not on your wrist until later that evening. In the meantime, Loulou finds your bracelet in the parking lot and wears it home. This bracelet may be classified as **lost property,** because you did not voluntarily give up the item and you have no idea where it is now. Lost property occurs when the owner involuntarily parts with it through carelessness, negligence, or inadvertence. Here, Loulou, as the finder of lost property, has acquired title and rights to this necklace against everyone else but the true owner—you. Assume that Loulou is a student at your school, and therefore the following week, you spot your bracelet on Loulou's wrist. If you are readily able to identify it, and prove that you are the true owner of this bracelet, then you may recover it from Loulou. Remember, Loulou acquired a valid claim to the bracelet when she found it, against everyone else in the world *except* the true owner.

mislaid property
Personal property that the owner has intentionally placed somewhere and then forgot about.

The second category of transferring property without the owner's knowledge or consent is called **mislaid property.** Here, the owner has inadvertently or carelessly placed the tangible object somewhere and then leaves, forgetting the item is there. Assume for example that Dilbert is in class and places his backpack on the floor next to his chair. At the end of class, Dilbert rushes out of the room, forgetting to pick up his backpack on the way out the door. In this case, the backpack is deemed mislaid property, as it is likely that Dilbert will return to the classroom to reclaim the property once he remembers where he left it or misplaced it. If Loulou finds the backpack when she comes to class later that evening, she does not acquire ownership rights in the backpack, because mislaid property carries the presumption that the true owner knows how to find the item and will return for it once he recalls where he intentionally placed it.

abandoned property
Personal property that the owner has intentionally discarded and to which the owner has relinquished ownership rights.

Finally, property may be transferred to another *intentionally* if the owner discards it, and this is called **abandoned property.** Property is abandoned where the owner voluntarily and intentionally relinquishes all rights to it. Assume that Mortimer is fed up with his cell phone service and throws his phone in the classroom trash can at the end of class, before leaving the room. Later that evening, Loulou spots the phone in the garbage can, takes it out, and puts it in her backpack. Loulou has acquired ownership rights to this phone, and her title to it is good against everyone, including Mortimer. Mortimer intentionally gave up any ownership rights to that phone, and it thus belongs to the first person who finds it. It makes no difference if Mortimer changes his mind a week later, he cannot reclaim the phone from Loulou.

Finders Keepers?

What are the duties or obligations of people who find lost, mislaid, or abandoned property? The answer is that it depends. First, it is necessary to be certain that the property is correctly classified in order to determine your rights as a finder. How does one determine whether something is lost, mislaid, or abandoned? The answer is determined by *where* the object is found. If you spot something in a dumpster, it will be considered abandoned property, because it is presumed that no one intentionally placed the object there and then forgot about it. Likewise, you would not presume that an item was lost in the dumpster unless someone was working inside the dumpster and unintentionally parted company with something. In the same respect, if you see a purse lying on a table, it should be presumed that this is mislaid property, since the purse would not have been dropped on a table without the owner realizing it. If you enter the restroom of your school and see a ring on the sink, it is presumed that this is mislaid property, intentionally placed there by the owner while she was washing her hands. Again, it is because of where it was found that indicates the classification of the property.

So, the classification of the property and *who* finds it governs the duties, if any, of the finder of this property. If it is abandoned property, the finder has absolutely no duty to try and find the true owner; the property now belongs to the finder. The finder of mislaid property does not automatically acquire title to the item. Rather, the finder must turn in the item to the owner of the premises where it was found. For example, if you find a ring in the restroom of your school, you are obligated to give it to a representative of the school so that they can attempt to find the rightful owner of the ring and return it. The owner of the premises becomes, in essence, a bailee of the item—a topic that will be discussed later in this chapter. Until the true owner is found, the bailee must take reasonable care to safeguard this item. The finder of the property has no ownership rights to something found on the premises of another. Finally, if it is lost property, the finder has a duty to attempt to locate the true owner. You may be obligated to turn the lost item in to the police, or maybe to the owner of the premises, so that reasonable efforts

You Be the Judge

Loulou went to the safe deposit vault at her bank to remove some savings bonds from her box at which time she discovered a diamond ring on the floor of the vault. Being honest, Loulou turned the ring over to the bank teller. The bank tried, but could not find the owner of the ring, despite placing advertisements for six months. Loulou asks for the ring back, as the true finder of the property, but the bank refuses. Loulou sues the bank. What is the likely result?

RESEARCH THIS!

Locate the following case and explain the court's reasoning and holding: *Commonwealth of Pennsylvania v. $7,000 in U.S. Currency,* 742 A.2d 711 (1999).

can be made to find the owner. However, when the property is found by a police officer in the performance of her duties, then that officer is ordinarily barred from asserting a claim to that property, if the true owner is not found. Whether the property is lost or abandoned is irrelevant, because the public faith in law enforcement would be undermined if the police were allowed to keep the property.

Bailment

bailment
The delivery of personal property from one person to another to be held temporarily.

bailor
The owner of the property transferring possession.

bailee
The recipient of the property, temporarily taking possession.

mutual benefit bailment
A bailment created for the benefit of both parties.

Personal property may be temporarily transferred to another person, usually for a limited, specific purpose, but ownership rights are not transferred. This temporary transfer of personal property by the owner is called a **bailment.** A bailment is created by the temporary transfer of possession (but not ownership) of personal property, from one person to another, to be held for the benefit of the bailee, the bailor, or both persons. Examples of a bailment include taking your car to the service station for an oil change or giving your suit to the dry cleaners to be cleaned and pressed. When you hand your car keys over to the mechanic, you are not cheerily giving him title to your car. You simply intend to temporarily deliver your car to him for the specific, limited purpose of getting your oil changed. Likewise, you are not donating your suit to the attendant at the local dry cleaners, you are merely delivering temporary possession of your suit for so long as it takes to get it cleaned. The owner of the car, the suit, or whatever property is being temporarily transferred, is called the **bailor** and the recipient of the property is called the **bailee.** Keep in mind that title to the property does not pass from the bailor to the bailee—only possession. It is this element of lawful possession, and duty to account for the thing as the property of someone else, that creates the bailment. While the bailee is keeping the item, that person has certain duties and obligations regarding the bailor's property, depending on which person stands to benefit from the contract.

While the bailor's property is in the possession of the bailee, that property must be reasonably safeguarded and protected, depending upon the type of bailment in that specific situation. In many cases involving a place of business, such as service stations or dry cleaners, these are considered **mutual benefit bailments.** This means that both parties to the transaction are receiving some benefit. For example, if you take your suit to be cleaned, the bailee receives cash in exchange for cleaning your suit. Thus, the bailee must exercise a duty of ordinary care; that is, she must take reasonable steps to ensure that the suit is not damaged, lost, or stolen because of her negligence.

Other types of bailments alter the degree of care that a bailee must assume. If the bailment is for the sole benefit of the *bailor,* then the bailee need only exercise a slight degree of care with the property. For example, assume that Susan is leaving town and asks her neighbor, June, to take care of her houseplants that week. Since June is doing this as a favor to Susan and receives no benefit for her diligence, she need exercise a slight degree of care over the houseplants. This

RESEARCH THIS!

Read the following two cases. Compare the facts and the holding of each case, and explain the different results, noting the court's reasoning.

Waterton v. Linden Motor, Inc., 810 N.Y.S.2d 319 (2006)

Ziva Jewelry, Inc. v. Car Wash Headquarters, Inc., 897 So.2d 1011 (Ala. 2004).

CASE IN POINT

Court of Appeals of Arizona,
Division 1, Department C.
CONTINENTAL TOWNHOUSES EAST UNIT ONE ASSOCIATION, an Arizona corporation;
Vincent Territo; Dorothea Waxman; and Jill Sampson, Plaintiffs-Appellees,
Cross Appellants,
v.
Roy R. BROCKBANK and Rita Brockbank, husband and wife, d/b/a Roy Brockbank
Enterprises, Defendants-Appellants, Cross Appellees.
No. 1 CA-CIV 8582.
Aug. 5, 1986.
Reconsideration Denied Dec. 5, 1986.
Review Denied March 11, 1987.

OPINION

CONTRERAS, Presiding Judge.

. . .

B. *Attorneys' Fees.*

We address two important issues regarding the attorneys' fee award at issue in this case:

(1) Whether the value of legal work performed by legal assistants may be recovered as an element of attorneys' fees under A.R.S. § 12-341.01; and

(2) The effect of the original contingency fee contract between counsel and the Association on the recovery of fees by the class.

The class requested an award of attorneys' fees under A.R.S. § 12-341.01(A). [FN6] It sought 40% of the jury verdict, or $124,981.96, pursuant to a contingency fee agreement signed by counsel and the President of the Association, the original plaintiff in the litigation. Counsel for the class contends that the same contingency fee agreement was expected to apply between it and the class when the class replaced the Association as plaintiff.

FN6. A.R.S. § 12-341.01(A) provides in part that "[i]n any contested action arising out of a contract, express or implied, the court may award the successful party reasonable attorney's fees." A.R.S. § 12-341.01(B) adds, "The award of reasonable attorney's fees awarded pursuant to subsection A should be made to mitigate the burden of the expense of litigation to establish a just claim or a just defense. It need not equal or relate to the attorney's fees actually paid or contracted, but such award may not exceed the amount paid or agreed to be paid."

The request for attorneys' fees included an itemization of hourly rates and time expended by counsel and legal assistants, totalling $73,977.00. The trial court awarded the class $58,485.00, and later increased the award to $61,795.00. All amounts requested for the legal tasks performed by legal assistants and law clerks were denied by the trial court. The trial judge set forth his reason:

> Absent specific Arizona authority to the contrary, this Court will not award attorney fees for work performed by non-lawyers. The only authorities cited to the Court are United States District Court holdings which are divided on the issue.

Until now, Arizona courts have not directly ruled on the recoverability of fees for legal work performed by legal assistants and law clerks. See the discussion in Stahl and Smith, *Paralegal Services and Awards of Attorneys' Fees Under Arizona Law,* Ariz. B.J., Oct.-Nov. 1984, at 21.

Courts which have permitted paralegal services to be recovered as an element of attorneys' fees have recognized that doing so promotes lawyer efficiency and reduces client costs. The Ninth Circuit has permitted recovery of paralegal services as part of the recovery of attorneys' fees under the Longshoremen's and Harbor Workers' Compensation Act for the assistance rendered by a claimant's lay representative to the claimant's attorney:

> One of the necessary incidents of an attorney's fee is the attorney's maintaining of a competent staff to assist him. . . . Paralegals can do some of the work that the attorney would have to do anyway and can do it at substantially less cost per hour, resulting in less total cost billed. . . .

Todd Shipyards Corp. v. Director, Office of Workers' Compensation Programs, 545 F.2d 1176, 1182 (9th Cir.1976).

The Arizona federal district court has agreed:

> Paralegal time has been included [in this case] as a part of the lodestar [fee] calculation rather than being allowed as costs . . . I realize this is an issue as to which courts differ. The use of paralegals, if properly supervised and directed, can be cost effective. It is reasonable to recognize and encourage a continuation of paralegal usage in appropriate circumstances.

State of Arizona v. Maricopa County Medical Society, 578 F.Supp. 1262, 1270 (D.Ariz.1984). *See also Pacific Coast Agricultural Export Assoc. v. Sunkist Growers, Inc.,* 526 F.2d 1196, 1210 n. 19 (9th Cir.1975), *cert. denied,* 425 U.S. 959, 96 S.Ct. 1741, 48 L.Ed.2d 204 (1976). [FN7] The Arizona federal district court has also refused to authorize compensation for lawyers performing services that could have been performed by a legal assistant, as well as for excessive or duplicated time incurred by both lawyers and legal assistants on routine tasks. *Metro Data Systems, Inc. v. Durango Systems, Inc.,* 597 F.Supp. 244 (D.Ariz.1984).

FN7. Several other cases and relevant articles are cited in the Arizona Appellate Handbook, vol. 1, ch. 1, p. 2 (Supp.1986).

[9] We conclude that legal assistant and law clerk services may properly be included as elements in attorneys' fees applications and awards pursuant to A.R.S. § 12-341.01, both in the trial court and on appeal. The purpose of awards based on that statute is to "mitigate the burden of the expense of litigation." A.R.S. § 12-341.01(B). Properly employed and supervised **legal assistants** and law clerks [FN8] can decrease litigation expense and improve lawyers' efficiency.

> FN8. Lawyers' **professional** responsibilities regarding supervision of nonlawyer **assistants** are stated in Rule of **Professional** Conduct 5.3.

Lawyers should not be required to perform tasks more properly performed by **legal assistants** or law clerks solely to permit that time to be compensable in the event an attorneys' fees application is ultimately submitted. Requiring such a misallocation of valuable resources would serve no useful purpose and would be contrary to the direction to interpret the Rules of Civil Procedure to serve the "just, speedy, and inexpensive determination of every action." Rule 1, Arizona Rules of Civil Procedure. Instead, proper **use** of **legal assistants** and law clerks should be encouraged to facilitate providing the most cost-effective **legal** services to the public. If compensation could not be obtained for **legal assistant** and law clerk services in appropriate cases, the fee-shifting objective of A.R.S. § 12-341.01 would also not be accomplished.

Use of **legal assistants** nationally has significantly increased in recent years. *See* Law Poll, 69 A.B.A.J. 1626 (1983); Ulrich, ***Legal Assistants*** *Can Increase Your Profits,* 69 A.B.A.J. 1634 (1983). **Legal assistants** are being employed increasingly both in Arizona and elsewhere, in many law practice categories, particularly in large firms. *See generally* Stahl and Smith, *supra;* National Law Journal, Sept. 30, 1985, at S4-S18; *Working with* ***Legal Assistants,*** *passim* (P. Ulrich and R. Mucklestone ed. 1980, 1981). Authoritative projections suggest the number of such positions will nearly double during the next years, from an estimated 53,000 in 1984 to 104,000 in 1995. U.S. Dept. of Labor, Bureau of Labor Statistics, *Occupational Outlook Quarterly,* at 19 (Spring 1986). Legal assistants have thus now become an essential element of legal services provided by many law offices. Lawyers have also employed law clerks for as long as there have been law students. They also can provide valuable assistance, particularly in legal research and preparing documents under the lawyer's supervision.

We do not believe such services should be considered part of taxable court "costs." They are instead properly considered as a component of attorneys' fees, since an attorney would have performed these services if a legal assistant was not employed instead. It also cannot be assumed legal assistant services are automatically included in lawyers' hourly billing rates as a standard law office operating expense. Instead, such services are often itemized and billed separately. Ulrich, *supra.* Moreover, lawyers should not be required to inflate their hourly rates to include **legal assistant** time as a general overhead component. Doing so would make fair allocation of the cost of such services impossible, since some clients and matters may require a much higher proportion of **legal assistant** and law clerk services than others.

The question then arises as to what categories of persons or tasks should be considered "**legal assistant**" for purposes of attorneys' fees applications. [FN9] In this regard, we believe the definition of "**legal assistant**" formulated by the American Bar Association's Standing Committee on **Legal Assistants** and approved as an official policy statement by its Board of Governors in February, 1986, is appropriate:

> FN9. We **use** the terms **legal assistant**, paralegal, and law clerk interchangeably in this opinion, and believe the ABA definition encompasses each of these titles.
>
> > A **legal assistant** is a person, qualified through education, training, or work experience, who is employed or retained by a lawyer, law office, governmental agency, or other entity in a capacity or function which involves the performance, under the ultimate direction and supervision of an attorney, of specifically-delegated substantive legal work, which work, for the most part, requires a sufficient knowledge of legal concepts that, absent such assistant, the attorney would perform the task.

Clearly, since the legal assistant must perform legal work and be supervised by an attorney, the fee application must contain enough details to demonstrate to the court that these requirements have been met, thereby comporting with the spirit of *Schweiger v. China Doll Restaurant, Inc.,* 138 Ariz. 183, 673 P.2d 927 (App.1983).

[10] Finally, we reiterate and emphasize the discretionary power of the trial judge in awarding attorneys' fees under A.R.S. § 12-341.01. *See, e.g., Associated Indemnity Corp. v. Warner,* 143 Ariz. 567, 694 P.2d 1181 (1985); *Solar-West, Inc. v. Falk,* 141 Ariz. 414, 687 P.2d 939 (App.1984). The trial judge is not required to, but may, consider the value of services rendered in a case by **legal assistants,** law clerks, and paralegals, applying the same standards as are **used** in evaluating lawyers' time.

Not only must this case be remanded to give the trial judge the opportunity to consider inclusion of **legal assistants,** 'services in the attorneys' fee award, but further evidence must be considered in order to determine whether the contingency fee agreement between counsel and the Association applies in favor of the class.

In the retainer agreement, the client agreed to pay counsel 40% of the net amount recovered if the case was tried. The client in the agreement was Continental Townhouses East Unit One Association. The client on appeal is the class of homeowners, represented by three individual homeowners. It is not clear to this court following oral argument whether the signed retainer agreement was intended to apply between counsel and the current plaintiff. The trial court is in a better position to determine, perhaps by way of further proceedings, the understanding between the parties with regard to the contingency fee agreement, and therefore whether it would be appropriate to award attorneys' fees pursuant to the fee agreement.

Thus, we remand with the following directions.

1. The original jury verdict must be reinstated, without pre-judgment interest.
2. The court should cons ider evidence of the parties' understanding with counsel regarding the continued viability of the retainer agreement after the lawsuit was converted to a class action.
3. If the court is convinced that the 40% fee recovery under the retainer agreement applies between counsel and the class, it may award up to 40% of the verdict as attorneys' fees. The 40% figure operates as a ceiling on the amount of attorneys' fees that may be recovered; the court need

not agree that 40% of the recovery is a reasonable sum for attorneys' fees in this case and may award less. In determining the amount to be awarded as attorneys' fees, the court may, in its discretion, consider and include the value of time spent by **legal assistants** on **legal** tasks. The hourly rate charged for time spent by **legal assistants** should reflect reasonable community standards of remuneration.

4. If the court determines that the retainer agreement was not intended to control the fee paid by the class, it may rely upon the itemized fee request submitted by counsel and also, in its discretion, consider the amounts requested for time spent on legal tasks by legal assistants.

Finally, the class requests an award of attorneys' fees on appeal pursuant to A.R.S. § 12-341.01. We grant the request. The class may establish the amount of its award by complying with Rule 21(c), Arizona Rules of Civil Appellate Procedure, and our decision in *Schweiger v. China Doll Restaurant, Inc.,* 138 Ariz. 183, 673 P.2d 927 (App.1983). In accordance with our decision today, the request for fees on appeal may include the value of legal work performed by legal assistants, if any.

The judgment of the trial court is affirmed in part, reversed in part and remanded with the foregoing directions.

Source: *Continental Townhouses v. Brockbank,* 152 Ariz. 537, 733 P.2d 1120 (St. Paul, MN: Thomson West). Reprinted with permission from Westlaw.

You Be the Judge

Ethel was traveling on a train with her three friends when the conductor discovered that her group of four passengers was short one ticket. The conductor informed Ethel that she must either pay the train fare or leave the car. Ethel insisted she had purchased a ticket, although she couldn't find it, so the conductor ordered her to leave. In the process, Ethel's camera was left behind. Ethel sues the train company for its loss. What is the likely result?

does not mean that June can be negligent or intentionally ignore the watering of these plants; she simply is not obligated to do more than a reasonable person would in that situation.

If the bailment is for the sole benefit of the *bailee,* then the bailee must exercise the highest degree of care in safeguarding the property. For example, assume Mortimer's car breaks down, and he needs transportation to get to classes. Loulou agrees to lend Mortimer her car for a week. If Mortimer carelessly drives with reckless disregard for Loulou's car and crashes into the side of the school building, this is not exercising the highest degree of care for the bailor's property. The law of bailments requires that the bailee exercise that degree of care necessary to safeguard property while it is under the control of the bailee.

A Day in the Life of a Real Paralegal

Property law is an area in which a paralegal will be constantly challenged and expected to undertake a variety of tasks in a relatively short time frame. Real estate law is also an area in which some states allow paralegals to represent clients at closings. Indeed, practicing in this area will require the ability to interact with a variety of people at different levels, and therefore paralegals that possess exceptional communication skills will enjoy this area of the law.

A significant aspect of work in this field entails the real estate closing. You must be able to maintain clear and accurate records and be knowledgeable about the steps in every property transaction. You will have the opportunity to draft real estate contracts, conduct title examinations, create title abstracts, review closing documents, schedule closings, and review the deed. In many cases, you will be attending the closing. Paralegals have extensive contact with clients, opposing counsel, banks, and title companies, and therefore the need to be familiar with current procedures and laws is important. Paralegals who practice in the area of property law may work for law firms that practice real estate, mortgage companies, and title insurance companies, as well as corporations. If you work in the legal department of a corporation, it is likely you will be responsible for drafting and reviewing lease agreements, as opposed to documents pertaining to property sales. Again, the opportunity arises for lots of client contact, and therefore your communication skills are important to success in this field.

Summary

Property ownership rights are fundamental to our society, forming the basis for our economy. As such, people are not only keenly interested in acquiring property, but in ensuring that their ownership rights are protected under the law. Property law sets forth who owns what, and what rights are associated with that ownership interest. Property law exists for the purpose of protecting the right of owners to sell, use, control, and dispose of their property as they will, without interference or trespassing by others. Property law ensures that this is accomplished without owners taking the law into their own hands and guarding their property with shotguns or building moats around their land.

In beginning an analysis of a property law question, you should first ascertain whether the subject matter concerns real property or personal property. Sometimes this classification changes, depending on the nature of the property, as in minerals in the ground. Issues that arise in property law often focus on whether the property has been legally transferred to another. If property has been transferred, an examination of the rights of ownership is often necessary in resolving a property law issue.

Key Terms

Abandoned property
Adverse possession
Bailee
Bailment
Bailor
Chattel
Deed
Donee
Donor
Easement
Estate in land
Fee simple absolute
Fee simple defeasible
Fixtures
Freehold estate
Future interest
Gift
Gift causa mortis
Gift inter vivos
Grantee
Grantor
Intangible property
Joint tenancy
Landlord
Life estate
Lost property
Marketable title
Mislaid property
Mutual benefit bailment
Non-freehold estate
Periodic tenancy
Quitclaim deed
Real property
Remainder
Reversion
Right of survivorship
Survey
Tangible property
Tenancy by the entirety
Tenancy for years
Tenancy in common
Tenant
Title insurance policy
Title search
Trade fixtures
Warranty deed

Discussion Questions

1. Think about the importance of property law as it relates to other substantive areas of the law, such as criminal law or tort law. Discuss.
2. Discuss the extent to which the burden of easements affects the enjoyment of land by the successors in title of those who created the easements.
3. How does the law of adverse possession reflect the logic of protecting a landowner's bundle of rights? Should the doctrine of adverse possession be abolished?
4. Explain whether the right to store furniture in your neighbor's basement can be considered an easement. What about the right to use a boundary fence for the erection of signage advertising a neighborhood grocery store?
5. Discuss whether you agree with the fault-based approach in the consideration of the ownership of an engagement ring after the termination of an engagement.

Exercises

1. Barney was the owner in fee simple of Blackacre Farm, which comprised a large house and garden, and the farm lands, which consisted of two large tracts commonly referred to as the "East Tract" and "West Tract." His will contained the following: "I bequeath my house and the garden to my daughters, Ann, Betty, and Charlotte. I bequeath East Tract and West Tract to be shared by my sons Abel and Ben. Barney died in 2002. All five siblings continued to live in the house and the two sons farmed the land. In 2003, Ann moved to Germany and needed money, so her sisters each gave her $100,000, agreeing in writing this was in exchange for her share of the inheritance. Meanwhile, Abel married Diane and Ben married Esther. They all lived in the house until quarrels occurred, at which time Abel and Diane moved out, into town. Ben farmed the land alone until his death in 2004. Then Abel took over the farm. Last month, Betty died. Who now has ownership of the house and the farm?
2. Dudley owns a large area of land, in fee simple, that includes a former hotel with tennis courts and a barn. The only access to the barn is via a path that runs across the hotel gardens to the main road in front of the hotel. In 1995, Dudley sold the barn to Smedley. Since moving in, Smedley has been using the path every day at 6 a.m. to access the barn from the main road, without any complaints from Dudley. In April of 2005, Dudley granted to Molly, by deed, the right to use the tennis court for 10 years. In May of 2005, Dudley sold the tennis courts to Smedley. In June of 2005, Dudley sold the rest of his property, including the former hotel and the remaining land to Mortimer. Mortimer immediately erects a large iron fence to stop Smedley from using the path across his grounds. What, if anything, can Smedley do about this?
3. Assume the same facts as in Exercise 2, but assume now that Smedley has erected an electrified fence to keep Molly from using the tennis courts. What if anything can Molly do about this?
4. Assume the same facts as in Exercise 2, but assume now that Smedley is planning to build on top of the stables, and Mortimer is afraid that this will obstruct the light to the hotel windows and interfere with his television reception in the hotel. What if anything can Mortimer do about this?
5. Portia leases her house to William, a carpenter. Upon moving in to the house, William immediately proceeds to make the house more like home by building bookshelves and nailing them to the wall, and then filling the shelves with heavy books such as the complete works of Shakespeare. He also erects a platform in the front entryway on which he places a marble statue of a Greek goddess. To feel safe in the house, William installs smoke alarms and a burglar alarm system. Finally, he affixes a stone water fountain onto the outside front wall of the house. At the expiration of his lease, William moves out, taking with him the bookcases and books, the fountain, the smoke alarms and burglar alarm, as well as his marble statue. He also takes the refrigerator, which was present in the house when he moved in. Removal of the fountain causes damage to the outer wall. Discuss Portia's rights and what, if anything, she can do.
6. Montague bought a house from Capulet. The sales contract specified that the property included "all fixtures at the property except for the storage shed in the backyard." Upon moving in to the house, Montague discovered that the shed, which was resting on a concrete slab, had not been removed. Montague contacts Capulet and inquires as to when he will be removing the shed. One month later, the shed remains. Does it belong to Montague now? Explain.
7. Sue owned two adjoining properties. There was a well-worn path across the land to get from one house to the other. Sue leased one of the houses to Peter, who proceeded to use the path as a shortcut to the Convenience Mart. Sue instructed him to not use this path, but he continued to do so. At the expiration of the one-year lease, Peter buys the house from Sue. Can Sue stop Peter from using the path after the purchase of the property? Did she have the right to stop him from using it during the period of the lease? Explain.

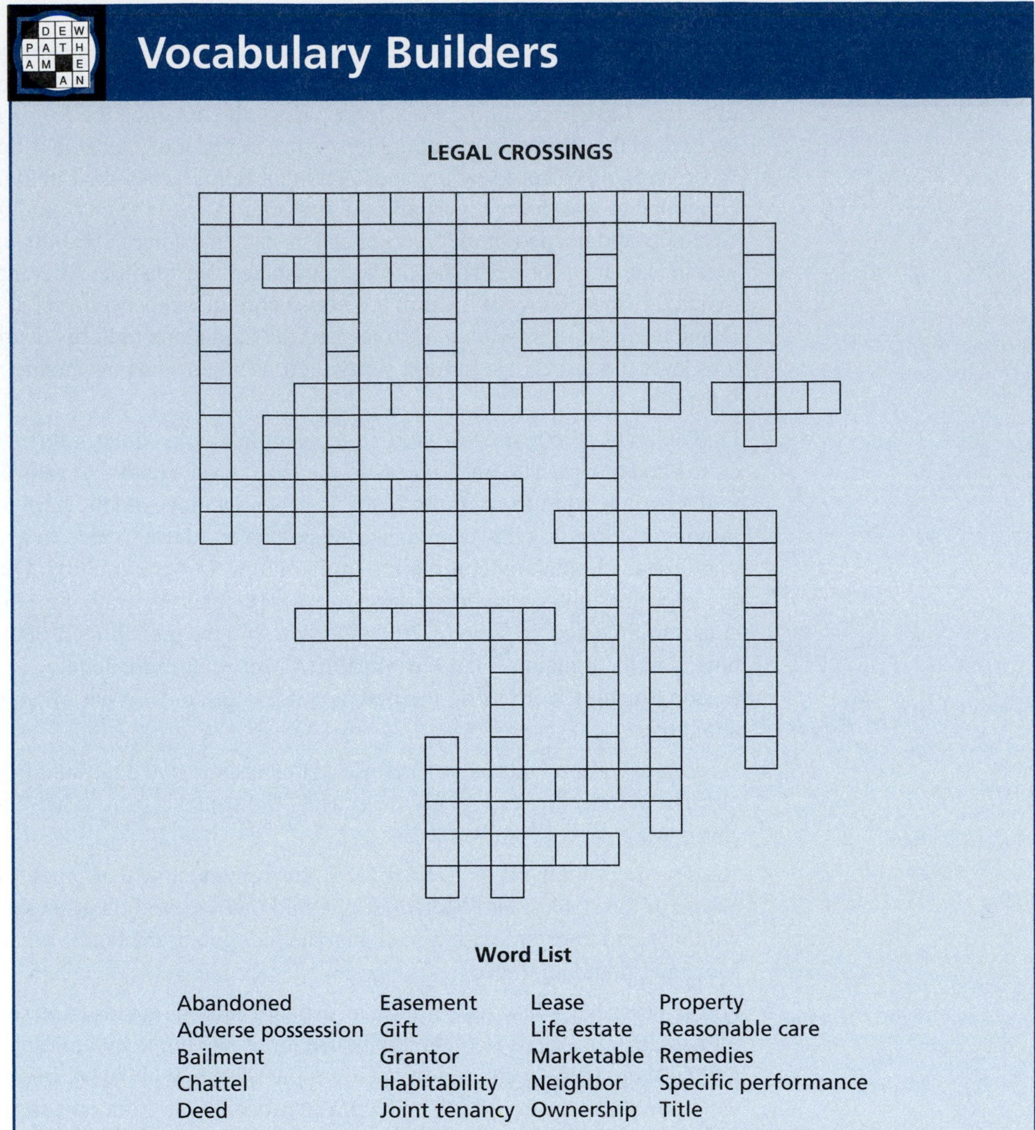
Vocabulary Builders
LEGAL CROSSINGS
Word List
Abandoned
Adverse possession
Bailment
Chattel
Deed
Easement
Gift
Grantor
Habitability
Joint tenancy
Lease
Life estate
Marketable
Neighbor
Ownership
Property
Reasonable care
Remedies
Specific performance
Title

Chapter 12

Wills and Estates

CHAPTER OBJECTIVES

After reading this chapter, you will be able to:

- List the common requirements of a valid will.
- Describe the kinds of gifts made in a will.
- Explain the probate process.
- Distinguish the types of intestate succession.
- Explain the purpose of a trust.

There are several ways in which property can be transferred between people. One of those ways is by inheritance. Upon a person's death, it is necessary to distribute whatever property was owned by that person at the time of death to another person or persons. Sometimes, when students are asked if they have a will, a common response is something similar to "Why should I? I don't own anything!" It is only after they are pressed to describe what is in their house or apartment, whether they have a cherished piece of jewelry from a grandparent, or even simply how they got to school that day that they are convinced that everyone has the need to decide precisely what should happen to their property upon their death. Even if it seems that the person owned nothing at death, in reality there is always some asset or possession for which its legal distribution will need to be ascertained. More importantly, the will serves other purposes beyond simply listing the distribution, or transfer, of tangible things. This chapter will discuss the use of both wills and trusts to distribute property. You will learn the typical requirements for a valid will, the reasons why a will may be challenged, and finally what happens when a person dies without a will.

ESTATE DISTRIBUTION

estate
The compilation of all a deceased's assets and debts.

testate
The state of having died with a valid will.

intestate
The state of having died without a will.

escheat
To pass property to the state, as is done with the assets of a person who dies without a will and without heirs.

probate
The court process of determining will validity, settling estate debts, and distributing assets.

The compilation of all a deceased's possessions and assets, along with his outstanding debts, is referred to as the **estate.** The settlement of the distribution of this estate depends on whether the transfer of the deceased's property will be testate or intestate.

Transferring property upon death can be accomplished by a will, and thus if a person dies with a valid will, then it is said that she died **testate.** Conversely, if a person dies **intestate**—without a will—then the method of dividing up the assets is done according to the relevant state statute. If a person dies intestate, with no identifiable surviving relatives, then his property transfers to the state. In this case, it is said that property **escheats,** or passes, to the state.

The process of distributing an estate's assets includes paying off the debts of the deceased as well as settling the division of assets, and this entire process is called **probate.** A specific division of our legal system exists for the purpose of administering the deceased's estates, and these probate courts, established in most states as a separate division of the civil courts, undertake the tasks of ensuring that the accounting and distribution is properly done, regardless of whether the person died testate or intestate. Where a person dies intestate, the court must ensure that the rules of intestate succession are followed.

WILLS

will
A document representing the formal declaration of a person's wishes for the manner and distribution of his or her property upon death.

testator/testatrix
The person who writes a will.

A **will** may be defined as the instrument representing a formal declaration of a person's wishes in the manner and distribution of her property upon her death. The person who writes the will is referred to as the **testator** or **testatrix.** In order to ensure that the will is valid, it is necessary for the person making the will to adhere to the exact rules dictated by her state of residence in terms of procedure and requirements to make a will. Although the requirements may vary from state to state, there are generally certain common factors in nearly all states. Be certain to consult your state statute for the specific rules and procedures.

Requirement of a Writing

First, the will typically must be in writing. Some states may still permit oral wills to be valid, provided that certain circumstances existed at the time of the oral will. For example, in the few states that may allow oral wills, it must be shown that the deceased believed death to be imminent, and in fact did die shortly after his declaration, and second, that the witnesses who heard his dying declaration were not substantially affected by the terms of his will. That is, the witnesses ought to be totally disinterested parties who did not stand to inherit under the oral will. Again, oral wills are not common, and paralegals should be certain to verify whether their state permits this verbal declaration to constitute a valid will. The rationale for disallowing oral wills is primarily common sense—there is no verification or proof that the verbal declarations were actually made nor that the professed statements truly reflected the intent of the deceased.

holographic will
A will entirely written and signed by the testator in that person's own handwriting.

nuncupative will
An oral will, usually made by the testator near death.

The written will may be either formal or informal, but again a few state statutes will specify what form this writing can take (see Figure 12.1 for a sample will). In general, the will should be typewritten. A will that is written by hand is called a **holographic will.** So long as this writing is signed by the person making the will, it is typically considered valid. It makes no difference on what the will is written or typed, so long as it is legible. Thus, the will may be composed on ordinary paper, a restaurant napkin, or the back of an envelope. A **nuncupative will** is a will that is not in writing and is declared by the testator as his or her will before witnesses. Where allowed, oral wills can usually be made only when the testator is in a last illness and near death.

The majority of states dictate that regardless if it is formal or informal, the will must be *signed* by the testator. Generally, this signature must come at the end of the document, so as to avoid any inference that later pages were added on after the original will had been signed. In addition, at the time of signing the document, the testator must *know* that the paper she is signing represents her will, her intent for the final distribution of her property. It will become obvious as this chapter progresses that such requirements, and the proof needed to establish that the requirements are met, only become a legal issue if someone is challenging the validity of the will at the time of the probate of the deceased's estate. For example, assume that Smedley dies testate and does not mention one of his three daughters, Loulou, by name in his will, leaving everything to his other two daughters, Endora and Glynda. The document purporting to be Smedley's will is presented to the court; it is possible that Loulou will challenge the document and assert that although it is Smedley's signature on the paper, in fact Smedley believed he was signing a lease agreement and not his will. If Loulou can prove that Smedley was deceived into thinking the paper was a lease, then the court will declare the will invalid.

Attestation Clause

attestation clause
The section of the will where the witnesses observe the act of the testator signing the will.

In addition, although state statutes vary, generally the will signing must be witnessed by at least two, sometimes three, disinterested people, and these witnesses must sign the document in each other's presence just after the testator has signed the will. When the witnesses sign the will, this is commonly called the **attestation clause.** This clause confirms that the witnesses have watched the testator sign the will in their presence and in the presence of each other, and they attest to the fact that the testator signed the document of her own free will. As wills generally contain more than one page, it is customary for the total number of pages to be noted on the signature page of the will, as well as having both the testator and the witnesses add their initials to the bottom of each page of the document. This ensures that later claims of added provisions or amended pages will not be substantiated.

The Uniform Probate Code, adopted in many jurisdictions, provides that any writing in existence when a will is executed may be incorporated by reference if the language of the will

FIGURE 12.1 Sample Will

LAST WILL AND TESTAMENT

This is the last will and testament of Romeo Montague, Squire, of 123 Castle Way in the City of Verona, California.

I hereby revoke all former wills and other testamentary dispositions by me at any time heretofore made and declare this to be and contain my last will and testament.

I nominate and appoint my wife, Juliet, of 123 Castle Way in the City of Verona, California, to be the sole executor and trustee of this my last will and testament, and I hereinafter refer to her as my trustee. In the event that Juliet shall be unable or unwilling for any reason whatsoever to act as my executor, I then appoint my cousin, Henry Montague of 125 Castle Way in the City of Verona, California, as executor and trustee of this last will and testament.

I give, devise, and bequeath all my estate, both real and personal, of every nature and kind and wheresoever located, including any property over which I may have a general power of appointment, to my wife, Juliet, if she survives me for a period of 30 days, for her own use absolutely.

If my said wife should predecease me, or die within a period of 30 days following my death, I give, devise, and bequeath all my estate, both real and personal, of every nature and kind and wheresoever located, to my Trustees to hold upon the following trusts:

a) to use their discretion in the realization of my estate, with power to my trustee to sell, call in and convert into money any part of my estate not consisting of money at such time or times, in such manner and upon such terms, and either for cash or credit as my said trustee in their discretion may decide upon as they may think best, and I hereby declare that my said trustee may retain any portion of my estate in the form in which it may be at my death for such length of time as my said trustee may in their discretion seem advisable, and my trustee shall not be held responsible for any loss that may happen to my estate by reason of their so doing.
b) to pay out of the capital of my general estate my just debts, funeral and testamentary expenses, and all succession duties and inheritance and death taxes, whether imposed by or pursuant to the law of this state or any jurisdiction whatsoever, that may be payable in connection with an insurance on my life or any gift or benefit given by me either in my lifetime or by survivorship or by this will.
c) to divide the rest and residue of my estate into equal shares, to be transferred and distributed equally among the following persons:
   1) My niece, Ophelia.
   2) My nephew, Henry.

If one of my above-named beneficiaries shall predecease me, then the equal share set apart for that deceased beneficiary shall instead be distributed to his or her descendants, equally share and share alike. If one of my above-named beneficiaries shall predecease me leaving no descendants surviving, then the equal share set apart for that deceased beneficiary shall be distributed to my other beneficiary, or if my other beneficiary has predeceased me, then to his or her descendants, equally share and share alike.

In witness whereof, I have hereunto set my hand to this and the preceding page at Verona, California, this 5th day of May, 2007.

Signed,

Romeo Montague

Romeo Montague

CASE IN POINT

Supreme Court of Appeals of
West Virginia.
Albert E. RUBLE, Administrator C.T.A. of the Estate of Mary Alverta Green,
Petitioner Below, Appellee
v.
Albert E. RUBLE, Betty Ruble, Jacob Mullett, Jeremy Potter, Mark Cappillini,
Brenda Cappillini, Steven Brannon, Christine Brannon, Robert Declerico, and
Philip Richel c/o Herod Funeral Home, Maude Copeland, Donald Copeland, Kathryn
Evans, Betty Lou Green, James Green, Mary M. Bishop, Raymond Abernathy, Mary
Margaret Sullivan, Martha Lancaster, Inez Deeley, and All Unknown Heirs of the
Estate of Mary Alverta Green, Respondent Below, Appellants.
No. 32506.
Submitted June 8, 2005.
Decided July 6, 2005.
Dissenting Opinion of Justice Starcher July 13, 2005.

PER CURIAM:

This case is before this Court upon appeal of a final order of the Circuit Court of Monongalia County entered May 7, 2004. In that order, the circuit court held that the residuary clause of a holographic will [FN1] was valid and that the residue of the decedent's estate was to be distributed to the appellees and petitioners below, Albert and Betty Ruble (hereinafter "the Rubles"), in accordance with the terms of the holographic will. [FN2] The appellants and respondents below, Donald Copeland and Maude Copeland (hereinafter, "the Copelands"), appeal the order believing that the circuit court erred in denying their motion for a proper expert handwriting analysis of the decedent's will. After reviewing the facts of the case, the issues presented, and the relevant statutory and case law, this Court reverses the decision of the circuit court.

FN1. A holographic will is a document that is "wholly in the handwriting of the testator," and, unlike non-holographic wills, does not require the attesting signatures of two witnesses to be valid. *See* W.Va.Code § 41-1-3 (1982); *see generally, In re Briggs' Estate,* 148 W.Va. 294, 134 S.E.2d 737 (1964).

FN2. A copy of the will in question is included in its entirety at the end of this opinion.

I.

FACTS

On September 15, 1999, Mary Alverta Green died in Monongalia County, West Virginia. On October 18, 1999, Albert E. Ruble was appointed Administrator C.T.A. of the estate of Ms. Green. On that same day, Mr. Ruble recorded Ms. Green's September 24, 1994, will in the Office of the Clerk of the County Commission of Monongalia County. Submitted with the will were the affidavits of two witnesses, Jerri S. Walls and Susan M. Johnson, verifying that they were acquainted with Ms. Green during her lifetime and were familiar with her handwriting and signature and that they believed the handwriting and signature on the holographic will was that of Ms. Green. Mr. Ruble and his wife Betty Ruble were also listed as potential beneficiaries with regard to a residuary clause contained in the final paragraph of the will.

On November 16, 2000, Mr. Ruble filed a Petition for Declaratory Judgment asking the circuit court to answer several questions regarding the validity and interpretation of the holographic will. Following a January 19, 2001, hearing, the circuit court entered an order on February 2, 2001, holding that the specific bequests set forth in the holographic will of Ms. Green were valid and immediately payable. Those specific bequests included: $5,000.00 for Jacob Mullett "for personal services during illness;" $5,000.00 to the Herod Funeral Home in Pt. Marion, Pennsylvania, for funeral expenses; and $500.00 each to the decedent's "caring neighbors," Mark Cappellini, Brenda Cappellini, Steve Brannon, Christine Brannon, Jeremy Potter, and Robert DeClerico. Those specific bequests are not the subject of this appeal.

Within that same order, the circuit court ordered Mr. Ruble to serve all ascertainable descendants of Ms. Green, thereby giving them notice of the pending action and giving them an opportunity to take part in a hearing to determine the validity of the residuary clause of Ms. Green's holographic will. On February 2, 2001, an Amended Petition for Declaratory Judgment was filed incorporating the circuit court's ruling and mailed to all ascertainable heirs. On March 8, 2001, a hearing was held to address the validity of the residuary clause.

The issue in question surrounds the last paragraph of Ms. Green's will which provides:

> I appoint the Huntington Bank as my administrator to hold monies not designated in a trust fund to pay all bills at 527 Martin for the heirs. Also in case of dire need they be alloted (sic) withdrawals as deemed nec. by the Adm.

Written under this paragraph with an arrow clearly connected to the word "heirs" in the above paragraph is the following designation: "Albert & Betty Ruble, 617 Elmina St. Morgantown." The issue before the circuit court was whether the above-quoted paragraph, combined with the designation of the Rubles, was sufficient to dispose of the residue of the estate and, if so, who was to receive the residue.

Maude Copeland and Donald Copeland, cousins of Ms. Green, argued that they along with several other heirs, should have been determined to be the proper distributees of the residue of Ms. Green's estate and therefore should have received such apportionments in accordance with the State's distribution statute. On May 7, 2004, however, the circuit court ruled that the residuary clause in the will was valid as to the Rubles and ordered that the residue of Ms. Green's estate be accordingly distributed to the Rubles. In doing so, the circuit court denied the Copelands' motion for a handwriting analysis by a handwriting expert of Ms. Green's will. The circuit court found that at the time of Ms. Green's death she was not close to any of her extended family, but that she had a close and warm relationship with her neighbors and friends, the Rubles, who provided her with care and companionship. This appeal followed.

III.

DISCUSSION

[2][3] We begin our review in this appeal with the Copelands' argument that the requirements of establishing a holographic will were not met in full in this case because the modified portion of Ms. Green's will was not sufficiently proven to have been in her own handwriting. The Copelands, however, do not dispute that holographic wills are permitted under West Virginia law as long as they are in compliance with the requirements of West Virginia Code § 41-1-3 (1923). [FN3] Moreover, "'[t]estamentary intent and a written instrument, executed in the manner provided by [W.Va.Code § 41-1- 3], existing concurrently, are essential to the creation of a valid will.' Syl. pt. 1, *Black v. Maxwell,* 131 W.Va. 247, 46 S.E.2d 804 (1948)." Syllabus Point 3, *Stevens v. Casdorph,* 203 W.Va. 450, 508 S.E.2d 610 (1998).

> FN3. W.Va.Code § 41-1-3, provides:
>
> No will shall be valid unless it be in writing and signed by the testator, or by some other person in his presence and by his direction, in such manner as to make it manifest that the name is intended as a signature; and moreover, unless it be wholly in the handwriting of the testator, the signature shall be made or the will acknowledged by him in the presence of at least two competent witnesses, present at the same time; and such witnesses shall subscribe the will in the presence of the testator, and of each other, but no form of attestation shall be necessary.

The Copelands also agree with the Rubles that it is clear Ms. Green intended to change portions of her one page will by scratching through nine lines located in the middle portion of the will, which was followed by the notation, "Corrected by M. Green 1/19/95." The Copelands, however, point out that there is no such notation of a correction, a date, or Ms. Green's signature or initials, on the section of the will in question where she drew an arrow connecting the Rubles' names to the residuary clause. The Copelands argue that the Rubles were not mentioned anywhere else in the will and clearly are not Ms. Green's statutory heirs. They assert that had Ms. Green intended to leave the balance of her estate to someone other than her natural heirs, she would have specified such in the same manner as she did with the eight specifically named beneficiaries whose bequests were previously ordered to be paid by the circuit court.

The Copelands believe this issue could have been resolved by a handwriting analysis conducted by a handwriting expert which was precluded by the circuit court. They assert that their motion was denied without explanation other than the circuit court's cursory conclusion that such analysis was not necessary because "the handwriting is wholly that of the deceased." They further believe a handwriting analysis was a reasonable request that would have provided the evidence necessary to make a full and informed ruling on the issue of the added notation surrounding Ms. Green's residuary clause.

Conversely, the Rubles contend that the Copelands' argument is presented completely out of context. They say that the action in the Circuit Court of Monongalia County was not a will contest. Instead, it was a declaratory judgment action requested by Attorney Raymond Frere as counsel for Albert E. Ruble in his capacity as the administrator of Ms. Green's estate. Mr. Ruble states that he remained neutral in that action and did not advocate for any particular interpretation of the holographic will. Moreover, the Rubles assert that the circuit court's order reflects an exhaustive analysis of the holographic will including consideration of the legal principles governing the validity and interpretation of holographic wills in the State of West Virginia.

The Rubles also maintain that the circuit court correctly denied the Copelands' motion for a handwriting analysis of Ms. Green's will. The Rubles say the Copelands only dispute the one line at the bottom of the will and admit that the remainder of the will was written by Ms. Green. Thus, the Rubles contend that the circuit judge, sitting as the trier of fact, obviously looked at the disputed line of handwriting, made his own comparison, and made an appropriate final determination of fact himself that the handwriting was that of Ms. Green.

[4][5] After fully reviewing the evidence, we believe that the circuit court erred in denying the Copelands' request for an expert handwriting analysis. Clearly, as we stated in Syllabus Point 8 of *In re Estate of Teubert,* 171 W.Va. 226, 298 S.E.2d 456 (1982), "[t]he law favors testacy over intestacy." Likewise, we have consistently held that decisions involving the construction of a will always begin with the recognition that: "The paramount principle in construing or giving effect to a will is that the intention of the testator prevails, unless it is contrary to some positive rule of law or principle of public policy." . . .

In *Hobbs v. Brenneman,* 94 W.Va. 320, 323, 118 S.E. 546, 549 (1923), we described the role of the judiciary in ascertaining the intention of the testator as follows:

> When the intention is ascertained from an examination of all its parts the problem is solved. The interpretation of a will is simply a judicial determination of what the testator intended; and the rules of interpretation and construction for that purpose formulated by the courts in the evolution of jurisprudence through the centuries are founded on reason and practical experience. It is wise to follow them, bearing in mind always that the intention is the guiding star, and when that is clear from a study of the will in its entirety, any arbitrary rule, however ancient and sacrosanct, applicable to any of its parts, must yield to the clear intention.

[6][7][8] Furthermore, in Syllabus Point 7 of *Weiss v. Soto,* 142 W.Va. 783, 98 S.E.2d 727 (1957), we held that: "In construing a will the intention must be ascertained from the words used by the testator, considered in light of the language of the entire will and the circumstances surrounding the testator when he made his will." We have explained that: "'Where a will is made it is

presumed that the testator intended to dispose of his whole estate, and such presumption should prevail unless the contrary shall plainly appear.' Moreover, "Where words are used in a will in a context which renders them doubtful or meaningless, they may be substituted by other words, if such substitution will carry into operation the real intention of the testator as expressed in the will, considered as a whole and read in the light of the attending circumstances." Syllabus Point 2, *In re Conley,* 122 W.Va. 559, 12 S.E.2d 49 (1940).

[9][10] More recently, in Syllabus Point 6, *Painter v. Coleman,* 211 W.Va. 451, 566 S.E.2d 588 (2002), this Court wrote that, "[i]n construing a will, effect must be given to every word of the will, if any sensible meaning can be assigned to it not inconsistent with the general intention of the whole will taken together. Words are not to be changed or rejected unless they manifestly conflict with the plain intention of the testator, or unless they are absurd, unintelligible or unmeaning, for want of any subject to which they can be applied." In Syllabus Point 2 of *Charleston Nat. Bank v. Thru the Bible Radio Network,* 203 W.Va. 345, 507 S.E.2d 708 (1998), we also explained: "'W.Va.Code, 41-1-3, provides that holographic wills are valid in this State if they are wholly in the handwriting of the testator and signed. The third and final requirement for a valid holographic will in our jurisdiction is that the writing must evidence a testamentary intent.' Syl. pt. 1, *In re Estate of Teubert,* 171 W.Va. 226, 298 S.E.2d 456 (1982)." 'Where a holographic will contains words not in the handwriting of the testator, such words may be stricken if the remaining portions of the will constitute a valid holographic will.' Syl. Pt. 2, *In re Estate of Teubert,* 171 W.Va. 226, 298 S.E.2d 456 (1982).

BOOK 98 PAGE 480

Sept. 24, 1994

"Last Will and Testament"

I, Mary Alverta Green, do hereby declare this document to be my will. This day Sat., Sept 24, 1994 being of sound mind,

~~I bequeath my real estate at 527 Martin~~ ~~Morgantown as follows:~~ [illegible]

corrected by M. Green 1/19/95

Monetary not designated on CD's to be alloted as follows: $5000.00 to Jacob Mullett 563 Martin St. City (for personal services during illness. $500. to Jeremy Potter (Jacob stepson) $500. ea to my caring neighbors, Mark + Brenda Cappellini, Steve + Christine Branson, Robert De Clerico. Funeral $5000 IN A CD to Philip Riehl % Herod Funeral Home, Pt Marion Pa.

I appoint the Huntington Bank as my administrator to hold monies not designated in a trust fund to pay all bills at 527 Martin for the heirs. Also in case of dire need they be alloted withdrawals as deemed nec. by the Adm.

Mary Alverta Green

Albert + Betty Ruble, 601 Preston St. Morgantown

In this case, neither party to this action contests the validity of Ms. Green's holographic will. The controversy centers completely around the final paragraph of Ms. Green's will which contains the residuary clause. Within that clause the word "heirs" is connected by an arrow to the notation "Albert & Betty Ruble, 617 Elmina St. Morgantown." The issue before the circuit court was whether the above-quoted paragraph combined with the designation of the Rubles, was sufficient to dispose of the residue of Ms. Green's estate and, if so, who was to receive the residue. The circuit judge wrote that he had "thoroughly read and studied the holographic will . . . and carefully examined and compared the handwriting [and that] from its review, the Court does not find it necessary to authorize any form of handwriting analysis." We disagree.

We believe that there was not sufficient evidence before the circuit court to prove that the modification to the bottom of the holographic will was in fact in Ms. Green's handwriting. We have reviewed Ms. Green's will and can only conclude that a proper expert handwriting analysis of the disputed portion was a reasonable request and should have been granted by the circuit court. We have recognized that there are often complications in ascertaining the validity of a will, particularly that of a holographic will, and in light of the fact that the residue of Ms. Green's estate rests entirely on the validity of this one short notation, the Copelands should have been given the opportunity to develop the evidence fully.

Given the specific facts of this case, we believe that the benefit of the opinion of persons who by training and experience are experts in dealing with the use of pen or pencil by another may have led to a more careful and informed result. The Copelands, therefore, should have had the opportunity to present expert testimony to test the genuineness of the notation in question. The testimony from persons of such skill commonly has been used as evidence in assisting courts and juries throughout the world in arriving at correct and accurate conclusions when presented with contested writings. Accordingly, it stands to reason that judges and juries should have the benefit of the opinions of expert witnesses possessing the peculiar skill in the department to which such questions relate. Thus, we are of the opinion that such testimony was desirable and admissible in this case and that the court below erred in denying the Copelands' motion.

Consequently, we order that this case be sent back to the Circuit Court of Monongalia County for a new hearing surrounding the issue of the residuary clause and the validity of the handwriting of the notation, "Albert & Betty Ruble, 617 Elmina St. Morgantown." We further order that the circuit court allow the Copelands, the Rubles, or both parties, to present evidence from expert witnesses with regard to the handwriting of that specific notation in Ms. Green's will.

. . .

IV.

CONCLUSION

For the reasons set forth above, the May 7, 2004, final order of the Circuit Court of Monongalia County is reversed. We also remand the matter to the Circuit Court of Monongalia County for further proceedings consistent with this opinion.

Reversed and Remanded With Directions.

Justice STARCHER dissents and files a dissenting opinion.

STARCHER, J., dissenting:

(Filed July 13, 2005)

The majority reversed this case by setting aside an experienced trial judge's evidentiary ruling, when the judge was sitting as the trier of the facts. Judge Stone found that a questioned notation in Mary Alverta Green's holographic will leaving the residuary of her estate to "Albert & Betty Ruble, 617 Elmina St, Morgantown" was Ms. Green's handwriting and therefore a valid portion of her will. This Court should have given deference to Judge Stone's years of experience as a trial judge, and not have reversed the case.

In this case, the trial judge compared the contested writing with writing to which the parties agreed as being that of Ms. Green. When a writing that has been admitted or proved to be that of the writer is available, it can be used as a standard of comparison by the trier of fact in making a determination of the authenticity of a contested writing, with or without the use of expert testimony. *Young v. Wheby,* 126 W.Va. 741, 30 S.E.2d 6 (1944). Ultimately, it is the trier of fact that determines the authenticity of disputed handwriting. *W.Va. Code,* 57-2-1 (1981).

The appellants failed to employ a handwriting expert during the proceedings below. The appellants allowed the trial judge to analyze the writing without the aid of an expert. Then, when receiving an adverse ruling, they appealed to this Court.

The majority opinion allows the appellants an undeserved second chance at making their case. Accordingly, I dissent.

Source: *Ruble v. Ruble,* 619 S.E.2d 226 (St. Paul, MN: Thomson West). Reprinted with permission from Westlaw.

manifests this intent and describes the writing sufficiently to permit its identification. Some states though have rejected the doctrine of incorporation by reference, stating that an unattested paper that is of a testamentary nature cannot be taken as part of a will even though referred to by that instrument.

Testamentary Capacity

testamentary capacity
The ability to understand and have the legal capacity to make a will.

Lastly, one of the most important requirements of a valid will is that the testator, at the time of signing, had **testamentary capacity** to make a will. In the reading of wills in television shows and movies, one often hears, "I, Testator, being of sound mind and memory, do hereby make and declare this to be my last will and testament . . ." In essence, this phrase is intended to represent that the testator had the intent to make a will and understood its significance.

CASE IN POINT

Court of Appeals of Ohio,
Seventh District, Monroe County.
ESTATE OF SNELL, Appellant,
v.
KILBURN, Exr., et al. Appellees.
Nos. 04 MO 16, 04 MO 17.
Decided Dec. 23, 2005.

DeGENARO, Judge.

¶ 1} These timely, consolidated appeals come for consideration upon the records in the trial court, the parties' briefs, and their oral arguments before this court. Plaintiff-appellant, Lanny Snell, appeals the decisions of the Monroe County Common Pleas Court, Probate Court Division, that granted summary judgment to defendant-appellee, Sharon Kilburn, as executor of the estate of Wayne Snell, on Lanny's will-contest action and dismissed his motion for a declaratory judgment to construe the will.

{¶ 2} Lanny argues that there were genuine issues of material fact as to whether Wayne Snell had testamentary capacity and whether the will was properly executed. However, the trial court properly granted summary judgment since Lanny provided no evidence supporting his allegations.

{¶ 3} Lanny also argues that the trial court erred by construing the will within the will-contest action. He contends that the will was properly construed in the declaratory-judgment action and that the ****575** issue should have been res judicata in the will-contest action. However, the trial court properly dismissed Lanny's will-contest action since both it and the declaratory-judgment action raised identical issues of construction and he has a similar interest in the outcome of both claims. Moreover, the trial court properly construed the will to determine that Wayne intended to disinherit Lanny. For all these reasons, the trial court's decision is affirmed.

Facts

{¶ 4} In the 1950s and 1960s Wayne was married to Beulah Snell and the couple had one child, Lanny. When the Snells divorced in the mid-1960s, Beulah retained custody of Lanny and moved to Mount Vernon, Ohio. Lanny testified that he maintained a relationship with his father at all times over the years since the divorce. Wayne remained in Monroe County, Ohio, until his death on May 17, 2003.

{¶ 5} Wayne's will bequeathed the remainder of his property, both tangible and intangible, to Rosa Mehler, a woman whom Wayne had been dating since the 1970s. According to the will, if Mehler died before Wayne, then the remainder of Wayne's property, both tangible and intangible, was to go to Kilburn, Mehler's niece.

{¶ 6} Wayne's will was admitted to probate and Kilburn was named executor. On June 25, 2003, Lanny commenced a will-contest action in the Monroe County Probate Court, claiming the will was deficient in four ways: (1) undue influence, (2) lack of testamentary capacity, (3) improper execution, and (4) improper construction. Kilburn subsequently moved for summary judgment, which the trial court granted. Lanny timely appealed that decision.

{¶ 7} Several months after the trial court granted summary judgment in that action, Kilburn filed her final account of Wayne's estate. Snell commenced another action objecting to the final account and asking for declaratory judgment to construe the will. The trial court overruled these objections on the basis that the same issues had been raised or should have been raised during the summary-judgment proceedings. Lanny also timely appealed this decision. We have consolidated Lanny's two appeals.

. . .

Will Contest

[1][2] {¶ 10} In his first four assignments of error, Lanny challenges various aspects of the trial court's decision to grant summary judgment to Kilburn in the will-contest action. The purpose of a will contest is to contest the validity of a will admitted to probate. R.C. 2107.71. The admission of a will to probate is prima facie evidence of its execution, attestation, and validity. R.C. 2107.74. With regards to prima facie evidence, the Ohio Supreme Court has stated that "prima facie evidence is not conclusive." *Krischbaum v. Dillon* (1991), 58 Ohio St.3d 58, 64, 567 N.E.2d 1291. The admission of a will to probate thus creates a presumption as to the will's validity; however, this presumption is not irrebuttable. Id. In order to rebut the presumption of validity created when a will is admitted to probate, a contestant must "produce evidence which furnishes a reasonable basis for sustaining his claim." *Kata v. Second Natl. Bank* (1971), 26 Ohio St.2d 210, 55 O.O.2d 458, 271 N.E.2d 292, paragraph two of the syllabus.

Testamentary Capacity

{¶ 11} In his first assignment of error, Lanny argues:

{¶ 12} "The trial court erred as a matter of law by dismissing the will contest on summary judgment upon the grounds that there was no evidence that decedent Wayne Snell lacked testamentary capacity."

[3] {¶ 13} Lanny contends that Wayne could not have had testamentary capacity when signing his will since there is no indication that he considered including his son as a beneficiary under the will. Without the requisite testamentary capacity, Lanny argues that the will is invalid.

[4][5] {¶ 14} "Testamentary capacity exists when the testator has sufficient mind and memory: First, to understand the nature of the business in which he is engaged; Second, to comprehend generally the nature and extent of his property; Third, to hold in his mind the names and identity of those who have natural claims upon his bounty; Fourth, [and] to be able to appreciate his relation to the members of his family." *Birman v. Sproat* (1988), 47 Ohio App.3d 65, 67–68, 546 N.E.2d 1354, citing *Niemes v. Niemes* (1917), 97 Ohio St. 145, 119 N.E. 503. The burden

of proof in determining testamentary capacity is on the party contesting the will. *Kennedy v. Walcutt* (1928), 118 Ohio St. 442, 161 N.E. 336, paragraph six of the syllabus.

{¶ 15} Lanny relies on *Springer v. Lee* (May 2, 1996), 3rd Dist. No. 5-95- 42, 1996 WL 223699, for the proposition that a genuine issue of material fact is created when a testator does not mention the names of the heirs of his body when executing a will. In *Springer,* the appellant, the son of the decedent, filed a will-contest action against the executor of the estate. The executor subsequently filed a motion for summary judgment. The appellant asserted that the decedent lacked the testamentary capacity to execute the will. This assertion was based on evidence that the decedent's memory was failing at the time he executed his will.

{¶ 16} Evidence of the decedent's memory failure came from two places. First, the appellee testified as to conversations he had had with the decedent about funeral arrangements. While the appellee stated that he believed the decedent to be of sound mind, his other testimony suggested otherwise. The appellee testified that during the funeral arrangement conversations, the decedent indicated to him only that he had a sister. No mention was made of the decedent's son or of numerous other siblings. Furthermore, the decedent also failed to inform the appellee that he had a number of grandchildren and great-grandchildren. The second piece of evidence presented was the decedent's form for funeral arrangements. In filling out this form, the decedent gave incorrect information about his date of birth, place of birth, and mother's name. After reviewing this evidence, the executor's motion for summary judgment was granted.

{¶ 17} On appeal, the appellant argued that the trial court improperly granted summary judgment on the issue of testamentary capacity. The court of appeals concluded that the decedent's failure to mention his son created an issue of fact under the *Niemes* test.

{¶ 18} This case is distinguishable from *Springer* because Kilburn introduced evidence showing that Wayne did, in fact, have testamentary capacity at the time he executed his will. Kilburn introduced the affidavits of three witnesses, Janet Valkovic, Ruth Valkovic, and Wayne's attorney, James W. Peters, each of whom averred that they believed Wayne to be of sound mind at the time he executed the will. Lanny offered no evidence contradicting the affidavits of these witnesses.

{¶ 19} Because Kilburn introduced evidence demonstrating Wayne's testamentary capacity, this case is similar to *Martin v. Dew,* 10th Dist. No. 03AP-734, 2004-Ohio-2520, 2004 WL 1109562. In *Martin,* the decedent's cousin filed a will-contest action after the decedent's will was admitted into probate. The appellant claimed an interest in the will as a cousin of the decedent (i.e., a lineal descendent of decedent's paternal grandparents). In the complaint, the plaintiff alleged that the decedent lacked testamentary capacity. The defendant moved for summary judgment, providing affidavits and deposition testimony reflecting that the witnesses believed the decedent to be fully aware of the nature and consequences of her actions on the day the will was executed. The trial court granted the defendants' motion for summary judgment.

{¶ 20} On appeal, the court held that "the evidence presented was insufficient to create a genuine issue of material fact as to whether [the] decedent lacked testamentary capacity" when she executed her will. Id. at ¶ 20. The court noted that "the only evidence in the record addressing the issue of [the] decedent's testamentary capacity at the time she executed her will was contained in the affidavits and deposition testimony of Gayton and his wife, and the affidavit of Dew." Id. Because the "appellant offered no evidence that [the] decedent was affected by dementia on the date she executed [her] will," the court determined that reasonable minds could come to only one conclusion. Id. at ¶ 20, 25. This reasoning was based on the fact that the "uncontradicted statements by the individuals who witnessed [the decedent] sign the will indicated [that] she * * * [had] testamentary capacity." Id. at ¶ 20.

{¶ 21} Given the evidence in this case, the trial court correctly concluded that Kilburn was entitled to summary judgment on this issue. In contrast to the testimony in *Springer,* the evidence in this case shows that Wayne was of sound mind when he executed his will. Lanny provided no evidence to the contrary, even within his own affidavit.

{¶ 22} Furthermore, Wayne's failure to mention his son's name is very different from the decedent's failure to do likewise in *Springer*. The decedent in *Springer* forgot to mention his son, grandchildren, and great-grandchildren while discussing funeral arrangements. Wayne did not mention his son while drafting and executing his will. This difference is important because the *Springer* decedent's failure was forgetful while Wayne's failure was intentional. Wayne executed four wills over a period of almost 22 years without ever mentioning his son.

{¶ 23} In this case, the evidence in the record demonstrates that there is not a genuine issue of material fact regarding Wayne's testamentary capacity at the time he executed his will. The trial court properly granted summary judgment on this issue. Wayne's first assignment of error is meritless.

Proper Execution of the Will

{¶ 24} In his second assignment of error, Lanny argues:

{¶ 25} "The trial court erred as a matter of law, by dismissing the will contest upon the grounds that Wayne Snell's will was properly executed according to law."

[6] {¶ 26} Lanny contends that the will was not properly attested to as required by R.C. 2107.03. That section provides:

{¶ 27} "Except oral wills, every last will and testament shall be in writing, but may be handwritten or typewritten. Such will shall be signed at the end by the party making it, or by some other person in such party's presence at his express direction, and be attested and subscribed in the presence of such party, by two or more competent witnesses, who saw the testator subscribe, or heard him acknowledge his signature."

{¶ 28} R.C. 2107.03 requires four things to create a valid will: (1) a written document, (2) signed at the end by the testator or the testator's agent, (3) in the presence of two witnesses, (4) who must observe the testator's signature or hear him acknowledge his signature. It is important to remember that in order to overcome the presumed validity of a will admitted to probate, the contestant in a will contest action must "produce evidence which furnishes a reasonable basis for sustaining his claim." *Kata,* 26 Ohio St.2d 210, 55 O.O.2d 458, 271 N.E.2d 292, paragraph two of the syllabus.

{¶ 29} In many ways, this case is similar to *In re Will of McGraw* (1967), 14 Ohio App.2d 87, 43 O.O.2d 207, 236 N.E.2d 684. In *McGraw,* a will was drafted by an attorney in a hospital room, during the last illness of the testator. The will bore an attestation clause, the testator's signature, and the signatures of two witnesses, one of which was the attorney's. Both witnesses testified that they were present when the testator signed the will. The will was denied admittance to probate since the attorney had improperly witnessed the will.

{¶ 30} The proponent of the will appealed, alleging that the trial court erred when it failed to admit the will to probate. The appellate court found that the will met the statutory requirements and should have been admitted to probate for three reasons. It first noted that the fact that the will was drawn by the attorney who was present at its execution was strong presumptive evidence that the execution of the will was regular. Id. at 89, 43 O.O.2d 207, 236 N.E.2d 684. It held that this presumption of due execution could be overcome only by other evidence, but not by a mere absence of evidence. Id. Finally, it relied on the fact that the attestation clause which recited compliance with all statutory requirements for the valid execution of the will. Id.

{¶ 31} Here, Wayne's will was similarly executed. It was drafted by the attorney who was present at its execution; the will was regular on its face and, therefore, was entitled to a presumption of proper execution; and the attestation clause was signed by two witnesses and recited compliance with the statutory requirements. Finally, the witnesses all signed affidavits stating that the will was properly executed. Lanny offered no evidence contradicting this evidence.

{¶ 32} Nevertheless, Lanny contends that the witnesses did not properly attest to the will since the attestation clause in the decedent's will does not comply with the technical requirements of R.C. 2107.03. Specifically Lanny argues that the clause in question is on a separate sheet of paper, the sheet is not numbered or dated, and the sheet has no reference to this particular will.

{¶ 33} No Ohio case has directly addressed this issue, but we find an Oklahoma case on this issue to be persuasive. In *In re Dunlap's Will* (1922), 87 Okla. 95, 209 P. 651, the mother of a deceased man challenged the admission of a will to probate. One of the issues raised was whether the will was properly attested to. The evidence showed that the will, including the signature of the testator, was entirely written on one sheet of paper, and the attestation clause and the signatures of the witnesses were on another sheet. There was not sufficient space on the first sheet of paper to include the attestation clause. The two sheets had been previously held together by a clipless fastener and were stapled at the time of trial. The will was admitted to probate over the widow's challenge, and appeal was taken all the way to the Oklahoma Supreme Court.

{¶ 34} The court held the separation of the will and the attestation clause to be immaterial. *Dunlap* at 652. The court's reasoning was based primarily on the fact that the statute did not forbid the use of separate sheets of paper or direct how they should be fastened together, nor did it require that the signature of the subscribing witnesses be upon the same sheet as the signature of the testator. Id. at 652. It was enough that the court could tell that the two sheets belonged together.

{¶ 35} Here, R.C. 2107.03 requires only that a will be attested to by two witnesses who saw the testator sign his name or heard him acknowledge his signature. There is no requirement that there be an actual attestation clause, that the signatures of the witnesses be on the same sheet as signature of the testator, that the pages be numbered, or that the attestation clause be dated. While these things would certainly entitle the will to a greater presumption of validity, the lack of them does not negate the presumption.

{¶ 36} Because Lanny has not met his burden of providing evidence to sustain his claim, and because Wayne's will complies with the statute, the trial court properly granted summary judgment to Kilburn on this issue. Lanny's second assignment of error is meritless.

. . .

Disinheritance of an Heir

{¶ 49} In Lanny's fourth assignment of error, he argues:

{¶ 50} "The trial court erred as a matter of law by failing to award Lanny Snell the remainder of his father's estate when his father failed to expressly disinherit him."

[13] {¶ 51} Lanny contends that Ohio courts should not allow a parent to disinherit a child without some kind of overwhelming evidence that the parent actually intended to do so. He contends that in order to have this type of overwhelming evidence, a parent must expressly state in the will that the parent intends to disinherit a child. According to Lanny, without this kind of express intent explicitly stated, courts should presume that a child inherits from a parent. Lanny's argument is not the law of Ohio.

[14][15][16] {¶ 52} It is a primary rule applicable to the construction of wills that the heir at law shall not be disinherited by conjecture, but only by express words or necessary implication. *Crane v. Doty's Exrs.* (1853), 1 Ohio St. 279, 283, 1853 WL 28. "That implication has been defined to be such a strong probability that an intention to the contrary cannot be supposed." Id. at 283. A testator cannot, by any words of exclusion used in his will, disinherit one of his lawful heirs, in respect to property not disposed of by that will. Id. at 283. "To allow a testator to leave his property undisposed of, and by will to control the course of descent and distribution, would be to allow him to repeal the law of the land." Id. at 283. However, it is important to note that Ohio law allows a testator to disinherit a child without specifically stating that he intends to disinherit that child. "[I]f [a] testator makes no mention of one of his children in his will and by such will disposes of all of his property, such child is as completely disinherited as if the testator had specifically so provided." *Birman v. Sproat* (1988), 47 Ohio App.3d 65, 69, 546 N.E.2d 1354.

{¶ 53} In *Birman,* the illegitimate daughter of a deceased man contested the execution and construction of his will. By will, the decedent made several small bequests and left the residue of his estate to his wife. The proponents of the will made a motion for summary judgment, and the motion was granted.

[17] {¶ 54} On appeal, the appellant argued that there is a presumption against disinheritance universally recognized by Ohio courts. The appellate court did not disagree with this argument. It did, however, hold that children, legitimate or not, can be completely disinherited by implication if a testator completely disposes of all his property by will. Id. at 69, 546 N.E.2d 1354. That disposition of property overcomes the presumption against disinheritance. Id.

{¶ 55} The facts in this case resemble those in *Birman*. Here, Wayne completely disposed of all his real and personal property. In the first clause of his will, Wayne stated: "I direct that all my just debts and funeral expenses be paid out of my estate as soon as practicable after the time of my decease." In the fourth clause of his will, Wayne stated, "In the event that Rosa A. Mehler, should predecease me, I give all the remainder of my property, tangible and intangible, of every kind, nature and description and wheresoever situated, which I may have or own, to Sharon Kilburn." Because Mehler predeceased Wayne, the remainder of all his property was to go to Kilburn after Wayne's debts were paid.

{¶ 56} In this case, Wayne clearly intended to disinherit Lanny. Wayne's will completely disposes of his property and makes no mention of his son. This disposition of his property overcomes the presumption against disinheritance. Accordingly, Lanny's fourth assignment of error is also meritless.

Conclusion

{¶ 57} In these cases, Lanny has challenged the validity of the will, how it is construed, and whether his father validly disinherited him. Lanny provided no evidence that his father lacked testamentary capacity when he executed his will. Moreover, the will is valid on its face since it has the testator's signature and was attested to by two witnesses. Additionally, the trial court had the authority to construe the will during the will-contest action and that construction had preclusive effect on Lanny's declaratory-judgment action. Finally, the words in Wayne's will show that he intended to disinherit Lanny and overcome the presumption against disinheritance. For all these reasons, the judgment of the probate court is affirmed.

Judgment affirmed.

Source: *Estate of Snell v. Kilburn,* 165 Ohio App.3d 352, 846 N.E.2d 572 (St. Paul, MN: Thomson West). Reprinted with permission from Westlaw.

Testamentary capacity generally involves two requirements. First, if the testator has legal capacity, it means that she is able to enter into legal contracts and thus has the mental capacity to understand that she is creating a valid, enforceable will. Legal capacity for contracts refers to being of a certain minimum age, according to state statute. In many states, this minimum age is 18. The person must have the ability, or capacity, to comprehend that he is executing a valid legal document. Second, testamentary capacity refers to the testator possessing a clear understanding of the value and extent of his whole estate. In other words, he must be able to appreciate the value of his assets and the effects of the provisions that distribute such assets to the named **beneficiaries,** the people who are named in the will to receive the testator's assets.

beneficiaries
The persons named in a will to receive the testator's assets.

CYBER TRIP

You might be interested in accessing this link to discover what information is available in the area of estate planning: www.estateplanninglinks.com.

Assume that Fred dies testate and has one million dollars in estate assets. Fred states in his will that he intends to divide his entire estate equally among his three beloved daughters. Fred leaves his castle to his daughter Pebbles, his six antique cars to his daughter Hanna, and his collection of sandpaper to his daughter Wilma. Assume that Fred never mentions in his will other significant assets such as three yachts and diamond rings. It is possible for Wilma, who otherwise inherits only sandpaper, to establish that Fred lacked testamentary capacity because he failed to evenly divide his assets and neglected to mention other assets of value. Wilma will contend that Fred failed to appreciate the value and extent of the assets in his estate.

Consider also a testator, Gandalf, who writes a will and leaves his collection of toothbrushes to his nephew, Frodo, and a box of canned tuna to his niece, Hermione. If Gandalf died with significant assets of value that are not noted in his will, it may be argued that the testator lacked the required mental capacity at the time of writing.

TYPES OF WILLS

mutual will
Joint wills executed by two or more persons.

Apart from the holographic and nuncupative wills discussed earlier, there are two other types of wills you may encounter as a paralegal in an estate planning firm. First, there is a **mutual will.** Mutual wills are those executed pursuant to an agreement between two or more persons to dispose of their property in a particular manner, each in consideration of the other. A mutual will consists of separate documents, involving more than one testator. When a mutual, or joint, will is executed, each person is bound to dispose of the property as agreed upon in each of their own wills. In creating a joint and mutual will, the testators are executing a contract to dispose of their property in a certain way. This contract prevents the surviving testator from disposing of the property by some other way than as contemplated by the joint will. The contract becomes irrevocable upon the death of the first testator. Thus, joint wills are not only testamentary but also contractual in nature. Upon the death of the first testator to die, the joint will is subject to probate as that specific testator's will. The same will is probated again upon the death of the surviving testator.

reciprocal will
Wills in which testators name each other as beneficiaries under similar plans.

Another kind of will is a **reciprocal will.** Reciprocal wills are when the testators name each other as beneficiaries under similar testamentary plans. The terms of the wills are reciprocal, meaning each person disposes of the property to the other person.

TYPES OF GIFTS BY WILL

bequest
Gift by will of personal property.

specific gift
A gift of a particular described item.

general gift
Gift of property that is not exactly identified, as in furniture.

residuary gift
Gift of the remaining property of an estate after expenses and specific gifts have been satisfied.

devise
A disposition of real property by will.

ademption
Failed bequest in a will because the property no longer exists.

Once it is established that the requirements of a will are met, the actual **bequests,** or gifts of personal property by will, are determined. There are three basic types of testamentary gifts: **specific, general,** and **residuary.** Specific gifts are exactly that—the testator names a particular item of personal property to be given to a designated beneficiary. For instance, Grandma Moses may want to be sure that her favorite niece, Loulou, receives her valuable wedding ring upon her death. So, rather than simply state, "I give my jewelry to my niece, Loulou," Grandma may avow, "I give my gold wedding ring to my niece, Loulou, and all my other jewelry to my niece, Marylou." In not specifically identifying the other pieces of her jewelry, this gift of jewelry is referred to as a general gift. A general gift is where the exact property is not identified, such as furniture or a sum of money. Lastly, residuary gifts are those in which the testator declares that any assets not definitively named thus far in her will are combined in one final bequest, as in: "All the rest, remainder and residue of my estate I leave to my uncle Boris." This means that once all creditors are paid and all specific and general gifts are distributed, anything left will be transferred to Boris. This may include gifts that for some reason have failed to be distributed according to the terms of the will.

Testators have the right to place conditions upon any transfers of property. For example, Herman may specify that "My niece, Marilyn, shall receive my antique automobile, only if Marilyn graduates from my alma mater, Transylvania College." At the time of Herman's death, Marilyn may have already graduated from a different university or Transylvania College may no longer exist. In this situation, the condition of the bequest has not been met, and therefore the gift shall not pass to Marilyn. Consider also the situation where Dean, a dedicated animal-rights lover, **devises,** or bequeaths "a thousand shares in Soy Bean Corporation to Sunshine City, to build a no-kill animal shelter at the corner of Main Street and First Avenue in Sunshine City." If it is impossible to build the shelter at that specific location, then the bequest will fail and the city will not receive the gift of the stock.

Another example of a bequest that cannot be satisfied according to the terms of the will is when the item no longer exists. At the time of writing his will, Herman owns a tractor, and declares, "I leave my tractor to my wife, Lily." At the time of Herman's death, the tractor no longer exists, having been destroyed by fire six months prior to Herman's death. In this situation, the bequest must fail and Lily receives nothing. This is referred to as the doctrine of **ademption.** Similarly, assume that Herman leaves 100 shares of Mortuary Casket Company to his son, Eddie. However, after writing his will, Herman sells the 100 shares of stock. Again, the gift is no longer in Herman's estate. Finally, assume that Herman devises a 1966 Champion Hearse to his uncle Fester. Six months prior to his death, Herman is forced to sell his beloved hearse to Igor, the local funeral home director, because he desperately needs the cash. Since the gift had already been sold, it is no longer part of his estate and uncle Fester gets nothing.

Now assume that Herman devises, "I give a thousand shares in Beechwood Casket Company to my son, Eddie." However, Eddie predeceases Herman, and the will is never changed. In this situation, the intended gift fails because the beneficiary is no longer living, and thus the thousand shares of stock fall into the residuary estate. The beneficiary designated in the residuary clause will receive the stock, along with any other failed bequests and items not specifically bequeathed elsewhere in the will.

You Be the Judge

In his will, Nigel left "my savings account at Fourth National Bank of Sunrise, Virginia, to my nephew, Todd." Two years after executing his will, Nigel moved to Illinois and closed his bank account in Virginia. He used the proceeds of that account to open a new account at the Commerce Bank of Illinois. Shortly thereafter, Nigel dies. What is the likely result if Todd seeks to collect the $150,000 that was in Nigel's account?

Eye on Ethics

You are a paralegal for an estate planning law firm. You typically assist your supervising attorney with the collection of decedent's assets, locating beneficiaries, and settling estate debts. A new client comes in to your office when the attorney is out of the office, wanting to write a will. What tasks are you able to undertake in the attorney's absence regarding this particular client? See the following Web site: www.legalethics.com.

Significant changes may occur between the time that the testator writes her will and the time of her death. There are specific rules that apply regarding altering a will or making a new will, in case of major changes.

SPECIAL ISSUES

From the time a will is written until the moment of the testator's death, the will may be revoked, amended, or altered at any time. Changes in life circumstances often dictate the necessity for revision or revocation of a will, and the enormity of those circumstances usually determines what the testator should do with the original will.

After writing a will, a testator may continue living for many years, during which time the assets in his possession might change, as well as the significant people in his life whom he originally intended to be beneficiaries of his estate upon his death. For example, it is not uncommon for a spouse to predecease the testator. If this happens, the testator may need to decide who will receive the gifts that were originally intended for the spouse. Likewise, the testator may remarry. Consider Fred's will, which in part states, "I leave my cars and stock to my wife, Wilma." If Fred divorces Wilma shortly after writing his will and never changes his will, might Wilma contest the will upon Fred's death, claiming that he intended her to receive that property, despite the fact that she is no longer his wife? If Fred subsequently marries Betty after his divorce, then might Betty contest the will to receive property previously bequeathed to a named former wife? Circumstances such as these are persuasive reasons why a testator should be certain that his will is always current as to intended beneficiaries as well as estate assets.

It may be preferable to revoke a will if there have been significant changes in the testator's life. A will can be revoked by certain acts of the testator, such as writing a paper that states that the will, dated on a specified date, is no longer valid. Alternatively, the testator may simply destroy all copies of the will. If a second will is executed at any time, then by operation of law, the first will is deemed revoked. In addition, it should be noted that in the preceding example of testator Fred, a divorce operates to revoke that part of the will giving the former spouse any property under the will, leaving the rest of the will intact and valid. Any time a subsequent will is drafted, keep in mind that all the state requirements for executing a valid will still apply. It may be necessary to state in any subsequent will that any prior wills executed before the date of the present will are specifically revoked, so as to avoid any possible legal issues.

codicil
A provision that amends or modifies an existing will.

Rather than revoke the entire will when minor circumstances change, a testator may prefer to execute a **codicil.** This is an independent legal document that specifically names the existing dated will, as well as the amendments to that prior document. Because the codicil operates as a part of the original will, and is read as one, all the requirements of executing a valid will still apply here. Once the codicil is signed by the testator and witnessed, it becomes incorporated into the original will, but the date of the will is now amended to reflect the new date of the codicil. It should be noted that simply deleting or crossing out provisions of an existing will do not effectively amend that will, which is why either a revocation or codicil is necessary to execute changes. Note that since virtually all wills can be word processed on a computer, the need for the execution of a codicil has become practically nonexistent, as it is a relatively simple matter to make an online change to an existing will and then execute that new will instead.

You Be the Judge

Nicholas recently died, leaving a will that had been originally typed and properly executed but which also contained several gifts that had been crossed out with a permanent marker. A new amount had been written above each of the typed provisions that had been crossed out. In addition, the original signatures in the attestation clause had been crossed out and both witnesses had re-signed and dated it. Discuss the validity of this modified will.

Sometimes a testator may not update her will, and the assets in her estate change dramatically over time. For example, assume that Jethro continues to live many years beyond the execution of his will, and in that time, his bank accounts are depleted due to simple living expenses. In this time, Jethro is also forced to sell his house and car in order to pay his bills. If he fails to update his will that had been executed 20 years prior to his death, the doctrine of **abatement** may apply. Where an estate is insufficient to pay the final debts of the testator, then all the bequests under the will may not be fulfilled, with unintended results.

abatement
Doctrine in which will bequests may fail due to insufficient estate funds at the time of testator's death.

For example, assume that Jethro gives specific gifts to his niece, Ellie Mae, and his nephew, Jed, in the amount of $5,000 cash. The residuary clause of his estate specifies that everything remaining in the estate goes to his favorite uncle Don. At the time of drafting his will, Jethro's estate was valued at a million dollars, and Jethro intended that nearly all of that go to Uncle Don. However, due to the circumstances outlined above, Jethro dies with $15,000 in his bank account. If he has $2,000 in debts, the creditors are paid first, followed by the specific gifts, that is the $10,000 to Ellie and Jed. As a result, Jethro's favorite uncle Don will end up with $3,000. Therefore, Jethro might have revised his will to ensure that only general gifts are made, or beneficiaries are changed, thus ensuring a more equal distribution of assets in case of financial difficulties.

Once the testator has died, the estate must be settled in order for debts to be paid, taxes collected, and assets distributed. This settlement process is referred to as probate.

PROBATING AN ESTATE

Nearly every state has a special division of the court system specifically assigned the duty of settling the estates of those who have died. If not, then the civil division of the court system in that state handles probating estates. The courts are charged with the responsibility of administering the estates and ensuring that the legal procedures contained in state statutes are properly followed. Typically, the testator would have named in his will the person he wants to handle the final affairs in winding up his estate. This person is called the **executor** or **executrix** or administrator of the estate. The executor may be represented by an attorney, on behalf of the estate, and may become necessary if the will is contested.

executor/ executrix
The administrator of the estate.

When the testator dies, the will is presented to the court that is probating the deceased's estate. The court oversees the executor who is responsible for paying final debts and taxes and distributing assets according to the terms of the will. Notices are sent to creditors and beneficiaries while an accounting is done of the estate. Hearings are scheduled in order to present creditor claims, pay such claims, and finally proceed with the distribution of estate assets. This probate process may take months or even years, depending on the size of the estate and whether there are any disputes. In some cases, the validity of a will may be challenged on various grounds, prolonging the settlement of the estate.

CONTESTED WILLS

Once a will is presented to the court for probate, the possibility arises that one or more individuals may contest the validity of that will. The person challenging the will has the burden of proving that the will is invalid, based upon several common legal grounds.

CASE IN POINT

Court of Appeals of Tennessee,
Eastern Section, at Knoxville.
In re ESTATE OF Kathleen Lee MEADE, Deceased,
L. Grady Lee,
v.
Helen Jo Gilliam.
No. E2003-02629-COA-R3-CV.
June 8, 2004 Session.
Aug. 30, 2004.
Permission to Appeal Denied by
Supreme Court Feb. 28, 2005.

HERSCHEL PICKENS FRANKS, P.J., delivered the opinion of the court, in which CHARLES D. SUSANO, JR., J., WILLIAM H. INMAN, Sr. J., joined.

OPINION

HERSCHEL PICKENS FRANKS, P.J.

A typewritten document and a handwritten document prepared later in time were offered for probate. The Trial Court rejected the handwritten document and admitted the typewritten document to probate as the Last Will and Testament of Deceased. On appeal, we reverse.

In this action, the issue before the Trial Court, as well as this Court, is which of two Wills was the last Will of the Testatrix, Kathleen Lee Meade, ("decedent"). Decedent was a widow with no children, who died on May 4, 2002, at age 79.

The petitioner Grady Lee, presented for probate a typewritten Will prepared by an attorney and executed on March 15, 2001. Lee, the brother of the decedent, was named as executor in the Will. Respondent, Jo Gilliam, niece of the testatrix, offered for probate a handwritten Will that she propounds as the decedent's last Will, executed subsequent to the typewritten Will. [FN1]

> FN1. Two other handwritten documents of similar intent, entitled Will, were found in Deceased's papers.

Following an evidentiary hearing, the Trial Court concluded the typewritten Will was the Last Will and Testament of decedent, and in his Opinion said:

> I think every witness testified the truth as they believed it at time . . . There's no doubt in my mind that what's been filed as Exhibit # 2, the so-called "handwritten will," was written by Decedent after the execution of Exhibit # 1, which was executed on the 5th day of March, 2001. No doubt in my mind at all. But that's not sufficient to answer the problem here. The document written in the Decedent's handwriting, there must be an intent that it be a will. And I find that it was not her intent for Exhibit # 2 to be her will. I find that her brother was not available due to his wife's illness at the time, to come at her beck and call like previously. That her niece here was at her beck and call and Jo Gilliam was the primary care giver in the last months of her life. And I have no doubt that she told Ms. Gilliam that she was going to leave things to her. And unconsciously she did a very cruel act here, I think, in hoping to keep someone taking care of her. Exhibit # 2 is found in Exhibit # 6 in a tablet in the kitchen drawer. The proof is that the Decedent, Ms. Meade, was very meticulous, a good business woman, very meticulous in everything she did . . . [s]he formed in her mind ahead of time what she wanted in the will before she went to the lawyer's office. She knew that she needed a good, valid will prepared, and she had prepared, was Exhibit # 1. I hold the Exhibit # 2 is something she used to show her niece to make sure her niece continued to take care of her but she never reached the point of adopting it as her will. Very strong circumstantial evidence of this, she would attempt, if she had intended for that to be a will to couch it in terms more like the attorney-prepared will. It was a thought she had but it never reached fruitation[sic] here, and for that reason I find that the Exhibit # 1 is the will controlling her estate and that Exhibit # 2 is not her will.

Exhibit # 2, as found by the Trial Court, is in the handwriting and signed by deceased.

It reads:

Will

> [1] Jo and Ron Gilliam, my (niece) & her husband said they would take care of me, and not put me in a rest home. They have said if they had to they would move in my home and take care of me.
>
> Grady Lee (brother) $20.00 and my car. Jo Gilliam (niece) & (Ron) husband the rest of my house & furniture except a few items.
>
> Cecil Lee (brother) the rest of my life ins. After burial is pd.
>
> Bertha Mae Cox (niece) mama's old sewing machine, pink wash bowl and pitcher (Xmas dishes), to Jo red ruby ring & diamond necklas[spelling?] ear rings.
>
> Jo Gilliam (niece) all my gold chains, lg. Diamond ring & holder.

Kimberly Dalton (niece) white luggage, sewing machine, pink iron, glasses, stone dishes, & pink crystal. Paul Revere stainless ware, punch bowl, & lg. dimon[spelling?] ring & band.

David Lee (nephew) rocking chair, luggage, camester [spelling?] & grand ma Lee's quilt. Leslie Tinter (great niece) blue safire [spelling] rg.

Gary Vicars (gardner) $500.00.

I'll divide the rest of my clothes & jewelry. I want my house to keep in the family & don't change the way it's brick. Just keep it up.

Kathleen (Lee) Meade.

The construction of wills is a question of law for the court. *Presley v. Hanks,* 782 S.W.2d 482, 487 (Tenn.Ct.App.1989). The validity of a will is a question of fact, as determined from all the evidence, intrinsic or extrinsic, as to whether the testatrix intended the writing to operate as a will. Tenn.Code Ann. § 32-4-107(a); *In re Estate of Cook,* 2002 WL 1034016 at * 2 (Tenn.Ct.App.2002), *citing, Scott v. Atkins,* 44 Tenn.App. 353, 314 S.W.2d 52, 56–56 (1957).

[2] The authenticity of the document offered here is not in dispute. The question before the Court is whether the decedent did, in fact, intend the holograph to be a final expression of her wishes that resulted in the revocation of the earlier typewritten will. (Prior will may be revoked expressly "or by inconsistency". Tenn.Code Ann. § 32-1-201(1)), or, as concluded by the Trial Court, whether it was mere notes and memoranda of an intent to make a formal will in the future.

[3] At the outset of our analysis, we note that it is immaterial whether a testatrix necessarily understands that by executing a particular document she is making a will, so long as the document demonstrates it was her clear intention to dispose of her property after her death, and the statutory formalities are satisfied. *Smith v. Smith,* 33 Tenn.App. 507, 232 S.W.2d 338, 341 (1949); *Carver v. Anthony,* 35 Tenn.App. 306, 245 S.W.2d 422, 424 (1951).

[4] A holographic will need not be dated or name an executor to be valid. *Nicley v. Nicley,* 38 Tenn.App. 472, 276 S.W.2d 497, 500 (1954); *Pulley,* 137 S.W.2d at 340. The statutory requirements for a holographic will are that the document's provisions be entirely in the testator's handwriting, and authenticated by 2 witnesses. *Tenn.Code Ann. § 32-1-105.* In this case, the parties have stipulated that the handwritten document is the decedent's handwriting and that the requirements of the statute are met.

[5][6][7][8][9][10][11] When the statutory requirements are met, a holographic will is of the same dignity as a will attested by subscribing witnesses. *Campbell v. Henley,* 172 Tenn. 135, 110 S.W.2d 329 (1937), and a properly proven holographic will supercede a formal will. *See, First Christian Church of Guthrie, Kentucky v. Moneypenny,* 59 Tenn.App. 229, 439 S.W.2d 620, 623 (1968). Testamentary intent "must be determined from what he has written and not from what it is supposed he intended." *Presley,* 782 S.W.2d at 488, *citing, Burdick v. Gilpin,* 205 Tenn. 94, 325 S.W.2d 547, 551 (1959); *First American Nat'l Bank v. Dewitt,* 511 S.W.2d 698, 706 (Tenn.1972).

> If the words of the will are plain and unambiguous the Court cannot, under the rules of construction, adopt a theory of some secret or reserved intention upon the part of the testator.
>
> . . .
>
> It is true the intention of the testator is to prevail, as in all cases of the construction of will. But this intention can only be learned from the words used in the will. Indeed, it may appear morally certain that the testator may have in his mind intended a certain thing; but, unless he has expressed that intention either by writing it into his will in express terms or by necessary implication and construction, it can not prevail. The question is not what the testator intended in his mind, but what is the meaning of his words and his intention, as shown by them?
>
> . . .
>
> The intention of the testator to be ascertained is not that which by inference may be presumed to have existed in his mind, but that which, by the words used in the will he has expressed.

City of Memphis v. Union Planters Nat'l Bank & Trust Co., 30 Tenn.App. 554, 208 S.W.2d 758, 764 (1947). *Also see, Richberg v. Robbins,* 33 Tenn.App. 66, 228 S.W.2d 1019, 1022 (1950).

In this case, the Trial Court imputed a secret intention to the mind of the testatrix which was not expressed in the Will itself. He characterized the holograph as a deception to coax the Respondent to care for her. The Trial Court erred when it delved into the "unconscious" design of the testatrix, which is nowhere expressed in any of the testamentary instruments. Moreover, there was nothing in the record to support the inference. The image of the testatrix that arises from the testimony portrays a gentle, generous aunt and sister, who was beloved by family. The proof is uncontroverted that respondent was raised with her aunt all of her life and they were very close, much like sisters. Nothing in the record suggests she took care of decedent grudgingly or needed to be bribed.

Even if the Trial Court's analysis were appropriate, such intent ascribed to the testatrix would not destroy the Will's validity:

> The law justly regards with peculiar tenderness the wills of the aged. The power to dispose of their property by will is often the only means which they possess of securing that attention and care for which they appeal in vain to human and natural affection. It then becomes the sole remaining staff of their declining years.

Pritchard on Wills and Administration of Estates, 5th ed., § 121, *citing, Van Huss v. Rainbolt,* 42 Tenn. 139 (Tenn.1865).

[12] The Trial Court's reference to the testatrix's prior Will prepared by an attorney in evaluating the holographic Will, was inappropriate. Whether a document meets the criteria for a testamentary instrument is derived from the document itself. The Trial Court cited as "very strong circumstantial evidence" that the decedent would have couched the language in more attorney-like terms, because she was a meticulous "business type" person, and in this context appellee argues that the decedent was a "business person" and "meticulous" and quite scrupulous in her affairs, and she would not have written a holograph but would have engaged legal counsel.

The evidence establishes the testatrix was a factory worker at Tennessee Eastman for 45 years and had an 8th grade education, and she did draft the document at issue without the benefit of counsel. Her concern about its validity was exhibited by her asking her great niece more than once if she thought the handwritten Will would be ok, and her great niece assured her that it was fine. While the holograph does not explicitly revoke the prior Will, decedent took several concrete actions that demonstrate revocation of the first Will. She wrote the second will and signed it and titled it a Will. She changed her life insurance beneficiary consistent with the second Will. She showed other persons where the Will was located, an act that would be unlikely if it were merely a draft or notes of future plans without present testamentary intent. She gave away some items consistent with the document's provisions before she died. There is no evidence that she stated she intended to make a will in the future or was just thinking about it. The evidence clearly preponderates that the handwritten will embodies the decedent's final wishes.

Finally, the widely disparate versions presented in evidence are reconcilable by noting that Petitioner's witnesses in large part testified to conversations with testatrix prior to or around the execution of the first Will. The record reveals that relatively little evidence more proximate to the testatrix' death supports the typewritten Will. Respondent's witnesses testified to testatrix' declarations that were uttered much closer to her death. In other words, the Trial Court's finding that all the witnesses were credible can be justified because the differing versions presented by the parties are not mutually exclusive, i.e., decedent did, at one time, have a typewritten will favoring the petitioner. Noting the sequencing of the conversations as related by the witnesses it can be seen that as time went on and testatrix became more ill, she changed her mind and took definite steps to implement that change. Of significance, Arlene Bear, who had no knowledge of the Will, was the only witness with no interest in the estate, and testified that a week before testatrix died, she told Bear that she wanted Gilliam to have her property, if she wasn't put in a nursing home.

For the foregoing reasons, we conclude that the handwritten Will was the Last Will and Testament of deceased, reverse the Judgment of the Trial Court, and remand, with the cost of the appeal assessed to the Estate of Kathleen Lee Meade.

Source: *Estate of Meade*, 156 S.W.3d 841 (St. Paul, MN: Thomson West). Reprinted with permission from Westlaw.

CYBER TRIP

In the area of wills and trusts, state law is important, as well as knowing procedural rules for probating estates. Access these Web sites for probate laws:
www.law.cornell.edu/uniform/probate.html
www.ca-probate.com/wills.htm

First, the will may be challenged based on the allegation that the testator lacked testamentary capacity. The mental capacity of the testator is judged based on her state of mind at the time she executed the will. For example, if the deceased specifies in the first paragraph of her will that she intends to divide her estate equally among her four children, and then subsequently fails to specifically name one of her four children in the will, only leaving specific bequests to three of the children, the fourth child might raise the presumption that the testator was not of sound mind and memory at the time of executing the will. The reasoning behind this argument is that if the testator doesn't even remember that she has four children, then the likelihood exists that other mistakes were made in the execution of the will.

Alternatively, a person may challenge a will's validity by attacking the premise that the testator voluntarily executed the will. Just like in contract law, a will may be declared invalid if the challenger to the document asserts that it was the product of duress or undue influence. The person making this challenge must demonstrate by substantial evidence surrounding the making of the will that the testator did not have free will but that one person who benefited greatly under the present will took advantage of the testator's physical or emotional weaknesses. The evidence must be clear and convincing that the testator was highly susceptible to the influence of a particular beneficiary who caused the will to benefit himself to the detriment of others. Mere suspicion or conjecture is not enough to support a finding that the testator was the victim of undue influence by one of the beneficiaries.

Finally, a will may be challenged on the basis of fraud. Once again, just like in a contract case, the allegation of fraud surmises that the testator was influenced to sign a document purporting to be something other than her will or that some other misleading statements were made that induced the testator to affix her signature to the document. The challenger must present clear evidence that the terms of the will are so inconsistent with the facts that the testator would not have reasonably executed such a will but for some false or misleading statements made by one of the beneficiaries.

TRUSTS

A trust is an arrangement in which property is transferred by one person to another for the benefit of a third party. The legal requirements for a trust are that (1) there is an intent to create a trust, (2) a trustee is named, (3) there is trust property, (4) there is at minimum one beneficiary of the trust, and (5) the trust has a purpose. For example, Tabitha conveys her house to Jones Bank to be held for the benefit of her sons. In this case, Jones Bank is the trustee. Trusts are created for a number of reasons, such as the desire to preserve assets, the protection of a disabled relative, or the desire to manage one's assets even after death. Generally, there are two kinds of trusts—testamentary trusts and living trusts.

A testamentary trust is a trust that is created by the will document and does not take effect until the grantor's death. The trustee for the trust may be named in the will. The advantage of establishing a trust is that in the event that there are minor children, their assets will then be managed by an independent trustee, acting on their behalf. The second type of trust, a living trust, is sometimes called an inter vivos trust, meaning between or among the living. It is created during the grantor's lifetime and is effective during the grantor's lifetime. Property conveyed in this way is not included in the grantor's estate upon death.

INTESTATE SUCCESSION

Up to this point, this chapter has focused on the deceased who dies with a will. However, a significant number of deceased die intestate, meaning without a will. The probate courts still serve an important role in ensuring that the debts of the deceased are paid. But, the courts' role is even more complex, as they are also charged with applying state statutes pertaining to intestate succession, in order to properly ascertain the rightful **heirs,** those individuals who inherit the property of the deceased. If no heirs can be found, then under most intestate statutes, the property escheats, passing to the state itself.

heirs
Persons entitled to receive property based on intestate succession.

STATUTORY RULES

By having a properly executed will, the testator is able to determine who shall receive his property upon death. However, in some cases, the deceased has failed to make a will and therefore has essentially entrusted this decision to the state in which he resides. Fortunately, it is not mere whim by which a deceased's assets are divided and distributed, as every state has intestacy statutes that govern how the property is transferred upon the person's death.

You should be careful to consult the statute in your state to familiarize yourself with intestate succession. Generally, basic rules are similar in every state. Statutes typically specify that once the net assets of the estate are determined, that property passes according to certain rules, with the spouse receiving the entire estate if there are no children of the deceased from a previous marriage. For example, if Darren dies intestate, survived by his wife, Samantha and their daughter Tabitha, then Samantha will receive the entire estate since Tabitha is the surviving issue of both of them. However, if Darren had a child, Mary, from a previous marriage, then Mary is entitled to one-half of the estate that is not considered to be marital property.

Depending upon who are the living relatives at the time of the person's death, intestate succession statutes generally progress from completely disposing of the entire estate to the spouse, then to surviving children equally, and the to other lineal heirs, such as grandchildren, parents, or siblings. For example, if Tabitha marries Dudley, and then she predeceases both her parents, then her parents will normally receive nothing under the rules of intestate succession.

In most statutes, special rules apply where the deceased is a murder victim. According to these statutes, if the person who murders the victim is a relative according to intestate succession rules, that person may not inherit property from the victim, pursuant to the murder disqualification rule. The reasoning is clear; the law does not favor those who might benefit from their own wrongdoing. In such cases, the rules state that property that ordinarily would pass to that wrongdoing heir will be disposed of as if the heir predeceased the victim.

In most statutes, there is a provision anticipating the death of a person with no surviving lineal heirs. In such situations, the rules state that the deceased's property escheats to the state, sometimes to be added to the capital of the state's school fund.

METHODS OF DISTRIBUTION

Generally, states have enacted two specific methods to determine the distribution of shares of an estate to surviving relatives. **Per capita distribution,** not commonly used,

RESEARCH THIS!

Locate the intestate succession statute for your state. Compare it to the succession statute of a neighboring state.

per capita distribution
The equal division of assets according to the number of surviving heirs with the nearest degree of kinship.

per stirpes distribution
The division of assets according to rights of representation.

requires that all surviving relatives are identified, and then the lineal descendants all share in the property *equally,* without any regard for their degree of relationship to the deceased. Under the *per capita* method, it is easy to see that inequities result. For example, assume that Mary dies intestate and the state law specifies a per capita distribution method. The state identifies 10 surviving lineal descendants, comprised of two siblings, one parent, three aunts, and four third cousins. Under this method, each person listed will receive a one-tenth share of the estate.

The second and most common method specified by state statutes is a **per stirpes distribution.** Here, the lineal descendants are identified, but the percentage of the estate that they receive is based upon their proximate relationship to the deceased. Hence, in the preceding example, the cousins would take nothing. However, if there is more than one relative in a specific category, such as five grandchildren, then these five individuals will receive an equal share, based on the percentage allocated to grandchildren as a whole. Assuming, though, that there is a surviving spouse, most statutes will not reach the level whereby a share of the estate will pass to grandchildren.

Because of the fact that many people die without a will, state statutes are quite clear as to the methods used in determining heirs and intestate succession. Any case law in this area clarifies questions pertaining to intestacy and generally arises in situations such as half-blood relationships or later-born children. However, as emphasized earlier, it is far preferable to not leave this important decision of property distribution to the state, but to instead depend on the individual's true wishes as expressed in a valid will.

A Day in the Life of a Real Paralegal

Probate and estate law provides ample opportunities for paralegals, as there is always a need for legal professionals in this field. One of the roles that a paralegal might assume in a law firm that practices in estate planning would be to prepare questionnaires and gather financial information of clients who desire to make a will. The paralegal is able to follow this process through from the very beginning and, under the supervision of the attorney, may draft the will based on the information gathered at the initial client interview stage. Moreover, paralegals serve an active role in handling the administrative details associated with probating the client's estate.

In many cases, settling an estate requires significant amounts of paperwork, tracking progress, locating beneficiaries and creditors, and preparing specific documents for probate. You may be asked to research the law in your state regarding such issues as the viability of nuncupative wills or the statute related to intestate succession. You may also work with the executor and attorney to prepare the estate accounting, as well as manage the estate assets. The responsibilities for an estate law paralegal are considerable, as following the timely progress of settling an estate requires an eye for detail and excellent management skills.

Summary

Probate and estates is an area of the law that is chiefly governed by state statutes. When a person dies, the case comes into one of two categories: testate or intestate. As noted, a valid will is the best method of ensuring that the deceased's wishes are fulfilled. Thus, this chapter reviewed the basic rules pertaining to making a valid will and the proper methods of changing that will. Specific situations pertaining to gifts under a will were discussed. In addition, the pitfalls related to challenging a will's validity were noted. If a will is declared invalid, or the person died intestate, then the rules regarding intestate succession are applied. In either case, the probate courts are entrusted with the responsibility of administering and supervising the proper settlement of the estates of persons recently deceased. This affects a significant segment of people, and thus the important role that the probate court serves in ensuring that the assets of an estate are efficiently distributed can be readily appreciated.

Key Terms

Abatement
Ademption
Attestation clause
Beneficiaries
Bequest
Codicil
Devise
Escheat
Estate
Executor/executrix
General gift
Heirs
Holographic will
Intestate
Mutual will
Noncupative will
Per capita distribution
Per stirpes distribution
Probate
Reciprocal will
Residuary gift
Specific gift
Testamentary capacity
Testate
Testator/testatrix
Will

Discussion Questions

1. Discuss whether you believe mutual wills are useful in preventing fraud.
2. What are the advantages of videotaping an oral will?
3. Locating heirs and beneficiaries is a common task for paralegals. Identify at least three sources on the Internet that will assist you in your search. Have a look at this Web site: www.heirsearch.com.
4. Explain the purposes of probating an estate rather than allowing family members to divide the deceased's assets on their own.
5. Given the fact that do-it-yourself will kits are readily available for purchase in many bookstores, do you think that paralegals should be able to draft wills for clients without supervision?

Exercises

1. Using the statute on intestate succession in your state, determine the distribution of the estates in the following situations:
   a. Blake dies with an estate valued at $100,000. He had no surviving wife but has two children, Amy and Beth. His mother, as well as two nephews, are still alive. How will his estate be divided?
   b. Mary dies with an estate valued at $80,000. She leaves behind two grandchildren, Cain and Abel, who are the children of her deceased son, Ben. She also has two grandchildren, Lila and Olivia, who are the children of her deceased stepdaughter, Frieda. How will Mary's estate be divided?

   c. John dies with an estate valued at $200,000. He is survived by his wife, Cindy. There are no surviving children, but there are two granddaughters, Susan and Beth, issue of his deceased daughter, Lorie. How will John's estate be divided?
   d. Rosa dies with an estate valued at $500,000. She is survived by just her three nephews, Huey, Dewey, and Louie.

2. Tony went on vacation in Europe. While he was on a train between Paris and Vienna, the train derailed, instantly killing him. In his will, Tony left his lakefront cottage to Maureen, who was his wife at the time he made the will two years ago, but they had divorced three months prior to the train accident. The residuary clause of his will leaves everything to his best friend, Oscar. Who is likely to inherit the cottage and why?
3. Hansel died, leaving a will with the following provisions:
   a. "to my wife, Gretel, my collection of coins and stamps;"
   b. "to my nephew Red, $100,000 to be used for his education;"
   c. "to my cousin Rapunzel, some of my paintings."

   Gretel predeceased Hansel. Hansel also has another nephew, Jack. Discuss the effect of each of these provisions in Hansel's will.
4. Christopher drafted his own will in his handwriting, designating that $50,000 be given to the Hundred Woods Charity and 20 bottles of Chateau Loire wine go to his best friend Ellen. The remainder of his estate was to be "divided among those of his relatives who are good people deserving financial assistance." What will be the effect of this will upon Christopher's death?
5. Alexandra was an eccentric old spinster who died, leaving a will that contained the following provisions:
   a. "$500 to each of my charming relatives;"
   b. $10,000 to the University of Coffee to be distributed among the fine students to be chosen at the discretion of the University president;"
   c. "my home in Smalltown to my niece Irene, so long as she does not marry until she is 40 years old."

   Discuss the effects of these provisions in Alexandra's will.

Vocabulary Builders

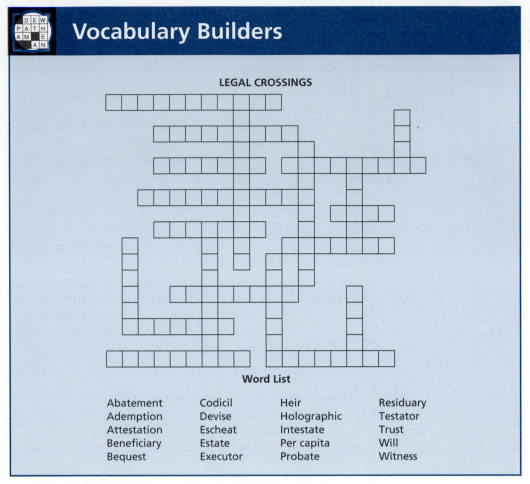

LEGAL CROSSINGS

Word List

Abatement	Codicil	Heir	Residuary
Ademption	Devise	Holographic	Testator
Attestation	Escheat	Intestate	Trust
Beneficiary	Estate	Per capita	Will
Bequest	Executor	Probate	Witness

Chapter 13

Family Law

CHAPTER OBJECTIVES

After reading this chapter, you will be able to:

- Explain the requirements of a valid marriage.
- Describe the common methods of terminating a marriage.
- Discuss the criteria used in awarding custody and support.
- Define key aspects of prenuptial agreements.
- Identify ethical considerations in domestic relations cases.

This chapter presents an overview of the legal principles commonly encountered in the substantive area referred to as "family law." Topics generally included in this area are marriage, dissolution of marriage, and the legal aspects of the parent-child relationship. Sometimes this substantive area is labeled "domestic relations." Within each subcategory of this topic are numerous issues that arise, including prenuptial agreements, child custody and support, adoption, and spousal abuse. This chapter will address the most common concepts related to the status of a family. Paralegals who work in this field will often discover that this is one area of the law that is never the same each day. There are many personal and emotional issues inherent in this area of the law, and consequently this area of practice requires diligence in separating the legal issues from the less tangible matters such as societal norms and the psychological facets of the situation.

Family law issues typically arise under state law, and therefore many states have separate domestic relations and juvenile law divisions in their court system. Although general legal principles may be identified in family law, you should take care to locate the applicable family law statutes in your state. In addition, many state and local bar associations have published guidelines in conjunction with the family law courts. You should consult these statutes and guidelines for your jurisdiction when reading this chapter, as the text material will focus on the uniform acts, as well as selected states' statutes, utilized here simply as examples of the law on a particular topic.

Because of the constant struggle of society to define a family unit, the law in this area is frequently changing. For example, as of the writing of this book, only two states—Vermont and Massachusetts—allow same-sex marriages, but this topic is being discussed in other states as well. Similarly, grandparents are seeking to establish visitation rights in some cases, and thus this is another evolving legal issue, which will be discussed later in this chapter. Examining the topic of family law from a historical perspective is helpful to an understanding of the rights and responsibilities that arise in this complex area.

HISTORICAL PERSPECTIVE

If you examine laws and trends in society against a historical background, it becomes readily apparent that the family unit has always been at the center of society. It was once considered that a bride was property that could be transferred from the bride's family to the groom, so long as an appropriate compensation, or dowry, was paid to the bride's family in advance of the marriage. Since women were customarily treated as property, they had very few legal rights regarding property, and even less rights when it came to spousal abuse. As society evolved, women gained a certain status, although the man was still treated as the head of the household for many legal purposes. In nineteenth century laws, courts recognized that an engagement, or promise to marry, was a contract, and therefore if the man backed out of the marriage, the woman had a cause of action for breach of contract. Today, family relationships have developed to the point that all parties are viewed on more equal terms. Changes in societal norms, and the resulting legislation, has led to redefining members of the family unit and a strengthening of the parent-child relationship. For example, it can no longer be assumed that the woman is automatically deemed the "preferred" parent granted custody of minor children, without regard to both parents' individual circumstances.

MARRIAGE

common law marriage
A form of marriage that is legally recognized in certain states, if the two people have been living together for a long period of time, have represented themselves as being married, and have the intent to be married.

Although there are many subsets of family law, the one concept that is the focus of most legal issues is marriage. A marriage is commonly defined as the legal union between a man and a woman, acquiring several legal rights and duties. Nearly all states have recognized that this union cannot legally be between two people of the same sex. The legal system does recognize that, with certain exceptions, everyone has the right to marry. In relying on common law cases, state statutes have explicitly set forth the other requirements that must be met in order to legally marry in the state. Restrictions on marriage are enforced by state requirements that the man and woman obtain a license to marry before the marriage can be legally recognized. In some states, parties can enter into a **common law marriage** which does not require a marriage license; however, as of this writing, only 14 states today recognize this type of marriage.

In order to obtain a marriage license, the following are typical regulations in all states:

CYBER TRIP

See the Web site www.familylaw-source.com. What kinds of information can be located on this site? Find your state and look for links to laws and guidelines in your jurisdiction.

1. The parties must be a man and a woman.
2. The parties must be of a certain age, typically 18 years of age, although this age restriction varies depending on whether it is a male or female.
3. The parties must be competent to marry, that is, capable of giving consent.
4. The parties must not be too closely related by blood to their spouse.
5. The parties may need some type of premarital medical testing such as blood tests.

consanguinity
The relationship between blood relatives, such as brothers and sisters.

solemnization
A formalization of a marriage, as in for example a marriage ceremony.

In considering the second requirement, keep in mind that every state statute varies as to the minimum legal age to give consent to marry; if one of the parties is too young, that party must obtain the consent of a parent to marry. In the third requirement listed, the state wants the assurance that both parties are entering into the marriage with a complete understanding of the nature and consequences of such a union. Therefore, mental incapacity may render a marriage invalid, as well as intoxication in certain situations. Fourth, states prohibit the persons from being too closely related by blood, otherwise referred to as **consanguinity** statutes. You should locate the relevant statute in your state, since some states permit marriage between first cousins or between step-relatives. If parties violate this state statute, they may be liable for criminal action involving incest. Finally, states typically require testing for AIDS or other blood tests to determine if either party possesses any certain communicable diseases noted in the statute or if there is evidence of incompatible blood types.

If the requirements to enter into a valid marriage are met, the parties must also demonstrate some formality or **solemnization** of the marriage, such as a marriage ceremony. This ceremony need not occur in a church, but may be held in any government office by an officer of the court or minister licensed to perform such ceremonies and recognize the parties' public acknowledgment of their union. The exception to this requirement of a solemnization of the marriage occurs in those few states that recognize common law marriages. In these situations, the parties cohabitate and hold themselves out to the public as husband and wife, but their marital relationship is informal and has not been solemnized, nor have the parties obtained a marriage license. Presently, there are just 13 states that recognize this type of marriage, and paralegals should consult their state statutes to determine whether this type of civil contract, without the normally required formalities, is legal in their state. Note that other states may recognize the validity of the common law marriage if the parties had entered into this marital relationship in a state that specifically allows such unions. However, keep in mind that some states may still not recognize a common law marriage, regardless of whether such a marriage was validly formed in a state where this is permissible.

Many state statutes specify other kinds of marriages, besides common law marriages, that are prohibited in that state. For example, most states will prohibit marriage between two people if one of the parties is still married and the dissolution of marriage decree in the prior marriage is not yet final. State statutes as well as established case law specify that a purported marriage between two living persons, "where one of the parties at the time has a husband or wife living, is void, absolutely and in all its aspects." Such marriages are deemed to be **void ab initio,** that is, "from the inception." In such a situation, if the parties marry, honestly believing that the one party's dissolution decree was final, then the second marriage will be declared invalid. It is not likely that criminal charges will result for bigamy, as the parties lacked the requisite criminal intent to enter into an invalid marriage.

void ab initio
Marriages that are void from the inception.

CONTRACT ISSUES—MARRIAGE

It has previously been noted in this chapter that early courts once recognized a promise to marry as an enforceable contract, and therefore if the man backs out of the marriage, then the woman has a valid cause of action for breach of promise to marry. Today, two contract situations arise in the marriage context. First, the parties may enter into an agreement before marriage that restricts property rights in the event of a divorce. Referred to as **prenuptial agreements,** or antenuptial agreements, these contracts are documents that prospective spouses enter into before marriage to set forth financial settlements, choice of law, and other rights or duties of the parties in case the marriage ends in divorce. At one point, courts used to look on such agreements with disfavor, as it seemed to suggest that the parties entered a marriage with the intent or expectation to later dissolve the marriage, and this was in contrast with societal norms at that time. However, recent courts have recognized that these types of contracts are enforceable so long as certain criteria are met.

prenuptial agreement
An agreement made by parties before marriage that controls certain aspects of the relationship, such as management and ownership of property.

According to the Uniform Prenuptial Agreement Act (UPAA), parties may seek to specify exactly how assets will be distributed, precise terms regarding spousal support, ownership rights in the death benefits of life insurance policies, and other rights and duties of each prospective spouse as to any other property, so long as the provision does not violate public policy or any criminal statute. In order to be enforceable should dissolution of the marriage occur, most courts will require that the agreement be in writing, signed by both parties, that there is a fair distribution of assets, so as to avoid claims of unconscionability, and that both parties have made a full and complete disclosure of assets. Furthermore, the UPAA also looks at whether the agreement violates public policy and whether one party entered into the agreement as the result of such inducement or duress at the last minute.

The second type of contract that arises in the marriage context is **cohabitation agreements.** This contract sets forth the rights of two people who decide to live together for an unspecified duration, without any intent of marrying. The most well-known case to illustrate this type of agreement arose in *Marvin v. Marvin*, 557 P.2d 106 (Cal. 1977). That case established the concept of **palimony,** in which support can be owed to a live-in individual, even though the two were never married. Most states are reluctant to embrace this type of agreement, as it does even more than prenuptial agreements to offend public policy in that parties are entering into a relationship with the expectation that it will not last. Here, the cohabiting partners are not holding themselves out as husband and wife, as in common law marriages, but rather are giving credence to the inference that the relationship is based on some sexual aspect, and this is seen as violating public policy. Since the *Marvin* case, some states have reluctantly accepted the validity of this type of contract, comparing it to prenuptial agreements.

cohabitation agreement
A contract setting forth the rights of two people who live together without the benefit of marriage.

palimony
A division of property between two unmarried parties after they separate or the paying of support by one party to the other.

You Be the Judge

Herman and Lily have lived together for 15 years without being married. They consider each other as spouses and hold themselves out to the community as husband and wife. Everyone who knows them believe them to be married. However, Lily's husband, Lester, has been living in another town and just recently died. The state in which they live recognizes common law marriage. It is now important to establish whether Lily and Herman are married. What will be the likely result?

TERMINATION OF MARRIAGE

annulment
Court procedure dissolving a marriage, treating it as if it never happened.

There are two primary ways in which marriages might be terminated. The first is called an **annulment.** This is a formal legal proceeding in which the ultimate result is the court returns both parties to their former status, as if the marriage had never occurred. The marriage is declared invalid, as if it had never taken place, and is retroactive to the date that the marriage was allegedly entered into. In order to have a marriage annulled, most state statutes require that the marriage was either voidable or void. Marriages are declared void if one of the parties lacked the legal ability to enter into a valid marriage. Assume Delbert marries Roxanne in Las Vegas, thinking that his marriage to Suzette had been legally dissolved and the dissolution decree entered. If Delbert is still legally married to Suzette, even if Delbert was under the mistaken belief that this was not the case, the marriage between him and Roxanne is void. You cannot legally marry someone if you are already married to someone else. Technically, the void marriage never existed, and thus can effectively be ignored without court intervention. It is in essence a legal nullity. However, a voidable marriage may present grounds for an annulment.

In order to successfully contend that a marriage should be annulled because it is voidable, most state statutes require the following:

1. One of the parties had a mental incapacity at the time the marriage was entered into; the aggrieved party must show that he was incapable of giving consent at the time of marriage.
2. One of the parties lacks the physical or psychological ability to consummate the marriage.
3. One of the parties is lacking in legal capacity according to the requirements of a valid marriage in the relevant state.
4. One of the parties was the victim of fraud or duress before the marriage took place.

Keep in mind that a voidable marriage, just like a voidable contract, means that the marriage remains valid unless or until one party seeks to obtain court intervention to declare the contract voided. The proceedings for an annulment do just this, and the court that grants the annulment is asserting that the marriage had never occurred. In some cases, parties may find that state statutes have less stringent grounds in which to have a marriage terminated by dissolution, rather than by annulment.

Should one of the parties allege fraud or duress in the inducement to marry, that party must demonstrate that the other party misrepresented a material fact and that the aggrieved party relied on that misrepresentation. For example, if Mary represents to her prospective spouse, John, that she is a virgin when in fact she is actually pregnant with Melvin's child at the time of the marriage, then John would likely be granted an annulment for this fraud. Cases in which annulments have *not* been granted based on fraud include the situation where one party misrepresents the size of their bank account, as wealth is not an element central to the model of marriage, or where one party fraudulently represents their virginity, absence any fact of pregnancy at the time of the marriage.

In determining proper grounds for an annulment, courts have looked to issues such as the professed religion of each party as valid grounds, since this element goes straight to the heart of a marriage. Similarly if one party represents to the other party that she has the ability to bear lots of children, when in fact she is medically unable to do so, this may also be grounds for annulment.

Duress is a similar basis for granting an annulment. In this case, one of the parties alleges that he would never have entered into the marriage voluntarily were it not for some external force or pressure brought against him by another person. For example, if the parent of a minor child threatens the child with a shotgun unless the child marries his pregnant partner, it is likely a court will find that the marriage was entered into under duress. Mere threats of legal action, such as someone threatening to seek criminal charges for statutory rape, however, are generally deemed insufficient to constitute duress.

If a party is seeking an annulment, the proper jurisdiction in which to pursue this process is where the parties are domiciled. Then, the court may apply the law of the state *where the marriage was created* for purposes of determining valid grounds. You should be aware that the legal process of annulment is completely separate and distinct from the religious annulment that parties may pursue within the Church. In both cases, a decision is rendered that leaves the parties as if a valid marriage had never existed. Note, however, that state statutes endeavor to protect children born of a void or voidable marriage; hence, children are deemed to be legitimate issue, thus ensuring the child's rights to support and minimizing any stigma of illegitimacy.

CASE IN POINT

Court of Appeals of North Carolina.
Cheryl W. MAYO, Plaintiff
v.
Frank E. MAYO, Defendant.
No. COA04-1334.
Aug. 16, 2005.

CALABRIA, Judge.

Cheryl W. Mayo ("plaintiff") appeals from a judgment of annulment of her marriage to Frank E. Mayo ("defendant"). We affirm.

On 17 February 1999, plaintiff and defendant applied for a marriage license in Georgia. Each of them represented, in the block designated "number of previous marriages," two previous marriages. Plaintiff and defendant married on 9 April 1999. In 2001, defendant learned and later confirmed plaintiff had been previously married seven times rather than two times. Subsequently, defendant accepted employment and moved to California and then communicated to plaintiff that he considered the marital relationship at an end.

Plaintiff filed for a divorce from bed and board, abandonment, indignities, and adultery in Transylvania County on 3 September 2002, seeking post-separation support, alimony, and equitable distribution. In plaintiff's complaint, she alleged the existence of a lawful marriage. Defendant admitted the existence of a valid marriage in his answer. After protracted litigation dealing with, *inter alia,* post-separation support in favor of plaintiff and interim distributions, a separate judgment of absolute divorce was entered on 25 March 2003. Thereafter on 11 March 2004, defendant submitted a motion in the cause for an annulment of the marriage. After conducting a hearing on the issues, the trial court entered a judgment annulling the marriage between the parties. From that judgment, plaintiff appeals, asserting the trial court erred in (1) permitting defendant to seek an annulment after earlier taking the position that the parties were legally married and (2) annulling the marriage on grounds of fraud when the only misrepresentation concerns the number of prior marriages.

I. Contrary Positions

Plaintiff asserts in her first assignment of error that defendant's pleadings include admissions of a lawful marriage, and annulment should not have been allowed in light of these admissions. We disagree.

At the hearing, plaintiff raised two initial challenges to the annulment proceeding: jurisdiction and standing. With respect to the standing argument, plaintiff argued defendant lacked standing to seek an annulment on the grounds that he was seeking to have the marriage annulled after a judgment of absolute divorce was entered. Specifically, plaintiff argued the following at the hearing:

> So here you have a Movant who is trying to ask the Court for an annulment . . . but has already gotten a divorce from the person he's asking the Court to render the Annulment for. So I think there's a serious issue of standing to even raise that. . . . I've never heard of anyone coming in later after a divorce has been granted and then . . . asking that . . . the prior marriage be declared null. . . . I don't think there is [standing to do that].

In her brief to this Court, however, plaintiff does not argue defendant lacked standing. Rather, plaintiff argues "defendant's ready admission that the parties were lawfully married in his pleadings, coupled with his lengthy silence on his alleged ground for an annulment necessarily demonstrate that the defendant was precluded from seeking an annulment." In so doing, plaintiff has impermissibly sought to change the theory presented in the instant appeal (defendant is bound by the representations in his pleadings) from that which was presented to the trial court for determination (defendant cannot seek an annulment because a judgment of divorce had already been entered). *See Weil v. Herring,* 207 N.C. 6, 10, 175 S.E. 836, 838 (1934) (noting our courts do not permit the submission of new theories, not previously argued, because "the law does not permit parties to swap horses between courts in order to get a better mount [on appeal]").

Moreover, plaintiff cites and primarily relies on this Court's holding in *Fungaroli v. Fungaroli,* 53 N.C.App. 270, 280 S.E.2d 787 (1981), involving a plaintiff husband who filed a complaint for divorce in North Carolina and, after being ordered by a North Carolina court to pay alimony and transfer custody of the child to the defendant wife, sought a decree of annulment in the courts of Virginia. The Virginia court annulled the parties' marriage, and this Court subsequently declined to give effect to the Virginia decree. Along with other reasons given, this Court noted it would violate North Carolina's public policy to give full faith and credit to the Virginia decree where plaintiff went to another state and sought an annulment in contradiction to his previous representations of a valid marriage solely to extinguish the defendant wife's right to alimony. *Id.,* 53 N.C.App. at 279, 280 S.E.2d at 793. This case does not implicate the full faith and credit clause or the public policy in favor of it; accordingly, *Fungaroli* does not preclude defendant's right to seek an annulment of the marriage. This assignment of error is overruled.

II. Grounds for Annulment

In her second assignment of error, plaintiff argues the trial court erred in annulling the marriage because "plaintiff's alleged concealment of the number of her prior marriages [does] not rise to the level of fraud that is necessary to sustain an annulment." Initially, we note the parties sought and the trial court applied Georgia law in determining substantively whether an annulment should be granted the parties, who were married and lived a portion of their married life in Georgia.

Under Georgia law, the nature of consent by the parties required to constitute an actual contract of marriage is voluntary consent "without any fraud practiced upon either." Ga.Code Ann. § 19-3-4 (2004). "Marriages of persons . . . fraudulently induced to contract shall be void" unless there occurs by the party so defrauded "a subsequent consent and ratification of the marriage, freely and voluntarily made, accompanied by cohabitation as husband and wife[,]" which renders the marriage valid. Ga.Code Ann. § 19-3-5 (2004). An annulment, under Georgia law, operates in the same manner as "a total divorce between the parties of a void marriage and shall return the parties thereto to their original status before marriage." Ga.Code Ann. § 19-4-5 (2004). The parties have not cited, nor can we find, a Georgia case concerning the effect of a misrepresentation concerning the number of prior marriages on the validity of the marriage. However, we do note that the Georgia application for a marriage license requires the bride and groom to disclose, under oath, the number of previous marriages, the method by which those marriages were dissolved, the grounds for dissolution, and the date and place. We hold plaintiff's argument, that her concealment of five of her seven previous marriages does not "constitute[ ] sufficient fraud to serve as a basis to annul a marriage," is erroneous for two reasons.

First, the statutory law of Georgia is couched in terms of "any" fraud. The relevant question, therefore, is whether there exists fraud, not whether the existing fraud is sufficient. We do not read the term "any" to mean that there might not exist some *de minimis* standard in Georgia which would not justify annulling a marriage; however, a misrepresentation hiding five previous marriages while disclosing two does not, in our opinion, fall within such a *de minimis* standard.

Second, none of the cases from other jurisdictions cited by plaintiff involve a party hiding as many previous marriages as in the instant case. Certainly, the greater the concealed number of marriages, the more force has the argument of the injured party. The application for a marriage license in Georgia further evinces that state's interest in the circumstances of previous marriages, which are given under oath. In light of the statutory language of Georgia, the requirements of disclosure on the application for a marriage license in Georgia, and the comparison between the number of concealed versus the number of revealed marriages, we perceive no error in the trial court's annulment of the marriage in the instant case. This assignment of error is overruled.

Affirmed.

Judges McGEE and ELMORE concur.

Source: *Mayo v. Mayo,* 617 S.E.2d 672 (St. Paul, MN: Thomson West). Reprinted with permission from Westlaw.

divorce/dissolution
The legal termination of a marriage.

The second primary method of terminating a marriage is by **dissolution** or **divorce.** The essential difference between the two options is that the granting of an annulment is judged based on facts that existed *at the time* the marriage occurred, whereas dissolutions are judged from facts that occurred either *before* or *during* the marriage. Divorce is probably the most common proceeding to legally terminate a marriage. Even though different states may have some right to determine issues related to a divorce, and thus diversity of jurisdiction exists, family law is unique because federal courts do *not* hear divorce cases. Jurisdiction rests with the state where the parties were domiciled. **Domicile** is the place where the party is physically present and where the party intends to make that place the permanent home.

domicile
the permanent home of the party.

A divorce proceeding is initiated when one party files a petition in the appropriate state court, requesting a dissolution of the marriage and specifying the reasons why the divorce should be granted. Relevant information that must be included in the petition are the names of the parties, date and place at which the marriage took place, names and ages of all minor children, and the length of time each party lived in the state where the petition is filed. Note that years ago, state statutes required that the parties allege fault in order for a divorce to be granted. Such grounds included allegations of cruelty, abandonment, or abuse. Today, many states have adopted **no-fault divorces.** The Uniform Marriage and Divorce Act (UMDA), adopted in most states, stipulates that parties need not prove grounds or fault in order for a divorce to be granted. The parties need only allege reasons such as incompatibility, irreconcilable differences, or irretrievable breakdown of the marriage. Keep in mind, however, that fault may still be alleged in no-fault states, as it is relevant to the granting of custody and support.

no-fault divorce
A divorce in which one spouse does not need to allege wrongdoing by the other spouse as grounds for the divorce.

Eye on Ethics

Locate the case *People v. Milner,* 35 P.3d 670 (2001). This is a stunning illustration of the implications of the unauthorized practice of law by paralegals and an attorney's failure to supervise. Identify the primary issues and discussion in this case related to paralegals.

No-fault divorces mean that a party may simply claim irreconcilable differences or irretrievable breakdown of the marriage as the reason for the court to grant the divorce. As the name implies, neither party has to assess blame for the marriage breakdown, nor must both parties consent to the divorce.

separation agreements
Contract between husband and wife to live apart; the document outlines the terms of the separation.

Although technically not a final termination of marriage, **separation agreements** are a way for couples to determine by a court declaration their respective property rights. Though they remain married, the parties might live apart, and at a minimum have issues such as custody of children and property division sorted out with a court decree. Some couples may never divorce, but continue to live apart, though neither is free to marry someone else since all marital rights and duties still pertain to each party.

DIVORCE PROCEEDING

Remember that you should be certain to consult your state statutes for specific procedures to be followed in divorce proceedings (see Figure 13.1 for a summary of state-by-state grounds for divorce and residency requirements). There are similarities among the statutes. Once the party seeking the divorce has filed a petition outlining the requirements, as discussed earlier, including any relevant affidavits noted in the statute, the petition must be filed with the court and served on the opposing spouse. The spouse then has a statutory period of time within which to file an answer to the petition. Sometimes a divorce is wanted by both parties, in which case they voluntarily and mutually agree to appear in court and present a negotiated settlement document reflecting property division, support, and custody agreements. While not obligated to accept the agreement as it stands, the court may take the parties' wishes into consideration when granting the divorce decree, doing so if the proposed settlement agreement appears reasonable under the circumstances.

temporary restraining order
A court order barring a person from harassing or harming another.

mediation
A dispute resolution method in which a neutral third party meets with the opposing parties to help them achieve a mutually satisfactory solution without court intervention.

If the divorce is not amicable, then typically the state statute will require service on the other spouse once the petition for dissolution is filed with the court. Keep in mind that divorces are civil proceedings. However, there may be other issues involved, and motions by either party may be filed while the petition is pending. For example, one party may request that a **temporary restraining order** be granted, in which one spouse is ordered to stay away from the other spouse and the children due to the tension and risk of domestic violence in that specific case. This order, also referred to as protection orders, is issued by the court in order to minimize conflict during the course of the proceedings, especially where minor children are involved, but sometimes these orders continue long after the divorce decree is final. The court holds an initial hearing on the petition for dissolution just so parties may file any such motions and also be ordered to **mediation,** if the judge believes that property issues and issues pertaining to minor children can be resolved during the waiting period.

Each statute specifies a particular length of time that parties must wait to have a final dissolution decree issued, even where the divorce is uncontested. This "waiting period" is designed to ensure that all procedures have been properly followed and gives the parties time to consider the terms of the settlement agreement, reflecting on the final outcome that is pending. During this time, and at the initial hearing on the petition, the court may deal with matters pertaining to bill payments and living arrangements, as it might be six months or more before a final decree might be issued.

Eye on Ethics

Sylvester Cat, an attorney, is representing Anne Gables in a dissolution of marriage action. When filing pleadings with the court, Gables completed and filed an affidavit purporting to list all her assets. Two months later, Sylvester discovers that his client owned $50,000 worth of stock in Acme Technologies Corporation, which she failed to list on the affidavit. Sylvester confronts Anne, who refuses to change her affidavit and insists that Sylvester keep quiet about it. "My ex-husband is going to get more than his fair share of my money," she argues. Anne tells Sylvester to proceed with the case and forget about mentioning the stock. What should Sylvester do?

FIGURE 13.1
Grounds for Divorce and Residency Requirements

Source: "Chart 4: Grounds for Divorce & Residency Requirements," by Elizabeth Brandt, published in *Family Law Quarterly,* Volume 39, No. 4, Winter 2006. © 2006 by the American Bar Association. Reprinted with permission.

State	No Fault Sole Ground	No Fault Added to Traditional	Incompatibility	Living Separate and Apart	Judicial Separation	Durational Requirements
Alabama		x	x	2 years	x	6 months
Alaska	x	x	x	2 years	x	6 months
Arizona	x	x[1]			x	90 days
Arkansas		x		18 months	x	60 days
California	x				x	6 months*
Colorado	x				x	90 days
Connecticut		x		18 months	x	1 year
Delaware		x	x	6 months		6 months
District of Columbia	x			1 year	x	6 months
Florida	x					6 months
Georgia		x				6 months
Hawaii				2 years[3]	x	6 months[4]
Idaho		x			x	6 weeks
Illinois		x		2 years	x	90 days
Indiana			x		x	60 days
Iowa	x				x	1 year
Kansas			x		x	60 days
Kentucky	x			60 days	x	180 days
Louisiana		x[1]		6 months[2]	x	6 months
Maine		x			x	6 months
Maryland		x		1 year	x	1 year
Massachusetts		x			x	None
Michigan	x				x	6 months
Minnesota	x				x	180 days
Mississippi		x				6 months
Missouri		x		1–2 years	x	90 days
Montana	x		x	180 days	x	90 days
Nebraska	x				x	1 year
Nevada			x	1 year	x	6 weeks
New Hampshire		x		2 years		1 year
New Jersey		x		18 months		1 year
New Mexico		x	x		x	6 months
New York		x		1 year	x	1 year
North Carolina		x		1 year	x	6 months
North Dakota		x			x	6 months
Ohio		x	x	1 year		6 months
Oklahoma			x		x	6 months
Oregon	x				x	6 months
Pennsylvania		x		2 years		6 months
Rhode Island		x		3 years	x	1 year
South Carolina		x		1 year	x	3 months (both residents)
South Dakota		x			x	None
Tennessee		x		2 years	x	6 months
Texas		x		3 years		6 months
Utah		x		3 years	x	90 days
Vermont		x		6 months		6 months
Virginia		x		1 year	x	6 months
Washington	x					1 year
West Virginia		x		1 year	x	1 year
Wisconsin	x				x	6 months
Wyoming		x	x		x	60 days

* California requires domicile as distinguished from residency for jurisdictional purposes.

1. Covenant marriage statutes establish specific grounds for divorce for covenant marriages.
2. Two years for covenant marriages.
3. Grounds are either marriage irretrievably broken or two years separation.
4. Six months in state and three months in circuit waiting for divorce itself, but can file as soon as residency established.

You Be the Judge

Fred and Wilma Stone have been married for 28 years, and Wilma has stayed at home to care for their two children. She has not worked outside of the home since they were married. Fred informs Wilma that he wants a divorce. Wilma is concerned that she won't be able to find a job as her only past employment was as a switchboard operator 30 years ago. What is the likelihood that Wilma will receive spousal support?

alimony
Court-ordered money paid to support a former spouse after termination of a marriage.

Sometimes, a divorce decree may include a provision for one spouse to receive financial support from the other, commonly referred to as **alimony.** Alimony is a specific sum of money paid to support a former spouse after the termination of the marriage. You must consult your state statute to determine whether court-ordered alimony may be awarded in your state, as some states prohibit this. Because of the change in societal standards, many couples today are dual-wage earners, and therefore court-awarded alimony, or maintenance, payments are not as prevalent as when the husband was typically the only wage earner. The purpose of granting alimony was to ensure that the former spouse, usually the wife who didn't work outside of the home, was able to maintain a similar standard of living. Today, most states will evaluate the ability of each spouse to support themselves after the termination of the marriage, along with other determining factors such as whether one spouse had supported the other during college or graduate school.

Either temporary or permanent alimony may be awarded. Permanent alimony is typically awarded to older spouses who have never held a job outside of the home and have limited prospects of supporting themselves. Permanent alimony is ordered until such time as the former spouse either remarries or dies. Temporary alimony may be awarded if the court determines that the former spouse needs rehabilitative support, which is financial support until the spouse can establish a new career or receive education or training. The type and form of alimony awarded is usually based on factors such as age, education, work background, and incomes of the parties.

Where minor children are involved, the courts are especially careful to engage the parties in mediation. Public policy dictates that the children are clearly not at fault for the breakdown of marital relations, and therefore society is eager to protect the best interests of the innocent parties in the family unit. Mediation often gives the parties an opportunity to save the time and expense of a lengthy trial in determining the issues that must be resolved before a settlement agreement can be approved and the decree issued. In the case of minor children, it must be determined who will have legal and physical custody, as well as the amount of support to be provided by the other spouse. This is certainly the most contested and volatile issue arising out of the divorce proceedings, typically because both parties act selfishly and are very emotional, typically ignoring arrangements that might be in the best interests of the child.

CHILD CUSTODY AND SUPPORT

custody
The legal authority to make decisions concerning a child's interests.

The issues of custody, visitation, and support are typically what compel the court to order the parties into mediation, even where it appears that a pre-arranged settlement agreement seems reasonable on its face. The court is always eager to ensure that the parents are acting in an emotionally and financially responsible manner where the children are concerned, since minors are innocent victims of a family breakup. Although the legal term **custody** *implies* the responsibility for raising the child, in many states there are two separate kinds of custody: legal and physical. Physical custody describes who the child resides with on a daily basis. The parent who is ultimately responsible for supervising day-to-day activities is the custodial parent. Legal custody refers to who has authority to make decisions on behalf of the child in all matters including education and health care. When custody is determined, the court must decide who has physical custody and legal custody and whether the parties will share custody. Joint custody refers to the legal custody aspect, granting *both* parents a say in matters such as health care and education. Traditionally, courts were reluctant to award joint custody, reasoning that if the parents can't get along, and are now divorcing, it is unlikely they will be able to agree about important matters relating to the care of the children. In these cases, courts typically awarded sole legal and physical custody to the mother, as the law once presumed that only the mother could be the best parent in terms of caring for a child "of tender years." Unless it was proved that the mother was unfit, the courts almost always awarded the mother custody. In that situation, the court would then award the father **visitation rights.** The noncustodial parent was granted the right to reasonable visits with the children. Today, however, the trend has changed to the presumption that either parent could be fit to care for minor children; moreover, joint legal custody is the preferred option, regardless of which parent has the primary physical custody. Sometimes, the court may also consider split custody, in which one parent has physical and legal custody during the school year, and the other parent has both types of custody during other designated times of the year, such as summers and holiday periods.

visitation rights
The right to legally see a child, where physical custody is not awarded.

In determining custody today, all states have adopted the **Uniform Child Custody Jurisdiction Act (UCCJA)** (see Figure 13.2). In 1968, the Uniform Law Commissioners drafted the UCCJA, which was subsequently adopted by all 50 states by 1981. The UCCJA was designed to discourage the kidnapping of children by noncustodial parents. Previously, noncustodial parents might transport children across state lines in the hopes of finding a sympathetic jurisdiction that might reverse court custody orders, and this happened quite frequently, until the UCCJA. First, the UCCJA operates to establish which state has jurisdiction to hear a child custody case. Then, the Act operates to protect the decision and order of that state court from modification by the court of any other state, so long as the original state retains jurisdiction over the entire case. Thus, parents are effectively discouraged from "forum shopping," and the incentive to flee with the child is greatly minimized.

Uniform Child Custody Jurisdiction Act (UCCJA)
An act that resolves jurisdictional issues related to child custody.

The child's presence in the state may not be sufficient to establish jurisdiction, given the possibility that one parent has kidnapped the child and moved to a state that has no connection to the family unit. The **Parental Kidnapping Protection Act (PKPA),** adopted in 1981, becomes relevant when states are asked to modify an existing child custody decree because of just such a situation. There are two primary differences between the PKPA and the UCCJA, mostly centered on disagreements over the application of jurisdictional principles. The UCCJA does not give first priority to the home state of the child in determining which state may exercise jurisdiction over a child custody dispute. The PKPA does. The PKPA also provides that once a state has exercised jurisdiction, that jurisdiction remains the continuing, exclusive jurisdiction until every party to the dispute has exited that state. The UCCJA simply states that a legitimate exercise of jurisdiction must be honored by any other state until the basis for that exercise of jurisdiction no longer exists. In practice, the two acts tend to work together for the most part, but the differences do confuse the adjudication and settlement of child custody disputes in certain cases.

Parental Kidnapping Protection Act (PKPA)
An act related to jurisdictional issues in applying and enforcing child custody decrees in other states.

CYBER TRIP

The National Conference of Commissioners on Uniform State Laws is 115 years old and provides states with nonpartisan, carefully drafted legislation that brings a clear understanding and stability to critical areas of the law, seeking to establish rules that are consistent from state to state. Look on the Web site www.nccusl.org and see!

In the UCCJA, there are four principles, or bases, for a state to take jurisdiction over a child custody dispute:

1. It is the child's home state.
2. There is a significant connection between the state and the parties to a child custody dispute.
3. The child is present in the state and there is the need for emergency jurisdiction because the child's welfare is threatened.
4. The child is present in the state and there is no other state with another sound basis for taking jurisdiction.

(*To take jurisdiction* simply means that a state's courts have a good reason for summoning the contestants to come before them to adjudicate the dispute no matter where they reside. If there is jurisdiction, the court's orders are valid and enforceable.)

The UCCJA sets forth several criteria for ascertaining jurisdiction, including what is the "home state" of the child six months before the legal proceeding and which state has a significant connection to the family unit. In all cases, the UCCJA establishes rules for determining jurisdiction based on what is in the best interests of the child. However, in the 1997 amended version, the "best interest" language of the UCCJA was eliminated, because the phrase tended to create confusion between the jurisdictional issue and the substantive custody determination. Since the language was not necessary for the jurisdictional issue, it was removed.

FIGURE 13.2
Excerpt from the UCCJA

Source: Uniform Child Custody Jurisdiction and Enforcement Act (1997), drafted by the National Conference of Commissioners on Uniform State Laws. Copyright © 1997 by National Conference of Commissioners on Uniform State Laws.

UNIFORM CHILD CUSTODY JURISDICTION AND ENFORCEMENT ACT (1997)

Drafted by the
NATIONAL CONFERENCE OF COMMISSIONERS
ON UNIFORM STATE LAWS
COPYRIGHT© 1997
By
NATIONAL CONFERENCE OF COMMISSIONERS
ON UNIFORM STATE LAWS
Approved by the American Bar Association
Nashville, Tennessee, February 4, 1998

****

[ARTICLE] 2

JURISDICTION

SECTION 201. INITIAL CHILD-CUSTODY JURISDICTION.

(a) Except as otherwise provided in Section 204, a court of this State has jurisdiction to make an initial child-custody determination only if:

(1) this State is the home State of the child on the date of the commencement of the proceeding, or was the home State of the child within six months before the commencement of the proceeding and the child is absent from this State but a parent or person acting as a parent continues to live in this State;

(2) a court of another State does not have jurisdiction under paragraph (1), or a court of the home State of the child has declined to exercise jurisdiction on the ground that this State is the more appropriate forum under Section 207 or 208, and:

(A) the child and the child's parents, or the child and at least one parent or a person acting as a parent, have a significant connection with this State other than mere physical presence; and

(B) substantial evidence is available in this State concerning the child's care, protection, training, and personal relationships;

(3) all courts having jurisdiction under paragraph (1) or (2) have declined to exercise jurisdiction on the ground that a court of this State is the more appropriate forum to determine the custody of the child under Section 207 or 208; or

(4) no court of any other State would have jurisdiction under the criteria specified in paragraph (1), (2), or (3).

(b) Subsection (a) is the exclusive jurisdictional basis for making a child-custody determination by a court of this State.

(c) Physical presence of, or personal jurisdiction over, a party or a child is not necessary or sufficient to make a child-custody determination.

Comment

This section provides mandatory jurisdictional rules for the original child custody proceeding. It generally continues the provisions of the UCCJA ? 3. However, there have been a number of changes to the jurisdictional bases.

Once the appropriate court is ascertained, then certain factors are considered in granting custody to one or both parents:

1. The parent's ability to provide for the child's emotional and physical needs
2. The parent's ability to provide a stable home environment
3. The parent's willingness to provide for the child's needs
4. The wishes of the child (keeping in mind this factor is dependent upon the age of the child)
5. Any other factors the court deems appropriate under the circumstances

See Figure 13.3 for a state-by-state custody criteria.

It should be noted that many states have taken a liberal view in deciding who the best parent is to have custody of a child, and thus issues such as the parent's sexual orientation or a parent's lifestyle may not have a bearing on their "fitness" to raise the child. Again, the courts have adopted the view that the best interests of the child outweigh other factors that may not impact or affect a child adversely. Since custody is an emotionally charged topic, the court may decide to appoint a **guardian ad litem** to represent the child. The guardian ad litem is a person, often an attorney, who is selected to represent the best interests of the child before the court.

guardian ad litem
A person appointed by the court to represent the best interests of the child in a custody determination.

Some states have statutes that allow the court to grant reasonable visitation rights to a grandparent upon proper showing that visitation would be in the best interests of the child. For example, the Idaho Code section 32-719 states that a court may grant "reasonable visitation rights to grandparents or great-grandparents upon a proper showing that the visitation would be in the best interests of the child." Acknowledging the United States Supreme Court decision regarding the fundamental rights of parents to make parenting decisions with regard to their children, including with whom the child may associate, the Idaho courts have required a clear and convincing standard of proof by grandparents seeking visitation rights under section 32-719. As of the date of this writing, the Idaho courts have not yet been required to consider the constitutionality of statute 32-719, as some other state courts have already done.

CHILD SUPPORT

child support
The right of a child to financial support and the obligation of a parent to provide it.

Once the courts award custody, and possibly also visitation rights if joint custody has not been granted, then the courts also determine **child support.** Each state maintains strict guidelines in calculating child support. It is important to note that a parent's desire to relinquish custody or reject visitation rights does *not* impact the duty and obligation to pay support. Similarly, a parent's failure to pay support does not permit the custodial parent to deny visitation rights to that parent.

Noncustodial parents are obligated to support their children by providing financial contributions toward the cost of food, clothing, housing, education, and similar necessities. Where joint custody has been awarded, the parent with the greater income must contribute a larger share of these costs to the other parent. Each state's guidelines provide detailed formulas to be used in calculating the amount of support, and typically this support continues until the child reaches the age of majority, except in special circumstances, such as if a child is physically challenged. Federal legislation has been enacted to ensure that child support obligations are met. For example, automatic wage withholding will be instituted in order to prevent the noncustodial parent from disregarding support obligations. In addition, some states will withhold the granting or renewal of certain licenses, such as a driver's license, if support payments are not being made. The Revised Uniform Reciprocal Enforcement of Support Act (RURESA) provides methods of enforcing child support orders where the parents live in different states. It is used to enforce spousal maintenance orders as well.

RESEARCH THIS!

Locate the statute in your state pertaining to visitation rights. Determine if your state code has a section pertaining to the visitation rights of grandparents. If so, conduct further research to ascertain if your state court has considered the constitutionality of this provision.

FIGURE 13.3

Custody Criteria

Source: "Chart 2: Custody Criteria," by Elizabeth Brandt, published in *Family Law Quarterly,* Volume 39, No. 4, Winter 2006. © 2006 by the American Bar Association. Reprinted with permission.

State	Statutory Guidelines	Children's Wishes	Joint Custody*	Cooperative Parent	Domestic Violence	Health	Attorney or GAL
Alabama	x	x	x		x		
Alaska	x	x	x		x		x
Arizona	x	x	x	x	x	x	x
Arkansas					x		
California	x	x		x	x	x	x
Colorado	x	x	x^{1}	x	x	x	x
Connecticut		x	x				x
Delaware	x	x	x		x	x	x
District of Columbia	x	x	x	x	x	x	x
Florida	x	x	x	x	x	x	x
Georgia	x	x	x		x		x
Hawaii	x^{2}	x^{8}	x^{7}		x		x^{9}
Idaho	x	x	x		x	x	
Illinois	x	x	x	x	x	x	x
Indiana	x	x	x	x	x	x	x
Iowa	x	x	x	x	x	x	x
Kansas	x	x	x	x	x	x	
Kentucky	x	x	x	x	x	x	x
Louisiana	x	x	x		x		
Maine	x	x	x		x		x
Maryland		x	x	x	x	x	x
Massachusetts			x		x		x
Michigan	x	x	x	x	x	x	x
Minnesota	x	x	x		x	x	x
Mississippi	x		x			x	x^{2}
Missouri	x	x	x	x	x	x	x
Montana	x	x	x		x		x
Nebraska	x	x	x		x	x	x
Nevada	x	x	x	x	x		x
New Hampshire	x	x	x		x		x
New Jersey	x	x	x	x	x	x	x
New Mexico	x	x	x	x	x	x	x
New York		x			x^{2}		x
North Carolina		x^{2}	x		x	x	
North Dakota	x	x	x	x^{3}	x	x	
Ohio	x^{2}	x	x^{10}		x	x	x
Oklahoma	x	x	x	x	x		x^{4}
Oregon	x	x	x	x	x		x^{3}
Pennsylvania	x	x	x	x	x	x	x
Rhode Island		x	x	x	x	x	x
South Carolina		x	x	x	x	x	x
South Dakota		x	x	x	x		
Tennessee	x	x^{5}	x^{6}	x	x		x
Texas	x	x	x	x	x	x	x
Utah	x	x	x	x			x
Vermont	x		x		x		x
Virginia	x	x^{2}	x	x	x	x	x^{4}
Washington	x	x			x	x	x
West Virginia	x	x	x		x		
Wisconsin	x	x	x	x	x	x	x
Wyoming	x	x	x	x	x	x	

* Court in the exercise of its sound discretion shall consider the best interests and welfare of the minor child.

1. Now uses term "parental rights and responsibilities."
2. Considered if child is old enough.
3. By case law.
4. Not mandatory.
5. The court must listen to the reasonable preferences of a child age twelve or older, giving greater weight to the preferences of older children. The court may at its discretion hear the reasonable preference of children under the age of twelve.
6. In divorce, courts no longer use "custody" terminology, instead, separately allocating between the parents (1) residential time and (2) parental responsibility in specific areas such as nonemergency health care, religion, education and extracurricular activities.
7. Emphasizes "best interest of child."
8. If child is of sufficient age and capacity to reason and form intelligent preference.
9. Appointment of custody evaluators and guardians *ad litem* authorized by administrative rule.
10. Now uses the term "shared parenting."

CASE IN POINT

Missouri Court of Appeals,
Western District.
Jonathan Michael BRYAN, Appellant,
v.
Stephanie GARRISON, Respondent,
and
Debra Howard, Respondent.
No. WD 64888.
April 11, 2006.

Before HARDWICK, P.J., BRECKENRIDGE and SPINDEN, JJ.

PATRICIA BRECKENRIDGE, Judge.

Jonathan Michael Bryan appeals the judgment of the trial court modifying the paternity judgment's provisions for visitation of his son, Jordin Matthew Bryan, with Debra Howard, Jordin's maternal grandmother. On appeal, Mr. Bryan claims the trial court erred in three respects. First, Mr. Bryan asserts that the trial court failed to make the requisite statutory findings in its modification judgment that visitation with Ms. Howard was in Jordin's best interests and that visitation with Ms. Howard would not endanger Jordin physically or emotionally. Second, Mr. Bryan contends the trial court erred because the visitation awarded to Ms. Howard in the modification judgment was excessive. Finally, Mr. Bryan claims the trial court erred because awarding unsupervised visitation to Ms. Howard was against the weight of the evidence. This court finds that the trial court made all necessary statutory findings and the trial court's judgment was supported by substantial evidence and was not against the weight of the evidence. Because the trial court's award of visitation to Jordin's maternal grandmother was excessive, the provisions in the trial court's judgment modifying visitation between Jordin and Ms. Howard are reversed, and the case is remanded to the trial court to enter a judgment with more restrictive visitation for Ms. Howard. The trial court's judgment is affirmed in all other respects.

Factual and Procedural Background

Jordin was born to Stephanie Garrison on March 17, 2001. When Jordin was first born, he lived with his mother. After approximately a month, however, Ms. Howard and James Howard, Jordin's maternal step-grandfather, became Jordin's primary caregivers. After Jordin's birth, Mr. Bryan filed a petition for a determination of paternity and for custody and support. The trial court found Mr. Bryan to be Jordin's natural father, and entered a judgment of custody and support on March 27, 2002. This judgment adopted a parenting plan submitted by Mr. Bryan and awarded Mr. Bryan sole legal and physical custody of Jordin. Mr. Bryan and Ms. Garrison have never been married. The judgment provided that Ms. Garrison would have visitation with Jordin "[e]very other weekend of each and every month from 6:00 P.M. Friday until 6:00 P.M. Sunday" and from 4:00 P.M. until 8:00 P.M. each Tuesday and Thursday evening. The judgment further provided that Ms. Garrison was to have visitation with Jordin for two weeks each summer and established a holiday visitation schedule. Ms. Garrison's visitation was to be supervised by her mother, Ms. Howard, or her step-father, Mr. Howard. The judgment stated that, if Ms. Garrison failed to exercise her visitation, Ms. Howard could exercise visitation with Jordin in her daughter's place.

On September 9, 2003, Mr. Bryan filed a motion to modify the trial court's judgment of March 27, 2002, by modifying the visitation arrangement. Specifically, Mr. Bryan alleged that Jordin had been sexually abused while in the care of the Howards. Because of the alleged abuse, Mr. Bryan's motion sought to modify visitation to protect Jordin's safety and welfare. Mr. Bryan also filed a motion seeking to terminate or restrict the visitation rights of Ms. Garrison and Ms. Howard, until such time as the court could determine their fitness to continue visitation. Both motions included a request for the court to appoint a guardian ad litem.

Ms. Howard filed an answer to Mr. Bryan's motion to modify, denying the allegations of abuse, and a countermotion to modify in which she requested "primary care, custody and control of" Jordin. In support of her countermotion, Ms. Howard alleged that awarding her custody of Jordin would be in Jordin's best interests because Mr. Bryan changed his residence frequently; failed to keep a safe, clean, and healthy home; made false accusations against her and her husband; and kept Jordin from seeing her and her husband with whom he had developed a bond. The countermotion further requested that Mr. Bryan's visitation with Jordin be supervised and that the court appoint a guardian ad litem. The trial court appointed a guardian ad litem.

At the end of the trial, the trial court found "no sufficient evidence" that Jordin had been abused "in any way." Nevertheless, the trial court found that, due to the fact that the Howards had recently moved to Colorado, a modification in visitation between Ms. Howard and Jordin was necessary. The trial court awarded Ms. Howard two separate two-week visitation periods during June, July and August of each year. In the trial court's findings, the court also awarded Ms. Howard two separate one-week periods of visitation in Colorado when Jordin is not in school. [FN1] Further, the trial court's order also provided that, whenever Ms. Howard is in the state of Missouri, she is entitled to see Jordin, provided she gives seven days notice to Mr. Bryan and the visitation does not interfere with Jordin's school plans or with holidays. The trial court did not change the terms of Ms. Garrison's visitation as set out in the Judgment of Paternity dated March 27, 2002. Consequently, the terms of visitation as originally set out in the March 27, 2002 judgment, including Ms. Howard's right to visitation with Jordin in the event Ms. Garrison fails to exercise visitation, remain in full force and effect. Mr. Bryan filed this appeal.

FN1. In the portion of the judgment where the trial court made its orders, however, the trial court did not include these additional one-week visitation periods. This court will assume that the trial court intended to award Ms. Howard the two separate one-week periods of visitation and that the trial court could correct its scrivener's omission by a judgment nunc pro tunc.

Standard of Review

[1][2][3][4][5] A grandparent visitation case is governed by the same standard of review as in other court-tried civil cases . . . To prevail on his claim, Mr. Bryan must overcome this court's presumption that the judgment of the trial court is in Jordin's best interest. *Id.* Where evidence on an issue is disputed, or where there is contradictory evidence, this court defers to the trial court's credibility determinations. *Doynov,* 149 S.W.3d at 922. This court grants the trial court's judgment greater deference in child custody cases than in other types of cases. *Id.*

Findings Sufficient

[6] In his first point on appeal, Mr. Bryan claims the trial court erred by failing to make findings required under section 452.402.2, RSMo 2000, Cum.Supp.2005. [FN2] Specifically, Mr. Bryan claims the trial court erred in failing to determine whether visitation with Ms. Howard was in Jordin's best interests and whether visitation with Ms. Howard would "endanger [Jordin's] physical health or impair [Jordin's] emotional development."

FN2. All statutory references are to the Revised Statutes of Missouri 2000, Cum.Supp.2005, unless otherwise indicated.

Ms. Howard intervened in the original paternity action. Under the terms of the parenting plan agreed to by the parties and adopted by the court, Ms. Howard was granted the right to supervise Ms. Garrison's visitation. In the event Ms. Garrison failed to exercise her right to visit Jordin, the original judgment awarded Ms. Howard visitation rights in Ms. Garrison's place. In his motion to modify, Mr. Bryan sought to modify Ms. Garrison and Ms. Howard's visitation rights, based on alleged sexual abuse during court-ordered visitation.

. . .

While Mr. Bryan's motion to modify sought a modification of both Ms. Garrison and Ms. Howard's visitation, in his point on appeal, Mr. Bryan only asserts error regarding the trial court's modification with respect to Ms. Howard. Therefore, this court will consider Mr. Bryan's alleged error solely in terms of a modification of grandparent visitation.

In determining whether to initially award a grandparent visitation rights under section 452.402.2, Mr. Bryan correctly notes that the trial court is required to "determine if the visitation by the grandparent would be in the child's best interest or if it would endanger the child's physical health or impair the child's emotional development." Moreover, "[v]isitation may only be ordered when the court finds such visitation to be in the best interests of the child." Section 452.402.2. Mr. Bryan's motion to modify visitation, however, is not an initial determination of visitation rights. Rather, Mr. Bryan's motion seeks a modification of visitation. Therefore, this case is governed by the applicable standards for a modification of visitation. As this court held in *Noakes,* section 452.400 governs and under that section, "*modification* of grandparent visitation rights requires only a reasonable finding that such modification is in the child's best interests." 168 S.W.3d at 596.

In this case, the trial court specifically found:

> 6. Since the date of the Judgment of Paternity, there have been changed circumstances so substantial and continuing as to make the terms of said Judgment and Decree unreasonable regarding the health, safety, welfare and best interests of [Jordin].
>
> 7. As a result of said circumstances, a modification of the judgment is necessary to serve the best interests of [Jordin].

. . .

Thus, the trial court found that awarding Ms. Howard unsupervised visitation with Jordin was in Jordin's best interests. Moreover, in regard to Mr. Bryan's allegation that Mr. Howard sexually abused Jordin, the trial court specifically found that there was insufficient evidence to support this claim. Rather, the changed circumstance that the trial court found justified modification was the Howards moving to Colorado.

The trial court's findings under section 452.402.2 are sufficient. The trial court found that the modification was in Jordin's best interests as required by *Noakes.* 168 S.W.3d at 596. In addition, the trial court found insufficient evidence to support the allegations of abuse. The statute does not require more detailed findings. . . . Mr. Bryan's first point is denied.

. . .

Award of Visitation to Ms. Howard Was Excessive

[10] In his second point on appeal, Mr. Bryan claims the trial court erred by awarding Ms. Howard excessive visitation. Specifically, Mr. Bryan claims that section 452.402 does not contemplate visitation for a grandparent in amounts consistent with parental visitation. Rather, Mr. Bryan claims visitation awarded to a grandparent under section 452.402 must be minimally intrusive to the family. Mr. Bryan claims that, because the visitation awarded to Ms. Howard by the trial court was not minimally intrusive, the trial court erred.

In this case, Ms. Howard was permitted to intervene pursuant to section 452.402.1(1), which allows a grandparent to file a motion to modify the original decree of dissolution and seek visitation when the grandparent has been denied visitation. The version of section 452.402 in effect at the time of the judgment provided, in pertinent part:

> 1. The court may grant reasonable visitation rights to the grandparents of the child and issue any necessary orders to enforce the decree. The court may grant grandparent visitation when:
>
> (1) The parents of the child have filed for a dissolution of their marriage. A grandparent shall have the right to intervene in any dissolution action solely on the issue of visitation rights. Grandparents shall also have the right to file a motion to modify the original decree of dissolution to seek visitation rights when visitation has been denied to them. . . .

In *Herndon v. Tuhey,* section 452.402 was challenged as violating the United States Constitution. 857 S.W.2d 203 (Mo. banc 1993). There, the grandparents were awarded visitation for nine hours on the first and third Saturday of each month, to be followed, after three months, with a schedule of nine hours visitation on the first Saturday of each month and an overnight stay on the third weekend of each month. *Id.* at 206. Additionally, the grandparents were awarded five hours of visitation on or around Thanksgiving Day and five hours of visitation on December twenty-third for Christmas. *Id.* Finally, the grandparents were awarded two days of visitation during the child's Christmas vacation, with an overnight stay, and one week during summer vacation. *Id.* In addition to this scheduled visitation, the parents were required to inform the grandparents regarding activities in which the child was involved so the grandparents could attend. *Id.*

The parents challenged section 452.402, claiming they possessed a constitutional right to raise their children without intervention from the state. *Id.* at 207. They argued that, by forcing them to permit visitation with the grandparents, the statute violated their constitutional rights. *Id.* The Missouri Supreme Court disagreed, finding subsections 452.402.1(3) and 452.402.2 constitutional. *Id.* at 208. The Court found that "[e]ven given the fact that parents have a constitutional right to make decisions affecting the family, the magnitude of the infringement by the state is a significant consideration in determining whether a statute will be struck down as unconstitutional." *Id.* The Court found that subsections 452.402.1(3) and 452.402.2 did not require a substantial enough encroachment on the family to be unconstitutional. *Id.* at 209. Rather, the visitation contemplated by the statute was "occasional, temporary visitation, which may only be allowed if a trial court finds visitation to be in the best interest of the child and does not endanger the child's physical or emotional development." *Id.*

Nevertheless, the Court did find that the specific visitation awarded was excessive. *Id.* at 210. The Court "interpret[ed] the language of section 452.402, which requires as a prerequisite to ordering visitation an unreasonable denial of visitation for ninety days, to mean that visitation is to be much more limited than what was granted by the trial judge." *Id.* Further, the Court found "that visitation should not be excessive, should not be on a par with parental visitation in custody matters, and should not necessarily be commensurate with the contact between the grandparents and grandchild prior to the deterioration of relations between the parties." *Id.* The Court remanded the case to the trial court to reassess the visitation. *Id.* at 211.

Several years after *Herndon,* however, the United States Supreme Court held a Washington statute permitting grandparent visitation unconstitutional as applied by the Washington courts. *Troxel v. Granville,* 530 U.S. 57, 73, 120 S.Ct. 2054, 2064, 147 L.Ed.2d 49 (2000). The constitutionality of section 452.402 was subsequently challenged again in *Blakely v. Blakely,* 83 S.W.3d 537 (Mo. banc 2002). The parents in *Blakely* claimed that, under the Supreme Court's decision in *Troxel,* section 452.402 was unconstitutional because it does not require a finding that lack of grandparent visitation will cause harm to the child. *Id.* at 543. The Court in *Blakely* determined *Troxel,* which found the Washington statute unconstitutional as applied, was based on the "'breathtakingly broad'" wording of the statute, the trial court's failure to give deference to the parent's decision regarding visitation, and the trial court's failure to take into account the parent's willingness to permit limited visitation. 83 S.W.3d at 542-43 (quoting *Troxel,* 530 U.S. at 67, 71, 120 S.Ct. 2054).

The Court, in *Blakely,* found that the United States Supreme Court's concerns in *Troxel* were not applicable to section 452.402. 83 S.W.3d at 543-44. *Blakely* found that, under *Troxel,* "the constitutionality of any standard for awarding visitation should turn on the specific manner in which that standard was applied." 83 S.W.3d at 543. *Blakely* found critical distinctions between the Washington statute and section 452.402. First, section 452.402 is more limited in terms of who may seek visitation. *Id.* at 544. While the Washington statute permitted anyone to seek visitation, section 452.402 is limited to the child's grandparents. *Id.* Second, *Blakely* found that, under section 452.402.1(3) [FN7], a grandparent must be denied visitation entirely for a period of ninety days before the statute takes effect. *Id.* Under this standard, the grandparents in *Troxel* would not have been able to obtain a visitation order under section 452.402 because the parent in *Troxel* was willing to allow limited visitation. *Id.* at 545. Third, *Blakely* found that, unlike the Washington statute, section 452.402.1(3) places "the burden of proving that [the] denial of visitation was 'unreasonable'" on the grandparents. *Id.* Finally, *Blakely* found that section 452.402, "unlike the Washington statute, does not simply leave the best interests issue to the unfettered discretion of the trial judge." *Id.* Rather, section 452.402 provides for "procedural safeguards that assist the judge in making the best interests determination, including providing for a home study, for consultation with the child regarding his or her wishes, and for appointment of a guardian ad litem." *Id.*

> FN7. The version of section 452.402 in effect at the time when *Blakely* was decided read:
> "1. The court may grant reasonable visitation rights to the grandparents of the child and issue any necessary order to enforce the decree. The court may grant grandparent visitation when:
> (1) The parents of the child have filed for a dissolution of their marriage. A grandparent shall have the right to intervene in any dissolution action solely on the issue of visitation rights. Grandparents shall also have the right to file a motion to modify the original decree of dissolution to seek visitation rights when such rights have been denied to them;
> (2) One parent of the child is deceased and the surviving parent denied reasonable visitation rights;
> (3) A grandparent is unreasonably denied visitation with the child for a period exceeding ninety days; or
> (4) The child is adopted by a stepparent, another grandparent or other blood relative.
> 2. The court shall determine if the visitation by the grandparent would be in the child's best interest or if it would endanger the child's physical health or impair the child's emotional development. Visitation may only be ordered when the court finds such visitation to be in the best interests of the child. The court may order reasonable conditions or restrictions on grandparent visitation."

Blakely "reaffirm[ed] the narrow interpretation of Missouri's statute adopted in *Herndon.*" 83 S.W.3d at 544. The Court found that such an interpretation met the standard set out in *Troxel. Id.* In so doing, the *Blakely* court affirmed *Herndon's* holding "that the statute contemplates only *'occasional, temporary visitation,* which may only be allowed if a trial court finds visitation to be in the best interest of the child and does not endanger the child's physical or emotional development.'" *Id.* at 543-44 (quoting *Herndon,* 857 S.W.2d at 209). Consequently, *Blakely* reiterated that section 452.402 "permitted only a '*minimal intrusion* on the family relationship.'" *Id.* at 544 (quoting *Herndon,* 857 S.W.2d at 210). Ultimately, the Court found that two hours of visitation every ninety days was not unconstitutionally excessive under the statute. *Id.* at 548.

Although *Herndon* and *Blakely* were construing the constitutionality of [section] 452.402.1(3) and not the remaining subsections of [section] 452.402.1, it is clear that the occasional, minimal restriction recognized by the *Herndon* court is necessary for all of section 452.402 to be constitutional. [FN8] *Hampton,* 17 S.W.3d at

604. [FN9] While recognizing that what may constitute a minimal intrusion will vary according to circumstances, the *Hampton* court noted that a parent does not lose the parent's fundamental right to direct the upbringing of [the parent's child] upon the dissolution of the parent's marriage. *Id.* at 605. *Hampton* concluded that visitation amounting to "more than a minimal intrusion on the family relationship" was "unconstitutional and prohibited."

FN8. Section 452.402 has been amended since the *Herndon* decision. Nevertheless, the substance of the statute has not been changed so as to impact the Court's decisions in *Herndon* or *Blakely.*

FN9. Both *Herndon* and *Blakely* dealt with section 452.402.1(3). This court's Southern District has held that *Herndon's* constitutional analysis does not control section 452.402.1(1) or 452.402.1(2). *Whoberry v. Whoberry,* 977 S.W.2d 946, 950 (Mo.App. S.D.1996). Both this court's Western District and Eastern District, however, have held that the constitutional analysis of *Herndon* applies to section 452.402.1(1) and 452.402.1(2).

. . .

In *Hampton,* the father was awarded primary physical custody of the child, subject to the mother's right to reasonable visitation. 17 S.W.3d at 601. Specifically, the mother was awarded visitation on alternate weekends, alternate major holidays, and two two-week periods in the summer. *Id.* The father subsequently filed a motion to modify requesting that the mother's visitation be supervised, and requesting sole legal custody and modified physical custody. *Id.* One changed circumstance cited by the father was the mother's impending incarceration. *Id.* The maternal grandparents intervened. *Id.* The trial court's judgment awarded the father sole legal custody, but awarded grandparents visitation every other weekend from 6:00 P.M. on Friday until 6:00 P.M. on Sunday, while Mother was incarcerated. *Id.* The trial court further ordered that, after Mother was released, her visitation would be supervised. *Id.* On appeal, this court found that requiring visitation every other weekend from 6 P.M. on Friday to 6 P.M. on Sunday is not minimal. *Id.* Consequently, the court in *Hampton* reversed the judgment of the trial court as an unconstitutional application of section 452.402. *Id.*

This court agrees with the analysis set forth in *Hampton* that visitation awarded under section 452.402 must be minimally intrusive on the family to be constitutional. Here, the trial court awarded Ms. Howard "two (2) separate two (2) week periods during the summer months of June, July and August of each and every year." The trial court also found she should have two one-week periods of visitation when Jordin was not in school. Additionally, the trial court's judgment states "[t]hat on such occasions when [Ms. Howard] is in the State of Missouri she shall be allowed to have a visitation period with [Jordin] for so long as she provides [Mr. Bryan] seven (7) days advance notice and that said period of visitation shall not interfere with [Jordin's] school attendance nor holidays."

. . .

As with *Herndon* and *Hampton,* the visitation awarded here is not a minimal intrusion on the family relationship. *Herndon,* 857 S.W.2d at 210; *Hampton,* 17 S.W.3d at 605. Because this court finds the trial court misapplied the law by awarding excessive visitation, the provisions for visitation by Ms. Howard are reversed, and this case is remanded back to the trial court to award visitation consistent with Missouri law. While the circumstances of this case are that Ms. Howard has custody of Dylon, Jordin's half-brother, and was the primary caregiver of Jordin for six months, the visitation order must still be only occasional, temporary visitation that is not commensurate with parental visitation and is only a minimal intrusion on the family relationship. The trial court's award in this case was excessive. The judgment is affirmed in all other respects.

All concur.

Source: *Bryan v. Garrison,* 187 S.W.3d 900 (St. Paul, MN: Thomson West). Reprinted with permission from Westlaw.

MAINTENANCE OR ALIMONY

You should be certain to review applicable state statutes pertaining to the award of financial support to one spouse, typically called maintenance or alimony payments. Traditionally, the court awarded permanent alimony because the woman was usually a stay-at-home mother who had no independent means of financial support once the marriage ended. Today, nearly all states will still award support to a spouse, but it is typically limited to a specific period of time, with the intention to give the recipient time to enter the workforce and maybe also to receive an education in order to qualify for a job and help the person become financially independent. Keep in mind that maintenance is no longer restricted to the woman, and thus courts have made such awards to the man also.

PROPERTY SETTLEMENTS

marital property
The property accumulated by a couple during marriage, called community property in some states.

When a marriage is terminated, the couple must decide how jointly owned property will be divided. Often this division is uncertain because it may not be absolutely clear what may be classified as marital property. **Marital property** is that which is acquired during the marriage. It does not matter if only one person worked outside the home and only that person financially contributed to the purchase of property during the marriage. If it was acquired while the parties were married, it is still marital property. In this case, the property will be divided equally, or under some other arrangement if both parties agree and the court determines it is equitable and fair to both spouses.

Specific property may be in the name of only one spouse, possibly because it was acquired before the marriage by that person. However, if that property is then brought into the marriage and not kept separate, then it becomes marital property. For example, if a woman owns a house prior to marriage, and it is titled in just her name, once she marries and the spouses live in that house during the marriage, it becomes marital property. However, assume Fiona owns undeveloped lakefront property that she inherited from her parents prior to marrying Ian. If Fiona and Ian live together as a married couple in a condominium purchased together after the marriage, and the lakefront property remains undeveloped, then upon divorce, Fiona retains sole ownership and rights to that property, as it was never commingled. Similarly, if the individual bank accounts of two people are merged into one joint savings account upon marriage, then each spouse's share loses its separate identity and is now classified as joint marital property.

In arriving at an equitable division of assets, the court must first ascertain what those assets are and then classify them as marital or separate property. In addition, liabilities and debts must also be identified, as these must also be divided fairly. In deciding what is fair, the court considers such factors as the relative contribution of the spouses, the length of the marriage, and the ages of the two parties. Division of marital property is entirely discretionary, and thus the court will often order mediation in hopes that the parties themselves will arrive at reasonable and equitable distribution agreements.

community property
All property acquired during marriage in a community property state, owned in equal shares.

Keep in mind that a handful of states are classified as **community property** states. Here, all property, except gifts and inheritance, is deemed marital property, and hence the court divides all of it equally without regard to who bought it or how it is titled. If the property is not subject to division easily, such as a house, then typically the court will require that it be sold and its proceeds divided. If there are minor children, then the custodial parent may be allowed to keep the house, so long as there is cash or some other property equal in value to the price of the house. If one spouse dies, the other spouse is entitled to receive one-half of the community property.

PARENT-CHILD ISSUES

Two specific issues arise in the context of the relationship between a parent and a child that will be discussed in this chapter: *adoption* and *paternity*. In both cases, states and family law courts ascertain the legal relationship between the parties. Legal proceedings are instituted usually because the parent is contesting rights and duties associated with the relationship.

adoption
The taking of a child into the family, creating a parent-child relationship where the biological relationship did not exist.

Adoption is the process by which a party becomes the legal parent of a child who is not biologically related to them. This situation may arise in several cases: where the biological parents are deceased or unable to care for the child, where the court has terminated rights due to abuse or neglect, or where the parents legally and voluntarily give up the child for adoption.

Adoption is a complex and typically lengthy process that is governed by state statutes, and these vary greatly. In every situation, the court is striving to determine what is in the child's best interests. Normally, there are three minimum requirements for an adoption. First, the biological parents must give up their legal rights, either by consent, death, or order of the court. Second, the adoptive parents must follow the court procedures of their state. Finally, the adoption must be formally approved by a judge. Other requirements may exist, so you should be certain to consult the statute in your state.

Adoptions can occur either through a social service agency recognized by the state or by independent adoption. The procedures for adoption will vary based on whether the child is coming through private adoption or otherwise. Independent adoption is where the biological parents and the adoptive parents mutually and privately agree to transfer parental and legal rights to the child. In these types of adoptions, there is still a large measure of court supervision and involvement of a social service agency in the state, as authorities want to ensure that the adoption is not the result of illegal "baby brokering" or the "sale" of the child

RESEARCH THIS!

Locate the statute in your state pertaining to adoption proceedings. Identify the requirements for an adoption to be approved. In addition, review the classified advertisements in your local newspaper. Are there ads for private adoptions? Are adoption agencies listed?

for financial gain. Hence, all adoptions, whether independent or through an agency, must be approved by the court.

In an agency adoption, an adoption agency licensed by the state acts as an intermediary, screening and thoroughly investigating prospective parents to determine if the parents are willing and able to meet the demands of assuming the role of a parent. Factors that an agency will consider in screening potential adoptive parents include whether there are already other children in the home, the financial stability of the parents, their health, their ages, and their religious background. It is intended that gathering such information will hopefully ensure that the adoptive parents are a good match and it is in the best interests of the child.

paternity action
A lawsuit to identify the father of a child born outside of marriage.

The second issue arising out of the parent-child relationship is a **paternity action.** This proceeding is instituted with the goal of ascertaining the true identity of a baby's father. This is a civil action, usually brought by the mother of a baby born out of wedlock. Paternity actions are brought because the mother wants to establish parental rights and seek child support from the putative father. In certain cases, it may be the father bringing the paternity action, sometimes to prove that he is *not* the father, but sometimes also to establish custody or visitation rights. In many states, the law presumes that the husband is the legal father of the child, and thus a father can bring a paternity action to prove he is *not* the biological father of the baby. However, note that some states will not allow fathers to overcome this presumption, even through DNA testing, as these states conclusively assert that husbands are the legal fathers.

Uniform Parentage Act
An act defining legal parentage and establishing parental rights.

In 1973, the National Conference of Commissioners on Uniform State Laws, the "Uniform Law Commissioners," drafted the **Uniform Parentage Act,** last amended in 2002. This Act was promulgated as a follow-up to U.S. Supreme Court decisions regarding illegitimacy and parentage that were decided in the 1960s and 1970s. Under common law, a child whose mother was not married was deemed to be an illegitimate child, and therefore the father of such a child was free of any burdens or obligations concerning that illegitimate child. The child had no right to financial support, and the father had no custodial rights. The U.S. Supreme Court eliminated illegitimacy as a legal barrier, and subsequently the Uniform Parentage Act was promulgated. In effect, the parent-child relationship now extended equally to every child and parent, regardless of the parent's marital status. The Act's purpose was to identify the natural father of any child, for purposes of ordering child support and establishing parental rights. Paternity actions included the use of blood tests to adjudicate parenthood for the alleged mother or father. The revised Act in 2002 established modern genetic testing as an efficient means to establish legal parentage.

CYBER TRIP

The following Web site is an excellent resource for information related to adoption, as it is a national adoption information clearinghouse: www.calib.com/naic/laws/index.cfm.

Lastly, an issue that unfortunately may arise in the context of a parent-child relationship is the legal responsibility that parents have to properly care for their children. To this end, parents are prohibited from physically abusing their children, and in such cases, civil law becomes intertwined with criminal law to resolve the situation. Criminal actions for child abuse and neglect may be instituted

A Day in the Life of a Real Paralegal

Paralegals have a significant role in this area of the law, as they are often responsible for interviewing the parties, gathering personal and financial information about them, and then preparing and filing petitions and motions. Paralegals that specialize in family law will have a variety of duties involving both document preparation as well as client contact. Sometimes the most difficult task will be balancing the emotional needs with the practical needs of the firm's clients. You may be asked to sit in on the initial client interview. At this stage, you have a fact-gathering role, and thus your firm will likely use a client questionnaire to ascertain information about the client's spouse, children, property, and debts. You will use this information to open the client's file and draft the relevant documents, such as a prenuptial agreement, a petition for dissolution of marriage, or settlement agreements. In addition to drafting documents, you may be asked to research the law in your state, as family law is largely governed by statutes. You may also want to consult the family law guidelines that are frequently published by your local bar association. In this respect, the desire for knowledge is crucial, particularly since this is a constantly evolving area of law. Finally, you will likely assist the attorney in mediation or pretrial preparation, or even the private adoption process for a client. Though family law is an emotionally charged area of the law, it is also extremely challenging and rewarding.

against the accused parent(s) after the state has investigated such allegations. At the same time, the state social service agency steps in to remove the child from the home pending the outcome of the criminal proceedings. Whether the child is temporarily or permanently removed from a parent's custody is dependent upon the resolution of criminal proceedings as well as the ability of the state to secure a court order authorizing permanent removal from the home. The state must provide clear and convincing evidence that the parent has negligently failed to provide the necessaries of life to a child or that the parent has intentionally harmed the child physically and/or emotionally. After evidence is presented, the court may decide to involuntarily terminate parental rights, should it find that one or both parents did nothing to protect the child's best interests or prevent abuse.

Summary

Family law, or domestic relations, is a wide-encompassing area that centers on the family unit. Relationships between husband and wife, and between parent and child, are all within the scope of this area. Since family law is predominantly governed by state statutes, as well as certain federal acts, you should know the applicable rules and procedures in your state. Many states have enacted statutes that adopt uniform acts such as the UCCJA. Keep in mind that this area of the law is constantly changing. Therefore, issues such as the legal requirements to marry or the criteria for awarding support or custody should be examined closely in light of your state's most current case law and statutes.

Key Terms

Adoption
Alimony
Annulment
Child support
Cohabitation agreement
Common law marriage
Community property
Consanguinity
Custody
Divorce/dissolution
Domicile
Guardian ad litem
Marital property
Mediation
No-fault divorce
Palimony
Parental Kidnapping Protection Act (PKPA)
Paternity action
Prenuptial agreement
Separation agreements
Solemnization
Temporary restraining order
Uniform Child Custody Jurisdiction Act (UCCJA)
Uniform Parentage Act
Visitation rights
Void ab initio

Discussion Questions

1. Some people suggest that too many marriages end in divorce, and therefore the institution of traditional solemnized marriages is no longer preferred, and thus more states should recognize common law marriages. Discuss the legal rights and benefits of each form of marriage and the implications of this argument.
2. In some states, grandparents are able to obtain visitation rights with their grandchildren. Do you think the courts should take into account the interests of the parents regarding with whom their child should have contact? Does it matter if the grandparents have had significant relationships with the child prior to the parents' divorce?
3. The "best interests of the child" is the prevailing standard when determining custody, but to what extent should the court take into consideration the interests of the parents? Discuss your view on the constitutionality of state statutes granting grandparents visitation rights.
4. "No-fault divorce laws that deny divorcees the opportunity to apportion blame for the breakdown of the marriage can never be successful in today's society." Discuss your views on this statement, taking into account your state's laws.

Exercises

1. Samantha and Darren have been married for 10 years. During the past three years, Darren has become increasingly depressed and physically abusive toward Samantha. He has broken her jaw on one occasion and her arm on another. However, in the past few months, his assaults have been verbal rather than physical. Their two children, Tabitha and Agnes, who are nine and seven, respectively, have been in the house when the assaults have occurred and witnessed some violence and heard Darren's verbal assaults. But, Darren has never physically assaulted the children and is generally a loving and devoted father. Samantha has, however, finally decided that she has had enough and has left the family home with the children. She is now living in her parents' house, which is a large, comfortable home, and her parents are very happy for her to stay indefinitely. However, Samantha wants to return home with the children to reside. What might be the likely result? What if she had shown no interest in the children residing with her? Would your answer be different if the family home is in Darren's name only? What if Darren had repeatedly telephoned Samantha's parents' home while she was living there, 20 or more times each day?
2. Henry and Amanda have cohabitated together for almost 15 years in a state that recognizes common law marriages. They have no children. Their best friends, Rachel and Tony, have also lived together for about 10 years and have no children. One day, Rachel discovers that she is pregnant and is horrified by what her parents will think, and thus convinces Amanda and Henry to raise the baby as their own once he is born. All four parties agree to this, and so when Duncan is born, Rachel immediately hands him over to Amanda. Five months later, Rachel is reading an article in Home Life magazine about surrogate parents and starts thinking about Duncan. She becomes depressed and asks Tony to write Amanda and Henry a letter, notifying them that she has made a terrible mistake and wants Duncan back. However, Amanda refuses, stating that they have become attached to Duncan and plan to formally adopt him. Discuss the likely result.
3. Nick and Jessica have lived together for 15 years but never married. They have two children, Anne, aged 9, and Marty, aged 7. Nick leaves Jessica to move to New Zealand to start a new life with his partner, Andy. Although extremely happy, Nick misses the children and writes and calls them on the telephone every week. He pays for their visits to New Zealand every summer to stay with him and Andy. Jessica has been taking depression medication since the separation and is now addicted to pain killers. They agree that Mona, Jessica's mother, should care for Anne and Marty until Jessica is able to resume a normal life and receive treatment. However, six months later, Nick receives a letter from Anne in which she expresses anger and hurt about the living arrangements and how she and Marty feel abandoned by both parents. Nick is devastated and wants to immediately bring the children to New Zealand to live with him. Jessica objects and demands that Mona return the children to her at once. Mona believes that the children are happy and better off with her, insisting that both Nick and Jessica are irresponsible and selfish parents. Discuss the issues here, consulting your own state statutes for guidance.

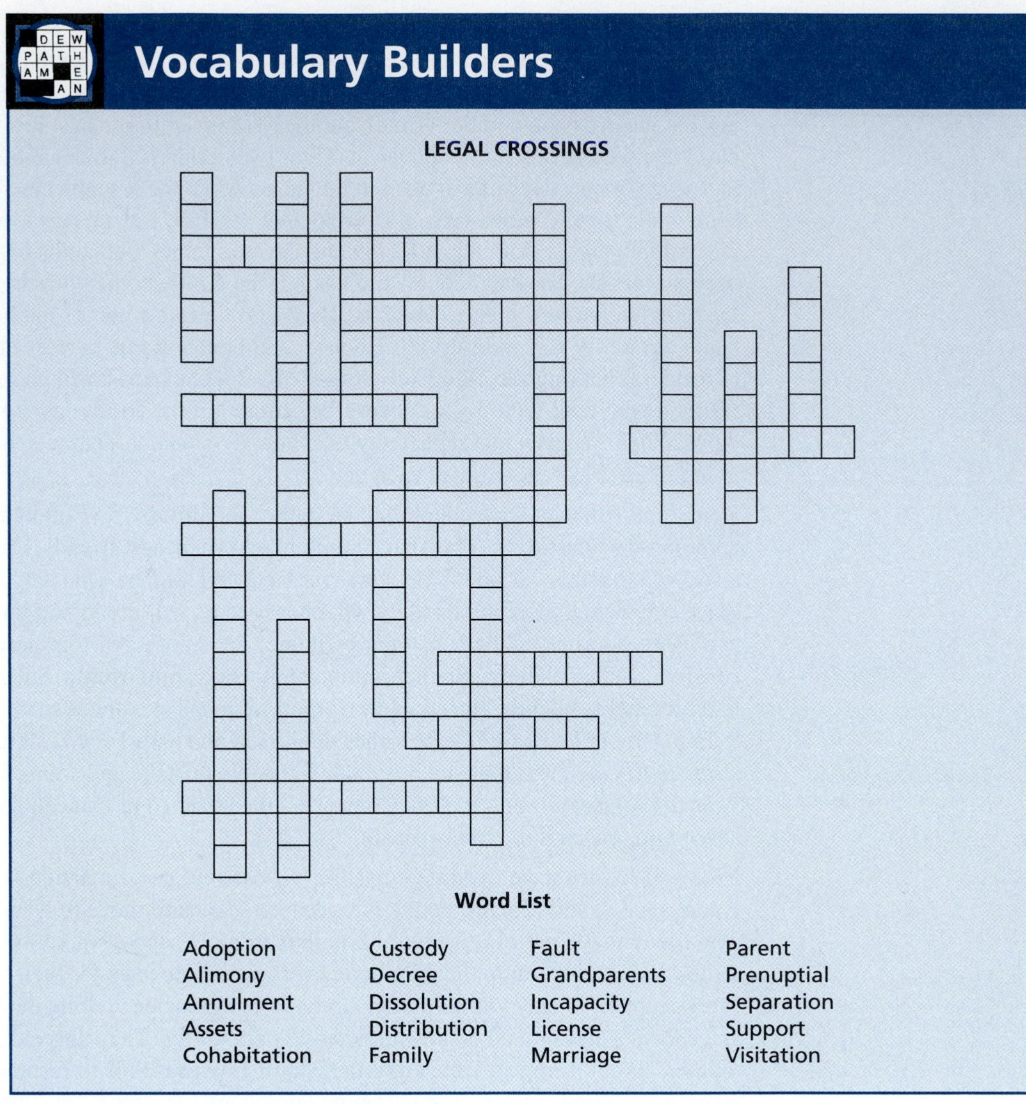
Vocabulary Builders
LEGAL CROSSINGS
Word List
Adoption
Alimony
Annulment
Assets
Cohabitation
Custody
Decree
Dissolution
Distribution
Family
Fault
Grandparents
Incapacity
License
Marriage
Parent
Prenuptial
Separation
Support
Visitation

Appendix A

CRIMINAL LAW

Model Penal Code—Selected Provisions[1]

§ 1.13 General Definitions.

In this Code, unless a different meaning plainly is required:

(1) "statute" includes the Constitution and a local law or ordinance of a political subdivision of the State;

(2) "act" or "action" means a bodily movement whether voluntary or involuntary;

(3) "voluntary" has the meaning specified in Section 2.01;

(4) "omission" means a failure to act;

(5) "conduct" means an action or omission and its accompanying state of mind, or, where relevant, a series of acts and omissions;

(6) "actor" includes, where relevant, a person guilty of an omission;

(7) "acted" includes, where relevant, "omitted to act";

(8) "person," "he" and "actor" include any natural person and, where relevant, a corporation or an unincorporated association;

(9) "element of an offense" means (i) such conduct or (ii) such attendant circumstances or (iii) such a result of conduct as
 (a) is included in the description of the forbidden conduct in the definition of the offense; or
 (b) establishes the required kind of culpability; or
 (c) negatives an excuse or justification for such conduct; or
 (d) negatives a defense under the statute of limitations; or
 (e) establishes jurisdiction or venue;

(10) "material element of an offense" means an element that does not relate exclusively to the statute of limitations, jurisdiction, venue or to any other matter similarly unconnected with (i) the harm or evil, incident to conduct, sought to be prevented by the law defining the offense, or (ii) the existence of a justification or excuse for such conduct;

(11) "purposely" has the meaning specified in Section 2.02 and equivalent terms such as "with purpose," "designed" or "with design" have the same meaning;

(12) "intentionally" or "with intent" means purposely;

(13) "knowingly" has the meaning specified in Section 2.02 and equivalent terms such as "knowing" or "with knowledge" have the same meaning;

(14) "recklessly" has the meaning specified in Section 2.02 and equivalent terms such as "recklessness" or "with" have the same meaning;

(15) "negligently" has the meaning specified in Section 2.02 and equivalent terms such as "negligence"' recklessness or "with negligence" have the same meaning;

(16) "reasonably believes" or "reasonable belief" designates a belief which the actor is not reckless or negligent in holding.

[1] Copyright 1985 by the American Law Institute. Reprinted with permission. All rights reserved.

2.01 Requirement of Voluntary Act; Omission as Basis of Liability; Possession as an Act.

(1) A person is not guilty of an offense unless his liability is based on conduct which includes a voluntary act or the omission to perform an act of which he is physically capable.

(2) The following are not voluntary acts within the meaning of this Section:
  (a) a reflex or convulsion;
  (b) a bodily movement during unconsciousness or sleep;
  (c) conduct during hypnosis or resulting from hypnotic suggestion;
  (d) a bodily movement that otherwise is not a product of the effort or determination of the actor, either conscious or habitual.

(3) Liability for the commission of an offense may not be based on an omission unaccompanied by action unless:
  (a) the omission is expressly made sufficient by the law defining the offense; or
  (b) duty to perform the omitted act is otherwise imposed by law.

(4) Possession is an act, within the meaning of this Section, if the possessor knowingly procured or received the thing possessed or was aware of his control thereof for a sufficient period to have been able to terminate his possession.

2.02 General Requirements of Culpability.

(1) Minimum Requirements of Culpability. Except as provided in Section 2.05, a person is not guilty of an offense unless he acted purposely, knowingly, recklessly or negligently, as the law may require, with respect to each material element of the offense.

(2) Kinds of Culpability Defined.
  (a) Purposely.
  A person acts purposely with respect to a material element of an offense when:
    (i) if the element involves the nature of his conduct or a result thereof, it is his conscious object to engage in conduct of that nature or to cause such a result; and
    (ii) if the element involves the attendant circumstances, he is aware of the existence of such circumstances or he believes or hopes that they exist.
  (b) Knowingly.
  A person acts knowingly with respect to a material element of an offense when:
    (i) if the element involves the nature of his conduct or the attendant circumstances, he is aware that his conduct is of that nature or that such circumstances exist; and
    (ii) if the element involves a result of his conduct, he is aware that it is practically certain that his conduct will cause such a result.
  (c) Recklessly.
  A person acts recklessly with respect to a material element of an offense when he consciously disregards a substantial and unjustifiable risk that the material element exists or will result from his conduct. The risk must be of such a nature and degree that, considering the nature and purpose of the actor's conduct and the circumstances known to him, its disregard involves a gross deviation from the standard of conduct that a law-abiding person would observe in the actor's situation.
  (d) Negligently.
  A person acts negligently with respect to a material element of an offense when he should be aware of a substantial and unjustifiable risk that the material element exists or will result from his conduct. The risk must be of such a nature and degree that the actor's failure to perceive it, considering the nature and purpose of his conduct and the circumstances known to him, involves a gross deviation from the standard of care that a reasonable person would observe in the actor's situation.

(3) Culpability Required Unless Otherwise Provided. When the culpability sufficient to establish a material element of an offense is not prescribed by law, such element is established if a person acts purposely, knowingly or recklessly with respect thereto.

(4) Prescribed Culpability Requirement Applies to All Material Elements. When the law defining an offense prescribes the kind of culpability that is sufficient for the

commission of an offense, without distinguishing among the material elements thereof, such provision shall apply to all the material elements of the offense, unless a contrary purpose plainly appears.

(5) Substitutes for Negligence, Recklessness and Knowledge. When the law provides that negligence suffices to establish an element of an offense, such element also is established if a person acts purposely, knowingly or recklessly. When recklessness suffices to establish an element, such element also is established if a person acts purposely or knowingly. When acting knowingly suffices to establish an element, such element also is established if a person acts purposely.

(6) Requirement of Purpose Satisfied if Purpose Is Conditional. When a particular purpose is an element of an offense, the element is established although such purpose is conditional, unless the condition negatives the harm or evil sought to be prevented by the law defining the offense.

(7) Requirement of Knowledge Satisfied by Knowledge of High Probability. When knowledge of the existence of a particular fact is an element of an offense, such knowledge is established if a person is aware of a high probability of its existence, unless he actually believes that it does not exist.

(8) Requirement of Wilfulness Satisfied by Acting Knowingly. A requirement that an offense be committed willfully is satisfied if a person acts knowingly with respect to the material elements of the offense, unless a purpose to impose further requirements appears.

(9) Culpability as to Illegality of Conduct. Neither knowledge nor recklessness or negligence as to whether conduct constitutes an offense or as to the existence, meaning or application of the law determining the elements of an offense is an element of such offense, unless the definition of the offense or the Code so provides.

(10) Culpability as Determinant of Grade of Offense. When the grade or degree of an offense depends on whether the offense is committed purposely, knowingly, recklessly or negligently, its grade or degree shall be the lowest for which the determinative kind of culpability is established with respect to any material element of the offense.

2.04 Ignorance or Mistake.

(1) Ignorance or mistake as to a matter of fact or law is a defense if:
  (a) the ignorance or mistake negatives the purpose, knowledge, belief, recklessness or negligence required to establish a material element of the offense; or
  (b) the law provides that the state of mind established by such ignorance or mistake constitutes a defense.

(2) Although ignorance or mistake would otherwise afford a defense to the offense charged, the defense is not available if the defendant would be guilty of another offense had the situation been as he supposed. In such case, however, the ignorance or mistake of the defendant shall reduce the grade and degree of the offense of which he may be convicted to those of the offense of which he would be guilty had the situation been as he supposed.

(3) A belief that conduct does not legally constitute an offense is a defense to a prosecution for that offense based upon such conduct when:
  (a) the statute or other enactment defining the offense is not known to the actor and has not been published or otherwise reasonably made available prior to the conduct alleged; or
  (b) he acts in reasonable reliance upon an official statement of the law, afterward determined to be invalid or erroneous, contained in (i) a statute or other enactment; (ii) a judicial decision, opinion or judgment; (iii) an administrative order or grant of permission; or (iv) an official interpretation of the public officer or body charged by law with responsibility for the interpretation, administration or enforcement of the law defining the offense.

(4) The defendant must prove a defense arising under Subsection (3) of this Section by a preponderance of evidence.

2.05 When Culpability Requirements Are Inapplicable to Violations and to Offenses Defined by Other Statutes; Effect of Absolute Liability in Reducing Grade of Offense to Violation.

(1) The requirements of culpability prescribed by Sections 2.01 and 2.02 do not apply to:
  (a) offenses which constitute violations, unless the requirement involved is included in the definition of the offense or the Court determines that its application is consistent with effective enforcement of the law defining the offense; or
  (b) offenses defined by statutes other than the Code, insofar as a legislative purpose to impose absolute liability for such offenses or with respect to any material element thereof plainly appears.

Discussion

The Model Penal Code (MPC) is a statutory text developed by the American Law Institute in 1962 in an effort to standardize the penal law of the United States of America. As of the date of this writing, 37 states have adopted revised versions of the MPC, in part, and several states, such as New York and Pennsylvania, have enacted almost all its provisions. Selected provisions of the New York statute follow, as they are representative of the MPC.

Selected Criminal Statutes of the State of New York

120.10 Assault in the first degree.
A person is guilty of assault in the first degree when:

1. With intent to cause serious physical injury to another person, he causes such injury to such person or to a third person by means of a deadly weapon or a dangerous instrument; or
2. With intent to disfigure another person seriously and permanently, or to destroy, amputate or disable permanently a member or organ of his body, he causes such injury to such person or to a third person; or
3. Under circumstances evincing a depraved indifference to human life, he recklessly engages in conduct which creates a grave risk of death to another person, and thereby causes serious physical injury to another person; or
4. In the course of and in furtherance of the commission or attempted commission of a felony or of immediate flight therefrom, he, or another participant if there be any, causes serious physical injury to a person other than one of the participants.

Assault in the first degree is a class B felony.

§ 140.30 Burglary in the first degree.
A person is guilty of burglary in the first degree when he knowingly enters or remains unlawfully in a dwelling with intent to commit a crime therein, and when, in effecting entry or while in the dwelling or in immediate flight therefrom, he or another participant in the crime:

1. Is armed with explosives or a deadly weapon; or
2. Causes physical injury to any person who is not a participant in the crime; or
3. Uses or threatens the immediate use of a dangerous instrument; or
4. Displays what appears to be a pistol, revolver, rifle, shotgun, machine gun or other firearm; except that in any prosecution under this subdivision, it is an affirmative defense that such pistol, revolver, rifle, shotgun, machine gun or other firearm was not a loaded weapon from which a shot, readily capable of producing death or other serious physical injury, could be discharged. Nothing contained in this subdivision shall constitute a defense to a prosecution for, or preclude a conviction of, burglary in the second degree, burglary in the third degree or any other crime.

Burglary in the first degree is a class B felony.

155.05 Larceny; defined.

1. A person steals property and commits larceny when, with intent to deprive another of property or to appropriate the same to himself or to a third person, he wrongfully takes, obtains or withholds such property from an owner thereof.

2. Larceny includes a wrongful taking, obtaining or withholding of another's property, with the intent prescribed in subdivision one of this section, committed in any of the following ways:
   (a) By conduct heretofore defined or known as common law larceny by trespassory taking, common law larceny by trick, embezzlement, or obtaining property by false pretenses;
   (b) By acquiring lost property.

A person acquires lost property when he exercises control over property of another which he knows to have been lost or mislaid, or to have been delivered under a mistake as to the identity of the recipient or the nature or amount of the property, without taking reasonable measures to return such property to the owner;

(c) By committing the crime of issuing a bad check, as defined in section 190.05;
(d) By false promise.

A person obtains property by false promise when, pursuant to a scheme to defraud, he obtains property of another by means of a representation, express or implied, that he or a third person will in the future engage in particular conduct, and when he does not intend to engage in such conduct or, as the case may be, does not believe that the third person intends to engage in such conduct.

In any prosecution for larceny based upon a false promise, the defendant's intention or belief that the promise would not be performed may not be established by or inferred from the fact alone that such promise was not performed. Such a finding may be based only upon evidence establishing that the facts and circumstances of the case are wholly consistent with guilty intent or belief and wholly inconsistent with innocent intent or belief, and excluding to a moral certainty every hypothesis except that of the defendant's intention or belief that the promise would not be performed;

(e) By extortion.

A person obtains property by extortion when he compels or induces another person to deliver such property to himself or to a third person by means of instilling in him a fear that, if the property is not so delivered, the actor or another will:

(i) Cause physical injury to some person in the future; or

(ii) Cause damage to property; or

(iii) Engage in other conduct constituting a crime; or

(iv) Accuse some person of a crime or cause criminal charges to be instituted against him; or

(v) Expose a secret or publicize an asserted fact, whether true or false, tending to subject some person to hatred, contempt or ridicule; or

(vi) Cause a strike, boycott or other collective labor group action injurious to some person's business; except that such a threat shall not be deemed extortion when the property is demanded or received for the benefit of the group in whose interest the actor purports to act; or

(vii) Testify or provide information or withhold testimony or information with respect to another's legal claim or defense; or

(viii) Use or abuse his position as a public servant by performing some act within or related to his official duties, or by failing or refusing to perform an official duty, in such manner as to affect some person adversely; or

(ix) Perform any other act which would not in itself materially benefit the actor but which is calculated to harm another person materially with respect to his health, safety, business, calling, career, financial condition, reputation or personal relationships.

§ 160.00 Robbery; defined.
Robbery is forcible stealing. A person forcibly steals property and Commits robbery when, in the course of committing a larceny, he uses or Threatens the immediate use of physical force upon another person for The purpose of:

1. Preventing or overcoming resistance to the taking of the property Or to the retention thereof immediately after the taking; or
2. Compelling the owner of such property or another person to deliver up the property or to engage in other conduct which aids in the Commission of the larceny.

§ 156.10 Computer trespass.
A person is guilty of computer trespass when he knowingly uses or causes to be used a computer or computer service without authorization and:

1. he does so with an intent to commit or attempt to commit or further the commission of any felony; or
2. he thereby knowingly gains access to computer material. Computer trespass is a class E felony.

§ 110.00 Attempt to commit a crime.
A person is guilty of an attempt to commit a crime when, with intent To commit a crime, he engages in conduct which tends to effect the commission of such crime.

§ 35.05 Justification; generally.
Unless otherwise limited by the ensuing provisions of this article defining justifiable use of physical force, conduct which would otherwise constitute an offense is justifiable and not criminal when:

1. Such conduct is required or authorized by law or by a judicial decree, or is performed by a public servant in the reasonable exercise of his official powers, duties or functions; or
2. Such conduct is necessary as an emergency measure to avoid an imminent public or private injury which is about to occur by reason of a situation occasioned or developed through no fault of the actor, and which is of such gravity that, according to ordinary standards of intelligence and morality, the desirability and urgency of avoiding such injury clearly outweigh the desirability of avoiding the injury sought to be prevented by the statute defining the offense in issue. . . .

Appendix B

FAMILY LAW

Kansas Legislature
23-804
Chapter 23.–DOMESTIC RELATIONS
Article 8.–UNIFORM PREMARITAL AGREEMENT ACT

23-804. Same; areas with respect to which parties may contract; right of child to support not to be adversely affected. (a) Parties to a premarital agreement may contract with respect to all of the following:

(1) The rights and obligations of each of the parties in any of the property of either, or both, whenever and wherever acquired or located;

(2) the right to buy, sell, use, transfer, exchange, abandon, lease, consume, expend, assign, create a security interest in, mortgage, encumber, dispose of or otherwise manage and control property;

(3) the disposition of property upon separation, marital dissolution, death or the occurrence or nonoccurrence of any other event;

(4) the modification or elimination of spousal support;

(5) the making of a will, trust or other arrangement to carry out the provisions of the agreement;

(6) the ownership rights in and disposition of the death benefit from a life insurance policy;

(7) the choice of law governing the construction of the agreement; and

(8) any other matter, including their personal rights and obligations, not in violation of public policy or a statute imposing a criminal penalty.

(b) The right of a child to support may not be adversely affected by a premarital agreement.

History: L. 1988, ch. 204, § 4; July 1.

Kansas Legislature
38-1114
Chapter 38.–MINORS
Article 11.–DETERMINATION OF PARENTAGE

38-1114. Presumption of paternity. (a) A man is presumed to be the father of a child if:

(1) The man and the child's mother are, or have been, married to each other and the child is born during the marriage or within 300 days after the marriage is terminated by death or by the filing of a journal entry of a decree of annulment or divorce.

(2) Before the child's birth, the man and the child's mother have attempted to marry each other by a marriage solemnized in apparent compliance with law, although the attempted marriage is void or voidable and:

(A) If the attempted marriage is voidable, the child is born during the attempted marriage or within 300 days after its termination by death or by the filing of a journal entry of a decree of annulment or divorce; or

(B) if the attempted marriage is void, the child is born within 300 days after the termination of cohabitation.

(3) After the child's birth, the man and the child's mother have married, or attempted to marry, each other by a marriage solemnized in apparent compliance with law, although the attempted marriage is void or voidable and:

(A) The man has acknowledged paternity of the child in writing;

(B) with the man's consent, the man is named as the child's father on the child's birth certificate; or

(C) the man is obligated to support the child under a written voluntary promise or by a court order.

(4) The man notoriously or in writing recognizes paternity of the child, including but not limited to a voluntary acknowledgment made in accordance with K.S.A. 38-1130 or 65-2409a, and amendments thereto.

(5) Genetic test results indicate a probability of 97% or greater that the man is the father of the child.

(6) The man has a duty to support the child under an order of support regardless of whether the man has ever been married to the child's mother.

(b) A presumption under this section may be rebutted only by clear and convincing evidence, by a court decree establishing paternity of the child by another man or as provided in subsection (c). If a presumption is rebutted, the party alleging the existence of a father and child relationship shall have the burden of going forward with the evidence.

(c) If two or more presumptions under this section arise which conflict with each other, the presumption which on the facts is founded on the weightier considerations of policy and logic, including the best interests of the child, shall control.

(d) Full faith and credit shall be given to a determination of paternity made by any other state or jurisdiction, whether the determination is established by judicial or administrative process or by voluntary acknowledgment. As used in this section, "full faith and credit" means that the determination of paternity shall have the same conclusive effect and obligatory force in this state as it has in the state or jurisdiction where made.

(e) If a presumption arises under this section, the presumption shall be sufficient basis for entry of an order requiring the man to support the child without further paternity proceedings.

(f) The donor of semen provided to a licensed physician for use in artificial insemination of a woman other than the donor's wife is treated in law as if he were not the birth father of a child thereby conceived, unless agreed to in writing by the donor and the woman.

History: L. 1985, ch. 114, § 5; L. 1994, ch. 292, § 5; July 1.

Kansas Legislature
38-1121
Chapter 38.–MINORS
Article 11.–DETERMINATION OF PARENTAGE

38-1121. Judgment or order. (a) The judgment or order of the court determining the existence or nonexistence of the parent and child relationship is determinative for all purposes, but if any person necessary to determine the existence of a father and child relationship for all purposes has not been joined as a party, a determination of the paternity of the child shall have only the force and effect of a finding of fact necessary to determine a duty of support.

(b) If the judgment or order of the court is at variance with the child's birth certificate, the court shall order that a new birth certificate be issued, but only if any man named as the father on the birth certificate is a party to the action.

(c) Upon adjudging that a party is the parent of a minor child, the court shall make provision for support and education of the child including the necessary medical expenses incident to the birth of the child. The court may order the support and education expenses to be paid by either or both parents for the minor child. When the child reaches 18 years of age, the support shall terminate unless: (1) The parent or parents agree, by written agreement approved by the court, to pay support beyond that time; (2) the child reaches 18 years of age before completing the child's high school education in which case the support shall not automatically terminate, unless otherwise ordered by the court, until June 30 of the school year during which the child became 18 years of age if the child is still attending high school; or (3) the child is still a bona fide high school student after June 30 of the school year during which the child became 18 years of age, in which case the court, on motion, may order support to continue through the school year during which the child becomes 19 years of age so long as the child is a bona fide high school student and the parents jointly participated or knowingly acquiesced in the decision which delayed the child's completion of high school. The court, in extending support pursuant to subsection (c)(3), may impose such conditions as are appropriate and shall set the child support utilizing the guideline table category for 16-year through 18-year old children. Provision for payment of support and educational expenses of a child after reaching 18 years of age if still attending high school shall apply to any child subject to the jurisdiction of the court, including those whose support was ordered prior to July 1, 1992. If an agreement approved by the court prior to July 1, 1988, provides for termination of support before the date provided by subsection (c)(2), the court may review and modify such agreement, and any order based on such agreement, to extend the date for termination of support to the date provided by subsection (c)(2). If an agreement approved by the court prior to July 1, 1992, provides for termination of support before the date provided by subsection (c)(3), the court may review and modify such agreement, and any order based on such agreement, to extend the date for termination of support to the date provided by subsection (c)(3). For purposes of this section, "bona fide high school student" means a student who is enrolled in full accordance with the policy of the accredited high school in which the student is pursuing a high school diploma or a graduate equivalency diploma (GED). The judgment may require the party to provide a bond with sureties to secure payment. The court may at any time during the minority of the child modify or change the order of support, including any order issued in a title IV-D case, within three years of the date of the original order or a modification order, as required by the best interest of the child. If more than three years has passed since the date of the original order or modification order, a requirement that such order is in the best interest of the child need not be shown. The court may make a modification of support retroactive to a date at least one month after the date that the motion to modify was filed with the court. Any increase in support ordered effective prior to the date the court's judgment is filed shall not become a lien on real property pursuant to K.S.A. 60-2202, and amendments thereto.

(d) If both parents are parties to the action, the court shall enter such orders regarding custody, residency and parenting time as the court considers to be in the best interest of the child.

If the parties have an agreed parenting plan it shall be presumed the agreed parenting plan is in the best interest of the child. This presumption may be overcome and the court may make a different order if the court makes specific findings of fact stating why the agreed parenting plan is not in the best interest of the child. If the parties are not in agreement on a parenting plan, each party shall submit a proposed parenting plan to the court for consideration at such time before the final hearing as may be directed by the court.

(e) In entering an original order for support of a child under this section, the court may award an additional judgment to reimburse the expenses of support and education of the child from the date of birth to the date the order is entered. If the determination of paternity is based upon a presumption arising under K.S.A. 38-1114 and amendments thereto, the court shall award an additional judgment to reimburse all or part of the expenses of support and education of the child from at least the date the presumption first arose to the date the order is entered, except that no additional judgment need be awarded for amounts accrued under a previous order for the child's support.

(f) In determining the amount to be ordered in payment and duration of such payments, a court enforcing the obligation of support shall consider all relevant facts including, but not limited to, the following:

(1) The needs of the child.

(2) The standards of living and circumstances of the parents.

(3) The relative financial means of the parents.

(4) The earning ability of the parents.

(5) The need and capacity of the child for education.

(6) The age of the child.

(7) The financial resources and the earning ability of the child.

(8) The responsibility of the parents for the support of others.

(9) The value of services contributed by both parents.

(g) The provisions of K.S.A. 23-4, 107, and amendments thereto, shall apply to all orders of support issued under this section.

(h) An order granting parenting time pursuant to this section may be enforced in accordance with K.S.A. 23-701, and amendments thereto, or under the uniform child custody jurisdiction and enforcement act.

History: L. 1985, ch. 114, § 12; L. 1985, ch. 115, § 39; L. 1986, ch. 138, § 5; L. 1986, ch. 137, § 22; L. 1988, ch. 137, § 1; L. 1991, ch. 171, § 3; L. 1992, ch. 273, § 1; L. 1994, ch. 292, § 10; L. 1997, ch. 182, § 5; L. 2000, ch. 171, § 10; L. 2001, ch. 195, § 5; July 1.

Kansas Legislature
60-1601
Chapter 60.–PROCEDURE, CIVIL
Article 16.–DIVORCE AND MAINTENANCE

60-1601. Grounds for divorce or separate maintenance. (a) The district court shall grant a decree of divorce or separate maintenance for any of the following grounds: (1) Incompatibility; (2) failure to perform a material marital duty or obligation; or (3) incompatibility by reason of mental illness or mental incapacity of one or both spouses.

(b) The ground of incompatibility by reason of mental illness or mental incapacity of one or both spouses shall require a finding of either: (1) Confinement of the spouse in an institution by reason of mental illness for a period of two years, which confinement need not be continuous; or (2) an adjudication of mental illness or mental incapacity of the spouse by a court of competent jurisdiction while the spouse is confined in an institution by reason of mental illness. In either case, there must be a finding by at least two of three physicians, appointed by the court before which the action is pending, that the mentally ill or mentally incapacitated spouse has a poor prognosis for recovery from the mental illness or mental incapacity, based upon general knowledge available at the time. A decree granted on the ground of incompatibility by reason of mental illness or mental incapacity of one or both spouses shall not relieve a party from contributing to the support and maintenance of the mentally ill or mentally incapacitated spouse. If both spouses are confined to institutions because of mental illness or mental incapacity, the guardian of either spouse may file a petition for divorce and the court may grant the divorce on the ground of incompatibility by reason of mental illness or mental incapacity.

History: L. 1963, ch. 303, 60-1601; L. 1965, ch. 354, § 14; L. 1967, ch. 327, § 1; L. 1969, ch. 286, § 1; L. 1982, ch. 152, § 1; Jan. 1, 1983.

Kansas Legislature
60-1602
Chapter 60.–PROCEDURE, CIVIL
Article 16.–DIVORCE AND MAINTENANCE

60-1602. Grounds for annulment. (a) The district court shall grant a decree of annulment of any marriage for either of the following grounds: (1) The marriage is void for any reason; or (2) the contract of marriage is voidable because it was induced by fraud.

(b) The district court may grant a decree of annulment of any marriage if the contract of marriage was induced by mistake of fact, lack of knowledge of a material fact or any other reason justifying recission of a contract of marriage.

History: L. 1963, ch. 303, 60-1602; L. 1982, ch. 152, § 2; Jan. 1, 1983.

Kansas Legislature
60-1603
Chapter 60.–PROCEDURE, CIVIL
Article 16.–DIVORCE AND MAINTENANCE

60-1603. Residence. (a) *State.* The petitioner or respondent in an action for divorce must have been an actual resident of the state for 60 days immediately preceding the filing of the petition.

(b) *Military residence.* Any person who has been a resident of or stationed at a United States post or military reservation within the state for 60 days immediately preceding the filing of the petition may file an action for divorce in any county adjacent to the post or reservation.

(c) *Residence of spouse.* For the purposes of this article, a spouse may have a residence in this state separate and apart from the residence of the other spouse.

History: L. 1963, ch. 303, 60-1603; L. 1969, ch. 287, § 1; L. 1974, ch. 241, § 1; L. 1982, ch. 152, § 3; Jan. 1, 1983.

Kansas Legislature
60-1611
Chapter 60.–PROCEDURE, CIVIL
Article 16.–DIVORCE AND MAINTENANCE

60-1611. Effect of a decree in another state. A judgment or decree of divorce rendered in any other state or territory of the United States, in conformity with the laws thereof, shall be given full faith and credit in this state, except that, if the respondent in the action, at the time of the judgment or decree, was a resident of this state and did not personally appear or defend the action in the court of that state or territory and that court did not have jurisdiction over the respondent's person, all matters relating to maintenance, property rights of the parties and support of the minor children of the parties shall be subject to inquiry and determination in any proper action or proceeding brought in the courts of this state within two years after the date of the foreign judgment or decree, to the same extent as though the foreign judgment or decree had not been rendered. Nothing in this section shall authorize a court of this state to enter a child custody determination, as defined in K.S.A. 38-1337 and amendments thereto contrary to the provisions of the uniform child custody jurisdiction and enforcement act.

History: L. 1963, ch. 303, 60-1611; L. 1965, ch. 355, § 7; L. 1978, ch. 231, § 31; L. 1982, ch. 152, § 10; L. 2000, ch. 171, § 80; July 1.

Kansas Legislature
60-1616
Chapter 60.–PROCEDURE, CIVIL
Article 16.–DIVORCE AND MAINTENANCE

60-1616. Parenting time; visitation orders; enforcement. (a) *Parents.* A parent is entitled to reasonable parenting time unless the court finds, after a hearing, that the exercise of parenting time would seriously endanger the child's physical, mental, moral or emotional health.

(b) *Grandparents and stepparents.* Grandparents and stepparents may be granted visitation rights.

(c) *Modification.* The court may modify an order granting or denying parenting time or visitation rights whenever modification would serve the best interests of the child.

(d) *Enforcement of rights.* An order granting visitation rights or parenting time pursuant to this section may be enforced in accordance with the uniform child custody jurisdiction and enforcement act, or K.S.A. 23-701, and amendments thereto.

(e) *Repeated denial of rights, effect.* Repeated unreasonable denial of or interference with visitation rights or parenting time granted pursuant to this section may be considered a material change of circumstances which justifies modification of a prior order of legal custody, residency, visitation or parenting time.

(f) *Court ordered exchange or visitation at a child exchange and visitation center.* (1) The court may order exchange or visitation to take place at a child exchange and visitation center, as established in K.S.A. 75-720 and amendments thereto.

(2) Any party may petition the court to modify an order granting visitation rights or parenting time to require that the exchange or transfer of children for visitation or parenting time take place at a child exchange and visitation center, as established in K.S.A. 75-720 and amendments thereto. The court may modify an order granting visitation whenever modification would serve the best interests of the child.

History: L. 1982, ch. 152, § 15; L. 1984, ch. 213, § 2; L. 1986, ch. 138, § 6; L. 1996, ch. 188, § 2; L. 2000, ch. 171, § 19; July 1.

Kansas Legislature
60-607
Chapter 60.–PROCEDURE, CIVIL
Article 6.–VENUE

60-607. Domestic relations actions. (a) An action for divorce, annulment of marriage or separate maintenance may be brought in:

(1) The county in which the petitioner is an actual resident at the time of filing the petition;

(2) the county where the respondent resides or where service may be obtained; or

(3) if the petitioner is a resident of or stationed at a United States post or military reservation within the state at the time of filing the petition, any county adjacent to the post or reservation.

(b) For the purposes of this section, a spouse may have a residence separate and apart from the residence of the other spouse.

History: L. 1963, ch. 303, 60-607; L. 1983, ch. 196, § 1; July 1.

Child Support Worksheet

IN THE ____________________ JUDICIAL DISTRICT

____________________ COUNTY, KANSAS

IN THE MATTER OF:

____

and **CASE NO. ____________**

____

CHILD SUPPORT WORKSHEET OF ______________________________________
(name)

		MOTHER		FATHER
A. INCOME COMPUTATION—WAGE EARNER				
1. Domestic Gross Income (Insert on Line C.1. below)*		$ ________		$ ________
B. INCOME COMPUTATION—SELF-EMPLOYED				
1. Self-Employment Gross Income*		________		________
2. Reasonable Business Expenses	(−)	________		________
3. Domestic Gross Income (Insert on Line C.1. below)		________		________
C. ADJUSTMENTS TO DOMESTIC GROSS INCOME				
1. Domestic Gross Income		________		________
2. Court-Ordered Child Support Paid	(−)	________		________
3. Court-Ordered Maintenance Paid	(−)	________		________
4. Court-Ordered Maintenance Received	(+)	________		________
5. Child Support Income (Insert on Line D.1. below)		________		________
D. COMPUTATION OF CHILD SUPPORT				
1. Child Support Income		________	+	________
			=	________
2. Proportionate Shares of Combined Income (Each parent's income divided by combined income)		________ %		________ %
3. Gross Child Support Obligation** (Using the combined income from Line D.1., find the amount for each child and enter total for all children)				

Age of Children	0–6		7–15		16–18		Total
Number Per Age Category	______	+	______	+	______	=	
Total Amount	______		______		______		______

*Interstate Pay Differential Adjustment? ______ Yes ______ No

**Multiple Family Application? ______ Yes ______ No

Case No. ____________

	MOTHER		FATHER
4. Health and Dental Insurance Premium	$ ________	+ =	$ ________ ________
5. Work-Related Child Care Costs Formula: Amt. 2 ((Amt. × %) + (.25 × (Amt. × %))) for each child care credit Example: 200 − ((200 × .30%) + (.25 × (200 3 .30%)))	________	=	________ ________
6. Parents' Total Child Support Obligation (Line D.3. plus Lines D.4. & D.5.)			________
7. Parental Child Support Obligation (Line D.2. times Line D.6. for each parent)	________		________
8. Adjustment for Insurance and Child Care (Subtract for actual payment made for items D.4. and D.5.)	(−) ________		________
9. Basic Parental Child Support Obligation (Line D.7. minus Line D.8.; Insert on Line F.1. below)	________		________

E. CHILD SUPPORT ADJUSTMENTS

APPLICABLE	N/A	CATEGORY	AMOUNT ALLOWED MOTHER	AMOUNT ALLOWED FATHER
1. ☐	☐	Long Distance Parenting Time Costs	(+/−) ________	(+/−) ________
2. ☐	☐	Parenting Time Adjustment	(+/−) ________	(+/−) ________
3. ☐	☐	Income Tax Considerations	(+/−) ________	(+/−) ________
4. ☐	☐	Special Needs	(+/−) ________	(+/−) ________
5. ☐	☐	Agreement Past Majority	(+/−) ________	(+/−) ________
6. ☐	☐	Overall Financial Condition	(+/−) ________	(+/−) ________
7. TOTAL (Insert on Line F.2. below)			________	________

F. DEVIATION(S) FROM REBUTTABLE PRESUMPTION AMOUNT

		AMOUNT ALLOWED MOTHER	AMOUNT ALLOWED FATHER
1. Basic Parental Child Support Obligation (Line D.9. from above)		________	________
2. Total Child Support Adjustments (Line E.7. from above)		(+/−) ________	________
3. Adjusted Subtotal (Line F.1. +/− Line F.2.)		________	________
4. Enforcement Fee Allowance** (Applied only to Nonresidential Parent) ((Line F.3. × Collection Fee %) × .5) or (Monthly Flat Fee × .5)	Percentage Flat Fee	________ % $ ________ (+) ________	(+) ________
5. Net Parental Child Support Obligation (Line F.3. + Line F.4.)		________	________

**Parent with nonprimary residency

____
Judge/Hearing Officer Signature

____
Date Signed

____
Prepared By

____
Date Approved

Two Child Families: Child Support Schedule
Dollars Per Month Per Child

Combined Gross Monthly Income	Support Amount ($ Per Child) Age Group			Combined Gross Monthly Income	Support Amount ($ Per Child) Age Group			Combined Gross Monthly Income	Support Amount ($ Per Child) Age Group		
	Age 0–6	Age 7–15	Age 16–18		Age 0–6	Age 7–15	Age 16–18		Age 0–6	Age 7–15	Age 16–18
50	6	7	7	**2400**	255	295	327	**6700**	592	683	759
100	12	13	15	**2500**	264	305	338	**6800**	599	691	768
150	17	20	22	**2600**	273	314	349	**6900**	606	699	777
200	23	27	30	**2700**	281	324	360	**7000**	613	708	786
250	29	33	37	**2800**	290	334	371	**7200**	628	724	805
300	35	40	44	**2900**	298	344	382	**7400**	642	741	823
350	40	46	52	**3000**	306	354	393	**7600**	656	757	841
400	46	53	59	**3100**	315	363	404	**7800**	670	773	859
450	52	60	66	**3200**	323	373	414	**8000**	684	789	877
500	58	66	74	**3300**	331	382	425	**8200**	698	805	895
550	63	73	81	**3400**	339	392	435	**8400**	712	822	913
600	69	80	89	**3500**	348	401	446	**8600**	726	837	931
650	75	86	96	**3600**	356	410	456	**8800**	740	853	948
700	81	93	103	**3700**	364	420	466	**9000**	753	869	966
750	86	100	111	**3800**	372	429	477	**9200**	767	885	983
800	92	106	118	**3900**	380	438	487	**9400**	781	901	1001
850	98	113	125	**4000**	388	447	497	**9600**	794	916	1018
900	104	120	133	**4100**	396	457	507	**9800**	808	932	1036
950	109	126	140	**4200**	404	466	517	**10000**	821	948	1053
1000	115	133	148	**4300**	411	475	528	**10200**	835	963	1070
1050	121	139	155	**4400**	419	484	538	**10400**	848	979	1087
1100	127	146	162	**4500**	427	493	548	**10600**	861	994	1004
1150	132	153	170	**4600**	435	502	557	**10800**	875	1009	1121
1200	138	159	177	**4700**	443	511	567	**11000**	888	1024	1138
1250	144	166	184	**4800**	450	520	577	**11200**	901	1040	1155
1300	150	173	192	**4900**	458	528	587	**11400**	914	1055	1172
1350	155	179	199	**5000**	466	537	597	**11600**	927	1070	1189
1400	161	186	207	**5100**	473	546	607	**11800**	940	1085	1206
1450	167	193	214	**5200**	481	555	616	**12000**	953	1100	1222
1500	173	199	221	**5300**	488	563	626	**12200**	966	1115	1239
1550	178	206	229	**5400**	496	572	636	**12400**	979	1130	1256
1600	183	211	235	**5500**	503	581	645	**12600**	992	1145	1272
1650	188	217	241	**5600**	511	589	655	**12800**	1005	1160	1289
1700	192	222	247	**5700**	518	598	664	**13000**	1018	1175	1305
1750	197	227	253	**5800**	526	607	674	**13200**	1031	1189	1322
1800	202	233	259	**5900**	533	615	684	**13400**	1044	1204	1338
1850	206	238	264	**6000**	541	624	693	**13600**	1056	1219	1354
1900	211	243	270	**6100**	548	632	702	**13800**	1069	1234	1371
1950	215	248	276	**6200**	555	641	712	**14000**	1082	1248	1387
2000	220	254	282	**6300**	563	649	721	**14200**	1094	1263	1403
2100	229	264	293	**6400**	570	658	731	**14400**	1107	1277	1419
2200	238	274	305	**6500**	577	666	740	**14600**	1119	1291	1434
2300	247	284	316	**6600**	584	674	749				

*2002 Poverty Level is $1550.

To determine child support at higher income levels:

Age 16–18: Raise income to the power .6994644 and multiply the result by 1.7529778849.
Age 7–15: Determine child support for Age 16–18 and then multiply by 0.90.
Age 0–6: Determine child support for Age 16–18 and then multiply by 0.78.

Domestic Relations Affidavit

IN THE ________________ JUDICIAL DISTRICT
________________ COUNTY, KANSAS

IN THE MATTER OF

____

and **Case No.** ____________

____

DOMESTIC RELATIONS AFFIDAVIT OF ________________________________
(name)

1. Mother's Residence ____

   Mother's ____________ __________________ ____________
   Date of Birth Social Security Number Home Telephone

2. Father's Residence ____

   Father's ____________ __________________ ____________
   Date of Birth Social Security Number Home Telephone

3. Date of Marriage: ________________

4. Number of Marriages: __________ ____________
   Mother Father

5. Number of children of the relationship: ______________

6. Names, Social Security Numbers, birthdates, and ages of minor children of the relationship:

Name	Social Security No.	Date of Birth	Age	Custodian
__________	__________	__________	____	__________
__________	__________	__________	____	__________
__________	__________	__________	____	__________
__________	__________	__________	____	__________

7. Names, Social Security Numbers, and ages of minor children of previous relationships and facts as to custody and support payments paid or received,if any.

Name	Social Security No.	Age	Custodian	Support Payment	Paid or Rec'd
__________	__________	____	__________	$__________	________
__________	__________	____	__________	$__________	________
__________	__________	____	__________	$__________	________
__________	__________	____	__________	$__________	________

8. Mother is employed by ____
   ____

   Father is employed by ____
   ____
   (Name and address of employer)

with monthly income as follows:

A. Wage Earner	Mother	Father
1. Gross Income	$__________	$__________
2. Other Income	$__________	$__________
3. Subtotal Gross Income	$__________	$__________
4. Federal Withholding (Claiming __________ exemptions)	$__________	$__________
5. Federal Income Tax	$__________	$__________
6. OASDHI	$__________	$__________
7. Kansas Withholding	$__________	$__________
8. Subtotal Deductions	$__________	$__________
9. Net Income	$__________	$__________

B. Self-Employed	Mother	Father
1. Gross Income from self-employment	$__________	$__________
2. Other Income	$__________	$__________
3. Subtotal Gross Income	$__________	$__________
4. Reasonable Business Expenses (Itemize on attached exhibit)	$__________	$__________
5. Self-Employment Tax	$__________	$__________
6. Estimated Tax Payments (Claim __________ exemptions)	$__________	$__________
7. Federal Income Tax	$__________	$__________
8. Kansas Withholding	$__________	$__________
9. Subtotal Deductions	$__________	$__________
10. Net Income (Line B.3. minus Line B.9.)	$__________	$__________

Pay period: ____________________ (Mother) ____________________ (Father)

9. The liquid assets of the parties are:

Item	Amount	Joint or Individual (Specify)
A. Checking Accounts:		
__________________	$__________________	__________________
__________________	$__________________	__________________
B. Savings Accounts:		
__________________	$__________________	__________________
__________________	$__________________	__________________
C. Cash		
Mother	$__________________	__________________
Father	$__________________	__________________
D. Other		
__________________	$__________________	__________________
__________________	$__________________	__________________

10. The monthly expenses of each party are: (Please indicate with an asterisk all figures which are estimates rather than actual figures taken from records.)

A.

Item	Mother (Actual or Estimated)	Father (Actual or Estimated)
1. Rent (if applicable)*	$__________	$__________
2. Food	$__________	$__________

Item	Mother (Actual or Estimated)	Father (Actual or Estimated)
3. Utilities:		
Trash Service	$__________	$__________
Newspaper	$__________	$__________
Telephone	$__________	$__________
Gas	$__________	$__________
Water	$__________	$__________
Lights	$__________	$__________
Other	$__________	$__________
4. Insurance:		
Life	$__________	$__________
Health	$__________	$__________
Car	$__________	$__________
House/Rental	$__________	$__________
Other	$__________	$__________
5. Medical and dental	$__________	$__________
6. Prescriptions drugs	$__________	$__________
7. Child care (work-related)	$__________	$__________
8. Child care (non-work-related)	$__________	$__________
9. Clothing	$__________	$__________
10. School expenses	$__________	$__________
11. Hair cuts and beauty	$__________	$__________
12. Car repair	$__________	$__________
13. Gas and oil	$__________	$__________
14. Personal property tax	$__________	$__________
15. Miscellaneous (Specify)		
____________________	$__________	$__________
____________________	$__________	$__________
____________________	$__________	$__________
____________________	$__________	$__________
16. Debt Payments (Specify)		
____________________	$__________	$__________
____________________	$__________	$__________
____________________	$__________	$__________
____________________	$__________	$__________
Total	$__________	$__________

*Show house payments, mortgage payments, etc., in Section 10.B.

B. Monthly payments to banks,loan companies or on credit accounts: (Indicate actual or estimated, use asterisk for secured.) DO NOT LIST ANY PAYMENTS INCLUDED IN PART 10.A ABOVE.

Creditor	When Incurred	Amount of Payment	Date of Last Payment	Balance	Responsibility Mother	Father
__________	______	______	______	$________	$________	$________
__________	______	______	______	$________	$________	$________
__________	______	______	______	$________	$________	$________
__________	______	______	______	$________	$________	$________
__________	______	______	______	$________	$________	$________
__________	______	______	______	$________	$________	$________
			Subtotal of Payments		$________	$________
			Total		$________	$________

C. Total Living Expenses

	Mother (Actual or Estimated)	Father (Actual or Estimated)
1. Total funds available to Mother and Father (from No. 8)	$__________	$__________
2. Total needed (from No. 10.A and B)	$__________	$__________
3. Net Balance	$__________	$__________
4. Projected child support	$__________	$__________

D. Payments or contributions received, or paid, for support of others. Specify source and amount.

Source	Mother	Father
__________(+/−)	$__________	$__________
__________(+/−)	$__________	$__________
__________(+/−)	$__________	$__________
__________(+/−)	$__________	$__________

11. How much does the party who provides health care pay for family coverage?

$__________ per __________.

How much does it cost the provider to furnish health insurance only on the provider?

$ __________ per __________.

FURNISH THE FOLLOWING INFORMATION IF APPLICABLE.

12. Income and financial resources of children.

Income/Resources	Amount
____________________	$__________
____________________	$__________
____________________	$__________
____________________	$__________

13. Child support adjustments requested.

	Mother	Father
Long Distance Visitation Costs	$__________	$__________
	$__________	$__________
Visitation Adjustments	$__________	$__________
Income Tax Considerations	$__________	$__________
Special Needs	$__________	$__________
Agreement Past Minority	$__________	$__________
Overall Financial Condition	$__________	$__________

14. All other personal property including retirement benefits (including but not limited to qualified plans such as profit-sharing, pension, IRA, 401[k], or other savings-type employee benefits, nonqualified plans, and deferred income plans), and ownership thereof (joint or individual), including policies of insurance, identified as to nature or description, ownership (joint or individual), and actual or estimated value.

	Amount	Joint or Individual (Specify)
______________	$__________	__________
______________	$__________	__________
______________	$__________	__________
______________	$__________	__________

THE FOLLOWING NEED NOT BE FURNISHED IN POST JUDGMENT PROCEDURES.

15. List real property identified as to description, ownership (joint or individual) and actual or estimated value.

Property Description	Ownership	Actual/Estimated Value

16. Identify the property, if any, acquired by each of the parties prior to marriage or acquired during marriage by a will or inheritance.

Property Description	Ownership	Source of Ownership	Actual/ Estimated Value

17. List debt obligations, including maintenance, not listed in Section 10.A or 10.B above, identified as to name or names of obligor or obligors and obligees, balance due and rate at which payable; and, if secured, identify the encumbered property.

Debt Obligation	Obligor	Obligee	Balance Due	Payment Rate	Encumbered Property

18. List health insurance coverage and the right, pursuant to ERISA §§ 601-608, 29 U.S.C. §§ 1161-1168 (1986), to continued coverage by the spouse who is not a member of the covered employee group.

Health Insurance	COBRA Continuation		
	Yes	No	Unknown
____________	______	______	______
____________	______	______	______
____________	______	______	______
____________	______	______	______
____________	______	______	______
____________	______	______	______

AFFIANT

/s/______________________________

VERIFICATION

State of ________________________, County of ________________________.

I swear or affirm under penalty of perjury that this affidavit and attached schedules are true and complete.

/s/__________________________

Subscribed and sworn this ________ day of ____________ 20 _________.

/s/______________________________
Notary Public
My Appointment Expires:

Appendix C

ETHICS

National Association of Legal Assistants
Model Standards and Guidelines for Utilization of Legal Assistants*
Introduction

The purpose of this annotated version of the National Association of Legal Assistants, Inc. Model Standards and Guidelines for the Utilization of Legal Assistants (the "Model," "Standards" and/or the "Guidelines") is to provide references to the existing case law and other authorities where the underlying issues have been considered. The authorities cited will serve as a basis upon which conduct of a legal assistant may be analyzed as proper or improper.

The Guidelines represent a statement of how the legal assistant may function. The Guidelines are not intended to be a comprehensive or exhaustive list of the proper duties of a legal assistant. Rather, they are designed as guides to what may or may not be proper conduct for the legal assistant. In formulating the Guidelines, the reasoning and rules of law in many reported decisions of disciplinary cases and unauthorized practice of law cases have been analyzed and considered. In addition, the provisions of the American Bar Association's Model Rules of Professional Conduct, as well as the ethical promulgations of various state courts and bar associations have been considered in the development of the Guidelines.

These Guidelines form a sound basis for the legal assistant and the supervising attorney to follow. This Model will serve as a comprehensive resource document and as a definitive, well-reasoned guide to those considering voluntary standards and guidelines for legal assistants.

I
Preamble

Proper utilization of the services of legal assistants contributes to the delivery of cost-effective, high-quality legal services. Legal assistants and the legal profession should be assured that measures exist for identifying legal assistants and their role in assisting attorneys in the delivery of legal services. Therefore, the National Association of Legal Assistants, Inc., hereby adopts these Standards and Guidelines as an educational document for the benefit of legal assistants and the legal profession.

Comment

The three most frequently raised questions concerning legal assistants are (1) How do you define a legal assistant; (2) Who is qualified to be identified as a legal assistant; and (3) What duties may a legal assistant perform? The definition adopted in 1984 by the National Association of Legal Assistants answers the first question. The Model sets forth minimum education, training and experience through standards which will assure that an individual utilizing the title "legal assistant" or "paralegal" has the qualifications to be held out to the legal community and the public in that capacity. The Guidelines identify those acts which the reported cases hold to be proscribed and give examples of services which the legal assistant may perform under the supervision of a licensed attorney.

These Guidelines constitute a statement relating to services performed by legal assistants, as defined herein, as approved by court decisions and other sources of authority. The purpose of the Guidelines is not to place limitations or restrictions on the legal assistant profession. Rather, the Guidelines are intended to outline for the legal profession an acceptable course of conduct. Voluntary recognition and utilization of the Standards and Guidelines will benefit the entire legal profession and the public it serves.

II
Definition

The National Association of Legal Assistants adopted the following definition in 1984:

> *Legal assistants, also known as paralegals, are a distinguishable group of persons who assist attorneys in the delivery of legal services. Through formal education, training, and experience, legal assistants have knowledge and expertise regarding the legal system and substantive and procedural law which qualify them to do work of a legal nature under the supervision of an attorney.*

In recognition of the similarity of the definitions and the need for one clear definition, in July 2001, the NALA membership approved a resolution to adopt the definition of the American Bar Association as well. The ABA definition reads as follows:

> *A legal assistant or paralegal is a person qualified by education, training or work experience who is employed or retained by a lawyer, law office, corporation, governmental agency or other entity who performs specifically delegated substantive legal work for which a lawyer is responsible. (Adopted by the ABA in 1997)*

Comment

These definitions emphasize the knowledge and expertise of legal assistants in substantive and procedural law obtained through education and work experience. They further define the legal assistant or paralegal as a professional working under the supervision of an attorney as distinguished from a non-lawyer who delivers services directly to the public without any intervention or review of work product by an attorney. Such unsupervised services, unless authorized by court or agency rules, constitute the unauthorized practice of law.

Statutes, court rules, case law and bar association documents are additional sources for legal assistant or paralegal definitions. In applying the Standards and Guidelines, it is important to remember that they were developed to apply to the legal assistant as defined herein. Lawyers should refrain from labeling those as paralegals or legal assistants who do not meet the criteria set forth in these definitions and/or the definitions set forth by state rules, guidelines or bar associations. Labeling secretaries and other administrative staff as legal assistants/paralegals is inaccurate.

For billing purposes, the services of a legal secretary are considered part of overhead costs and are not recoverable in fee awards. However, the courts have held that fees for paralegal services are recoverable as long as they are not clerical functions, such as organizing files, copying documents, checking docket, updating files, checking court dates and delivering papers. As established in *Missouri v. Jenkins*, 491 U.S.274, 109 S.Ct. 2463, 2471, n.10 (1989) tasks performed by legal assistants must be substantive in nature which, absent the legal assistant, the attorney would perform.

There are also case law and Supreme Court Rules addressing the issue of a disbarred attorney serving in the capacity of a legal assistant.

III
Standards

A legal assistant should meet certain minimum qualifications. The following standards may be used to determine an individual's qualifications as a legal assistant:

1. Successful completion of the Certified Legal Assistant (CLA)/Certified Paralegal (CP) certifying examination of the National Association of Legal Assistants, Inc.;
2. Graduation from an ABA approved program of study for legal assistants;

3. Graduation from a course of study for legal assistants which is institutionally accredited but not ABA approved, and which requires not less than the equivalent of 60 semester hours of classroom study;
4. Graduation from a course of study for legal assistants, other than those set forth in (2) and (3) above, plus not less than six months of in-house training as a legal assistant;
5. A baccalaureate degree in any field, plus not less than six months in-house training as a legal assistant;
6. A minimum of three years of law-related experience under the supervision of an attorney, including at least six months of in-house training as a legal assistant; or
7. Two years of in-house training as a legal assistant.

For purposes of these Standards, "in-house training as a legal assistant" means attorney education of the employee concerning legal assistant duties and these Guidelines. In addition to review and analysis of assignments, the legal assistant should receive a reasonable amount of instruction directly related to the duties and obligations of the legal assistant.

Comment

The Standards set forth suggest minimum qualifications for a legal assistant. These minimum qualifications, as adopted, recognize legal related work backgrounds and formal education backgrounds, both of which provide the legal assistant with a broad base in exposure to and knowledge of the legal profession. This background is necessary to assure the public and the legal profession that the employee identified as a legal assistant is qualified.

The Certified Legal Assistant (CLA)/Certified Paralegal (CP) examination established by NALA in 1976 is a voluntary nationwide certification program for legal assistants. (*CLA and CP are federally registered certification marks owned by NALA.*) The CLA/CP designation is a statement to the legal profession and the public that the legal assistant has met the high levels of knowledge and professionalism required by NALA's certification program. Continuing education requirements, which all certified legal assistants must meet, assure that high standards are maintained. The CLA/CP designation has been recognized as a means of establishing the qualifications of a legal assistant in supreme court rules, state court and bar association standards and utilization guidelines.

Certification through NALA is available to all legal assistants meeting the educational and experience requirements. Certified Legal Assistants may also pursue advanced certification in specialty practice areas through the APC, Advanced Paralegal Certification, credentialing program. Legal assistants/paralegals may also pursue certification based on state laws and procedures in California, Florida, Louisiana and Texas.

IV
Guidelines

These Guidelines relating to standards of performance and professional responsibility are intended to aid legal assistants and attorneys. The ultimate responsibility rests with an attorney who employs legal assistants to educate them with respect to the duties they are assigned and to supervise the manner in which such duties are accomplished.

Comment

In general, a legal assistant is allowed to perform any task which is properly delegated and supervised by an attorney, as long as the attorney is ultimately responsible to the client and assumes complete professional responsibility for the work product.

ABA Model Rules of Professional Conduct, Rule 5.3 provides:

> *With respect to a non-lawyer employed or retained by or associated with a lawyer:*
>
> *(a) a partner in a law firm shall make reasonable efforts to ensure that the firm has in effect measures giving reasonable assurance that the person's conduct is compatible with the professional obligations of the lawyer;*

(b) a lawyer having direct supervisory authority over the non-lawyer shall make reasonable efforts to ensure that the person's conduct is compatible with the professional obligations of the lawyer; and

(c) a lawyer shall be responsible for conduct of such a person that would be a violation of the rules of professional conduct if engaged in by a lawyer if:

1. the lawyer orders or, with the knowledge of the specific conduct ratifies the conduct involved; or

2. the lawyer is a partner in the law firm in which the person is employed, or has direct supervisory authority over the person, and knows of the conduct at a time when its consequences can be avoided or mitigated but fails to take remedial action.

There are many interesting and complex issues involving the use of legal assistants. In any discussion of the proper role of a legal assistant, attention must be directed to what constitutes the practice of law. Proper delegation to legal assistants is further complicated and confused by the lack of an adequate definition of the practice of law.

Kentucky became the first state to adopt a Paralegal Code by Supreme Court Rule. This Code sets forth certain exclusions to the unauthorized practice of law:

> *For purposes of this rule, the unauthorized practice of law shall not include any service rendered involving legal knowledge or advice, whether representation, counsel or advocacy, in or out of court, rendered in respect to the acts, duties, obligations, liabilities or business relations of the one requiring services where:*
>
> *A. The client understands that the paralegal is not a lawyer;*
>
> *B. The lawyer supervises the paralegal in the performance of his or her duties; and*
>
> *C. The lawyer remains fully responsible for such representation including all actions taken or not taken in connection therewith by the paralegal to the same extent as if such representation had been furnished entirely by the lawyer and all such actions had been taken or not taken directly by the attorney. Paralegal Code, Ky.S.Ct.R3.700, Sub-Rule 2.*

South Dakota Supreme Court Rule 97-25 Utilization Rule a(4) states:

The attorney remains responsible for the services performed by the legal assistant to the same extent as though such services had been furnished entirely by the attorney and such actions were those of the attorney.

Guideline 1

Legal assistants should:

1. Disclose their status as legal assistants at the outset of any professional relationship with a client, other attorneys, a court or administrative agency or personnel thereof, or members of the general public;
2. Preserve the confidences and secrets of all clients; and
3. Understand the attorney's Rules of Professional Responsibility and these Guidelines in order to avoid any action which would involve the attorney in a violation of the Rules, or give the appearance of professional impropriety.

Comment

Routine early disclosure of the paralegal's status when dealing with persons outside the attorney's office is necessary to assure that there will be no misunderstanding as to the responsibilities and role of the legal assistant. Disclosure may be made in any way that avoids confusion. If the person dealing with the legal assistant already knows of his/her status, further disclosure is unnecessary. If at any time in written or oral communication the legal assistant becomes aware that the other person may believe the legal assistant is an attorney, immediate disclosure should be made as to the legal assistant's status.

The attorney should exercise care that the legal assistant preserves and refrains from using any confidence or secrets of a client, and should instruct the legal assistant not to disclose or use any such confidences or secrets.

The legal assistant must take any and all steps necessary to prevent conflicts of interest and fully disclose such conflicts to the supervising attorney. Failure to do so may jeopardize both the attorney's representation of the client and the case itself.

Guidelines for the Utilization of Legal Assistant Services adopted December 3, 1994 by the Washington State Bar Association Board of Governors states:

> *"Guideline 7: A lawyer shall take reasonable measures to prevent conflicts of interest resulting from a legal assistant's other employment or interest insofar as such other employment or interests would present a conflict of interest if it were that of the lawyer."*

In Re Complex Asbestos Litigation, 232 Cal. App. 3d 572 (Cal. 1991), addresses the issue wherein a law firm was disqualified due to possession of attorney-client confidences by a legal assistant employee resulting from previous employment by opposing counsel.

In Oklahoma, in an order issued July 12, 2001, in the matter of *Mark A. Hayes, M.D. v. Central States Orthopedic Specialists, Inc.*, a Tulsa County District Court Judge disqualified a law firm from representation of a client on the basis that an ethical screen was an impermissible device to protect from disclosure confidences gained by a non-lawyer employee while employed by another law firm. In applying the same rules that govern attorneys, the court found that the Rules of Professional Conduct pertaining to confidentiality apply to non-lawyers who leave firms with actual knowledge of material, confidential information and a screening device is not an appropriate alternative to the imputed disqualification of an incoming legal assistant who has moved from one firm to another during ongoing litigation and has actual knowledge of material, confidential information. The decision was appealed and the Oklahoma Supreme Court determined that, under certain circumstances, screening is an appropriate management tool for non-lawyer staff.

In 2004 the Nevada Supreme Court also addressed this issue at the urging of the state's paralegals. The Nevada Supreme Court granted a petition to rescind the Court's 1997 ruling in *Ciaffone v. District Court.* In this case, the court clarified the original ruling, stating "mere opportunity to access confidential information does not merit disqualification." The opinion stated instances in which screening may be appropriate, and listed minimum screening requirements. The opinion also set forth guidelines that a district court may use to determine if screening has been or may be effective. These considerations are:

1. substantiality of the relationship between the former and current matters
2. the time elapsed between the matters
3. size of the firm
4. number of individuals presumed to have confidential information
5. nature of their involvement in the former matter
6. timing and features of any measures taken to reduce the danger of disclosure
7. whether the old firm and the new firm represent adverse parties in the same proceeding rather than in different proceedings.

The ultimate responsibility for compliance with approved standards of professional conduct rests with the supervising attorney. The burden rests upon the attorney who employs a legal assistant to educate the latter with respect to the duties which may be assigned and then to supervise the manner in which the legal assistant carries out such duties. However, this does not relieve the legal assistant from an independent obligation to refrain from illegal conduct. Additionally, and notwithstanding that the Rules are not binding upon non-lawyers, the very nature of a legal assistant's employment imposes an obligation not to engage in conduct which would involve the supervising attorney in a violation of the Rules.

The attorney must make sufficient background investigation of the prior activities and character and integrity of his or her legal assistants.

Further, the attorney must take all measures necessary to avoid and fully disclose conflicts of interest due to other employment or interests. Failure to do so may jeopardize both the attorney's representation of the client and the case itself.

Legal assistant associations strive to maintain the high level of integrity and competence expected of the legal profession and, further, strive to uphold the high standards of ethics.

NALA's Code of Ethics and Professional Responsibility states "A legal assistant's conduct is guided by bar associations' codes of professional responsibility and rules of professional conduct.

Guideline 2

Legal assistants should not:

1. Establish attorney-client relationships; set legal fees; give legal opinions or advice; or represent a client before a court, unless authorized to do so by said court; nor
2. Engage in, encourage, or contribute to any act which could constitute the unauthorized practice [of] law.

Comment

Case law, court rules, codes of ethics and professional responsibilities, as well as bar ethics opinions now hold which acts can and cannot be performed by a legal assistant. Generally, the determination of what acts constitute the unauthorized practice of law is made by state supreme courts.

Numerous cases exist relating to the unauthorized practice of law. Courts have gone so far as to prohibit the legal assistant from preparation of divorce kits and assisting in preparation of bankruptcy forms and, more specifically, from providing basic information about procedures and requirements, deciding where information should be placed on forms, and responding to questions from debtors regarding the interpretation or definition of terms.

Cases have identified certain areas in which an attorney has a duty to act, but it is interesting to note that none of these cases state that it is improper for an attorney to have the initial work performed by the legal assistant. This again points out the importance of adequate supervision by the employing attorney.

An attorney can be found to have aided in the unauthorized practice of law when delegating acts which cannot be performed by a legal assistant.

Guideline 3

Legal assistants may perform services for an attorney in the representation of a client, provided:

1. The services performed by the legal assistant do not require the exercise of independent professional legal judgment;
2. The attorney maintains a direct relationship with the client and maintains control of all client matters;
3. The attorney supervises the legal assistant;
4. The attorney remains professionally responsible for all work on behalf of the client, including any actions taken or not taken by the legal assistant in connection therewith; and
5. The services performed supplement, merge with and become the attorney's work product.

Comment

Paralegals, whether employees or independent contractors, perform services for the attorney in the representation of a client. Attorneys should delegate work to legal assistants commensurate with their knowledge and experience and provide appropriate instruction and supervision concerning the delegated work, as well as ethical acts of their employment. Ultimate responsibility for the work product of a legal assistant rests with the attorney. However, a legal assistant must use discretion and professional judgment and must not render independent legal judgment in place of an attorney. The work product of a legal assistant is subject to civil rules governing discovery of materials prepared in anticipation of litigation, whether the legal assistant is viewed as an extension of the attorney or as another representative of the party itself. Fed.R.Civ.P. 26 (b) (3) and (5).

Guideline 4

In the supervision of a legal assistant, consideration should be given to

1. Designating work assignments that correspond to the legal assistant's abilities, knowledge, training and experience;
2. Educating and training the legal assistant with respect to professional responsibility, local rules and practices, and firm policies;

3. Monitoring the work and professional conduct of the legal assistant to ensure that the work is substantively correct and timely performed;
4. Providing continuing education for the legal assistant in substantive matters through courses, institutes, workshops, seminars and in-house training; and
5. Encouraging and supporting membership and active participation in professional organizations.

Comment

Attorneys are responsible for the actions of their employees in both malpractice and disciplinary proceedings. In the vast majority of cases, the courts have not censured attorneys for a particular act delegated to the legal assistant, but rather, have been critical of and imposed sanctions against attorneys for failure to adequately supervise the legal assistant. The attorney's responsibility for supervision of his or her legal assistant must be more than a willingness to accept responsibility and liability for the legal assistant's work. Supervision of a legal assistant must be offered in both the procedural and substantive legal areas. The attorney must delegate work based upon the education, knowledge and abilities of the legal assistant and must monitor the work product and conduct of the legal assistant to insure that the work performed is substantively correct and competently performed in a professional manner.

Michigan State Board of Commissioners has adopted Guidelines for the Utilization of Legal Assistants (April 23, 1993). These guidelines, in part, encourage employers to support legal assistant participation in continuing education programs to ensure that the legal assistant remains competent in the fields of practice in which the legal assistant is assigned.

The working relationship between the lawyer and the legal assistant should extend to cooperative efforts on public service activities wherever possible. Participation in pro bono activities is encouraged in ABA Guideline 10.

Guideline 5

Except as otherwise provided by statute, court rule or decision, administrative rule or regulation, or the attorney's rules of professional responsibility, and within the preceding parameters and proscriptions, a legal assistant may perform any function delegated by an attorney, including, but not limited to the following:

1. Conduct client interviews and maintain general contact with the client after the establishment of the attorney-client relationship, so long as the client is aware of the status and function of the legal assistant, and the client contact is under the supervision of the attorney.
2. Locate and interview witnesses, so long as the witnesses are aware of the status and function of the legal assistant.
3. Conduct investigations and statistical and documentary research for review by the attorney.
4. Conduct legal research for review by the attorney.
5. Draft legal documents for review by the attorney.
6. Draft correspondence and pleadings for review by and signature of the attorney.
7. Summarize depositions, interrogatories and testimony for review by the attorney.
8. Attend executions of wills, real estate closings, depositions, court or administrative hearings and trials with the attorney.
9. Author and sign letters providing the legal assistant's status is clearly indicated and the correspondence does not contain independent legal opinions or legal advice.

Comment

The United States Supreme Court has recognized the variety of tasks being performed by legal assistants and has noted that use of legal assistants encourages cost-effective delivery of legal services, *Missouri v. Jenkins*, 491 U.S.274, 109 S.Ct. 2463, 2471, n.10 (1989). In *Jenkins*, the court further held that legal assistant time should be included in compensation for attorney fee awards at the market rate of the relevant community to bill legal assistant time.

Courts have held that legal assistant fees are not a part of the overall overhead of a law firm. Legal assistant services are billed separately by attorneys, and decrease litigation expenses. Tasks performed by legal assistants must contain substantive legal work under the direction or supervision of an attorney, such that if the legal assistant were not present, the work would be performed by the attorney.

In *Taylor v. Chubb*, 874 P.2d 806 (Okla. 1994), the Court ruled that attorney fees awarded should include fees for services performed by legal assistants and, further, defined tasks which may be performed by the legal assistant under the supervision of an attorney including, among others: interview clients; draft pleadings and other documents; carry on legal research, both conventional and computer aided; research public records; prepare discovery requests and responses; schedule depositions and prepare notices and subpoenas; summarize depositions and other discovery responses; coordinate and manage document production; locate and interview witnesses; organize pleadings, trial exhibits and other documents; prepare witness and exhibit lists; prepare trial notebooks; prepare for the attendance of witnesses at trial; and assist lawyers at trials.

Except for the specific proscription contained in Guideline 1, the reported cases do not limit the duties which may be performed by a legal assistant under the supervision of the attorney.

An attorney may not split legal fees with a legal assistant, nor pay a legal assistant for the referral of legal business. An attorney may compensate a legal assistant based on the quantity and quality of the legal assistant's work and value of that work to a law practice.

Conclusion

These Standards and Guidelines were developed from generally accepted practices. Each supervising attorney must be aware of the specific rules, decisions and statutes applicable to legal assistants within his/her jurisdiction.

Addendum

For further information, the following cases may be helpful to you:

Duties

Taylor v. Chubb, 874 P.2d 806 (Okla. 1994)
McMackin v. McMackin, 651 A.2d 778 (Del.Fam Ct 1993)

Work Product

Fine v. Facet Aerospace Products Co., 133 F.R.D. 439 (S.D.N.Y. 1990)

Unauthorized Practice of Law

Akron Bar Assn. V. Green, 673 N.E.2d 1307 (Ohio 1997)
In Re Hessinger & Associates, 192 B.R. 211 (N.D. Calif. 1996)
In the Matter of Bright, 171 B.R. 799 (Bkrtcy. E.D. Mich)
Louisiana State Bar Assn v. Edwins, 540 So.2d 294 (La. 1989)

Attorney/Client Privilege

In Re Complex Asbestos Litigation, 232 Cal. App. 3d 572 (Calif. 1991)
Makita Corp. V. U.S., 819 F.Supp. 1099 (CIT 1993)

Conflicts

In Re Complex Asbestos Litigation, 232 Cal. App. 3d 572 (Calif. 1991)
Makita Corp. V. U.S., 819 F.Supp. 1099 (CIT 1993)
Phoenix Founders, Inc., v. Marshall, 887 S.W.2d 831 (Tex. 1994)
Smart Industries v. Superior Court, 876 P.2d 1176 (Ariz. App. Div.1 1994)

Supervision

Matter of Martinez, 754 P.2d 842 (N.M. 1988)
State v. Barrett, 483 P.2d 1106 (Kan. 1971)
Hayes v. Central States Orthopedic Specialists, Inc., 2002 OK 30, 51 P.3d 562

Liebowitz v. Eighth Judicial District Court of Nevada Nev Sup Ct., No 39683, November 3, 2003 clarified in part and overrules in part *Ciaffone v. District Court,* 113 Nev 1165, 945. P2d 950 (1997)

Fee Awards

In Re Bicoastal Corp., 121 B.R. 653 (Bktrcy.M.D.Fla. 1990)
In Re Carter, 101 B.R. 170 (Bkrtcy.D.S.D. 1989)
Taylor v. Chubb, 874 P.2d 806 (Okla.1994)
Missouri v. Jenkins, 491 U.S. 274, 109 S.Ct. 2463, 105 L.Ed.2d 229 (1989) 11 U.S.C.A.'330
McMackin v. McMackin, Del.Fam.Ct. 651 A.2d 778 (1993)
Miller v. Alamo, 983 F.2d 856 (8th Cir. 1993)
Stewart v. Sullivan, 810 F.Supp. 1102 (D.Hawaii 1993)
In Re Yankton College, 101 B.R. 151 (Bkrtcy. D.S.D. 1989)
Stacey v. Stroud, 845 F.Supp. 1135 (S.D.W.Va. 1993)

Court Appearances

Louisiana State Bar Assn v. Edwins, 540 So.2d 294 (La. 1989)

In addition to the above referenced cases, you may contact your state bar association for information regarding guidelines for the utilization of legal assistants that may have been adopted by the bar, or ethical opinions concerning the utilization of legal assistants. The following states have adopted a definition of "legal assistant" or "paralegal" either through bar association guidelines, ethical opinions, legislation or case law:

Legislation

California
Florida
Illinois
Indiana
Maine
Pennsylvania

Supreme Court Cases or Rules

Kentucky
New Hampshire
New Mexico
North Dakota
Rhode Island
South Dakota
Virginia

Cases

Arizona
New Jersey
Oklahoma
South Carolina
Washington

Guidelines

Colorado
Connecticut
Georgia
Idaho
New York
Oregon
Utah
Wisconsin

Bar Association Activity

Alaska
Arizona
Colorado
Connecticut
Florida
Illinois
Iowa
Kansas
Kentucky
Massachusetts
Michigan
Minnesota
Missouri
Nevada
New Mexico
New Hampshire
North Carolina
North Dakota
Ohio
Oregon
Rhode Island
South Carolina
South Dakota
Tennessee
Texas
Virginia
Wisconsin

NALS
Code of Ethics*

Members of NALS are bound by the objectives of this association and the standards of conduct required of the legal profession.

Every member shall

- Encourage respect for the law and the administration of justice;
- Observe rules governing privileged communications and confidential information;
- Promote and exemplify high standards of loyalty, cooperation, and courtesy;
- Perform all duties of the profession with integrity and competence; and
- Pursue a high order of professional attainment.

Integrity and high standards of conduct are fundamental to the success of our professional association. This Code is promulgated by the NALS and accepted by its members to accomplish these ends.

Canon 1. Members of this association shall maintain a high degree of competency and integrity through continuing education to better assist the legal profession in fulfilling its duty to provide quality legal services to the public.

Canon 2. Members of this association shall maintain a high standard of ethical conduct and shall contribute to the integrity of the association and the legal profession.

Canon 3. Members of this association shall avoid a conflict of interest pertaining to a client matter.

Canon 4. Members of this association shall preserve and protect the confidences and privileged communications of a client.

Canon 5. Members of this association shall exercise care in using independent professional judgment and in determining the extent to which a client may be assisted without the presence of a lawyer and shall not act in matters involving professional legal judgment.

Canon 6. Members of this association shall not solicit legal business on behalf of a lawyer.

Canon 7. Members of this association, unless permitted by law, shall not perform paralegal functions except under the direct supervision of a lawyer and shall not advertise or contract with members of the general public for the performance of paralegal functions.

Canon 8. Members of this association, unless permitted by law, shall not perform any of the duties restricted to lawyers or do things which lawyers themselves may not do and shall assist in preventing the unauthorized practice of law.

Canon 9. Members of this association not licensed to practice law shall not engage in the practice of law as defined by statutes or court decisions.

Canon 10. Members of this association shall do all other things incidental, necessary, or expedient to enhance professional responsibility and participation in the administration of justice and public service in cooperation with the legal profession.

---

* Reprinted with permission of NALS.

The National Federation of Paralegal Associations†
Position Statement on Non-Lawyer Practice

The National Federation of Paralegal Associations (NFPA) believes it is in the best interest of the NFPA to be prepared to respond to potential legislation or court rules providing for non-lawyer practice.

---

† Reprinted by permission from The National Federation of Paralegal Associations, Inc., www.paralegals.org.

NFPA has adopted a position on the regulation of paralegals which is set forth in its Model Act for Paralegal Licensure. This position statement sets forth NFPA's position as it pertains to guidelines and criteria specific to non-lawyer practice and does not change NFPA's current position on the regulation of paralegals working under the supervision of an attorney.

NFPA believes that paralegals can and should play an integral role in the delivery of cost-effective legal and law-related services. Therefore, the NFPA adopts the following position statement regarding Non-Lawyer Practice, to be implemented consistent with the NFPA Resolution 01S-04 which imposes certain limits on advocacy efforts in those states with the NFPA voting member associations:

The NFPA supports legislation and adoption of court rules permitting non-lawyers to deliver limited legal services provided that such legislation or court rules include:

1. Exceptions from the unauthorized practice of law.
2. That non-lawyer practice rules contain minimum criteria as set forth herein.
3. Advanced competency testing as to specialty practice area and limitation of practice as prescribed by laws, regulations, or court rules.
4. Notwithstanding the foregoing, paralegals who choose to work in a traditional setting under the supervision of an attorney shall be specifically exempt from any such non-lawyer practice laws, regulations, or court rules.

Background

Over twenty years ago, the NFPA stated that "In examining contemporary legal institutions and systems, the members of the NFPA recognize that a redefinition of the traditional delivery of legal services is essential in order to meet the needs of the general public. We are committed to increasing the availability of affordable, quality legal services, a goal which is served by the constant reevaluation and expansion of the work that paralegals are authorized to perform. Delivery of quality legal services to those portions of our population currently without access to them requires innovation and sensitivity to specific needs of people"[1] The growing gap between those few citizens who can afford quality legal services and those who must proceed without any legal representation whatsoever has gained increased prominence in recent years. Many observes now recognize the desirability and fairness of increasing the availability of basic legal services to a much broader portion of our community. Certain states have adopted or are considering legislation or judicial rules allowing non-lawyers to provide limited legal and law-related services directly to the public (such non-lawyers are commonly referred to as Legal Document Preparers ("LDP")).[2]

Recommendations

In order to facilitate improved access to the legal system, qualified non-lawyers must be permitted to provide limited legal and law-related services directly to the public, including guidance and/or direction within a certain scope, according to their expertise, experience, and education. To be effective, any new non-lawyer regulation plan must include authority for qualified non-lawyers to provide a limited scope of legal advice under conditions which balance public protection with consumers' individual needs.

However, the NFPA believes that the following four areas must to be addressed in any non-lawyer practice regulation plan: 1) minimum licensing criteria; 2) practice state; 3) exemptions for traditional paralegals working under the supervision of an attorney; and. 4) specific exceptions from unauthorized practice of law (UPL) statutes (if any).

---

[1] Legal Assistant Today/Winter 1985.

[2] Arizona Code of Judicial Administration § 7-208; California Business and Professions Code §§ 6400-6401.6; 2005 IL S.B. 335, Illinois 94th General Assembly.

1. Minimum Registration Criteria

Currently, the educational standards in the State of Arizona for a person to become an LDP[3] are far below what NFPA and the American Association for Paralegal Education (AAfPE) deem acceptable for entry into the paralegal profession. The Department of Labor, Bureau of Labor Statistics, recognizes that it is no longer common for a person to become a paralegal *without formal paralegal education*.[4] The North Carolina Bar Association and the North Carolina Supreme Court recently adopted a plan for certification of paralegals, which provides very broad authority for non-lawyer practice for those who meet the certification standards. 27 N.C. Administrative Code, Subchapter 1G, Paralegal Regulation.

Because paralegals often perform the same functions as an attorney, it is recommended that paralegals attain a certain level of education and specifically, paralegal education. If this is the case for paralegals who work under the direct supervision of an attorney, then it is certainly necessary for those working directly with the public to attain at least the same. In fact, non-lawyers practicing directly to the public should be held to a higher standard than those working under the supervision of an attorney.

NFPA has resolved that any non-lawyer delivering legal and law-related services directly to the public meet the following minimum criteria:

a. Minimum post-secondary education standards as further described on the attached Appendix A; and

b. Continuing Legal Education criteria consistent with NFPA's, the standards of which are described in the attached Appendix B; and

c. Attestation by an attorney licensed to practice law in that state as to the non-lawyers experience and work history; and

d. Fitness and Character criteria as further described on the attached Appendix C; and

e. Bonding or Insurance Requirements.

---

[3] *Arizona minimum criteria*. 3. Initial Certification a. Eligibility for Individual Certification. The board shall grant an initial certificate to an individual applicant who meets the following qualifications: (1) A citizen or legal resident of this country; (2) At least 18 years of age; (3) Of good moral character; and (4) Comply with the laws, court rules, and orders adopted by the supreme court governing legal document preparers in this state. (5) The applicant shall also possess one of the following combinations of education or experience: (a) a high school diploma or a general equivalency diploma evidencing the passing of the general education development test and a minimum of two years of law related experience in one or a combination of the following situations: (i) under the supervision of a licensed attorney; (ii) providing services in preparation of legal documents prior to July 1, 2003; (iii) under the supervision of a certified legal document preparer after July 1, 2003; or (iv) as a court employee; (b) a four-year bachelor of arts or bachelor of science degree from an accredited college or university and a minimum of one year of law-related experience in one or a combination of the following situations: (i) under the supervision of a licensed attorney; (ii) providing services in preparation of legal documents prior to July 1, 2003; (iii) under the supervision of a certified legal document preparer after July 1, 2003; or (iv) as a court employee; (c) a certificate of completion from a paralegal or legal assistant program that is institutionally accredited but not approved by the American Bar Association, that requires successful completion of a minimum of 24 semester units, or the equivalent, in legal specialization courses; (d) a certificate of completion from an accredited educational program designed specifically to qualify a person for certification as a legal document preparer under this code section; 6 (e) a certificate of completion from a paralegal or legal assistant program approved by the American Bar Association; (f) a degree from a law school accredited by the American Bar Association: or (g) a degree from a law school that is institutionally accredited but not approved by the American Bar Association.

[4] While some paralegals train on the job, employers increasingly prefer graduates of postsecondary paralegal education programs; college graduates who have taken some paralegal courses are especially in demand in some markets. There are several ways to become a paralegal. The most common is through a community college paralegal program that leads to an associate's degree. The other common method of entry, mainly for those who have a 'college degree, is through a certification program that leads to a certification in paralegal studies. A small number of schools also offer bachelor's and master's degrees in paralegal studies. Some employers train paralegals on the job, hiring college graduates with no legal experience or promoting experienced legal secretaries. Other entrants have experience in a technical field that is useful to law firms, such as a background in tax preparation for tax and estate practice, criminal justice, or nursing or health administration for personal injury practice. *See* http://www.bls.gov/oco/ocos114.htm#training.

2. Practice Area and Practice State

The types of services being provided by LDP's in the States of Arizona and California require specific practice are knowledge. However, the current laws and/or rules are for general certification. If LDP's represent themselves as specialists in specific practice areas as Wills & Estates, Family Law, etc., then how will the consumer know that the LDP "specializing" in such areas has received only a general certification based on undefined law related experience? Further, with the growing use of the Internet and software technology there is a risk of LDP's, including businesses, so certified, extending beyond the jurisdiction in which they are licensed to practice to offer legal and law-related services to unsuspecting residents of other states.

Therefore, practice area and jurisdictional restrictions should be LDP Rule disclosure requirements. Additionally, any such LDP Rule should provide for disciplinary action of the LDP and consumers with remedies in the event the consumer is harmed by an LDP working outside the scope of his or her knowledge and jurisdiction.

3. Exemption for Paralegals Working Under the Supervision of an Attorney

Historically, paralegals work under the supervision of an attorney and unless such paralegal applies and obtains licensure under a non-lawyer practice rule, he or she must be specifically exempt from such rule. Many traditional paralegals perform substantive legal work with very few restrictions because the work product is the responsibility of the supervising attorney. Attorneys have been able to provide lower cost services to their clients through the increased utilization of their paralegals. Without a specific exemption for traditional paralegals who work for and under the supervision of an attorney, there are substantial risks that the scope of work performed by traditional paralegals could exceed the limitations established by the non-lawyer practice laws and/or rules. Consequently, the fees associated with such work may be deemed non-recoverable. Equally important, the use of paralegals in a traditional setting may become limited by the parameters set forth in non-lawyer laws. Non-lawyer practice rules must be limited to those non-lawyers who deliver legal and law related services directly to the public without the supervision of an attorney.

4. UPL

If the intent of non-lawyer laws and/or rules is to create more choices for consumers to obtain legal and law related services by providing an additional level of service provider, then it is imperative that the non-lawyer laws and/or rules include specific exemptions from unauthorized practice of law statutes or court rules. Since some states rely on court interpretations of broad practice of law definitions and unauthorized practice of law, the activities permitted under any non-lawyer practice law and/or rule, would be subject to interpretation by state courts. This is counterintuitive to the intent of the creation of non-lawyer laws and may prevent consumers from receiving the services required to effectively resolve their legal issues. For example, in the State of Arizona, an LDP can "prepare or provide legal documents without an attorney's supervision." In certain instances, the mere provision of a legal document may require a degree of legal judgment. Alternatively, if a consumer chooses the wrong legal document for his or her situation, what responsibility does the LDP have to advise against the use of such document? The activity (preparing and providing legal documents) is authorized by Arizona's LDP Rule; however, the application of this activity is subject to interpretation by state courts. If a non-lawyer is practicing in accordance with the laws and/or rules enabling such practice, it is in the best interest of the consumer that the non-lawyer be permitted to fully provide services without fear of prosecution for the unauthorized practice of law.

Conclusion

NFPA wants to avoid the creation of a legal document preparer profession where people purport to be paralegals, *but who have neither the requisite education nor training recommended by paralegals and paralegal educators for entry into the paralegal profession.*

NFPA desires to expand paralegal roles where qualified paralegals have alternate career paths.

NFPA desires to maintain the integrity of the paralegal profession and together with AAfPE, has worked to establish appropriate minimum paralegal education criteria, ethical standards, and Continuing Legal Education requirements.

NFPA desires to keep high standards intact. Allowing non-lawyers who have not met the minimum standards for entry into the paralegal profession to deliver legal and law-related services directly to the public or to identify themselves as paralegals may jeopardize the integrity of the entire paralegal profession.

It has taken many years of hard work for paralegals to be recognized as professionals and to establish paralegal industry standards that are becoming widespread today.

Any state seeking to regulate non-lawyers is to be commended for attempting to address the access to legal services crisis with the increased utilization of paralegals as an additional level of service providers.

Prepared for the National Federation of Paralegal Associations by the Ad Hoc Committee on Non-Lawyer Practice. The Ad Hoc Committee on Non-Lawyer Practice was created by Resolution 05-08, passed by the delegation at the 2005 Policy Meeting in Las Vegas, Nevada. The committee presented their draft position statement to the Board of Directors at the Summer Board Meeting held July 22-23, in Rochester, New York. The final position statement was presented to the Board of Directors via e-mail and published in the Inside on December 23, 2005.

[Text omitted]

Appendix A

Post-Secondary Education and Experience Standards

A candidate applying for certification under a non-lawyer practice rule shall:

(a) Have graduated from a paralegal/legal assistant program that consists of a minimum of 90 quarter hours (900 clock hours or 60 semester hours) of which at least 45 quarter hours (450 clock hours or 30 semester hours) are substantive legal courses; or and that is approved by the American Bar Association (ABA) or a program which is in substantial compliance with ABA guidelines and shall have six (6) years substantive paralegal experience; or

(b) A bachelor's degree in any course of study obtained from an institutionally accredited school and three (3) years of substantive paralegal experience;

(c) A bachelor's degree and completion of a paralegal program which said paralegal program may be embodied in a bachelor's degree; and two (2) years substantive paralegal experience or

(d) A post-baccalaureate certificate program in paralegal/legal assistant studies, or

(e) Four (4) years substantive paralegal experience on or before December 31, 2000.

Appendix B

The National Federation of Paralegal Association Continuing Legal Education (CLE) Standards

NFPA accepts the following definition of Continuing Legal Education:

> *Continuing Legal Education shall include seminars on substantive legal topics, or topics applicable to substantive law issues, or must be oriented to the specific nature of the paralegal profession, such as enhancing computer skills or research techniques, increasing paralegal management skills, issues related to, or affecting, the paralegal profession.*
>
> *Further, Continuing Legal Education includes authorship of articles by an individual paralegal, including research time; and/or speaking to paralegals regarding substantive law issues or topics oriented to the specific nature of the paralegal profession, including preparation time for such presentation; and attendance and successful completion of law-related classes at community colleges, colleges and universities.*

NFPA recognizes continuing legal education offered by the following groups to be approved without further review by NFPA or a designated Coordinator: all bar associations, either mandatory or voluntary; National Association of Legal Assistants, Inc.; American Alliance of Paralegals, Inc.; Inns of Court; and Courts of all jurisdictions within the United States.

Appendix C

Fitness and Character Model

Applicants should be of good moral character based upon the following circumstances:

Whether the applicant has been convicted of a felony or comparable crime as defined by an individual state that does not have felony designations; OR

Whether the applicant has been suspended or disbarred from the practice of law in any jurisdiction; OR

Whether the applicant has been convicted of the unauthorized practice of law in any jurisdiction; OR

Whether the applicant has been convicted of any of the acts described in Section X below; OR

Whether the applicant is, for reasons of misconduct, currently under suspension, termination, or revocation of a certificate, registration, or license to practice by a professional organization, court, disciplinary board, or agency in any jurisdiction.

An applicant shall be rejected if any of the acts set forth in paragraphs 1-5 immediately above apply. An applicant should have the right to appeal a denial based on the provisions of these criteria. When considering the appeal, it should be considered, but shall not be limited to, the nature of the act, rehabilitation, the time that has transpired since the act, and any other extraordinary circumstances.

Appendix D

CAREER CONSIDERATIONS

Paralegals and Legal Assistants*

- Nature of the Work
- Working Conditions
- Training, Other Qualifications, and Advancement
- Employment
- Job Outlook
- Earnings
- Related Occupations
- Sources of Additional Information

Significant Points

- About 7 out of 10 work for law firms; others work for corporate legal departments and government agencies.
- Most entrants have an associate's degree in paralegal studies, or a bachelor's degree coupled with a certificate in paralegal studies.
- Employment is projected to grow much faster than average, as employers try to reduce costs by hiring paralegals to perform tasks formerly carried out by lawyers.
- Competition for jobs should continue; experienced, formally trained paralegals should have the best employment opportunities.

Nature of the Work

While lawyers assume ultimate responsibility for legal work, they often delegate many of their tasks to paralegals. In fact, paralegals—also called legal assistants—are continuing to assume a growing range of tasks in the Nation's legal offices and perform many of the same tasks as lawyers. Nevertheless, they are still explicitly prohibited from carrying out duties that are considered to be the practice of law, such as setting legal fees, giving legal advice, and presenting cases in court.

One of a paralegal's most important tasks is helping lawyers prepare for closings, hearings, trials, and corporate meetings. Paralegals investigate the facts of cases and ensure that all relevant information is considered. They also identify appropriate laws, judicial decisions, legal articles, and other materials that are relevant to assigned cases. After they analyze and organize the information, paralegals may prepare written reports that attorneys use in determining how cases should be handled. Should attorneys decide to file lawsuits on behalf of clients, paralegals may help prepare the legal arguments, draft pleadings and motions to be filed with the court, obtain affidavits, and assist attorneys during trials. Paralegals also organize and track files of all important case documents and make them available and easily accessible to attorneys.

In addition to this preparatory work, paralegals perform a number of other vital functions. For example, they help draft contracts, mortgages, separation agreements, and instruments of trust.

* Source: Bureau of Labor Statistics, U.S. Department of Labor, Occupational Outlook Handbook, 2006-07 Edition, Paralegals and Legal Assistants, on the Internet at *www.bls.gov/oco/ocos114.htm* (visited May 27, 2006).

They also may assist in preparing tax returns and planning estates. Some paralegals coordinate the activities of other law office employees and maintain financial office records. Various additional tasks may differ, depending on the employer.

Paralegals are found in all types of organizations, but most are employed by law firms, corporate legal departments, and various government offices. In these organizations, they can work in many different areas of the law, including litigation, personal injury, corporate law, criminal law, employee benefits, intellectual property, labor law, bankruptcy, immigration, family law, and real estate. As the law has become more complex, paralegals have responded by becoming more specialized. Within specialties, functions often are broken down further so that paralegals may deal with a specific area. For example, paralegals specializing in labor law may concentrate exclusively on employee benefits.

The duties of paralegals also differ widely with the type of organization in which they are employed. Paralegals who work for corporations often assist attorneys with employee contracts, shareholder agreements, stock-option plans, and employee benefit plans. They also may help prepare and file annual financial reports, maintain corporate minutes' record resolutions, and prepare forms to secure loans for the corporation. Paralegals often monitor and review government regulations to ensure that the corporation is aware of new requirements and is operating within the law. Increasingly, experienced paralegals are assuming additional supervisory responsibilities such as overseeing team projects and serving as a communications link between the team and the corporation.

The duties of paralegals who work in the public sector usually vary within each agency. In general, paralegals analyze legal material for internal use, maintain reference files, conduct research for attorneys, and collect and analyze evidence for agency hearings. They may prepare informative or explanatory material on laws, agency regulations, and agency policy for general use by the agency and the public. Paralegals employed in community legal-service projects help the poor, the aged, and others who are in need of legal assistance. They file forms, conduct research, prepare documents, and, when authorized by law, may represent clients at administrative hearings.

Paralegals in small and medium-size law firms usually perform a variety of duties that require a general knowledge of the law. For example, they may research judicial decisions on improper police arrests or help prepare a mortgage contract. Paralegals employed by large law firms, government agencies, and corporations, however, are more likely to specialize in one aspect of the law.

Familiarity with computers use and technical knowledge have become essential to paralegal work. Computer software packages and the Internet are used to search legal literature stored in computer databases and on CD-ROM. In litigation involving many supporting documents, paralegals usually use computer databases to retrieve, organize, and index various materials. Imaging software allows paralegals to scan documents directly into a database, while billing programs help them to track hours billed to clients. Computer software packages also are used to perform tax computations and explore the consequences of various tax strategies for clients.

Working Conditions

Paralegals employed by corporations and government usually work a standard 40-hour week. Although most paralegals work year round, some are temporarily employed during busy times of the year and then are released when the workload diminishes. Paralegals who work for law firms sometimes work very long hours when they are under pressure to meet deadlines. Some law firms reward such loyalty with bonuses and additional time off.

These workers handle many routine assignments, particularly when they are inexperienced. As they gain experience, paralegals usually assume more varied tasks with additional responsibility. Paralegals do most of their work at desks in offices and law libraries. Occasionally, they travel to gather information and perform other duties.

Training, Other Qualifications, and Advancement

There are several ways to become a paralegal. The most common is through a community college paralegal program that leads to an associate's degree. The other common method of entry, mainly for those who already have a college degree, is through a program that leads to a certification in paralegal studies. A small number of schools also offer bachelor's and master's degrees in paralegal studies. Some employers train paralegals on the job, hiring college graduates with no legal experience or promoting experienced legal secretaries. Other entrants have experience in a technical field that is useful to law firms, such as a background in tax preparation for tax and estate practice or in criminal justice, nursing, or health administration for personal injury practice.

An estimated 1,000 colleges and universities, law schools, and proprietary schools offer formal paralegal training programs. Approximately 260 paralegal programs are approved by the American Bar Association (ABA). Although many programs do not require such approval, graduation from an ABA-approved program can enhance one's employment opportunities. The requirements for admission to these programs vary. Some require certain college courses or a bachelor's degree, others accept high school graduates or those with legal experience, and a few schools require standardized tests and personal interviews.

Paralegal programs include 2-year associate degree's programs, 4-year bachelor's degree programs, and certificate programs that can take only a few months to complete. Most certificate programs provide intensive and, in some cases, specialized paralegal training for individuals who already hold college degrees, while associate's and bachelor's degree programs usually combine paralegal training with courses in other academic subjects. The quality of paralegal training programs varies; the better programs usually include job placement services. Programs generally offer courses introducing students to the legal applications of computers, including how to perform legal research on the Internet. Many paralegal training programs also offer an internship in which students gain practical experience by working for several months in a private law firm, the office of a public defender or attorney general, a bank, a corporate legal department, a legal aid organization, or a government agency. Experience gained in internships is an asset when one is seeking a job after graduation. Prospective students should examine the experiences of recent graduates before enrolling in a paralegal program.

Although most employers do not require certification, earning a voluntary certificate from a professional society may offer advantages in the labor market. The National Association of Legal Assistants (NALA), for example, has established standards for certification requiring various combinations of education and experience. Paralegals who meet these standards are eligible to take a 2-day examination, given three times each year at several regional testing centers. Those who pass this examination may use the Certified Legal Assistant (CLA) designation. The NALA also offers an advanced paralegal certification for those who want to specialize in other areas of the law. In addition, the Paralegal Advanced Competency Exam, administered through the National Federation of Paralegal Associations, offers professional recognition to paralegals with a bachelor's degree and at least 2 years of experience. Those who pass this examination may use the Registered Paralegal (RP) designation.

Paralegals must be able to document and present their findings and opinions to their supervising attorney. They need to understand legal terminology and have good research and investigative skills. Familiarity with the operation and applications of computers in legal research and litigation support also is important. Paralegals should stay informed of new developments in the laws that affect their area of practice. Participation in continuing legal education seminars allows paralegals to maintain and expand their knowledge of the law.

Because paralegals frequently deal with the public, they should be courteous and uphold the ethical standards of the legal profession. The National Association of Legal Assistants, the National Federation of Paralegal Associations, and a few States have established ethical guidelines for paralegals to follow.

Paralegals usually are given more responsibilities and require less supervision as they gain work experience. Experienced paralegals who work in large law firms, corporate legal departments, or government agencies may supervise and delegate assignments to other paralegals and clerical staff. Advancement opportunities also include promotion to managerial and other law-related positions within the firm or corporate legal department. However, some paralegals find it easier to move to another law firm when seeking increased responsibility or advancement.

Employment

Paralegals and legal assistants held about 224,000 jobs in 2004. Private law firms employed 7 out of 10 paralegals and legal assistants; most of the remainder worked for corporate legal departments and various levels of government. Within the Federal Government, the U.S. Department of Justice is the largest employer, followed by the Social Security Administration and the U.S. Department of the Treasury. A small number of paralegals own their own businesses and work as freelance legal assistants, contracting their services to attorneys or corporate legal departments.

Job Outlook

Employment for paralegals and legal assistants is projected to grow much faster than average for all occupations through 2014. Employers are trying to reduce costs and increase the availability and efficiency of legal services by hiring paralegals to perform tasks formerly carried out by lawyers. Besides new jobs created by employment growth, additional job openings will arise as people leave the occupation. Despite projections of rapid employment growth, competition for jobs should continue as many people seek to go into this profession; however, experienced, formally trained paralegals should have the best employment opportunities.

Private law firms will continue to be the largest employers of paralegals, but a growing array of other organizations, such as corporate legal departments, insurance companies, real estate and title insurance firms, and banks hire paralegals. Corporations in particular are boosting their in-house legal departments to cut costs. Demand for paralegals also is expected to grow as an expanding population increasingly requires legal services, especially in areas such as intellectual property, health care, international law, elder issues, criminal law, and environmental law. Paralegals who specialize in areas such as real estate, bankruptcy, medical malpractice, and product liability should have ample employment opportunities. The growth of prepaid legal plans also should contribute to the demand for legal services. Paralegal employment is expected to increase as organizations presently employing paralegals assign them a growing range of tasks and as paralegals are increasingly employed in small and medium-size establishments. A growing number of experienced paralegals are expected to establish their own businesses.

Job opportunities for paralegals will expand in the public sector as well. Community legal-service programs, which provide assistance to the poor, elderly, minorities, and middle-income families, will employ additional paralegals to minimize expenses and serve the most people. Federal, State, and local government agencies, consumer organizations, and the courts also should continue to hire paralegals in increasing numbers.

To a limited extent, paralegal jobs are affected by the business cycle. During recessions, demand declines for some discretionary legal services, such as planning estates, drafting wills, and handling real estate transactions. Corporations are less inclined to initiate certain types of litigation when falling sales and profits lead to fiscal belt tightening. As a result, full-time paralegals employed in offices adversely affected by a recession may be laid off or have their work hours reduced. However, during recessions, corporations and individuals are more likely to face other problems that require legal assistance, such as bankruptcies, foreclosures, and divorces. Paralegals, who provide many of the same legal services as lawyers at a lower cost, tend to fare relatively better in difficult economic conditions.

Earnings

Earnings of paralegals and legal assistants vary greatly. Salaries depend on education, training, experience, the type and size of employer, and the geographic location of the job. In general, paralegals who work for large law firms or in large metropolitan areas earn more than those who work for smaller firms or in less populated regions. In addition to earning a salary, many paralegals receive bonuses. In May 2004, full-time wage and salary paralegals and legal assistants had median annual earnings, including bonuses, of $39,130. The middle 50 percent earned between $31,040 and $49,950. The top 10 percent earned more than $61,390, while the bottom 10 percent earned less than $25,360. Median annual earnings in the industries employing the largest numbers of paralegals in May 2004 were as follows:

Federal Government	$59,370
Local government	38,260
Legal services	37,870
State government	34,910

Related Occupations

Among the other occupations that call for a specialized understanding of the law and the legal system, but do not require the extensive training of a lawyer, are law clerks; title examiners, abstractors, and searchers; claims adjusters, appraisers, examiners, and investigators; and occupational health and safety specialists and technicians.

Sources of Additional Information
Disclaimer: Links to non-BLS Internet sites are provided for your convenience and do not constitute an endorsement.

General information on a career as a paralegal can be obtained from:

- Standing Committee on Paralegals, American Bar Association, 321 North Clark St., Chicago, IL 60610. Internet: http://www.abanet.org/legalservices/paralegals

For information on the Certified Legal Assistant exam, schools that offer training programs in a specific State, and standards and guidelines for paralegals, contact:

- National Association of Legal Assistants, Inc., 1516 South Boston St., Suite 200, Tulsa, OK 74119. Internet: http://www.nala.org

Information on a career as a paralegal, schools that offer training programs, job postings for paralegals, the Paralegal Advanced Competency Exam, and local paralegal associations can be obtained from:

- National Federation of Paralegal Associations, 2517 Eastlake Ave. East, Suite 200, Seattle, WA 98102. Internet: http://www.paralegals.org

Information on paralegal training programs, including the pamphlet *How to Choose a Paralegal Education Program*, may be obtained from:

- American Association for Paralegal Education, 19 Mantua Rd., Mt. Royal, NJ 08061. Internet: http://www.aafpe.org

Information on obtaining positions as occupational health and safety specialists and technicians with the Federal Government is available from the Office of Personnel Management through USAJOBS, the Federal Government's official employment information system. This resource for locating and applying for job opportunities can be accessed through the Internet at http://www.usajobs.opm.gov or through an interactive voice response telephone system at (703) 724-1850 or TDD (978) 461-8404. These numbers are not tollfree, and charges may result.

Glossary

A

abandoned property Personal property that the owner has intentionally discarded and to which the owner has relinquished ownership rights.

abatement Doctrine in which will bequests may fail due to insufficient estate funds at the time of testator's death.

acceptance The offeree's clear manifestation of agreement to the exact terms of the offer in the manner specified in the offer.

actus reus The guilty act.

ademption Failed bequest in a will because the property no longer exists.

Administrative Law The body of law governing administrative agencies, that is those agencies created by Congress or state legislatures, such as the Social Security Administration.

adoption The taking of a child into the family, creating a parent-child relationship where the biological relationship did not exist.

adverse possession The legal taking of another's property by meeting the requirements of the state statute, typically open and continuous use for a period of five years.

alimony Court-ordered money paid to support a former spouse after termination of a marriage.

alter ego doctrine A business set up to cover or be a shield for the person actually controlling the corporation, and thus the court may treat the owners as if they were partners or a sole proprietor.

alternative dispute resolution (ADR) Method of settling a dispute before trial in order to conserve the court"s time.

American Bar Association (ABA) A national organization of lawyers, providing support and continuing legal education to the profession.

American Law Institute A nongovernmental organization composed of distinguished judges and lawyers in the United States.

annulment Court procedure dissolving a marriage, treating it as if it never happened.

answer The defendant"s response to the plaintiff's complaint.

appellate court The court of appeals that reviews a trial court's record for errors.

arraignment A court hearing where the information contained in an indictment is read to the defendant.

arrest The formal taking of a person, usually by a police officer, to answer criminal charges.

articles of incorporation The basic charter of an organization, written and filed in accordance with state laws.

articles of partnership Written agreement to form a partnership.

assault Intentional voluntary movement that creates fear or apprehension of an immediate unwanted touching; the threat or attempt to cause a touching, whether successful or not, provided the victim is aware of the danger.

assumption of the risk The doctrine that releases another person from liability for the person who chooses to assume a known risk of harm.

attempt To actually try to commit a crime and have the actual ability to do so.

attestation clause The section of the will where the witnesses observe the act of the testator signing the will.

attractive nuisance doctrine The doctrine that holds a landowner to a higher duty of care even when the children are trespassers, because the potentially harmful condition is so inviting to a child.

B

bailee The recipient of the property, temporarily taking possession.

bailment The delivery of personal property from one person to another to be held temporarily.

bailor The owner of the property transferring possession.

battery An intentional and unwanted harmful or offensive contact with the person of another; the actual intentional touching of someone with intent to cause harm, no matter how slight the harm.

bench trial A case heard and decided by a judge.

beneficiaries The persons named in a will to receive the testator's assets.

bequest Gift by will of personal property.

bilateral contract A contract in which the parties exchange a promise for a promise.

binding authority (mandatory authority) A source of law that a court must follow in deciding a case, such as a statute or federal regulations.

board of directors Policy managers of a corporation, clected by the shareholders, who in turn chose the officers of the corporation.

breach of contract A violation of an obligation under a contract for which a party may seek recourse to the court; a party's performance that deviates from the required performance obligations under the contract.

breach of duty The failure to maintain a reasonable degree of care toward another person to whom a duty is owed.

briefing a case Summarizing a court opinion.

burglary Breaking and entering into a structure for the purpose of committing a crime.

business judgment rule The rule that protects corporate officers and directors from liability for bad business decisions.

business organization A form of conducting business.

bylaws Corporate provisions detailing management structure and operating rules.

C

capacity The ability to understand the nature and significance of a contract; to understand or comprehend specific acts or reasoning.

case law Published court opinions of federal and state appellate courts; judge-created law in deciding cases, set forth in court opinions.

case of first impression A case in which no previous court decision with similar facts or legal issue has arisen before; a case with a legal issue that has not been heard by the court before in a specific jurisdiction.

case on all fours A case in which facts, issues, parties, and remedies are analogous to the present case.

case on point A case involving similar facts and issues to the present case.

case reporters Sets of books that contain copies of appellate court opinions.

challenge An attorney's objection, during voir dire, to the inclusion of a specific person on the jury.

chattel A term for tangible personal property or goods.

child support The right of a child to financial support and the obligation of a parent to provide it.

Chinese wall The shielding, or walling off, of a new employee from a client in the new firm with whom there may be a conflict of interest.

circuit One of several courts in a specific jurisdiction.

civil cause of action A claim for damages that is based on the relevant substantive area of law and has facts that support a judicial resolution.

civil law The legal rules regarding offenses committed against the person.

closely held corporation A business that is incorporated with limited members, typically related family members.

closing argument A statement by a party's attorney that summarizes that party's case and reviews what that party promised to prove during trial.

codicil A provision that amends or modifies an existing will.

cohabitation agreement A contract setting forth the rights of two people who live together without the benefit of marriage.

common law Judge-made law, the ruling in a judicial opinion.

common law marriage A form of marriage that is legally recognized in certain states, if the two people have been living together for a long period of time, have represented themselves as being married, and have the intent to be married.

community property All property acquired during marriage in a community property state, owned in equal shares.

compensatory damages A payment to make up for a wrong committed and return the nonbreaching party to a position where the effect or the breach has been neutralized.

competence The ability and possession of expertise and skill in a field that is necessary to do the job.

complaint The document that states the allegations and the legal basis of the plaintiff"s claims.

concurrent jurisdiction Jurisdiction over the subject matter exists in both state and federal court, unless statutorily prohibited.

confidentiality Lawyer's duty not to disclose information concerning a client.

conflict check A procedure to verify potential adverse interests before accepting a new client.

consanguinity The relationship between blood relatives, such as brothers and sisters.

consent All parties to a novation must knowingly assent to the substitution of either the obligations or parties to the agreement.

consequential damages Damages resulting from the breach that are natural and foreseeable results of the breaching party's actions.

consideration The basis of the bargained for exchange between the parties to a contract that is of legal value.

conspiracy By agreement, parties work together to create an illegal result, to achieve an unlawful end.

contract A legally binding agreement between two or more parties.

corporation An organization formed with state government approval to act as an artificial person to carry on business and issue stock.

counterclaim A countersuit brought by the defendant against the plaintiff.

counteroffer A refusal to accept the stated terms of an offer by proposing alternate terms.

criminal law The legal rules regarding wrongs committed against society.

cross-claim Plaintiffs or defendants suing each other.

custody The legal authority to make decisions concerning a child's interests.

D

deed The written document transferring title, or an ownership interest in real property, to another person.

defamation An act of communication involving a false and unprivileged statement about another person, causing harm.

default judgment A judgment entered by the court against the defendant for failure to respond to the plaintiff"s complaint.

defendant The party against whom a lawsuit is brought.

deposition A discovery tool in a question-and-answer format in which the attorney verbally questions a party or a witness under oath.

devise A disposition of real property by will.

disaffirm Renounce, as in a contract.

discovery The process of investigation and collection of evidence by litigants.

diversity jurisdiction Authority of the federal court to hear a case if the parties are citizens of different states and the amount at issue is over $75,000.

dividends Portion of profits, usually based on the number of shares owned.

divorce/dissolution The legal termination of a marriage.

domicile The place where a person maintains a physical residence with the intent to permanently remain in that place; citizenship; the permanent home of the party.

donee A party to whom a gift is given.

donor The person making a gift.

duress Unreasonable and unscrupulous manipulation of a person to force him to agree to terms of an agreement that he would otherwise not agree to.

duty A legal obligation that is required to be performed.

E

easement A right to use another's property for a specific purpose, such as a right of way across the land.

entrapment An act of a law enforcement official to induce or encourage a person to commit a crime when the defendant expresses no desire to proceed with the illegal act.

escheat To pass property to the state, as is done with the assets of a person who dies without a will and without heirs.

estate The compilation of all a deceased's assets and debts.

estate in land An ownership interest in real property.

ethics Standards by which conduct is measured.

exclusive jurisdiction Only one court has the authority to hear the specific case; for example, only a federal court can decide a bankruptcy case.

executor/executrix The administrator of the estate.

exemplary damages Punitive damages, awarded as a punishment and a deterrent.

F

false imprisonment Any deprivation of a person's freedom of movement without that person's consent and against his or her will, whether done by actual violence or threats.

federal question The jurisdiction given to federal courts in cases involving the interpretation and application of the U.S. Constitution or acts of Congress.

Federal Rules of Civil Procedure The specific set of rules followed in the federal courts.

fee simple absolute A property interest in which the owner has full and exclusive use and enjoyment of the entire property.

fee simple defeasible An interest in land in which the owner has all the benefits of a fee simple estate, except that property is taken away if a certain event or condition occurs.

felony A crime punishable by more than a year in prison or death.

fixtures Personal property that has become permanently attached or associated with the real property.

foreign corporation A business that is incorporated under the laws of a different state, doing business in multiple states.

forum shopping Plaintiff attempts to choose a state with favorable rules in which to file suit.

fraud A knowing and intentional misstatement of the truth in order to induce a desired action from another person.

freehold estate An estate interest that includes both ownership and possessory interests.

future interest Right to property that can be enforced in the future.

G

general gift Ggift of property that is not exactly identified, as in furniture.

general intent An unjustifiable act; reckless conduct.

gift Bestowing a benefit without any expectation on the part of the giver to receive something in return and the absence of any obligation on the part of the receiver to do anything in return.

gift causa mortis A gift made by the donor in contemplation of death.

gift inter vivos Gift made during the lifetime of the donor.

grantee The person receiving the property.

grantor The person transferring the property.

guardian ad litem A person appointed by the court to represent the best interests of the child in a custody determination.

H

headnotes An editorial feature in unofficial reporters that summarizes a single legal point or issue in the court opinion.

heirs Persons entitled to receive property based on intestate succession.

holographic will A will entirely written and signed by the testator in that person's own handwriting.

I

illegal contract A contract that is unenforceable because the subject matter of the agreement is prohibited by state or federal statutory law and thus void.

implied contract An agreement whose terms have not been communicated in words, but rather by conduct or actions of the parties.

impossibility of performance An excuse for performance based upon an absolute inability to perform the act required under the contract.

in personam jurisdiction A court's authority over a party personally.

in rem jurisdiction A court's authority over claims affecting property.

inchoate offenses Uncompleted crimes.

indictment A written list of charges issued by a grand jury against a defendant in a criminal case.

injunction A court order that requires a party to refrain from acting in a certain way to prevent harm to the requesting party.

insanity defense A defendant's claim that he or she was insane when the crime was committed, even if temporarily insane.

intangible property Personal property that has no physical presence but is represented by a certificate or some other instrument, such as stocks or trademarks.

intent Having the knowledge and desire that a specific consequence will result from an action.

intentional infliction of emotional distress Intentional act involving extreme and outrageous conduct resulting in severe mental anguish.

intentional torts An intentional civil wrong that injures another person or property.

interrogatories A discovery tool in the form of a series of written questions that are answered by the party in writing.

intestate The state of having died without a will.

invitation to treat A person is expressing willingness to enter into negotiations, inviting another to make an offer.

J

joint tenancy The shared ownership of property, giving the other owner the right of survivorship if one owner dies.

judgment The court's final decision regarding the rights and claims of the parties.

judicial precedent A court decision in which similar facts are presented; provides authority for deciding a subsequent case.

jury instructions The relevant laws that the jury uses to apply to the facts of a case.

jury trial Case is decided by a jury.

L

landlord The lessor of property.

larceny The common law crime of taking property of another without permission.

law A set of rules and principles that govern any society.

legal analysis The process of examining prior case law and comparing it to your case.

legal assistant Individual qualified to assist an attorney in the delivery of legal services.

legal issue The point in dispute between two or more parties in a lawsuit.

life estate An ownership interest in property for a designated period of time, based on the life of another person.

limited liability company A hybrid business formed under state acts, representing both corporation and partnership characteristics.

limited partnership A partnership of two or more persons, consisting of limited partners, who provide only financial backing, and general partners, who manage the business and have unlimited liability.

liquidated damages An amount of money agreed upon in the original contract as a reasonable estimation of the damages to be recovered by the nonbreaching party.

litigants A party to a lawsuit.

lost property Personal property with which a person has involuntarily parted possession.

M

M'Naghten Rule The defendant alleges he or she lacked capacity to form criminal intent.

malice Person's doing of any act in reckless disregard of another person.

malice aforethought The prior intention to kill the victim or anyone else if likely to occur as a result of the actions or omissions.

malum in se An act that is prohibited because it is "evil in itself."

malum prohibitum An act that is prohibited by a rule of law.

manslaughter The unlawful killing of a human being without premeditation.

marital property The property accumulated by a couple during marriage, called community property in some states.

marketable title The title transfers full ownership rights to the buyer.

mediation A dispute resolution method in which a neutral third party meets with the opposing parties to help them achieve a mutually satisfactory solution without court intervention.

meeting of the minds A legal concept requiring that both parties understand and ascribe the same meaning to the terms of the contract; a theory holding that both parties must both objectively and subjectively intend to enter into the agreement on the same terms.

mens rea "A guilty mind"; criminal intent in committing the act.

minimum contacts The test, based on the case *International Shoe v. Washington,* that courts use to ascertain if a defendant has some contact with the state of which he or she is not a resident.

mirror image rule A requirement that the acceptance of an offer must exactly match the terms of the original offer.

misdemeanor A lesser crime punishable by less than a year in jail and/or a fine.

mislaid property Personal property that the owner has intentionally placed somewhere and then forgot about.

mistake in fact An error in assessing the facts, causing a defendant to act in a certain way.

Model Penal Code (MPC) A comprehensive body of criminal law, adopted in whole or in part by most states.

motion A procedural request or application presented by the attorney in court.

motion for a directed verdict A request by a party for a judgment because the other side has not met its burden of proof.

motion for a summary judgment A motion by either party for judgment based on all court documents.

motion in limine A request that certain evidence not be raised at trial, as it is arguably prejudicial, irrelevant, or legally inadmissible evidence.

murder The killing of a human being with intent.

mutual benefit bailment A bailment created for the benefit of both parties.

mutual will Joint wills executed by two or more persons.

N

National Association of Legal Assistants (NALA) A legal professional group that lends support and continuing education for legal assistants.

necessaries of life Generally legally considered to be food, clothing, and shelter; necessities.

negligence The failure to use reasonable care to avoid harm to another person or to do that which a reasonable person might do in similar circumstances.

no-fault divorce A divorce in which one spouse does not need to allege wrongdoing by the other spouse as grounds for the divorce.

non-freehold estate A lease agreement.

nuncupative will An oral will, usually made by the testator near death.

O

offer A promise made by the offeror to do (or not to do) something provided that the offeree, by accepting, promises or does something in exchange.

offeree The person to whom the offer is made.

offeror The person making the offer to another party.

official reporters Government publications of court decisions (for example, 325 Ill.3d 50).

opening statement An initial statement by a party's attorney explaining what the case is about and what that party's side expects to prove during the trial.

option contract A separate and legally enforceable agreement included in the contract stating that the offer cannot be revoked for a certain time period.

original jurisdiction Authority of a court to hear a case first.

P

palimony A division of property between two unmarried parties after they separate or the paying of support by one party to the other.

paralegal A person qualified to assist an attorney, under direct supervision, in all substantive legal matters with the exception of appearing in court and rendering legal advice.

Parental Kidnapping Protection Act (PKPA) An act related to jurisdictional issues in applying and enforcing child custody decrees in other states.

partnership Business enterprise owned by more than one person, entered into for profit.

paternity action A lawsuit to identify the father of a child born outside of marriage.

per capita distribution The equal division of assets according to the number of surviving heirs with the nearest degree of kinship.

per stirpes distribution The division of assets according to rights of representation.

peremptory challenge An attorney's elimination of a prospective juror without giving a reason; limited to a specific number of strikes.

periodic tenancy Tenancy in which the tenant is a holdover after the expiration of a tenancy for years.

persuasive authority A source of law or legal authority that is not binding on the court in deciding a case but may be used by the court for guidance, such as law review articles.

piercing the corporate veil To show that a corporation exists as an alter ego for a person or group of individuals to avoid liability.

plain meaning rule Courts will use the traditional definition of terms used if those terms are not otherwise defined.

plaintiff The party initiating legal action.

pleadings The complaint, answer to complaint, and reply.

precedent The holding of past court decisions that are followed in future judicial cases where similar facts and legal issues are present.

pre-existing duty An obligation to perform an act that existed before the current promise was made that requires the same performance presently sought.

prenuptial agreement An agreement made by parties before marriage that controls certain aspects of the relationship, such as management and ownership of property.

pretrial conferences The meeting between the parties and the judge to identify legal issues, stipulate to uncontested matters, and encourage settlement.

pretrial stage The steps in the litigation process before trial, to accomplish discovery and encourage settlement.

prima facie case A case with the required proof of elements in a tort cause of action; the elements of the plaintiff's (or prosecutor's) cause of action; what the plaintiff must prove.

probate The court process of determining will validity, settling estate debts, and distributing assets.

procedural law The set of rules that are used to enforce the substantive law.

professional corporation Business form organized as a closely held group of professional intellectual employees such as doctors.

promissory estoppel A legal doctrine that makes some promises enforceable even though they are not compliant with the technical requirements of a contract.

promoter A person, typically a principal shareholder, who organizes a business.

proximate cause The defendant's actions are the nearest cause of the plaintiff's injuries.

publicly held corporation A business held by a large number of shareholders.

Q

quitclaim deed A deed transferring only the interest in property of the grantor, without guarantees.

R

real property Land and all property permanently attached to it, such as buildings.

reasonable person standard The standard of conduct of a person in the community in similar circumstances.

reciprocal will Wills in which testators name each other as beneficiaries under similar plans.

remainder Right to receive property interest at some point in the future.

res ipsa loquitur Doctrine in which it is assumed that a person's injuries were caused by the negligent act of another person as the harmful act ordinarily would not occur but for negligence.

rescission and restitution A decision by the court that renders the contract null and void and requires the parties to return to the wronged party any benefits received under the agreement.

rescue doctrine Doctrine in which a tortfeasor is liable for harm caused to a person who is injured while rescuing the original victim.

residuary gift Gift of the remaining property of an estate after expenses and specific gifts have been satisfied.

Restatement of the Law of Torts, Second An authoritative treatise that is a compilation of the key principles of tort law.

reversion Right to receive back property in the event of the happening of a certain condition.

revoke To take back, as in to retract an offer at any time prior to it being accepted.

right of survivorship The right of a surviving joint tenant to take ownership of a deceased joint tenant's share of the property.

robbery The direct taking of property from another through force or threat.

rules of construction The rules that control the judicial interpretation of statutes.

S

self-defense A defendant's legal excuse that the use of force was justified.

separation agreements Contract between husband and wife to live apart; the document outlines the terms of the separation.

separation of powers The doctrine that divides the powers of government among the three branches established under the U.S. Constitution.

shareholder The owner of one or more shares of stock in a corporation.

sole proprietorship A business owned by one person.

solemnization A formalization of a marriage, as in for example a marriage ceremony.

solicitation The crime of inducing or encouraging another to commit a crime.

specific gift A gift of a particular described item.

specific intent The mental desire and will to act in a particular way.

specific performance A court order that requires a party to perform a certain act in order to prevent harm to the requesting party.

stare decisis The judicial process of adhering to prior case decisions; general legal principle in which a court abides by the prior decisions in settling cases; the doctrine of precedent whereby once a court has decided a specific issue one way in the past, it and other courts in the same jurisdiction are obligated to follow that earlier decision in deciding cases with similar issues in the future.

Statute of Frauds Rule that specifies which contracts must be in writing to be enforceable.

statutes Written laws enacted by the legislative branches of both federal and state governments.

statutory law Primary source of law consisting of the body of legislative law.

strict liability The defendant is liable without the plaintiff having to prove fault.

subject matter jurisdiction A court's authority over the *res*, the subject of the case.

subpoena An order issued by the court clerk directing a person to appear in court.

substantive law Legal rules that are the content or substance of the law, defining rights and duties of citizens.

summons The notice to appear in court, notifying the defendant of the plaintiff's complaint.

survey A description of the boundaries of a piece of property.

syllabus An editorial feature in unofficial reporters that summarizes the court's decision.

T

tangible property Personal property that can be held or touched, such as furniture or jewelry.

temporary restraining order A court order barring a person from harassing or harming another.

tenancy by the entirety A form of ownership for married couples, similar to joint tenancy, where the spouse has right of survivorship.

tenancy for years A lease with fixed beginning and ending dates; for example, a lease may be for one year.

tenancy in common A form of ownership between two or more people where each owner's interest upon death goes to his or her heirs.

tenant A person, or corporation, who rents real property from an owner; also called a lessee.

testamentary capacity The ability to understand and have the legal capacity to make a will.

testate The state of having died with a valid will.

testator/testatrix The person who writes a will.

third-party claim A suit filed by the defendant against a party not originally named in the plaintiff's complaint.

title insurance policy The insurance provided by a title company; it protects the lender and buyer in case it is discovered that the title is imperfect.

title search A search of the abstract of title, the short history of a piece of property including ownership interests and liens.

tort A civil wrongful act, committed against a person or property, either intentional or negligent.

trade fixtures Pieces of equipment on or attached to the property being used in a trade or business.

transferred intent doctrine The doctrine that holds a person liable for the unintended result to another person not contemplated by the defendant's actions.

trespass to land Intentional and unlawful entry onto or interference with the land of another person without consent.

U

unauthorized means The offeree accepts the offer by a method that is not the same as specified by the offeror.

unconscionable contract A contract so completely unreasonable and irrational that it shocks the conscience.

undue influence Using a close personal or fiduciary relationship to one's advantage to gain assent to terms that the party otherwise would not have agreed to.

Uniform Child Custody Jurisdiction Act (UCCJA) An act that resolves jurisdictional issues related to child custody.

Uniform Parentage Act An act defining legal parentage and establishing parental rights.

uniform statute Model legislation drafted by the National Conference of Commissioners on Uniform State Laws, dealing with areas of the law such as sales transactions.

unilateral contract A contract in which the parties exchange a promise for an act.

United States Constitution The fundamental law of the United States of America, which became the law of the land in March of 1789.

unjust enrichment The retention by a party of unearned and undeserved benefits derived from his own wrongful actions regarding an agreement.

unofficial reporters Private publications of court decisions (for example, 525 N.E.2d 90).

V

venue County in which the facts are alleged to have occurred and in which the trial will take place.

visitation rights The right to legally see a child, where physical custody is not awarded.

void ab initio Marriages that are void from the inception.

voir dire The process of selecting a jury for trial.

warranty deed A deed guaranteeing clear title to real property.

will A document representing the formal declaration of a person's wishes for the manner and distribution of his or her property upon death.

writ of certiorari Granting of petition, by the U.S. Supreme Court, to review a case.

Index

A

B

C

D

E

J

K

L

M

N

O

P

Q

R

S

T

U

V

W

Z